Kim Ki-duk

## Contemporary Film Directors

Edited by James Naremore

The Contemporary Film Directors series provides concise, well-written introductions to directors from around the world and from every level of the film industry. Its chief aims are to broaden our awareness of important artists, to give serious critical attention to their work, and to illustrate the variety and vitality of contemporary cinema. Contributors to the series include an array of internationally respected critics and academics. Each volume contains an incisive critical commentary, an informative interview with the director, and a detailed filmography.

*A list of books in the series appears at the end of this book.*

# Kim Ki-duk

Hye Seung Chung

UNIVERSITY
OF
ILLINOIS
PRESS
URBANA,
CHICAGO,
AND
SPRINGFIELD

Frontispiece: Kim Ki-duk


Manufactured in the United States of America
1 2 3 4 5 C P 5 4 3 2 1
∞ This book is printed on acid-free paper.

Library of Congress Cataloging-in-Publication Data
Chung, Hye Seung, 1971–
Kim Ki-duk / Hye Seung Chung.
p. cm.
Includes bibliographical references and index.
Includes filmography.
ISBN 978-0-252-03669-9 (cloth : alk. paper)
ISBN 978-0-252-07841-5 (pbk. : alk. paper)
1. Kim, Ki-duk, 1960 —Criticism and interpretation.
I. Title.
PN1998.3.K585C58 2012
791.4302'33092—dc23 [B] 2011034800

# Contents

*Acknowledgments* | ix

BEYOND "EXTREME": THE CINEMA OF *RESSENTIMENT* | 1

Kim Ki-duk: Towards a More Perfect Imperfection 1

An Auteur Is Born: Fishhooks, Critical Debates, and Transnational Canons 12

On Suffering and Sufferance: Postcolonial Pain and the "Purloined Letter" in *Address Unknown* 26

Reconciling the Paradox of Silence and Apologia: *Bad Guy, The Isle,* and *3-Iron* 45

Neofeminist Revisions: Female Bodies and Semiotic *Chora* in *Birdcage Inn* and *Samaritan Girl* 69

The Bodhisattva Inner-Eye: Inwardly Drawn Transcendence in *Spring, Summer, Fall, Winter . . . and Spring* 104

INTERVIEW WITH KIM KI-DUK: FROM *CROCODILE* TO *ADDRESS UNKNOWN*, BY KIM SO-HEE | 127

*Filmography* | 141

*Bibliography* | 147

*Index* | 155

# Acknowledgments

First, I am thankful for the insights provided by my former students at the University of Michigan, Hamilton College, and the University of Hawaii at Manoa, who watched Kim Ki-duk's films in my classes and shared their thoughtful responses. Their enthusiasm and appreciation for Kim's often misunderstood and maligned cinema solidified my conviction about this project over the past few years. I also want to acknowledge the financial support provided by the University of Hawaii's Research Council, whose generous summer grant enabled my research trip to Seoul, South Korea, in 2009. LJ Film America granted permission for reprinting the Korean critic Kim So-hee's interview with Kim Ki-duk. Although I was not able to conduct a formal interview with him, I am grateful for the generosity of the filmmaker, who came to see me at Ewha Woman's University during a short conference trip to Seoul in November 2008. I will always cherish the memory of our engaging conversation, which is presented toward the end of this book.

David Scott Diffrient, my life companion and intellectual sparring partner, deserves a special thank-you for watching Kim Ki-duk's films with me and sharing many thought-provoking insights. He also went over the manuscript with me page by page and improved its quality immensely with his editorial acumen. I am also deeply indebted to Daniel Martin, who closely read the manuscript and offered invaluable advice for revisions. Last, but not least, I wish to thank James Naremore, the editor of the Contemporary Film Directors series, and Joan Catapano, the former editor-in-chief of the University of Illinois Press, for their patience and encouragement throughout the long process of writing this book.

| | |

The author and editor acknowledge permission from the University of Illinois Press to reprint an earlier portion of this book published under the title “Beyond ‘Extreme’: Rereading Kim Ki-duk’s Cinema of *Ressentiment*” in the *Journal of Film and Video* 62.1–2 (Spring/Summer 2010): 96–111.

Note: The Romanization of Korean names in this book follows the McCune-Reischauer system, which is the academic standard endorsed by the Library of Congress. Exceptions to this rule are a handful of names (notable filmmakers and political leaders) whose spellings are known to English-speaking readers, such as Chun Doo Hwan, Im Kwon-taek, Jang Sun-woo, Kim Ki-duk, Park Chan-wook, and Park Chung Hee. Whenever Korean authors’ works that have been published in English are cited, their names are presented the way they are printed in source materials. Korean and other East Asian names appear in their native standard, with surname first (except for names printed otherwise in English-language publications). Finally, all quotations from Korean-language sources are presented in my own translation.

# Kim Ki-duk

# Beyond "Extreme"

## The Cinema of *Ressentiment*

### Kim Ki-duk: Towards a More Perfect Imperfection

Alongside Park Chan-wook (Pak Ch'an-uk), famous for his Vengeance Trilogy of films comprising *Sympathy for Mr. Vengeance* (*Poksu nŭn na ŭi kŏt*; 2002), *Oldboy* (*Oldŭ poi*; 2003), and *Lady Vengeance* (*Ch'ingŏlhan Kŭmjassi*; 2005), Kim Ki-duk is one of the most acclaimed Korean filmmakers in the Western world. As of 2011, an unprecedented ten of Kim's seventeen feature-length motion pictures are commercially available in the U.S. home-video market: *The Isle* (*Sŏm*; 2000), *Real Fiction* (*Siljae sanghwang*; 2000), *Bad Guy* (*Nappŭn namja*; 2001), *Address Unknown* (*Such'wiin pulmyŏng*; 2001), *The Coast Guard* (*Haeansŏn*; 2002), *Spring, Summer, Fall, Winter . . . and Spring* (*Pom yŏrŭm kaŭl kyŏul kŭrigo pom*; 2003), *Samaritan Girl* (*Samaria*; 2004), *3-Iron* (*Pinjip*; 2004), *The Bow* (*Hwal*; 2005), and *Time* (*Sigan*; 2006).[1] Among these thematically linked yet stylistically disparate films, his award-winning Buddhist fable *Spring, Summer, Fall, Winter . . . and Spring* became an international art-house hit in April and May 2004, breaking all previous box-office records for South Korean films receiving theatrical distribution in the United States and Europe. Around the time of this film's U.S. debut on April 2, Kim was beginning to make his way into Western critics' East Asian film canons by winning two prestigious Best Director awards from the Berlin and Venice International Film Festivals, for *Samaritan Girl* and *3-Iron,* respectively. As the mother of all tributes to a maverick filmmaker whose "sensuous, sensational imagery and wild and haunting narratives" have enthralled film-festival juries and "extreme cinema" aficionados around the world, the New York Museum of Modern Art (MoMA) held a retrospective of Kim's fourteen films to date between April 23 and May 8, 2008 (Kardish).[2]

As a self-trained visual artist with little formal training in filmmaking, Kim Ki-duk is a distinctive talent in world cinema, someone whose oeuvre spills over with painterly landscapes—from placid lakes and sun-bleached seashores to mist-shrouded mountains and windswept fields. Yet those sometimes serene evocations of the natural world contrast sharply with the agitated mental state of his films' anguished characters. Exposing the dark underbelly of Korean society and training an unforgiving lens on the actual as well as imagined spaces where criminal activities proliferate and corruption or vice is a fact of life, Kim's cinema simultaneously respects and deconstructs conventional codes of realism through the incorporation of metaphysical elements and fantasy sequences. Film after film, in narratives of alienation, cruelty, obsession, and transcendence that shift between Brechtian distanciation techniques and coercive strategies of affective suture, immersing the viewer in a world that is both comfortably familiar and strangely foreign or "exotic," Kim has consistently invited audiences to question the distinctions between morality and immorality, love and hatred, happiness and misery, reality and fantasy. Shifting effortlessly from the sublime spiritual symbolism of Robert Bresson and Andrei Tarkovsky to the interclass angst of Oshima Nagisa or Rainer Werner Fassbinder, Kim's diverse yet unified body of work—seventeen feature-length motion pictures thus far, all of which were written by him between 1996 and 2011—has left an indelible mark on global art cinema.

Kim's high profile among cinephiles in North America and Europe as well as his thoroughgoing attempts to take chances as an experimental filmmaker—mixing Japanese and Korean dialogue in *Dream* (*Pimong*; 2008) and shooting large sections of *Real Fiction* in a single take, without conventional cuts[3]—are not the only reasons why his body of work deserves a book-length treatment. While his expressive and painterly visual style merits critical attention as a sign of his ability to conjure up thoughts of "pure cinema," his life story is filled with enough drama and controversy to pique the interest of casual readers outside film studies. Indeed, his unique personal background sets Kim Ki-duk apart from other world directors whose names are referenced in this introductory section for the sake of aesthetic and thematic comparisons.

Born December 20, 1960, in the remote mountain hamlet of Bonghwa, north of Kyŏngsan Province (southeast of Seoul), Kim experienced numerous setbacks—including class discrimination and harassment based on his lowly status—as a young boy forced to fit into an elitist system that privileged industrial growth, capitalist development, educational achievement, and personal wealth during the Park Chung Hee (Pak Chŏng-hŭi) era. When he was nine years old, his family moved to Ilsan, on the outskirts of Seoul. After graduating from elementary school, Kim enrolled in Samae Industrial School, an agricultural training institute, but had to drop out in accordance with his father's orders. Having grown disappointed by the academic failings of his eldest son, who was expelled from school, Kim's father forced his second son to abandon hopes of upward mobility through formal education and to instead focus his efforts on landing work in factories. For six years starting in 1976, Kim took up various menial jobs, working at an auto junkyard, various construction sites, a button factory, and for electronics manufacturers. At the age of seventeen, while working for a semiconductor manufacturer, he built his own machine that was capable of assembling 2,300 transistors a day. The gifted laborer was promoted to foreman as a result of his ingenuity. During his spare time between working hours at factories and junkyards, Kim made several makeshift guns, which soon landed him in hot water with local police (who arrested him and allegedly tortured him over the course of a week).

To escape from his abusive father, Kim volunteered to join the Marine Corps in 1982, two years after the repressive, militarist Chun Doo Hwan (Chŏn Tu-hwan) regime came into power. After five years of service in the most physically and mentally demanding military division in the Republic of Korea, the ex-marine turned to volunteer work for a Baptist church in the Namsan area in Seoul and attended nighttime seminary classes with the intention of becoming a preacher. During his three-year residency at this church for the visually impaired, Kim nurtured his love of painting, a lifelong hobby that he had developed as a child. In 1990, Kim cashed in his savings and flew to Paris, eventually spending three years in the City of Lights and in a seaside village near Montpellier, in the South of France, as a sidewalk artist. Besides making a meager living from sketching portraits of passersby, the self-taught artist put together a collection of over twenty semi-abstract oil paintings and toured nearly a dozen European cities to exhibit his work in public squares. During his tenure in Europe, Kim finally took time out from producing images to become a consumer of images, soaking up the intangible elixir of light and shadow that washed over him in cine-clubs and movie theaters. He was particularly activated by the visceral thrills on display in such films as Jonathan Demme's *The Silence of the Lambs* (1991) and Leos Carax's *Les Amants du Pont-Neuf* (*The Lovers on the Bridge*; 1991), which, by his own account, represented his first serious exposure to the world of cinema (Merajver-Kurlat 10–11).

Inspired by those and other motion pictures, he took up screenwriting after returning to South Korea in 1993. Having taken a six-month course in screenwriting offered by the Korea Scenario Writers Association, Kim wrote several scripts and started to submit his work to semi-annual contests sponsored by the government-subsidized Korean Film Council (KOFIC, then the Korean Motion Picture Promotion Corporation). After several misfires, he won the top prize in 1995 with a script entitled *Illegal Crossing* (*Mudan hoengdan*), which tells a love story involving a portrait artist afflicted with lung cancer (given the name "I") and an adult-magazine model by day, call-girl by night (named "Skirt"). Skirt seduces and manipulates I, leading him to kill her stepfather, who has sexually abused her since her childhood. After reporting their whereabouts to the police, Skirt takes I to the seaside, where the ill-fated couple is surrounded by officers of the law. The woman stages a fake hostage show and exhorts I to end her miserable life with a bullet. However, he is shot by a police sniper, which puts him out of his own misery. Devising the action in a way that might evoke melodrama, Kim has I and the sniper pull the triggers of their guns simultaneously, and the mortally shot lovers tumble down a cliff together in a final embrace.

As a loose mosaic of plotlines and tropes found in several of Kim's films, including *Wild Animals* (*Yasaeng tomgmul pohoguyŏk*; 1997), *Birdcage Inn* (*P'aran taemun*; 1998), *Real Fiction, Bad Guy,* and *Samaritan Girl,* the script for *Illegal Crossing* is significant for the way it anticipates thematic motifs to come. Although the project was shelved and never went into production (having been sold to a production company that would eventually go bankrupt), it paved the way for Kim's entry into the exclusive Ch'ungmuro film industry, located in downtown Seoul. However, Kim did not adjust well to the constrictive environment of Ch'ungmuro, where he worked for two major film companies (Hanmaek Films and Ha Myŏng-jung Films), and he quickly returned to independent screenwriting in the mid 1990s.

Kim's first feature project, *Crocodile* (*Agŏ*; 1996), was inspired by a news report he fortuitously encountered: a group of homeless individuals living under a bridge were managing to survive by fishing out and selling the bodies of suicide victims—people who had jumped into the Han River—to bereaved families. The film's male protagonist is nicknamed "Crocodile." The narrative premise hinges on an act of combined altruism and selfishness, when one day Crocodile saves a woman from drowning in the river only to rape her while she is still unconscious. Such behavior effectively sets the tone for what will develop into often crude forms and primitive displays of masculinity in Kim's cinema, a tendency or trajectory for which the director has been heavily criticized, particularly from feminist camps. As a depressing tale in which virtually every major character dies—both the male antihero and the woman he saves and eventually falls in love with commit suicide—*Crocodile* was a tough sell in the profit-oriented Ch'ungmuro, South Korea's version of the Hollywood film industry. Initially rejected by all of the established producers he had contacted, the no-name screenwriter finally got his lucky break when two first-time producers, Kim Pyŏng-su and Kim Sun-yŏng, expressed interest in purchasing a script from him. When Kim Ki-duk demanded that he be allowed to direct his own script of *Crocodile,* the nervous producers reluctantly agreed to give him the green light if he could pass the cinematographer Yi Tong-sam's "test." After learning of

Kim's background in painting, Yi gave his consent to work with him and, as a result, the untested screenwriter with no academic or professional training in filmmaking made his debut as a full-fledged filmmaker (Kim Ki-duk 80–81).

As this brief biography suggests, there is a direct correlation between Kim's films and his life, which has supplied his scripts with the kind of autobiographical richness of detail that helps substantiate claims of his auteur status. Much like Chi-hŭm, one of the many troubled characters in *Address Unknown,* Kim grew up fearing his authoritarian father, a Korean War veteran who was wounded in combat during the early stages of that so-called police action. Another parallel between Kim's life and that of the protagonist in that film relates to his adolescent years. As a teenager, he had an Amerasian friend who would later commit suicide, and Kim was frequently bullied by village thugs. During his service in the marines, Sergeant Kim was wrongly court-martialed for failing to report a North Korean spy ship (in place of his superior, who was reportedly responsible) and detained in a military prison for months. This experience served as the basis for the narrative in *The Coast Guard.*

Religious overtones in *Bad Guy, Spring, Summer, Fall, Winter . . . and Spring,* and *Samaritan Girl* are imbued with additional relevance in light of an especially pious period of Kim's early adulthood, the time in his life that followed military service, when he was deeply involved in church activities and took seminary classes to become a minister. Perhaps most significant is the fact that several of his central characters are unsuccessful sketch artists, as in *Crocodile, Wild Animals, Real Fiction,* and *Address Unknown.* This diegetic inscription of figures driven by their creative urges yet sometimes stymied by their artistic failings as well as material paucity reflects the writer-director's own experience in Europe. Moreover, the mute protagonist of *3-Iron* who fixes broken objects (toy guns, scales, clocks) in other people's houses that he has snuck into might remind one of Kim's adolescence as a factory mechanic.

Kim's cinema is shaped by his own life experiences and propelled by underdog protagonists—socially marginalized and oppressed subalterns or "shadow figures" such as homeless people, thugs, prostitutes, camptown residents, Amerasians, the disabled, and prison inmates—whose only means of communication is a shared sense of corporeal pain resulting from extreme acts of violence. Kim's necessarily brutal cinema, which reflects the cruelty of a classist society blind or indifferent to the misfortunes of others, is often misinterpreted by Western critics and cult fans as simply another example of East Asian "extreme cinema," an umbrella term referring to a variety of films characterized by an exploitative or sensationalistic use of sex, violence, and horror/terror. In South Korea, Kim is likewise misunderstood by his compatriots, occasionally referred to as a "psychopath" and a "misogynist" (Kim So-hee, "Biography" 1). The disturbing images of violence in his films—from murder and cannibalism to animal cruelty and body mutilation to rape and sadomasochistic sex—continue to upset mainstream sensibilities and undermine middle-class notions of propriety and "good taste" in the (cinematic) arts.

The primary impulse of my project is to challenge various misunderstandings of Kim's cinema among Korean and Western critics and to initiate a new set of inquiries reflecting the director's own transnational movements across literal and figurative borders. That East-West valence, that oscillatory movement of an artist who frustrates the classificatory desire of critics to delineate the boundaries of his boundlessly inventive cinema, reflects my own liminal identity as a Korean-born scholar trained in Western film theory and cultural criticism who conducts research in both English and Korean. Borrowing Friedrich Nietzsche's concept of *ressentiment,* which refers to a particular type of anger and resentment that results from sustained periods of subordination and oppression, I argue that Kim's cinema can be read as a politically poetic, poetically political statement about social marginalization. Taking Nietzsche's concept as a theoretical springboard, I investigate how and why Kim's cinema of *ressentiment* is often misunderstood as something else, as something *other*—from "sexual terrorism" to cheap thrills—inside and outside South Korean institutional and cultural contexts. The subversive power of Kim's films rests in their ability to capture, channel, and convey the raw emotions of subaltern protagonists who live on the bottom rungs of Korean society, an aspect that links his work to that of Ken Loach in Great Britain and Rainer Werner Fassbinder in West Germany.[4] It is also possible to recuperate Kim's deeply personal films as productive case studies that attest to the continued relevancy and explanatory power of auteurism, despite its seemingly outdated status in postmodernist film studies, in this age of global media flows, increased conglomeration, shrinking art-house markets, and the ceaseless move toward effects-driven cinema.

Ironically, Kim's commercial failures and his perpetual outsider status in the Korean film industry have reinforced his authenticity and integrity and lent legitimacy to his reputation as an uncompromising auteur. As Myung Ja Kim perceptively points out, "The mainstream does not seem to be willing to shake hands with [Kim Ki-duk]. . . . Ironically, the very reason he was rejected makes him one of the most important film directors in contemporary Korean cinema" (260). Unable to attract large funds or top-notch stars due to his poor track record at the box office (local admissions for his first three films, *Crocodile, Wild Animals,* and *Birdcage Inn,* were a mere 3,300, 5,400, and 5,800, respectively), Kim was forced to put together his own stock company of little-known theater actors or new talent beginning in the late 1990s. There are notable exceptions to his rule of making films with fresh, untested actors, such as *The Coast Guard* (which features Jang Dong-gun [Chang Tong-gŭn], one of the biggest South Korean male stars) and *Breath* (*Sum*; 2007) and *Dream* (which feature the internationally celebrated East Asian stars Chang Chen and Odagiri Jo, respectively). However, for the most part, Kim's millennial mode of hands-on production is a testament to his ability to make films outside the star system that, like Alfred Hitchcock's midcentury masterpieces (including *Rope* [1948], *Strangers on a Train* [1951], and *Rear Window* [1954]), frequently downplay and subsume acting talent within an overall directorial vision, positing performance as merely one aspect of mise-en-scène to be manipulated, like a prop on a set. Here it is important to consider the director's own words: "[T]o me [during the shooting of *Isle*], the boat was more important than the female character and the floating yellow house more significant than the male character. . . . The ideal acting to me is when the actor/actress presents the character in a documentary-like style, as if he/she is actually living that life" (Interview with Kim So-hee reprinted in this volume).

The prolific director has often resorted to multitasking to lower production costs and maintain creative control over his projects. In addition to writing original scripts for all of his films (among his contemporary compatriot directors with comparable standing, only Lee Chang-dong [Yi Ch'ang-dong] can boast the same credit), Kim has served as producer (*Samaritan Girl, 3-Iron, The Bow, Time, Breath, Dream, Arirang,* and

*Amen*), art director (*Crocodile, Wild Animals, Birdcage Inn, The Isle, Real Fiction, Address Unknown,* and *Samaritan Girl*), editor (*Spring, Summer, Fall, Winter, and . . . Spring, Samaritan Girl, The Bow, Time, Dream, Arirang, Amen*), and actor (*Spring, Summer, Fall, Winter, and . . . Spring, Breath, Amen*). The breadth and depth of his creative control, which encompasses the stages of preproduction, production, and postproduction, might remind audiences of the operational practices associated with New American Cinema and stateside experimental film movements of the 1950s and 1960s, particularly the dynamic, improvisational motion pictures made by John Cassavetes, referred to by one critic as the "American auteur in its most pure and unadulterated form" (Tzioumakis 175). A similar claim can be made about Kim Ki-duk in the context of Korean cinema.

And yet, in terms of his efficiency and speed in making films, Kim's production process has more in common with Hollywood's studio-era factory output or Roger Corman's quickly and cheaply shot B-movies, especially those unleashed by American International Pictures at the height of the youth craze during the late 1950s and early 1960s. Kim's films are typically shot in two or three weeks and made on budgets that rarely exceed four hundred thousand dollars. With their six-hundred-thousand-dollar production costs, *Bad Guy* and *3-Iron* are considered "big budget" films in Kim's body of work. This on-the-fly, off-the-cuff, in-your-face style of filmmaking—combined with Kim's lack of formal training—partially accounts for the rawness of his early motion pictures: their flaws, inconsistencies, and fissures. As the Italian film scholar Andrea Bellavita puts it, praise for Kim's films often stems from their "imperfections" (149). In this way, his cinema might be said to share certain traits with the Cuban director-theorist Julio Garcia Espinosa's notion of "imperfect cinema" and the Argentinean film directors Fernando Solanas and Octavio Getino's concept of "Third Cinema."

In his 1969 manifesto "For an Imperfect Cinema," Espinosa resists the pull of "perfection" found in reactionary cinemas of the West in defense of an "imperfect" cinema that would thematize the struggles of oppressed people seeking social change through revolutionary means. Unlike the technologically dependent perfect cinema associated with Hollywood studio output, imperfect cinema can be made "equally well with a Mitchell or with an 8mm camera, in a studio or in a guerrilla camp in the middle of the jungle" (Espinosa 33). Solanas and Getino transport Espinosa's ideas into the militant arena, and in their own manifesto ("Towards a Third Cinema"), the authors divide world cinemas into three categories: the First Cinema (commercial Hollywood movies and their analogs around the world); the Second Cinema (the author's cinema, or high-modernist avant-garde art films); and the Third Cinema ("a cinema outside and against the System . . . a cinema of liberation") (Solanas and Getino 51–52). The Third Cinema is a revolutionary cinema or a "cinema of the masses" produced by a "film-guerrilla group" and distributed and exhibited through underground networks in avoidance of governmental censorship. Mobilizing warfare metaphors, Solanas and Getino compare the camera to an "expropriator of image-weapons" and metaphorize the projector as "a gun that can shoot 24 frames per second" (58). Although Kim's films are not overtly directed against the state or anti-imperial in their content, his guerrilla-style approach to filmmaking and his confrontational attitude toward mainstream society and loci of hegemonic power can be likened to Third Cinema aesthetics. Appropriately, Kim Ki-duk has called himself a "proletarian director" who, instead of wasting time on meetings with prospective financiers or stars' agents, begins looking for locations as soon as the idea for a motion picture sprouts in his mind and then proceeds to shoot footage with whatever funds, resources, and actors that are available at that moment (Kang, "Kim Ki-duk" 37). A by-product of proletarian work ethics and his instinctual grasp of the poetic potential in color design, Kim's oeuvre is an anomaly in international cultural production, evincing the potential to blur or perhaps even eradicate the boundaries between Second (auteurist) and Third (subaltern) Cinemas.

Rather than simply brandish auteurism and its attendant terminology as a way of elevating Kim Ki-duk's films to a canonical level of appreciation, it behooves us to turn our attention to the context in which Western canons of South Korean films have been constructed and perpetuated, with film festivals and art-house circuits being privileged sites of international cultural brokerage. The controversial Korean director's fortunes and misfortunes lie precisely in the different modes of transnational film reception attending his work. Kim is already an established name in contemporary world cinema, and his films have been embraced by global audiences, particularly in North America, Europe, and Asia. Over the past few years, a number of American film scholars have shared with me their newfound admiration for South Korean cinema after viewing *Spring, Summer, Fall, Winter . . . and Spring* and *3-Iron. Spring, Summer, Fall, Winter . . . and Spring* in particular seems to have left an indelible imprint on several American audience members outside of academia, as testified by Kim Ki-duk himself:

> I showed it at the Lincoln Center. . . . And there was a woman well into her eighties—a very pale white American woman who stayed long after the screening and didn't leave and . . . begged the staff if she could please meet the director so she could hold his hand. And when we met, she thanked me for letting her see such a wonderful film before she died. (Canavese)

Seen by 370,000 theatergoers in the United States and grossing $2.4 million for its distributor, Sony Pictures Classics, *Spring, Summer, Fall, Winter, and . . . Spring* garnered a mere thirty thousand admissions in Kim's home country and is currently unavailable in the South Korean DVD market due to a lack of commercial demand.

In the press conference for his thirteenth film, *Time,* Kim expressed frustration over the continued neglect and unpopularity of his films in South Korea: "I hope that two hundred thousand people will come see [*Time* in South Korea]. More than three hundred thousand American moviegoers saw *Spring, Summer, Fall, Winter . . . and Spring.* And *3-Iron* was seen by two hundred thousand in France and another two hundred thousand in Germany. My mind [about the Korean market] might change if domestic admissions [for *Time*] exceed two hundred thousand" (Chu Sŏng-ch'ŏl 8). Despite Kim's threat to stop "exporting" his new films (the distribution rights for which belong to his foreign investors and/or himself) to his own country should his goal not be met, *Time* fell short of thirty thousand admissions. In his July 13, 2005, interview with *Time Out,* Kim speculates on the cause for his continued commercial failures in South Korea: "I make movies that I want to see. The reason most Korean people don't see my movies is because they don't want to see the movies that I want to see" ("Film Q&A" 84). Why do Western art-house patrons accept so willingly films that have little commercial appeal in the country of their origin? This question should be contextualized within the larger history of the Western reception of East Asian cinema.

## An Auteur Is Born: Fishhooks, Critical Debates, and Transnational Canons

Beginning in the 1950s and 1960s, the films of Kurosawa Akira, Ozu Yasujiro, and Mizoguchi Kenji entered the Western canon of East Asian cinema under the various rubrics associated with auteurism and art cinema. Throughout the 1980s and 1990s, Fifth Generation Chinese filmmakers such as Zhang Yimou and Chen Kaige rose to international fame for their exotic, ethnographic films, sparking critical debates about self-orientalism, among other things (Chow 142–72). In recent years, however, the dominant mode of East Asian canon-formation in the West appears to have shifted into an area that can be (and has been) described as "extreme cinema." Although it is unclear when and by whom the critical term "extreme cinema" was first coined, at least in the context of marketing Asian cinema, credit should be given to Hamish McAlpine, the founder and proprietor of the now-defunct U.K.-based Tartan Films, who created the popular "Asia Extreme" brand in 2002 and subsequently distributed numerous Asian horror films, thrillers, and erotic films to British and American markets.[5] Under this blood-soaked banner are assembled some of the most iconoclastic auteurs in East Asia, including Fruit Chan, Kurosawa Kiyoshi, Kim Ki-duk, Miike Takashi, the Pang brothers, and Park Chan-wook, who are all enjoying a spike in international recognition and cult fandom thanks in part to the visceral nature of their disturbing yet engrossing films, which frequently shuttle between tranquility and terror, the sublime and the grotesque.

Constructed and sustained by Western distributors, critics, and fanboys, extreme cinema is a geographically, culturally ambiguous concept that neglects intra-Asian differences and presupposes the morbid aesthetic essence of Eastern cultural productions from different national, ethnic, linguistic backgrounds. It is a Eurocentric classification, a marketing structure that indexes a variety of Asian films under the same category based on presumed Western tastes and standards as to what constitutes cinematic extremism. As Chi-Yun Shin points out in her study of Tartan's "Asia Extreme" label, "[T]he output of the label, and indeed the name of the label itself, invoke and in part rely on the western audiences' perception of the East as weird and wonderful, sublime and grotesque" ("Art of Branding").

Regardless of the ceaseless controversy surrounding Kim Ki-duk at home and abroad, MoMA's endorsement and showcasing of his entire oeuvre in the spring of 2008—the first of its kind granted to a Korean filmmaker[6]—demonstrates that Korean cinema can now boast its own Kurosawa Akira, its own Zhang Yimou, its own visionary auteur whose border-crossing reputation promises to boost the status of the nation's earlier and future cultural productions in the global arena. Such rhetorical maneuvers by critics may prove to be problematic, however, given that the pigeonholing of Kim as a "Korean Kurosawa"—and, by extension, the labeling of Korean cinema as something derivative (or, in the words of Anthony C. Y. Leong, "the New Hong Kong")[7]—has the potential to reproduce dominant ideological positions vis-à-vis the abstracted Asian "other," with an attendant risk of rendering diverse cultural traditions as interchangeable elements within a monolithically conceived canon endorsed by Western scholars and Euro-American institutions. Moreover, these kinds of ahistorical analogies threaten to reduce a centralized yet discursive national cinema to a mere handful of exceptional filmmakers, an auteurist folly criticized by several scholars in the context of classical Hollywood cinema but rarely challenged in the context of East Asian cinema.

A social outcast and autodidact, Kim Ki-duk has a very different background from that of Kurosawa or Zhang, who were trained in prestigious film institutions, Toho Studios and the Beijing Film Academy, respectively. In addition, this ex–sidewalk artist continues to operate in an expressive, "semi-abstract" realm (to borrow his own words),[8] departing from the primarily realistic diegetic worlds and classical narratives found in Kurosawa's and Zhang's films. And yet, despite their apparent dissimilarities, one can detect reception-based parallels among the three directors, each one at least partly responsible for "instituting" a passion for Asian genre films in the West, from Kurosawa's samurai films of the 1950s and 1960s to Zhang's historical melodramas three decades later, to the extreme cinema being grinded out by Kim and his contemporaries in the new millennium. At the risk of being reductive, one can argue that a pervasive orientalism—far from being consigned to the grave by some postcolonial scholars—links the Western reception of "exotic" East Asian cinemas across national borders and increasingly porous genres over the course of the past six decades.

More specifically, by lumping Kim Ki-duk's socially conscious, if also exploitative, dramas with assorted East Asian genre films—from supernatural horror flicks like Nakata Hideo's *Ringu* (1998) and the Pang brothers's *The Eye* (*Gin gwai*; 2002) to psychological thrillers like Miike Takashi's *Audition* (*Odishon*; 1999) to science-fiction spectacles like Min Pyŏng-ch'ŏn's *Natural City* (2003)—under the inclusive umbrella of extreme cinema, one is likely to gloss over the cultural specificity and thematic profundity of his necessarily brutal films. Although the excessively coded and deeply felt corporeal effects (from vomiting to fainting) of his visceral psychosexual thriller *The Isle* are what made Kim an overnight sensation in the West, a complete hermeneutic picture of his films—a full understanding of their complex social meanings—would be lost if aesthetic celebration or condemnation of such effects were to take precedence over a culturally specific analysis of cinematic pain and violence as a form of therapeutic *ressentiment*, a concept that will be addressed in depth later in this section.

A landmark achievement in this controversial auteur's prolific career and the winner of the Best Picture Award at the 2004 Grand Bell Awards (Taejongsang) Awards, the Korean equivalent to the Oscars, *Spring, Summer, Fall, Winter . . . and Spring* includes an autobiographical scene in the penultimate "Winter" chapter. After serving time in prison for murder, a former monk (played by the director himself) returns to a floating temple in the middle of a lake, the film's idyllic central setting. In one of his physically rigorous training sessions, the ex-monk, seeking atonement and spiritual rebirth, drags a heavy stone Buddha up to the summit of one of the surrounding mountains, which commands a panoramic view of the world beneath him. This scene is significant insofar as it connotes, in allegorical fashion, Kim's own life journey: his ultimate ascendancy in the world of filmmaking as well as his artistic introspection and maturation. Like his onscreen character, before climbing to such heights of fame, before gaining recognition as a world-class auteur, Kim had to overcome enormous obstacles and hardships, the likes of which would be unthinkable to his contemporaries from privileged backgrounds. As a middle-school dropout victimized by domestic violence, an exploited factory worker, a wrongly court-martialed marine, a vagabond street artist in Paris, and a self-educated screenwriter lacking the familial, educational, and professional connections necessary to succeed in South Korea, Kim encountered one setback or difficulty after another. Yet, like the monk, he has risen above it all.

Kim Ki-duk's international fame did little to improve the box-office performance of his independently produced art films in his homeland or to assuage the critical controversy plaguing this iconoclastic director, who apparently got under the skin of members of the Korean press as early as 1997, a year after the release of his widely neglected debut feature, *Crocodile.* In the wake of the negative critical and commercial reception of his second feature, *Wild Animals,* Kim sent a provocative fax to South Korean dailies, declaring his outright "hatred" toward indifferent, dismissive, or hostile journalists who, in his opinion, were responsible for keeping audiences away from his films. The critical reception of Kim's films has since been divided into polemical positions and diametrically opposed extremes. While there has been a steady stream of accolades from domestic critics and cult film fans who have followed Kim's career since the early days, a majority of the public has either ignored or denounced his films, primarily because of their disturbing images of violence—from murder and cannibalism to animal cruelty and body mutilation to rape and sadomasochistic sex—and their often discontinuous, discombobulating narratives filled with ellipses, fissures, contradictions, and fantasies. The vicious rhetoric adopted by some of his detractors, who went so far as to call Kim Ki-duk a "psychopath," attests to the fact that such films not only upset or alienate mainstream sensibilities but also undermine middle-class conformity in South Korea and unleash the kind of invectives that reveal more about the speaker than the receiver.

In *Primitive Passions: Visuality, Sexuality, Ethnography, and Contemporary Chinese Cinema,* Rey Chow lays out several accounts of critics who have criticized the films of Zhang Yimou, mainland China's most celebrated yet controversial filmmaker who, like Kim, is known for his distinctive visual style:

> First, we hear that Zhang's films lack depth, a lack that critics often consider as *the reason* why his films are beautiful. . . . Second, Zhang's

> "lack of depth" is inserted in what become debates about the politics of cross-cultural representations. The beauty of Zhang's films is, for some critics, a sign of Zhang's attempt to pander to the tastes of foreigners. . . . Even though Zhang and his contemporaries are "orientals," then, they are explicitly or implicitly regarded as producing a kind of orientalism. Third, this lack of depth, this orientalism, is linked to yet another crime—that of exploiting women. Zhang's films are unmistakably filled with sexually violent elements. (150–51)

Chow's summary reflects the kinds of criticism that Kim Ki-duk has also encountered at home and abroad despite critical consensus endorsing his painterly aesthetic sensibilities—his predilection for primary colors and water imagery. As with Zhang, the integrity and sincerity of the Korean filmmaker have been questioned by suspicious or skeptical critics who accuse him of having "sold out" to North American and European festival programmers, juries, and art-house patrons who are drawn to exotic visuals or shock-filled material.

Two leading Korean film magazines—*Cine 21* and *Film 2.0*—have devoted many pages to the heated critical debates surrounding Kim Ki-duk, discourse that only further fuels the fire of his detractors and defenders. Those who complain most vociferously about Kim's cinema typically target his films' implausible narratives, their shallow characterizations, their on-the-fly aesthetics, their misanthropic displays of violence, and their superficial gloss of an anger that is said to lack deep historical insight or social relevance.[9] In other words, the perceived failures of Kim's films have been measured by mainstream standards of well-crafted, narrative-based motion-picture production, the kinds of works that are thought to be nonthreatening and filled with humanistic messages capable of sparking personal reflection or social change. Korean feminists have delivered the most cohesive, sustained critique of Kim Ki-duk and his "misogynistic" films, which are often populated with prostitute characters and frequently feature scenes of sexual violence. For example, Yu Chi-na called *Crocodile* a "rape movie" (qtd. in Kim Ki-duk 85), and Chu Yu-sin deemed his most commercially successful film, *Bad Guy,* an example of "dangerous penis fascism" ("His Film Is a Terror to Women" 34). The feminist critic and psychiatrist Sim Yŏng-sŏp accused Kim Ki-duk of "annihilating the presence of women altogether" in his films, except for women-as-genitals or sexual objects for men (69). Echoing the reactions of their Korean counterparts, some American female journalists have been offended by Kim's films, as exemplified by Carina Chocano's review of *Bad Guy* in the *Los Angeles Times.* Describing the film's plot, in which a vengeful underworld pimp turns a middle-class college student into a sex worker, Chocano labels it "a metaphor only a Marxist critic could love," which suggests that "you can take the middle class out of the girl, but you can't take the whore out of the woman" (E6).

Despite its seemingly misogynistic premise, which has been frowned upon by female critics such as Chu and Chocano, *Bad Guy* is a far cry from conventional sexploitation fare. In fact, sex scenes often take place offscreen and, when depicted within the frame, are presented in long shots and long takes to emphasize the *pain,* rather than the pleasure, experienced by female characters. There is no implication of a sexual relationship between the two protagonists, the brothel thug Han-gi and the college student–turned-prostitute Sŏn-hwa, who gradually falls in love with the man responsible for her social downfall. Upon closer scrutiny, *Bad Guy* is a multilayered text that skillfully interweaves reality and fantasy as well as soft-porn melodrama and indictments against Korea's class system. Closing with a bittersweet "happy ending" (which may be a mortally stabbed Han-gi's dying dream) in which the interclass couple makes a living from roadside prostitution, *Bad Guy* should be taken as a reverse-*Pygmalion* social allegory, the flip side of George Bernard Shaw's play wherein the erudite Professor Higgins transforms the cockney-speaking flower girl Eliza Doolittle into a dignified lady. In a 2002 interview, Kim elaborates on the intention behind *Bad Guy*: "People look at the world of prostitutes and hoodlums and say, 'This is trash, we need to clean this up.' But these people's lives deserve to be treated with respect" (Paquet, "Close-Up" 14).

Kim's most vocal "nemesis" in the English-speaking world seems to be the British critic Tony Rayns, an influential advocate of East Asian cinema and a supporter of several Korean directors, most notably Jang Sun-woo [Chang Sŏn-u], the subject of his 2001 documentary, *The Jang Sun-Woo Variations.* In a controversial essay published by *Film Comment* in the winter of 2004, Rayns indicts not only Kim Ki-duk but also his "duped" champions (film-festival jurors and sympathetic critics).

Rayns goes so far as to call *3-Iron* a "shameless plagiarism" of Tsai Ming-liang's *Vive l'amour* (*Ai quin wan sui*; 1994). He also refers to *The Isle, Bad Guy*, and *Samaritan Girl* as examples of "sexual terrorism." Moreover, he denounces *Spring, Summer, Fall, Winter . . . and Spring* as a faux-Buddhist film that would appeal only to orientalist Western critics who know nothing about Buddhism and whose "bullshit detectors [have stopped] working" when it comes to East Asian films (50–52). Unintentionally, Rayns's condescending bashing of the factory worker–turned-director generated controversy online among cinephilic members of particular Web communities and ended up converting some former detractors into defenders.

Kim responded with uncharacteristic nonchalance, stating, "[T]he way I see it is that recently I've been doing extremely well, and Tony's giving me an opportunity to look back and reexamine my work. . . . We need not only sun but also rain for agriculture" (qtd. in Smith N9). However, less forgiving bloggers passionately protested Rayns's "hatchet job." For example, in his blog post titled "Tony Reigns," Ben Slater opines, "[I]ts main argument—that Kim has somehow fooled people into believing his terrible films are good—reveals that Rayns's target isn't actually Kim himself, but rather all the critics, curators, programmers, juries and audiences who have apparently committed the ultimate, unforgivable mistake. They didn't listen to Tony." The Singapore-based blogger persuasively argues, "Rayns has made his position clear—only people who don't know anything about Asian cinema would embrace Kim Ki-duk. Where this leaves Asian critics who admire him, and programme him into their festivals, and the Asian audiences who admire his work, I have no idea." To this list can be added a host of Asian producers who, over the past few years, have invested in his work (*3-Iron, The Bow*, and *Time* were financed by the Japanese company Happinet Pictures).

In response to the online hullabaloo sparked by Rayns's three-page article, Chuck Stephens, an editor of *Film Comment* who had commissioned the piece, published his justification in a 2005 issue of *Cinema Scope*. In this ostensible review of *3-Iron*, Stephens makes his editorial intentions clear: "My initial hope in asking Rayns to rework his already-familiar-in-Korea thesis was to sound a cautionary note at precisely the moment Kim stood on the verge of greatly expanding his American profile. . . . The umpteenth incarnation of exportable Asian cinema was the last thing anyone needed, with Kim cast as a more scabrous variation on Zhang Yimou." This admission ironically confirms Slater's suspicion that Rayns (and his editor) "[seem] to be wishing that [Kim] Ki-duk had remained obscure, that no one in the West had ever heard of him, and to take that desire further, that Kim had been unable to continue making films (which given his lack of success in South Korea is a likely scenario)." Despite Rayns's and Stephens's efforts to diminish his Euro-American profile, Kim's international reputation remained intact, culminating in *Breath*'s entry into the competition section at the 2007 Cannes Film Festival, the 2008 MoMA retrospective, and more recently his latest film *Arirang*'s winning of the Best Picture award in the Un Certain Regard section at the 2011 Cannes Film Festival .

Although Kim Ki-duk is best known to mainstream American and European cinephiles for glossier, more meditative, modern Zen fables such as *Spring, Summer, Fall, Winter . . . and Spring* and *3-Iron,* an intense cult fandom for his brutal *yŏpgi* (bizarre, grotesque, or horrific) aesthetics first sprang up with the 2000 release of *The Isle,* a psychological thriller set against the backdrop of a deceptively peaceful waterscape. One gruesome scene in particular, in which the fugitive male protagonist swallows a ball of fishhooks in an attempt to evade capture by the police, led some audience members to faint or vomit in theaters worldwide, from Venice to New York, turning the little-known South Korean independent filmmaker into an overnight sensation and earning him a spot in international extreme film canons.

For the screenings of *The Isle* as a part of the 2001 New York Korean Film Festival at the Anthology Film Archives, the following disclaimer was advertised: "*The Isle* contains scenes of a graphic nature. Incidents, including fainting (see 'Viewing Peril' below), have occurred. Attend at your own risk. Management of the Anthology Film Archives cannot be held responsible" (qtd. in "When Korean Cinema Attacks"). The tie-in "viewing peril" bulletin was taken from the August 5, 2001, issue of the *New York Post*: "Being a movie critic isn't as easy as you might think. Joshua Tanzer . . . found a scene in the Korean feature *The Isle* so disturbing, he blacked out during a screening at the Anthology Film Archives the other day." In June 2004, the *New Yorker* retrospectively reported this notorious incident in a more graphic way: "*The Isle* contains . . . 'a moment of extreme fishhook penetration,' and it was shortly after this part of the film that a critic emerged into the lobby, made a high-pitched gurgling noise, and passed out on the floor. . . . The story was reprinted in [the *Post* and] other newspapers, and soon *The Isle* acquired a reputation as the most dangerous movie around" (Agger 37).

Tanzer's gagging and fainting upon seeing the scene of "extreme fishhook penetration" in *The Isle* is a perfect example of powerful corporeal effects on the viewer induced by what film theorists sometimes call the "body genre." According to Linda Williams, there are three major body genres: (1) pornography, characterized by gratuitous sex and nudity; (2) horror films, characterized by gratuitous violence and terror; and (3) melodramas, characterized by gratuitous emotion and affect (603–7). Body genres prompt the spectator's physical self to enact an "almost involuntary mimicry of the emotion or sensation of the body on the screen" (605). As a unique art-house remix of various traits found in all three types of the body-genre formula, Kim's visceral cinema provides intense sensory stimulation—a potential source of spectatorial pleasure as much as repulsion and shock—for adventurous cinephiles in the West.

Figure 1. A moment of "extreme fishhook penetration" in *The Isle* induced a fainting spell among certain audiences in European and American art-house theaters and film festivals.

Writing for the *Village Voice,* Michael Atkinson celebrates the sensorial audience participation induced by Kim's gory aesthetics:

> You'd have to look back to the theater-lobby barf-bag heyday of *Night of the Living Dead, Mark of the Devil,* and *The Exorcist* for this kind of fun. In every case, however, the ostensible trauma begins with the offscreen, or just vaguely glimpsed, suggestion of physical violation. . . . It's refreshing to see that audiences are still vulnerable enough to lose their consciousness or their lunch thanks to a film, but thanks to what a film doesn't show? That's entertainment. ("Ace in the Hole" 126)

Particularly noteworthy is Atkinson's choice of two words: "fun" and "entertainment." Kim's films (with the exception of *Bad Guy,* which garnered 750,000 admissions) flopped one after the other at the domestic box office precisely because they denied the kinds of fun and entertainment that mainstream moviegoers generally pursue, forcing them to confront the torturous, harsh realities of subalterns living on the bottom rungs of Korean society. Chŏng Sŏng-il, one of the few Korean critics to consistently post favorable reviews of Kim Ki-duk since his debut, commented, "I become sad when I see a Kim Ki-duk film. . . . There are people who say they become angry. I wonder why. I do not intend to fight with them. But I do want to understand their anger. And I want them to understand my sadness" ("Why Kim Ki-duk?" 36–37). As Adrian Martin puts it in a post to the online *Film-Philosophy Salon,* Kim "is a director who evokes love and/or hate in viewers—certainly not indifference!" From the disdain and indignation of Tony Rayns to the amusement and exhilaration of Michael Atkinson, from the pathos and sympathy of Chŏng Sŏng-il to the outrage of Chŏng's feminist counterparts, Kim's emotionally wrought films have prompted diametrically opposed yet equally passionate reactions (whether positive or negative) from viewers around the world.

In his essay "Kim Ki-duk's Cinema of Cruelty: Ethics and Spectatorship in the Global Economy," Steve Choe vividly reports the audience's discomfort and disgust at the screenings of Kim's films in the context of international film festivals:

> A screening of *The Isle* . . . in Philadelphia . . . began with an in-person disclaimer by the festival programmer stating that it was unquestionably

> the most graphic of all the films being screened and advising the audience to leave the theater if the intensity of images became unbearable. . . . In Rotterdam . . . *Address Unknown* also began with a disclaimer, stating that "No animal was harmed in any way during the making of this film." . . . A static melancholy and seemingly endless cycle of violence does pervade *Address Unknown* (it seems that every ten minutes or so someone or some animal is battered) which, coupled with the film's increasingly morbid imagery, endangered the security of the voyeuristic audience. As the film depicted more brutality and scenes of blatant disregard for others, viewers became increasingly uncomfortable . . . some were audibly disgusted . . . [o]thers nervously shuffled at their seats. . . . Frustrated audience members left the theater altogether. (65–66, 69)

Choe dubs the extreme corporeal effects of Kim's cinema "spectatorial terrorism" (67), or "a form of 'cruel and unusual punishment'" (80) that defamiliarizes the safe, voyeuristic filmgoing experience and raises ethical questions about spectatorship.

The extreme nature of Kim's films, however, should not be misunderstood as merely a sensorial provocation or exploitative sleight-of-hand to "hook" the audience with repulsive images. Rather, it can be seen as a desperate (and desperately needed) exclamation point—a kind of corporeal exclamation point—emphasizing the excruciating pain suffered by heroes who often serve as semiautobiographical portraits of the filmmaker himself. To gain a deeper understanding of Kim's cinema, it is vital that audiences interject an auteuristic interpretation of its "abject hero,"[10] to borrow a phrase coined by the literary critic Michael A. Bernstein. Literally and figuratively silent underdogs populating Kim's cinema—from Han-gi in *Bad Guy* to T'ae-sŏk in *3-Iron* to Chang Chin in *Breath*—are semiautobiographical portraits of the director himself, who, before becoming an award-winning filmmaker, lived a subaltern existence as an undereducated factory worker in South Korea. In an interview with Kim So-hee, Kim Ki-duk equated filmmaking with the metaphorical act of "kidnapping those of the mainstream into [his] own space, and then introducing [himself] to them as a human being" ("Biography" 5), rather than as a lowlife.

As a Nietzschean cinema of *ressentiment,* Kim's films derive their vitality and momentum from raw emotions such as angst, frustration, envy, and resentment—emotions felt and exhibited by disenfranchised individuals ill-equipped to survive in an ultracompetitive society where exclusive college connections or family networks are prerequisites for upward mobility. Translated into "resentment" or "hostility," the French term *ressentiment* is central to Friedrich Nietzsche's understanding of morality. In his landmark philosophical treatise on the historical evolution of Judeo-Christian moral values, *On the Genealogy of Morality*, Nietzsche defines *ressentiment* as a process by which disempowered and injured parties "*anaesthetize pain through emotion* . . . a tormenting, secret pain that is becoming unbearable with a more violent emotion of any sort" (93). According to the German philosopher, this state of mind arises when the powerless and oppressed, who are "denied the proper response for action, compensate for it only with imaginary revenge" (20). Whereas Nietzsche identifies the ancient Jews as a "priestly nation of *ressentiment par excellence*" (32), Max Scheler adds woman (particularly, the "old maid" and the mother-in-law) as well as the older generation, the arsonist, and the disappearing class of artisans to the list of those who are susceptible to such emotion (42–47).

Though *ressentiment* was denounced as a vengeful and poisonous "slave morality" by Nietzsche, affirmative possibilities of the concept have been recuperated by contemporary scholars and philosophers. For example, M. J. Bowles argues, "*Ressentiment* in fact marks the potentiality of a tremendous energy source. . . . To exploit human *ressentiment* is something of an art" (14–15). Rebecca Stringer sees *ressentiment* as "an inevitable and potentially positive force in feminism" that is partly responsible for shaping such institutional practices as affirmative action and women's studies (266–67). Countering Wendy Brown's call for "a feminist politics without *ressentiment*," Stringer recuperates feminist *ressentiment* as a regenerative force that can give rise to creativity, agency, responsibility, and new power (266–69). Jeffrey T. Nealon calls *ressentiment* a "political anger of transformation" that might "open a space for us to respond to subjective or communal expropriation in other than resentful ways" (277). According to Nietzsche, a profound comprehension of *ressentiment* is possible only by and among those who share the same ailments and agonies. The sick are in need of "doctors and nurses *who are sick themselves*. . . . [The man of *ressentiment*] must be sick himself, he must really be a close relative of the sick and the destitute in order to understand them" (92).

Themes and characters that derive from the writer-director's *lived* experiences make Kim Ki-duk's cinema of *ressentiment* so potent. In this regard, Kim's corpus can be described as a *necessarily* brutal cinema, one that accurately reflects and symbolically avenges the cruelty of a classist, conformist society. Although such New Wave filmmakers as Park Kwang-su [Pak Kwang-su], Jang Sun-woo, and Chung Ji-young [Chŏng Chi-yŏng] have explored the wretched situations of the Korean underclass in the throes of state-initiated modernization under military regimes (1961–92), their films typically privilege intellectual male protagonists who speak for subaltern characters. A good example of this cross-class ventriloquism occurs in Park Kwang-su's biopic *A Single Spark* (*Arŭmdaun ch'ŏngyŏn Chŏn T'ae-il*; 1995), in which the life of the martyred union activist Chon T'ae-il—who immolated himself in 1970 at the age of twenty-two in protest against the exploitation of sweatshop workers—unfolds from the perspective of his biographer, a fugitive law-school graduate. In contrast, Kim's cinema is propelled by underdog protagonists—socially marginalized and oppressed subalterns such as homeless people, thugs, prostitutes, camptown residents, Amerasians, the disabled, inmates, and so on—whose only means of communicating their *ressentiment* is a shared sense of corporeal pain resulting from sadistic or masochistic acts of violence. As Steve Choe persuasively argues, "In the world of Kim's film, violence becomes the sole means of interaction for individuals who are atomized from discoursing human beings into their lowest common denominator, at the level of the body" (72). As defined by Kim Ki-duk himself, the violence of his characters is "a kind of body language" or a "physical expression rather than just negative violence" (Hummel).

As a Korean-born woman who has firsthand knowledge of gender discrimination in my native country, I am more sympathetic to the feminist criticism directed against Kim Ki-duk's alleged misogyny than to Tony Rayns's outrage at Kim's supposed lack of authenticity as an artist and his "undeserving" canonical standing as South Korea's preeminent provocateur. From a feminist perspective, it is indeed problematic that male-focalized class warfare is waged over the bodies of middle-class women in such films as *Crocodile*, *Bad Guy*, and *3-Iron*. However, Kim's oeuvre constitutes a visceral, bottom-to-top critique of social stratification in South Korea and cannot be fully grasped from a feminist perspective alone. As the Chinese American critic Sheng-mei Ma observes in his insightful essay on Kim's films, the director's "ritualization of violence dangles between sadomasochism that debases and reifies human beings and mysticism that negates [the] demarcation of human and non-human" (37–38). As Ma perceptively argues, Kim's cinema centers on voiceless, traumatized, or sometimes bodiless "nonpersons" who, regardless of their gender, are subject to various forms of unspeakable physical, social, or sexual violence. It is true that many female characters in Kim's films are beaten, raped, or coerced into prostitution. However, as the Korean film critic Kyung Hyun Kim observes, Kim Ki-duk's films "are no more misogynistic than the Korean society itself that has adopted its masculine hegemonic values by fusing neo-Confucian ethics and military rule and structure that stem from decades—if not centuries—of foreign occupation and martial violence" (135).

Moreover, Korean society does not have a monopoly on patriarchy and misogyny, for there have been numerous shocking depictions of sexual violence in the annals of world cinema (particularly in the films of Pier Paolo Pasolini, Imamura Shohei, Oshima Nagisa, and Miike Takashi), the likes of which far surpass anything that Kim's tormented imagination has churned out. What is unique about Kim's version of extreme cinema is the vivid nature of the psychological wounds apparent therein, caused by or leading to further violence, not violence in and by itself.

In his interview with Darcy Paquet, Kim Ki-duk reveals the authorial intentions of his cinema: "It's not my purpose to offend people, but the things I show in my films are genuine problems in our society. If mainstream society distances itself from the class of people I show in my films, it will only cause deeper conflicts. With my films, I want to help both sides understand each other" (Paquet, "Close-Up" 14). Kim's cinema creates an allegorical and often fantastical space where men and women from different class backgrounds encounter one another and reconcile their antagonisms. Several metaphysically imbued moments in Kim's cinema—such as the penultimate scene of *Birdcage Inn*, in which summer snow falls as a middle-class college student voluntarily takes a client as a stand-in for her sick sex-worker friend, or the final shot of *3-Iron*, wherein an upper-class housewife and a ghostly homeless man embrace one another on top of a weight scale pointing toward zero—suggest faint yet discernible hopes of interclass communication, against all odds and despite social prejudices. Kim's films can indeed promote interclass communication, but only when it is embraced by an open-minded audience.

As Kim So-hee puts it, "What Kim Ki-duk truly longs for is a gentle touch that will soothe his ragged inner world, yet keep his spirit intact. Sincere criticism along with encouragement from the heart" ("Biography" 6). Like the silent protagonist of *Breath,* a prisoner on death row (played by the Taiwanese actor Chang Chen) who is visited by a kindhearted stranger (an unhappily married, middle-class woman with whom the inmate bonds spiritually), Kim Ki-duk is awaiting a sympathetic audience who can recognize the vulnerable and innocent soul beneath the surface of his "extreme" cinema.

## On Suffering and Sufferance: Postcolonial Pain and the "Purloined Letter" in *Address Unknown*

In his seminar on Edgar Allan Poe's 1845 short story "The Purloined Letter," Jacques Lacan examines the psychoanalytic implications of the American author's titular epistle, around which much ill-directed investigation has gathered. In Poe's text, the Queen's secretive letter is purloined by Minister D in the royal *boudoir,* in the presence of the King (whose sudden appearance has allowed his spouse no time to hide the document from her table). Although the Queen witnesses the act of stealing, she has no choice but to keep silent, lest she draw her unsuspecting husband's attention. Commissioned by the Queen, the Prefect of the Parisian Police and his men ransack the Minister's hotel room to locate the private letter, but to no avail. Desperate and clueless, the Prefect enlists the help of the renowned private eye Dupin. The latter succeeds in retrieving the object (which has been purposely exposed in a stack of miscellaneous letters to evade the police's attention) by switching letters the same way that the Minister did on the earlier occasion. Calling attention to the repetitive scenes of letter-stealing, Lacan identifies three gazes/subjects in each scenario. The first gaze/subject is commanded by the King (scene 1) and the police (scene 2), who see nothing. The second belongs to the Queen (scene 1) and the Minister (scene 2), who see that the first individuals see nothing. The third gaze, that of the Minister (scene 1) and Dupin (scene 2), is one that is *all-seeing*, penetrating the first and second glances. The purloined letter is thus emblematic of an unspoken desire that connects all of these subject positions. Lacan refers to the object as "a letter which has been diverted from its path: one whose course has been *prolonged* . . . or, to revert to the language of the post office, *a letter in sufferance*" (43). According to the French theorist, "[T]he sender . . . receives from the receiver his own message in reverse form. Thus it is that what the 'purloined letter,' nay, the 'letter in sufferance,' means is that a letter always arrives at its destination" (53). As in Lacan's seminar and the short story upon which it is based, Kim Ki-duk's *Address Unknown* revolves around the metaphor of the "letter in sufferance."

Although Lacanian psychoanalysis may seem like an unexpected theoretical paradigm with which to approach Kim's cinema, I wish to suggest that *Address Unknown*—the filmmaker's sixth and most overtly political feature to date—can serve as a useful case study wherein psychoanalytic and postcolonial theories productively converge. The film's overarching narrative device is a letter whose delivery has been prolonged for an unidentified period of time. The sender of this letter is simply called Ch'ang-guk's mother, a middle-aged woman of a *kijich'on* (camptown) who lives with her biracial son, the offspring of an offscreen African American G.I. simply known to her as Michael (he is given no last name in the film). The only evidence of his existence is a framed photograph of the once-happy family that decorates their cramped makeshift home, a refurnished bus. Blood-red and bearing the insignia of the U.S. Air Force, the bus not only signifies the traces of American military dominance in South Korea but also is an extension of many "mobile homes" in Kim's cinema (from boat houses in *Wild Animals* and *The Bow* to colorfully-painted fishing shacks in *The Isle* and the temple in the lake in *Spring, Summer, Fall, Winter. . . . and Spring*). Michael apparently left the Korean woman and their son, Ch'ang-guk, years ago with the promise that he would send an invitation for them to immigrate to the United States. Desperately waiting for good news from her American "husband," the woman repeatedly sends a letter of inquiry, which keeps returning to her provisional residence with the U.S. postal message "address unknown" stamped on it. Confirming Lacan's thesis that "a letter always arrives at its destination," the reply from the United States finally *does* arrive at

Figure 2. Ch'ang-guk's mother, a camptown woman, repeatedly writes to her nonresponsive American "husband" in *Address Unknown*.

the end of the film, but it is too late. By the time it arrives, Ch'ang-guk and his mother have put an end to their suffering, having individually opted to take their own miserable lives.

Lacan's tripartite model of looking relations applies to *Address Unknown*, a bleak yet bewitching film set in a remote camptown during the 1970s. Paralleling Ch'ang-guk's mother's initially happy, eventually troubled relationship with Michael—a shared set of experiences lived outside the filmic frame and consigned to the past—is the high-school student Ŭn-ok's onscreen/present relationship with James, an alienated American soldier suffering emotional problems in a foreign land. In a way that might recall Rainer Werner Fassbinder's post–World War II period piece *The Marriage of Maria Braun* (*Die Ehe der Maria Braun*; 1979) or Brian De Palma's Vietnam War epic *Casualties of War* (1989), Kim situates their relationship within the larger context of U.S. military dominance from the opening sequence onward.

The thirty-second precredit montage shows close-up shots of a toy gun being made out of a wooden plank with a U.S. military logo. An extreme close-up of a boy's hand loading a steel pellet into the gun is followed by a medium close-up reaction shot of a ponytailed young girl who has been crowned with a C-ration can, presumably placed on her head by the same boy (her brother, we soon learn). The camera cuts to a long shot in which the boy on the left side of the frame directly (mis)fires at his sister, who, from the right side of the frame, thrusts her hands up to her face and makes visible her physical pain. The flashback montage fades out, and the screen is blanketed by a harsh overexposed light, an image of combined serenity and cruelty that segues to the bilingual title card, "Address Unknown." Rendered in Korean and English, the title is set against a tricolor fabric (green, brown, and black), suggesting an abstracted kind of camouflage patterned after U.S. military garb. The establishing shot reveals a rural shantytown, recessionally situated in the background, behind a vast field sprinkled with autumnal colors. Against the opening credits, the next image, a medium shot, shows two G.I.s raising an American flag to the tune of *The Star Spangled Banner.* After cutting to a long shot of the Camp Eagles front gate, the camera zooms in on the American flag, which fills the entire screen. In the shot that immediately follows, a group of G.I.s (including James) are seen jogging around the town in unison, chanting a marching song. This two-minute credit sequence concludes with an image of a jet departing from the camp, initiating a recurring visual motif throughout the film.

Figure 3. Ŭn-ok's brother injures his sister's eye with a toy gun made out of U.S. camp supplies in the opening flashback sequence of *Address Unknown.*

The camptown is an example of what the French philosopher Michel Foucault terms "heterotopia," a space riveted with visible difference and characterized by jarring juxtapositions, bringing together ideas and identities that might seem "incompatible with each other" (354). Neither the United States nor Korea but rather a hybridized mixture of the two, the heterotopic *kijich'on* is a neocolonial space filled with bilingual signage where state-of-the-art armaments and agricultural livestock sit side by side, and where the boundaries between the military and civilian quarters are blurred. While the barbed-wire fence surrounding the camp prominently displays a sign declaring "U.S. Government Property: No Trespassing," barring local residents from the American territory of Camp Eagles, U.S. military personnel enjoy unilateral access to the Korean town and its surrounding mountains for the purpose of training, policing, and R&R.

It is notable that James first spots Ŭn-ok while practicing basketball at her high-school playground and reencounters her during armed training on the mountain road that serves as the commute passage for students. Although the coy young girl initially recoils from the advances of the blue-eyed G.I. (mediated by offers of material goods, such as Coke and ice cream), she ultimately agrees to be his "sweetheart" in exchange for an eye-surgery operation in a U.S. military hospital. Ironically, she regains the sight of the eye that had been damaged by a toy gun (the object, mentioned earlier, recycled from camp supplies) thanks to American medical technology that is otherwise off-limits to Korean civilians. However, Ŭn-ok's American benefactor is quickly revealed to be a schizophrenic drug addict who goes from buying her a ring to suddenly slapping her hours later when the high-school girl refuses to take LSD with him.

Observing this mismatched couple's love-hate relationship from afar is Ŭn-ok's brokenhearted admirer Chi-hŭm, an effeminate apprentice sketch artist who is repeatedly bullied and robbed by two high-school thugs. Just as the violence endured by Ŭn-ok can be said to "originate" in the U.S. military, the bullies who harass Chi-hŭm are culturally positioned as "would-be Americans" who purchase *Playboy* magazines from camp guides and pose English questions to the dropout Chi-hŭm (whose inability to answer back in English is the ostensible reason for his "punishment"). Like Chi-hŭm, the dark-skinned Ch'ang-guk is another oppressed denizen of the camptown who, despite his fluent English, cannot obtain a job other than that of an apprentice in the dog slaughterhouse owned by a violent man named "Dog-eye" (a longtime boyfriend of Ch'ang-guk's mother). Ch'ang-guk transfers the abuse he receives from Dog-eye to his own mother, whom he curses and beats regularly.

Comparable to two scenes of self-inflicted flesh-mutilation in *The Isle*—"gross-out" moments involving sensitive body parts, the throat and the vagina—there are several shots and scenes in *Address Unknown* in which violence, accidental and intended, is directed at the eye. Ŭn-ok gets a glass eye as a young girl when her brother's makeshift gun accidentally sends a pellet into her optical tissues; Chi-hŭm hurts his own eye when his gun aimed at bullies misfires; and Ch'ang-guk's eye is pierced when Ŭn-ok attacks it with a pencil upon his peeping through a hole in her door. The final and most traumatic eye injury occurs when James, Ŭn-ok's neurotic G.I.-boyfriend-gone-AWOL, visits her in a state of panic and attempts to violate her body. When James tries to tattoo his name on the eighteen-year-old Korean girl's bosom as a marker of his ownership, Ŭn-ok knifes her own cured eye to absolve her debt to the American G.I. and to end their abusive relationship once and for all. The

Figure 4. Ch'ang-guk (background), Chi-hŭm (middleground), and Ŭn-ok (foreground) each experience eye injuries and social alienation in *Address Unknown*.

subaltern woman's masochistic act of violence shocks her neocolonial abuser, who flees the scene of the crime in fear, only to be shot in his groin area by avenging local archers, including Chi-hŭm. Earlier in the film, the camera captures the three social outcasts with eye injuries in a single long shot (Ch'ang-guk in the background, Chi-hŭm in the middle ground, and Ŭn-ok in the background), emphasizing the intersubjectivity of subaltern men and women in a postcolonial space dominated by U.S. military masculinity.

Like Poe's "The Purloined Letter," the narrative of *Address Unknown* is impregnated with "repetition automatism," to borrow Lacan's expression (32). The rondo manner in which violence is enacted against the eye involves different characters (Ŭn-ok's brother, Ŭn-ok, Ch'ang-guk, Chi-hŭm, bullies, James), and is summarized below:

| | | | | |
|---|---|---|---|---|
| Primal scene | Ŭn-ok's injury: | Ŭn-ok's brother (perpetrator) | → | Ŭn-ok (victim) |
| Scene 2 | Ch'ang-guk's injury: | Ŭn-ok (perpetrator) | → | Ch'ang-guk(victim) |
| Scene 3 | Chi-hŭm's injury: | bullies (indirect perpetrators) | → | Chi-hŭm (self-perpetrator) |
| Scene 4 | Ŭn-ok's injury: | James (indirect perpetrator) | → | Ŭn-ok (self-perpetrator) |

As Minister D's position in Poe's story shifts from what Lacan refers to as "the third gaze" (which takes in both the King's and Queen's positions) to "the second gaze" (which sees through the police's impotence and displays the letter in the open, only to be divulged as a result of Dupin's "third gaze"), Ŭn-ok's position slips from victim to perpetrator to self-perpetrator. Having lost sight in one eye due to a childhood accident, Ŭn-ok is literally the "blinded one," recalling the King and the police in Poe's story.

The love triangle involving Ŭn-ok, Chi-hŭm, and James parallels the familial/Oedipal triangle of Ch'ang-guk's mother, Ch'ang-guk, and Michael (the absent father). Ch'ang-guk's mother is metaphorically blinded in that she does not see the futility of her perpetually postponed American Dream and keeps on sending a letter to the unresponsive other, an act that Ch'ang-guk cannot bear to watch. Her obsession with America morphs into a make-believe fantasy to the extent that the wannabe-immigrant gives her order in English to local grocers, who in turn refuse to serve her. The extremity of the mother's blindness (which may be a kind of psychological self-defense measure) provokes Ch'ang-guk's violent fury, which reaches its climax when the son returns to their vehicular home after killing Dog-eye in revenge. In that hybridized space of cultural intermixing and combined movement and stasis, he knifes the father's tattoo from his mother's breast. Both couples—Ŭn-ok and Chi-hŭm as well as the mother and Ch'ang-guk—eventually reconcile in tears, but only after the foreign men's traces (Ŭn-ok's cured eye and the mother's love mark) have been removed from these female bodies. Such moments of catharsis are fleeting, for the narrative soon plunges into a tragic dénouement in which Chi-hŭm is sent to prison for injuring an American G.I., while Ch'ang-guk and his mother commit suicide without receiving the long-awaited letter from the United States.

Following Lacan's tripartite model of positing different gazes and subjectivities based on Poe's "The Purloined Letter," both Ŭn-ok and Ch'ang-guk's mother are confined to the first position, that of "blindness." Before her eye surgery, Ŭn-ok is warned twice by Korean men—Dog-eye and Chi-hŭm—not to receive favors from James. Paying the price for neglecting their foresight, she later returns to her original state of disability by harming her repaired eye voluntarily. The male characters Chi-hŭm and Ch'ang-guk are the bearers of the second gaze insofar as they are able to see the "sight-challenged" women with pathos (in Chi-hŭm's case) or rage (in Ch'ang-guk's case). Chi-hŭm is ultimately a *meta-seer* thanks to his "third gaze" positionality as someone who observes both Ŭn-ok's relationship with James and Ch'ang-guk's relationship with the mother from a distance. To borrow Kim Ki-duk's own words, "Ŭn-ok represents the 1960s, when Korean children were delighted by ice creams handed out by American G.I.s, while Ch'ang-guk symbolizes the 1970s, as a mixed-race child between one of those G.I.s and a Korean woman. Chi-hŭm is a portrait of ourselves in the 1980s and 1990s, seeing everything from a macro perspective" (Kim So-hee, "Film Director Kim Ki-duk"). As the bearer of the third, all-encompassing gaze, Chi-hŭm functions as the audience's primary identificatory conduit as well as an autobiographical stand-in for the director himself. It is no coincidence that Kim Ki-duk used the pseudonym Kim Chi-hŭm when entering the KOFIC screenwriting contest of 1995 (for which he received the top prize, an honor that opened the doors for his directorial career). In his interview with Kim So-hee, reprinted in this volume, Kim compares Chi-hŭm, Ch'ang-guk, and Ŭn-ok—characters based on his own adolescent self and friends—to "abandoned letters" bearing unknown addresses that were scattered on the ground during his childhood. The director goes on to call them "children of an 'era which is yet to be received.'"

As seen in *Address Unknown,* U.S. militarism has significantly altered the lives of Koreans since the first American troops entered the liberated Japanese colony in 1945 and staked out a three-year military occupation. Following the Korean War (1950–53), U.S. troops became permanently installed in South Korea on the pretext of protecting the host country from Communist threats from the North. As a result, over one million Korean women have served as "entertainment hostesses" to accommodate the R&R needs of American G.I.s, VIPs of the South Korean government. As Katharine H. S. Moon asserts in her book *Sex among Allies,* U.S. military prostitution in South Korea (as well as other Asian-Pacific regions) is not simply a matter of international transactions involving women's bodies but also a state-intervening system, a site of negotiations and tensions between the two involved governments (1). As Cynthia Enloe asserts, "None of these institutions—multilateral alliances, bilateral alliances, foreign military assistance programmes—can achieve their militarizing objective without controlling women for the sake of militarizing men" (qtd. in Moon 11). Institutionalized prostitution and camptown-building indeed played significant roles in maintaining the U.S.–Republic of Korea (ROK) joint-defense alliance during and after the Korean War. Although prostitution is nominally illegal in South Korea, the bars, clubs, and brothels in *kijich'on* sites have been endorsed and regulated by the government. Multifariously exploited by the Korean authorities (translating the women's earnings of U.S. dollars into a contribution to the nation's economic development while granting little in the way of social benefits), pimps and bar owners (who often coerce the women into prostitution, confiscate large percentages of their income, and slave-trade them through a debt-bond system), and U.S. military men (many of whom abuse the women physically and psychologically), *kijich'on* women and their mixed-race children typically have been abandoned by G.I. fathers and treated as outsiders by a Korean society prizing female virtues and a racially homogenous citizenry.

One of the most common Korean terms to designate a *kijich'on* sex worker is *yanggongju* (foreign princess or Western princess), a term applied to Ch'ang-guk's mother by bullies in *Address Unknown*. This derogatory expression exudes a high degree of cynicism and irony because *gongju* ("princess") is a common word to describe middle-class Korean girls' and women's perceived norm of excessive femininity, maintained and displayed by conformist modes of consumption, clothing, hairstyles, accessories, make-up, and cosmetic surgery (the latter is the subject of Kim Ki-duk's thirteenth film, *Time*). The mainstream media has encouraged and capitalized on this social phenomenon, which is popularly known as *gongju pyŏng* (princess fever), by disseminating grossly exhibitionistic, cosmetically coated, floridly decorated doll images through the major pipelines of popular culture: sitcoms, dramas, variety shows, and commercials. While the college-educated, middle-class, "good" *gongju* inhabits a privileged position within the rigidly circumscribed ideal of femininity constructed for the pleasure of Korean males, the undereducated, working-class, "bad" *yanggongju* poses a threat to Korean patriarchy precisely because she bears the traces of and thus represents the infiltration and domination of Western (specifically American) masculinity in South Korea. As Katharine H. S. Moon points out, "[K]ijich'on women are [not only] living symbols of the destruction, poverty, bloodshed, and separation from family of Korea's civil war [but also] living testaments of Korea's geographical and political division into North and South and of the South's military insecurity and consequent dependence on the United States" (8). Therefore, it should come as no surprise that the *yanggongju* occupies a precarious yet iconographic place in Korean literature and film as an allegorical personification of the divided nation thrown headfirst into modernization and Westernization and faced with the eternal specter of U.S. military intervention/occupation as well as unabated cultural imperialism.

Throughout South Korean cinema's Golden Age of the 1950s and 1960s, *yanggongju* figures were depicted either as temptresses equivalent to the dangerous, powerful, and hypersexual femmes fatales of American film noir or tragic "fallen women" forced to sell their bodies out of economic urgency and familial obligations. While in Shin Sang-ok (Sin Sang-ok)'s crime thriller *Hell Flower* (*Chiokwha*; 1958), the *yanggongju* Sonya is an egoistic "spider woman" who is responsible for seducing her own brother-in-law and gets killed by the avenging husband, in Yu Hyun-mok (Yu Hyŏn-mok)'s realist classic *The Stray Bullet* (*Obalt'an*; 1961), Myŏng-suk becomes a *yanggongju* to alleviate the burden of her underpaid accountant brother Ch'ŏr-ho, who is singlehandedly supporting the extended Song family (their demented mother, Ch'ŏr-ho's pregnant wife and young daughter, and his three siblings) in poverty-stricken postwar Seoul.

In the wake of the 1980 Kwangju Massacre, which is responsible for the rise of anti-Americanism in South Korea due largely to the alleged complicity of the U.S. military,[11] the anti-authoritarian labor-student demonstrations comprising the *minjung* (people) movement of the 1980s and early 1990s instigated a new perception and interest in *kijich'on* sex workers. Having long been neglected and despised as the lowest of the low, these women emerged as the victimized "sisters and daughters" of the nation enslaved by American imperialists, so long as their legacy was couched within the rhetoric of nationalist activism and political dissidence. One case in particular—the brutal rape and murder in 1992 of a barwoman, Yun Kŭm-i, by Private Kenneth Markle (who stuffed two beer bottles into Yun's womb, a cola bottle into her uterus, and an umbrella into her anus after killing her)—flamed nationwide rage and protests against the U.S. military. In the Korean New Wave filmmaker Chung Ji-young's maternal melodrama *Silver Stallion* (*Ŭnma nŭn toraoji atnŭnda*; 1990), the peasant widow Ollye becomes a "Yankee wife" after being brutally raped by two American G.I.s and then ostracized by villagers during the Korean War. In Yi Kwang-mo's lyrical art film *Spring in My Hometown* (*Arŭmdaun sijŏl*; 1998), Ch'ang-hŭi's mother, a *kijich'on* laundry woman, is forced to have sex with an African American officer as payment for G.I. garments that have been stolen. It is even suggested that some rough G.I.s might have murdered Ch'ang-hŭi in revenge for the death of one of their men, who perished as a result of the arson committed by the young boy (who burned down the abandoned mill where his mother had a sexual encounter with the G.I. after witnessing the traumatic scene). In each of these films, focalized through the son's perspective, the *yanggongju* mother serves as a corporeal metaphor of the oppressed nation and a textual symptom of a male trauma that necessitates physical externalizing for it to be dealt with and ultimately overcome.

Unlike their Golden Age counterparts made under the dictatorial Park Chung Hee regime, which prohibited "films that might profit the enemy countries or any country that is in conflict with the Republic of Korea" (explicitly negative portrayals of American allies were to be inversely interpreted as encouragements of the communist enemy), post-authoritarian films such as *Silver Stallion* and *Spring in My Hometown* do not shy away from directly confronting U.S. military crimes against Korean women and children.[12] For the most part, *Address Unknown* inherits the double-edged representational strategy of the aforementioned films in which the violated female body is cast as the allegory of the (neo)colonized nation and the abject sign of male trauma.

Because Kim's film is focalized through the male gaze, which subjugates female characters as the object of sexual fantasy or disciplinary reform, it appears to conform to Laura Mulvey's oft quoted, frequently debated scopic paradigm of narrative cinema, which can be bifurcated into active/male/gaze and passive/female/spectacle. However, unlike Euro-American male protagonists, disempowered Korean male characters are unable to indulge in fetishistic or voyeuristic scopophilia (pleasure in looking) due to sociopolitical conditions that undercut their visual pleasure and/or impair their vision. In her study of *The Stray Bullet,* Eunsun Cho calls this unique phenomenon "scopophobia" (fear of/in looking), a condition that is exemplified by Ch'or-ho's averted gaze away from Myŏng-suk's act of prostitution in the bus scene where the brother accidentally spots his sister with an American G.I. from the window (103–4). Despite his privileged status as the "third gazer" (the one who sees all from a detached position), Chi-hŭm likewise bears the traces of scopophobia, particularly in relation to Ŭn-ok, the object of his forlorn affection who is raped by bullies in the greenhouse (where the two were on the verge of having consensual sex) and who enters into a kind of contractual relationship with James. For Chi-hŭm, these are humiliating situations that he has no choice but to watch helplessly.

Ŭn-ok, however, is not simply a passive victim. The aforementioned eye-gouging scene may seem to be another gratuitous *yŏpgi* or "gross-out" moment prevalent within Kim's cruel universe, wherein the masochistic woman enacts senseless self-mutilation. However, the postcolonial significance of its resistant message cannot be overemphasized. Ŭn-ok's eye-knifing is a symbolic act of "speaking back" to the cruelty of the physical and mental violence committed by U.S. military personnel against countless Korean women during and after the Korean War. James can finally *see* the atrocious nature of his own violence when Ŭn-ok fearlessly exhibits its mechanism, using her own eye as the target. Only then does he cower and turn away from his victim in shame and perhaps abject horror. It should also be noted that, though frequently directed at female bodies, excessive corporeal violence in Kim's films is not gender-specific. Although it appears that Chi-hŭm and other Korean men have come to Ŭn-ok's rescue belatedly and that they punish James by figuratively castrating him, Chi-hŭm is arrested for injuring an American G.I. and shot in his knee by a policeman (for resisting transport to a prison) toward the film's end.

Although Ch'ang-guk habitually releases his frustration and anger by beating his mother and even cuts away his black father's tattoo from her breast, it is his demented mother who cannibalizes the son's frozen body after his peculiar head-dive suicide in the wintry rice field. The mother immolates her son's remains and then herself shortly after this extreme

Figure 5. A scene of violent confrontation between the neocolonial abuser (James) and the subaltern woman (Eŭn-ok) in *Address Unknown.*

act of necrophilic cannibalism. As Myung Ja Kim observes, the literally devouring mother "symbolically unbirths" her son and "erases all traces of them both" in fire (259). The disturbing yet comically inflected image of Ch'ang-guk's half-buried, half-visible body planted headlong in the mud—a shot that might recall the image of a framed painting plugged into a sandy beach near the beginning of *Birdcage Inn*—is a fitting visual correlative of the character's inability to belong to the homeland, a country that persists in rejecting him even after his death.

*Address Unknown* illustrates how the national and the postcolonial can be "inserted" into Poe's purloined letter and Lacan's psychoanalytically driven reading of it. The persistent letter of *yanggongju* represents a failed, missed, or denied chance at communication not only between an American military man and his abandoned Korean wife and son, but also between the two nations that they represent. The delayed and prolonged communication between the (neo)colonizer/dominator and the colonized/dominated evinces quite clearly the historical snarls and schisms subtending (post)colonial double temporality. The Bengali subaltern-studies scholar Dipesh Chakrabarty articulates the temporal struggle between the colonizer and the colonized as that of the "not yet" and the "now" (8–9). Whereas the colonizer continues to delay the emancipation of the colonized through the "waiting room" mantra of "not yet," the anticolonial nationalist countervenes this moratorium on political independence by emphasizing the urgency of the "now." Like Ch'ang-guk and his mother, many *kijich'on* women and biracial children experience the immediacy of the "now," as they are desperate to escape the harsh realities of poverty, discrimination, and ostracism, while G.I.s returning home typically evade their paternal responsibilities with the colonizer's rhetoric of the "not yet" (wait . . . I will send for you and the baby later . . . ), making the women and children patiently—pointlessly—await the never-to-come invitation from the United States.

Translated into national terms, as early as November 1943, representatives of the world's three superpowers—the United States, Great Britain, and the Republic of China—proclaimed, in the Cairo Declaration, that "in due course Korea shall become free and independent." The "not now" rhetoric in the controversial phrase "in due course" did not escape the attention of Korean nationalists. On August 11, 1945, four days prior to the Japanese surrender, the Truman administration proposed to Joseph Stalin a division of Korea along the thirty-eighth parallel, a hasty decision propelled by fear of postwar Soviet expansion in the Asia-Pacific region (Cumings 186–87). Although the American military occupation in southern Korea was considerably shorter than what Franklin D. Roosevelt had originally envisioned during World War II,[13] the national division was made indefinite as the Soviet-American Joint Commission failed to agree on the terms of reunification due to the mounting cold-war rivalry. The United States subsequently secured its long-term hegemony in the Republic of Korea—the new capitalist regime it defended during the Korean War—with the signing of the Mutual Defense Treaty in October 1953 (under which the United States maintained two infantry divisions and several air force squadrons in South Korea until 1971, when the number of troops was reduced to thirty-seven thousand).[14] Just as South Korea has technically been at war with the North for the past six decades, the U.S. promise of protection has likewise been prolonged, perpetuating its military/economic/cultural dominance in the region.

This impossible (post)colonial convergence not only implies a temporal paradigm (the perpetual delay of South Korea's military sovereignty and reunification with northern brethren) but also evokes a spatial dynamic of estrangement and alienation (caused by the periodic shipment of thousands of young American soldiers to rural Korea, where most camps are located). James, a G.I. who suffers loneliness and claustrophobia in the mountainous Korean countryside (nothing like his open prairie home), bursts into hysteria during military training, frantically yelling, "Where is the fucking enemy? What are we doing in somebody else's backyard?" Through ghostly scenes of the G.I.s' combat maneuvers and recurring shots of combat planes patrolling the peaceful village, the film exposes the emptiness and futility of the U.S. military excursion in South Korea against invisible Communists residing on the other side of the Demilitarized Zone (DMZ). While remaining critical of the hegemonic "military-industrial complex" (to use Dwight D. Eisenhower's famous expression), Kim's *Address Unknown* cleverly finds a way to personify the U.S.'s double-faced foreign policy in South Korea (which can be termed as "limited commitment" or "self-serving benevolence") in the contradictory character of James, who shuttles between protector and perpetrator over the course of the film.

In his reading of Lacan's seminar on "The Purloined Letter," Slavoj Žižek argues that in the realm of the real,

> "[A] letter always arrives at its destination" equals what "meeting one's fate" means: "we will all die" . . . the only letter that nobody can evade, that sooner or later reaches us, i.e., the letter which has each of us as its infallible addressee, is death. . . . [T]he closing of the letter's circuit equals its consumption. The crucial point here is the imaginary, the symbolic, and the real dimension of "a letter always arrives at its destination" are not external to each other: at the end of the imaginary as well as the symbolic itinerary, we encounter the Real. (20–21)

The repressed real of the postcolonial letter relentlessly returns toward the end of the film. Immediately before Ch'ang-guk's mother immolates herself, the long-awaited letter from the other arrives at her door as if it were a death warrant. The letter addressed to the now-dead woman is carried away by the wind to the field where a G.I. performing maneuvers picks it up and begins reading it aloud: "Dear Ch'ang-guk's mother, How are you? My name is Clint and I own a small deli in California. Are you. . . ." The closing music and credits steal into the scene, muting his voice.

This enigmatic ending may have left some viewers confused, as evidenced by the utter bewilderment confessed by the otherwise astute film critic Chuck Kleinhans:

> What should we make of it? Has she begun to write a "mail order bride" service? But the salutation is strange. . . . Has she been writing to try to get not herself but her son relocated to the United States? We don't know, but the film ends by opening up another door, a lost chance. (195)

Apparently, neither of Kleinhans's conjectures is what Kim Ki-duk originally intended. In the earlier script, the sender is identified as a neighbor conveying the news of Michael's death and wishing happiness to Ch'ang-guk and his mother ("I Met the Director Kim Ki-duk"). According to this scenario, both letters—from Ch'ang-guk's mother to Michael as well as from his neighbor to Ch'ang-guk's mother—are impossible signifiers addressed to an absent/deceased party. They cannot be imaged in the realm of the imaginary, nor can they be linguistically signified in the realm of the symbolic. The enigmatic letter from the United States (whose sender is unknown, just as in Poe's detective story) remains unread to the audience as well as its addressee. The sole reader of the letter is a ghostlike G.I. in a white coat whose painted face is pale and lifeless. The physical existence of the soldier is further questioned in the final long shot: The spectral figure is seen alone on the misty field, a space from which his fellow trainees have (magically?) disappeared. The abstracted colonial other is the *ultimate* blind one, a spectral presence whose perpetual unknowing of the traumatic histories of the *yanggongju* and her "tragic mulatto" son aggravates rather than relieves spectatorial mourning.

Going into the production of *Address Unknown*, Kim Ki-duk posed the question, "Where does our cruelty come from?" (Kim So-hee interview reprinted in this volume). He apparently found a partial answer in modern Korean history itself, which is punctuated with many violent ruptures, including national division, civil war, and cold-war military confrontations—themes that recur in a few of his other films, such as *Wild Animals* (which depicts a friendship between a South Korean street artist and an AWOL North Korean solider exiled in Paris) and *The Coast Guard* (set along the heavily armed coastal border between the two Koreas). The latter film opens with a caption that overtly situates its narrative in the cold-war context:

> The Korean peninsula is the only divided country on earth. After the Korean War, South Korea's coastline has been surrounded by barbed-wire fences to block any attack from North Korea. Since the armistice, twenty cases of North Korean spy infiltration have taken place. Even now, whoever enters the coast after sunset can be considered a spy and be killed.

Reminiscent of the boot-camp sequence in Stanley Kubrick's Vietnam War film *Full Metal Jacket* (1987), *The Coast Guard* begins by introducing the audience to a group of marines who are undergoing physical training on the muddy shore and whose individuality is rendered indiscernible through an image of military collectivism. The coast guards are also seen being indoctrinated by their anti-Communist commander, who instills an ideological fear of spies' ambush tactics and encourages his men to ready themselves for an enemy attack. The film's protagonist, Private Kang, is a mentally unbalanced antihero who is obsessed with the prospect of killing North Korean spies. One night, he spots a human figure moving in the restricted coastal area and wipes out what he believes to be a northern spy through a rapid shower of bullets followed by a grenade attack. However, the suspected spy turns out to be an inebriated village punk who had been copulating with his girlfriend. Instead of being disciplined for his (accidental) civilian killing, the marine is awarded a special seven-day vacation for his "proper measures to stop an infiltrator."

Guilt and paranoia plunge the man deeper into dementia and thoughts of aggression. Diagnosed as being "unfit for duty" by a psychiatrist, Kang is discharged only to return to his camp begging to be readmitted, literally enacting the famous slogan, "once a marine, always a marine." Although, as a civilian, Kang is denied access to military facilities, he hovers outside the barbed-wired gate and makes ghostly, nocturnal intrusions into his ex–platoon buddies' barracks and guard posts, provoking skirmishes among marines that escalate into fatal shooting incidents. Mirroring his haunting presence is that of Yŏng-mi, the dead man's bereaved girlfriend who has slipped into insanity after witnessing the corporeal dismemberment of her loved one. Traumatized, she sleeps with several marines, including the platoon leader, mistaking them for her dead boyfriend. After the madwoman is impregnated by one of the marines, the platoon leader arranges for his inexperienced medic to perform an abortion, eliminating his and his men's paternal responsibilities. After the forced abortion takes place in a camp shack, Yŏng-mi returns to her brother's sushi restaurant with an open wound and bathes herself in a fish tank, turning the water red with her blood. Transferring the violence that she has received from military men, the violated woman bites the heads of live fish in the tank, killing them. As in *Address Unknown,* here Kim Ki-duk draws parallels between state-to-citizen military violence, male-to-female gendered violence, and human-to-animal interspecies violence.

*The Coast Guard* closes with a fish-out-of-water scene involving Private Kang, who performs a one-man military exercise in the heart of Seoul's shopping district, Myŏngdong. Initially, his mannequin-like wielding of the gun induces curiosity and derision among the circling crowd until the armed ex-marine stabs a spectator with his bayonet. As the crowd screams in panic, five armed policemen rush to the scene and circle around the crazed marine, who appears to have lost contact with reality. The camera zeroes in on the demented ex-solder's face, shown in close-up, as he aims his gun directly at the offscreen police/crowd/audience, as if indicting anyone and everyone for their complicity in South Korea's defense-oriented, militaristic culture. The screen becomes blank with the sound of a gunshot, only to segue into a happier flashback image of several marines (including Private Kang) playing volleyball across a net that divides the court, its shape like that of the Korean peninsula engraved in stones. An overhead shot captures the digitally generated disappearance of the demarcation net, projecting Kim Ki-duk's ideal vision of the reunified peninsula, with no border violence or unrest in sight.[15]

The extremity of Kim's cinema should not—indeed, *cannot*—be divorced from its historical and social context, as evidenced by *Address Unknown* and *The Coast Guard.* It is tempting to point toward the long history of U.S. military domination as the origin of cruelty and misery in Korean camptowns in the former film. For example, the audience is invited to conjecture that Dog-eye's extreme violence and anger derives partially from his offscreen past as a laborer in the U.S. camp. In his rare compassionate moments, the dog butcher shares words of wisdom with his Amerasian apprentice, Ch'ang-guk, telling him, "To speak good English is no good thing—you've gotta do everything those Yankees tell you to. Everything!" However, except for James, the "Yankees" are relegated to the background as depersonalized bystanders, just as Korean characters function in such American films as Robert Altman's *MASH* (1970), Spike Lee's *Do the Right Thing* (1989), Joel Schumacher's *Falling Down* (1993), and Paul Haggis's *Crash* (2004). While not entirely devoid of anticolonial subtexts (particularly in scenes involving James's violence against Ŭn-ok), *Address Unknown* seems more critical of the "local complicity in neo-colonialism" (Kleinhans 184) and the circular nature of violence as a whole. Although the neocolonial presence of the United States remains unseen (or offscreen) in *The Coast Guard,* the South Korean government's complicity in the construction of a U.S. cold-war empire is subtly criticized in a line delivered by a supporting character, who alludes to the recreational killing of soldiers in the Vietnam War, where South Korean troops fought and committed atrocities alongside Americans from 1965 to 1973. Neocolonial violence is only one part of "a continuous cycle of violence, humiliation, and abuse at every level and for every character" (Kleinhans 186)—a cycle that includes rape, bullying, domestic violence, dating abuse, animal cruelty, and racial discrimination, and which begets more violence in the form of murders, suicides, and self-mutilation. As Steve Choe rightly points out, "a form of the community is secured through this circle of cruelty" in the narrative, its palpable pathos stemming "from the inescapable repetition of this violence, both horizontally throughout the community and vertically from one generation to another, and from an inability to 'work through' the past trauma" (67, 72).

According to the American studies scholar Christina Klein, the term "ambivalent" aptly describes "South Korea's relationship with the United States," a relationship "that its supporters characterize as a close alliance and its critics as neocolonial" (874). As if eloquently translating such historical and geopolitical ambivalence into visual terms, *Address Unknown* ends on an ambiguous note with a static long shot of an innocent, if oblivious, G.I. stranded in a Korean field. The film's inconclusive dénouement accentuates the director's own equivocal statement about the political issue attending U.S.-Korean relations: "[T]he position I take in *Address Unknown* is at the conjunction between 'pro-U.S.' and 'anti-U.S.' sentiments" (Kim So-hee interview reprinted in this volume). Like Dupin in Poe's story, Kim Ki-duk applies a clairvoyant "third gaze" to the postcolonial history of his nation and the many missed moments of possibly reciprocal communication between colonizer and colonized, doing so without passing simplistic judgments.

## Reconciling the Paradox of Silence and Apologia: *Bad Guy*, *The Isle*, and *3-Iron*

As many observers have noted, silence is a recurring motif in Kim Kiduk's cinema. According to the French critic Cédric Lagandré, Kim's films hinge on "the impossibility of language itself: impossibility, consequently, of adapting to the social world, of polishing one's vices, of softening them through relationships with fellow humans" (60). Lagandré goes on to state,

> Because of that original wound, because of those "unkept promises," about which Kim Ki-duk repeats in his interviews that they are the origin of all violence . . . everybody withdraws into a stubborn silence. . . ."The characters in my films are not mute," said Kim Ki-duk. "They just don't believe in verbal communication." It is not that they cannot speak, it's that they don't want to speak. They are not silent through the inability to speak, but through the inability to believe in words. (67)

Like his characters, Kim withdrew into a bubble of "stubborn silence" after being "wounded" by the words of unsympathetic critics and after having become exhausted from defending his films, controversy after controversy.

In August 2006, Kim Ki-duk broke his two-year media silence and held a press conference arranged by Sponge, the Korean distributor of his film *Time,* produced by the Japanese company Happinet Pictures.[16] This otherwise uneventful thirty-minute publicity gig for a small art film generated unexpected scandal when two comments by Kim were sensationalized by the mainstream media and within various Web communities. First, when asked about his opinion on the success of the mega-blockbuster *The Host* (*Koemul*; 2006), which had opened in an unprecedented 620 theaters and would become the highest-grossing domestic film of all time, Kim ambiguously described the phenomenon as "a perfect meeting between the level of Korean audience and the level of Korean cinema" (qtd. in Paquet, "Helmer Ignites" 16). Second, in an outburst of frustration over considerably lower admissions for his films in South Korea (as opposed to North America and Europe), the director suggested that he might stop "exporting" his films to South Korea should *Time* sink at the box office. These angst-ridden statements should be contextualized within the oligopolistic market conditions of the Korean film industry, where the Big Three investor-distributor-exhibitor majors—CJ-CGV, Showbox-Megabox, and Lotte Entertainment-Cinema—dominate approximately 60 percent of the total market share, driving independent art films such as Kim's into near-extinction (Howard 94). (Mis)interpreting Kim's remarks as a sign of his condescension and hostility toward Korean audiences, however, thousands of "netizens" (or Internet citizens) posted invectives against the director in online discussion boards and chat rooms.[17]

This sudden burst of public frenzy led to Kim Ki-duk's official apology to the production crew of *The Host* as well as to national audiences, a message that was e-mailed to major South Korean media institutions. In his statement, Kim evaluates his films in a self-deprecating way:

> My movies are lamentable for uncovering the "genitals" that everyone wants to hide; I am guilty for contributing only incredulity to an unstable future and society; and I feel shame and regret for having wasted time making movies without understanding the feelings of those who wish to avoid excrement. . . . I apologize for making the public watch my films under the pretext of the difficult situation of independent cinema, and I apologize for exaggerating the hideous and dark aspects of Korean society and insulting excellent Korean filmmakers with my works that ape art-house cinema but are, in fact, self-tortured pieces of masturbation, or maybe they're just garbage. Now I realize I am seriously mentally challenged and inadequate for life in Korea. (qtd. in Jamier)

Kim's choice of extreme vocabulary—"excrement," "garbage," and "mentally challenged"—once again captured the media's attention, granting the director a nearly unprecedented amount of publicity. Several domestic critics reacted to the apology in a cynical way. For example, Sŏng Ŭn-ae states, "It's uncertain where the sincerity in Kim Ki-duk's radical masochism ends and where the ridicule of audiences or his 'performance' begins" (317). What Sŏng fails to openly consider is the *irony* of the director's apology, in which Kim defines himself and frames his films from the perspective of his worst detractors. The whole situation is uncannily reminiscent of several scenes in Kim's motion pictures, where outlaw protagonists are pressed by social elites to confess or apologize for their supposed sins.

Take the notorious six-minute opening sequence of *Bad Guy*, for instance. A quintessential Kim hero, played by Cho Chae-hyŏn (referred to by Tony Rayns as "the De Niro to Kim's Scorsese"), sluggishly enters the heart of Seoul's commercial district, Myŏngdong. In front of the upscale Lotte Department Store, the only thing that this lowlife thug dressed in black can afford to eat is a skewer of processed fish, purchased from a makeshift food stand. While navigating passersby on the street, Cho's character (Han-gi) spots a beautiful college girl (Sŏn-hwa) in a blue polka-dot dress and a white cardigan sitting on a department-store bench, a member of the middle class clearly beyond his reach. Nevertheless, Han-gi approaches the bench and sits awkwardly by her side as if demanding equal status.

After phoning her boyfriend, for whom she is waiting, Sŏn-hwa notices this stranger sitting beside her and moves to an adjacent bench, disgust etched on her face. After her boyfriend arrives, the college couple avoids Han-gi, glancing derisively at him. Only when the unwelcome intruder walks away does the couple begin to feel at ease. Provoked by their innocent yet mindless sweet-nothings, Han-gi turns back and snatches Sŏn-hwa, planting a forceful kiss on her lips. The boyfriend intervenes, banging Han-gi's body with a nearby garbage can and punching him in the face. An enraged Sŏn-hwa stops Han-gi, when he starts to withdraw, barking at him, "Where are you going? Apologize! In front of everybody." Emerging from the crowd that begins to circle around, three marines block the way of Han-gi's exit. They order him to "apologize to the lady." When Han-gi resists, the marines gang up and beat him, calling him a "gangster." The marines force the bloody, apparently unrepentant culprit to kneel in front of the insulted college girl and demand that he apologize. As the defiant offender continues to remain silent, Sŏn-hwa

Figure 6. The underclass antihero Han-gi dares to desire the beautiful college student Sŏn-hwa in the controversial opening sequence of *Bad Guy.*

spits on him, calling him "a crazy bastard." After the crowd dissipates, Han-gi turns his face to the side, at ninety degrees, displaying his profile on the left side of the frame. The film's title, "Bad Guy," appears next to the frozen close-up of the socially branded outlaw.

This confrontational opening is reminiscent of a passage from Frantz Fanon's *The Wretched of the Earth*, in which the Martinique-born philosopher describes the psychology of the dominated native in colonial society:

> The look that the native turns on the [white] settler's town is a look of lust, a look of envy; it expresses his dreams of possession—all manner of possession: to sit at the settler's table, to sleep in the settler's bed, with his wife if possible. The colonized man is an envious man. And this the settler knows very well; when their glances meet he ascertains bitterly, always on the defensive, "They want to take our place." (39)

Although the class antagonism depicted in this opening scene may appear to be distinct from the racially mediated colonial tensions elaborated in Fanon's treatise, the dark clothing and facial complexion symbolically encode Han-gi's character as a "black man," an internally colonized subject who belongs to "the Negro village, the medina, the reservation . . . a place of ill fame, peopled by men of evil repute." His encroachment on the "well-fed town, an easygoing town . . . always full of good things" (Fanon 39), is rendered an unpardonable offense. However, what is more threatening is his envy and *ressentiment,* his insolent desire to look at and possess the other man's girlfriend.

Not unlike the colonial power structure explained by Fanon, postcolonial South Korean society can be characterized by the decades-long collusion between militaristic, educational, and capitalistic powers, which together exert a hegemonic hold on the populace. The soldiers intervene to safeguard privileged members of the consumption-driven middle class who possess material and cultural capital. Seen from a subaltern perspective, the arrogance of the college girl (who forces a lower-class man to speak despite his throat injury) partially justifies his vengeful scheme to bring her down to his depressed station in life. Despite his despicable act of luring Sŏn-hwa into the world of prostitution, Han-gi is no ordinary "bad guy." Not only does he eventually display remorse and agony in witnessing Sŏn-hwa's degradation, but he is also altruistic and self-sacrificial in protecting his underlings (he voluntarily goes to prison for the murder committed by Chŏng-t'ae and buries a knife after being stabbed with it by a jealous Myŏng-su, to eliminate evidence of his own murder).

Kim's cinema puts forth a unique variation on the oppressed subaltern who, according to the postcolonial critic Gayatri Chakravorty Spivak, "cannot be heard or read . . . [and] cannot speak" (104). Significantly, Kim's muted subaltern characters *can* but *will not* speak, as is the case for T'ae-sŏk of *3-Iron,* a harmless housebreaker who remains silent despite his repeated beatings at the hands of a police officer who attempts to extract a false confession of rape. The same goes for Hŭi-jin of *The Isle,* a gatekeeper of a remote fishing resort who, after sexually servicing one of the customers, refuses to humor him verbally in exchange for a big tip. In both cases, subaltern characters—a homeless man and a part-time sex worker, respectively—challenge the authority of the dominant class by *not* speaking what others wish to hear from them (and by extension, not speaking at all, to the consternation of their impatient listeners).

In *The Isle,* Kim Ki-duk deliberately makes it explicit that his heroine's muteness is a choice, not a physical impairment. Hŭi-jin's penny-pinching client (who is pushed to pay the woman for her service to him and his gambling partner) complains, "I know that you can talk. You moaned while doing it." Because she does not capitulate and continues to maintain her silence, the irritated fisherman throws five ten-thousand-won bills (approximately forty-five dollars) on the lake's surface, which Kim's camera captures in close-up. The woman picks up the money stoically and rows away from the floating fishing shack. In a low-key long shot, Hŭi-jin is seen washing her groin area. She sits on her boat, surrounded by water that has been contaminated by human waste (there are no flushing toilets on the bright yellow, green, and lavender floats for overnight fishermen). In the next interior shot, the humiliated woman dries the hard-earned bills with a newspaper. Her shame pushes her to strangle herself with a steel wire tied to a fishhook on the wooden window panel. The suicide attempt fails when the hook is loosened and falls off without sustaining the tension of the tightening wire.

This brutal Hitchcockian scene in *The Isle* consists of seven shots: a close-up of the wet newspaper, a tilted medium shot of the woman looking down at the bills underneath the paper, a long shot of the woman looking out the window, an extreme close-up of the wire being pulled from the window area, a mirror image of the woman strangling herself, an extreme close-up of the loosening hook, and a medium shot of the window from which the hook springs. Kim's use of montage conveys the heroine's desperate emotions as well as her physical strains through a kind of "sounding" of silence.

"Sounding silence" is a concept theorized by Matilde Nardelli, who—in her reading of Michelangelo Antonioni's *La notte* (1961)—refers to the self-reflexive commentary brought forth by the subdued heroine Valentina (Monica Vitti). At one point in the film, Valentina muses, "The park is full of silence made of noises." This prompts Nardelli to stress the point that silence is sonorous in Antonioni's cinema, since it magnifies "a spectrum of [non-dialogue] sounds" such as ambient noises (19, 21). Although, unlike Antonioni (whose *La notte* features diegetic music only, save for the opening-credits sequence), Kim uses relatively hushed, nondiegetic string music in the background, the dramatic tension of the attempted-suicide scene derives from the scratching sound of the fishhook as it is pressed by the tightening wire, a nerve-wracking noise that can be heard over shots four to seven but which is replaced by an emancipatory popping sound (that of the falling hook/steel wire) at the end of the montage. In the next scene, the insulted woman attacks the bare hide of the rude client, a hypocritical family man who, in mid-defecation, phones his kindergarten-aged daughter and who will be punished when the woman nearly drowns him in the moments that follow.

Hŭi-jin is drawn to a new fisherman, Hyŏn-sik, who has apparently murdered his unfaithful wife and her paramour—a piece of information conveyed visually in a fleeting dream sequence. The dream sequence shows an unidentified intruder witnessing a copulating couple. The couple turns into two corpses (being dragged away by the offscreen murderer) in the following shot. In a similar fashion, Kim inserts a visual clue about Hŭi-jin's own painful past in a later scene, where the sobbing woman longingly watches an abandoned black motorcycle submerged in the mud and presumably belonging to her dead or separated lover. The two wounded souls with troubled pasts silently watch over each other, after Hŭi-jin prevents the suicidal man from offing himself with a gun. On a rainy day, drunken Hŭi-jin boldly advances and shows up in his shack with a soju (vodka) bottle. The two loners fail to connect physically, however, and Hyŏn-sik nearly rapes her—a violent rupture captured in static long shot, with ironically lyrical nondiegetic music silencing sounds of struggle. After pushing Hyŏn-sik into the water, Hŭi-jin returns to her manager's cabin on the dock, where she is seen making a phone call, which is silenced by the sound of rain. The nature of her call is revealed in the next shot. A "coffee delivery girl" arrives with complaints about the pouring rain. As this call girl, named Chŏng-a, falls for Hyŏn-sik and visits him again in a nonprofessional capacity, Hŭi-jin develops an extreme jealousy and even spies on their lovemaking. Hŭi-jin finally seizes her chance of possessing Hyŏn-sik when she saves him after he mutilates his throat with fishhooks in a bizarre suicide attempt.

It is worth noting that the two consummate their passion in a moment of extreme sadomasochistic agony, immediately after Hŭi-jin performs non-anesthetized "surgery," removing the hooks from Hyŏn-sik's throat with a wrench. It is as if they can accept each other's bodies only after Hyŏn-sik's voice organ is damaged, turning him (temporarily) into a mute—Hŭi-jin's equal. Their relationship is tested when Chŏng-a reappears and Hŭi-jin leaves her bound in a remote shack overnight to keep her away from Hyŏn-sik. The unfortunate captive accidentally drowns

Figure 7. On a rainy day, the two loners—Hŭi-jin and Hyŏn-sik—yearn for communication yet fail to connect physically in *The Isle*.

herself in her ill-fated struggle to escape. After burying her body and scooter in the lake, Hŭi-jin kills another person, the call girl's pimp, who gets into a fight with Hyŏn-sik and falls into the lake (where the nymphlike woman pulls him down to his death).

After healing and regaining his voice, Hŭi-jin's reluctant accomplice Hyŏn-sik becomes increasingly violent and abusive, declaring, "I am not your man. I can leave whenever I want to, you whore." During an early-morning episode, after intense sadomasochistic lovemaking, the volatile man gently caresses Hŭi-jin's face as she sleeps and rows away to the land with his suitcase. The woman wakes up and, in a desperate attempt to stop him from leaving her, places fishhooks underneath her skirt and pulls the wire just as Hyŏn-sik did to his throat. An intense close-up of Hŭi-jin's pained face segues to a long shot of the rowing man who, upon hearing her sharp scream, turns around and heads back to the floating shack. In extreme pain, Hŭi-jin staggeringly stands up on the deck to display her bloody skirt right in front of Hyŏn-sik on the boat. The shared experience of unspeakable physical pain brings the couple back together. Soon they will motor the float toward the sea in an apparent double-suicide voyage.

In the otherworldly, wordless, yet sonorous epilogue, Hyŏn-sik emerges from the water and vanishes into aquatic weeds in a thick fog, an enigmatic image superimposed with a long overhead shot of the nude Hŭi-jin's dead body (with miniature weeds in her pelvic area, symbolically containing Hyŏn-sik) on the submerged boat-coffin. The film's not-so-subtle "back-to-the-womb" metaphor in its final scene may well be the origin for a popular, slangy expression directed at the filmmaker in his home country, where he is known as "a person who cultivates religious truth in the woman's womb" (chagung aesŏ to ttaknŭn saram).

Unlike anti-Kim factions of female critics (such as Chu Yu-sin, Sim Yŏng-sŏp, and Yu Chi-na), the critic Paek Mun-im offers a refreshing feminist interpretation of Hŭi-jin's self-mutilation. According to Paek, the woman's masochistic action should be interpreted as a self-administered ritual of "genital purification." This reading is supported by textual evidence in which the purified woman displays her "virginal" blood on a white skirt as proof of her sexual innocence ("Fishing Education" 225). In the process, Hŭi-jin is refuting Hyŏn-sik's phallocentric interpellation[18] of her identity ("you whore") with her body, not words. As Paek points

Figure 8. The enigmatic final shot of *The Isle*, which shows Hŭi-jin's dead body symbolically containing her lover Hyŏn-sik.

out, Hŭi-jin's silent self-mutilation constitutes a corporeally inscribed "resistance to masculine language" ("Fishing Education" 226).

Hŭi-jin's subaltern body language (communicating her innocence through blood) is strikingly reminiscent of Spivak's example in her famous essay, "Can the Subaltern Speak?" Toward the end of the essay, Spivak introduces the case of Bhuvaneswari Bhaduri, who hanged herself in North Calcutta in 1926 at the age of sixteen or seventeen. She was a member of a militant independence group and was entrusted with the duty of a political assassination. Instead of taking another person's life, she decided to take her own, but waited until the onset of her menstruation to prove that her suicide was not a result of illicit pregnancy (Spivak 103). Although Spivak rightly concludes that "[t]he subaltern cannot speak" (104), her ambiguous example belies her premise by suggesting a possibility of alternative communication on the part of a subaltern woman. Both Hŭi-jin and Bhuvaneswari reject masculine violence and verbosity in favor of silence and corporeal communication.

Just as Bhuvaneswari proved her sexual innocence with her menstrual blood in Spivak's story, Hŭi-jin does the same with her blood-stained white skirt displayed in front of the man she loves.

If silence connotes female subaltern resistance to masculine violence in *The Isle*, it also signifies male subaltern resistance in the face of military/police brutality in *Bad Guy* and *3-Iron* (the latter distantly evoking the political dissidence and martyrdom of the 1970s and 1980s). Translated into auteuristic terms, silence is a manifestation of Kim Ki-duk's own mistrust of language-based discourse and the signifying systems that are controlled and manipulated by members of the intelligentsia (including journalists). It is not difficult to discern a parallel between the filmmaker and his silent protagonists, such as Han-gi and T'ae-sŏk. These rebels with hearts of gold are mistaken as "bad guys" as a result of their provocative actions and unapologetic demeanors. However, unlike his muted characters who maintain their silence in the face of violent force, Kim caved in and *spoke*. He apologized publicly, an act demanded repeatedly of his alter-ego Han-gi in the opening sequence of *Bad Guy*. Through his "extreme" words of masochism and apologia, however, the filmmaker turned the tables and exposed the cruelty or thoughtlessness of his "persecutors." In an editorial for *Chosun Daily* (*Chosŏn Ilbo*), the musician Sin Tae-ch'ŏl correctly interprets Kim's apology as a "masochistic act of resistance against mass lynching directed against him." Sin goes on to warn against the culture of collective violence directed toward a nonconforming minority.

Kim Ki-duk's aesthetics of silence reaches its apex in *3-Iron*, which, despite its tonal austerity and air of solemnity, has been compared to the silent-era classics of Charlie Chaplin and Buster Keaton by American film critics (Scott, "Man Breaks" 16; Klein, "Invisible" 36). Throughout the film, the male protagonist, T'ae-sŏk, a mysterious motorcyclist and home-breaker, does not say a word, while the female protagonist, Sŏn-hwa (an abused housewife who, not coincidentally, has the same name as the protagonist of Kim's earlier film, *Bad Guy*), utters only two lines—"I love you" and "Breakfast is ready"—toward the end of the film. Unlike the loquacious, quarrelsome middle-class couples whose houses are broken into throughout the film, however, these two central characters communicate harmoniously in nonverbal forms.

Kim Ki-duk's use of silence in *3-Iron* and other films evokes the Hungarian film theorist Belá Balázs's writing on sound in *Theory of the*

*Film*. Defining silence as "one of the most dramatic effects of the sound film" (205), Balázs elaborates:

> [S]ilence can be extremely vivid and varied, for although it has no voice, it has very many expressions and gestures. A silent glance can speak volumes; its soundlessness makes it more expressive because the facial movements of a silent figure may explain the reason for the silence, makes us feel its weight, its menace, its tension. In the film, silence does not halt action even for an instant and such silent action gives even silence a living face. The physiognomy of men is more intense when they are silent. More than that, in silence even things drop their masks and seem to look at you with wide-open eyes. (207)

In addition to the aforementioned interpretations of muteness or quietude in Kim Ki-duk's cinema (mistrust in words and political resistance), Balázs's theory and *3-Iron* suggest another potential of screen silence as an active agent and facilitator of communication. Just as a rejection of language based on its negative functions (lies, distortions, slandering) is motivated by Kim's many disappointments with words, the director's predilection for nonverbal communication derives partly from his own experience in Paris, where he could get by without learning to speak French by observing people's "expressions and behavior" (Merajver-Kurlat 16).

The director has advocated and elaborated his philosophy of muted communication in various interviews. In his discussions with Marta Merajver-Kurlat, Kim opined, "I consider silence to be words [as well]. Silence is words in the most varied sense. And then, I consider laughter and tears to be very brilliant dialogue [next to silence]. Words coming out of a mouth have nuance . . . more than one meaning. Depending on the topic of a film, I think that the meanings of dialogues always differ" (31). Similarly, in his 2005 interview with *Time Out*, the filmmaker explained his motivation behind the suppression of dialogue in *3-Iron*: "I want the audience to watch the characters more closely by reducing the dialogue as much as possible. Most movies have too much dialogue; I don't think words make everything understandable" ("Film Q&A" 84). In another interview, Kim stated: "[I]t's a strategy to force the audience to fill in the blanks themselves. So in some ways they insert sort of their own dialogue throughout the film: imagining what they would say—imagining what might be said when there is silence in the film" (Canavese).

Just as the French philosopher Jacques Derrida acknowledges the centrality of phonocentrism (the privileging of speech over writing) in the Western philosophical tradition with his project of grammatology, inadvertently gesturing toward "a *deaf-mute philosophy*" (Bauman), Kim Ki-duk's muted cinema destabilizes the hierarchy between dialogue (verbal communication) and silence (nonverbal communication) in filmmaking. As Marta Merajver-Kurlat rightly interprets,

> Precisely because of their multiple meanings, of their connotations, words can mislead and distract. On the other hand . . . [silence] draws attention to a thesaurus brimming with all the words available to the speaker of a language. It is up to the interlocutor to take his/her pick. You may argue that, supposing they share the same wavelength, communication will occur. . . . [I]n Kim's films, words tend to foster miscommunication or absence of communication. (34)

Let us take, for instance, the extended sequence in which T'ae-sŏk and Sŏn-hwa, the silent protagonists of *3-Iron,* first encounter one other and communicate without words. Mistaking it as an "empty house" (the Korean title of the film), T'ae-sŏk breaks into Sŏn-hwa's richly decorated upper-class mansion in search of temporary shelter, a place to clean up, eat, and rest. Bruised and traumatized by spousal violence, Sŏn-hwa has withdrawn to the shadowy corner of her room and is initially unnoticed by the curious intruder, who takes a tour of his borrowed "home." He flips through a nude picture book of Sŏn-hwa (who is apparently an ex-model, having now become the trophy wife of a wealthy businessman). He then eavesdrops on her husband's pleading on the answering machine, a message in which the latter asks his wife to answer his call. The battered wife silently spies on the uninvited guest making himself at home—taking a digital photo of himself in front of her glamour portrait, fixing lunch, doing laundry, watering the plants, practicing golf in the garden, taking a bath, and fixing a broken weight scale. The mistress of the home finally reveals herself to the trespasser, who has been masturbating in bed. She does so by opening the bedroom door and standing at the threshold silently. Their wordless exchange of glances is interrupted

Figure 9. The mysterious housebreaker T'ae-sŏk makes his own digital "family portrait" in *3-Iron.*

when the irritated husband calls again. The wife picks up the phone only to emit a long hysterical scream and hang up. After intently gazing at her face, bearing physical and emotional scars, T'ae-sŏk quietly takes off, only to turn his motorcycle around and return to the housewife, who has been crying in the bathtub.

The enigmatic yet sympathetic stranger "speaks" to her indirectly: he plays the Belgian singer Natacha Altas's Arabic love song "Gafsa" (Cage) on a CD and displays a feminine pink outfit (picked up from her closet) on the floor while she is still in the bathroom. Reversing sides, it is now T'ae-sŏk who silently gazes at her putting on clothes from a distance. Hidden on the other side of the partitioned living room, T'ae-sŏk initiates a timid "conversation" with Sŏn-hwa by gently sending a golf ball to her way, which the woman picks up and rolls back in his direction. The playful banter between the muted strangers is cut short when the husband returns to admonish his recalcitrant wife, whom he slaps and molests. Like a knight in shining armor, T'ae-sŏk intervenes and punishes the high-class man with his own golf club (the "iron" of the film's English-language title) by shooting balls directly at his stomach and groin. Without uttering a single word, he waits for Sŏn-hwa on his motorcycle parked outside the house, the vehicle's engine roaring as if it were a mating call. Accepting the invitation to join his nomadic life, the woman leaves her home and loveless marriage without saying a word to her fallen husband, who futilely tries to stop his wife by holding on to her shoes.

In this sequence, Kim Ki-duk employs a variety of cinematic devices (close-ups of facial expressions, diegetic music, point-of-view shots, proximate spatial arrangements, costumes, props) to narrativize nonverbal communication and underscore the intersubjective reciprocity between "two ghostlike people," to borrow Seungho Yoon's phrase. According to Yoon, in *3-Iron,* "[T]he empty houses . . . are not literally void but rather haunted by people or ghosts who are only spectrally present. . . . Kim himself has become a kind of ghost . . . [who] has made a film about ghosts and haunted spaces" (60). T'ae-sŏk and Sŏn-hwa are symbolic ghosts who do not exist socially. The former is homeless and does not seem to have any job other than breaking into empty houses using a low-tech scheme (he hangs a Chinese-restaurant menu over each house's front doorknob lock and returns to the neighborhood later to locate a vacated home marked by an unremoved flyer outside and a vacation message on the answering machine inside). He is a ghostly housesitter who eats other people's food, does other people's chores (washing laundry, gardening, making repairs, and so forth), takes photos in front of other people's portraits, wears other people's pajamas, and sleeps in other people's beds.

His lack of a discernable social identity is poignantly expressed in a line delivered by a professional pugilist who returns home and finds an unknown couple—Sŏn-hwa and T'ae-sŏk—occupying his bed. When his wife reports no signs of theft, the bewildered homeowner exclaims, after beating up T'ae-sŏk, "What the hell are you doing in my house if you're not even a thief?" A young police detective echoes the confusion in a later scene, when the vagabond couple is arrested and taken to the station for interrogation. T'ae-sŏk is accused of illegal entries, kidnapping, rape, and even the murder of an old man (whose tenement apartment the couple breaks into only to find the owner dead). Reporting the cause of death as lung cancer and pointing out T'ae-sŏk's care in dressing and burying the body, the junior detective defends the accused (whom he says is "not a bad guy") to his superior.

Neither a thief nor a bad guy, T'ae-sŏk nevertheless inherits the outlaw mentality of Kim's earlier heroes. However, he is an anomalous figure who has a clean-cut, handsome look; drives a BMW motorcycle; and is identified as "a college graduate" in the aforementioned police scene. The free-spirited nomad is thus distinct from the crude petty criminals and rugged working-class men and women who populate Kim's early films, from *Crocodile* and *Wild Animals* to *Address Unknown* and *Bad Guy*. Two-thirds of the way into the narrative, *3-Iron* turns into a surrealist drama in which T'ae-sŏk literally becomes invisible after mastering the ability to hide in the shadowy jail cell, outside the purview of human vision, through metaphysical "ghost practice" (*yuryŏng yŏnsŭp*, a term coined by Kim himself and used in various local interviews about the film). A frustrated warden yells at the prisoner, who is prone to "vanish" in his tidy cell (climbing onto the wall, hiding behind the back of another person, and so on): "Why do you keep hiding? Do you want to disappear from the world altogether?" After a series of trials and errors, T'ae-sŏk's corporeal immaterialization is perfected before his release from prison. Having tested his ability to break into occupied houses without being detected by their owners, T'ae-sŏk infiltrates Sŏn-hwa's house, where the scorned husband keeps a vigilant eye on his returned wife. Invisible to the husband, T'ae-sŏk reveals himself to Sŏn-hwa in a mirror and shares a secret kiss with her behind the back of her husband, who embraces

Figure 10. Forbidden lovers—Sŏn-hwa and T'ae-sŏk—steal a kiss behind the back of the married woman's oblivious husband in *3-Iron*.

his wife after hearing her say "I love you" (a remark meant for the man behind him). The next morning, after the husband leaves for work, the reunited lovers stand on a scale together. The scale displays a weight of zero, implying their mutual transcendence of bodily existence. Over the final close-up shot of the scale, a cryptic caption reads: "It's hard to tell whether the world we live in is either a reality or a dream."

In his lengthy interview with Kim Ki-duk for the October 6, 2004, issue of *Cine 21,* Chŏng Sŏng-il interprets T'ae-sŏk as "Sŏn-hwa's fantasy," an interpretation corroborated by the writer-director. Kim also suggests an alternative reading that Sŏn-hwa may be a figment of T'ae-sŏk's imagination, as the object of rescue in his solitary visits to empty houses. Whether one takes the two characters as literal or figurative embodiments, *3-Iron* is distinct insofar as Kim makes class *ressentiment* abstract through a transcendental tale of love and human existence where the inaudible and (later) invisible are characters of liminal class affiliations. One can even conjecture that T'ae-sŏk might be the disillusioned son of a rich family who rebels against the materialist lifestyle into which he is born. Although one can assume that Sŏn-hwa is from a not-so-well-to-do family (from dialogue that reveals the husband's wiring of money to her family during her absence), her premarital career as a model as well as her interclass marriage likewise complicates the character's social status. Instead of externalizing class antagonism, as he had in the dramatic opening scene of *Bad Guy,* Kim quietly explores issues of marginality, voicelessness, and invisibility in an allegorical fashion.

Moreover, T'ae-sŏk's jail-cell disappearance—his ability to move to the other side of a 180-degree sphere of human vision—is a significant metaphor of the motion-picture medium, which is often constrained by a 180-degree-axis rule through which mainstream filmmakers are able to ensure screen direction and suture the spectator into the diegesis without creating disorientation. Taking this metaphor further, Kim's cinema as a whole can be interpreted as a coherent effort to expose the unseen "flip side" of South Korean society, the "other" 180-degree side that is largely suppressed and neglected in mainstream commercial filmmaking. Replacing the dominant cinematic spaces of urban middle-class work, leisure, and consumption—offices, apartments, cafes, shopping malls, upscale restaurants—in Kim's cinema are alternative spaces of invisibility, exile, and alienation, such as homeless shelters on the bank of the Han River (*Crocodile*), crime-ridden back alleys of Paris (*Wild Animals*), red-light motel districts (*Birdcage Inn, Bad Guy, Samaritan Girl*), U.S. military camptowns (*Address Unknown*), prisons (*Bad Guy, 3-Iron, Breath*), and remote countryside areas (*The Isle, Spring, Summer, Fall, Winter . . . and Spring, Samaritan Girl, The Bow*).

Although *3-Iron* shows upper-class and middle-class residential areas, it is ultimately a traditional Korean house (*hanok*)—another space of marginality in the hypermodern metropolis of Seoul—where two social outcasts feel most at home and consummate their love. Unlike the paranoid owners of upscale apartments and mansions, people who are obsessed with protecting their property and asserting their ownership, the couple living in the *hanok* and wearing modernized *hanbok* (traditional Korean dress) is depicted as being loving and open, going so far as to let Sŏn-hwa, a complete stranger, enter their home and take a nap on their sofa without any explanation. It might be tempting to interpret the utopian space of Korean traditional environs as a manifestation of Kim's nativist nostalgia for a premodern past, but the blissful home in question is an already hybridized space where Western antique-style furniture and accessories—canapés, cushions, and teapots—blend into the traditional architecture and garden.

Kim's nativist aesthetics can be most notably found in *The Bow* and *Spring, Summer, Fall, Winter, . . . and Spring,* two films that are exclusively set in remote traditional spaces—a fishing boat house and a floating temple on the lake, respectively—where primitive/spiritual ways of life have been left intact. Like the incorporation of Zen mysticism and Buddhist iconography in *Spring, Summer, Fall, Winter . . . and Spring,* the ravishingly photographed exotic rituals in *The Bow* (including a traditional wedding ceremony and the telling of fortunes through the shooting of arrows in the Buddhist painting on the hull of the vessel), combined with the anomalous ethnographic scene of the protagonist dressing an old man's body in *3-Iron,* may appear to warrant suspicion. The audience might be led to suspect Kim of exhibitionist self-orientalism, staged for the Western gaze. However, unlike the films of the veteran Korean director Im Kwon-taek (Im Kwŏn-t'aek), such as *Sopyonje* (*Sŏp'yŏnje*; 1993), *Chunhyang* (*Ch'unhyangdŏn*; 2000), and *Chihwaseon* (2004), which explicitly foreground unadulterated forms of Korean tradition and culture, Kim defamiliarizes traditional iconographies in his hybridizing, transnational cinema. For example, in the fleeting scene of *3-Iron* that shows Sŏn-hwa and T'ae-sŏk wrapping and knotting the stranger's body with cloth and rice paper, dissonant string music—reminiscent of the Austrian composer Arnold Schoenberg's twelve-tone works of the 1920s—fills the sound track. Although fragmented close-up shots of the mummy-like corpse being dressed in accordance of the traditional Korean funeral practice verge toward narratively unmotivated visual ethnography, the clash between the modern soundscape and the traditional image as well as the brevity of the scene—lasting one minute—undermines its fetishistic potential. The incongruity between the painstaking burial preparation and the absence of the dead man's family (who are on vacation while, unbeknownst to them, their dead father is being buried in a random site by two complete strangers) further separates the scene from the original cultural context of family-centric Korean funerals.

The occasional "Koreanness" of Kim's mise-en-scène is a whimsical aesthetic variant rather than a consistent thematic quest for culture, tradition, and identity. Kim's fifteenth film, *Dream*, is set almost entirely in a *hanok* district of Seoul despite the lack of narrative necessity for such a specialized setting. In this surrealist psychological drama, Chin (played by the Japanese actor Odagiri Jo) is a sculptor whose girlfriend has left him for another man. After waking up from a vivid nightmare involving a hit-and-run accident in which he absconds from the scene of a fatal car crash, Chin discovers that the misfortune in his dream has taken place in the real world, with striking similarities. Indeed, all but one of the details of the real accident had been anticipated by those in his dream: it is a woman named Ran (played by Yi Na-yŏng), not he, who is behind the wheel of the vehicle. Having undergone a disastrous breakup with her boyfriend, who now dates Chin's ex-girlfriend, Ran suffers from sleepwalking and mysteriously enacts Chin's dreams (the aforementioned auto accident, sexual reunions with the ex-lover, a jealousy murder) in a trance, apparently against her will. When not sleepwalking, the *hanbok* designer is seen attending a showing of her collection of French couture–inspired silk gowns in traditional color palettes (red, orange, yellow, green). Appropriately, her living quarter is a hybridized *hanok* whose interiors mix antique doors and window panels with Western-style furniture. The female protagonist's East-meets-West aesthetic sensibility reflects Kim's own taste in juxtaposing the gritty realism of Korean settings with modernist conventions of European art cinema: a mixture of reality and fantasy, elliptical storytelling, open-ended finales, and so forth. The director also harbors a predilection for incorporating tropes and actual images of Western art, such as the paintings of Egon Schiele (*Birdcage Inn* and *Bad Guy*) and the sculptures of Camille Claudel (*Wild Animals*), as well as "exotic" foreign-language songs such as "Gafsa" (Arabic) in *3-Iron* and Etta Scollo's "I Tuoi Fiori" (Italian) in *Bad Guy*.

Kim's linguistic experiments in *Dream* are as uncanny as its metaphysical narrative of two doppelganger-like individuals inexplicably connected through dreams. Although Odagiri Jo delivers his dialogue in Japanese and Yi Na-yŏng and other actors speak Korean, they manage to seamlessly communicate with one another in the diegesis, as if there were no linguistic differences. Kim is certainly not the first filmmaker to cinematically realize such a fall-of-Babel-defying vision of multilingual vocality in the context of art cinema. Five years prior to *Dream*'s release, the Portuguese director Manoel de Oliveira released *A Talking Picture* (*Um Filme Falado*; 2003) with a dinner scene set on a cruise ship in which the American captain (John Malkovich) and three female passengers of French, Italian, and Greek origins (Catherine Deneuve, Stefania Sandrelli, and Irene Papas) all speak their mother tongues and yet understand one another with no barriers whatsoever (going so far as to reflexively comment on their own ability and the dropping away of language barriers). In addition to implicitly critiquing the centrality of the English language in Hollywood films through a multinational cast and several foreign settings, *A Talking Picture* suggests an idealistic future of a multilingual European Union.

The mixing of Japanese and Korean languages in *Dream* is perhaps more provocative, given the historical animosities between two nations/linguistic communities dating back to the colonial period (1910–45), when bilingualism was forced upon Koreans who lost their country to Japan. One should not overlook the covert political undertones, whether intended or not by Kim, in this notion of understanding the (colonial) other's language. The film's underlying premise—that Chin's happiness (dreams of kissing and making love to his ex-girlfriend) hinges upon Ran's misery (unwanted sexual relationships with her ex, whom she despises)—remotely echoes conventional representations of adverse Japan-Korea relations. For example, the director Yi Si-myŏng's futuristic time-travel film *2009: Lost Memories* (2002), a subjunctive narrative of alternative history wherein Korea remains under the control of the Japanese imperial government in the new millennium, features heavy-handed crosscutting between slow-motion images of a Japanese girl celebrating fireworks with her parents and those of a Korean guerrilla boy being killed by Japanese police. The initially combative relationship between Chin and Ran, however, gradually transforms from one overridden with guilt (on the part of Chin) and hostility (on the part of Ran) to one in which empathy and love predominate, offering an oblique allegory of emotional antidotes to prolonged traumas of the colonial past. The film ends with a vague suggestion of the redemptive afterlife union of the Japanese- and Korean-speaking couple after they have both committed suicide. After hanging herself in prison, where she has been sent for killing her ex-lover, Ran reincarnates as a butterfly and lands on the lifeless hand of Chin, who has just jumped from a bridge to protect her from his uncontrollable dreams.

In his interview with Hwang Chin-mi, Kim frankly professes the market logic behind his "Koreanist mise-en-scène" and use of experimental bilingualism in *Dream.* To Hwang's comment, "It seems that you insisted on showing Korean traditional houses, colors, and designs, targeting Western audiences," Kim replies:

> Some people are sarcastically saying that my films are made for European film festivals. It is true that the biggest patrons of my films are Europeans. Partially I did intend to maintain my primary market by providing Korean mise-en-scène to Western audiences. At the same time, I aimed to show the "beauty of Korea." . . . Those who have a negative view called me "arrogant" for letting Odagiri Jo speak Japanese with the European market in mind. In fact, for European audiences who cannot distinguish between Korean and Japanese, it would not be strange at all. For Korean audiences, it can be weird . . . but I thought it wouldn't matter if each performer spoke his/her mother tongue since the film has universal themes and an oneiric atmosphere (Hwang, "Director Kim Ki-duk of *Dream*").

In his review of *Dream,* the film critic An Si-hwan succinctly states, "In [Kim's] film, the specific traces of Korea as a geotemporal entity are disappearing. . . . There is no reason why Korea should be the setting and why Korean or Japanese actors should be cast in *Dream*" ("Wishing Unity"). In other words, despite the conspicuous foregrounding of Korean props and other elements within the mise-en-scène, *Dream* is a radically transnational text that transcends linguistic/ethnic barriers of any one national cinema and explores timeless existential questions—concerning dreams, love, jealousy, death, and guilt—unfettered by cultural specificity.

*Dream* contains a crucial scene that provides a hermeneutic key to understanding not only the film's overarching themes but also Kim Ki-duk's oeuvre in general. Twenty minutes into the film, Chin and Ran visit a spiritually inclined female psychiatrist who cryptically tells the doppelganger duo: "The two of you are one. . . . Remember white and black are the same color." At the end of his interview with the *Dis Voir* editors who published the French-English monograph *Kim Ki-duk*, the director likewise philosophizes, "My answer to all questions is this, and this alone: 'Black and white are the same color'" (Rivière 117). In his subsequent interview with Merajver-Kurlat, Kim elaborates on his maxim in a slightly different way: "This is sort of a kind of philosophy of mine, but it's this idea that the colors of black and white are actually the same color. You can only explain black by pointing to what's white. You can only explain white by pointing to what's black" (46–47). In a sense, Kim's cinema is a decentering site of signification wherein a litany of binary oppositions—silence versus speech, reality versus fantasy, truth versus deception, morality versus immorality, tenderness versus violence, love versus hate, happiness versus misery, hope versus despair, victim versus perpetrator, modernity versus tradition, West versus East, masculinity versus femininity, young versus old, life versus death, corruption versus redemption, normalcy versus extremity, cruelty versus mercy—are consistently questioned and capsized.

Kim's is a cinema of paradoxes and ironies. *3-Iron* has a deceptive happy ending that belies the cruel fate faced by two lovers whose phantomlike cohabitation is compromised by the existence of Sŏn-hwa's husband, the owner of the house as well as the breadwinner. T'ae-sŏk and Sŏn-hwa can stay and live as a couple in another man's house as long as T'ae-sŏk hides in the shadowy space outside or beyond human vision, and as long as Sŏn-hwa maintains the façade of a good wife.

Like all framed family portraits festooning the walls of middle-class and upper-class households (with the exception of the *hanok* house), images of the happy domicile in the high-key-lit, penultimate breakfast scene are lies. Sŏn-hwa's bright smile, loving gaze, and tending hands are not intended for her husband (as the cuckolded man mistakenly believes) but for T'ae-sŏk, who is standing right behind him. It is a paradoxical happy end, one that reassures yet leaves a bitter aftertaste.

The dénouement of *3-Iron* is reminiscent of the ambivalent ending of *Bad Guy*, in which it is unclear where reality ends and fantasy begins. After being stabbed by his resentful underling, Myŏng-su, multiple times and hemorrhaging blood by the riverside, the protagonist Han-gi miraculously resurrects and heads to the seaside, where he had earlier witnessed, along with Sŏn-hwa, a mysterious woman (whose back was turned to the camera) drowning. Having been freed from the red-light district by Han-gi and left to go wherever she wishes, Sŏn-hwa arrives at the waterfront first. There she finds the missing pieces of two torn pictures, which the drowned woman had buried in the sand. When she fits the missing parts to the now-complete pictures that she has kept, the couple depicted turns out to be none other than Sŏn-hwa and Han-gi, not the dead woman and her lover, as conventional wisdom has led the audience to believe. The duo reunites just like the couple in the pictures—wearing the same clothing and leaning toward each other in the same way—and their image is momentarily frozen before fading out in overexposure. As the next scene fades in, Han-gi is seen preparing a makeshift bed in the back of his truck while being watched by Sŏn-hwa in the passenger seat. An ensuing static long shot captures the waterfront setting of a rural fishing village, where Han-gi approaches a couple of fishermen. One of them responds to his solicitation and is taken to the back of the truck where Sŏn-hwa awaits. After the fisherman pays and disappears into the truck, Han-gi walks toward the foreground, where he squats and smokes a cigarette while waiting for his partner to complete her "business" (insinuated by the jerky movements of the truck in the background). After her customer leaves, Sŏn-hwa silently joins Han-gi and shares his cigarette on the waterfront. Against a sound track of Carola Häggkvist's Swedish rendition of the hymn "Day by Day" (Blott en Dag), an overhead shot shows the truck containing the world-weary couple pull away from the sea village and hit the open road.

As several Korean critics have pointed out, the final two scenes of *Bad Guy*—depicting the couple's metaphysical reunion on the beach and their nomadic life together on the road—lack narrative causality and can be interpreted as the dying Han-gi's fantasy or dream (Song 156–57; Kim Kyŏng-uk 321–22). It is another ending befitting the caption at the end of *3-Iron*: "It's hard to tell whether the world we live in is either a reality or a dream." The hymn on the sound track indirectly expresses an unspoken desire for redemption on the part of the titular hero in the otherwise morally foggy dénouement. However, Kim intentionally obstructs the film's religious subtext by opting to include an untranslated Swedish version of the song. As the case of Odagiri Jo's Japanese dialogue in *Dream* (which was subtitled in Korean for local audiences), multilingualism in Kim's cinema destabilizes and denaturalizes spoken language as the primary purveyor of meanings. The closure of *Bad Guy* has radically different nuances, depending on the audience's ability to identify the gospel song and its meanings, transmitted through its lyrics:

> Day by day, and with each passing moment
> Strength I find, to meet my trials here;
> Trusting in my Father's wise bestowment,
> I've no cause for worry or for fear.
> He Whose heart is kind beyond all measure
> Gives unto each day what He deems best—
> Lovingly, it's part of pain and pleasure,
> Mingling toil with peace and rest.

Regardless of whether the viewer interprets it as a chauvinistic vision of female sexual enslavement or as a redemptive romance between the interclass couple, the withholding of religious lyrics enhances the ambiguity of the already ambivalent ending, which might be nothing but a dream. If it is indeed Han-gi's dying dream, it is a sad, humble fantasy. Even in his dream, the upwardly mobile middle-class life filled with material comforts and steeped in social status eludes him. All that the underclass hero can envision is a tough life on the road with his de facto wife, whose sexual labor provides the couple's meager means of sustaining themselves. *Bad Guy*'s bittersweet final scene perhaps epitomizes the central concept of Kim's paradoxical cinema: "black and white are the same color."

## Neofeminist Revisions: Female Bodies and Semiotic *Chora* in *Birdcage Inn* and *Samaritan Girl*

Few Korean directors in recent years have provoked such diametrically opposed critical responses as Kim Ki-duk, who has been criticized by his compatriots for many reasons and as a result of several highly publicized occurrences, from his "I hate journalists" fax to major national dailies in 1997 to his derogatory comments about the blockbuster monster movie *The Host* and the apparently diminished standards of Korean audiences in 2006. No issue has provoked more passionate uproar from his detractors—domestic and international critics—than the director's alleged misogyny, which has been branded as everything from "sexual terrorism" to "dangerous penis fascism." In her review of *Bad Guy*, one incensed critic, Chu Yu-sin, even declared figurative war against not only the much-maligned director but also his supporters when she wrote, "The fact that this kind of film exists in Korean society itself is a threat to women. If anyone supports this film for any reason, it is an insult to all women" ("It Is a Bad Film" 8). Reviewing *The Isle*, the feminist film critic Sim Yŏng-sŏp harshly criticizes Kim's "aesthetics of rape," which is said to derive from psychotic rage—not only that of the characters but also that of the director (70). In a retaliatory rhetorical maneuver, a male film critic, Kang Sŏng-yul, deplores the status of "fascist feminism," which has launched a "witch hunt" against Kim Ki-duk while letting other Korean directors off the hook for equally, if not more, offensive female images in such films as Im Kwon-taek's *Chihwaseon* and Lee Chang-dong's *Oasis* (2002) (175–77).

In his aptly titled article, "From Prostitutes to Holy Women: Women as Objects of Male Desire," Kim Sŏn-yŏp summarizes the major tendencies among feminist complaints and divides female images in the director's films into three groups: holy prostitutes, dangerous prostitutes, and parasitical prostitutes. The writer laments the fact that Kim's love stories uniformly spread "the gospel of the holy-prostitute fantasy" as a sort of redemptive-religion or spiritual-salvation fantasy (183). From Chin-a in *Birdcage Inn* to Sŏn-hwa in *Bad Guy* to Yŏ-jin and Chae-yŏng in *Samaritan Girl*, female characters are burdened with the responsibility of having to convert and redeem morally reprehensible or unstable men by sleeping with them. *Samaritan Girl* explicitly makes a connection between prostitution and religion by opening with a story-within-the-story about an Indian courtesan-deity named Vasumitra whose clients, as legend goes, were turned into devout Buddhists after their sexual encounter with her. Telling the story to her pimp, Chae-yŏng (who is also her best friend), while being prepped for her own sexual liaison, the elfish teen prostitute Yŏ-jin nicknames herself Vasumitra.

Femmes fatales of the second category include the Hungarian street-performance artist Corinne and the Korean adoptee peepshow girl Laura in *Wild Animals,* which depicts the hardened (low) lives of the Korean diaspora in Paris. The petty criminal Ch'ŏng-hae, who once nurtured the dream of becoming a painter, joins the French mafia after falling in love with Corinne, an illegal immigrant at the mercy of her abusive French boyfriend-pimp (who demands a large sum of money in exchange for her freedom). Unable to keep absorbing the habitual beatings meted out by the jealous Frenchman, the Hungarian woman snaps one night and stabs her pimp to death with a frozen mackerel. Corrine enlists Ch'ŏng-hae's help in disposing of the body in the Seine. Ch'ŏng-hae's partner, the North Korean defector and martial artist Hong-san, is a secret admirer of Laura, whose peepshow joint in the red-light district of Pigalle he frequents as a customer. Unbeknownst to Hong-san, Ch'ŏng-hae murders Laura's boyfriend Emil on behalf of his mafia boss and gives the dead man's gold watch as a gift to his North Korean partner. Oblivious, Hong-san pops up in Laura's peepshow performance space one day with Emil's watch on his wrist. The grieving strip-dancer notices the familiar object and wrongly suspects Hong-san as the murderer of her lover. She ultimately avenges Emil's death by gunning down Ch'ŏng-hae and Hong-san in a Parisian back alley—a surprise attack that is reserved for the film's initially hopeful but ultimately tragic dénouement.

According to Kim Sŏn-yŏp, Hŭi-jin, the female protagonist of *The Isle,* is another "dangerous prostitute" whose possessive attachment to the fugitive fisherman Hyŏn-sŏk leads to the killing of two people—a call girl, who falls for Hyŏn-sŏk on her "professional" visit to his fishing shack, and her pimp, who searches for her after her disappearance. Hŭi-jin goes so far as to violate herself physically, mutilating her vagina with fishhooks to stop Hyŏn-sŏk from leaving her. Sharing Hŭi-jin's wayward sexuality is Mi-yŏng in *The Coast Guard,* who convinces her reluctant boyfriend to sneak into the off-limits military zone on the beach for their nocturnal tryst. Eventually, the woman's transgressive desire costs not only the life of her boyfriend (whose body is ripped apart by machine-gun fire and grenades) but also her own sanity. Similarly, in *Spring, Summer, Fall, Winter . . . and Spring,* a fragile girl with no name visits the lake temple for healing, and in the process stirs up the sexual desire of the adolescent monk. Although their physical relationship helps to cure her sickness, the teen seductress is responsible for derailing the once-pious boy from his spiritual journey and luring him to join her in the secular world. Blinded by the promise of carnal pleasure, the young monk leaves the temple only to return ten-odd years later as a fugitive from the law after murdering his wife in a fit of jealousy.

Ŭn-ok in *Address Unknown,* Sŏn-hwa in *3-Iron,* and the unnamed Girl in *The Bow* belong to the third category in Kim Sŏn-yŏp's taxonomy: "parasitical" femininity/sexuality that is subjugated to a patriarchal "host." Although they are neither forced to prostitute themselves professionally nor presented as fatal threats to their romantic interests, they are minors or homemakers lacking the ability to become socially secure and financially independent. These "parasitical" women are in need of male protection, and their bodies are offered as rewards for such protection. In *3-Iron* and *The Bow,* the female protagonists—the abused housewife Sŏn-hwa and the sixteen-year-old girl who is engaged to a sixty-year-old man (who has raised her in his boat house)—are freed from the lecherous clutches of an oppressive older man only to be guided by a comparatively more youthful, gentler form of patriarchy represented by the house breaker T'ae-sŏk and the unnamed college boy/fisherman, respectively.

There is great validity in Kim Sŏn-yŏp's critique of Kim Ki-duk's female images, a view shared by the majority of feminist critics and female movie audiences in South Korea. Like other alleged "antifeminist" auteurs, such as Alfred Hitchcock, Brian De Palma, Spike Lee, Imamura Shohei, Zhang Yimou, and Lars von Trier, Kim often resorts to diegetic inscriptions of various forms of sadomasochistic violence (from rape and spousal abuse to corporeal mutilation and coerced prostitution). To the chagrin of many female viewers, the women's bodies in these diegetically contained yet extradiegetically excessive images become a figurative battlefield where a Korean-specific class warfare between upper/middle-class husbands and boyfriends and underclass men is waged—a confrontation suffused with *ressentiment* at the heart of such films as *Crocodile, Bad Guy,* and *3-Iron.* Unlike these and other semi-autobiographical films focusing on socially marginalized and oppressed male protagonists, however, *Birdcage Inn* and *Samaritan Girl* collectively offer surprisingly female-centered narratives that I wish to offer up—at the risk of further antagonizing Kim's detractors—as some of the most powerfully *feminist* evocations of sisterly solidarity to be found in contemporary Korean cinema, exclusive of issue-oriented woman's documentaries such as Pyŏn Yŏng-ju's acclaimed "Comfort Women" trilogy (*The Murmuring* [*Najŭn moksori*; 1995], *Habitual Sadness* [*Najŭn moksori* 2; 1997], and *My Own Breathing* [*Sumkyŏl*; 2000]). In fact, if asked to describe these films, I would use the term "neofeminist" to differentiate my position from the negatively charged readings of Kim's portrayals of women as articulated in the traditional feminist camp as well as the revisionist interpretations of commercialized female images in mainstream media offered by Euro-American "postfeminist" critics, many of whom uncritically espouse the neoliberal agency of white, middle-class, professional women in an age of relative equality.

Although, at this point, I probably do not need to remind readers that the purpose of this book is neither to naively defend Kim Ki-duk's cinema nor to attack it from a traditional feminist perspective, it is important to underscore my reasoning for a neofeminist reinterpretation of his controversial female images. It is not my intention to defensively position the director himself as a feminist against conventional wisdom. Rather, I would like to utilize the broad definition of women's pictures so eloquently put forth by the British film critic Annette Kuhn: "A feminine text . . . has no fixed characteristics, precisely because it is a relationship: it becomes a feminine text in the moment of its reading" (13). If we accept Kuhn's sensible premise and follow her inclusivist advice, then the obstinate, myopic blindness to the neofeminist potential in Kim's globally distributed films can be understood as a disservice, rather than contribution, to transnational feminist film criticism inside and outside the Korean context.

Two aspects of Kim's unique neofeminist poetics can be framed or interpreted from a transnational perspective in which French feminist discourse provides conceptual anchors for exploring the female body and feminine textuality. First, *Birdcage Inn* and *Samaritan Girl* in particular (and arguably Kim's cinema in general) are filmic exemplars of Julia Kristeva's notion of the pre-Oedipal, preverbal *semiotic,* a feminine discourse of language linked to the maternal body. Along with James Joyce, Antonin Artaud, Stéphane Mallarmé, Comte de Lautréamont, Arnold Schoenberg, and John Cage (whom Kristeva extolled as successful practitioners of *semiotic* discourses), Kim Ki-duk can be marshaled into the ranks of male artists who have privileged the unfettered libidinal drives of the feminine/maternal *semiotic* (rhythms, musicality, ruptures, repetitions, movements) over the Oedipal/phallic system of the *symbolic,* which is regulated by paternal laws and order (grammar, logic, syntax). Even Kim's ostensibly male-centered films such as *The Isle* and *The Bow* privilege the feminine/maternal space, or in Kristeva's words, "the semiotic *chora*" ("Semiotic and the Symbolic" 47–49), represented by the womblike water engulfing the male protagonist at the decisive moment of narrative closure. Perhaps it is Kim's "feminine" predilection for the repressed *semiotic* drive for subversive energies and narrative fissures that antagonizes and alienates mainstream Korean audiences, who are accustomed to the unified *symbolic* language of big-budget blockbusters and crowd-pleasing romantic comedies.

Second, Kim's synthesis of corporeality and communication ("speaking through the body" instead of through verbal enunciation) evokes French poststructuralist feminist concerns, in particular Hélène Cixous's and Luce Irigaray's notion of *l'écriture féminine* (feminine writing). In their seminal works "The Laugh of Medusa" and *This Sex Which Is Not One,* respectively, Cixous and Irigaray advocate feminine writing and speech acts that emanate directly from the woman's body, a locus of multiple, fluid sexual modalities brimming with desire and language. Opposing the phallocentric symbolic order, they insist on feminine writing practice armed with subversive tactics such as identity dispersal, word-play and punning, syntactical disjuncture, and heterogeneity of meaning. Although Kim's emphasis on body language is not limited to female images, it is most effectively mobilized in the interclass "female twin" narratives of *Birdcage Inn* and *Samaritan Girl.*

It is possible, therefore, to think of these films as neofeminist texts wherein gentle sisterly love serves as a beacon of hope and warmth—a redemptive haven in Kim's otherwise cold universe of cruelty and despair, where dysfunctional male bonding culminates in violence, bloodshed, destruction, and madness (as in *Crocodile, Wild Animals, Address Unknown, The Coast Guard,* and *Bad Guy*). In opposition to Western postfeminist media productions (*Sex and the City* [1998–2004], *Bridget Jones's Diary* [2001], and so forth), in which the freedom and power of Caucasian career women are celebrated through an emphasis on dating, shopping sprees, and girl talk in glittering spaces of a global metropolis, Kim's neofeminist texts portray more desperate working women trapped in seedy Korean red-light districts who sell their bodies out of economic necessity. These characters' relief and agency derive from their unusual bonding with other women—middle-class members of an increasingly affluent, upwardly mobile society. In each film, the latter's willingness to put themselves in the former's shoes, or rather bodies, is an ultimate expression of cross-class female bonding: in *Birdcage Inn,* a frigid college student sleeps with a customer of her weary sex-worker friend; in *Samaritan Girl,* a high-school girl meets old customers of her dead friend (whom she reluctantly pimped), one-by-one, to sleep with them and return the monies they paid to the other girl. Kim's provocative vision of female solidarity—obliquely suggestive of lesbianism and mediated through prostitution—is understandably open to criticism and debate. However, one should also acknowledge the subversive possibilities of his scenarios, wherein seemingly meaningless, interchangeable male bodies serve as sites of exchange and as conduits that facilitate deep emotional and spiritual camaraderie between two women across class boundaries.

In *Birdcage Inn* and *Samaritan Girl,* heterosexual relationships are depicted as dysfunctional or abusive. Although male characters—boyfriends, pimps, customers, and fathers—intervene and obstruct, it is ultimately the female narrative that triumphs: *Birdcage Inn* closes with a reflection of a female twin (whose social difference as prostitute and college student has been eradicated) on the ocean; *Samaritan Girl* ends with a long shot of the lone teenaged girl who is left to drive (and survive) on her own after her widowed father has been taken by the police for murdering one of the adult men she has slept with. Kim's choice of dénouement in each film opens up the possibility of freedom, emancipating a female character from male influence (expressed through heterosexual relationships and paternal surveillance) and restoring the primacy of female subjectivity in the process.

One of the most forcefully argued feminist complaints about Kim Ki-duk's films is tied to the fact that most of his female characters (with few exceptions, such as affluent housewives in *3-Iron* and *Breath* as well as the professional dress designer in *Dream*) are either prostitutes by profession or engage in some type of monetarily compensated sexual activities. More specifically, many female critics lament the ways in which Kim's films reduce women to (sexualized) bodies/genitals. Kim Ŭn-jin goes so far as to define Kim's cinema as "pornography," a culturally debased mode of cine-exploitation that "demeans, objectifies, and oppresses women" (187). Such a limited definition of pornography, foreclosing its potential for expressing female desire through excessive acts of "polymorphous perversity," is in itself problematic. As the revisionist feminist scholar Linda Williams points out, "[P]ornography has historically been one of the few types of popular film that has not punished women for actively pursuing their sexual pleasure" (610). More fundamentally, it is difficult to sustain the argument that Kim's films, which are devoid of pleasure-oriented sex scenes and libidinally satisfying "money shots," constitute pornography. Often, the audience is positioned to identify with joyless or pained female characters who are shown engaging in sex acts that are presented in static, decidedly deglamorized scenes. Such scenes, usually filmed in long shot, are more likely to induce cringes or feelings of discomfort, nudging pleasure and arousal out of the equation for both male and female viewers.

What baffles me most, though, is why and how Kim's decision to foreground underclass sex workers—ubiquitous heroines of South Korean Golden Age film melodramas of the 1950s and 1960s as well as the soft-porn "hostess" genre of the 1970s—automatically qualifies his films as misogynist. Such a view seems to be class-biased, insofar as it implicitly prescribes an ideal form of femininity in the guise of well-educated, middle-class professional women—female protagonists who function as onscreen surrogates for many of the journalists and critics writing film reviews. I am equally skeptical about the assumption that the association of femininity and the body as a site of cultural negotiation, cross-gender contestation, and externalized violence is inherently antifeminist, a presupposition that neglects the dominant role of corporeality in Kim's cinema. In his interview with Chŏng Sŏng-il, the director elaborates on his politics of the body:

> The mainstream society teaches us how to make a living through the brain, not the body. But there are groups of people who must use their bodies for a living. Gangsters are one example. Women of red-light districts are another. Ethics, morality, and notions of right and wrong are applied to judge their lives. . . . Our society endorses the pure use of body for the purpose of transportation, but tends to look at the mobilization of one's body to contact another person's in a negative light. I am arguing that there is no difference in these two modes of body use. That's simply how people live, depending on their situations. There is a mainstream way of life, and there is a corporeal way of life. I mean to show there is little difference between these two ways. (Chŏng, *Kim Ki-duk* 348)

To understand the affirmative potential of Kim Ki-duk's use of the female body in his films, it is helpful to examine the notion of "corporeal feminism" put forth by Elizabeth Grosz in *Volatile Bodies.* In this important book, Grosz charts out three trends of feminist thought with regard to different conceptions about the body. Termed "egalitarian feminism," the first category of thinkers—including such pioneering feminists as Mary Wollstonecraft, Simone de Beauvoir, and Shulamith Firestone—commands negative views of the female body, which they see as a limit to "women's capacity for equality and transcendence . . . a hindrance to be overcome, an obstacle to be surmounted if equality is to be attained" (15). For "egalitarian feminists," gender equality can only be achieved in the public sphere, and the containment of women in private, corporeal, and reproductive spheres leads to patriarchal oppression. The second category includes theorists whom Grosz refers to as "social constructionists," women like Juliet Mitchell, Julia Kristeva, Michèle Barrett, and Nancy Chodorow. Harboring a more positive attitude toward the body compared to the first group, this camp problematizes "the social system [that] organizes and gives meaning to biology," rather than biology per se (17). In other words, what oppresses women is not the body itself but the ideological and sociopolitical formations of gender that are based on perceived biological differences.

For the purpose of analyzing Kim Ki-duk's women, perhaps the third group, or what Grosz terms a "sexual difference" camp, is most relevant. Represented by such feminists as Luce Irigaray, Hélène Cixous, Gayatri Chakravorty Spivak, Jane Gallop, Moira Gatens, Vicki Kirby, Judith

Butler, Naomi Schor, and Monique Wittig, this group is most affirmative about the body as a locus of female identity. As Grosz elaborates:

> For them, the body is crucial to understanding woman's psychical and social existence, but the body is no longer understood as an ahistorical, biologically given, acultural object. They are concerned with the *lived body*, the body insofar as it is represented and used in specific ways in particular cultures. For them, the body is neither brute nor passive but is interwoven with and constitutive of systems of meaning, signification, and representation. On one hand, it is a signifying and signified body; on the other, it is an object of systems of social coercion, legal inscription, and sexual and economic exchange. . . . The body is regarded as the political, social, and cultural object par excellence. . . . As sexually specific, the body codes the meanings projected onto it in sexually determinant ways. These feminists do not evoke a precultural, presocial, or prelinguistic pure body but a body as social and discursive object, a body bound up in the order of desire, signification, and power. (19)

Most feminist critics who denounce Kim Ki-duk's films seem to subscribe to the somewhat antiquated notion of the body put forth by egalitarian feminists. It would appear that, to them, the "lived body"—or, to borrow Kim's own idea, the body "as a means of living"—is inferior to the cerebral work performed by white-collar women. To appreciate the multilayered meanings of the female body in Kim's cinema, it is imperative to move beyond the conventional hierarchy that situates the mind over the body, masculinity over femininity. In his interview with Chŏng Sŏng-il, Kim professes his desire to "iron the human body" out to eradicate differences at the level of genitalia (Chŏng, *Kim Ki-duk* 350). This admittedly grotesque metaphor attests to the fact that Kim has no vested interest in representing the sexualized body: for him, the focus lies in "a signifying and signified body" (to borrow Grosz's words) that might serve to externalize psychic traumas and perform social identities that he believes to be significant sites of meaning.

Perhaps no other work in Kim Ki-duk's filmography foregrounds the "lived body" of a working-class woman as prominently as *Birdcage Inn*. It is a small miracle that this—Kim's third film—was put into production at all, given the dismal failures (commercial and critical) of his debut and sophomore films, *Crocodile* and *Wild Animals*. The demoralized director was just about to toss in the towel and fly back to France when he received news that the state-subsidized KOFIC would award special production grants to select scenarios at its annual screenwriting contest. Kim hurriedly drafted a screenplay for a story set in P'ohang, an industrial seaport where he served in the marines for five years. His scenario was awarded the second-place prize, and KOFIC bankrolled the project, albeit within the financial constraints of its grant (approximately $260,000). The state subsidy served to alleviate the director's commercial burdens, the pressure that he might have felt to perform well at the box office, and thus gave birth to what can be considered Kim's first full-fledged "auteur film"—one that would travel the international festival circuit, from Berlin to Moscow to Montreal to Los Angeles.

*Birdcage Inn*'s first image is a medium close-up shot of two green turtles crawling on a pile of junk, which consists of a red telephone, a sex magazine, some bricks, and a capsized, broken fishbowl containing a couple of fish, among other things. The camera zooms in on one of the turtles, which starts to navigate a space of busy human and automobile traffic, as indicated by close-ups of many pedestrians' shoes and the wheels of cars. A close-up of a woman's hand, her fingernails painted purple, enters from the left side of the frame and picks up the turtle before it becomes roadkill. The next image, an underwater shot, captures the reflection of the turtle's benefactor—a young woman, seen from a low angle, dressed in a purple skirt and white cardigan. She releases the animal onto the reflective surface. Following a Korean-language title-card shot (with the words *P'aran taemun* [Blue Gate] in blue letters against the blank screen), a 360-degree panning shot establishes the film's primary setting, Songdo Beach of P'ohang, home to South Korea's steel industry. A thirtysomething woman in a black cardigan and arrow-patterned skirt walks toward the camera on the beach, which is scarcely populated save for a handful of fishermen and empty seafront sushi restaurants. The setting's desolation is accentuated by the Pohang Iron and Steel Company (POSCO)'s sprawling steel-refinery facilities, visible in the distant background, as well as a rusted steel diving tower in the middle of the water. When the camera completes its circular panning motion, a yellow taxi comes into view. After the vehicle approaches the beachfront, a young woman—the one who has saved the turtle in the prologue scene—hops out of it.

At this point, the two women—one exiting the beach, the other entering—bump into one another, an act that anticipates many mutually reciprocal female interactions throughout the narrative. This physical convergence results in a plastic bag with goldfish (which the slightly older woman in black has been carrying) dropping onto the sand. After the women exchange perplexed looks, the younger one calmly takes a water bottle from her purse and fills the flattened bag with the liquid before putting the fish back into it. The older woman retrieves the bag without saying a word and departs in the same taxi that brought this stranger. Without being discouraged by the other woman's silent treatment, the out-of-towner sits down to enjoy the ocean in a blue chair, positioned somewhat precariously on the shoreline. Propped up behind her on the sand is a framed print of a female nude, a replica of a painting by the Austrian expressionist Egon Schiele. The print appears to be this woman's only possession besides her small handbag. A muscular young man in black tank top and marine's pants, who has been attending to his speedboat behind this woman, notices her and rushes to her rescue when she accidentally tips over while dozing in the chair. Without uttering a word of gratitude or kindness (recalling the nonresponse of the woman in the black cardigan), she leaves the beach hurriedly.

From the precredit prologue and the opening scene, the protagonist Chin-a is depicted as a free-spirited, independent woman. Her compassion for others, her charitable disposition, is clearly demonstrated through the benevolent act of saving the turtle and fish. She is a typical Kim protagonist, a wounded soul who carries "a symbol of hope," manifested in "vulnerable life forms such as a bird, a goldfish, and a turtle" (Kim So-hee, "Biography" 2). Adorned in frilly clothing (a flower-patterned purple dress and a light pink cardigan) and wearing make-up, she provocatively invades a masculine space dominated by steel manufacturers, fishermen, and ex-marines, carrying with her a large, conspicuous sign of the female body: Schiele's 1910 painting *Black-Haired Nude Girl Standing* (*Schwarzhaariges Mädchen*). The portrait is no ordinary female nude, however, insofar as it combines the beautiful, melancholic face of a black-haired young woman with a grotesquely emaciated, hollowed-out body (which appears to be that of a malnourished older woman). The Austrian painter's strategy of deflating the image's erotic potential through expressionistic distortion of the form resembles Kim's unconventional treatment of "brothel narratives," from *Birdcage Inn* to *Bad Guy*. In a slow-motion medium-close-up shot set on the beach, the filmmaker captures, on the right side of the frame, the face of Chin-a (who gradually slips into a trance as an ocean breeze gently caresses her hair) and, on the left side, Schiele's black-haired girl, her head resting on the left hand. Not only does this "two shot" foreground the film's central theme of female doubling and twinned sisterhood, but it also distills Kim's aesthetic sensibilities and interest in bringing together disparate things or binary oppositions: solidity and fluidity, stillness and movement, beauty and grotesquery.

A profile shot of Chin-a's slowly tilting head, framed against a horizon of phallic towers and chimneys jutting up into the sky, juxtaposes the hardness of the steel plants and the softness of the female body and also gestures toward the rapid speed of South Korea's "compressed modernization" (the so-called Miracle of the Han River achieved during military regimes of the 1960s to 1980s), which is similarly set off against the leisured pace of life associated with those who are barred from white-collar jobs. Later in the film, after starting her nighttime job as a sex worker, Chin-a is shown filling up her snail-paced daytime life (when,

Figure 11. The working-class heroine Chin-a boldly invades a masculine space of steel refineries with her feminine emblem—Egon Schiele's nude portrait—in *Birdcage Inn*.

by her own account, she has "nothing to do") with drawing classes and trips to the beach for sketching. In the opening beach scene, the decelerated film speed—the slow motion—mimics Chin-a's existential state, her *tempo adagio* descent into sweet daytime reverie, which serves as a much-needed oasis from her nocturnal labor. When the well-meaning boatman, so obviously associated with speed, reaccelerates the narrative in his rush to Chin-a (whom he carries away from the water in his arms), the defiant woman immediately rejects this moment of interpellation, or ideological hailing,[19] and leaves this space that has been reclaimed by a masculine *tempo allegro*.

In the following shot, Chin-a is seen arriving at a shabby guesthouse in the back alley behind the beach, with a sign in green and red letters that reads "Birdcage Inn."[20] Although its name conjures up negative associations of entrapment and exploitation, the place is not some impersonal, multistory sex motel in the city. It is fronted by an open "blue gate" (the Korean title of the film) that leads to a dilapidated, traditional-style Korean house, complete with an open courtyard with cement floor that the entire family shares for the purposes of washing, exercise, and home gardening. On the left side of the house is the residential area with three family rooms, which are located across from a few guest rooms. Without knocking or ringing a bell, Chin-a steps into the setting and washes her wet hair at the outdoor faucet. When the angle is reversed, a middle-aged woman is shown looming over, looking down on her new employee from the left wing of the house. With no introduction or greeting, this matronly figure asks the young woman, "How old are you?" to which Chin-a answers, "Twenty-two." The inn owner comments, "Like my daughter," and points out a room in the corner that, she warns, "needs a little cleaning." Inside the lightly furnished yet untidy room, the new occupant picks up a half-torn picture of her predecessor: none other than the woman in black that she has just run into on the beach. Chin-a hangs the print of the nude on the wall, as if claiming the space as her own, and looks out to the window, which commands a rear view of the beach.

The first seven minutes of the film establish the female-centric discourse of the narrative. In the long shot that captures dialogue between Chin-a and her new boss, the patriarch of the house (the older woman's husband) is visible in the background, where he is reduced to the status of a silent observer, situated outside of the female interactions taking place in the foreground. Following her predecessor and boss, Chin-a encounters a third woman—the boss's daughter, who is of her age and with whom she forms the most important relationship—in the next scene.

Hae-mi, the college student, enters the scene as she steps out of her boyfriend's car in the middle of the road amid busy traffic (after refusing his offer to deposit her in front of her house). After his sedan is out of sight, Hae-mi catches a taxi and heads home, an act that showcases the shame that she feels for the family business. Walking toward Birdcage Inn after disembarking from the taxi, Hae-mi notices that a stranger, Chin-a (who is returning from her short trip to a convenience store), is heading in the same direction. Finally realizing that Chin-a is the new "service girl in residence" for her parents' business, Hae-mi coldly gazes at her and closes the gate halfway behind her, blocking Chin-a's entrance. From this icy first encounter onward, the college student takes every opportunity to exhibit her contempt and feeling of superiority to Chin-a—shying away from the side dish the sex worker has touched at the dinner table and refusing to share toothpaste with her, as if she has a disease. On a rainy day, Chin-a offers to share her yellow umbrella

Figure 12. The college student Hae-mi coldly shuts the gate and blocks Chin-a's entrance, expressing her class antagonism against the sex worker, in *Birdcage Inn*.

when the two women encounter one another outside the clinic (where the former has been given an abortion). This kind gesture prompts the college woman to declare her hostility to the sex worker, exploding, "Let's make this clear: Our class is different! So don't you ever talk to me and pretend that we're friends."

Although the rest of Hae-mi's family accept Chin-a as a surrogate member, it becomes clear that she is nevertheless a secondary outsider. Hae-mi's mother lets Chin-a call her "Mom" but admonishes her for wasting condoms and tissues. Hae-mi's father directs his disapproving gaze to his own daughter, who is disrespectful toward Chin-a at the dinner table. But one day he takes advantage of his wife's absence and rapes his employee. Hae-mi's younger brother, a would-be photographer named Hyŏn-u, is kind to Chin-a. But he eavesdrops on her as she performs sexual labor in an adjoining room. The high-school boy persuades a hesitant Chin-a not only to pose nude for his contest pictures but also to help him lose his virginity (a request that she reluctantly accepts after initially rejecting him). The overstretched sex worker is also harassed by her abusive pimp, nicknamed Dog-nose (Kaek'o), who hunts her down after being released from prison and confiscates her money. On top of all of this, a couple of clients endanger her safety: an overnight guest forces unprotected morning sex on her; and a middle-aged pervert dresses her in a high-school uniform and attempts to rape her from behind, only to be stopped by Hae-mi's father (a former gangster nicknamed "the wild dog of P'ohang," who beats the man to a pulp).

Paralleling Chin-a's oppression at the hands of lustful men is Hae-mi's troubled relationship with her boyfriend, Chin-ho, who persistently demands intercourse against her desire to save herself for marriage. After being rejected and slapped by Hae-mi one night, the drunken boyfriend visits Birdcage Inn (without knowing it is his girlfriend's house) and pays for Chin-a's service. However, it is unclear whether or not he leaves prematurely after getting Hae-mi's beeper message. Soon thereafter, Hae-mi officially brings her boyfriend to her home—something she has been avoiding thus far, despite Chin-ho's insistence. For the guest's visit, Chin-a has been asked to stay out late by Hae-mi's mother, who for the first time denies her surrogate daughter's right to family dinner (something she has been adamant about despite Hae-mi's expressed aversion to eating with Chin-a). Feeling betrayed and abandoned, Chin-a drinks heavily and shows up uninvited for dinner in "slutty" makeup, to the embarrassment of Hae-mi and her parents.

When Hae-mi tells Chin-ho that Chin-a is her cousin who is helping her parents' business, the sex worker boldly declares that her business is selling sex to lonely travelers. Hae-mi walks out and is followed by her equally embarrassed boyfriend (who is apparently nervous about being recognized from his recent visit as a client). After the couple leaves, Hae-mi's mother slaps Chin-a, who then forcefully feeds rice to herself while uncontrollably weeping. Later that night, when Hae-mi returns home (after being consoled by her understanding boyfriend), she confronts Chin-a, who is quietly grieving outside of her room: "You think everything is so easy. Anybody can live like you." The woman talks back defiantly, "I live easily? How do you know how I feel?" Without backing down, Hae-mi furthers her antagonism: "Don't try to make an excuse. You dug your own grave. Your sentimental look of movie-heroine sadness disgusts me."

At the midpoint of the film, the deepening conflict between the two women reaches its climax when a suspicious Hae-mi confronts her boyfriend (based on her mother's observation that he looks familiar and her own spotting of his shoes outside Chin-a's room on the night of his first visit). The boyfriend, in turn, confesses that he made a prior visit to this locale but insists that he did not have sex with Chin-a. Upon his request, Chin-a is called as a witness, but she contradicts his account in front of Hae-mi and confirms that they indeed did have sex twice that evening. The enraged girlfriend insults Chin-a, returning a Walkman the latter has secretly bought for Hae-mi (who initially mistakes it as a present from her mother) and telling her that she cannot accept a gift bought with "dirty" money. Subsequently, Hae-mi does everything she can to get rid of the in-house sex worker, informing her mother of Hyŏn-u's relationship with Chin-a (which she has learned of as an auditory voyeur, overhearing a conversation between the two) and even reporting her own parents' illegal business transactions to the police, which results in the overnight incarceration of Hae-mi's father and Chin-a.

Despite these explosive conflicts, a major turning point in the two women's antagonistic relationship occurs when Hae-mi enters Chin-a's room to return her luggage. She does so in accordance with her mother's wishes (since the old woman has impulsively laid off the worker, only to change her mind immediately thereafter for practical reasons: she has no replacement). In Chin-a's room, Hae-mi notices things about the woman that had earlier escaped her vision: going through her belongings, she spots a stuffed bear, a pet goldfish, and a sketchbook filled with drawings of her and her family members. Hae-mi smiles in recognition of her own angry expression, which has been captured in Chin-a's lifelike pencil portrait. Out on the beach, and gazing toward the diving tower, the college student witnesses the intense lovemaking between Chin-a and the boatman, the only man who has consistently treated the socially ostracized woman with respect. From this point on, Hae-mi's negative perception of Chin-a and her sexual activities changes. In this reverse-gender Oedipal scenario, the primal scene of the nurturing Chin-a's lovemaking awakens the latent sexuality of a character who might be thought of as her "prodigal daughter," someone who has previously defied that kinship. Captured in dynamic circular crane shots from multiple angles and accompanied by swelling orchestral music, this is the only sex scene in the film that Kim opts to stylize (the other moments of intercourse are treated either as offscreen noises that disturb frigid Hae-mi and excite her young brother, or as emotionless business transactions briefly glimpsed from the perspective of stoic Chin-a, who quietly bears the weight of her insensitive, overexcited client).

In lieu of the normative, heterosexual male gaze (a privileged looking position in Hollywood and South Korean mainstream cinema), Kim's film foregrounds Hae-mi's *female gaze* in a couple of reaction-shot close-ups that register a complex combination of confusion, shock, and excitement. The elegantly shot and simply edited love scene is followed by an abstract, low-angle shot of two women: Hae-mi gazing meditatively at the water, and Chin-a standing behind her. This unstable image fluctuates as waves fill the bottom half of the screen.

The destabilization of social barriers dividing the two women (foreshadowed in the aforementioned image) is further evidenced in an intriguing "tailing" sequence, a moment when a pantomimic game of role-reversal occurs. In the scene that immediately precedes this sequence, Hae-mi receives a card with a reprinted picture of Egon Schiele's *Two Little Girls* (*Zwei kleine Mädchen*; 1911), given to her by Chin-a. The picture shows two sister-like girls in matching dresses—a blonde in black and red, and a brunette in black and blue—sitting side by side. A close-up shot of Hae-mi scrutinizing the picture leads to a point-of-view long shot of Chin-a (in a feminine green-blue, square-patterned dress) exiting her private art school. As the camera tracks Chin-a's movement to the right, the identity of the looker is revealed in the foreground. Hae-mi, wearing a masculine white shirt, gray tie, and gray pants, can be seen observing Chin-a from the window of a fashion boutique across the street, her back turned to the camera. The next shots show Hae-mi following and watching Chin-a as she flips through art-history tomes in a bookstore, eats snacks in a makeshift restaurant, sings at a karaoke by herself, and tries on a green flower hairpin picked up from a street vendor. The direction of the gaze suddenly shifts after Chin-a sees Hae-mi's reflection in the hand mirror while trying the pin on her hair. Chin-a quickly ducks into a back-alley restroom and disappears from sight. The second half of this tailing sequence unfolds from Chin-a's point of view; she assumes the role of the subject rather than object of surveillance. Not suspecting that she is being watched by Chin-a, Hae-mi stops by the exact locations—the bookstore, the restaurant, the karaoke, and the pin vendor—and mimics the activities of the other woman. While trying on a hairpin (albeit a pink rather than green one), Hae-mi sees the reflection of her follower in the mirror. The college student turns

Figure 13. Hae-mi recognizes her "twin sister" Chin-a in a symbolic mirror shot toward the end of the trailing sequence of *Birdcage Inn*.

her head and gazes directly at Chin-a with an embarrassed expression. The reverse close-up shows Chin-a acknowledging Hae-mi's look with a coy yet friendly smile. The scene ends with a static overhead shot of the two women facing one other from opposite sides of the street.

This sequence might remind many cinephiles of a more famous, yet similarly silent and uncanny, tailing sequence in Alfred Hitchcock's *Vertigo* (1958). In this classic mystery-thriller, the policeman-turned-private eye John "Scottie" Ferguson (James Stewart) follows his old college pal's allegedly possessed wife, Madeleine Elster (Kim Novak), who in one famous sequence wanders throughout the city of San Francisco while in an apparent trance. Focalized through Scottie's perspective, this long travelling sequence takes us from one destination to another. First he (and we, the audience) visit a flower shop, and from there he makes his way to a graveyard at a Spanish mission. Then he follows the woman to an art gallery in the Palace of the Legion of Honor, and then to a vintage hotel, where the enigmatic woman vanishes without a trace. Early in the sequence, Scottie follows Madeleine to a drab back alley of the cityscape, where the object of his investigation disappears into a building. As the detective follows the woman's path through a dark storage room and then opens a back door, the jarring sight of a soft-focused, well-lit space filled with vibrantly colored flowers (in the midst of which Madeleine stands) catches the hero/audience off guard. Here, Hitchcock and his cinematographer, Robert Burks, insert an intriguing shot in which the male looker and the object of his gaze are captured in a single frame. As the feminist critic Tania Modleski describes it,

> Madeline turns around and comes toward the camera, and with the cut we expect the reverse shot to show that, as is usual in classical cinema, the man is in visual possession of the woman. Quite startlingly, however, it turns out that the door has a mirror attached to it, so this shot shows both Scottie, as he looks at Madeleine, *and* Madeline's mirror image. Donald Spoto says of this shot, "by implication he (and we) may be seen as her reflection." . . . The shot is in many ways prophetic: despite all his attempts to gain control over Madeleine, Scottie will find himself repeatedly thrown back into an identification, a mirroring relationship, with her and her desires. . . . It is as if he were continually confronted with the fact that woman's uncanny otherness has some relation to himself, that he resembles her in ways intolerable to contemplate—in-

> tolerable because this resemblance throws in question his own fullness of being. (92)

If we were to change the pronouns *he, himself,* and *his* to *she, herself,* and *her,* Modleski's description would evoke Hae-mi's relationship with Chin-a in *Birdcage Inn.*

Like Hitchcock, Kim Ki-duk has a penchant for scenes of voyeurism wherein one character (usually male) secretively watches another character (usually female) through two-way mirrors, windows, doors, or other Peeping Tom devices, on view in such films as *Wild Animals, Address Unknown,* and *Bad Guy.* As Kim Kŭm-dong states,

> In Kim Ki-duk's films, the act of peeping is not a means of releasing voyeuristic desire but an identification process through which the watcher recognizes identicalness between him/herself and the person being watched. . . . Through peeping, Hae-mi realizes Chin-a is the same as herself despite her preconceived notion of differences. The relationship between the two changes as if they were sisters, friends, or the two little girls in Egon Schiele's painting. (22)

Even in Kim's other films that focus on heterosexual relationships, that act of engaging in Peeping Tom behavior rarely, if ever, offers voyeuristic pleasure for the onscreen male viewing subject.

In *Bad Guy,* the gangster Han-gi watches Sŏn-hwa's room through a two-way mirror on the wall as the virgin prostitute is forced to receive her first client. Unable to bear witnessing her physical struggle, accompanied by pained screams, the soft-hearted pimp gives a call to his underling, who forcefully intervenes to remove the bewildered would-be rapist. The following night, Han-gi lets the fearful woman be deflowered by a different man, after his attempt at issuing another intervention is blocked by the proprietor of the brothel. However, he masochistically watches the painful rape scene through the window, with visible agony accentuated by shadows cast on his face, shown in close-up with low-key lighting. The window in the adjacent room functions as a movie screen-like apparatus through which the titular "bad guy" identifies with female pain and transforms his initial social *ressentiment* into interclass, cross-gender empathy. Forty minutes into the film, the first tender moment between the two characters occurs when the tormented Sŏn-hwa leans her cheek against the mirror, and Han-gi, on the other side of the glass in the next room, gently caresses and kisses her face unbeknownst to the woman (who nevertheless closes her eyes as if receiving solace from the cold reflective surface).

After narrowly escaping execution for the murder he did not commit, an acquitted Han-gi returns from prison and once again faces Sŏn-hwa (who, during his absence, has developed feelings for him) with only the glass wall separating them. Kim Ki-duk's static camera lingers on a long mirror shot of Sŏn-hwa—an image that, this time, also includes an overlapping reflection of Han-gi's face and torso. In the same vein as the partially reflected two-shot in *Vertigo,* Kim's dual-reflection shot emphasizes an "identification, a mirroring relationship" between Sŏn-hwa and Han-gi, who have come to understand each other's misery and suffering, transcending the gender and class schisms dividing them.[21] Unlike Hitchcock's Ferguson, however, Kim's hero voluntarily gives up his position as a voyeur by igniting a lighter, the glow of which exposes his presence to Sŏn-hwa on the other side of the mirror.[22] The surprised woman breaks the mirror with an ashtray, and the two characters gaze intensely at each other through the cracks before being united and sharing an emotionally charged embrace in her room. Han-gi frees Sŏn-hwa from the brothel in the following scene, attesting to the significance of this mirror scene in the development of the odd couple's relationship.

In *Birdcage Inn* and *Bad Guy,* voyeurism functions in a way that differs considerably from Laura Mulvey's definition in her seminal essay "Visual Pleasure and Narrative Cinema." Drawing upon Freudian psychoanalysis, Mulvey sees male voyeurism in cinema as inherently sadistic, where "pleasure lies in ascertaining guilt, . . . asserting control and subjecting the guilty [woman] through punishment or forgiveness" (718). In her essay "A Closer Look at Scopophilia: Mulvey, Hitchcock, and *Vertigo,*" Marian E. Keane debunks Mulvey's argument that *Vertigo* "focuses on the implications of the active/looking, passive/looked-at split in terms of sexual difference and the power of the male symbolic encapsulated in the hero" (Mulvey 720). As Keane perceptively points out, "Mulvey describes the Stewart figure as possessing, branding, and relishing a position of active power in relation to the woman, but the truth is that he suffers throughout *Vertigo*" (236). She goes on to criticize Mulvey's account of *Vertigo,* saying that it "is blind to the woman's role within the film and to Hitchcock's allegiance with her" (246). Perhaps the same charges can be directed to blanket dismissals of Kim Ki-duk's cinema as misogynistic—charges that too often fail to account for male suffering and female subjectivity therein.

Throughout Kim's oeuvre, the male body is subject to various forms of physical affliction and degradation, including beatings, stabbings, gunshot wounds, mutilations, torture, and incarceration. As Sheng-mei Ma points out, some of the ingredients of Kim's controversial "themes of 'non-person' torment effecting transcendence" include "physical violence against males, sexual violence against females, and voicelessness/bodilessness" (36). In his discussion of violence against the male body in Kim's cinema, Ma raises an intriguing objection to the director's sexual politics from a queer, rather than feminist, perspective:

> One is immediately struck by the fact that sexual violence is never perpetrated against males. If repeated beatings and copious bleeding so predictable in Kim aim to undo characters' manhood, why do they not culminate in the ultimate form of emasculation, homosexual anal penetration that reduces a man to a woman? That homosexuality never occurs despite overwhelming physical violence among males suggests the integrity of masculinity even within Kim's iconoclastic dramaturgy. On the contrary, physical violence against males without sexual subjugation serves paradoxically to highlight macho-ness. (36)

There are indeed a couple of demeaning images of marginalized gay characters in Kim's films. In his debut feature, *Crocodile,* a homosexual police sketch-artist makes sexual advances on the titular hero, only to be beaten and humiliated by the homophobe, who binds his face with unspooled videotape and stuffs a cucumber in his anus. The sketch-artist is portrayed as a malicious individual who frames the "Crocodile" and clubs him in revenge, a representational strategy that indirectly exonerates the heterosexual hero's explicit homophobia. In *Breath,* another effeminate gay man—a more sympathetic figure this time—leers after and is rejected by his straight cellmate, the suicidal male protagonist on death row, whose libidinal desire is awakened by a housewife who visits him regularly after watching news concerning him on television. The unwanted gay man ends up strangling the male protagonist with tears in his eyes at the end of the film, after all his advances have been for naught.

Despite the inclusion of such problematic, less-than-desirable gay images, it might be a leap of logic to associate Kim Ki-duk's films with machismo on the basis that there is no representation of "the ultimate form of emasculation, homosexual anal penetration that reduces a man to a woman." First, it is problematic to assume that gay sexual activity is the "ultimate form of emasculation," or a reference to the "feminization" of males. Such a simplified definition conflates homosexual masculinity and femininity without considering subtle gender and sexual differences. Second, I believe that Kim Ki-duk's films, far from being homophobic, are conducive to the articulation and expression of bisexual desires and identificatory modes.

Drawing upon Teresa de Lauretis's study of "feminine" narrative structures, Tania Modleski argues that Hitchcock's *Vertigo* not only solicits a "double desire" (homosexual and heterosexual) from female spectators but also a "masculine bisexual identification because of the way the male character oscillates between a passive mode and an active mode, between a hypnotic and masochistic fascination with the woman's desire and a sadistic attempt to gain control over her, to possess her" (99). Devoid of such an internally divided yet centrally focalizing male narrator, *Birdcage Inn* almost exclusively foregrounds female desire, subjectivity, and identification. The desires and actions of supporting male characters—Hae-mi's father and her brother Hyŏn-u, Hae-mi's boyfriend Chin-ho, Chin-a's pimp, Chin-a's clients, and the boatman—intermittently intrude within the narrative, but they are revealed to be ineffective and insignificant at best, or reprehensible and idiotic at worst. With a sense of black humor, Kim Ki-duk gently ridicules pompous or inappropriate male desires in several scenes: when Hae-mi's father takes his shoes to Chin-a's room lest his wife return during his adulterous rape; when Hyŏn-u celebrates his loss of virginity with an exaggerated, open-armed victory scream, which contrasts comically with his precoital kneeling and begging in front of Chin-a; when Chin-ho lures Hae-mi into a motel, making the empty promise that he will lay beside her without touching her body (after being rejected by his frigid girlfriend in bed, Chin-ho blames uncontrollable male hormones for his ungentlemanly behavior).

It is noteworthy that Kim Ki-duk uses dress codes and hairstyles to contrast Chin-a's femininity (long hair, painted nails, colorful dresses and skirts) with Hae-mi's boyishness (crew-cut hair, white shirts, and dark pants). After the trailing sequence, Hae-mi assumes the masculine role of Chin-a's protector, shielding her from the abusive pimp and saving her life by stopping a suicide attempt. During the night that Chin-a returns from hospital, the two women consummate their "coupling" on a boat at the waterfront: Hae-mi puts a green flower hairpin in Chin-a's hair, rests her head on Chin-a's lap, and tells her that she does not care about what happened between her boyfriend and Chin-a. By this point, heterosexual romantic interests for these women—Chin-ho and the boatman—have dropped out of the narrative or are rendered insignificant.

Interclass homosocial bonding and sisterhood are ultimately tested and confirmed in the controversial penultimate scene of the film. For the first time, Hae-mi invites Chin-a to her room while it is snowing in the summer night, foreshadowing a miracle that is about to happen. When a voice is heard from outside, Hae-mi volunteers to go out and check, telling Chin-a (who is still recovering from her wrist wound) to rest. Entering his guest room, the middle-aged client asks the college student if she is "the girl" and how much she charges. Hae-mi asks the guest to wait and heads to her room (where Chin-a awaits), her hesitant steps accentuated in a close-up shot of her blue shoes. In the middle, she stops, squats, and makes a snowball, which she rolls in the direction of her room and Chin-a. The camera cuts to the interior of Hae-mi's room, where Chin-a is going through her friend's books and pictures to kill time. Finding it odd that Hae-mi is not returning, Chin-a opens the door to look for her friend and spots Hae-mi's shoes and footprints in the snow outside the guest room across the garden. The next shot is a close-up reflection of Chin-a's curious, peeping face outside the window of the guest's room. Suppressing such anticipated images as a point-of-view shot of the guestroom (the scene of Hae-mi's surrogate prostitution) and Chin-a's reaction shot (one that registers shock), Kim's camera tastefully cuts to a slow-motion pillow shot of Hae-mi's snowball in a close-up.

Subsequently, the screen goes to white/blank before transitioning to a close-up of the Birdcage Inn's blue gate, which opens magically—much like a theatrical curtain—to reveal a happy portrait of Hae-mi and Chin-a's family opening the morning together in the garden. The three children are washing and brushing their teeth while the mother peels vegetables and the father burns trash, including a sex magazine with Chin-a's nude photos. Filling the sound track is Richard Schönherz's instrumental rendition of "Ruhe Sanft" from Wolfgang Amadeus Mozart's unfinished opera *Zaide*, the same cheerful yet elegant minuet-style music that accompanied the opening beach scene. After a series of frontal close-ups of family members looking directly at the camera and lighting up with big smiles (with the exception of Hae-mi's father, whose attention is distracted by a nude picture that he is in the process of burning), the film takes us back to the beach where the narrative began. The camera cranes in to show Chin-a and Hae-mi sharing a friendly conversation—albeit one that is muted by nondiegetic music—while sitting side-by-side on the diving tower, their proximity reminiscent of Egon Schiele's little girls.

The film concludes with another low-angle reflection shot. Reminiscent of a similar shot with Chin-a and the turtle (from the precredit prologue), this final shot shows the two smiling women looking down at a goldfish in the ocean. The image is squeezed as the screen is split in two and credits roll on the left side against the black background. In slow motion, the image of Chin-a and Hae-mi distorts and disintegrates as the waves hit the reflective surface. The final freeze-frame shows the faces of Chin-a and Hae-mi, their visages slipping and sliding as if they are in the process of melting into one another.

This final shot of *Birdcage Inn* epitomizes Kristeva's notion of "semiotic *chora*," which the French feminist defines as "the *mobile-receptacle site of the process* . . . a representation of the subject in process" ("Subject in Process" 134). Kristeva borrows the concept of *chora* (*khora*) from Plato's *Timaeus*, "where it has several possible meanings, including womb, enclosed space, nurse, receptacle and mother" (Robbins 130). It is a preverbal, pre-Oedipal space structured around the maternal body—a space of perpetual motion and infinite renewal. The *chora* is further characterized by the dissolution of boundaries and "partitions in which the subject might shelter in order to constitute itself" (Kristeva, "Subject in Process" 134). In the final shot of *Birdcage Inn*, the water/ocean functions as a regenerative, pulsating space of semiotic *chora* wherein the two female subjects are in the process of becoming one,

Figure 14. The faces of Chin-a (left) and Hae-mi (right) are in the process of blending into one another in the abstract final shot of *Birdcage Inn*.

unfettered by language and largely outside the symbolic order (note that the entire epilogue sequence is rendered without dialogue, and the father figure is marginalized as a distracted outsider).

Although it may seem that Kim Ki-duk idealizes the utopian potential of such a feminine space free from patriarchal oppression and surveillance, the distorted final image of two women makes one feel ambivalent about the subversive power of the semiotic. This imagistic ambivalence aptly captures the spirit of Kristeva's theory, regardless of whether Kim intended it or not. The unstable, mobile *chora* is a space in which the signifying subject is both generated and negated. Thus, Kristeva believes that the desire to return to the repressed drive is a dangerous inclination for female writers, since women's over-identification with the pre-Oedipal maternal force can lead to the loss of identity and an embrace of the death drive. She links female writers' semiotic obsession with the risk of suicide, exemplified in the case of the English author Virginia Woolf, "who sank wordlessly into the river . . . [h]aunted by voices, waves, lights, in love with colours—blue, green" (Kristeva, "About Chinese Women" 157). In fact, the drowning woman is a kind of archetypal figure or recurring trope in Kim Ki-duk's films, including *Crocodile, The Isle, Bad Guy,* and *Spring, Summer, Fall, Winter . . . and Spring. Birdcage Inn* also features a soft-filtered fantasy sequence in which Hae-mi finds the drowned body of Chin-a buried in the beach sand—a nightmare that prompts the college student to raid the guest's room at night just in time to save the sex worker who has slashed her wrist out of despair.

Along with *Birdcage Inn, Samaritan Girl* is among the most "feminine" of all Kim Ki-duk's films. It explores the promiscuous behaviors associated with ambivalent female teen sexuality with probing psychological insights. From its outset, *Samaritan Girl* establishes a mirroring relationship between two high-school girls who set up an online escort service to save up money for a summer trip to Europe. Reminiscent of the early scenes in the Romanian film *4 Months, 3 Weeks, and 2 Days* (2007), in which the young female character Otilia arranges an illegal abortion for her college friend Gabriella, the middle-class girl Yŏ-jin (doted on by her widowed detective father) functions as a backstage manager and bookkeeper for her less privileged friend Chae-yŏng's online chat-room-based prostitution business. Just as Otilia fronts for Gabriella and contacts the abortionist Mr. Bebe on her behalf in *4 Months, 3 Weeks, and 2 Days,* Yŏ-jin calls prospective clients and makes appointments pretending to be Chae-yŏng, who is reliant on her managerial skills. Despite this hierarchical brain/body division of labor and apparent class difference, from the beginning of the film the two girls share deep friendship and even latent homosexual desire, insinuated in a couple of intimate bath scenes in which Yŏ-jin admires Chae-yŏng's beauty and curses the "filthy men" she sleeps with. This, among other things, sets *Samaritan Girl* apart from *Birdcage Inn,* despite their obvious similarities.

The mise-en-scène in *Samaritan Girl* often emphasizes the characters' horizontal camaraderie by capturing both girls in two shots, sitting side by side, running hand in hand, and walking arm in arm in identical school uniforms. Consisting of three roughly half-hour segments (titled "Vasumitra," "Samaria," and "Sonata"), the first part of the film ends with the tragic death of Chae-yŏng, who jumps out of a motel window to escape capture by the raiding police. In the second part of the film, Yŏ-jin assumes the name and identity of Chae-yŏng to meet her former clients one by one and relive the dead girl's sexual experiences in ritualistic fashion. Right before receiving her first client, Yŏ-jin looks out of the same window from which her friend jumped and sees the apparition of Chae-yŏng waving to her. All sex acts occur offscreen, and, when fleetingly glimpsed, the insignificant male body is apparently little more than an empty vessel for the bereaved teen, who goes to extreme lengths to reach a spiritual communion with her dead friend and alleviate her guilt complex. After her sexual encounters with older men, to their surprise Yŏ-jin pays them money—or, more correctly, she returns the money they paid to Chae-yŏng—and thanks them as if she is *their* client. In fact, she inadvertently becomes the Vasumitra of Chae-yŏng's story and reforms her pedophilic clients, who, after their transformative liaisons with Yŏ-jin, atone in one way or another (by calling their daughters or praying for Yŏ-jin in utmost sincerity).

Forty minutes into the narrative, *Samaritan Girl* undergoes a radical shift in the point of view, as Yŏ-jin's father Yŏng-gi emerges as our central identifactory conduit, intercepting female narration midway. The

Figure 15. An intimate two shot of Chae-yŏng (left) and Yŏ-jin (right) in *Samaritan Girl* accentuates the deep friendship and latent homosexual desire of the two teens.

hardened detective who is also a gentle father discovers his daughter's double life as he accidentally spots Yŏ-jin with a client from the window of another motel, where he is investigating a murder case. As Sheng-mei Ma asserts, from this point, "the detective father and the realistic realm he represents intrude into the symbolic and mystical context" of female sexuality (41). Unlike Hae-mi's disempowered father in *Birdcage Inn*, the detective father in *Samaritan Girl* is endowed with both symbolic/patriarchal and public/state powers. He is an unlikely hero in Kim's universe, where law-enforcement figures along with the rich and affluent are typically depicted as corrupt and abusive (in both *Bad Guy* and *3-Iron*, a police detective misuses his professional power for personal gain). However, the middle-class hero Yŏng-gi descends into an abyss of maddening rage as he runs surveillance on his own daughter and blocks any planned sexual liaisons, behind her back, by resorting to various bullying tactics on her partners (from punching and slapping to vandalism on cars and verbal insults). After pushing a middle-aged patriarch to suicide by humiliating him in front of his family, the vengeful father arrives too late to block another tryst and ruthlessly kills a thirtysomething man who has just had quick car sex with Yŏ-jin in a public park.

Just when the film has started to look like a masculine thriller in which the father dominates as a brutal disciplinary force, the third chapter—titled "Sonata" (the name of a Hyundai that the detective drives)—begins, and the narrative takes an unexpected turn. The father and daughter travel to a remote countryside area to visit the dead wife/mother's grave. It is there—in the maternal space of *chora*—where symbolic language and order (which dominates the middle section of the film) gradually disintegrates. This major transformation occurs by a river, where the father parks his Sonata and calls his colleague to turn himself in while Yŏ-jin is sleeping. The "realistic realm" of the father/symbolic bleeds into the semiotic world, and the point of view shifts back to Yŏ-jin. In a surreal dream sequence shot in semi-black-and-white, the daughter wakes up and looks for her father, shouting "Appa" ("Dad"). The detective/father attacks her from behind, strangles her, and buries her body in the riverbank. He puts headphones on her before covering her body with soil. He then pulls out the cord to connect it to the CD player above ground. He presses the play button, and Erik Satie's "Gymnopédie No. 1" fills the sound track (which is audibly focalized through the dead girl's perspective or posthumous sensorium). The father's action repeats an earlier scene in which he wakes his daughter by playing Satie's music the same way at her bedside. The eerie dream sequence not only brings to light the complex psychological state of Yŏ-jin (a combination of guilt for her actions and fear for paternal punishment) but also hints that she may have sensed that her father knew about her secrets and that she may have suspected all along that it was him who sabotaged her recent dates and murdered the guy in the park (whose mangled body in the public restroom so traumatized her).

Back in full color, Yŏ-jin wakes up from the nightmare with a gasp of relief. She then sees her father painting rocks in yellow to make traffic lines for driving practice (in an earlier scene, he offers her a driving lesson when she shows an interest in steering the car). After giving her basic instructions, the father tells her to try it on her own. The director crosscuts between close-ups of Yŏ-jin engrossed in the wonder of driving and long shots of a white jeep approaching from afar and the father turning himself in to his fellow detectives. After a successful run through the makeshift test course on the riverbank, the teen pops her head out of the car window and calls to her father proudly, only to see a departing police jeep. A bird's-eye-view aerial shot shows Yŏ-jin's Sonata following the white jeep on a curvy, muddy country road. Several long shots track the inexperienced Yŏ-jin chasing the jeep, which disappears offscreen in the foreground as the black Sonata falls behind in the background. Yŏ-jin's sedan gets struck in the muddy swamp and becomes immobile. A point-of-view shot shows the jeep quickly speeding forward, away from Yŏ-jin's position. The novice driver struggles to accelerate, but she is unable to pull the car out of the mud.

Widening shots situate the stranded black Hyundai, a masculinized sign of South Korea's modernization, in the peaceful, foggy, rural landscape against a sound track of lyrical music with subdued yet decisively female background chorus. In the striking final image, an extreme long shot, Yŏ-jin's tiny, lost figure outside the car (looking around at her surroundings aimlessly) becomes part of the grand semiotic *chora,* where the female subject is in the process of regeneration and renewal outside the phallocentric, symbolic order. As a woman and as a film scholar drawn to many different national cinemas, rarely have I seen a more powerfully affective image than this transcendental final shot of

Figure 16. The final extreme long shot of *Samaritan Girl* shows Yŏ-jin's tiny, lost figure in the space of the "semiotic *chora*," where the female subject is in the process of regeneration and renewal.

*Samaritan Girl.* It poetically captures the essence of feminine writing, as described by Hélène Cixous: "A feminine textual body is recognized by the fact that it is always endless, without ending: there is no closure" ("Castration or Decapitation?" 53).

The etymological root of the term *semiotic* is the Greek word *sema,* which means "distinctive mark, trace, index, precursory sign, proof, engraved or written sign, imprint . . . figuration" (Kristeva, "Semiotic and the Symbolic" 47). I propose that the neofeminist elements in Kim Ki-duk's cinema can be seen in the same capacity as mark, trace, index, sign, imprint, and figuration. The final image of *Samaritan Girl* is one of the most powerful feminist signs in contemporary South Korean cinema, albeit one that has been neglected by feminist critics at home and abroad. Kim's semiotic poetics are charged with subversive energies, rhythms, ruptures, and musicality and can break down the unifying symbolic language of mainstream South Korean cinema. Kim himself is a perfect candidate for the Kristevan *sujet en procés* (subject in process), an individual who is continually developing, as evidenced by his versatility as a factory worker, a soldier, a would-be-priest, a street artist, a screenwriter, and a film director. To understand the relevance of

Kristeva's concept to Kim's directorial career, one needs only to compare the "crude," uneven quality of his early works (such as *Crocodile* and *Wild Animals,* both of which contain moments of visual brilliance undercut by implausible, discombobulated narratives) with the aesthetic polish and narrative sophistication of his internationally acclaimed works such as *Spring, Summer, Fall, Winter . . . and Spring, Samaritan Girl,* and *3-Iron.*

There are pitfalls and risks involved in generalizing feminine writing and female identity via French feminist theory, which has been criticized in its own right for biological essentialism, ahistoricism, utopianism, and romanticism, among other things.[23] More specifically, Cixous and Kristeva have been criticized for privileging European avant-garde male writers. In her influential article "French Feminism in an International Frame," the postcolonial feminist Gayatri Chakravorty Spivak states, "Kristeva seems to suggest that if women can accede to the avant-garde in general, they will fulfill the possibilities of their discourse. . . . Cixous privileges poetry . . . and suggests that a Kleist or a Rimbaud can speak as women do" (142). According to Kristeva, the two modalities of semiotic/feminine/maternal and symbolic/Oedipal/paternal are not mutually exclusive. As she elaborates, "[T]he subject is always *both* semiotic *and* symbolic, no signifying system . . . can be either 'exclusively' semiotic or 'exclusively' symbolic, and is instead necessarily marked by an indebtedness to both" ("Semiotic and the Symbolic" 47). Despite the theoretical persuasiveness of Kristeva's fluid, deconstructive thinking, there is good reason to feel ambivalent about celebrating already canonized male artists as model practitioners of feminine/semiotic writing.

The issue is particularly relevant in film studies, since historians and critics have long embraced male-directed films as "women's pictures"—from the classical Hollywood melodramas and romantic comedies of George Cukor to postmodern period pieces and fantasy films directed by the Hong Kong auteur Stanley Kwan—due to the severe shortage of female directors in mainstream film industries.[24] In the context of South Korean cinema, Soyoung Kim takes an inclusive approach and refers to both male-directed commercial films and female-directed documentaries as *yŏsŏng yŏnghwa* (woman's film) (187–89). Here I concur with the British feminist critic Annette Kuhn, who insists that a feminine or feminist text is created in the moment of reception, rather than production, through "feminist [critical] intervention" (13–14). She goes on to argue that "to write 'in the feminine' is in itself to challenge the ideological constitution of dominant modes of representation. It is in this respect that such a cultural practice may be considered as feminist" (18). Like her French contemporaries—Kristeva, Cixous, and Irigaray—Kuhn does not equate "writing in the feminine" (*l'écriture féminine*) with female writers/directors (*femmes auteurs*).

In his interview with Marta Merajver-Kurlat, Kim Ki-duk voices his thoughts about feminist debates surrounding his films:

> [T]here are people who consider my films as antifeminist and derogatory to females in general. There are many diverse feminists, ranging from just a female to a female activist to a female college [student]. When it is a group, some movies become their flag or, in my films' case, it becomes their political target. There are times when a cut from my movies is required for their ideology, but if you watch my entire film, you may consider me to be a feminist. Therefore, I think there are various possible interpretations. (26–27)

Although it may be naïve to accept Kim's self-appellation as a "feminist" at face value, feminist film criticism can indeed benefit from being open to "various possible interpretations" of the female images in his cinema rather than blindly attacking the director and rashly foreclosing possibilities for constructive dialogue.

As in the cases of Alfred Hitchcock, Robert Altman, Brian De Palma, and Lars von Trier, Kim has been singled out as an "antifeminist" auteur partly because many of his films center on women who suffer physically and psychologically. Taking Altman as an example, Robin Wood eloquently articulates why a male director's travestied identification with his suffering heroines can be problematic in spite of benign intentions:

> Obviously, Altman's identification with a female (never feminist) position is extremely problematic: it is limited almost exclusively to the notion of woman-as-victim, to sensation of pain, humiliation and breakdown. If one reads it as the expression of Altman's own "femininity," then it is centered upon masochism and self-punishment; if one reads it as an effort to understand how actual women within patriarchal culture *feel*, then the masochism begins to look suspiciously like its counterpart, sadism. (44)

It is precisely this convergence of masochism and sadism that disturbs many feminist/female viewers of Kim Ki-duk's films. However, (mis) directing spectatorial outrage to the text and its author rather than to the patriarchal system/culture that the text exposes is, in my view, neither a mature nor a sophisticated mode of reception.

The feminist debate surrounding Kim Ki-duk reminds me of the ironic finale of Alexander Payne's satirical comedy *Citizen Ruth* (1996), in which an irresponsible, glue-addicted Ruth Stoops and her unborn baby (whom she is ordered to abort by a judge in her drug trial) accidentally become a political symbol of the abortion battle being fought in America's heartland. Toward the end of the film, Ruth's high-profile case draws hundreds of protesters from both sides of the issue to the clinic where she is supposed to get an abortion (unbeknownst to the crowd, Ruth has had a miscarriage but pretends to be pregnant still to take advantage of monetary offers from both pro-life and pro-choice factions). After collecting fifteen thousand dollars from a security guard at the clinic (an advocate of personal freedom who has cashed in on his veteran's compensation to match the bid from a pro-life group), Ruth passes by a large crowd of oblivious protesters, who are self-absorbed in their political fervor, and spirits away. Likewise, in the heated critical debate between pro- and anti-Kim factions, the celluloid female body has been appropriated as evidence to advance the political agendas of individual critics. Too much critical energy has been squandered on debating whether or not Kim Ki-duk is an antifeminist, rather than unpacking the wide range of women's social issues depicted in his films—prostitution, rape, abduction, abortion, domestic violence, marital infidelity, teenage sexuality, cosmetic surgery, and so forth—and raising feminist consciousness *through,* not against, his films.

There is no better way to wrap up this attempt at a revisionist neofeminist discussion of Kim Ki-duk's work than by introducing dialogue between the director and Lim Soon-rye (Im Sun-rye), a prominent Korean female director who recently produced *Forever the Moment* (*Uri saengae ch'oego ŭi sungan*; 2008), an inspiring feminist sports film about the Olympic women's handball team. KOFIC's Korean Film Directors series, in its entry on Lim Soon-rye, features dialogue between Kim Ki-duk—an alleged antifeminist—and the bona-fide feminist director.

Arranged by the film magazine *Cine 21*, the interview is prefaced by a disclaimer-like foreword:

> The apprehension that their worlds might be miles apart turned out to have been groundless. Director Lim Soon-rye and director Kim Ki-duk, who seem to have little in common, in fact had many things in common. Lim's third-rate band wandering around night clubs (in *Waikiki Brothers* [2001]) and Kim's Amerasians around brothels near an American military camp are not that distant. Although the method of narration—simplistic realism, on the one hand, and pictorial image, on the other hand—may be different, the picture they draw is . . . of marginalized individuals. These films have made their mark in the niche of mainstream cinema and have stayed away from large capitalistic or star-ranking systems. Making a film that has a small but firm voice, a film that shows their unique views rather than being dominated by the market order, is another common denominator between these two directors. (Lee Yoo-ran 75–76)

Toward the end of their conversation, which reveals commonality between their filmmaking styles as well as shared thematic preoccupations, Kim Ki-duk asks Lim Soon-rye if she is "really a woman." "The reason I ask this," Kim goes on to state, "is because I think you would understand me better than some female critics do" (Lee Yoo-ran 82). Lim diplomatically replies,

> Rather than that I totally agree with your depiction of women, I think I should look at it from a different angle because I'm a director. The facility that you use as the means to understand the world and humans, even if that facility is different from many women, I think it is necessary to look at it with a broad view. I depicted women too . . . [a]nd the way I expressed women . . . isn't different from the way I expressed men . . . I just used men as the subject matter. I depicted all the characters in my film with the same view and weight. (Lee Yoo-ran 82)

Lim's advocacy of macro-perspectives on social marginalization is relevant to a balanced understanding of Kim Ki-duk's cinema and the portrayals of women therein. If Lim's early "feminist" cinema explores gender oppression in a masculinist society from the perspective of alienated and disenfranchised men (nonconforming, effeminate, or obese teenaged boys who have failed in college entrance exams in *Three Friends* [*Se ch'ngu*; 1996], as well as the titular traveling band that encounters one humiliation after another while shortchanging their musical ambition in provincial nightclubs and karaoke bars in *Waikiki Brothers*), Kim's cinema does much the same thing with his sympathetic portrayals of women in a patriarchal society: female characters are subject to male violence and aggression, yet they remain strong, resilient, and resistant. Thus, it is counterproductive to address identity politics in Lim Soonrye's and Kim Ki-duk's films based solely on the biological foundation of sex, since both filmmakers are inclined to expose the cruelty of an elitist and materialist society that continues to oppress *all* nonconforming dreamers and dropouts regardless of their age or gender.

## The Bodhisattva Inner-Eye: Inwardly Drawn Transcendence in *Spring, Summer, Fall, Winter . . . and Spring*

My first encounter with Kim Ki-duk's films was at the 1999 Los Angeles AFI Film Festival, where *Birdcage Inn* was among the many screenings. My initial reaction was mixed. While I appreciated the director's visual style and his film's symbol-laden mise-en-scène, the premise of a college student sleeping with a client of her prostitute friend was too bizarre, too sensational, for me to give it the necessary attention that I now believe it deserves. Even though I could make out the film's underlying Marxist political commentary, my sensibilities were challenged in a way that I was not prepared to reflexively examine, and I quickly forgot about this new, relatively unknown filmmaker. During my graduate studies at UCLA, despite my initially unsatisfying first encounter with Kim's work, I undertook a writing project related to his latest film, *Address Unknown,* and began serious research on the director for the first time. However, my interest in that film mainly derived from its subject matter—Korean women's relationships with American G.I.s—rather than the auteur. *Address Unknown* was an even more uncomfortable film-viewing experience than that of *Birdcage Inn,* and I ended up leveling a negative critique against it from a feminist perspective. I was shocked by the extreme violence in the film, particularly the infamous eye-knifing scene.

While doing research about Kim and talking to Korean film students in Los Angeles, I began to realize that many people hate him with a passion. A Korean BFA student at UCLA told me how the director's claim of an "art education" in France is bogus, suggesting that Kim had been nothing more than a street vagabond who, as a filmmaker, only intended to repulse his audience. Again, after writing that piece on *Address Unknown,* I stopped paying attention to Kim Ki-duk and had little interest in pursuing research related to his other films. I would probably have maintained my dismissive attitude toward the director—like most middle-class Korean women—had I not seen him speak at a film festival in Paris.

While living and studying in Paris in 2002 and 2003, I had the good fortune of being able to attend the Etrange Film Festival, held at the Forum des images Cinémathèque in September 2002. The festival organizers were hosting a retrospective of five Kim Ki-duk films—*Crocodile, Wild Animals, Birdcage Inn, Real Fiction,* and *Address Unknown.* Despite my initial disregard of the filmmaker, I went to a screening of *Crocodile,* which was followed by a question-and-answer session in which the director fielded inquiries from his generally receptive audience. It was during this session that my perception of Kim Ki-duk changed. The filmmaker talked about his experience living in Paris in the early 1990s, when he made many Middle Eastern friends (some of whom had experienced French racism, according to Kim, who made a sly comment that people from the Arab world were good to him no matter what French people thought).

I was particularly moved to hear him say that the happiest time in his life had been when he immersed himself in painting while residing in a small seaside village near Montpellier, in the South of France. He recounted walking the seaside for hours each day, meditating and exhibiting his paintings on the boardwalk where few passersby bothered to give him or his work notice. Although he had few worldly possessions, that time was the freest and most relaxing of Kim's life, a time when he remained free from the pressures and conformist ideals of Korean society, where he had endured an inferiority complex due to his lack of formal education. The director told his audience that he returned to his home country with fear because, as he confided elsewhere, "[Korean] society's elite class consists of those who graduate from college and find employment in such conglomerates as Hyundai and Samsung, [whereas his] undereducated background prevented [him] from even submitting applications for decent jobs" (Chŏng, *Kim Ki-duk* 47).

Hearing his life story, spoken by him in his native tongue (which was translated for the French audience by an interpreter), I felt the pain and suffering he underwent and understood where the rage and violence—as well as the predilection for water imagery—in his films originated from. Immediately thereafter, I went to a Korean grocery in Paris and rented videos of other Kim Ki-duk films that I had missed. I can still recall watching *The Isle* on a small thirteen-inch screen in the tiny Parisian studio that my husband and I rented—both of us cringing through the infamous fishhook-mutilation scenes. However, unlike my prior viewing of *Birdcage Inn* and *Address Unknown,* I could now appreciate the transcultural meaning and affective value of cinematic pain as a crucial mode of communication.

Back in the United States, I decided to assign *Bad Guy* as the first film screening of a Gender and Korean Cinema course that I was teaching at the University of Michigan in the fall of 2004. As a novice teacher, I was nervous that my students might get upset by the level of misogyny in the film. These misgivings turned out to be groundless, however. I was pleasantly surprised when one of my students, an African American woman, approached me after the screening and told me that she knew she would love the film from the first scene—a moment in the narrative that frequently turns off many Korean female audiences. From that point forward, whenever I assigned Kim Ki-duk's films in different classes, they consistently ranked among the students' favorites in the questionnaires distributed at the end of the semester. One student, a film-production major at the University of Michigan who had seen *Bad Guy* and *3-Iron,* told me how much he appreciated Kim's instinctual rather than cerebral filmmaking style. Another student, a Japanese anime *otaku* (fanboy), reflected on how much he identified with the misunderstood male protagonist in *3-Iron.* A year later, when I was teaching film courses at Hamilton College, a female comparative-literature major selected *Samaritan Girl* as her favorite screening of the class, one whose gentle depiction of female friendship was unrivaled by any other recent film. More recently, in a graduate seminar on global popular culture at the University of Hawaii, one student—a professional writer—admitted to being amused by the irony of "suffering spectatorship" applied to mainstream American audiences of Kim's films. Another biracial graduate student saw great value in *Address Unknown* as a transnational text, despite its retooling of a familiar "tragic mulatto" narrative.

As a member of a diaspora currently residing and teaching in the United States, I have encountered Kim Ki-duk films primarily through DVD releases, with the exception of *Birdcage Inn, Crocodile,* and *Spring, Summer, Fall, Winter . . . and Spring.* It was a memorable experience when the latter film played in an art-house theater in downtown Ann Arbor in 2004. Like the colleague who saw the film with me on a peaceful Sunday afternoon, I was enthralled by the stunning beauty of its landscapes and the simple profundity of its narrative; but what struck me most was the visible maturation of Kim Ki-duk as an artist. As A. O. Scott states in his review for the *New York Times,* "[T]he film's lyrical plainness is the sign of a profound and sophisticated artistic sensibility" ("Buddhist Observes" B3)—a description that few Korean critics would offer when asked to recall the comparatively "unrefined" early works in the career of Kim Ki-duk.

It is only a slight exaggeration to say that *Spring, Summer, Fall, Winter . . . and Spring* is to Kim Ki-duk what *Dreams* (*Yume*; 1990) is to Kurosawa Akira. Several common characteristics link these two films: both feature autobiographical elements (*Dreams* is reportedly based on Kurosawa's actual dreams, and Kim's film is sort of a "spiritual confession" on his part); both films foreground nativist aesthetics, landscapes, and rituals; both films are episodic, or comprised of discrete yet linked narrative episodes (*Dreams* consists of eight separate segments, and *Spring, Summer, Fall, Winter . . . and Spring* has five seasonal segments); both films follow the human life-cycle, presenting a different stage of life in each episode (incrementally progressing from childhood to adulthood to old age); both films privilege symbolic imagery over dialogue; both films have fantastical/spiritual elements that transcend the physical constraints of reality. The main difference between them, however, is related to the age of the two directors: Kurosawa made *Dreams* at the age of eighty (nearly forty years after his directorial debut in 1943); and Kim Ki-duk produced *Spring, Summer, Fall, Winter . . . and Spring* at the age of forty-two (only seven years after his debut in 1996). It seems that "Kim's inner octogenarian," to borrow Scott Foundas's words ("Why

Dharma and Dames Don't Mix" 35), crafted an exquisitely designed film that closely matches the Japanese master's late-career meditation on the inner life of the artist.

In his review for *Film Quarterly*, Michael Sofair argues that *Spring, Summer, Fall, Winter . . . and Spring* "is typically 'Western,' conforming to the Hollywood tradition of fantasy resolutions while its spirituality becomes a retreat into abstraction and contrivance that parallels the movement of Western religions before similar challenges" (37). Ever the auteurist, Andrew Sarris puts forth an opposing position in his review for the *New York Observer*: "*Spring*, which the 43-year-old director also wrote and edited, probably represents the purest and most transcendental distillation of the Buddhist faith ever rendered on the screen" (P21). In his all-out attack on Kim Ki-duk in the pages of *Film Comment*, Tony Rayns disagrees: "Those commentators who sincerely believed that *Spring, Summer* was a profound meditation on Buddhist expiation and the natural cycle not only know nothing about Buddhism; they're also oblivious to the existence of the Korean classics from which Kim borrowed many of his ideas, Im Kwon-taek's *Mandala* (81) and Bae Yong-kyun's *Why Has Bodhi-Dharma Left for the East?* (89)" ("Sexual Terrorism" 52). Writing for the *Village Voice*, Michael Atkinson defines *Spring, Summer, Fall, Winter . . . and Spring* as "a meta-Buddhist fable, entirely connected with the quotidian of work and human vice, and in total thrall to the philosophy's poetic juxtapositions," although he does acknowledge that Kim, raised as a Christian, "invented most of the rituals and totems" ("Celestial Seasons" 54).

My interest in *Spring, Summer, Fall, Winter . . . and Spring* does not reside in debating whether or not it is a "Buddhist film," or whether it is more "Western" than "Eastern." It is a well-documented fact that Kim did not intend the film to be received as a religious text and deliberately avoided reading any books on Buddhism or soliciting the technical advice of Buddhist experts during production. In his interview with *Cine 21*, Kim explains that his film approaches Buddhism as "traditional culture" and that it does not claim any authority on Buddhism as a set of religious practices (Nam 63).[25] In his interview with the *Los Angeles Times*, however, Kim calls the film "a meditation" and expresses his wish that people "think about the meaning of their life after watching this film." The director goes on to say, "While I was making this film, I realized that life isn't all sad, life isn't only suffering, but life is also very graceful and beautiful" (Cheng E14). The latter statement is significant insofar as it offers a glimpse into Kim's softening inner psyche and his (partial) sublimation of *ressentiment,* which had permeated his early work. While Western criticism of *Spring, Summer, Fall, Winter . . . and Spring* focuses on the film's Buddhist religiosity, or lack thereof, Korean criticism targets its decisiveness as a transitional, transformative moment in Kim's career, marking a significant shift in his worldview and aesthetic sensibility.

Kim pulls his camera back from the "action" to expose a deeply recessional space, a remote forest setting severed from civilization. The narrative takes place within a floating Buddhist monastery on the lake, with the surrounding mountains towering above this site of conflict, longing, and resignation. It is a timeless space, far removed from modern-day attractions and taken-for-granted amenities, such as electricity, cellular phones, television, radio, and the Internet. In a manner that breaks from his earlier films, Kim uses copious establishing shots as well as extreme long shots to capture the changing seasonal colors within the landscape and provide multiperspectival views of the majestic setting and diminutive human figures.

When the first "Spring" chapter begins, three separate establishing shots ensue. First, a wooden gate bearing a nativist mural at the lake's entrance opens with a creaking sound, its movement suggesting the parting of theatrical curtains. An extreme long shot reveals a frontal view of the floating temple, partially hidden by the fog rising above the water and drifting toward the mountainous backdrop. The shot that follows is of a three-hundred-year-old tree's reflection in the lake. The camera tilts up to reveal another, slightly closer view of the monastery through the ancient tree's twisted branches. The third shot includes the free-floating gate—it has no walls—in the foreground, the tree in the middle ground, and the temple in the distant background, the latter now bathed in bright sunlight. Following these establishing shots, the camera shifts to the interior of the monastery, where an old monk is praying to a Buddha statue placed atop a miniature pond base—one that visually mimics the aquatic environment of the temple itself. A door divides the tiny worship hall and the adjoining bedroom, where a small boy monk is sleeping. However, there are no walls between these spaces (again, this suggests the main gateway at the lake entrance). And yet all of the characters in this film—monks and the few visitors who stop by—will observe these nominal doors, opting out of the seemingly easy means of passing through nonexistent "walls." Much like Lars von Trier does in *Dogville* (2003), Kim approaches his setting from a minimalist perspective, using Brechtian devices such as free-standing doors that call attention to the artificiality of the film's mise-en-scène. Such textual "violations" break the illusion of reality and invite a more active participation and reflection on the part of the spectator.

This first "Spring" chapter introduces an important life lesson that will ripple or reverberate throughout the remaining narrative. Bored by his idle day in the lake monastery, the mischievous boy monk (the sole living mate of the aforementioned old monk) makes an excursion into the neighboring woods where he plays a cruel game with animals—a fish, a frog, and a snake—tying a small stone to each of them before releasing them back into their natural habitat. The little monk laughs when he observes the creatures struggling with the weight they are forced to carry. Observing the innocent yet merciless child from afar is the stern-faced old master, who collects a large stone from the forest and ties it to the young monk's back while he is asleep. When the boy wakes up the next morning and complains about the heaviness of the stone, he is reminded

Figure 17. A picturesque establishing shot of the floating Buddhist monastery in *Spring, Summer, Fall, Winter . . . and Spring.*

Figure 18. The old monk imparts an important life lesson to his mischievous discipline in the first "Spring" episode of *Spring, Summer, Fall, Winter . . . and Spring.*

of his own mistreatment of the fish, frog, and snake. The master orders the repentant youngster to release the animals, warning him that if any of them have died, he will "carry the stone in [his] heart for the rest of [his] life." The boy returns to the valley, only he is too late: although the frog is alive, the fish and the snake have become casualties of his meaningless game. The old monk watches with a sympathetic gaze, as his tearful disciple learns a hard lesson.

The old monk's presence as an omnipresent observer in these "lesson scenes" set within the mountains is inexplicable, since there is only one rowboat capable of taking residents of the lake-bound temple to the gated (yet wall-less) dock leading to the surrounding areas. After the boy is ordered to release the animals, we see him ride the boat and head to the valley by himself. As a metaphysical figure, the master could be said to symbolize Kim Ki-duk's "inner eye," his searching self, transcendently "watching over" the sin and repentance of his other, guilty self. As the director explains, autobiographical elements in *Spring, Summer, Fall, Winter . . . and Spring* are "psychological, rather than situational" (Pak). Although the setting and characters are all human archetypes stripped of social and cultural identities, the film captures the director's spiritual mind and his longing for inner peace and transcendence—otherworldly qualities embodied in the guise of the old monk.

In the "Summer" chapter, the boy is seventeen. Over the course of this episode, he falls in love with an ailing high-school girl who temporarily stays in the temple in an attempt to recover from her unnamed illness. When the old master finds out about the two teens' sexual liaison, he warns his disciple, "Lust awakens the desire to possess. And that awakens the intent to murder." These cautionary words turn out to be prophetic, as evidenced in the next segment of the film.

This third chapter, "Fall," comes after another substantial gap in time. Now in his thirties and with fully grown hair, the young monk is revealed to be a fugitive, having run away after murdering his unfaithful wife—presumably the same girl from the "Summer" chapter—in a fit of jealousy. The protagonist's previously mild expressions of his childhood and adolescence are nowhere to be seen, for the young man is now full of bitterness and enmity. At this stage of life, the young monk is a familiar figure in Kim Ki-duk's cinema: a man of *ressentiment.* He spews his rage in the form of curses, shouts, wild gesticulations, and the masochistic roping of his body. He even attempts suicide, taping his eyes and mouth shut with rice paper, a bizarre act of desperation that the old monk brings to an end through intervention. To help his prodigal disciple restore his inner peace, the master orders him to carve the Prajnaparamita Sutra scripture on the temple's wooden deck. While the young monk is engraving the letters that his master has written (using a live cat's tail as his brush), two detectives arrive on the scene, their obvious intention being to capture him. Initially the murderer resists with his knife, his murder weapon-turned–sculpting tool. Wielding it, he threatens the two detectives, who are pointing their guns at him, but he soon returns to his task of carving upon the master's intervention. The old man humbly pleads to the policemen, who agree to wait until their prisoner finishes carving the holy text. In the process of performing this labor overnight, the young monk regains emotional equilibrium and is ready to peacefully leave the temple in police custody the next morning.

After their departure, the old monk performs an act of self-immolation on the rowboat, covering his mouth, eyes, and ears in the same way that the disciple had done in his suicide attempt while waiting for the funeral logs to catch fire beneath his crossed legs. It is significant that the disciple and master both write the Chinese character "door" on the piece of rice paper that blocks their sense organs, the orifices that connect their bodies to the world. The paper closes off the physical world while opening up these men to a spiritual world in a moment of self-sacrifice. If we accept several critics' interpretation of this film as a Christian text in "Buddhist clothing,"[26] then the old monk's enigmatic act of suicide can be conceptually framed within the doctrine of transferred guilt, which is at the heart of Christian morality. However, the master's exit can be also understood as a part of the natural cycle of life, as his post must be made vacant so that his disciple can return from prison and take it over in the subsequent chapter.

The "Winter" chapter is the most important segment of the film in terms of its autobiographical implications. Here, distinctions between character, actor, and director evaporate, as Kim Ki-duk himself plays the now-slightly-older adult monk who, returning to the monastery after years of incarceration, finds his former home in a literal and figurative state of suspension, a distant reminder of his past, surrounded on all sides by frozen water. Becoming the new master of the abandoned temple, the monk practices martial arts and trains his body in the wintry landscape. One day, the solitary man is visited by an unknown woman, whose face is covered by a scarf. The mysterious woman is carrying her baby boy whom she intends to abandon, as we soon learn. After praying in front of the Buddha statue with tears soaking her scarf-mask, the guilt-ridden woman flees at night, leaving her child in the temple only to drown by falling in a hole on the frozen lake, a negative space that had been carved out by the monk for the purpose of washing.

Feeling guilty for the woman's death, which reminds him of his killing of another woman, the monk embarks on a self-punitive trek up the mountain, carrying a large stone grinder roped to his waist and a bronze Buddha statue in his arms. The character/director slides, falls down, drops the statue, and struggles to climb a steep slope with the heavy stone weighing him down. Kim uses montage during this sequence and inserts close-up shots of the tortured fish, frog, and snake from the "Spring" chapter—images that are intercut with his own images of self-inflicted physical hardship. Kim's monk reaches the summit with difficulty and from it commands a view of the monastery far below in the valley. Following the direction of his gaze, the camera pans left to provide a point-of-view overhead shot of the temple, which fills the screen. This meta-POV shot further conflates character/actor/director, suggesting that their shared look in the single person of Kim are one and the same with the camera's gaze. The camera cuts back to the monk/Kim, who sits next to the Buddha statue, praying piously, and then to a panoramic view of the temple. A frontal close-up of the statue gives way to the chapter's final image: a zoom-in long shot of the temple, held for nine seconds.

Kim Ki-duk's centralizing gaze—as protagonist, actor, and director—dominates this "Winter" sequence, which is steeped in cinéma vérité–style documentary elements despite its overt abstraction and philosophical suggestiveness. In his interview with *Cine 21,* he describes the process of shooting the mountain-climbing scene: "It was not in the original script. During lunch hours, I told the production staff that I am going to climb up to the summit [of Chuhwang Mountain], 3,600 feet high. No one believed me, but I did it. . . . I carried the grinding stone, and my staff carried the camera. And it was minus-twenty-two degrees Fahrenheit" (Pak). The director/actor indeed hiked half-naked (in thin cotton pants with no shirt or jacket) for four hours to the top of

Figure 19. Kim Ki-duk plays the adult monk who seeks atonement on mountain top in the "Winter" episode of *Spring, Summer, Fall, Winter . . . and Spring.*

Chuhwang Mountain, carrying the heavy stone all the way and playing himself rather than a character. As the columnist Yi Tong-jin aptly puts it in his review of the film, "At that moment, Kim Ki-duk ceases to be the monk character in his film but is just himself, a filmmaker and nature man who is reflecting back on his life" ("Three Questions").

Kim was never coy about the semiautobiographical elements of his films, explicitly identifying with his abject heroes such as Chi-hŭm in *Address Unknown* and the titular homeless man in *Crocodile* (Kim So-hee, "Biography" 2). However, the "Winter" sequence of *Spring, Summer, Fall, Winter . . . and Spring* is the most directly autobiographical of all his narrative fiction films in an ontological sense, as there is no distinction between the nameless monk character and Kim Ki-duk as a subject-in-process who seeks transcendence and atonement. What is notable about the final four shots of the "Winter" episode is that Kim's gaze collapses onto the stone Buddha's gaze through editing. Kim's profile, shown in long shot in a moment of prayer, is followed by an extreme long shot of the temple, which supposedly represents his point of view. Instead of cutting back to the expected reaction shot of Kim, however, the third shot is a medium close-up of the Buddha statue facing directly at the camera/audience. A zoom-in is used in the following overhead shot of the temple, suggesting the ocular perspective of the statue—the Buddha's gaze.

In the final chapter, "And . . . Spring," Kim once again associates his looking position with that of the Buddha. The abandoned baby of the preceding episode has grown into an adolescent boy whose playfulness is reminiscent of the now-gray-haired master's previous self in the original "Spring" episode (significantly, the two boys are played by the same actor, Kim Chong-ho). Kim, ever true to himself, is seen drawing a portrait of his young disciple in pencil on the temple deck. However, Kim disappears after this brief appearance and is nowhere to be seen when the male child rows the boat to the land by himself and tortures a fish, a frog, and a snake, repeating the actions from the first episode. The film thus cyclically turns in on itself, with this episode repeating the first yet also departing from it insofar as Kim's character is not present and thus unable to intervene during the boy's cruel act. The final shot shows the back of the Buddha statue on top of the mountain, appearing to peer down at the temple below and replacing Kim's anticipated reaction shots with a thoroughly abstract, transcendental gaze.

Figure 20. Kim Ki-duk collapses his own transcendent inner-eye onto the stone Buddha's gaze in the abstract final shot of *Spring, Summer, Fall, Winter . . . and Spring.*

*Spring, Summer, Fall, Winter . . . and Spring* ends on a pessimistic, yet elegiac, note, accentuated by gloomy nondiegetic music. It is as if the auteur has given up his fight to change society and forsaken the will to communicate with others. Ultimately, there is no lesson (as there was in the original "Spring"), no passion (as in "Summer"), no *ressentiment* (as in "Fall"), and no transcendence (as in "Winter"). There is only repetition and a sense of resignation at the end. Perhaps Chŏng Sŏng-il, the Korean critic most sympathetically aligned with the director, is right when he argues, against the critical consensus, that Kim Ki-duk's films have been getting progressively "colder" after *Spring, Summer, Fall, Winter . . . and Spring* ("Flesh, Meat, Bones" 187). In a 2004 article, Chŏng correctly predicted that Kim's films were going to become increasingly abstract—a result, he argued, of the filmmaker's waning interest in communicating with members of Korean society.

Despite its commercial failure, *Spring, Summer, Fall, Winter . . . and Spring* was well-respected in the director's native country, garnering the coveted Grand Bell (Taejong) Best Picture Award and being selected as South Korea's entry into the Academy Award competition for Best Foreign Language Film in 2004. Hard-won critical recognition at home was soon displaced by another controversy, when Kim refused to offer advance press screenings of *The Bow,* which ended up becoming the least popular of his films (drawing only two thousand admissions in South Korea). After nearly retiring from the film industry in the wake of the fiasco surrounding his controversial remarks about the director Bong Joon-ho (Pong Jun-ho)'s *The Host* in a press conference for *Time,* Kim managed to come back with *Breath,* an entirely self-funded project in which he plays another godlike character: a prison warden who, situated near a closed-circuit television screen, silently watches the interactions on view in the visitors' room, one of the main settings where the film's two protagonists—a prisoner and a betrayed housewife—initiate an intense love affair.

Kim's fifteenth film, *Dream,* initially raised high hopes for a commercial breakthrough, since it cast two high-profile stars, Yi Na-yŏng and Odagiri Jo, in the lead roles. However, its modest theatrical admissions (hovering around ninety thousand) were a sign that this was another disappointment in his career, reaffirming Kim's reputation as box-office poison. Kim did, however, achieve relative commercial success as the producer and writer of the low-budget action film *Rough Cut* (a.k.a. *Movie Is a Movie*; *Yŏnghwa nŭn yŏnghwada*; 2008), which was seen by over a million theatergoers in South Korea, more than the combined admission of all fifteen of his previous films. Directed by Kim's protégé, Chang Hun (who worked as his assistant director on *The Bow* and *Time*), the film tells a satirical story of a movie actor who, rejected by his fellow performers for his on-set antics, is forced to play opposite a professional gangster and enact a series of violent scenes for real to salvage his career.

In lieu of a formal conclusion, I would like to end this commentary with an anecdotal account of my face-to-face encounter with Kim Ki-duk. As mentioned earlier, I first saw Kim in person as an audience member in the post-screening question-and-answer session at the Etrange Film Festival, held in Paris in September 2002. Six years later, in November 2008, I conducted an interview with him in Seoul shortly after the release of *Dream.* After agreeing to a meeting (arranged by a common friend), Kim graciously came to a conference venue at Ewha Woman's University, my alma mater and the center of feminist scholarship in South Korea. Realizing the irony, I was protectively conscious about the potential for disapproving looks, but no one seemed to recognize him (or at least they ignored him) at a campus-center coffee shop, an underground space designed by a French architect (which I did not forget to point out to Kim). Although it was a casual meeting rather than a formal interview, I asked him a few questions that had been plaguing me for years: "Did you really see, as legend goes, a film in a theater for the first time in Paris in your early thirties?" He replied that he in fact had seen biblical epics such as *Ben Hur* (1959) with his church group in his teens; but *The Silence of the Lambs* and *Les amants du Pont-Neuf*—two films he references most as inspirational sources of influence (which he saw in Paris in 1991)—represent his first serious exposure to cinema as an art form.

"Do you still feel that your vagabond days in Montpellier were the happiest time of your life, even after receiving awards at Venice and Berlin Film Festivals?" He nodded. "It was the most primitive yet carefree time of my life," he replied. I also explained that, when I first viewed *Samaritan Girl,* I was shocked to see a middle-class male hero rather than a working-class protagonist. He admitted that he began to introduce middle-class characters into his films after *Spring, Summer, Fall, Winter . . . and Spring,* a work that he considers a turning point in his career. From this film on, he explained, his primary subject matter shifted from national and societal issues to contradictions of life and existential anguish. He even insinuated that he himself might have entered the mainstream as represented by his affluent, middle-class protagonists in recent films. When I referred to the characters in early films as "outsiders living on the bottom rungs of Korean society," he was quick to correct me, saying that he believed that they were people who lived their lives most fully and intensely. They were most sensorially alive to the world. I asked if he was not considering a move toward more mainstream filmmaking, and he reminded me of his producer credit on *Rough Cut,* a low-budget sleeper. However, he did acknowledge the increasingly rigorous tendency in his own auteur style, which had shifted away from realism to semifantasy to formal abstraction. In the abstract stage of his career, words were becoming obsolete, as meanings could be conveyed more effectively through nuanced emotional expressions and allegories. Kim also mused that his latest films could be interpreted as more cruel and pessimistic than his earlier ones, unlike the argument put forth by many critics.

As we were about to wrap up our meeting over coffee, Kim encouraged me to continue writing and offered a little life lesson in a manner that recalled the old monk counseling his young disciple in *Spring, Summer, Fall, Winter . . . and Spring.* Pointing toward a college student seated nearby, he stated, "Take her as an example. You might think that she is goofing off without studying. You might see her again later and tell her that you saw her not focusing on her studies in the coffee shop the other day. The girl might say, 'That was the day when I had just heard the news of my best friend's death. So I could not focus.'" Kim seemed to be telling me how he himself had been misunderstood by critics who seemed unable to overcome their prejudices and who refused to see beyond the surface of his films.

The following summer I returned to Seoul to teach a course in Korean cinema at Ewha Woman's University. I wanted to invite Kim Ki-duk to my class and give my mixed-group students (Korean, Japanese, Chinese, American, and German) a chance to engage him in conversation. However, the number of his cell phone had been disconnected, and he did not reply to my e-mails. After the summer session ended, I contacted him again to briefly report my students' interest in *3-Iron* and to express my regret about not being able to see him again before my return to the United States. I received a short response from him, apologizing for having been unable to make it to my class. Apparently, he was not ready to "stand up in public" again. As I did in the Parisian theater a few years earlier, I could sense in the filmmaker's typed comment a self-conscious recognition of internalized pain, one that ran deep. That was the last time I heard from him.

In his interview with *Cine 21* at the time of *Dream*'s release in the fall of 2008, Kim indicated that he had taken up farming in Kangwŏn Province as a pastime, choosing a quiet pastoral life over one spent mentoring his former assistant directors and helping members of his production staff to launch their own directorial careers (Hwang). While doing Korean-language research for this book, I struggled to find any records or accounts of Kim's current exploits after 2008, when he was still receiving media exposure for his dual role as producer (for *Beautiful* [*Arŭmdapda*] and *Rough Cut*) and writer/director (*Dream*). Toward the final stages of my writing, however, I happened across the online reporter Chŏng Sŏng-gi's article, "Ch'ungmuro's Hit Formula Is 'More Cruel': What Has Kim Ki-duk Been Doing Recently?" on the *Break News* Web site. This August 18, 2010, article opens with a discussion of the general gravitation toward violence, cruelty, and revenge in recent Korean box-office hits such as *The Man from Nowhere* (*Ajŏssi*; 2010) and *I Saw the Devil* (*Agma rŭl poatda*; 2010). The author goes on to establish a connection between these new films and those of Kim Ki-duk:

> These films are no less cruel than *The Isle, Samaritan Girl, Time,* and *3-Iron,* films by a director who is often dubbed the "Sam Peckinpah" of Korean cinema, and who frequently used the subject matter of "cruel revenge" that has recently become a hit formula of the Ch'ungmuro film industry. We have no news of Kim Ki-duk's new project, but he seems to be focusing his energy on being a producer-mentor for the "Kim Ki-duk platoon," consisting of his former assistant directors.

I was relieved to learn that Kim Ki-duk is still active in the industry, albeit away from the director's chair. However, the explicitly masculine, fraternal images conjured up in such words as "cruel revenge," "Sam Peckinpah," and "Kim Ki-duk platoon" contradicted my decidedly feminine memory of conversing with him on the all-woman campus of Ewha University.

It was not until I had completed the writing of my manuscript and was waiting for the copyedited proofs when I heard the news that Kim Ki-duk had been "living like a zombie" in the remote mountains after withdrawing from the media spotlight in late 2008. Apparently I had missed another controversy about the director, one that caught fire in December 2010, when a Korean online newspaper reported Kim's distressed state and divulged the cause for his self-imposed solitary exile: a shock from the "betrayal" by his protégé Chang Hun, who entered a contract with a major film company without his mentor's knowledge and left Kim in the midst of working on their second collaborative project—*Poongsan* (*P'ungsan kae*; 2011), aimed at reviving the success of *Rough Cut*. In contrast to the *Host* controversy four years earlier, public opinion swayed in favor of Kim Ki-duk, who in turn issued a public letter in which the reclusive filmmaker explained his situation and defended his estranged mentee (who had apologized to him and contributed partial funding for *Poongsan,* now being directed by Chŏn Chae-hong, who stepped in after Chang's premature departure). On May 13, 2011, Kim Ki-duk made his first public appearance in nearly three years at the Cannes Film Festival, where he premiered *Arirang*, an entirely self-made digital video that he had written, shot, edited, directed, and produced.

The film consists largely of cinéma vérité-style recordings of the director's daily routines in and around a mountaintop shack (collecting water, chopping wood, bathing in a plastic container, preparing simple meals, drinking soju, singing the titular folk song, and so on) where he had taken shelter for an extended period. It is no ordinary documentary, however, as Kim reflects on his life and career in an experimental fashion, intercutting footage in which he plays three distinct roles: one asking questions, one answering, and the other observing. In tearful close-ups, the director confesses to a traumatic accident on the set of *Dream* where the actress Yi Na-yŏng nearly lost her life while shooting a suicide-hanging scene, an incident that triggered his crippling depression and prolonged inactivity. In front of his camcorder, Kim does not hold back his raw emotions, including bitterness over the high-profile breakup with his once trusted disciple Chang Hun, who "left [him] because of capitalistic seduction." Chang is not the only target of his videographic venting, as the inebriated filmmaker goes on to attack several random individuals, from an actor who specializes in evil roles to government bureaucrats who awarded Kim national medals of honor for his achievements at international film festivals (without recognizing his subversive messages). However, the artist blames himself most while also self-aggrandizing his legacy via montage sequences showing his oil paintings and film posters. Despite the media attention directed toward Kim Ki-duk's comeback from an uncharacteristically long hiatus, he declined to give any press interviews at the Sixty-fourth Cannes International Film Festival, where *Arirang* was honored with a top award in the Un Certain Regard category. Kim was likewise absent from a Korean press conference for *Poongsan* (which he wrote and produced) prior to the film's domestic release on June 23, 2011, and is rumored to be staying in Europe temporarily.[27]

At this point, it is difficult to imagine where Kim Ki-duk is headed professionally. Will the artistic exorcism that is *Arirang* bring an end to the auteur's spiritual wandering and usher in a new creative period? Will he steer clear of the director's chair to continue his mentoring role, lending his support to talented younger filmmakers such as Chŏn Chae-hong, a former music student who helmed *Beautiful* and *Poongsan* under his tutelage? Will he turn his attention to writing and producing more indie genre films in the vein of *Poongsan,* a dark comedy-cum-action-drama about a mysterious courier who is capable of smuggling any object or person across the militarized border of South and North Korea? Considered by many critics to be the most crowd-pleasing of all nineteen films written by Kim to date, *Poongsan* broke even in the first five days of its domestic release (with 320,000 admissions), a rare achievement in his career, which prompted the writer-producer to release, through major media outlets, a handwritten, open letter of gratitude addressed to the film's audiences. It is particularly ironic that this modest box-office breakthrough arrived just over one month after Kim showcased at Cannes his most solipsistic and experimental film, *Arirang,* for which no theatrical distribution is planned in South Korea. Only time will tell which of these two films is a more prophetic harbinger of Kim's future output.

This admittedly sentimental end to the commentary might strike some readers as a shameless auteurist romanticization of the director and his films. As a media scholar, I am aware of the pitfalls and shortcomings of auteurism as an interpretative paradigm. Nevertheless, I find it necessary to share with readers my up-close and personal encounters with Kim Ki-duk because without them, my own understanding and evaluation of his films would be considerably different. With the possible exception of Lars von Trier, few contemporary directors in world cinema have generated such impassioned responses. To his "platoon" of future guerilla filmmakers, he is an inspirational force who has refused to capitulate to the mainstream industry and maintains his artistic vision and integrity despite repeated commercial failures. For observers of South Korea's class system, his is a Cinderella story representing an alternative model of social mobility without the benefit of college education. For some film critics, it may be a cautionary tale of indulgences as well as obstinacy that has resulted in almost irreconcilable schisms between mass audiences and the socially withdrawn artist. Ultimately, Kim Ki-duk is a contradictory figure whose body of work illustrates how difficult it is to sustain a deeply personal cinema in today's commercialized industrial environment, even as he reaffirms its possibility for similarly committed filmmakers.

## *Notes*

1. No other Korean filmmaker has achieved such a commercial presence in the North American home-video/DVD market. After Kim, Park Chan-wook ranks a distant second, with six of his eight features (*Joint Security Area* [*Kongdong kyŏngbi kuyŏk*; 2000], *I'm a Cyborg, But That's OK* [*Ssaibogŭjiman Kwaench'ana*; 2006], *Thirst* [*Pakjwi*; 2009], and the Vengeance Trilogy) available on DVD in the United States.

2. Prior to the MoMA retrospective, there had been a couple of European retrospectives devoted to Kim Ki-duk: the 2002 Etrange Film Festival in Paris and the 2002 Karlovy Vary International Film Festival in the Czech Republic. According to a report issued by the Korean Film Council (KOFIC), the government-subsidized organization receives more overseas requests for assistance with Kim Ki-duk retrospectives than all other Korean film-related events combined (Rayns, "Sexual Terrorism" 50).

3. Kim's experimental fifth feature, *Real Fiction,* was shot in two hundred minutes nonstop, using eight 35mm cameras and ten digital cameras. Although a far cry from the one hundred cameras used by Lars von Trier's production crew during the shooting of the musical numbers in *Dancer in the Dark* (2000), such a proliferation of tools at Kim's disposal suggests some of the contradictions bound up in this and his other films, which are at once minimal and maximal, simple yet excessive, stripped down yet extravagant.

4. While the British critic Tony Rayns identifies Kim as the most conspicuous "wayward primitive" in world cinema since Ken Loach ("Calculated Mannerism of a Primitive" 43), the Korean critic Paek Mun-im points out that Kim is often considered a "Korean Fassbinder" in the international festival circuit ("Hong Sang-soo vs. Kim Ki-duk" 186).

5. Tartan Films went bankrupt in the summer of 2008. For detailed information about the Tartan Asia Extreme line of DVDs, see Shin, "Art of Branding."

6. Although various Korean studies programs at U.S. universities have held retrospectives on important Korean directors (Im Kwon-taek [Im Kwŏn-t'aek], Lee Myung-se [Yi Myŏng-se], Park Kwang-su [Pak Kwang-su], Hong Sang-soo [Hong Sang-su], etc.), and although MoMA introduced selective works of Shin Sang-ok [Sin Sang-ok], Yu Hyun-mok [Yu Hyŏn-mok], and Im Kwon-taek under the title "Three Korean Master Filmmakers" in 1996, a complete MoMA retrospective of Kim Ki-duk's fourteen films is an unprecedented honor in terms of its scope and prestige.

7. Leong argues that "South Korea is even being likened to the new 'Hong Kong,' with its homegrown film industry on the verge of exploding onto the world stage, similar to how 'Hong Kong New Wave' catapulted the former British colony and its groundbreaking directors into the international spotlight" (2). Recapitulating the term in his online review of *New Korean Cinema,* edited by Chi-Yun Shin and Julian Stringer, Mike Walsh states that the "startling factor

in the success of recent Korean film has been not only the growth of domestic box office, but the exponential growth in export sales, particularly throughout East Asia. Truly, Korea is the new Hong Kong in this respect."

8. Kim Ki-duk defines "semi-abstract" as "the juncture between reality and the imaginary" and singles out his film *3-Iron* as illustrative of this concept (Rivière 114).

9. Notable critical debates include "Support or Criticize"; "Problems of Kim Ki-duk"; and "Why Do I Support or Criticize Kim Ki-duk."

10. Exemplified by antiheroes in the literary works of Diderot, Dostoevsky, and Céline, as well as the real-life serial killer Charles Manson, the abject hero is both victim and murderer, "servile and satanic." According to Bernstein, "abjection could lead directly to a *ressentiment* embittered enough to erupt into murder" (9). Many of Kim Ki-duk's onscreen heroes are likewise criminals of some sort—murderers, rapists, gangsters, and so on—who are themselves victims of circumstance and often evoke our sympathy.

11. For more information about the Kwangju Uprising and anti-Americanism in South Korea, see Cumings 382–91.

12. According to official records, between 1967 and 1998, 56,904 American soldiers committed 50,082 crimes in South Korea. Based on this statistic, scholars and activists infer that over a hundred thousand crimes were committed by U.S. soldiers stationed in Korea between September 8, 1945 (the inaugural date for the U.S. military occupation), and 1999. Under the Status of Forces Agreement (SOFA), American G.I.s on duty are exempt from prosecution by Korean courts for any crimes against Korean civilians. See Anti–U.S. Military Crime Movement Headquarters.

13. At the Yalta Conference in February 1945, Franklin D. Roosevelt met with Joseph Stalin and proposed a four-power trusteeship (involving the United States, the Soviet Union, Great Britain, and China) of postwar Korea for up to thirty years. The Soviet leader agreed on the trusteeship but recommended a shorter period. See Hart-Landsberg 37.

14. Under the joint-forces defense system, a four-star U.S. commander retained operational control of the Republic of Korea (ROK) Army until 1994, when the South Korean government regained peacetime command of its own troops. At the request of the South Korean government, the United States subsequently agreed to transfer wartime command (which it, under the U.N. banner, had taken over in 1950) by 2012. However, the date has been postponed to 2015 by the Obama administration and Lee Myung-bak (Yi Myŏng-bak)'s government, to reflect the "current security condition on the Korean peninsula." See "U.S. Forces, Korea."

15. In the theatrical release prints, Kim included a caption: "I ardently pray for the nation's reunification." The heavy-handed text provoked many complaints from audiences and critics and has been removed from the South Korean DVD release.

16. Kim had initially given up the Korean release of *Time*, which was being exported to thirty countries. An online petition demanding its release in South Korea was partly responsible for Sponge's purchase of the film's Korean distribution rights.

17. The situation became aggravated when Kim appeared on a television panel (MBC's "100 Minutes Special") debating the screen monopoly on August 17, eleven days after the controversial press conference. In this rare TV appearance, Kim defended himself against the online attacks and restated his controversial remark about *The Host*.

18. A term coined by the French Marxist philosopher Louis Althusser, *interpellation*, or "hailing," refers to the process by which ideology addresses the individual. Althusser uses an example of the policeman hailing, "Hey, you there!" When at least one individual turns around and answers that call, he or she becomes a subject in relation to ideology. For an elaboration on the concept of interpellation, see Althusser.

19. In the beach scene, I interpret the boatman's action as an interpellation of Chin-a as a "damsel in distress."

20. The building of the same name appears in the background of fantastical beach scenes in *Bad Guy*, another Kim Ki-duk film that thematizes prostitution.

21. The DVD jacket of *Bad Guy*—both Korean and U.S. releases—features an image of a naked Sŏn-hwa (whose back is turned) holding up a mirror on a Western-style antique bench. The mirror shows the tormented face of Han-gi, who is standing behind the woman's back. Although this promotional cover may appear to be a cheap promotional scheme to provoke audience expectations about the adult sexual content, it is a fitting image that foregrounds the cross-gender, interclass identification between Sŏn-hwa and Han-gi (which is mediated by mirrors throughout the narrative).

22. *Wild Animals* includes an almost identical scene in which the North Korean refugee Hong-san ignites a lighter and reveals himself from the other side of the peep-show window to comfort the uncontrollably weeping striper Laura, a Korean adoptee who has recently lost her lover.

23. For more information about the various Anglo-American critiques of these three French feminist theorists (Kristeva, Cixous, and Irigaray), see Bray; Huffer; and Schor and Weed.

24. According to Mary Ann Doane, woman's films "deal with a female protagonist . . . treat problems defined as feminine . . . and, most crucially, are directed toward a female audience" (3). Doane's study of the Hollywood woman's films of the 1930s and 1940s focuses exclusively on male-directed works such as *Dark Victory* (1939), *Rebecca* (1940), *Now, Voyager* (1942), *Gaslight* (1944), and *Dragonwyck* (1946), rather than films by female directors such as Dorothy Arzner and Ida Lupino.

25. Despite his lack of interest in representing Buddhist religious disciplines, Kim strove for aesthetic authenticity and hired art experts to re-create interior

mural paintings and design the set of the lake-bound monastery. He also borrowed a three-hundred-year-old, authentic antique Buddhist statue as a prop (Nam 63).

26. For example, Yi Tong-jin argues that the metaphorical stone that the monk has to carry in his heart for the rest of his life signifies Original Sin, a conceptual centerpiece of Christianity ("Three Questions").

27. On September 17, 2011, Kim Ki-duk unveiled his latest film *Amen* at the San Sebastian Film Festival in Spain. Shot entirely in Europe (Paris, Venice, and Avignon), the low-budget HD film follows the border-crossing journey of a girl in search of her missing boyfriend. As in the case of *Arirang*, Kim handled most of production and postproduction single-handedly, and also played the role of a mysterious rapist/thief whose face is hidden behind a gas mask.

# Interview with Kim Ki-duk

## From *Crocodile* to *Address Unknown*

By Kim So-hee

This interview was originally published in a promotional booklet, edited by Lee Hae-jin, entitled *Kim Ki-duk: From Crocodile to Address Unknown* (Seoul: LJ Film, 2001). It is reprinted here with permission of LJ Film America. Although the interview only covers Kim Ki-duk's first six feature films, many of the issues, themes, and ideas presented here apply to his later films as well. Several Korean-language interviews about Kim's more recent films are quoted in the main essay to supplement this interview.

### Where Does Our Cruelty Come From?

KIM SO-HEE: The title of your film, *Address Unknown*, is quite unique.

KIM KI-DUK: When I was growing up in the countryside, I remember many letters scattered on the ground, undelivered because they were sent to unknown addresses. Most of them were stuck in mailboxes for the longest time until they were swept away by the wind and thrust into the bottom of rice fields or a filthy ditch. Whenever I would see them, I was always overcome with the desire to open them, which in fact I [attempted to do] a number of times. Quite a few contained sad, desperate tales. To me, the three characters in this film are just like the abandoned letters of my childhood. They are children of an "era which is yet to be received." In the desolate plains, Ch'ang-guk has been entirely violated; Ŭn-ok is halfway to that point; and Chi-hŭm will rise up, like a weed.

KS: Going into this film, you raised the question, "Where does our cruelty come from?"

KK: By dealing with the lives surrounding the U.S. military base, I wanted to ruminate on the history of the Korean War down to the time of Japanese imperialism. Perhaps the cruelest scene of this film is when the father repairs the gun found in the front yard of the family's house and shoots the chicken he has been raising. The violence repeated through generations—I believe this is the most uniquely Korean form of violence.

KS: How did you come up with the extraordinary episodes in *Address Unknown*?

KK:This is actually a story from the time my friends and I were seventeen. Chi-hŭm's experiences are taken from mine, and the stories about his friend who commits suicide at the age of twenty-seven and another friend who has only one eye are exactly how they really happened.

KS: The relationship between Ch'ang-guk and his mother is quite unique.

KK: There are actually many similar cases around the U.S. military base. After the Korean War, many children of mixed heritage were adopted into America, but the ones left behind had to lay low, suffering along with their own mothers. I remember the headquarters of Holt Children's Services, Inc., next to my elementary school. Perhaps that was the reason why there were always two or three kids of mixed heritage in our class. At the time, I was quite afraid of them, and they were, in fact, violent. Among them were those who lived in small wooden shacks, just like the red bus that Ch'ang-guk and his mother live in, who beat their mothers like Ch'ang-guk did his. I was a fourth or fifth grader at the time, and I remember it as vividly shocking. Now I can understand where this friend of my childhood was coming from. Nothing has changed as the pain and anguish continues.

KS: The U.S. soldier in *Address Unknown* seems to go beyond the dichotomy between pro- and anti-U.S. sentiments that, as a whole, have defined our attitude towards the United States.

KK: The U.S. military may be a familiar presence, yet it is an uncomfortable one as well. They create small and large incidents, including sex crimes, which should be done away with, the sooner the better. However, the deep-seated military culture and the imperialistic sentiments that this projects cannot just be a matter of one or two U.S. soldiers causing problems. I was quite critical of the U.S. military at the time I was writing this script. However, as I was hunting for shooting locations, I began to feel a kind of sadness, looking at the shabby and filthy clubs surrounding the military bases in great numbers. It was isolation and loneliness I felt from the G.I.s wretchedly returning to their military base after spending time with Russian or Filipino girls they bought for a couple of dollars. For the first time, I asked myself if I had ever tried to understand them. It dawned on me that these men were just like the Korean soldiers dispatched to the Middle East. It made me see another side to the issue of sex crimes committed by U.S. soldiers. What could they really do in the extraterritorial jurisdiction area around the military base? They were only young men spending their youth in a foreign country. In this sense, I would like to say that the position I take in *Address Unknown* is at the conjunction between "pro-U.S." and "anti-U.S." sentiments.

KS: Unlike in your previous works, you place politics and history at the forefront of this film.

KK: I think I have always talked about political issues in every one of my films. For example, *Crocodile* focuses on issues of normality and abnormality, and *Birdcage Inn* examines class distinctions. Perhaps it is the lyrical rather than political approach that separates those films from this one.

## Amazing Images that Jump from the Screen

KS: Based on your distinction between abstract and realist films, you define your works as "semi-abstract." What do you mean by that?

KK: Film is created out of a point where fantasy and reality meet. But because cinema depends on the photographic image, the cinematic medium is most often regarded as the domain of realism. Cruel class distinctions and a lack of compassion permeate the reality I have experienced throughout my entire life. How can I possibly show a beautiful, positive world that could be cured of its problems in a single day? For me, the first step toward healing is in revealing our sicknesses as they really are. My definition of "semi-abstract film" reflects my own desire to present the borderline where the painfully real and the hopefully imaginative meet.

KS: The British film critic Tony Rayns commented on your extraordinary visual talents; even if there are weaknesses in other areas of your films, your ability to crystallize ideas, emotions, moods and implications in images of great intensity is startling.[1]

KK: I guess I have a tendency to develop my films around a specific image. For example, when I want to suggest to people that they should "be good," I try to express the inexpressible feeling of happiness instead of referring to specific dialogue or narrative. However, I am also aware that images in a film can only be a fragment of a larger picture. It is true that some have commented on a few shots in my films as extraordinary images; however, I still feel that I have not reached a point where I can consider these images to be satisfactory. Besides, I'm not fit for words.

KS: You are known to start from a specific image when you are making a film.

KK: To give *Birdcage Inn* as an example, my main principle was to begin and to end with the routines of daily life. The next point was irony. Four years ago [1997], while I was travelling through the coast of the East Sea, I stayed in a motel located in front of the Pohang train station for a week. There was a red-light district nearby. There was a girl who escorted me to my room. Obviously I thought she was a prostitute, but I found out the next day that she was the daughter of the motel owner and also a college student. I was taken by surprise. It was quite odd and ironical to me that an ordinary family lived near the red-light district. In fact, no prostitutes were living in that motel. And then, an image came up to me at the last moment.

KS: Please comment on the spectacular colors of the fishing seats in your film *The Isle*.

KK: The fishing seat of the main character is yellow. For me, this color represents paleness, a kind of surrealistic and fantastic sensibility. Yellow is also the color of the mentally sick. The scene showing the man and the woman embracing each other while still attached to the fishhook, out-of-focus for around ten seconds, suggests that they have gone mad.

## My Films Are a Gesture for Reconciling the World

KS: You often show a dichotomy between characters living in different worlds.

KK: This is because I wanted to create a dialogue with people who are from worlds unfamiliar to mine. The recurrent themes in my films are space and captivity. Specific examples of the first theme are the abduction of "those other than I" to a space that is considered "mine" such as the [the lake resort] in *The Isle* or the Han River in *Crocodile.* If my spaces are those of the marginal, then the spaces of the other are those of the mainstream. Women in *Crocodile* and men in *The Isle* are the captives. They become prisoners through violence that is ironically beautiful. My world is presented to them, and they slowly become entwined into it, accepting and identifying with it. I introduce myself as a human being, urging them to forgive my threatening position. To make the people standing on the Tower of Babel come down and shake my hand, this is the gesture I make to the world, a handshake that is truly made out of modesty. Filmmaking is my attempt to understand the world, which I have failed to understand, a world of kindness and warmth overlooked by my habitual ignorance with different perspectives.

KS: You have an extraordinary talent to describe the lives of the marginal.

KK: I am opposed to people calling the characters in my film "marginal." What does it mean to be in the mainstream? Does it refer to the middle-class people living in Seoul? To me, it is the people in my films who are the mainstream.

KS: Do you identify with other filmmakers who call themselves anti-elitist?

KK: The voices in those films (made by the so-called anti-elitist filmmakers) are all voices of intellectuals. I recall the time of the Kwangju

Massacre, during which the film *A Petal,* made by filmmaker Jang Sun-woo, was set. A few days before this atrocity of history, a great rally took place in Seoul Station where a mass of students gathered with pickets protesting against the dictator Chun Doo-Hwan.[2] This was the first time I acknowledged this name. I was nineteen and perhaps on my way to the factory. No, I may have been heading towards a car junkyard to get a job there. However, I was caught in the bus due to the protestors crowding the streets. I didn't understand why people were protesting; I was just angry at the fact that I couldn't move forward to reach my destination. I had to agree with the people complaining that "those students should be beaten to death."

## The Desperate Message behind All the Violence and Sex

KS: There is an ongoing controversy over the level of violence in your films.

KK: Once in a while, I ask myself why I have to express things so violently. However, I believe this is an issue of convention—a convention of life, and a convention of looking at life. I may as well be trying to resist any kind of contemporary and general form of conventionality.

KS: Sex in particular is often expressed within the boundaries of sadism and masochism.

KK: In *Birdcage Inn* I wanted to bring sex out from the confines of conflict and power and into being a part of our everyday lives. In *The Isle* I wanted to dispose of any fear of the world and reach a peaceful state by presenting the rigorous conflict between the man and the woman through their repetitive sadomasochism. When the man attempts to leave the woman, she self-inflicts pain by impaling herself with a fish-hook. These types of psychic energy, which include intensive attachment, love, anger, and jealousy, are the unique energy our society carries. The dominant image in this film is the two fishhooks facing each other in the shape of a heart.

KS: Do you see *The Isle* as a beautiful love story?

KK: I've been told that I shouldn't have had the woman kicked. People often try to imagine love as a pure emotional extreme or exchange. But to go beyond the surface, there is a passion, even some other power that exists to sustain this feeling of love. What the man and woman in *The Isle* represent isn't simply anger but the frightening nature of the human relationship itself. The man will drown if he refuses to hang onto the thin fishing line, but excruciating pain follows when he does. I wanted to present the seemingly cruel, yet fragile and inevitable, qualities of relationships. I believe that behind the contempt and destructiveness of it lies something so alluring, the most beautiful love of them all.

KS: Describe the epilogue of *The Isle*.

KK: An "island" is to a woman as a woman is to a man. The last scene in this film's epilogue defines the entire image of this film. I wanted to convey my desire to return to a supernatural state by means of a love story.

KS: It was quite surprising that you refused any sexually explicit images in this film.

KK: I wanted to use Korea's censorship to my advantage. This doesn't mean that I am laying any blame on it, either. Searching for a different means of expression with this institutional practice in mind is also a process of creativity. Obviously the purpose of filmmaking isn't to show everything.

KS: Why is it that most of your female characters are prostitutes or women in similar positions?

KK: It may be because I haven't found a better answer: However, I do believe that it is worth understanding the process and practice of class distinction. Most of the characters in my films do not explain their past. But can one assume that a woman who is a prostitute now has always been a prostitute since childhood? Is it impossible to see their lives as one out of many? Can't we accept the fact that selling one's body was the only means of living for that person? Only when this is possible can we enter the inner world of that person.

KS: You are a filmmaker often criticized by feminist film critics.

KK: I express what I feel in my own unique way. I am comfortable with this. I am aware that this can be perceived as being sadistic. However, I am disappointed by the narrow-mindedness that claims me as the public enemy of everything, when in fact I may be another victim of the patriarchal environment surrounding me. I agree that there are elements in my film that may anger them. But why can't they see that these are merely pieces of reality that become events, moving and turning our lives? It could be that these people are unable to identify with my own experiences.

KS: Are you willing to respond to the feminist critiques through film?

KK: Some female film critics call me "psycho" or a "good-for-nothing filmmaker within the Korean film community." I wanted to ask them if they have actually seen the lives of those presented in my films or wholeheartedly tried to understand their desperate messages. It could be an inevitable result of their own political stance, yet I am suspicious that this position may have created an anger that easily concludes, that readily disregards different perspectives. Their opinions lack the edge that could persuade and inspire most filmmakers. Why do they refuse to enter the core of a film and explore every angle of it? It could be that they tend to see films from their own idle reality. The main issue is that there is a market that caters to these film critics. The only answer and means of defending myself is to continue my work as freely as possible.

KS: The awkwardness of your films may gear film critics towards freely critiquing them.

KK: A filmmaker isn't someone who picks up things and technically assembles them. When you work hard at something, the word "skillful" tends to come up. You are commended when making thirty products when in fact you are supposed to make twenty products. "Skillful labor"—I abhor these words. The films I encounter in international film festivals convey a carefree energy. In comparison, Korean films tend to be too formulaic.

## The World of Water, Its Peacefulness and Anxiety

KS: The space in your films is abstract and unrealistic.

KK: Space is the priority when I start working on a film script because it is the environment in which the characters breathe. However, the spaces that I choose are generally depressive, damp, and closed. I believe that, below the surface, everything is persistent and severe. People may see the spaces in my films as abstract and unrealistic, but I am convinced that they are quite similar to our daily lives.

KS: Water has always been a significant background in your films, but in *The Isle* it finally emerges as a space where life and dream intertwine.

KK: I always start from a certain feeling. By instinct, I determine a space, but once this is decided, I try not to stray from it. When I am on a film shoot, I am happy when on water. However, this sense of bliss is also accompanied by anxiety. Peacefulness, no direction, and unlimited escape . . . in addition, water represents continuous movement, like life itself.

KS: Unlike the perfect control you present as an art director, you don't really profess any particular characteristic in your selection of music.

KK: I am not quite confident in this field. Furthermore, the way in which I use music is a bit different from the norm. For example, I wanted to use Arabic music in the saddest scene of *Address Unknown*. I encountered too much opposition, as people couldn't understand why I wanted to use such music for a tragic Korean story. But in my opinion, there was a similarity between the mental pains of Arabic women enduring a society practicing polygamy and the inner pains of a woman living in Korea with her son of mixed heritage.

KS: Do you insist on your own style during the editing process as well?

KK: Whether it is editing or shooting, I tend to rely on my own instincts. Many people think that it is this style that determines everything about my films. But I believe that it is during the process of writing the film script and recording the movements of the characters through the camera that a large portion of the film is determined. If a considerable amount of energy isn't put into this process, it is no use, regardless of whether the editing and music are done to perfection.

KS: What kind of director are you to your actors?

KK: Once, the actress in *The Isle* asked me if the characters were actually [lower] than the dog starring in the film. I answered by saying that I see them the same as the dog, if not [lower]. In fact, to me, the boat was more important than the female character and the floating yellow house more significant than the male character. Even if I had to compromise I would have considered them the same. This is why I tried to inject more life into the overall visual aspect of the film, when it seemed that the acting was not getting any better. The ideal acting to me is when the actor/actress presents the character in a documentary-like style, as if he/she is actually living that life.

## Who is Kim Ki-duk? The Function of a Malfunction

KS: Unlike *Crocodile* or *Wild Animals, Birdcage Inn* is impressive in that it reaches a point of reconciliation between two totally different worlds.

KK: It could be that my view of the world is slowly changing. This also means that I have developed an attitude of fairness when I look at the world. I was aggressive in *Crocodile* due to my strong resistance to forgiveness. I was able to tone this down in *Wild Animals.* For *Birdcage Inn,* I was determined to see it through to the end, which was one of reconciliation. It was my own proposition that maybe different social views should be something like that. The scornful glares that Hae-mi continues to send her father represent a reality that permeates our lives. I wanted to insist that we have to overcome this as well. Looking back, the significant aspect of this film is that I have begun to raise questions, finally attempting to initiate a dialogue.

KS: Reflecting on *Birdcage Inn,* which seeks reconciliation and hope, it seems that *The Isle* returns to the wild world of *Crocodile.*

KK: Rather than considering this as a return, I want to see it as the surfacing of a thought, among the many within me, similar in sensibility to something I had in the past. Instead of following a systematic and consistent structure of consciousness, my sensory and nerve systems immediately respond by jumping out as in *Crocodile* and *Birdcage Inn.* But if *Crocodile* challenges the absolute power of the world of rules and regulations, *The Isle* focuses on one individual attempting to approach the feelings of love.

KS: *Real Fiction* is an inquiry into the form and nature of film. It was a unique attempt in the Korean film industry, but more than a few critics raised the issue that the film failed to initiate worthwhile debate and became a mere happening instead.

KK: It is true that I feel frustrated that this film could have been better if only I had the time and budget of *The Isle* or *Birdcage Inn.* But paradoxically, I was taken by this idea to shoot as quickly as possible. In order to persuade myself into believing that the month and a half I set myself up for was actually an incredible amount of time, my idea progressed into this desire to be free of any form or convention such as the rules of drama, camera positions, mise-en-scène, and aesthetics of editing. One take, one mistake, it is the accumulation of such things that have made our one hundred years of film history. If there are one hundred film directors in Korea, one filmmaker like Kim Ki-duk could have a different attitude to film, couldn't he? I'm a malfunction or a foreign substance anyway. I wanted this malfunction to function. But the conclusion I reached was the importance of the cinematic, in other words, cinematic expressions and the significance of drama. I have succeeded in shooting a film in an amazing time span of three hours. Now I had to free myself of my obsession towards time constraints and focus on the fundamental nature of the cinema. However, instead of evaluating my attempt as a success or failure, I would like people to understand this as "something different."

KS: The turtle crawling on the asphalt in the prologue of *Birdcage Inn* recalls the turtle in *Crocodile.*

KK: The scene in *Birdcage Inn* where Chin-a releases the turtle is the exact location where Crocodile in *Crocodile* paints a blue line on the back of a turtle. Likewise, the frozen mackerel in *Wild Animals* appears as the softened mackerel that represents father's greed in *Birdcage Inn.* If I am able to continue making films, you will be able to discover a structure similar to *Pulp Fiction,* not just in one film but throughout my body of work. If I were to make ten films, then *Birdcage Inn* will be one sequence, while *The Isle* will be another. My next film, *Bad Guy,* . . . will be the prequel to *Birdcage Inn,* as it will explain why Chin-a in *Birdcage Inn* had no other choice but to become a prostitute. In this light, *Real Fiction* will be the trailer to every sequence. This is not what I have planned but what has happened by itself.

KS: For those who expect the unique and attractive sensibility of *The Isle,* how would you think they would accept the course that begins with *Real Fiction* and *Address Unknown* and leads to your next feature, *Bad Guy*?

KK: I consider *Real Fiction,* in this aspect, a great film. In my own way, I tried to make it with consistency, but it is hard to predict how people will accept it. I'm just always open to the idea of going back to the beginning and starting over.

## An Enigma Anxiously Hovering Around

KS: Opinions of your film are always divided into extremes. This is quite extraordinary in Korea. On the other hand, the international response has been very positive.

KK: No film can be perfectly interpreted and understood by one critic. However, I would like to point out that Korean film critics have the tendency to generalize their opinion of a film based on their personal moral values. I clearly want to create a world that exists outside the boundaries of "morality and common sense." For those who attempt to view my films from within their own set of personal rules, my films become bad or foul, even losing the qualification to be a film. On the other hand, during last year's Venice Film Festival [2000], when I encountered the description of myself as a "filmmaker with an extraordinary talent for poetic expression," I was overwhelmed with happiness that *The Isle* was not understood as grotesque but as beautiful poetry.

KS: After you made your second feature, a fax you sent to a daily newspaper became the center of controversy. You attacked the journalist's indifferent or critical attitude toward your film by stating, "I hate journalists. From Kim Ki-duk." What is your position now?

KK: At one point, I wanted to be part of the center, receiving the spotlight. But now, I am more laid-back. Meanwhile, my resistance towards humanity and my sense of solidarity with social underdogs has become stronger. The majority of filmmakers are people who have received higher education, while I am far from any normal form of institutional education. Once in a while I am haunted by the thought that, as hard as I try, I may as well never be accepted.

KS: To mainstream Korean film criticism, or within elitist art discourses, you remain an enigma.

KK: The mainstream tends to carry an anxiety towards the non-mainstream. It is perhaps a relief to them that Kim Ki-duk maintains an awkwardness.

KS: In spite of tight budgets and a number of restrictions, it is truly a miracle that you continue making films at such speed.

KK: I am always confronted with the question of whether I will be able to make my next film. This is the reason why I cannot help but maintain a guerilla-type approach to filmmaking.

KS: Nineteen-ninety-six, the year that you began to make films, was the year that a new energy revitalized the Korean film industry. As a "low-budget filmmaker," do you actually feel a change taking place?

KK: I may not be in the center of all this so-called change, but it is true that to filmmakers like myself, there seems to be more leeway. Money piled up in the vaults is likely to go to stars, but as the Kim Ki-duk market grows, a small portion of capital comes my way.

KS: You have often been compared to the master of the Golden Age of Korean cinema of the 1950s and 1960s, Kim Ki-young [Kim Ki-yŏng].

KK: Could it be because our names are similar? I truly respect Kim Ki-young. When I first saw *Carnivore,* I understood that this kind of cinematic expression could only be made when the psychological dimension reaches an extreme that my films barely fumble to. The starting point for me is always hatred. I am driven by my failure to understand the most profound corners of my life. I want to think of my films as a process for transforming these numerous misunderstanding into something comprehensible. If the epitome of misunderstanding is hatred, my quest is to slowly but persistently move towards a point where I can understand the world. The wavelengths of my films are tracing towards these directions.

KS: Looking at your films, one cannot help but to despair of any possibility of redemption.

KK: The world will not change. What I truly want to show is a psychological liberation. We can find happiness only if we accept this and do not fear falling to the bottom.

KS: How would you describe yourself?

KK: Once in a while, I think of who and what I am. I think that without even being aware of any possible war, I have been making useless guns. I may have been odd to people when I finally brought these guns out and started shooting. I don't think that everyone is enjoying a "cultural life." There are the other half of people like myself who, just out of elementary school, went from factory to factory, barely having the time to see one or two films a year. For over thirty years, I have lived with these people, and likewise, I have been accustomed to a life quite different from other filmmakers. One day I woke to discover the world of cinema and jumped into it. Perhaps this personal experience is why my films are like a mixed breed, difficult for both sides to understand.

### *Notes*

1. This interview was conducted three years prior to Tony Rayns's publication of the controversial *Film Comment* article attacking Kim Ki-duk. Apparently, the British critic was relatively favorable, or at least neutral, to Kim at that early stage of his career, prior to his international breakthrough.

2. A military leader who seized executive power through a coup in December 1979 and whose regime was responsible for the Kwangju Massacre of May 1980, which claimed the lives of an estimated two thousand innocent citizens who rose up against Chun's dictatorship.

# Filmography

*Crocodile* (*Agŏ*; 1996)
South Korea
Production Company: Choyŏng Film
Producers: Kim Pyŏng-su, Kim Sun-yŏng
Screenplay: Kim Ki-duk
Cinematographer: Yi Tong-sam
Editor: Pak Kok-il
Art Director: Kim Ki-duk
Cast: Cho Chae-hyŏn (Yong-p'ae), U Yun-kyŏng (Hyŏn-jŏng), Chŏn Mu-song (Old Man), An Chae-hong (Boy)
Color
102 min.

*Wild Animals* (*Yasaeng tomgmul pohoguyŏk*; 1997)
South Korea
Production Company: Dream Cinema
Producers: Kwŏn Ki-yŏng, Ch'oe Hŭi-il
Screenplay: Kim Ki-duk
Cinematographer: Sŏ Chŏng-min
Editor: Pak Sun-dŏk
Art Director: Kim Ki-duk
Cast: Cho Chae-hyŏn (Ch'ong-hae), Chang Tong-sik (Hong-san), Chang Ryun (Laura), Sasha Rucavina (Corrine), Denis Lavant (Emil)
Color
103 min.

*Birdcage Inn* (*P'aran taemun*; 1998)
South Korea
Production Company: Pugŭi Film
Producers: Yi Kwang-min, Yu Hŭi-suk
Screenplay: Kim Ki-duk
Cinematographer: Sŏ Chŏng-min

Editor: Ko Im-p'yo
Art Director: Kim Ki-duk
Cast: Yi Chi-ŭn (Chin-a), Yi Ŭn-hae (Hae-mi), Chang Hang-sŏn (Father), Yi In-ok (Mother), An Chae-mo (Hyŏn-u)
Color
100 min.

*The Isle* (*Sŏm*; 2000)
South Korea
Production Company: Myŏng Film
Producer: Yi Ŭn
Screenplay: Kim Ki-duk
Cinematographer: Hwang Sŏ-sik
Editor: Kyŏng Min-ho
Art Director: Kim Ki-duk
Cast: Kim Yu-sŏk (Hyŏn-sik), Sŏ Chŏng (Hŭi-jin), Sŏ Wŏn (Chŏng-a), Cho Chae-hyŏn (Pimp)
Color
90 min.

*Real Fiction* (*Silje sahwang*; 2000)
South Korea
Production Company: Sin Sŏng-su Production
Producers: Yi Chŏng-su, Sin Sŏng-su
Screenplay: Kim Ki-duk
Cinematographer: Hwang Ch'ŏl-hyŏn
Editor: Kyŏng Min-ho
Art Director: Kim Ki-duk
Cast: Chu Chin-mo (I), Kim Chin-a (Girl)
Color
84 min.

*Address Unknown* (*Such'wiin pulmyŏng*; 2001)
South Korea
Production Company: LJ Film
Producer: Yi Sŏng-jae
Screenplay: Kim Ki-duk
Cinematographer: Sŏ Chŏng-min
Editor: Ham Sŏng-wŏn
Art Director: Kim Ki-duk
Cast: Yang Tong-gŭn (Ch'ang-gu), Pan Min-jŏng (Ŭn-ok), Kim Yŏng-min (Chi-hŭn), Cho Chae-hyŏn (Dog-eye), Pang Ŭn-jin (Ch'ang-guk's mother), Myŏng Kae-nam (Chi-hŭn's father), Mitch Mahlum (James)
Color
117 min.

*Bad Guy* (*Nappŭn namja*; 2001)
South Korea
Production Company: LJ Film
Producer: Yi Sŭng-jae
Screenplay: Kim Ki-duk
Cinematographer: Hwang Ch'ŏl-hyŏn
Editor: Ham Sŏng-wŏn
Art Director: Kim Sŏn-ju
Cast: Cho Chae-hyŏn (Han-gi), Sŏ wŏn (Sŏn-hwa), Kim Yun-t'ae (Chŏng-t'ae), Kim Min-jŏng (Madam)
Color
100 min.

*The Coast Guard* (*Haeansŏn*; 2002)
South Korea
Production Company: LJ Film
Producer: Yi Sŭng-jae
Screenplay: Kim Ki-duk
Cinematography: Hwang Ch'ŏl-hyŏn
Editor: Ham Sŏng-wŏn
Art Director: Kim Sŏn-ju
Cast: Chang Tong-gŭn (Private Kang), Kim Chŏng-hak (Private Kim), Pak Chi-a (Mi-yŏng), Yu Hae-jin (Mi-yŏng's brother)
Color
94 min.

*Spring, Summer, Fall, Winter . . . and Spring* (*Pom yŏrŭm kaŭl kyŏul kŭrigo pom*; 2003)
South Korea/Germany
Production Company: LJ Film, Pandora Filmproduktion
Producers: Yi Sŏng-jae, Park Baumgartner
Screenplay: Kim Ki-duk
Cinematographer: Paek Tong-hyŏn
Editor: Kim Ki-duk
Art Director: Kim Sŏn-ju
Cast: O Yŏng-su (Old Monk), Kim Ki-duk (Adult Monk), Kim Yŏng-min (Young Adult Monk), Sŏ Chae-kyŏng (Boy Monk), Kim Chong-ho (Child Monk), Ha Yŏ-jin (Girl)
Color
106 min.

*Samaritan Girl* (*Samaria*; 2004)
South Korea
Production Company: Kim Ki-duk Film
Producer: Kim Ki-duk
Screenplay: Kim Ki-duk
Cinematographer: Sŏn Sang-jae
Editor: Kim Ki-duk
Art Director: Kim Ki-duk
Cast: Yi Ŏl (Yŏng-gi), Kwak Chi-min (Yŏ-jin), Han Yŏ-rŭm (Chae-yŏng)
Color
95 min.

*3-Iron* (*Pinjip*; 2004)
South Korea
Production Company: Kim Ki-duk Film
Producer: Kim Ki-duk
Screenplay: Kim Ki-duk
Cinematographer: Chang Sŏng-baek
Editor: Kim Ki-duk
Art Director: Kim Hyŏn-ju
Cast: Yi Sŏng-hyŏn (Sŏn-hwa), Chae-hŭi (T'ae-sŏk), Kwŏn Hyŏk-ho (Min-gu)
Color
88 min.

*The Bow* (*Hwal*; 2005)
South Korea/Japan
Production Company: Kim Ki-duk Film, Happinet Pictures
Producers: Kim Ki-duk, Michio Suzuki
Screenplay: Kim Ki-duk
Cinematographer: Chang Sŏng-baek
Editor: Kim Ki-duk
Art Director: Kim Hyŏn-ju
Cast: Han Yŏ-rŭm (Young Girl), Chŏn Sŏng-hwang (Old Man), Sŏ Si-jŏk (College Student)
Color
90 min.

*Time* (*Sigan*; 2006)
South Korea/Japan
Production Company: Kim Ki-duk Film, Happinet Pictures
Producers: Kim Ki-duk, Michio Suzuki
Screenplay: Kim Ki-duk
Cinematographer: Sŏng Chong-mu
Editor: Kim Ki-duk
Art Director: Choe Kŭn-u

Cast: Sŏng Hyŏn-a (Sae-hŭi), Ha Chŏng-u (Chi-u), Pak Chi-yŏn (Se-hŭi), Kim Sŏng-min (Plastic Surgeon)
Color
97 min.

*Breath* (*Sum*; 2007)
South Korea
Production Company: Kim Ki-duk Film
Producer: Kim Ki-duk
Screenplay: Kim Ki-duk
Cinematographer: Sŏng Chong-mu
Editor: Wang Su-wan
Art Director: Hwang In-jun
Cast: Chang Chen (Chin), Pak Chi-a (Yŏn), Ha Chŏng-u (Husband), Kang In-hyŏng (Cellmate)
Color
84 min.

*Dream* (*Pimong*; 2008)
South Korea
Production Company: Kim Ki-duk Film
Producers: Kim Ki-duk, Cho Sŏng-gyu
Screenplay: Kim Ki-duk
Cinematographer: Kim Chi-t'ae
Editor: Kim Ki-duk
Art Director: Yi Hyŏn-ju
Cast: Odagiri Jo (Chin), Yi Na-yŏng (Ran), Kim T'ae-hyŏn (Ran's ex-lover), Pak Chi-a (Chin's ex-lover), Chang Mi-hŭi (Doctor)
Color
95 min.

*Arirang* (2011)
South Korea
Production Company: Kim Ki-duk Film
Producer: Kim Ki-duk
Screenplay: Kim Ki-duk
Cinematographer: Kim Ki-duk
Editor: Kim Ki-duk
Cast: Kim Ki-duk
Color
100 min.

*Amen* (2011)
South Korea
Production Company: Kim Ki-duk Film
Producer: Kim Ki-duk
Screenplay: Kim Ki-duk
Cinematographer: Kim Ki-duk, Kim Ye-na
Editor: Kim Ki-duk
Cast: Kim Ye-na (Girl), Kim Ki-duk (Gas-masked Rapist)
Color
72 min.

# Bibliography

Agger, Michael. "Gross and Grosser." *New Yorker,* June 28, 2004, 37.

Althusser, Louis. "Ideology and Ideological State Apparatuses." In *Lenin and Philosophy and Other Essays.* Trans. Ben Brewster. New York: Monthly Review Press, 1971. 173–77.

An, Si-hwan. "Wishing the Unity between Dream and Reality" [Kkum kwa hyŏnsil ŭi hapil ŭl Somanghada]. *Cine 21,* October 7, 2008; accessed July 9, 2011. http://www.cine21.com/do/article/article/typeDispatcher?mag_id=53137.

Anti-U.S. Military Crime Movement Headquarters. *A History of Unfinished Pain: U.S.Military Crimes* [*Kkŭtnaji anjŭn ap'ŭm ŭi yŏksa migun pŏmjoe*]. Seoul: Kaemasŏwŏn, 1999.

Atkinson, Michael. "Ace in the Hole." *Village Voice,* August 21–27, 2002, 126.

———. "Celestial Seasons." *Village Voice,* March 31-April 6, 2004, 54.

Balázs, Belá. *Theory of the Film: Character and Growth of a New Art. Trans. Edith Bone.* New York: Dover Publications, 1970.

Bauman, H-Dirksen. "Listening to Phonocentrism with Deaf Eyes: Derrida's Mute Philosophy of (Sign) Language." *Essays in Philosophy* 9.1 (2008); accessed May 25, 2011. http://commons.pacificu.edu/eip/vol9/iss1/2.

Bellavita, Andrea. "Films That Lack a Bit: Kim Ki-duk" ["Yaggan mojaran tŭthan yŏnghwa: Kim Ki-dŏk"]. In *Speaking about Seven Korean Directors* [*Han'guk ŭi yŏnghwakamdok ch'ilin ŭl malhada*]. Ed. Chu Chin-suk. Seoul: Bon Books, 2008. 129–49.

Bernstein, Michael A. *Bitter Carnival: Ressentiment and the Abject Hero.* Princeton, N.J.: Princeton University Press, 1992.

Bowles, M. J. "The Practice of Meaning in Nietzsche and Wittgenstein." *Journal of Nietzsche Studies* 26 (2003): 12–24.

Bray, Abigail. *Hélène Cixous.* New York: Palgrave MacMillan, 2004.

Canavese, Peter. "Kim Ki-duk—3-*Iron.*" *Groucho Reviews,* April 25, 2005; accessed May 25, 2011. http://www.grouchoreviews.com/interviews/118.

Chakrabarty, Dipesh. *Provincializing Europe: Postcolonial Thought and Historical Difference.* Princeton, N.J.: Princeton University Press, 2000.

Cheng, Scarlet. "Seasons of Change." *Los Angeles Times*, April 4, 2004. E14.
Cho, Eunsun. "*The Stray Bullet* and the Crisis of Korean Masculinity." In *South Korean Golden Age Melodrama: Gender, Genre, and National Cinema*. Ed. Kathleen McHugh and Nancy Abelmann. Detroit: Wayne State University Press, 2005. 99–116.
Chocano, Carina. "Love among Ruins." *Los Angeles Times*, April 1, 2005, E6.
Choe, Steve. "Kim Ki-duk's Cinema of Cruelty: Ethics and Spectatorship in the Global Economy." *Positions: East Asia Cultures Critiques*. 15.1 (2007): 65–90.
Chŏng Sŏng-gi. "Ch'ungmuro's Success Code Is 'More Cruel': What Is Kim Ki-duk Doing Recently?" ["Ch'ungmuro hŭnghaeng k'odŭ tŏ chanhok hagae: Kim Ki-dŏk ŭn yojŭm?"]. *Break News*, August 17, 2010; accessed May 24, 2011. http://www10.breaknews.com/sub_read.html?uid=141945.
Chŏng, Sŏng-il, ed. *Kim Ki-duk: A Wild Life or Sacrificial Lamb* [*Kim Ki-dŏk: yaseang hok ŭn sokjaeyang*]. Seoul: Haengbok han ch'aek ilgi, 2003.
———. "Why Kim Ki-duk?" ["Wae Kim Ki-dŏk inga?"]. Preface to *Kim Ki-duk: A Wild Life or Sacrificial Lamb* [*Kim Ki-dŏk: yaseang hok ŭn sokjaeyang*]. Ed. Chŏng Sŏng-il. Seoul: Haengbok han ch'aek ilgi, 2003. 34–38.
———. "Special: Everything about Kim Ki-duk and *3-Iron*" ["Sŭp'aesyŏl: Kim Ki-dŏk kwa Pinjip ae kwanhan modŭngŏt"]. *Cine 21*, October 6, 2004; accessed July 9, 2011. http://www.cine21.com/do/article/article/typeDispatcher?mag_id=26405.
———. "Flesh, Meat, Bones" ["Sal, kogi, ppyŏ"]. *Words* [*Mal*]. 221 (November 2004): 184–87.
Chow, Rey. *Primitive Passions: Visuality, Sexuality, Ethnography, and Contemporary Chinese Cinema*. New York: Columbia University Press, 1995.
Chu, Sŏng-ch'ŏl, "Broadcasting Kim Ki-duk's *Time* Press Conference" ["Kim Ki-duk *Sigan* Kijahoegyŏn Chisangjunggae"]. *Film 2.0*, August 15, 2006, 8.
Chu, Yu-sin. "His Film Is a Terror to Women" ["Kŭ ŭi yŏnghwa nŭn yŏsŏng ae taehan t'erŏda"]. *Cine 21*, January 22, 2002, 34–35.
———. "It Is a Bad Film" ["Nappŭn yŏnghwa ta"]. *Dong-a Daily* [*Tong-a Ilbo*], January 11, 2002. 8.
Cixous, Hélène. "Castration or Decapitation?" Trans. Annette Kuhn. *Signs* 7.1 (1981): 41–55.
———. "The Laugh of Medusa." In *Women and Language Debate: A Source Book*. Ed. Camille Roman, Suzanne Juhasz, and Christanne Miller. New Brunswick, N.J.: Rutgers University Press, 1994. 78–93.
Cumings, Bruce. *Korea's Place in the Sun: A Modern History*. Updated Ed. New York: W.W. Norton and Co., 2005.
Doane, Mary Ann. *The Desire to Desire: The Woman's Film of the 1940s*. Bloomington: Indiana University Press, 1987.
Espinosa, Julio Garcia. "For an Imperfect Cinema." In *Twenty-Five Years of New Latin American Cinema*. Ed. Michael Chanan. London: British Film Institute, 1983. 71–82.

Fanon, Frantz. *The Wretched of the Earth.* New York: Grove Press, 1963.

"Film Q&A: Kim Ki-Duk." *Time Out,* July 13, 2005, 84.

Foucault, Michel. "Of Other Spaces: Utopias and Heterotopias." In *Rethinking Architecture: A Reader in Cultural Theory.* Ed. Neil Leach. New York: Routledge, 1997. 350–56.

Foundas, Scott. "Why Dharma and Dames Don't Mix." *L.A. Weekly,* April 2, 2004. 35.

Grosz, Elizabeth. *Volatile Bodies: Toward a Corporeal Feminism.* Bloomington: Indiana University Press, 1994.

Hart-Landsberg, Martin. *Korea: Division, Reunification, and U.S. Foreign Policy.* New York: Monthly Review Press, 1998.

Howard, Chris. "Contemporary South Korean Cinema: 'National Conjunction' and 'Diversity.'" In *East Asian Cinemas: Exploring Transnational Connections on Film.* Ed. Leon Hunt and Leung Wing-Fai. London: I. B. Tauris, 2008. 88–102.

Huffer, Lynne. *Maternal Pasts, Feminist Futures.* Stanford, Calif.: Stanford University Press, 1998.

Hummel, Volker. "Interview with Kim Ki-duk." *Senses of Cinema* 18 (February 2002); accessed May 25, 2011. http://archive.sensesofcinema.com/contents/01/19/kim_ki-duk.html.

Hwang, Chin-mi. "Director Kim Ki-duk of *Dream*" ["*Pi-mong* ŭi Kim Ki-dŏk kamdok"]. *Cine 21,* October 7, 2008; accessed July 9, 2011. http://www.cine21.com/do/article/article/typeDispatcher?mag_id=53138.

"I Met the Director Kim Ki-duk on the Rocky Road" ["Sunt'anch'i mothan kamdok Kim Ki-dŏk ŭl mannada"]. *Kino,* May 30, 2001. Reposted and archived in *Yahoo Korea Blog*; accessed July 7, 2011. http://kr.blog.yahoo.com/first2168/10541.

Irigaray, Luce. "This Sex Which Is Not One." In *Women and Language Debate: A Source Book.* Ed. Camille Roman, Suzanne Juhasz, and Christanne Miller. New Brunswick, N.J.: Rutgers University Press, 1994. 94–100.

Jamier, Samuel. "The Strange Case of Director Kim Ki-Duk: The Past, the Persistent Problems, and the Near Future." *The Korea Society,* 2009; accessed May 25, 2011. http://www.koreasociety.org/film_blog/portraits/the_strange_case_of_director_kim_ki-duk_the_past_the_persistent_problems_and_the_near_future.html.

Kang, Han Sup. "Kim Kid-duk: A Film Director Who Dares to Challenge the Establishment." *Koreana* 19.3 (Autumn 2005): 34–39.

Kang, Sŏng-yul. *Korean Cinema: Addiction and Antidote* [*Han'guk yŏnghwa, chungdok kwa haedok*]. Seoul: Litopia, 2008.

Kardish, Laurence. "Kim Ki-duk." MoMA Film Exhibitions. April 23-May 8, 2008; accessed July 7, 2011. http://www.moma/org/visit/calendar/films/597.

Keane, Marian E. "A Closer Look at Scopophilia: Mulvey, Hitchcock, and *Vertigo.*" In *A Hitchcock Reader.* Ed. Marshall Deutelbaum and Leland Poague. Ames: Iowa University Press,1986. 234–49.

Kim, Ki-duk. "Film Is My Struggle" ["Yŏnghwa nŭn naegae t'ugaeng ida"]. In *Kim Ki-duk: A Wild Life or Sacrificial Lamb* [*Kim Ki-dŏk: yaseang hok ŭn sokjaeyang*]. Ed. Chŏng Sŏng-il. Seoul: Haengbok han ch'aek ilgi, 2003. 67–121.

Kim, Kŭm-dong. "Aesthetic Traits and the New Role of the Spectator in Kim Ki-duk's *Birdcage Inn*" ["Kim Ki-dŏk kamdok ŭi yŏnghwa <P'aran taemun> ae nat'ananŭn mihakjŏkt'ŭkjing kwa kangaek ŭi saeroun yŏkhwal"]. *Film Studies* [*Yŏnghwa yŏngu*] 25 (2005): 6–35.

Kim, Kyŏng-uk. "Please Send Me to My Place Now; or, Body and Soul Obsession" ["Ije kŭman che chariro ponae chuseyo, hokŭn yuksin kwa yŏnghon toch'akjŏng"]. In *Kim Ki-duk: A Wild Life or Sacrificial Lamb* [*Kim Ki-dŏk: yaseang hok ŭn sokjaeyang*]. Ed. Chŏng Sŏng-il. Seoul: Haengbok han ch'aek ilgi, 2003. 308–23.

Kim, Kyung Hyun. *The Remasculinization of Korean Cinema.* Durham, N.C.: Duke University Press, 2004.

Kim, Myung Ja. "Race, Gender, and Postcolonial Identity in Kim Ki-duk's *Address Unknown.*" In *Seoul Searching: Culture and Identity in Contemporary Korean Cinema.* Ed. Frances Gateward. Albany: State University of New York Press, 2007. 243–63.

Kim, Nam-in. "Film Director Kim Ki-duk" ["Yŏnghwa kamdok Kim Ki-dŏk"]. *Weekly Chosun* [*Chugan Chosŏn*], October 23, 2004; accessed July 9, 2011. http://www.chosun.com/culture/news/200410/200410230042.html.

Kim, So-hee, "Biography." In *Kim Ki-duk, from* Crocodile *to* Address Unknown. Ed. Lee Hae-jin. Seoul: LJ Film, 2001. 1–6.

———. "Film Director Kim Ki-duk, 'I Am Imperfect. So the World is Relieved.'" ["Yŏnghwa kamdok Kim Ki-dŏk, 'Na nŭn ŏsŏlp'ŭda. Tŏkpunae saesang ŭn andohanda'"]. *Cultizen*. September 15, 2001. Reposted and archived in *Tistory*; accessed July 7, 2011. http://pseudo.tistory.com/97.

Kim, Sŏn-yŏp. "From Prostitutes to Holy Women: Women as Objects of Male Desire" ["Ch'angnyŏ aesŏ sŏnyŏ kkaji: Namsŏng dŭl ŭi yongmang ŭi taesang ŏrosŏ ŭi yŏsŏng"]. *Korean Film Critiques* [*Yŏnghwa p'yŏngron*] 17 (2005): 179–93.

Kim, Soyoung. "Questions of Woman's Film: *The Maid, Madame Freedom,* and Women." In *South Korean Golden Age Melodrama: Gender, Genre, and National Cinema.* Ed. Kathleen McHugh and Nancy Abelmann. Detroit: Wayne State University Press, 2005. 185–200.

Kim, Ŭn-jin. "The Relationship among Women, Art, and Pornography" [Yŏsŏng kwa yesul p'orŭnograp'i ŭi kwangae]. *Thinkers and Thoughts* [*Inmul kwa sasang*] 55 (November 2002): 183–92.

Klein, Andy. "Invisible Visitor." *L.A. City Beat*, April 28-May 4, 2005, 36.

Klein, Christina. "Why American Studies Needs to Think about Korean Cinema, or, Transnational Genres in the Films of Bong Jun-ho." *American Quarterly* 60.4 (December 2008): 871–98.

Kleinhans, Chuck. "Dog Eat Dog: Neo-imperialism in Kim Ki-duk's *Address Unknown." Visual Anthropology* 22 (2009): 182–99.

Kristeva, Julia. "About Chinese Women." In *The Kristeva Reader.* Ed. Toril Moi. New York: Columbia University Press, 1986. 138–59.

———. "The Semiotic and the Symbolic." In *Women and Language Debate: A Source Book.* Ed. Camille Roman, Suzanne Juhasz, and Christanne Miller. New Brunswick, N.J.: Rutgers University Press, 1994. 45–55.

———. "The Subject in Process." In *The Tel Quel Reader.* Ed. Patrick French and Roland-Francois Lark. New York: Routledge, 1998. 133–78.

Kuhn, Annette. *Women's Pictures: Feminism and Cinema.* 2d Ed. London: Verso, 1994.

Lacan, Jacques. "Seminar on *The Purloined Letter.*" In *The Purloined Poe: Lacan, Derrida, and Psychoanalytic Reading.* Ed. John P. Muller and William J. Richardson. Baltimore: Johns Hopkins University Press, 1988. 28–54.

Lagandré, Cédric. "Spoken Words in Suspense." In *Kim Ki-duk.* Ed. Danièl Rivière. Paris: Dis Voir, 2006. 59–93.

Lee, Yoo-ran. *Lim Soon-rye.* Seoul: Korean Film Council, 2008.

Leong, Anthony C. Y. *Korean Cinema: The New Hong Kong.* Victoria, Can.: Trafford, 2003.

Ma, Sheng-mei. "Kim Ki-duk's Non-Person Films." *Asian Cinema* 17.2 (Fall/Winter 2006): 32–46.

Martin, Adrian. "Re: Kim Ki Duk." Message to *Film-Philosophy Salon* discussion list (film-philosophy@jiscmail.ac.uk), February 15, 2007.

Merajver-Kurlat, Marta. *Kim Ki-Duk: On Movies, the Visual Language.* New York: Pinto Books, 2009.

Modleski, Tania. *The Women Who Knew Too Much: Hitchcock and Feminist Theory.* New York: Routledge, 1988.

Moon, Katharine H. S. *Sex among Allies: Military Prostitution in U.S.-Korea Relations.* New York: Columbia University Press, 1997.

Mulvey, Laura. "Visual Pleasure and Narrative Cinema." In *Film Theory and Criticism.* 7th Ed. Ed. Leo Braudy and Marshall Cohen. Oxford: Oxford University Press, 2009. 711–22.

Nam, Tong-ch'ŏl. "Approaching Buddhism as Traditional Culture, Not Religion" ["Pulgyo rŭl sinangi anin chŏnt'ongmunhwa ro chŏpgŭn"]. *Cine 21,* April 15, 2003. 63.

Nardelli, Matilde. "Some Reflections on Antonioni, Sound, and the Silence in *La notte." The Soundtrack* 3.1 (2010): 11–23.

Nealon, Jeffrey T. "Performing Resentment: White Male Anger; or, 'Lack' and Nietzschean Political Theory." In *Why Nietzsche Still? Reflections on Drama, Culture, and Politics.* Ed. Alan D. Schrift. Berkeley: University of California Press, 2000. 274–92.

Nietzsche, Friedrich. *On the Genealogy of Morality.* Ed. Keith Ansell-Pearson. Trans. Carol Diethe. Cambridge: Cambridge University Press, 2004.

Paek, Mun-im. "Fishing Education, Relation-Making through Wounds" [Naksi kyouk, sangchŏ rŭl t'onghan kwangae maetgi]. In *Kim Ki-duk: A Wild Life or Sacrificial Lamb* [*Kim Ki-dŏk: yaseang hok ŭn sokjaeyang*]. Ed. Chŏng Sŏng-il. Seoul: Haengbok han ch'aek ilgi, 2003. 216–27.

———. "Hong Sang-soo vs. Kim Ki-duk: Auteurism In and Out" [Hong Sang-su vs. Kim Ki-dŏk: Chagga chuŭi an kwa pak]. *Social Criticism* [*Sahoe pip'yŏng*] 37 (Fall 2007): 176–87.

Pak, Hae-myŏng. "Probing into Director Kim Ki-duk's Change and Anguish" ["Kim Ki-dŏk kamdok ŭi pyŏnhwa wa komin ŭl k'aemutda"]. *Cine 21*, September 19, 2003; accessed July 9, 2011. http://www.cine21.com/do/article/article/typeDispatcher?mag_id=20907.

Paquet, Darcy. "Close Up: Kim Ki-duk." *Screen International*, April 19–25, 2002, 14.

———. "Helmer Ignites 'Time' Tussle." *Variety*, August 28, 2006, 16.

"Problems of Kim Ki-duk" ["Kim Ki-dŏk ŭi munje"]. *Film 2.0*, December 3–10, 2002. 40–45.

Rayns, Tony. "Calculated Mannerism of a Primitive" ["Wonsijuŭija ŭi kaesandoen maenŏr"]. *Film 2.0*, December 3–10, 2002, 42–44.

———. "Sexual Terrorism: The Strange Case of Kim Ki-duk." *Film Comment* 40.6 (November/December 2004): 50–52.

Rivière, Danièl, ed. *Kim Ki-Duk*. Paris: Dis Voir, 2006.

Robbins, Ruth. *Literary Feminisms*. New York: St. Martin Press, 2000.

Rohmer, Eric, and Claude Chabrol. *Hitchcock: The First Forty-Four Films*. New York: Ungar Publishing, 1979.

Sarris, Andrew. "The Four Seasons of Life Kim Ki-duk's Buddhism 101." *New York Observer*, April 26, 2004, P21

Schatz, Thomas. *The Genius of the System: Hollywood Filmmaking in the Studio Era*. New York: Pantheon Books, 1988.

Scheler, Max. *Ressentiment*. Milwaukee: Marquette University Press, 1994.

Schor, Naomi and Elizabeth Weed. *The Essential Difference*. Bloomington: Indiana University Press, 1994.

Scott, A. O. "A Buddhist Observes Humanity with Sharp and Stern Eyes." *New York Times*, March 31, 2004, B3

———. "A Man Breaks into Houses to Fill Them Up with Life." *New York Times*, April 29, 2005, 16.

Shaw, George Bernard. *Pygmalion*. New York: Washington Square Press, 1973.

Shin, Chi-Yun. "Art of Branding: Tartan 'Asia Extreme' Films." *Jump Cut: A Review of Contemporary Media* 50 (Spring 2008); accessed May 25, 2011. http://www.ejumpcut.org/archive/jc50.2008/TartanDist/text.html.

Shin, Chi-Yun, and Julian Stringer, eds. *New Korean Cinema*. New York: New York University Press, 2005.

Sim, Yŏng-sŏp. "The Crocodile Who Didn't Go to the Sea" ["Pada rŏ naagaji motha nŭn agŏ"]. *Cine 21*, May 16, 2000, 68–70.

Sin Tae-ch'ŏl. "Lynching Kim Ki-duk Is Collective Violence" ["Kim Ki-dŏk ttaerigi nŭn tasu ŭi hoengp'o"]. *Chosun Daily* [*Chosŏn Ilbo*], August 30, 2006; accessed July 9, 2011. http://www.chosun.com/editorials/news/200608/200608300488.html.

Slater, Ben, "Tony Reigns." *Gone to Persia,* November 26, 2004; accessed July 7, 2011. http://www.gonetopersia.com/downloads/dotc1.pdf.

Smith, Damon. "The Bad Boy of Korean Cinema." *Boston Globe,* May 1, 2005, N9.

Sofair, Michael. Rev. of *Spring, Summer, Fall, Winter . . . and Spring. Film Quarterly* 59.1 (Autumn 2005): 36–44.

Solanas, Fernardo, and Octavio Getino. "Toward a Third Cinema." In *Movies and Methods.* Vol. 1. Ed. Bill Nichols. Berkeley: University of California Press, 1976. 44–64.

Song, Ch'ang-sŏp. "A Symbolic Wing and a Truck of Desire (2)" ["Sangjing nalgae wa yongmang t'rŭk (2)"]. *Narrative* 7 (August 2003): 142–65.

Sŏng, Ŭn-ae. "*The Host* and Kim Ki-duk: Beyond the Monstrous Dialectics" ["Koemul kwa Kim Ki-dŏk: Kŭ koemul kat ŭn taehang ŭl nŭmŏ"]. *Criticism* [*Pip'yŏng*] 13 (Winter 2006): 310–23.

Spivak, Gayatri Chakravorty. "Can the Subaltern Speak?" In *Colonial Discourse and Post-Colonial Theory: A Reader.* Ed. Patrick Williams and Laura Chrisman. New York: Columbia University Press, 1994. 66–111.

———. "French Feminism in an International Frame." In *In Other Worlds: Essays in Cultural Politics.* New York: Routledge, 1988. 134–53.

Stephens, Chuck. "*3 Iron.*" *Cinema Scope* 22 (June 2005); accessed May 25, 2011. http://www.cinema-scope.com/cs22/cur_stephens_iron.htm.

Stringer, Rebecca. "'A Nietzschean Breed': Feminism, Victimology, *Ressentiment.*" In *Why Nietzsche Still? Reflections on Drama, Culture, and Politics.* Ed. Alan D. Schrift. Berkeley: University of California Press, 2000. 247–73.

"Support or Criticize: Six Perspectives on Kim Ki-duk" [Onghohal kŏtinga pip'anhal kŏtinga: Kim Ki-dŏk ŭl parabonŭn 6-gae ŭi sisŏn]. *Film 2.0,* January 23, 2002. 56–63.

Tzioumakis, Yannis. *American Independent Cinema: An Introduction.* New Brunswick, N.J.: Rutgers University Press, 2006.

"U.S. Forces, Korea/Combined Forces Command Combined Ground Component Command (GCC)." *GlobalSecurity*; accessed May 25, 2011. http://www.globalsecurity.org/military/agency/dod/usfk.htm.

Walsh, Mike. Rev. of *New Korean Cinema,* ed. Chi-Yun Shin and Julian Stringer. *Screening the Past,* March 7, 2006; accessed May 25, 2011. http://www.latrobe.edu.au/screeningthepast/19/new-korean-cinema.html.

"When Korean Cinema Attacks: New York Korean Cinema Festival 2001." *Subway Cinema*; accessed May 25, 2011. http://www.subwaycinema.com/kfest2001/theisle.htm.

"Why Do I Support or Criticize Kim Ki-duk" ["Na nŭn wae Kim Ki-dŏk ŭl chiji hanŭnga/pandae hanŭnga"]. *Cine 21,* January 22, 2002. 31–35.

Williams, Linda. "Film Bodies: Gender, Genre, and Excess." In *Film Theory and Criticism.* 7th Ed. Ed. Leo Braudy and Marshall Cohen. Oxford: Oxford University Press, 2009. 602–16.

Wood, Robin. *Hollywood from Vietnam to Reagan.* New York: Columbia University Press, 1986.

Yi, Tong-jin. "Three Questions about *Spring, Summer, Fall, Winter . . . and Spring* and Kim Ki-duk's Films" ["<*Pom yŏrŭm kaŭl kyŏul kŭrigo pom*> kwa Kim Ki-dŏk yŏnghwa ae taehan segae ŭi panmun"]. *Cine 21*, October 1, 2003; accessed July 9, 2011. http://www.cine21.com/do/article/article/typeDispatcher?mag_id=21102.

Yoon, Seungho. "Empty Houses Haunted: Hauntology of Space in Kim Ki-duk's *3-Iron.*" *Post Script: Essays in Film and the Humanities* 27.3 (Summer 2008): 59–68.

Žižek, Slavoj. *Enjoy Your Symptom! Jacques Lacan in Hollywood and Out.* New York: Routledge, 1992.

# Index


abject hero, 22, 115, 124n10
*Address Unknown*, 1, 6, 9, 22, 26–45, 60, 62, 71, 74, 88, 104–7, 115, 127–29, 135, 137, 142; cannibalism in, 38–39; double temporality of, 39; ending of, 41–42; eye injuries in, 31–32, 37–38; heterotopia of, 30; *kijich'on* (camptown) in, 27, 30, 34–36, 39; Kim Ki-duk on, 127–29; Lacanian analysis of, 26–28, 32–33, 41; postcolonial implications of, 32, 38–39, 41, 45; precredit montage and credit sequence in, 28–29; scopopobia in, 37; U.S.-Korean relations in, 34, 36, 39–40, 44–45; *yanggongju* (sex workers for American G.I.s) in, 35–36, 39, 42
AFI Film Festival, 104
Altas, Natacha, 58
Althusser, Louis, 125n18. *See also* interpellation
Altman, Robert, 44, 101
*Amants du Pont-Neuf, Les* (The Lovers on the Bridge), 4, 118
*Amen*, 8–9, 126, 146
An, Si-hwan, 65
Antonioni, Michelangelo, 51
*Arirang*, 8–9, 19, 121–22, 145
Artaud, Antonin, 73
Arzner, Dorothy, 125n24
Atkinson, Michael, 21, 108
*audition*, 14. *See also* Miike, Takashi
auteurism, 7, 10, 12, 122

*Bad Guy*, 1, 5–6, 9, 16–18, 21–22, 24, 47–50, 55, 60–62, 64, 67–69, 72, 74, 80, 88–89, 95, 97, 106, 125nn20–21, 137, 143; class warfare in, 24, 49, 71–72; "Day by Day" (hymn) played in, 67–68; ending of, 17, 67–68; feminist backlash against, 16–17, 69; "I Tuoi Fiori" (song) played in, 64; Kim Ki-duk on, 17; metaphysical beach scenes in, 67–68; opening sequence of, 47–49; religious overtones in, 6, 68; role of the military in, 48–49, 55; silent protagonist in, 22, 55; voyeurism in, 88–89
Balázs, Béla, 55–56
Barrett, Michèle, 76
*Beautiful*, 119, 122. *See also* Chŏn, Chae-hong
Beauvoir, Simone de, 76
Bellavita, Andrea, 9
Ben Hur, 118
Bernstein, Michael A., 22, 124n10. *See also* abject hero
*Birdcage Inn*, 5, 8–9, 25, 39, 62, 64, 69, 72–74, 77–89, 91–95, 97, 104–7, 129–30, 132, 136–37, 141–42; box-office record of, 8; *chora*, 93–94; class antagonism in, 82–83; comparison to *Bad Guy*, 88–89; comparison to *Vertigo*, 87–88; controversial surrogate prostitution scene in, 92; Egon Schiele's paintings in, 64, 79, 85; female-centric shot composition of, 81–82; female gaze in, 85–87; final shot of, 93–94; interclass female bonding in, 25, 73–74, 92–93; Kim Ki-duk on, 130, 132, 136–37; mockery of male desires

in, 91; as neofeminist text, 72–74; pre-credit prologue and opening scene in, 78–79; production history of, 77–78; tailing sequence in, 85–87; voyeurism in, 88–89
body genre, 20. *See also* Williams, Linda
Bong, Joon-ho, 117. See also *Host, The*
*Bow, The*, 1, 8–9, 18, 27, 62, 71, 73, 117, 144
Bowles, M. J., 23. See also *ressentiment*
*Breath*, 8–9, 19, 22, 26, 62, 75, 90, 117, 145
Bresson, Robert, 2
*Bridget Jones's Diary*, 74
Brown, Wendy, 23. See also *ressentiment*
Burks, Robert, 87. *See also* Hitchcock, Alfred; *Vertigo*
Butler, Judith, 76–77

Cage, John, 73
Cannes International Film Festival, 19, 120–22
*Carnivore*, 139
Cassavetes, John, 9
*Casualties of War*, 28. *See also* De Palma, Brian
Chakrabarty, Dipesh, 38
Chan, Fruit, 12
Chang, Chen, 8, 26
Chang, Hun, 117, 120–21. See also *Rough Cut*
Chaplin, Charlie, 55
Chen, Kaige, 12
*Chihwaseon*, 62, 69. *See also* Im, Kwon-taek
Cho, Chae-hyŏn, 47. See also *Bad Guy*
Cho, Eunsun, 37
Chocano, Carina, 17
Chodorow, Nancy, 76
Choe, Steve, 21–22, 24, 45
Chŏn, Chae-hong, 120–21. See also *Beautiful*; *Poongsan*
Chŏn, T'ae-il, 24. *See also* Park, Kwang-su
Chŏng, Sŏng-gi, 119
Chŏng, Sŏng-il, 21, 61, 75, 77, 116
*Chosun Daily* (Korean newspaper), 55
Chow, Rey, 12, 15–16. *See also* self-orientalism
Chu, Yu-sin, 16, 53, 69
Chun Doo Hwan, 3, 132, 140n2
Chung, Ji-young, 24, 36. See also *Silver Stallion*
*Chunhyang*, 62. *See also* Im, Kwon-taek
*Cine 21* (Korean film magazine), 16, 61, 103, 108, 114, 119
*Citizen Ruth*, 102
Cixous, Hélène, 73, 76, 99–101, 125n23; *l'écriture féminine* (feminine writing), 73, 101
Claudel, Camille, 64
*Coast Guard, The*, 1, 6, 8, 42–44, 70–71, 74, 143
Corman, Roger, 9
*Crash*, 44
*Crocodile*, 5–6, 8–9, 15–16, 24, 60, 62, 72, 74, 77, 90, 95, 100, 105, 107, 115, 129, 131, 136–37, 141; abject (anti) hero in, 5, 115; box-office record of, 8; class warfare in, 24, 71–72; feminist criticism of, 16; homophobia in, 90; Kim Ki-duk on, 131, 136–37; production history of, 5–6
Cukor, George, 100

*Dancer in the Dark*, 123n3. *See also* Von Trier, Lars
*Dark Victory*, 125n24
Demme, Jonathan, 4. See also *Silence of the Lambs, The*
Deneuve, Catherine, 64
De Palma, Brian, 28, 71, 101
Derrida, Jacques, 57; phonocentrism, 57
Doane, Mary Ann, 125n24. *See also* women's pictures
*Dogville*, 110. *See also* Von Trier, Lars
*Do the Right Thing*, 44. *See also* Lee, Spike
*Dream*, 3, 8–9, 63–66, 68, 75, 117, 119, 121, 145
*Dreams*, 107. *See also* Kurosawa, Akira

Eisenhower, Dwight D., 40
Enloe, Cynthia, 34

Espinosa, Julio Garcia, 9–10
Etrange Film Festival, 105, 117, 123n2
extreme cinema, 2, 7, 12–14, 19, 25–26
*Eye, The*, 14. *See also* Pang brothers

*Falling Down*, 44
Fanon, Frantz, 49
Fassbinder, Rainer Werner, 2, 7, 28, 123n4
Feminism, 23, 69, 76, 100; antifeminist, 71, 75, 101–2; corporeal, 76; feminist, 5, 16, 21, 23–24, 53, 69, 71–72, 75–77, 87, 90, 100–104, 117, 133–34; French, 72–73, 93, 100, 125n23; neofeminist, 72–74, 99, 102; postfeminist, 72, 74
*Film Comment*, 17–18, 108, 140n1
film festivals, 2, 9, 19, 104–5, 117–18, 120–22, 123n2, 138
*Film Quarterly*, 108
*Film 2.0* (Korean film magazine), 16
Firestone, Shulamith, 76
*Forever the Moment*, 102. *See also* Lim, Soon-rye
Foundas, Scott, 107
*4 Months, 3 Weeks, and 2 Days*, 95
*Full Metal Jacket*, 42

Gallop, Jane, 76
*Gaslight*, 125n24
Gatens, Moira, 76
Getino, Octavio, 9–10
Grosz, Elizabeth, 76–77

*Habitual Sadness*, 72
Haggis, Paul, 44
Häggkvist, Carola, 67
Happinet Pictures, 18, 46
*Hell Flower*, 35. *See also* Shin, Sang-ok
Hichcockian, 50. *See also* Burks, Robert; *Vertigo*
Hitchcock, Alfred, 8, 71, 87–91, 101
homosexuality, 90; bisexual desire, 91; gay images, 90–91; lesbianism, 74, 95
Hong, Sang-soo, 123n4, 123n6
*Host, The*, 46–47, 69, 117, 120, 125n17. See also *Time*
Hwang, Chin-mi, 65, 119

*Illegal Crossing* (screenplay), 4–5
Im, Kwon-taek, 62, 69, 108, 123n6
*I'm a Cyborg, But That's Okay*, 123n1. *See also* Park, Chan-wook
Imamura, Shohei, 25, 71
imperfect cinema, 9. *See also* Espinosa, Julio Garcia
interpellation, 53, 81, 125nn18–19
Irigaray, Luce, 73, 76, 101, 125n23; *l'écriture féminine* (feminine writing), 73, 101
*I Saw the Devil*, 120
*Isle, The*, 1, 8–9, 14, 18–21, 27, 31, 50–55, 62, 69–70, 73, 95, 106, 120, 130–38, 142; colors in, 130–31; corporeal effects (fainting) in, 14, 19–20; epilogue, 53, 133; feminist interpretations of, 53–55, 69; Hitchcockian montage in, 50–51; as love story, 132–33; self-mutilation in, 31, 52–54; silences subaltern resistance in, 50, 54–55; sound in, 51–52; suicide attempts in, 50–52; at the Venice Film Festival, 138; water in, 19, 50, 53, 73

Jang, Dong-gun, 8
Jang, Sun-woo, 17, 24, 132
*Jang Sun-Woo Variations, The*, 17
*Joint Security Area*, 123n1. *See also* Park, Chan-wook
Joyce, James, 73

Kang, Sŏng-yul, 69
Karlovy Vary International Film Festival, 123n2
Keane, Marian E., 89
Keaton, Buster, 55
Kim, Ki-duk: acting in his films, 9, 14, 113–15, 117, 126n27; autobiographical elements in his films, 6, 14–15, 22, 33, 107, 111–13, 115, 121; awards and grants, 2, 4, 14, 19, 78, 116, 118, 121; biography, 3–6; comparisons to other directors, 2, 7–9, 13–16, 19, 25, 107–8, 123n4, 139; confrontation with the Korean press, 11, 15, 69, 117, 138; controversial comments on *The Host*,

46–47, 69, 117, 120, 125n17; controversy about, 7, 15–19, 21–22, 46–47, 69, 117, 120, 125n17, 132, 138; directorial debut, 5–6; feminist critiques of, 5, 16–17, 24, 69–72, 75, 77, 101–2, 133–34; filmmaking style, 8–10, 13, 103, 106, 118, 124n8, 129–31, 134–35; influence on younger Korean filmmakers, 119–22; life in France, 4, 56, 105; MoMA retrospective, 2, 13, 19, 123n6; philosophy of colors, 10, 16, 66, 130–31; predilection for water imagery, 16, 73, 106, 134–35; producer credits, 8, 117–19, 122; public apology, 47, 55; queer critique of, 90–91; "Sam Peckinpah" of Korean cinema, 120; "semi-abstract" aesthetics, 4, 13, 124n8, 129–30; unconventional use of music, 52, 64, 135; views on filmmaking, 22, 136–39; views on the body, 75–77
Kim, Ki-young, 139
Kim, Kŭm-dong, 88
Kim, Kyung Hyun, 25
Kim, Myung Ja, 8, 39
Kim, So-hee, 7–8, 22, 26, 33, 42, 45, 79, 115, 127
Kim, Sŏn-yŏp, 69–71
Kirby, Vicki, 76
Klein, Christina, 45
Kleinhans, Chuck, 41, 44–45
Korean cinema, 8–9, 11, 13, 19, 35–6, 46, 72, 75, 99, 100, 106, 119, 120, 123n7, 139; censorship, 37, 133; feminist/women's films, 72, 100; Golden Age, 35, 75, 139; "hostess" genre, 75; Korean New Wave, 36; as the New Hong Kong, 13, 123n7; New York Korean Film Festival, 19
Korean Film Council (KOFIC) 4, 33, 78, 102, 123n2
Korean history: Cairo Declaration (1943), 39; civil war (the Korean War: 1950–53), 6, 34–36, 38, 40, 42, 128; division (1945), 35, 39–40, 42; Kwangju Massacre (1980), 36, 124n11, 131–32, 140n2; *minjung* (people) movement, 36; modernization under military regimes (1961–92), 24, 80; U.S. military occupation (1945–48), 34, 40, 124n12; U.S. operational control of the South Korean army, 124n14; U.S. policy about, 39–40; U.S. troops in, 34, 40, 124n12; Yalta Conference, (1945) 124n13
Kristeva, Julia, 73, 76, 93–95, 99–101, 125n23; *chora*, 73, 93–94, 97–98; semiotic, 73, 93–94, 97–100; subject in process, 93, 99, 115
Kubrick, Stanley, 42
Kuhn, Annette, 72, 100–101. *See also* women's pictures
Kurosawa, Akira, 12–13, 107
Kurosawa, Kiyoshi, 12
Kwan, Stanley, 100

Lacan, Jacques, 26–28, 32–33, 39, 41; letter in sufferance, 37; repetition automatism, 32; third gaze, 26, 32–33, 37, 45
Lady Vengeance, 1. *See also* Park, Chan-wook
Lagandré, Cédric, 45
Lauretis, Teresa de, 91
Lautréamont, Comte de, 73
Lee, Chang-dong, 8, 69
Lee, Myung-se, 123n6
Lee, Spike, 44, 71
Leong, Anthony C. Y., 13, 123n7
Lim, Soon-rye, 102–4
Loach, Ken, 7, 123n4
*Los Angeles Times*, 17, 108
Lupino, Ida, 125n24

Ma, Sheng-mei, 25, 90, 97
Malkovich, John, 64
Mallarmé, Stéphane, 73
Mandala, 108
Man from Nowhere, The, 120
Markle, Private Kenneth, 36
*Marriage of Maria Braun, The*, 28. *See also* Fassbinder, Rainer Werner
Martin, Adrian, 21
*MASH*, 44. *See also* Altman, Robert
McAlpine, Hamish, 12. *See also* Tartan Asia Extreme
melodrama, 4, 13, 17, 20, 36, 75, 100
Merajver-Kurlat, Marta, 56–57, 66, 101

Miike, Takashi, 12, 14, 25
Min, Pyŏn-ch'ŏn, 14
misogyny, 16–17, 24–25, 69, 90, 106
Mitchell, Juliet, 76
Mizoguchi, Kenji, 12
Modleski, Tania, 87–88, 91
Moon, Katharine H. S., 34–35
Mozart, Wolfgang Amadeus, 93
Mulvey, Laura, 37, 89
*Murmuring, The*, 72
*My Own Breathing*, 72

Nakata, Hideo, 14
Nardelli, Matilde, 51
*Natural City*, 14
Nealon, Jeffrey T., 23. See also *ressentiment*
*New Yorker*, 19
*New York Observer*, 108
*New York Post*, 19–20
*New York Times*, 107
Nietzsche, Friedrich, 7, 22–23. See also *ressentiment*
*Notte, La*, 51
*Now, Voyager*, 125n24

*Oasis*, 69. *See also* Lee, Chang-dong
Odagiri, Jo, 8, 63–65, 68, 117
*Oldboy*, 1. *See also* Park, Chan-wook
Oliveira, Manoel de, 64
Oshima, Nagisa, 2, 25
Ozu, Yasujiro, 12

Paek, Mun-im, 53, 123n4
Pang brothers, 12, 14
Papas, Irene, 64
Paquet, Darcy, 17, 25, 46
Park, Chan-wook, 1, 12, 123n1
Park, Chung Hee, 3, 37
Park, Kwang-su, 24, 123n6
Pasolini, Pier Paolo, 25
Payne, Alexander, 102
*Petal, A*, 132
Plato, 93
Poe, Edgar Allan, 26, 32–33, 39, 42, 45. *See also* "Purloined Letter, The"
*Poongsan*, 120–22. See also *Beautiful*
pornography, 20, 75
*Pulp Fiction*, 137
"Purloined Letter, The" (short story), 26–27, 32–33, 41. *See also* Poe, Edgar Allan
*Pygmalion* (novel), 17
Pyŏn, Yŏng-ju, 72

Rayns, Tony, 17–19, 21, 24, 47, 108, 123n2, 123n4, 130, 140n1
*Real Fiction*, 1, 3, 5–6, 9, 105, 123n3, 136–37, 142
*Rebecca*, 125n24
*ressentiment*, 7, 14, 22–24, 49, 61, 72, 88, 109, 112, 116, 124n10; cinema of, 7, 22, 24; class, 61, 72, 88; definitions of, 22–23, 124n10; man of, 23, 112; role in Kim Ki-duk's cinema, 24; sublimation of, 109
*Ringu*, 14
Roosevelt, Franklin D., 40, 124n13
*Rough Cut*, 117–20. *See also* Chang, Hun

*Samaritan Girl*, 1–2, 5–6, 8–9, 18, 62, 69–70, 72–74, 95–100, 106, 118, 120, 144; Best Director Award at the Berlin Film Festival, 2, 118; *chora* in, 97–98; disciplinary father in, 97–98; dream sequence in, 97–98; ending of, 74, 98–99; "Gymnopedie No. 1" (music) played in, 97; legend of Vasumitra in, 70, 96; lesbianism in, 74, 95; middle-class hero in, 96–97, 118; as neofeminist text, 72–74, 99; online prostitution in, 95; religious overtones of, 6, 70, 96; shifts in point of view in, 96–97; Sonata (Hyundai) in, 97–98; two-shots in, 95
Sandrelli, Stefania, 64
Sarris, Andrew, 108
Satie, Erik, 97–98
Scheler, Max, 23. See also *ressentiment*
Schiele, Egon, 64, 79–80, 85, 88, 93. See also *Birdcage Inn*
Schoenberg, Arnold, 63, 73
Schor, Naomi, 77
Schumacher, Joel, 44. See also *Falling Down*
Scollo, Etta, 64
Scott, A. O., 107

self-orientalism, 12, 16, 62. *See also* Chow, Rey; Zhang, Yimou
*Sex and the City* (TV series), 74
Shaw, George Bernard, 17
Shin, Chi-yun, 12, 123n7
Shin, Sang-ok, 35, 123n6
*Silence of the Lambs, The*, 4, 118
*Silver Stallion*, 36–37. *See also* Chung, Ji-young
Sim, Yŏng-sŏp, 16, 53, 69
Sin, Tae-ch'ŏl, 55
*Single Spark, A*, 24. *See also* Park, Kwang-su
Slater, Ben, 18–19
Sofair, Michael, 108
Solanas, Fernando, 9–10
Sŏng, Ŭn-ae, 47
*Sopyonje*, 62. *See also* Im, Kwon-taek
Soyoung Kim, 100
Spivak, Gayatri Chakravorty, 50, 54–55, 76, 100
*Spring, Summer, Fall, Winter . . . and Spring*, 1, 6, 9, 11, 14, 18–19, 27, 62, 71, 95, 100, 107–19, 143,125nn25–26; autobiographical elements in, 14–15, 113–15; awards given to, 14, 116; Brechtian effects in, 110; Buddha' gaze in, 115; Buddhist film debate surrounding, 18, 108; Christian subtext in, 113, 126n26; comparison to *Dreams*, 107–8; drowning in, 95, 113; establishing shots in, 109; international success of, 1–2, 11; old monk's lesson in, 110–11, 119; pessimism in, 116; representing a shift in Kim Ki-duk's worldview, 108–9, 118; self-immolation in, 112–13
*Spring in My Hometown*, 36–37
Stalin, Joseph, 40, 124n13
Stephens, Chuck, 18–19
*Stray Bullet, The*, 36–37. *See also* Yu, Hyun-mok
Stringer, Rebecca, 23. See also *ressentiment*
*Sympathy for Mr. Vengeance*, 1. *See also* Park, Chan-wook

*Talking Picture, A*, 64
Tanzer, Joshua, 19–20
Tarkovsky, Andrei, 2
Tartan Asia Extreme, 12, 123n5
Third Cinema, 9–10
*Thirst*, 123n1. *See also* Park, Chan-wook
*Three Friends*, 104. *See also* Lim, Soon-rye
*3-Iron*, 1–2, 6, 8–9, 11, 18–19, 22, 24–25, 55–64, 66–68, 71–72, 75, 97, 100, 106, 119–20, 124n8, 144; ambiguous social identity in, 59–61; Best Director Award at the Venice Film Festival, 2, 118; class warfare in, 24, 71–72; "Gafsa" (song) played in, 58, 64; "ghost practice" in, 60; Kim Ki-duk on, 61, 124n8; 180-degree sphere of vision in, 61; paradoxical happy end of, 66–67; plagiarism charge against, 18; police brutality and corruption in, 50, 55, 97; silence in, 55–59; silent protagonist in, 22, 55; traditional iconography in, 62–63
*Time*, 1, 8–9, 11, 18, 35, 46, 117, 120, 125n16, 144
*Time Out* (magazine), 11, 56
Tsai, Ming-liang, 18
*2009: Lost Memories*, 65

Venice International Film Festival, 2, 19, 118, 138
*Vertigo*, 87, 89, 91
*Village Voice*, 21, 108
violence, 6–7, 14–16, 20, 22, 24–25, 30–32, 38, 43–46, 54–55, 57, 66, 71, 74–75, 90, 102, 104, 106, 120, 128, 131–32; against the male body, 38, 90; animal cruelty, 7, 15, 43, 45; body mutilation, 7, 15, 45, 53–54, 70, 90, 106; cannibalism, 7, 15, 38–39; domestic, 14, 45, 102; extreme, 6, 44, 104; gendered, 43; Kim Ki-duk on, 24, 128, 131–32; as means of communication, 6, 24; military, 43; murder, 7, 14–15, 36, 45, 50–51, 59, 63, 70–71, 74, 89, 97–98, 112, 124n10; neocolonial, 45; rape, 5, 7, 15–16, 25, 36–37, 45, 50, 52, 59, 69, 71, 83, 88, 91, 102; sadomasochistic, 7, 15, 71, 132; sexual, 16, 25, 90; spousal abuse, 57–58, 71
Vitti, Monica, 51

*Vive l'amour*, 18
Von Trier, Lars, 71, 101, 110, 122, 123n3

*Waikiki Brothers*, 103–4. *See also* Lim, Soon-rye
*Why Has Bodhi-Dharma Left for the East?*, 108
*Wild Animals*, 5–6, 8–9, 15, 27, 42, 60, 62, 64, 70, 74, 77, 88, 100, 105, 125n22, 136–37, 141; box-office record of, 8; femme fatales in, 70; inter-Korean male bonding in, 42, 70; Kim Ki-duk's protest fax about, 15, 69, 138; Peeping Tom devices in, 88, 125n22
Williams, Linda, 20, 75
Wittig, Monique, 77
Wollstonecraft, Mary, 76
women's pictures, 72, 100, 125n24. *See also* Kuhn, Annette
Wood, Robin, 101

Yi, Kwang-mo, 36. See also *Spring in My Hometown*
Yi, Na-yŏng, 63–64, 117, 121. See also *Dream*
Yi, Si-myŏng, 65
Yi, Tong-jin, 115, 126n26
Yoon, Seungho, 59
Yu, Chi-na, 16, 53
Yu, Hyun-mok, 36, 123n6. See also *Stray Bullet, The*
Yun, Kŭm-i, 36

Zhang, Yimou, 12–13, 15–16, 19, 71. *See also* self-orientalism
Žižek, Slavoj, 41

**Hye Seung Chung** is an assistant professor of film and media studies in the department of communication studies at Colorado State University. She is the author of *Hollywood Asian: Philip Ahn and the Politics of Cross-Ethnic Performance*.

Books in the series
Contemporary Film Directors

*Nelson Pereira dos Santos*
Darlene J. Sadlier

*Abbas Kiarostami*
Mehrnaz Saeed-Vafa and
Jonathan Rosenbaum

*Joel and Ethan Coen*
R. Barton Palmer

*Claire Denis*
Judith Mayne

*Wong Kar-wai*
Peter Brunette

*Edward Yang*
John Anderson

*Pedro Almodóvar*
Marvin D'Lugo

*Chris Marker*
Nora Alter

*Abel Ferrara*
Nicole Brenez, translated by
Adrian Martin

*Jane Campion*
Kathleen McHugh

*Jim Jarmusch*
Juan Suárez

*Roman Polanski*
James Morrison

*Manoel de Oliveira*
John Randal Johnson

*Neil Jordan*
Maria Pramaggiore

*Paul Schrader*
George Kouvaros

*Jean-Pierre Jeunet*
Elizabeth Ezra

*Terrence Malick*
Lloyd Michaels

*Sally Potter*
Catherine Fowler

*Atom Egoyan*
Emma Wilson

*Albert Maysles*
Joe McElhaney

*Jerry Lewis*
Chris Fujiwara

*Jean-Pierre and Luc Dardenne*
Joseph Mai

*Michael Haneke*
Peter Brunette

*Alejandro González Iñárritu*
Celestino Deleyto and
Maria del Mar Azcona

*Lars von Trier*
Linda Badley

*Hal Hartley*
Mark L. Berrettini

*François Ozon*
Thibaut Schilt

*Steven Soderbergh*
Aaron Baker

*Mike Leigh*
Sean O'Sullivan

*D.A. Pennebaker*
Keith Beattie

*Jacques Rivette*
Mary M. Wiles

*Kim Ki-duk*
Hye Seung Chung

The University of Illinois Press
is a founding member of the
Association of American University Presses.

Designed by Paula Newcomb
Composed in 10/13 New Caledonia LT Std
with Helvetica Neue LT Std display
by Barbara Evans
at the University of Illinois Press
Manufactured by Thomson-Shore, Inc.

University of Illinois Press
1325 South Oak Street
Champaign, IL 61820-6903
www.press.uillinois.edu

Jens Petersen

# Max Webers Rechtssoziologie und die juristische Methodenlehre

Jens Petersen

# Max Webers Rechtssoziologie und die juristische Methodenlehre

RECHT

De Gruyter Recht · Berlin

♾ Gedruckt auf säurefreiem Papier, das die US-ANSI-Norm über Haltbarkeit erfüllt.

ISBN 978-3-89949-534-8

*Bibliografische Information der Deutschen Nationalbibliothek*

Die Deutsche Nationalbibliothek verzeichnet diese Publikation in der Deutschen Nationalbibliografie; detaillierte bibliografische Daten sind im Internet über <http://dnb.d-nb.de> abrufbar.



Printed in Germany

Datenkonvertierung/Satz: Werksatz Schmidt & Schulz, Gräfenhainichen
Druck und Bindung: Hubert & Co., Göttingen
Einbandgestaltung: Christopher Schneider, Berlin

*Detlef Leenen zugeeignet*

# Vorwort

Während über Max Webers Religionssoziologie ganze Bibliotheken geschrieben worden sind, gibt es zu seiner Rechtssoziologie vergleichsweise wenige Bände. Insbesondere ist sein Verhältnis zur juristischen Methodenlehre nahezu unberücksichtigt geblieben, obwohl er als promovierter und habilitierter Jurist im weitesten Sinne von ihr ausgegangen ist. Die vorliegende Abhandlung unternimmt daher einen ersten Versuch in diese Richtung. Sie steht zugleich in einem inneren Kausal- und Verweisungszusammenhang mit meinem Buch „Von der Interessenjurisprudenz zur Wertungsjurisprudenz" (2001), das sich auf die dogmatischen Einzelheiten des besagten Übergangs konzentriert, aber die rechtstheoretischen, rechtssoziologischen und rechtsphilosophischen Berührungen nur am Rande erörtert hat.

Ich widme das vorliegende Buch Herrn Professor Dr. *Detlef Leenen*, dessen Vorlesung „Methodenlehre" im Sommersemester 1991 an der Freien Universität Berlin mein Interesse an der juristischen Methodenlehre geweckt hat.

Potsdam, im Juni 2008 Jens Petersen

# Inhaltsverzeichnis


Einleitung . . . . . . . . . . . . . . . . . . . . . . . . . . . . 1

§ 1 Rechtsordnung und Wirtschaftsordnung . . . . . . . . . . . . . 11

I. Die Ordnung des Materials . . . . . . . . . . . . . . . . . . . 11
1. Webers und Nietzsches Historienvergleichung . . . . . . 12
2. Die Zurechnungsproblematik als Paradigma . . . . . . . 14
II. Juristische und soziologische Betrachtungsweise . . . . . . . . 16
1. Ideelle Geltung als Recht . . . . . . . . . . . . . . . . 16
2. „One right answer" als regulative Idee? . . . . . . . . . . 17
3. Recht und Sprache . . . . . . . . . . . . . . . . . . . 19
a) Sprachpragmatische Ansätze . . . . . . . . . . . . . 19
b) Verbindungslinie zur Sprachphilosophie . . . . . . . . 20
III. Rechtsdogmatik und Sozialökonomik . . . . . . . . . . . . 22
1. Webers Verständnis der Rechtsdogmatik . . . . . . . . 23
2. Heterogenität . . . . . . . . . . . . . . . . . . . . . . 24
a) Parallele zwischen Rechtssoziologie und Methodenlehre? . . . . . . . . . . . . . . . . . . . . . . . 24
b) Gefahr des Methodensynkretismus . . . . . . . . . . 26
3. Max Webers Methodenlehre . . . . . . . . . . . . . . . 28
a) Werturteilsstreit . . . . . . . . . . . . . . . . . . . . 29
b) Werturteil und Wertung . . . . . . . . . . . . . . . . 31
c) Relevanz des Streits für die Rechtswissenschaft . . . . 33
4. Ökonomische Analyse des Rechts . . . . . . . . . . . . 35
IV. Rechtsordnung als empirische Geltung . . . . . . . . . . . . 37
1. Bedeutung des Begriffs der Rechtsordnung . . . . . . . . 37
2. Parallelgedanken in den wissenschaftstheoretischen Aufsätzen . . . . . . . . . . . . . . . . . . . . . . . 38

§ 2 Rationalität des Rechts . . . . . . . . . . . . . . . . . . . 41

I. Rechtsfindung und Rechtsschöpfung . . . . . . . . . . . . . 42
1. Ableitung rationaler Rechtssätze . . . . . . . . . . . . 42
a) Zweckrationale Vereinbarungen . . . . . . . . . . . . 43

b) Mitwirkung gefühlsmäßiger Determinanten ..... 44
c) Rechtssoziologie und Interessenjurisprudenz ..... 45
2. Gewohnheitsrecht ..... 46
II. Entwicklung und „Herausläuterung" von Rechtssätzen ... 48
1. Reduktion auf Prinzipien ..... 49
2. Denkmanipulation (Weber) und Denkökonomie (Mach) ..... 51
III. Analytische Gewinnung von Rechtssätzen ..... 52
1. Wechselwirkung zwischen Prinzipien und Tatbestandsmerkmalen ..... 53
2. Analogie als „parataktisches Assoziieren" ..... 55
3. Anreicherung der Kasuistik ..... 57
IV. Synthetische Arbeit der juristischen Konstruktion ..... 58
1. Vergleich mit Hecks Interessenjurisprudenz ..... 58
a) Webers Affinität gegenüber der Begriffsjurisprudenz . 59
aa) „Zeitbedingtheit" der Rechtssoziologie Webers? . 60
bb) Webers methodologische Eigenständigkeit .... 61
b) Unklarheiten in der frühen Interessenjurisprudenz .. 62
c) Würdigung der Begriffsjurisprudenz ..... 62
d) Jherings Wandel ..... 63
e) Aussonderung der Rechtssoziologie ..... 65
2. Interdependenz von Analyse und Synthese ..... 66
a) Bewegliches System und Typusbegriff ..... 67
b) Rationalität trotz Wertungsspielraum ..... 68

§ 3 Systematisierung des Rechts ..... 69

I. Prinzipielle Lückenlosigkeit ..... 71
1. Webers Anspielung auf das Preußische Allgemeine Landrecht ..... 71
2. „Intern intellektualistische „Interessenkonstellation" .. 72
3. Systematisierung als Subsumierbarkeit logisch geordneter Normen ..... 74
II. Das Steuerrecht als Paradigma mangelnder Systematisierung 75
III. Äußeres Ordnungsschema und inneres System ..... 76
1. Inneres und äußeres System ..... 77
2. Maßgeblichkeit der Prinzipienebene ..... 78
IV. Folgerungen für das Verhältnis zwischen Rechtssoziologie und Interessenjurisprudenz ..... 79

1. Primat der Lebensforschung . . . . . . . . . . . . . . . . . . 79
2. Logische Sinndeutung und prinzipielle Konvergenz . . . 81
3. Unreflektierte Soziologisierung der Rechtsanwendung? . 82
V. Sinndeutende Abstraktion . . . . . . . . . . . . . . . . . . . 83
1. Höchstgrad methodisch-logischer Rationalität . . . . . . 84
a) Subsumtion mit den Mitteln der Rechtslogik . . . . . 84
b) Argumentum ad absurdum . . . . . . . . . . . . . . . . 85
c) Paradoxien . . . . . . . . . . . . . . . . . . . . . . . . 86
d) Naturrecht als Ersatz? . . . . . . . . . . . . . . . . . . 88
e) Ansprüche und Ermächtigungen . . . . . . . . . . . . 89
2. Juristischer Gutachtenaufbau als Abbildung . . . . . . . 89

§ 4 Logik und Berechenbarkeit des Rechts . . . . . . . . . . . . 91

I. Logik und Widerspruchsfreiheit . . . . . . . . . . . . . . . 92
1. Berechenbarkeit als Attribut des Rechts . . . . . . . . . 92
2. Denkbarkeit des Rechtsverhältnisses . . . . . . . . . . . 94
II. Verbindungslinien zwischen Rechtssoziologie und Rechtsphilosophie . . . . . . . . . . . . . . . . . . . . . . . . . 96
1. Logik bei Weber und Nietzsche . . . . . . . . . . . . . . 96
2. Webers Rezeption der Logik . . . . . . . . . . . . . . . . 98
a) Tertium non datur? . . . . . . . . . . . . . . . . . . . . 98
b) Unterschiedliche Überzeugungskraft von Sollenssätzen . . . . . . . . . . . . . . . . . . . . . . . . . . 99
c) Das zugrunde liegende Verständnis der Logik . . . . . 101
d) Unterschied zum Common Law . . . . . . . . . . . . 102
e) Bedeutungsdifferenz . . . . . . . . . . . . . . . . . . . 103
3. Naturrechtsdogmen und „Macht der Logik im Rechtsdenken“ . . . . . . . . . . . . . . . . . . . . . . . . . . . 103
a) Kontraintuitive Verbindungslinien . . . . . . . . . . . 104
b) Vernünftigkeit des positiven Rechts und Naturrechtsrenaissance . . . . . . . . . . . . . . . . . . . . . . . . 105
III. Verabsolutierung des „logisch richtigen“ Rechts . . . . . . . 107
1. Webers Skepsis gegenüber der Begriffsjurisprudenz . . . 107
2. Rechtsgeschäftslehre als Paradigma . . . . . . . . . . . . 108
IV. Zwischen Logisierung und Freirechtsbewegung . . . . . . . 110
1. Verdrängung des „Primats der Logik“? . . . . . . . . . . 110
2. Bedenken gegen die Freirechtsschule . . . . . . . . . . . 112
3. Richterliche Eigenwertung und ihre Grenzen . . . . . . . 114

4. Verhältnis von Rechtssoziologie und Rechtsdogmatik . . 115
a) Ehrlichs vergleichsweise radikale Rechtssoziologie . . 116
b) Luhmann und Weber . . . . . . . . . . . . . . . . . . . . 117
c) Rechtssoziologie und „soziologisierende“ Rechtswissenschaft . . . . . . . . . . . . . . . . . . . . . . . 118
V. Lebensfremdheit des logischen Rechts . . . . . . . . . . . 119
1. Paradoxe Irrationalität aus Sicht der Verkehrsinteressenten . . . . . . . . . . . . . . . . . . . . . . . . . 120
2. Rechtsbindung an Präjudizien? . . . . . . . . . . . . . 121
3. Drittschützende Wertungen . . . . . . . . . . . . . . . 122
a) Drittschutz bei Webers Ermächtigungsnormen . . . . 123
b) Beschränkungen der Interessenjurisprudenz . . . . . 124
c) Zuordnung zur Prinzipienjurisprudenz? . . . . . . . . 125
VI. Ausblick . . . . . . . . . . . . . . . . . . . . . . . . . . 127
1. Weitblick auf die Epochen der Jurisprudenz . . . . . . . 127
2. Zweckrationale Revolution rationalen Rechts . . . . . . 128
a) Missbrauchsanfälligkeit der juristischen Methode . . 129
b) Gefahr der „De-Institutionalisierung von Rationalitätskriterien“ . . . . . . . . . . . . . . . . . . . . . . . 129

§ 5 Typus und Rechtsfindung . . . . . . . . . . . . . . . . . . 133

I. Methodische Grundlegung des Idealtypus . . . . . . . . . 135
1. Ausschluss irrationaler Elemente . . . . . . . . . . . . 135
2. Herstellung vollständiger Sinnadäquanz . . . . . . . . . 136
II. Ideal als Maßstab der Dogmatik . . . . . . . . . . . . . . 137
1. Typenbildung in der Dogmatik . . . . . . . . . . . . . . 137
2. Der „ideale“ Fahrer als Paradigma . . . . . . . . . . . 138
III. Rationalisierung in Rechtssoziologie und Dogmatik . . . . . 139
1. Rechtssoziologie als ancilla iuris? . . . . . . . . . . . . 139
2. Die unterschiedlichen Erkenntnisinteressen . . . . . . . . 140
IV. Typisierung als Mittel der Rechtsanwendung und Reduktion von Komplexität . . . . . . . . . . . . . . . . . . . . . . 142
V. Typenarten . . . . . . . . . . . . . . . . . . . . . . . . . 143
1. Durchschnittstypus . . . . . . . . . . . . . . . . . . . 143
2. Häufigkeitstypus . . . . . . . . . . . . . . . . . . . . . 144
VI. Typus und Ermächtigungsnorm . . . . . . . . . . . . . . 145
1. Vertragsfreiheit und Typus . . . . . . . . . . . . . . . . 145
a) Typen von Vertragsvereinbarungen . . . . . . . . . . 146

b) Das Desiderat des „theoretischen Bezugsrahmens" . . 147
c) Rechtsrationalität und Formenreichtum . . . . . . . . 148
2. Vertragstypen und typenfremde Verträge . . . . . . . . . 148
VII. Begriff und Typus . . . . . . . . . . . . . . . . . . . . . 150
1. Bedingte Kompensierbarkeit . . . . . . . . . . . . . . . 150
2. Primäre und sekundäre Wertungen . . . . . . . . . . . . 151
VIII. Folgerungen . . . . . . . . . . . . . . . . . . . . . . . 152
1. Leistungsfähigkeit . . . . . . . . . . . . . . . . . . . . 153
2. Zusammenfassung von Beobachtungen unter dem Prinzip der Denkökonomie . . . . . . . . . . . . . . . . . . . . . 155
3. Bezug zum Wissenschaftsanspruch der Jurisprudenz . . . 156

§ 6 Rechtswissenschaft als Beruf . . . . . . . . . . . . . . . 159

Literaturverzeichnis . . . . . . . . . . . . . . . . . . . . . 167

Personenverzeichnis . . . . . . . . . . . . . . . . . . . . . 195

# Einleitung

Gegen Ende seiner Rechtssoziologie[1] sagt Max Weber über den juristischen Laien, dessen Rechtsdenken „wortgebunden“ sei: „Er pflegt vor allem ein Wortrabulist zu werden, wenn er ‚juristisch‘ zu argumentieren glaubt. Und daneben ist ihm das Schließen vom Einzelnen auf das Einzelne natürlich: die juristische Abstraktion des ‚Fachmanns‘ ist ihm fern.“[2] Solch herablassender Juristendünkel scheint nur der Feder eines habilitierten Juristen entspringen zu können.[3] In der Tat erscheint die so beschriebene laienhafte Vorgehensweise vor allem als Ausprägung eines tief eingewurzelten Misstrauens gegenüber fachjuristischer Argumentation und als trotzige Reaktion dagegen erklärlich.[4] Die nachvollziehbare Abwehrreaktion gegenüber einer als haarspalterisch empfundenen Auslegung kann leicht zu einer laienhaften Imitation eines ver-

1 Streng genommen sind es – mit den Worten *Niklas Luhmanns* (Rechtssoziologie, 3. Auflage 1987, S. 16 f.) „die als ‚Rechtssoziologie‘ herausgegebenen Bruchstücke des Weberschen Gesamtwerks“. Siehe auch *H. Baier/M. R. Lepsius/W. J. Mommsen/W. Schluchter*, Zur Edition von „Wirtschaft und Gesellschaft“. Allgemeine Hinweise der Herausgeber der Max Weber-Gesamtausgabe. Max Weber-Gesamtausgabe, Abteilung I: Schriften und Reden, Band 22-5: Max Weber, Wirtschaft und Gesellschaft. Die Wirtschaft und die gesellschaftlichen Ordnungen und Mächte. Nachlass. Teilband 5: Die Stadt (Hg. W. Nippel), 1999, S. VII–XVII; *W. Schluchter*, Max Webers hinterlassenes Hauptwerk: Die Wirtschaft und die gesellschaftlichen Ordnungen und Mächte. Entstehung und gedanklicher Aufbau, 1986; *ders.*, „Wirtschaft und Gesellschaft“ – Das Ende eines Mythos, in: Max Weber heute. Erträge und Probleme der Forschung (Hg. J. Weiß), 1989, S. 55.

2 *Max Weber*, Wirtschaft und Gesellschaft, 1. Auflage 1922, im Folgenden zitiert nach der von J. Winckelmann besorgten 5. revidierten Auflage, 1980, Zweiter Halbband, Kapitel VII, § 8, S. 510.

3 Er wurde 1892 in Berlin mit einer von August Meitzen betreuten Arbeit über „Die römische Agrargeschichte in ihrer Bedeutung für das Staats- und Privatrecht“ habilitiert. Näher *G. Dilcher*, JZ 2007, 105.

4 Zu entsprechenden Vorbehalten *B. Rüthers*, Institutionelles Rechtsdenken im Wandel der Verfassungsepochen, 1970, S. 9 ff.

meintlich juristischen Vorgehens führen.[5] Hinzu kommt ein nur scheinbar zugänglicher Fachjargon, welcher dem Alltagssprachgebrauch in Ermangelung einer Metasprache der Rechtswissenschaft ähnelt,[6] ohne mit ihm aber zwangsläufig gleichbedeutend zu sein.[7] So entbehrt Webers Beobachtung, zumal aus Sicht des Juristen, nicht einer gewissen alltagstheoretischen Plausibilität.

Das wirft freilich die Frage auf, was es eigentlich ist, das eine Begründung zu einer spezifisch juristischen erhebt und wodurch sie sich von dem laienhaften Missverständnis unterscheidet. Wäre es nur eine wortreiche Verbrämung, so dürfte sie auf keinerlei Anerkennung hoffen, und so ist nicht zuletzt der drohende Akzeptanzverlust das Skandalon,[8] das dem Dictum Webers zugrunde liegt. Die Jurisprudenz bedarf also einer besonderen und wissenschaftlichen Ansprüchen standhaltenden juristischen Methode,[9] deren universelle Geltung diesen Akzeptanzverlust überwinden kann, indem ein lege artis gewonnenes Ergebnis nicht nur dem Wortlaut, sondern auch dem Sinn der betreffenden Norm entspricht,[10] und darüber hinaus auch den Schluss vom Allgemeinen auf das Einzelne erlaubt.[11] Das entspricht im Übrigen einer Be-

[5] Vgl. auch *B. Rüthers*, Das Ungerechte an der Gerechtigkeit, 2. Auflage 1993, S. 66 ff.

[6] *U. Neumann*, Juristische Fachsprache und Umgangssprache, in: Sprachkultur als Rechtskultur (Hg. G. Grewendorf), 1992, S. 110.

[7] Vgl. *M. Weber*, Wirtschaft und Gesellschaft, S. 6. Zum Verhältnis von Sprache und Metasprache und dem Problem der Äquivokation *K. Röhl*, Allgemeine Rechtslehre, 2. Auflage 2001, § 8, S. 61; § 10, S. 75 ff.; *E. Oksaar*, Alltagssprache, Fachsprache, Rechtssprache, Zeitschrift für Gesetzgebung 3 (1989) 210.

[8] Hierzu auch *N. Luhmann*, Ausdifferenzierung des Rechts, 1981, S. 374 ff., 445 ff.; mit anderer Zielrichtung *G. Roellecke*, Wende der deutschen Rechtsphilosophie?, ARSP 1991, Beiheft 44, S. 287 ff.

[9] Nur um diese geht es im Folgenden und nicht um die methodischen Grundlagen, die Weber selbst seinem Werk (Wirtschaft und Gesellschaft, Kapitel I, § 1 I) voranstellt.

[10] Vgl. auch *K. Larenz*, Das Problem der Rechtsgeltung, 1929.

[11] Der umgekehrte Schluss wäre nach *K. Popper*, Logik der Forschung, 10. Auflage 1994, S. 4 f., nur auf der Grundlage eines in die Metaphysik bzw. in einen infiniten Regress führenden Induktionsprinzips möglich. Der Ge-

merkung Max Webers in seinem bahnbrechenden Vortrag über *Wissenschaft als Beruf*, die er Hermann von Helmholtz zugesprochen hat, wonach „sich der Dilettant vom Fachmann nur dadurch unterscheidet, dass ihm die feste Sicherheit der Arbeitsmethode fehlt."[12] Nicht von ungefähr findet sich dort sein berühmtes Wort von der „Entzauberung der Welt", das Niklas Luhmann zu Webers Rechtssoziologie in Beziehung setzt: „Die ‚Entzauberung der Welt', die Herstellung eines rationalen Weltverhältnisses und namentlich die Einrichtung einer ‚kapitalistischen' Wirtschaft haben ihre Voraussetzungen und Konsequenzen im Recht."[13] Vor diesem Hintergrund leuchtet ein, dass auch Webers Rechtssoziologie eine imaginäre Verbindungslinie zur juristischen Methodenlehre immanent ist,[14] die es im Folgenden nachzuverfolgen gilt.[15]

Die Problematik gewinnt zusätzliches Interesse dadurch, dass Philipp Heck, einer der großen Methodenlehrer des 20. Jahrhunderts,[16] Weber höchstwahrscheinlich gekannt hat, zumal beide

danke findet sich freilich schon bei *D. Hume*, An Enquiry Concerning Human Understanding, 1748 (deutsch: Eine Untersuchung über den menschlichen Verstand; übersetzt von R. Richter, Hg. J. Kulenkampff, 12. Auflage 1993).

12 *M. Weber*, Wissenschaft als Beruf, Geistige Arbeit als Beruf. Vier Vorträge vor dem Freistudentischen Bund, 1919, in: Gesammelte Aufsätze zur Wissenschaftslehre, 7. Auflage 1988, S. 582, 589 f. Das entspricht auch dem Verständnis von Methode als der Frage des allgemeingültigen Wissens aus Erfahrung (*W. Dilthey*, Die Entstehung der Hermeneutik, 1910, S. 334).

13 *N. Luhmann*, Rechtssoziologie, 3. Auflage 1987, S. 17.

14 Das spiegelt auch die Literaturauswahl Webers (ebenda, S. 15) wider, wo verwiesen wird auf *R. v. Jhering*, Der Zweck im Recht, 1877; *P. E. W. Oertmann*, Rechtsordnung und Verkehrssitte, 1914; *E. Weigelin*, Sitte, Recht und Moral, 1919; sowie implizit *R. Stammler*, Wirtschaft und Recht nach der materialistischen Geschichtsauffassung, 2. Auflage 1906 (dagegen *M. Weber*, Analyse des Begriffs der „Regel", Archiv für Sozialgeschichte XXIV (1907) 94; kritisch hierzu *A. v. Schelting*, Max Webers Wissenschaftslehre, 1934, S. 400 ff.).

15 Grundlegend aus dem älteren Schrifttum *H. Sinzheimer*, Die soziologische Methode in der Privatrechtswissenschaft, 1909; *ders.*, Die Aufgabe der Rechtssoziologie, 1935.

16 Näher *M. Wolf*, Philipp Heck als Zivilrechtsdogmatiker – Studien zur dogmatischen Umsetzung seiner Methodenlehre, 1996.

nahezu zeitgleich in engem Kontakt zu dem Handelsrechtler[17] Levin Goldschmidt standen,[18] bei dem Weber promoviert hat[19] und dessen Lehrverpflichtungen im Handels- und Wertpapierrecht er nach seiner eigenen Habilitation übernahm, als Goldschmidt schwer erkrankte.[20] Mag dieser Umstand für sich betrachtet, ein reines Kuriosum sein, gewinnt er dadurch an Brisanz, dass Weber und Heck nicht nur beide am ersten deutschen Soziologentag in Frankfurt im Jahre 1910 zusammengetroffen sind, sondern vor allem deswegen, weil sie sich nach dem Abschlussreferat von Kantorowicz[21] an der durchaus kontroversen Diskussion um die juristische Methodenlehre beteiligten,[22] im Rahmen derer Weber die Wertfreiheit der Wissenschaft betonte.[23] Da die von Heck begrün-

[17] *K. Schmidt*, Levin Goldschmidt (1829–1897). Der Begründer der modernen Handelsrechtswissenschaft, in: Deutsche Juristen jüdischer Herkunft (Hg. H. Heinrichs u. a.), 1993, S. 215. Näher *G. Dilcher*, JZ 2007, 105, 106.

[18] Monographisch *L. Weyhe*, Levin Goldschmidt. Ein Gelehrtenleben in Deutschland – Grundfragen des Handelsrechts und der Zivilrechtswissenschaft in der zweiten Hälfte des 19. Jahrhunderts, 1996. Seinen Doktorvater bezieht Weber bis in die Behandlung konkreter dogmatischer Fragen mit rechtsgeschichtlichem Hintergrund in seine Rechtssoziologie ein; vgl. *M. Weber*, Wirtschaft und Gesellschaft, S. 408; ähnlich ebenda, S. 466.

[19] Das Thema seiner ebenfalls juristischen Dissertation lautete „Die Entwicklung des Solidarhaftprinzips und des Sondervermögens der offenen Handelsgesellschaft aus den Haushalts- und Gewerbegemeinschaften in den italienischen Städten" (1889); vgl. *M. Weber*, Zur Geschichte der Handelsgesellschaften im Mittelalter, Schriften 1889–1894 (Hg. G. Dilcher/S. Lepsius), Max Weber-Gesamtausgabe I 1, 2008. Siehe auch *G. Dilcher*, JZ 2007, 105, 107 f.

[20] *H. N. Fügen*, Max Weber, 6. Auflage 2000, S. 46, 57, 134.

[21] *H. Kantorowicz*, Rechtswissenschaft und Soziologie. Verhandlungen des Ersten Deutschen Soziologentages 1910, Tübingen 1911, S. 275, mit der provokanten These, dass Rechtssoziologie nur von Juristen im Nebenamt fruchtbar betrieben werden könne; lakonisch *N. Luhmann*, Rechtssoziologie, 3. Auflage 1987, S. 1: „Die Fruchtbarkeit ist ausgeblieben."

[22] Vgl. die Niederschrift über die Diskussionsbeiträge zum Soziologentag, in: Verhandlungen des Ersten Deutschen Soziologentages, Tübingen 1910, S. 316–321 (Heck); S. 323–330 (Weber).

[23] *H. Schoppmeyer*, Juristische Methode als Lebensaufgabe, 2001, S. 160. Allgemein zu diesem Postulat *J. Cohn*, Die Erkenntnis der Werte und das Vorrecht der Bejahung. Betrachtungen angeknüpft an Max Webers Lehre von der Wertfreiheit der Wissenschaft, Logos X (1921) 195.

dete Interessenjurisprudenz sich besonders der Lebensforschung und Lebenswertung verpflichtet hat,[24] interessierte dieser sich auch für Webers Rechtssoziologie.[25] Die Interessenjurisprudenz stellt sonach eine wichtige Verbindungslinie zwischen Webers Rechtssoziologie und der Methodenlehre seiner Zeit dar.[26] Allerdings muss in diesem Zusammenhang immer auch berücksichtigt werden, dass die Lebensnähe auch der dogmatischen Jurisprudenz – und nicht nur die der Rechtssoziologie – an sich eine bare Selbstverständlichkeit ist, weil ihr Gegenteil, die Lebensfremdheit, überhaupt nicht zu rechtfertigen wäre,[27] so dass zumindest die Lebenswertung für sich betrachtet weder ein besonderes Verdienst noch ein Alleinstellungsmerkmal bedeuten kann.[28] Nach wie vor gilt Savignys klassisches Wort, wonach das Recht „das Leben der Menschen selbst ist, von einer besonderen Seite angesehen."[29]

Aber vielleicht konnte Weber auch nicht zuletzt deshalb so prägend auf die Methode seiner Wissenschaft Einfluss nehmen, weil er mit der juristischen Methodenlehre vertraut war,[30] deren Beherrschung sich in seiner Rechtssoziologie widerspiegelt.[31] Natür-

24 *Ph. Heck*, Begriffsbildung und Interessenjurisprudenz, 1932, S. 17: „Primat der Lebensforschung und Lebenswertung".

25 *H. Schoppmeyer*, Juristische Methode als Lebensaufgabe, 2001, S. 162.

26 *Ph. Heck* (AcP 142, 1936, 297, 299) hielt die Interessenjurisprudenz freilich für älter als die Rechtssoziologie.

27 *H. Eidenmüller*, Rechtswissenschaft als Realwissenschaft, JZ 1999, 55.

28 Süffisant *N. Luhmann*, Rechtssystem und Rechtsdogmatik, 1974, S. 15 (unter Verweis auf *C. Starck*, JZ 1972, 131): „Dass die Rechtsdogmatik nicht sich selber, sondern dem Leben (und das soll heißen: der Rechtsanwendung) zu dienen habe, wird von Juristen wohl übereinstimmend betont. Diese ‚Erkenntnis' sollte jedoch nicht am Ende, sondern am Anfang einer Untersuchung stehen."

29 *F. C. v. Savigny*, Vom Beruf unserer Zeit für Gesetzgebung und Wissenschaft, 1814, S. 30.

30 *St. P. Turner/R. A. Factor*, The Lawyer as Social Thinker, 1994. Siehe zum Ganzen auch *M. Rehbinder*, Weber und die Rechtswissenschaft, 1986; *ders.*, Max Weber und die Rechtswissenschaft, in: Max Weber als Rechtssoziologie (Hg. ders./K.-P. Tieck) 1987, S. 127; St. P. Turner/R. A. Factor, The Lawyer as Social Thinker, 1994.

31 Allgemein dazu *F. Loos*, Zur Wert- und Rechtslehre Max Webers, 1970;

lich darf daraus kein unbedingter Primat der juristischen Methodenlehre gegenüber anderen Wissenschaften hergeleitet werden. Vielmehr geht es umgekehrt um die Frage, welchen Nutzen die juristische Methodenlehre gegebenenfalls aus der Rechtssoziologie Webers ziehen kann, der sie verinnerlicht und reflektiert hat. Dabei beschränkt sich die Darstellung auf das Zivilrecht, weil Weber selbst gerade diesen Bereich für wirtschaftlich ausschlaggebend gehalten hat.[32]

Die Abhandlung konzentriert sich bewusst auf die klassische juristische Methodenlehre,[33] weil vor allem sie auch Weber noch vor Augen gestanden haben kann und daher auch insofern gemeinsame Verbindungslinien aufgezeigt werden können.[34] Behandelt werden jedoch auch angloamerikanische Strömungen, zumal Weber selbst das angelsächsische Präjudizienrecht immer wieder abgrenzend in die Betrachtung einbezogen hat, so dass die unterschiedlichen methodischen Wurzeln zu berücksichtigen sind. Auch im Hinblick auf die Interessenjurisprudenz sind parallele Entwicklungen aus den Vereinigten Staaten zweckmäßigerweise zu betrachten. Außen vor bleiben muss jedoch beispielsweise eine Untersuchung zur Rechtfertigung der Normsetzung durch bürokratisches Handeln der Verwaltung,[35] deren Bezug zu Max Weber als Entdecker der Gestalt bürokratischer Herrschaft mit Händen zu greifen ist,[36] aber zugleich das Feld seiner Rechtssoziologie im

*ders.*, Max Webers Wissenschaftslehre und die Rechtswissenschaft, in: Max Weber als Rechtssoziologe (Hg. M. Rehbinder/K.-P. Tieck), 1987, S. 169 (= JuS 1982, 87).

32 *M. Weber*, Wirtschaft und Gesellschaft, S. 394.

33 *K. Larenz*, Methodenlehre der Rechtswissenschaft, 6. Auflage 1991; *W. Fikentscher*, Methoden des Rechts in vergleichender Betrachtung, Band IV, 1977; *F. Bydlinski*, Juristische Methodenlehre und Rechtsbegriff, 2. Auflage 1991; *P. Raisch*, Juristische Methoden, 2. Auflage 1995.

34 Kritisch gegenüber der etablierten Methodenlehre mit gewichtigen Einwänden *A. Somek*, Gesetzesbindung als Problem der Demokratie, Journal für Rechtspolitik 6 (1998) 41.

35 *M. Seidenfeld*, A Civic Republican Justification for the Bureaucratic State, Harvard Law Review 105 (1992) 1511, 1542 ff.

36 *M. Weber*, Wirtschaft und Gesellschaft, S. 125 ff.; dazu *J. Winckelmann*, Legitimität und Legalität in Max Webers Herrschaftssoziologie. Mit

engeren Sinne verlassen würde, weil es vornehmlich die an anderer Stelle von ihm behandelten Typen der Herrschaft betrifft.[37] So unerlässlich diese aber – nicht zuletzt im Hinblick auf den auch für diese Untersuchung wichtigen Typusbegriff[38] – für das Verständnis der Soziologie Webers sind, würde ihre vertiefende Behandlung den hier gesetzten Rahmen sprengen, weil es auf Kosten der Behandlung paralleler Probleme der juristischen Methodenlehre gehen müsste.

Den soziologischen Laien überrascht, wie vergleichsweise kursorisch Weber in manchen rechtssoziologischen Gesamtdarstellungen abgehandelt wird, die selten über die paraphrasierende Wiederholung von Schlagworten („Charisma", „bürokratische Herrschaft") hinausgehen,[39] aber die eigentliche Rechtssoziologie Webers allenfalls kursorisch abhandeln. Aber auch innerhalb der Soziologie steht die eingehende wissenschaftliche Beschäftigung mit Webers Rechtssoziologie wohl überhaupt erst am Anfang. Mit Recht fordert Rainer Lepsius: „Notwendig ist daher auch eine Belebung der Rechtssoziologie, wie sie erst von Weber entfaltet wurde, nicht als einer Soziologie der Rechtsberufe und der Resozialisierung von Strafgefangenen – so wichtig auch dies ist –, sondern als einer Soziologie von Verfahrensordnungen und ihren Fol-

einem Anhang: Max Weber, Die drei Typen der legitimen Herrschaft, 1952; *H. Speer*, Herrschaft und Legitimität. Zeitgebundene Aspekte in Max Webers Herrschaftssoziologie, 1978; *W. Lübbe*, Legitimität kraft Legalität. Sinnverstehen und Institutionenanalyse bei Max Weber und seinen Kritikern, 1991. *M. R. Lepsius*, Interessen, Ideen und Institutionen, 1990, S. 7: „Max Webers Soziologie ist weitgehend Institutionenanlyse."

37 *M. Weber*, Wirtschaft und Gesellschaft, Erster Halbband, Kapitel III, S. 122 ff.

38 *D. Leenen*, Typus und Rechtsfindung, 1971.

39 Aus dem schier unüberschaubaren Schrifttum zum Charisma und der bürokratischen Herrschaft nur einige besonders wichtige Monographien: *W. Schluchter*, Aspekte bürokratischer Herrschaft, 1972; *St. Breuer*, Bürokratie und Charisma. Zur politischen Soziologie Max Webers, 1994. Unter den unzähligen Aufsätzen: *S. H. Udy*, „Bureaucracy" and „Rationality" in Weber's Organization Theory, American Journal of Sociology 24 (1959) 791; *H. D. Seibel*, Bürokratie und Charisma. Systemrationalität und Systemwandel, Jahrbuch für Sozialwissenschaft 27 (1976) 342.

gen."[40] An diesem Befund hat sich auch in den vergangenen dreißig Jahren nicht genügend geändert. In diesem Sinne versteht sich die vorliegende Abhandlung als ein bescheidener Versuch, dort anzusetzen, wo vielleicht auch Webers Methodologie ihren Ausgangspunkt nahm, ohne freilich den Anspruch zu erheben, dass man sie nur von daher erklären könne. Wohl nicht von ungefähr sieht der amerikanische Soziologe Talcott Parsons den „Kern der substantiellen Soziologie Webers weder in der Darstellung der ökonomischen und politischen Probleme noch in der Religionssoziologie (…), sondern in der Rechtssoziologie."[41] Etwas Vergleichbares findet man später womöglich nur noch bei dem gleichfalls von der Rechtswissenschaft herkommenden Niklas Luhmann,[42] dessen Beobachtungen zur Rechtsdogmatik hier nicht nur deshalb ausführlich mit berücksichtigt werden, weil er ein profunder Kenner der juristischen Methodenlehre war,[43] sondern auch deswegen,

[40] *M. R. Lepsius*, Interessen, Ideen und Institutionen, 1977, S. 30.

[41] *T. Parsons*, Wertgebundenheit und Objektivität in den Sozialwissenschaften. Eine Interpretation der Beiträge Max Webers, in: Max Weber und die Soziologie heute. Verhandlungen des 15. deutschen Soziologentages (Hg. O. Stammler), 1965, S. 39, 54 f. Weitere zentrale Werke, in denen er sich neben Emile Durkheim maßgeblich auf Weber beruft, um eine allgemeine Theorie zu entwickelt, „die sich als generalisierende Rechtssoziologie bezeichnen lässt" (*N. Luhmann*, Rechtssoziologie, S. 18), sind: *T. Parsons*, Unity and Diversity in the Modern Intellectual Disciplines. The Role of the Social Science, in: *ders.*, Sociological Theory and Modern Society, 1967, S. 166 ff.; vor allem *ders.*, The Structure of Social Action, 1937; *ders.*, The Place of Ultimate Values in Social Theory, The International Journal of Ethics 45 (1935) 282; *ders.*, Evolutionary Universals in Society, American Sociological Review 29 (1964) 339; *ders.*, Societies. Evolutionary and Comparatives Perspectives, 1966; *ders.*, The System of Modern Societies, 1971. Siehe zu beiden auch *B. S. Turner*, Lebensphilosophie und Handlungstheorie. Die Beziehungen zwischen Talcott Parsons und Max Weber innerhalb der Entwicklung der Soziologie, in: Max Webers Wissenschaftslehre. Interpretation und Kritik (Hg. G. Wagner/H. Zipprian) 1994, S. 310.

[42] In diese Richtung aus soziologischer Sicht *K. Gabriel*, Analysen der Organisationsgesellschaft. Ein kritischer Vergleich der Gesellschaftstheorien Max Webers, Niklas Luhmanns und der phänomenologischen Soziologie, 1979.

[43] *N. Luhmann*, Das Recht der Gesellschaft, 1985, S. 380 ff.

weil er trotz ähnlicher Provenienz einer genuin soziologischen Betrachtung das Wort redete,[44] die sich von der Rechtsdogmatik weitgehend abgelöst hat und ihr ein systemtheoretisches Fundament versprach, das zugleich die Wissenschaftlichkeit der Jurisprudenz gewährleisten könne.[45] Indes kann die Systemtheorie selbst hier unberücksichtigt bleiben, weil von ihr der Wissenschaftsanspruch der Jurisprudenz nicht abhängig ist und Weber kein Systemtheoretiker war.[46] Weber wie auch später Luhmann konnten der Jurisprudenz über die Rechtssoziologie eine Außensicht vermitteln, die von einer inneren Kenntnis zeugte und von daher Einsichten hervorbrachte, die auch für die Rechtsdogmatik bedeutsam sind.

[44] Gegenüberstellung bei *K. Grimm*, Niklas Luhmanns „soziologische Aufklärung" oder Das Elend der aprioristischen Soziologie. Ein Beitrag zur Pathologie der Systemtheorie im Licht der Wissenschaftslehre Max Webers, 1974.

[45] *N. Luhmann*, Rechtssystematik und Rechtsdogmatik, 1974, S. 13, 76; siehe auch *dens.*, Ausdifferenzierung des Rechtssystems, Rechtstheorie 7 (1976) 121. *G. Dilcher*, JZ 2008, 105, 109, hat die interessante These aufgestellt, dass sich schon von Webers Dissertation über seine Rechtssoziologie eine Linie bis zur Systemtheorie Luhmanns ziehen lässt.

[46] *M. R. Lepsius*, Max Weber (1864–1920) Begründer der modernen Sozialwissenschaften, in: München leuchtet für die Wissenschaft (Hg. U. Leutheusser/H. Nötz), 2007), S. 64, 69: „Weber war kein Systemtheoretiker und sah in der Nutzenabwägung nicht die elementaren Antriebe der Sebstdomestizierung des Menschen." Vgl. auch *dens.*, Max Weber in München. Rede anlässlich der Enthüllung einer Gedenktafel, Zeitschrift für Soziologie 6 (1977) 103.

## § 1 Rechtsordnung und Wirtschaftsordnung

Max Webers Rechtssoziologie, in der hier zitierten Ausgabe[47] ein hundertfünfundzwanzig großformatige, eng bedruckte Seiten langes Kapitel,[48] ist weniger aufgrund des Umfangs als vielmehr wegen seiner außergewöhnlichen Dichte, des überaus präzisen Stils,[49] der sehr komprimierten Darstellung und der nicht selten verschachtelten, alle Voraussetzungen und Ausnahmen klassifizierenden Ausführung,[50] ein schwer zu durchdringender Text.

### I. Die Ordnung des Materials

Vor allem der Detailreichtum historischer und vergleichender Erörterungen, der von einem schier enzyklopädischen Wissen zeugt,[51] wirkt nicht nur einschüchternd, sondern hat auch die wissenschaftliche Durcharbeitung nicht selten erlahmen lassen. Hans-Georg Gadamer spricht nicht von ungefähr von der „dämonischen Figur Max Webers, des letzten Polyhistors auf dem Gebiet der Kulturwissenschaften, den die Welt gesehen hat".[52]

47 Ebenso trotz aller berechtigten Bedenken bezüglich der Werkgeschichte *H.-P. Müller*, Max Weber, 2007, S. 228: „Angesichts dieser ‚normativen Kraft des Faktischen' folgen wir einstweilen der Fassung, in der dieses Werk weltweit bekannt geworden ist."

48 Es ist das VII. Kapitel des 2. Teils des postum veröffentlichten Bandes „Wirtschaft und Gesellschaft".

49 Anderer Ansicht *M. Rehbinder*, Max Weber und die Rechtswissenschaft, in: ders./K.-P. Tieck), 1987, S. 127: „Der Stil ist miserabel, und die Aussage ist dunkel."

50 Dementsprechend *H. Plessner*, in: Max Weber zum Gedächtnis (Hg. R. König/J. Winckelmann) 1963, S. 34, über Webers Münchener Vorlesung im Sommersemester 1919: „Pure Definitionen und Erläuterungen").

51 Näher *G. Abramowski*, Das Geschichtsbild Max Webers. Universalgeschichte am Leitfaden des okzidentalen Rationalisierungsprozesses, 1966.

52 *H.-G. Gadamer*, Philosophische Lehrjahre, 1977, S. 201. Siehe auch *A. Zingerle*, Max Webers Historische Soziologie. Aspekte und Materialien zur Wirkungsgeschichte, 1981.

Niklas Luhmann erblickte wohl nicht zuletzt in dem historischen Materialreichtum einen Schwachpunkt der Weberschen Rechtssoziologie: „Auch die Weberschen Analysen, die in ihrem konkreten Material reicher sind, als hier wiedergegeben werden kann, akzentuieren nach Maßgabe ihres leitenden Interesses einseitig und sind überdies in ihrem theoretischen Fundament unzureichend durchdacht.“[53]

## 1. Webers und Nietzsches Historienvergleichung

Einiges spricht dafür, dass Weber hier zum Teil dasjenige unternahm,[54] was Nietzsche der Rechtsphilosophie überantwortete,[55] nämlich die Historien- und Völkervergleichung, die für Nietzsche ein dringendes Desiderat der Rechtsphilosophie war,[56] das freilich die Juristen seiner Zeit schmählich vernachlässigt hätten.[57] Dieser Gedanke, der eine eigene Monographie füllen würde,[58] kann hier nur ganz am Rande verfolgt werden. Er steht im Zusammenhang mit der noch weiter gespannten Problematik des Einflusses, den Nietzsche auf Weber ausübte,[59] und von dem im Abschnitt über

53 *N. Luhmann*, Rechtssoziologie, 3. Auflage 1987, S. 17 f.

54 Siehe auch *H. Treiber*, Zur Genealogie einer „Science positive de la morale en Allemagne“. Die Geburt einer r(é)ealistischen Moralwissenschaft“ aus der Idee einer monistischen Naturkonzeption, Nietzsche-Studien 22 (1993) 165; *T. B. Strong*, „What have we to do with the morals?“ Nietzsche and Weber on history and ethics, History of the Human Sciences 5 (1992) 9. *O. G. Oexle*, Von Nietzsche zu Max Weber, in: *ders.*, Geschichtswissenschaft im Zeichen des Historismus, 1996.

55 Zu Max Weber als Rechtsphilosoph *K. Engisch*, Max Weber als Rechtsphilosoph und Rechtssoziologe, in: ders./B. Pfister/J. Winckelmann (Hg.), Max Weber. Gedächtnisschrift der Ludwigs-Maximilians-Universität München zur 100. Wiederkehr seines Geburtstags 1964, 1966, S. 67 ff.

56 Kursorisch *S. Kalberg*, Einführung in die historisch-vergleichende Soziologie Max Webers, 2001.

57 *F. Nietzsche*, Der Wille zur Macht, 747.

58 *J. Petersen*, Nietzsches Genialität der Gerechtigkeit, 2008, S. 1 ff.

59 Vgl. auch *H. Baier*, Die Gesellschaft – ein langer Schatten des toten Gottes. Friedrich Nietzsche und die Entstehung der Soziologie aus dem Geist der decadence, Nietzsche-Studien 10/11 (1981/82) 1.

die Logik noch ausführlicher die Rede sein wird. Eduard Baumgarten zitiert Weber mit dem folgenden aufschlussreichen Bekenntnis,[60] das er gegenüber seinen Studenten abgelegt haben soll, nachdem sich Oswald Spengler in seiner Gegenwart geringschätzig über Marx und Nietzsche geäußert hatte: „Die Redlichkeit eines heutigen Gelehrten, und vor allem eines heutigen Philosophen, kann man daran messen, wie er sich zu Nietzsche und Marx stellt. Wer nicht zugibt, dass er gewichtigste Teile seiner eigenen Arbeit nicht leisten könnte, ohne die Arbeit, die diese beiden getan haben, beschwindelt sich selbst und andere. Die Welt, in der wir selber geistig existieren, ist weitgehend eine von Marx und Nietzsche geprägte Welt."[61] Weber meint ersichtlich die „intellektuelle Rechtschaffenheit", die Nietzsche immer wieder anmahnt.[62] Gerade im Verhältnis zwischen formellem Juristenrecht und materiellem Volksrecht bestehen Parallelen,[63] die darauf hindeuten, dass Nietzsche und Weber von einer und derselben Sache sprechen,[64] wobei freilich Weber, dem zeitlichen Verhältnis entsprechend, in der Klassifizierung des Rechts weiter fortgeschritten ist.[65]

Es werden im Folgenden diejenigen Passagen, welche die Historien- und Völkervergleichung betreffen, weitgehend ausgeblendet, soweit sie nicht zur Exemplifizierung der die Methodenlehre berührenden Stellen vonnöten sind. Das ist freilich nicht zuletzt dort der Fall, wo der Gegenbegriff und das Gegenteil der von Weber begründeten Rationalität des Rechts waltet, nämlich bei der von

60 *E. Baumgarten*, Max Weber. Werk und Person, 1964, S. 554 f.

61 Vgl. dazu auch *H.-P. Müller*, Max Weber, 2007, S. 22 f.

62 *F. Nietzsche*, Der Wille zur Macht, 455, 460.

63 *M. Weber*, Wirtschaft und Gesellschaft, S. 408, 455, einerseits und *F. Nietzsche*, Menschliches, Allzumenschliches, I, 459 andererseits.

64 Zu den Spuren Nietzsches im Werk Webers *W. Hennis*, Nietzsche-Studien 16 (1987) 382; *W. Shapiro*, The Nietzschean Roots of Max Weber's Social Science, 1978; *D. Owen*, Maturity and Modernity. Nietzsche, Weber, Foucault and the Ambivalence of Reason, 1994; *ders.*, Autonomy and „inner distance": a trace of Nietzsche in Weber, History of the Human Sciences 4 (1991) 79.

65 Näher *J. Petersen*, Nietzsches Genialität der Gerechtigkeit, 2008, S. 92 f.

ihm so genannten „irrationalen Rechtsfindung".[66] Das veranschaulicht zugleich, dass auch unter diesem Gesichtspunkt die herkömmliche Unterscheidung zwischen Rechtsphilosophie, Rechtssoziologie und Rechtsdogmatik je nach der eingenommenen Perspektive[67] weniger strikt ausfallen kann und dass es dementsprechend Schnittstellen und Verbindungslinien gibt,[68] deren Verfolgung neue Horizonte öffnen kann, ohne einen wissenschaftstheoretischen Rückschritt bedeuten zu müssen.[69]

## 2. Die Zurechnungsproblematik als Paradigma

Weber hat beispielsweise im Rahmen der Erörterung objektiver Möglichkeit und adäquater Verursachung in der historischen Kausalbetrachtung[70] die diesbezüglichen rechtsdogmatischen Erkenntnisse eingehend gewürdigt und insbesondere die strafrechtliche Zurechnungslehre in den Vordergrund gestellt. Dort nimmt er

66 *M. Weber*, Wirtschaft und Gesellschaft, S. 394; siehe in diesem Zusammenhang *A. Sica*, Weber, Irrationality, and Social Order, 1988.

67 Zu diesem Moment im Recht *B. Rüthers*, Wissenschaft und Weltanschauung am Beispiel der Jurisprudenz, 1995.

68 Siehe nur *A. Kaufmann*, Rechtsphilosophie zum Mitdenken, Einführung in die juristische Methodenlehre, Jura 1992, 346.

69 Ähnlich wie hier von einem anderen Ausgangspunkt her *H. Eidenmüller*, JZ 1999, 53, 57: „Rechtswissenschaft als Realwissenschaft und die traditionelle Methodenlehre sind vielfältig miteinander verflochten und aufeinander angewiesen."

70 *M. Weber*, Objektive Möglichkeit und adäquate Verursachung in der historischen Kausalbetrachtung, Archiv für Sozialwissenschaften und Sozialpolitik 22 (1906) 143 ff. Siehe dazu *P. J. Bouman*, Kausalität und Funktionszusammenhang in der Soziologie Max Webers, Zeitschrift für die gesamte Staatswissenschaft 1949, S. 463; *K.-H. Nusser*, Kausale Prozesse und sinnerfassende Vernunft. Max Webers philosophische Fundierung der Soziologie und der Kulturwissenschaften, 1986; *I.-J. Oh*, Das Kausalproblem bei Max Weber und in der neueren Wissenschaftstheorie, 1998; *K. Knauthe*, Kausales Rechtsdenken und Rechtssoziologie, 1968, *W. Krawietz*, Juristische Entscheidung und wissenschaftliche Erkenntnis. Eine Untersuchung zum Verhältnis von dogmatischer Kausalwissenschaft und rechtswissenschaftlicher Grundlagenforschung, 1978.

auch auf die Methodenlehre der Sozialwissenschaften Bezug:[71] „In der Methodologie der Sozialwissenschaften ist bisher die Kriessche Gedankenreihe[72] bisher nur in der Statistik übernommen worden. Dass gerade die Juristen, in erster Linie die Kriminalisten, das Problem behandelten, ist naturgemäß, da die Frage nach der strafrechtlichen Schuld, insofern sie das Problem enthält: unter welchen Umständen man behaupten könne, dass jemand durch sein Handeln einen bestimmten äußeren Erfolg ‚verursacht' habe, reine Kausalitätsfrage ist, – und zwar offenbar von der gleichen logischen Struktur wie die historische Kausalitätsfrage ist."[73]

Es verdient Hervorhebung, dass Weber die Gleichartigkeit der logischen Struktur in den Vordergrund stellt, die auch für seine Rechtssoziologie einen erheblichen Stellenwert besitzt, wie weiter unten noch ausführlich behandelt wird.[74] Auch wenn es sich bei dem soeben zitierten Aufsatz um ein anderes Werk als seine Rechtssoziologie handelt, zeigt es, dass Weber naheliegenden Verbindungslinien zur Rechtsdogmatik nicht aus dem Wege geht und diese daher auch hier besonders betrachtet werden können.[75]

Weber erkannte das Zurechnungsproblem als universelles und nicht nur den Juristen vorbehaltenes: „Und ebenso wie bei der Frage nach der ursächlichen Bedingtheit eines konkreten, even-

71 *M. Weber*, Archiv für Sozialwissenschaften und Sozialpolitik 22 (1906) 143 ff., unter Berufung auf *G. Radbruch*, Die Lehre von der adäquaten Verursachung, N. F. Band 1, Heft 3, 1902.

72 Gemeint ist *J. v. Kries*, Über den Begriff der objektiven Möglichkeit und einige Anwendungen desselben, Vierteljahresschrift für wissenschaftliche Philosophie 12, 1888, 179.

73 Zur Zurechnung im Strafrecht *C. Jäger*, Zurechnung und Rechtfertigung als Kategorialprinzipien des Strafrechts, 2006; *ders.*, Der Rücktritt vom Versuch als zurechenbare Gefährdungsumkehr, 1996. Siehe dazu aus dem neueren Schrifttum *C. Rothenfußer*, Kausalität und Nachteil, 2003.

74 Unter § 4.

75 *M. Rehbinder*, Recht und Rechtswissenschaft im Werk von Max Weber, in: Max Weber heute (Hg. J. Weiß), 1989, S. 497; siehe auch *M. Rheinstein*, Preface and Introduction to Max Weber on Law in Economy and Society, in: *ders.*, Gesammelte Schriften, Band 1. Rechtstheorie und Soziologie. Rechtsvergleichung und Common Law (Hg. H. G. Leser) 1979, S. 27.

tuell strafrechtlich zu sühnenden oder zivilrechtlich zu ersetzenden Erfolges, richtet sich auch das Kausalitätsproblem des Historikers stets auf die Zurechnung konkreter Erfolge zu konkreten Ursachen, nicht auf die Ergründung abstrakter ‚Gesetzlichkeiten'."[76] Umgekehrt hat Philipp Heck von der Methodenlehre her die Kausalanalyse im Sinne Webers in den Vordergrund gestellt, so dass insoweit ein gemeinsames Erkenntnisinteresse bestand.[77]

## II. Juristische und soziologische Betrachtungsweise

Vor der eigentlichen Rechtssoziologie ist jedoch dasjenige zu behandeln, was Weber gleichsam vor der Klammer in einer Art allgemeinem Teil der Rechtssoziologie über die Rechtsordnung sagt, die er von der Wirtschaftsordnung abgrenzt. Er stellt der Rechtsordnung den Rechtssatz sowie das Recht selbst an die Seite, nicht um es gleichbedeutend zu verstehen, sondern um die sogleich zu behandelnden Ebenen der juristischen und soziologischen Betrachtungsweise auseinanderzuhalten. Nicht nur für Webers Vorhaben, sondern auch für den vorliegenden Zusammenhang wegweisend ist die Differenzierung, die Weber vor allem behandelt, um eine Vermengung von soziologischer und juristischer Betrachtungsweise, von Sein und Sollen sowie – für unsere Problematik besonders wichtig – von Rechtssoziologie und Rechtsdogmatik bereits im Ausgangspunkt zu vermeiden.

### 1. Ideelle Geltung als Recht

Während die soziologische Betrachtungsweise das faktische Geschehen untersucht, betrifft die juristische die normative Ebene

[76] Vgl. *M. Weber*, Archiv für Sozialwissenschaften und Sozialpolitik 22 (1906) 143 ff.: Wichtig zur Zurechnungsproblematik bei Max Weber *M. R. Lepsius*, Interessen, Ideen und Institutionen, 1977, S. 31 ff.

[77] *Ph. Heck*, Grundriss des Schuldrechts, 1929, S. 42 f., dort auch mit Bezug auf den von Weber zitierten v. Kries, dessen Arbeit Heck nach Ansicht von *E. Dorndorf* (ARSP 1995, 542, 561) gründlich gekannt haben dürfte. Siehe auch *Ph. Heck*, AcP 143 (1937), 129 f.

und fragt,[78] „was als Recht ideell gilt."[79] Schon an dieser Formulierung fällt auf, dass es nicht um die Frage geht, was Recht *ist*.[80] Die damit verbundene philosophisch-spekulative Problematik interessiert Weber ungeachtet des scheinbar darauf hindeutenden Adverbs („ideell") von vornherein nicht.[81] Zugleich handelt es sich nicht um eine bloße Fiktion, wie man vom Standpunkt der juristischen Methodenlehre meinen könnte („gilt als"). Vielmehr ist die prädikative Geltung als Recht gemeint, die durch das Wort „ideell" klargestellt wird; es geht eben nicht um das reelle Recht, mit dem es die Rechtssoziologie zu tun hat. Damit einher geht eine Neutralität gegenüber dem spezifischen Inhalt des jeweiligen Rechts, der ebenso gut ein anderer sein könnte, wie Weber später auch in seinem Vortrag Wissenschaft als Beruf verdeutlicht hat.[82]

## 2. „One right answer" als regulative Idee?

Die Frage der juristischen Betrachtungsweise ist mithin, „welche Bedeutung, und dies wiederum heißt: welcher *normative Sinn* einem als Rechtsnorm auftretenden sprachlichen Gebilde logisch *richtiger*weise zukommen *sollte*."[83] Auch insoweit geht es nicht um

[78] Dazu aus rechtsphilosophischer Sicht *J. Habermas*, Faktizität und Geltung, 1992; zur Unterscheidung zwischen faktischer und normativer Ebene in der juristischen Methodenlehre *J. Petersen*, Von der Interessenjurisprudenz, 2001, S. 54 ff.

[79] *M. Weber*, Wirtschaft und Gesellschaft, S. 181 ff.

[80] Zur sog. Rechtsontologie *G. H. Schäfer*, Die Rechtsontologie Werner Maihofers: Möglichkeiten und Grenzen einer Rechtsphilosophie im Anschluss an Martin Heidegger, 2004; *L. Philipps*, Zur Ontologie der sozialen Rolle, 1963.

[81] Lesenswert *A. Somek*, Der Gegenstand der Rechtserkenntnis – Epitaph eines juristischen Problems, 1996; siehe auch *dens.*, Rechtliches Wissen, 2006.

[82] *M. Weber*, Wissenschaft als Beruf, Geistige Arbeit als Beruf. Vier Vorträge vor dem Freistudentischen Bund, 1919, in: Gesammelte Aufsätze zur Wissenschaftslehre, 7. Auflage 1988, S. 582.

[83] *M. Weber*, Wirtschaft und Gesellschaft, S. 181; Hervorhebungen auch dort.

„richtiges Recht";[84] das wäre wiederum eine rechtsphilosophische Fragestellung. Mit dem Rekurs auf den normativen Sinn ist also die rechte Auslegung des Rechts gemeint, wobei das Moment des Normativen nicht von ungefähr hervorgehoben wird.[85] Die genannte Rechtsnorm ist nicht auf das gesetzte Recht beschränkt, sondern erfasst etwa auch alle privatautonom geschaffenen Vereinbarungen.

Wenn Weber fragt, welcher normative Sinn der Rechtsnorm *richtigerweise* zukommen sollte, so erinnert diese Betonung im Zusammenhang mit der soeben angesprochenen Auslegungsproblematik an die auf Ronald Dworkin zurückgehende[86] und auch in der deutschsprachigen Methodenlehre mitunter favorisierte[87] „one right answer-Thesis", die These also, dass es auf eine dogmatische Frage in einer als regulative Idee zugrunde zu legenden Weise nur eine richtige Antwort gibt, auch wenn diese nur von einem „juristischen Herkules" gefunden werden könnte.[88] Es ist klar, dass man Webers offener Formulierung kein Bekenntnis zu der seinerzeit noch nicht diskutierten Frage entnehmen kann. So sehr gerade die doppelte Betonung (*„richtiger*weise *sollte"*) für die einzig richtige Antwort zu streiten scheint, darf nicht übersehen werden, dass die Einsicht, wonach es nicht nur das Schicksal, sondern geradezu der Sinn der Wissenschaft ist, überboten zu werden,[89] für die gegentei-

[84] Im Sinne von *K. Larenz*, Richtiges Recht – Grundzüge einer Rechtsethik, 1979; *K. Engisch*, Wahrheit und Richtigkeit im juristischen Denken, 1963.

[85] Eine kontrastierende Sichtweise zum herkömmlichen Verständnis der Normativität bietet *St. L. Paulson*, The Weak Reading of Authority in Hans Kelsen's Pure Theory of Law, Law and Philosophy 19 (2000) 131; eher klassisch noch *D. M. Patterson*, Recht und Wahrheit, 1999.

[86] *R. Dworkin*, The Law's Empire, 1986; *ders.*, Taking Rights Seriously, 1977 (Bürgerrechte ernstgenommen, 1984, S. 122 ff., 145 ff.).

[87] In diese Richtung *C.-W. Canaris*, Richtigkeit und Eigenwertung in der richterlichen Rechtsfindung, Grazer Universitätsreden 50, 1993; *K. Langenbucher*, Die Entwicklung und Auslegung von Richterrecht, 1996.

[88] Skeptisch *H. Eidenmüller*, Rechtswissenschaft als Realwissenschaft, JZ 1999, 55 ff.; *B. Rüthers*, Rechtstheorie, 3. Auflage 2007, Rz. 491c; siehe auch *P. Koller*, Theorie des Rechts, 2. Auflage 1997, S. 172 ff.

[89] *M. Weber*, Wissenschaft als Beruf, Geistige Arbeit als Beruf. Vier Vorträge vor dem Freistudentischen Bund, 1919, in: Gesammelte Aufsätze zur Wissen-

lige Auffassung ins Feld geführt werden könnte. Denn die damit vorausgesetzt einzig „richtige" Lösung eines dogmatischen Problems basiert ihrerseits auf dogmatischen Annahmen[90] bzw. der Wirkungsweise von Wertungen und Prinzipien, die später als unzureichend oder unvollständig erkannt werden könnten.

### 3. Recht und Sprache

Methodologisch interessant ist, dass Weber von dem „als Rechtsnorm auftretenden sprachlichen Gebilde" spricht. Diese nüchterne Formulierung ist rechtstheoretisch durchaus bedeutsam.

#### a) Sprachpragmatische Ansätze

Auch wenn sich die vorliegende Untersuchung auf die klassische juristische Methodenlehre konzentriert,[91] sei am Rande eine modernere Richtung erwähnt, die veranschaulicht, wie unwillkürlich vorausschauend Webers möglichst allgemein gehaltene Wendung des „als Rechtsnorm auftretenden sprachlichen Gebildes" aus heutiger Sicht erscheint. Das entspricht in bemerkenswerter Weise einer aus dem angloamerikanischen Rechtskreis herrührenden methodologischen Richtung, die der Frage nachgeht, wie Recht erst durch den Gebrauch der Sprache hergestellt wird.[92] Diese

schaftslehre, 7. Auflage 1988, S. 582, 592 („jede wissenschaftliche ‚Erfüllung' bedeutet neue ‚Fragen' und *will* ‚überboten' werden und veralten"; Hervorhebung auch dort).

90 Zur Rolle solcher Basissätze für die Theoriebildung *K. Popper*, Objektive Erkenntnis, 4. Auflage 1984, S. 82; zu ihm *M. Schmid*, Rationalität und Theoriebildung. Studien zu Karl R. Poppers Methodologie der Sozialwissenschaften, 1966. Bezogen auf einzelne dogmatische Streitfragen *J. Petersen*, Von der Interessenjurisprudenz zur Wertungsjurisprudenz, 2001, S. 77 ff.

91 Aber auch dort wird dies diskutiert: *M. Herberger/H.-J. Koch*, Juristische Methodenlehre und Sprachphilosophie, JuS 1978, 810.

92 *R. B. Brandom*, Making it explicit. Reasoning, Representing & Discursive Commitment, 1994; *ders.*, Articulating Reasons. An Introduction of Inferentialism, 2000; dazu instruktiv *J. Habermas*, Wahrheit und Rechtfertigung, 2000, S. 11 ff. Zur sprachphilosophischen Grundlage *J. R. Searle*, Sprechakte,

sprachpragmatischen Ansätze,[93] die hier nicht näher behandelt werden können,[94] gehen nicht selten auf Jürgen Habermas zurück.[95] Für den vorliegenden Zusammenhang ist nur die Feststellung interessant, wie sich in den überaus präzisen Definitionen Webers moderne Antworten der juristischen Methodenlehre spiegeln und er den möglichen Zusammenhang zwischen Sprache, Rechts- und Wahrheitsfindung frühzeitig zugrunde gelegt hat: „Der Umstand andererseits, dass ein solches ideales ‚Gelten-Sollen' eines bestimmten *‚Rechtssatzes'* aus bestimmten *Wortverbindungen* von solchen empirischen Personen, welche *‚juristische Wahrheit'* wollen, faktisch erschlossen zu werden pflegt, ist seinerseits natürlich wieder keineswegs ohne empirische Konsequenzen, vielmehr von allergrößter empirisch-historischer Bedeutsamkeit."[96]

### b) Verbindungslinie zur Sprachphilosophie

Eine ähnliche Verbindungslinie lässt sich im Übrigen bereits bei Nietzsche feststellen,[97] wie überhaupt entsprechend dem in der Einleitung Gesagten eine – wenn auch nicht in dieser Abhandlung[98] – noch näher zu beleuchtende Beziehung zwischen Webers

1971; *J. L. Austin*, Zur Theorie der Sprechakte, 2. Auflage 1974; *E. v. Savigny*, Die Philosophie der normalen Sprache, 1974.

93 *R. Alexy*, Theorie der juristischen Argumentation, 1976; siehe auch *K. Günther*, Der Sinn für Angemessenheit, 1988.

94 *R. Christensen/H. Kudlich*, Theorie richterlichen Begründens, 2001 (vgl. nur S. 437: „Sprache ist ein Marktphänomen"; dazu interessant *A. Somek*, Juristische Expertise, Rechtshistorisches Journal 20, 2001, 698).

95 *J. Habermas*, Strukturwandel der Öffentlichkeit, 1962; zusammenfassend *ders.*, Faktizität und Geltung. Beiträge zur Diskurstheorie des Rechts und des demokratischen Rechtsstaates, 1992, S. 15 ff.

96 *M. Weber*, Analyse des Begriffs der „Regel", Archiv für Sozialwissenschaft und Sozialpolitik 24 (1907) 94 ff. Hervorhebung nur hier.

97 *J. Petersen*, Nietzsches Genialität der Gerechtigkeit, 2007, S. 129 ff.; *R. Schacht*, Philosophy as Linguistic Analysis: A Nietzschean Critique, Philosophical Studies 25 (1974) 153.

98 Ansatzweise *J. Petersen*, Nietzsches Genialität der Gerechtigkeit, 2007, S. 114, wonach bei Nietzsche (in: Menschliches, Allzumenschliches, II, 2, 33) das Recht mitunter als Rationalisierung des Archaischen erscheint.

Methode, insbesondere im Hinblick auf die Rechts- und Völkervergleichung und Nietzsches Postulaten im Hinblick auf die Rechtsphilosophie bestehen dürfte,[99] die nicht zuletzt darin zu sehen ist, wie dem Wortsinn unter Betonung des Logischen auf den Grund gegangen wird.[100] Darauf wird im Abschnitt über die Logik des Rechts noch zurückzukommen sein,[101] so dass es an dieser Stelle bei der Feststellung bewenden kann, dass die jeweiligen Probleme auch eine sprachphilosophische Komponente aufweisen, die mit zu berücksichtigen ist.[102] Der Zusammenhang ergibt sich nicht zuletzt aus der Formulierung der Anwendung des Rechtssatzes auf den Fall, den Weber seziert hat: „Tatsächlich ist denn auch neben die Doktrin von der unvermeidlichen Lückenhaftigkeit des Rechts und den Protest gegen die Fiktion seiner systematischen Geschlossenheit die weitergehende Behauptung getreten:[103] dass Rechtsfindung überhaupt prinzipiell nicht ‚Anwendung' genereller Normen auf einen konkreten Tatbestand sei (oder doch nicht sein sollte) – *so wenig der sprachliche Ausdruck ‚Anwendung' grammatischer Regeln sei* –, dass vielmehr der ‚Rechtssatz' das Sekundäre, durch Abstraktion aus den konkreten Entscheidungen Gewonnene sei, diese aber, die Produkte der Juristentätigkeit, der eigentliche Sitz des ‚geltenden' Rechts seien."[104] Diese Stelle ist auch rechtstheoretisch bedeutsam.[105] Jedenfalls hat Weber – wie vordem Nietzsche – einen Zusammenhang erkannt und bezeichnet, der bis in die moderne rechts- und sprachtheoretische Diskussion hineinreicht.

99 Vgl. *F. Nietzsche*, Der Wille zur Macht, 744.
100 Siehe nur *F. Nietzsche*, Menschliches, Allzumenschliches, I, 32; zu dieser Stelle weiterführend *J. Habermas*, Erkenntnis und Interessen, 1973, S. 363.
101 In § 4 unter II 1.
102 Siehe auch *R. Hegenbarth*, Juristische Hermeneutik und linguistische Pragmatik, 1982.
103 Zu den damit aufgeworfenen Fragen der systematischen Geschlossenheit und Lückenlosigkeit der Rechtsordnung noch weiter unten sub § 3.
104 *M. Weber*, Wirtschaft und Gesellschaft, S. 507 f.; Hervorhebung nur hier.
105 *B. Rüthers*, Rechtstheorie, Rz. 724 mit Fußnote 817.

## III. Rechtsdogmatik und Sozialökonomik

Weber verwirklicht die Gegenüberstellung von Recht und Wirtschaft im Folgenden durch einen Parallelismus, der zunächst von der Rechtsdogmatik ausgeht und ihr die Sozialökonomik gegenüberstellt. „Die letztere (sc. die soziologische Betrachtungsweise) dagegen fragt: was innerhalb einer Gemeinschaft *faktisch* um deswillen *geschieht*, weil die *Chance* besteht, dass am Gemeinschaftshandeln beteiligte Menschen, darunter insbesondere solche, in deren Händen ein sozial relevantes Maß von faktischem Einfluss auf dieses Gemeinschaftshandeln liegt, bestimmte Ordnungen als geltend *subjektiv* ansehen und praktisch behandeln, also ihr eigenes Handeln an ihnen orientieren."[106] Hier scheint im Übrigen der zentrale Begriff der Handlung auf, dessen Ausarbeitung Luhmann als wichtige Errungenschaft der Rechtssoziologie Webers bezeichnet[107] und der sich auch in Webers berühmter Begriffsbestimmung der Soziologie manifestiert: „Soziologie (...) soll heißen: eine Wissenschaft, welche soziales Handeln deutend verstehen und dadurch in seinem Ablauf und seinen Wirkungen ursächlich verstehen will. ‚Handeln' soll dabei ein menschliches Verhalten (...) heißen, wenn und insofern als der oder die Handelnden mit ihm einen subjektiven *Sinn* verbinden."[108]

[106] *M. Weber*, Wirtschaft und Gesellschaft, S. 181; Hervorhebung auch dort.
[107] *N. Luhmann*, Rechtssoziologie, 3. Auflage 1987, S. 18. Siehe auch *J. Berger*, Die Grenzen des handlungstheoretischen Paradigmas am Beispiel der „soziologischen Grundbegriffe" Max Webers, in: Materialien aus der soziologischen Forschung (Hg. K. M. Bolte) 1978, S. 108.
[108] *M. Weber*, Wirtschaft und Gesellschaft, S. 1; siehe auch *dens.*, Über einige Kategorien der verstehenden Soziologie, Logos 4 (1913) 253; *ders.*: (Hervorhebung auch dort). Dazu *T. Parsons*, On the Relation of Action to Max Weber's „Verstehende Soziologie", in: Verhalten, Handeln und System. Talcott Parsons' Beitrag zur Entwicklung der Sozialwissenschaft (Hg. W. Schluchter) 1980, S. 150.

## 1. Webers Verständnis der Rechtsdogmatik

Von daher fragt sich, was Weber demgegenüber unter Rechtsdogmatik versteht. Sein Begriffsverständnis ist deswegen so wichtig für den vorliegenden Zusammenhang, weil es den Weg zur juristischen Methodenlehre ebnet, die dasjenige erfasst und theoretisch untermauert, was Weber folgendermaßen beschreibt: „Die juristische, genauer: die rechtsdogmatische, Betrachtung stellt sich die Aufgabe: Sätze, deren Inhalt sich als eine Ordnung darstellt, welche für das Verhalten eines irgendwie bezeichneten Kreises von Menschen maßgebend sein soll, auf ihren richtigen Sinn, und das heißt: auf die Tatbestände, welche ihr, und die Art, wie sie ihr unterliegen, zu untersuchen.“[109] Es sind wohl Sätze wie dieser, die in ihrer unermüdlichen Präzision den Eindruck haben entstehen lassen, dass sich Webers Rechtssoziologie gerade in stilistischer Hinsicht mitunter beschwerlich für den Leser darstellt.[110]

Wichtiger ist aber der nachfolgende modale Aspekt: „Dabei verfährt sie in der Weise, dass sie die verschiedenen einzelnen Sätze jener Art, ausgehend von ihrer unbezweifelten empirischen Geltung, ihrem logisch richtigen Sinn nach dergestalt zu bestimmen trachtet, dass sie dadurch in ein logisch in sich widerspruchsloses System gebracht werden. Dies System ist die ‚Rechtsordnung‘ im juristischen Sinn des Wortes.“[111] Was mit der für Weber bedeutsamen empirischen Geltung gemeint ist, wird weiter unten behandelt.[112] Hier ist zunächst dasjenige zu betonen, was die zeitlos gültige Aufgabe der Dogmatik darstellt,[113] nämlich die Einordnung in ein logisch widerspruchsloses System. Diese Postulate werden in

[109] *M. Weber*, Wirtschaft und Gesellschaft, S. 181.

[110] *M. Rehbinder*, Rechtssoziologie, 1977, S. 59 f. („stilistisch schwierig geschrieben und inhaltlich nicht leicht überschaubar“).

[111] *M. Weber*, Wirtschaft und Gesellschaft, S. 181.

[112] Sub III.

[113] Aus soziologischer Sicht, freilich gleichfalls vor dem Hintergrund der erfahrenen rechtsdogmatischen Bildung, wenngleich mit durchaus eigenständiger systemtheoretischer Sicht, *N. Luhmann*, Rechtssystem und Rechtsdogmatik, 1974.

den nachfolgenden Paragraphen noch eingehend behandelt, so dass es hier bei der Feststellung bewenden kann, dass darin nach wie vor die Aufgabe der Rechtswissenschaft als solcher besteht.[114]

### 2. Heterogenität

Rechts- und Wirtschaftsordnung sind für Weber etwas fundamental Verschiedenes, weil beide auf verschiedenen Ebenen mit einem unterschiedlichen Erkenntnisinteresse angesiedelt sind,[115] so dass sich juristische und soziologische Betrachtungsweise nicht berühren.[116] Dieser methodologische Ausgangspunkt führt zu zwei möglichen Einwänden, denen sich die vorliegende Betrachtung ausgesetzt sieht und die sie zumindest mitberücksichtigen muss.

#### a) Parallele zwischen Rechtssoziologie und Methodenlehre?

Indem nämlich die Parallele bezüglich Webers Rechtssoziologie[117] und der juristischen Methodenlehre behandelt wird, muss zugleich

[114] *C.-W. Canaris*, Systemdenken und Systembegriff in der Jurisprudenz, 2. Auflage 1983, passim.

[115] An anderer Stelle (Archiv für Sozialwissenschaft und Sozialpolitik 24, 1907, 94, Fußnote 10) würdigt Weber *G. Jellinek*, System der subjektiven öffentlichen Rechte, 2. Auflage, Kapitel III, S. 12, der „naturalistische Eingriffe in das rechtsdogmatische Denken abzuwehren" suche (siehe auch *dens.*, Allgemeine Staatslehre, 3. Auflage 1959, S. 337 f., zur „normativen Kraft des Faktischen"), kritisch und vertritt den umgekehrten Standpunkt. Mit „naturalistisch" ist, wie weiter unten im Text (vor Fußnote 15) von Weber dargestellt wird, der Gegensatz zu dogmatisch gemeint. Dort findet sich im Übrigen ein wenig beachteter Exkurs zur Rechtsgeschichte, die für Weber ebenfalls und folgerichtig eine naturalistische und keine dogmatische Disziplin ist, „weil auch sie die *Faktizität* der Rechtsnormen und nicht ihren idealen *Sinn*, zum Objekt hat." (Hervorhebungen auch dort).

[116] *M. Weber*, Wirtschaft und Gesellschaft, S. 181.

[117] Zusammenfassend *M. Rehbinder*, Max Webers Rechtssoziologie: Eine Bestandsaufnahme, in: Max Weber zum Gedächtnis. Materialien und Dokumente zur Bewertung von Werk und Persönlichkeit 1963, S. 470. Zu den Grundzügen der Rechtssoziologie Max Webers *M. Baurmann*, JuS 1991, 97. Siehe auch *Th. Raiser*, Grundlagen der Rechtssoziologie, 4. Auflage 2006. Zur Relevanz der Soziologie Max Webers für die juristische Praxis und Juris-

dem Einwand begegnet werden, dass sich bei konsequentem Fortdenken die Linien selbst im Unendlichen nicht treffen würden, womit die Erörterung im Wortsinne gegenstandslos wäre. In der Tat muss immer berücksichtigt werden, dass das jeweilige Erkenntnisinteresse ein im Ansatz unterschiedliches ist, wie Weber selbst nicht nur hier, sondern auch an anderer Stelle beispielhaft zugrunde gelegt hat: „Die gattungsmäßigen Merkmale des Tausches, Kaufs usw. interessieren den Juristen, – was uns (sc. die Soziologen) angeht, ist die Aufgabe, eben jene Kulturbedeutung der historischen Tatsache, dass der Tausch heute Massenerscheinung ist, zu analysieren."[118] Es soll daher nicht bei der Herausstellung eines beziehungslosen Nebeneinander bewenden,[119] sondern das interdisziplinäre Ineinandergreifen dort veranschaulichen,[120] wo die juristische Methodenlehre von dem lernen kann,[121] der als ge-

tenausbildung *H. A. Hesse*, Zeitschrift für vergleichende Rechtswissenschaft 84 (1982) 242; siehe auch *A. Febbrajo*, Per una rilettura della sociologia del diritto weberiana, Sociologia del diritto 3 (1976) 1.

118 *M. Weber*, Die „Objektivität" sozialwissenschaftlicher und sozialpolitischer Erkenntnis, Archiv für Sozialwissenschaft und Sozialpolitik, 19 (1904), 22 ff.

119 *L. Kißler*, Recht und Gesellschaft. Einführung in die Rechtssoziologie, 1984, S. 80: „Die Fortschreibung der Dreidimensionalität des Rechts (Rechtsideal, Rechtsnorm, Rechtswirklichkeit) auf die disziplinäre Aufspaltung in Rechtsphilosophie, Rechtsdogmatik und Rechtssoziologie – wie sie von einem analytischen Wissenschaftsverständnis vorgenommen wird – erhöht nicht die interdisziplinäre Kommunikation, sondern zementiert die halbierte Rationalität innerhalb der Disziplinen."

120 Man mag dies „heuristisch" nennen; vgl. *W. Fikentscher*, Juristische Heuristik, Festschrift für C.-W. Canaris, 2007, S. 1091, 1093 f. Siehe auch *A. Heldrich*, Das Trojanische Pferd in der Zitadelle des Rechts?, Überlegungen zur Einbeziehung der Sozialwissenschaften in die juristische Ausbildung, JuS 1974, 281; *H. Schelsky*, Nutzen und Gefahren der sozialwissenschaftlichen Ausbildung von Juristen, JZ 1974, 410; *ders.*, Soziologiekritische Bemerkungen zu gewissen Tendenzen der Rechtssoziologen, Jahrbuch für Rechtssoziologie und Rechtstheorie 3 (1972) 603; *K. Hopt*, Rechtssoziologische und rechtsinformatorische Elemente im Wirtschaftsrecht, BB 1972, 1017.

121 Anderer Ansicht *St. Uecker*, Die Rationalisierung des Rechts. Max Webers Rechtssoziologie, 2005, S. 102: „Der Fortschritt der juristischen Methodenlehre hat Weber längst überholt."

lernter Jurist von ihr ausgegangen ist und in der von ihm mitbegründeten Disziplin dadurch wegweisend wurde,[122] dass er über die angewandte und anzuwendende Methode wie nur wenige Rechenschaft abgelegt hat. Vor diesem Hintergrund kann man mit Rainer Lepsius sagen: „Max Webers Methodologie ist zeitgenössische Wissenschaftskritik in der Absicht, sein eigenes Forschungsprogramm zu rechtfertigen und den Sozialwissenschaften wissenschaftspolitisch größere Autonomie zu verschaffen."[123] Webers Methodologie steht damit zugleich in einem unausgesprochenen Dialog mit der juristischen Methodenlehre, und sei es auch, um – ganz im Sinne des soeben Zitierten – im Wege der Reflexion und Abgrenzung die Eigenständigkeit der sozialwissenschaftlichen Methodenlehre unter Beweis zu stellen.

### b) Gefahr des Methodensynkretismus

Damit soll die gängige Unterscheidung zwischen Rechtssoziologie und Rechtsdogmatik durchaus nicht aufgehoben werden, es sei denn, man begreift dies in einem höheren – gleichsam hegelianisch gefärbten dialektischen[124] – Sinne: „Darin (sc. im Sinnverständnis) liegt der Unterschied der empirischen Wissenschaften vom Handeln: der Soziologie und der Geschichte, gegenüber allen *dogmatischen: Jurisprudenz*, Logik, Ethik, Ästhetik, welche an ihren Objekten den ‚richtigen', ‚gültigen' Sinn erforschen wollen."[125] Es geht also darum aufzuzeigen, welche Erkenntnisse die juristische Methodenlehre aus der für die Rechtssoziologie grundlegenden

[122] Als Gesamtdarstellung nach wie vor interessant *R. Bendix*, Max Weber, An Intellectual Portrait, 1960.

[123] *M. R. Lepsius*, Interessen, Ideen und Institutionen, 1977, S. 23; in diese Richtung auch *W. Schluchter*, Wertfreiheit und Verantwortungsethik, 1971, S. 20 ff.

[124] Zu diesem Zusammenhang allgemein *E. H. Flitner*, Revolte gegen den Rationalismus. Beziehungen zwischen Max Webers und Hegels Analysen zur Dialektik der Verwissenschaftlichung, Kölner Zeitschrift für Soziologie und Sozialpsychologie 35 (1983) 255.

[125] *M. Weber*, Wirtschaft und Gesellschaft, S. 1 f.; Hervorhebung nur hier. Zu dieser Stelle in rechtssoziologischer Hinsicht *W. Schluchter*, in: Rechtssoziologie am Ende des 20. Jahrhunderts (Hg. H. Dreier) 2000, S. 8, 21 f.

Darstellung Webers ableiten kann und wie sich in ihr ein in jeder – das heißt nicht nur soziologischer[126] oder philosophischer, sondern auch juristischer – Hinsicht methodengerechtes Vorgehen abbildet, das auch die Rechtsdogmatik befruchten kann,[127] an der Webers Denken ursprünglich geschult war.

Paradoxerweise ist für den vorliegenden Zusammenhang daher interessant und weiterführend, was Weber im rechtssoziologischen Schrifttum mitunter vorgeworfen wurde,[128] nämlich dass er sich zu engmaschig an der Rechtsdogmatik orientiere.[129] Wenn im Folgenden vereinfachend von der Methodenlehre gesprochen wird, ist die juristische gemeint, auch wenn sie mit Selbstverständlichkeit nicht beanspruchen kann, gleichsam als Oberbegriff die Methoden der Sozialwissenschaften zu umspannen.[130] Diese Klarstellung ruft die Gefahr eines „Methodensynkretismus" in Erinnerung,[131] vor der die vorliegende Abhandlung immer gewarnt sein muss.[132]

[126] Der Nutzen der operationalen Rechtssoziologie, die den Einfluss von Rechtsnormen auf die Gesellschaftsverhältnisse ermittelt (vgl. nur *R. Dahrendorf*, Homo Sociologicus, 11. Auflage 1972, S. 37 ff.), ist für die Rechtswissenschaft nach *H. Eidenmüller*, Rechtswissenschaft als Realwissenschaft, JZ 1999, 53, 55, bisher noch nicht hinreichend hoch.

[127] Siehe etwa *H. Rottleuthner*, Zur Rezeptivität der Rechtswissenschaft gegenüber soziologischem Wissen, Soziologie, Mitteilungsblatt der Deutschen Gesellschaft für Soziologie 2 (1978) 17 ff.

[128] In diese Richtung auch *N. Luhmann*, Rechtssoziologie, 3. Auflage 1987, S. 18 f. mit Fußnote 18.

[129] *G. Gurvitch*, Grundzüge der Soziologie des Rechts, 1960, S. 37 ff.

[130] *H. Rottleuthner*, Richterliches Handeln. Zur Kritik der juristischen Dogmatik, 1973, S. 3.

[131] Prägnant *G. Boehmer*, Grundlagen der Bürgerlichen Rechtsordnung, Zweites Buch, Erste Abteilung, Dogmengeschichtliche Grundlagen des Bürgerlichen Rechts, 1951, S. 163. Aus dem neueren Schrifttum *B. Rüthers*, Methodenrealismus in Jurisprudenz und Justiz, JZ 2006, 53.

[132] Vorbildhaft dagegen *H. Sinzheimer*, Über die soziologische und dogmatische Methode der Arbeitsrechtswissenschaft, 1922.

## 3. Max Webers Methodenlehre

So kann die vorliegende Untersuchung womöglich im interdisziplinären Diskurs über Methodenfragen einen Fingerzeig geben,[133] weil gerade Weber vor dem Hintergrund seiner juristischen Provenienz eine Methode zugrunde legte,[134] die dann für eine andere, von ihm maßgeblich entwickelte und mitbegründete Disziplin stilprägend wurde,[135] und die auch davon abgesehen ihresgleichen sucht.[136] Dieter Henrich, der die Methodenlehre Webers exemplarisch untersucht hat, gelangt zu der Einsicht, „dass der Sammelband der Aufsätze nicht nur (…) Einzelanalysen und Meinungen eines Spezialforschers versammelt, sondern eine theoretische Einheit ausdrückt, deren Geschlossenheit um so mehr in Verwunderung setzt, weil sie nicht offen sichtbar und vielleicht nicht einmal Max Weber selbst bewusst ist."[137] Natürlich kann nicht unbedarft

[133] Mit Recht warnt *H. Rottleuthner* (Richterliches Handeln. Zur Kritik der juristischen Dogmatik, 1973, S. 1) vor einer „interdisziplinären Attitude".

[134] Zur Entstehung *F. H. Tenbruck*, Die Genesis der Methodenlehre Max Webers, Kölner Zeitschrift für Soziologie und Sozialpsychologie 11 (1959) 573; siehe auch *W. Hennis*, Max Webers Fragestellung. Studien zur Biographie des Werks, 1987.

[135] Näher *H. Plessner*, Der Weg der Soziologie, 1960, S. 36 f.; *M. R. Lepsius*, Die Soziologie in der Zwischenkriegszeit: Entwicklungstendenzen und Beurteilungskriterien, in: Soziologie in Deutschland und Österreich 1918–1945, Materialien zur Entwicklung, Emigration und Wirkungsgeschichte (Hg. *ders.*), Sonderheft 23 der Kölner Zeitschrift für Soziologie und Sozialpsychologie, 1981, S. 7 ff.; *ders.*, Max Weber (1864–1920) Begründer der modernen Sozialwissenschaften, in: München leuchtet für die Wissenschaft (Hg. U. Leutheusser/H. Nötz), 2007), S. 64.

[136] Aus dem jüngeren amerikanischen Schrifttum wegweisend *F. Ringer*, Max Weber's Methodology. The Unification of the Cultural and Social Sciences, 1997; *ders.*, Max Weber. An intellectual biography, 2004.

[137] *D. Henrich*, Die Einheit der Wissenschaftslehre Max Webers, 1952, S. 2 und passim: „Die Interpretation will zunächst die Methodenlehre Max Webers darstellen, indem sie ihre hauptsächlichen Begriffe auf ein einziges Prinzip zurückführt." Ferner dazu *ders.*, Die Situation der Historie und Max Webers Methodenlehre, Archiv für Philosophie 3 (1949) 400; *A. v. Schelting*, Max Webers Wissenschaftslehre, 1934; *H. H. Brunn*, Science, Values and Politics in Max Weber's Methodology, 1972; *W. G. Runciman*, A Critique of Max Weber's Philosophy of Social Science, 1972.

davon ausgegangen werden, dass Weber nur diejenige Methode, die er in der Jurisprudenz erlernt hatte, ohne weiteres auf die Sozialwissenschaften angewandt hätte. Es versteht sich, dass dies nicht vermengt werden darf mit der im Hintergrund stehenden Problematik des Methodenstreits in den Sozialwissenschaften.[138] Jedoch ist dieser auch für die vorliegende Betrachtung von zumindest unterschwelliger Bedeutung.

### a) Werturteilsstreit

Im Werturteilsstreit, den Max Weber maßgeblich geprägt und beeinflusst hat,[139] ging es um die von ihm behauptete Wertfreiheit der Wissenschaften,[140] wonach Werturteile als nicht wahrheitsfähige Aussagen auch wissenschaftlich nicht weiterführend seien.[141] Über ein Werturteil ist, wie Weber durchaus plastisch formuliert, „im Hörsaal nichts auszusagen": „Ob unter solchen Verhältnissen die Wissenschaft wert ist, für jemanden ein ‚Beruf' zu werden und ob sie selbst einen objektiv wertvollen ‚Beruf' hat – das ist wieder ein Werturteil, über welches im Hörsaal nichts auszusagen ist. Denn für die Lehre dort ist die Bejahung *Voraussetzung.*"[142] Da-

[138] Aus dem früheren Schrifttum *Ch. Engel-Reimers*, Der Methodenstreit in der Soziologie, Schmollers Jahrbuch für Gesetzgebung, Verwaltung und Volkswirtschaft im Deutschen Reiche 56 (1932) 87; ferner *G. Dux*, Gegenstand und Methode. Am Beispiel der Wissenschaftslehre Max Webers, Festschrift für H. Plessner, 1974, S. 187.

[139] *M. Weber*, Der Sinn der ‚Wertfreiheit' der soziologischen und ökonomischen Wissenschaften, Logos 7 (1917) 40.

[140] Siehe auch *H. Albert*, Theorie und Praxis. Max Weber und das Problem der Wertfreiheit und der Rationalität, Festschrift für S. Moser, 1967, S. 264.

[141] *H. Albert/E. Topitsch* (Hg.), Werturteilsstreit, 3. Auflage 1990; *E. Topitsch* (Hg.), Logik der Sozialwissenschaften, 12. Auflage 1993; *ders.*, Das Wertfreiheitsproblem seit Max Weber, Zeitschrift für Nationalökonomie 13 (1952) 158; *Th. W. Adorno*, Zur Logik der Sozialwissenschaft, in: Der Positivismusstreit in der deutschen Soziologie (Hg. ders./Habermas/Dahrendorf/Popper/Albert/Pilot), 14. Auflage 1991.

[142] *M. Weber*, Wissenschaft als Beruf, Geistige Arbeit als Beruf. Vier Vorträge vor dem Freistudentischen Bund, 1919 in: Gesammelte Aufsätze zur Wissenschaftslehre, 7. Auflage 1988, S. 582, 608; Hervorhebung auch dort.

raus folgt allerdings nach Weber mitnichten, „dass Werturteile deshalb, weil sie in letzter Instanz auf bestimmten Idealen fußen und daher ‚subjektiven' Ursprungs sind, der wissenschaftlichen Diskussion überhaupt entzogen seien."[143]

Die Gegenmeinung[144] hält auch Werturteile für wissenschaftlich begründbar.[145] Für die Rechtswissenschaft ist diese letztgenannte Auffassung deshalb nicht folgenlos, weil damit die kategoriale Unterscheidung zwischen Sein und Sollen in Frage gestellt wird.[146] Damit – und mit der Problematik der Erkennbarkeit selbst[147] – erreicht die Problematik auch eine rechtsphilosophische Dimension,[148] und so nimmt es nicht wunder, dass die Wahrheitsfähigkeit von Werturteilen auch in der Philosophie teilweise für wenigstens begründbar gehalten wird.[149] Einige dieser so genannten Kognitivisten leiten die Begründbarkeit und Wahrheitsfähigkeit der Werturteile aus dem aufgeklärten Eigeninteresse rational handelnder Personen ab.[150] Jürgen Habermas hat dies wie folgt zusam-

143 *M. Weber*, Die Objektivität sozialwissenschaftlicher und sozialpolitischer Erkenntnis, Archiv für Sozialwissenschaft und Sozialpolitik 19 (1904) 22. Eine vergleichsweise frühe amerikanische Rezeption verdankt die Weber-Forschung *T. Parsons*, The Place of Ultimate Values in Sociological Theory, International Journal of Ethics 45 (1935) 282.

144 Differenzierend *J. Tiemeyer*, Zur Methodenfrage der Rechtssoziologie, 1969.

145 *J. Habermas*, Zur Logik der Sozialwissenschaften, 5. Auflage 1982; aus wissenschaftstheoretischer Sicht *P. Lorenzen*, Konstruktive Wissenschafts-dem rechtstheoretischen Schrifttum *M. Kriele*, Kriterien der Gerechtigkeit, 1963, S. 16 ff.

146 *B. Rüthers*, Rechtstheorie, 3. Auflage 2007, Rz. 290a.

147 Aus dem früheren Schrifttum bereits *J. Cohn*, Die Erkenntnis der Werte und das Vorrecht der Bejahung. Betrachtungen angeknüpft an Max Webers Lehre von der Wertfreiheit der Wissenschaft, Logos X (1921/22) 195.

148 *H. Putnam*, The Collapse of the Fact/Value Dichotomy and Other Essays, 2004, gibt zu bedenken, dass es unentbehrliche Wissenschaftsbegriffe gibt, die sowohl beschreibend als auch bewertend sind.

149 Für einen pluralistisch-kritischen Rationalismus *H. Albert*, Traktat über kritische Vernunft, 1968; skeptisch aus juristischer Sicht *W. Henke*, Kritik des kritischen Rationalismus, 1974.

150 Nachweise im Einzelnen bei *M. Quante*, Allgemeine Ethik, 2003; siehe nur *G. Weisser*, Zur Erkenntniskritik der Urteile über den Wert sozialer Ge-

mengefasst: „Seit der von Max Weber herbeigeführten Klärung im sogenannten Werturteilsstreit, und den präziseren Bestimmungen einer positivistischen ‚Logik der Forschung', [151] haben sich die Sozialwissenschaften von den normativen Elementen, dem schon vergessenen Erbe der klassischen Politik, ganz gelöst – so jedenfalls stellt es sich ihrem wissenschaftstheoretischen Selbstverständnis dar."[152]

## b) Werturteil und Wertung

Für den vorliegenden Zusammenhang ist das deshalb aufschlussreich, weil diese Richtung damit hinsichtlich ihres Erkenntnisinteresses in einem Näheverhältnis zur Interessenjurisprudenz steht,[153] wie im rechtstheoretischen Schrifttum erkannt worden ist.[154] Auch wenn dies ersichtlich nicht mit einem strikten Standpunkt der Interessenjurisprudenz gleichgesetzt werden kann, den diese schließlich auch zeitbedingt noch nicht einnehmen konnte, veranschaulicht es die Offenheit des Interessenbegriffs,[155] die bis zur Konturenlosigkeit reichen kann.[156] Am Beispiel von Webers

bilde und Prozesse. Weiterführung der „Werturteilsdebatte", Kölner Zeitschrift für Soziologie und Sozialpsychologie 6 (1953/54) 16.

[151] Mit Hinweis auf die Zusammenfassung von *H. Albert*, Probleme der Wissenschaftslogik in der Sozialforschung, in: Handbuch der empirischen Sozialforschung, Band I, ed. König, 1962, S. 38 ff. Siehe auch *H. Albert*, Plädoyer für einen kritischen Rationalismus, 1971.

[152] *J. Habermas*, Theorie und Praxis. Sozialphilosophische Studien, 1971 (1963), S. 50.

[153] Im frühen soziologischen Schrifttum nahmen Wertungen noch breiten Raum ein; vgl. *L. Gumplowicz*, Grundriss der Soziologie, 1885.

[154] *B. Rüthers*, Rechtstheorie, Rz. 118. Er spricht davon, dass sie „wie die Interessen- und Wertungsjurisprudenz an dem Interesse anknüpft", während nach der hier vertretenen Auffassung insoweit noch eine wissenschaftstheoretisch maßgebliche (*Th. Kuhn*, Die Struktur wissenschaftlicher Revolutionen, 12. Auflage 1993) Differenz besteht (*J. Petersen*, Von der Interessenjurisprudenz zur Wertungsjurisprudenz, 2001, S. 7 ff.).

[155] In der Diktion Hecks sind es teilweise „gesetzlich gewertete Interessen".

[156] Dazu und dem sogleich im Text näher beschriebenen Wandel etwa *O.A. Germann*, Probleme und Methoden der Rechtsfindung, 2. Auflage 1967.

Rationalitätsverständnis und der Rolle, die er dem Logischen im Recht beimisst, wird sich noch zeigen,[157] dass die Lebensforschung und Lebenswertung der Interessenjurisprudenz seiner Vorstellung der Rationalität des Rechts nur bedingt entgegenkam. So ist seine im Werturteilsstreit eingenommene Position auch hinsichtlich möglicher Konsequenzen aus dem Epochenwandel innerhalb der Jurisprudenz in sich folgerichtig. Zur Vermeidung von Missverständnissen ist darauf hinzuweisen, dass die Werturteile, die Weber als nicht wahrheitsfähig erachtet, und auch die Wertungen, von denen er spricht, nicht unbedingt etwas mit den Wertungen im Sinne der Wertungsjurisprudenz zu tun haben:[158] „Unter ‚Wertungen' sollen nachstehend, wo nicht ein anderes gesagt oder von selbst ersichtlich ist, *‚praktische'* Bewertungen einer durch unser Handeln beeinflussbaren Erscheinung als verwerflich oder billigenswert verstanden werden."[159] Es ist also ersichtlich etwas anderes gemeint, weil es in der Wertungsjurisprudenz zumindest *idealiter*[160] die Wertungen des Gesetzes in Gestalt gesetzgeberischer Basiswertungen sind.[161] Sie können gewichtet und unter Berücksichtigung der systematischen Verschränkungen innerhalb der Pri-

[157] Unter § 2 und § 3.

[158] Ungeachtet dessen ist die Feststellung von *B. Rüthers*, Rechtstheorie, Rz. 541, richtig: „Juristische Methoden dienen immer der Wertverwirklichung durch Rechtsnormen, haben also Bezüge zu den weltanschaulichen Grundlagen der Rechtsordnung."

[159] *M. Weber*, Der Sinn der „Wertfreiheit" der soziologischen und ökonomischen Wissenschaften, Logos 7 (1917) 40 ff.

[160] Realiter mag das Vorverständnis der Richter etc. hineinspielen (*B. Rüthers*, Rechtstheorie, Rz. 36 ff.; siehe auch *J. Esser*, Vorverständnis und Methodenwahl in der Rechtsfindung, 2. Auflage 1972; *H. Rottleuthner*, Richterliches Handeln, 1973. Es verhält sich insoweit ähnlich wie im Verhältnis des von Weber bewusst nicht zugrunde gelegten „Durchschnittstypus" zu seinem „Idealtypus" (*M. Weber*, Wirtschaft und Gesellschaft, S. 10 ff.); dazu noch näher unter § 5.

[161] Selbst wenn die Begründer der Wertungsjurisprudenz (vgl. nur *H. Westermann*, Interessenkollisionen und ihre richterliche Wertung bei den Sicherungsrechten an Fahrnis und Forderungen, 1954) die Interessenjurisprudenz wegen der Vielgestaltigkeit des Interessenbegriffs nur „umtaufen" (*B. Rüthers*, Rechtstheorie, Rz. 532) wollten, würde das wissenschaftstheore-

vatrechtsordnung zueinander ins Verhältnis gesetzt werden.[162] Damit würde dem Rationalitätsanspruch Webers Rechnung getragen, so dass dies auch vor dem Hintergrund seiner im Werturteilsstreit eingenommenen Haltung nicht zu einer Ablehnung der Wertungsjurisprudenz führen müsste.

### c) Relevanz des Streits für die Rechtswissenschaft

Auch wenn die Methodenlehre Webers mit Selbstverständlichkeit nicht mit der juristischen Methodenlehre gleichgesetzt oder gar aus ihr erklärt werden kann, ist der Werturteilsstreit umgekehrt nicht folgenlos für die Dogmatik[163] und das Wissenschaftsverständnis der Jurisprudenz,[164] so dass die Problematik einen jener in der Einleitung angedeuteten Fälle betrifft, in denen die Jurisprudenz womöglich von der Methodenlehre Webers lernen kann.[165] So ist im rechtstheoretischen Schrifttum bereits darauf aufmerksam gemacht worden,[166] dass etwa im Medienrecht zwischen Tatsachenbehauptung und Werturteil unterschieden werden muss, weil letztere der Meinungsfreiheit unterfallen[167] und insoweit nicht gerichtlich überprüft werden.[168] Die Relevanz des Werturteils-

tisch nicht dagegen sprechen, den betreffenden Wandel ex post als Paradigmenwechsel zu verstehen (*J. Petersen*, Von der Interessenjurisprudenz, 2001, passim).

162 Das entspricht der Sache nach der pointierten These von *R. Stammler*, Theorie der Rechtswissenschaft, 1923, S. 15, wonach der Rechtsanwender einer einzelnen Vorschrift in Wahrheit das ganze Gesetz oder sogar die gesamte Rechtsordnung anwendet.

163 Siehe nur *F.-J. Säcker*, Grundprobleme der kollektiven Koalitionsfreiheit, 1969, S. 69 Anmerkung 198.

164 *E. Hilgendorf/L. Kuhlen*, Die Wertfreiheit der Jurisprudenz, 2000.

165 Siehe aber auch *K. Röhl*, Allgemeine Rechtslehre, 2. Auflage 2001, S. 153: „Die verbreitete Ablehnung von Webers Konzeption ist nicht zuletzt eine Folge der unglücklichen Benennung als ‚wertfreie' Wissenschaft. Sie (sc. die Jurisprudenz) hätte es verdient, eine *wertbewusste Wissenschaft* genannt zu werden." Hervorhebung auch dort.

166 *B. Rüthers*, Rechtstheorie, Rz. 110.

167 BGHZ 34, 99.

168 *J. Petersen*, Medienrecht, 4. Auflage 2008, § 7.

streits für die Jurisprudenz geht aber über solche Einzelheiten hinaus,[169] weil sie ihren Wissenschaftsanspruch betrifft. Immerhin geht es letztlich um nicht weniger als die Ermittlung wahrheitsfähiger Aussagen.[170] Das Meinungsspektrum zur Erörterung der Wertdebatte,[171] das hier nur angedeutet werden kann, reicht vom Verdikt der Unwissenschaftlichkeit[172] bis zur Annahme eines „relativen Relativismus",[173] der zwar nicht in eine Begründung der Werturteile mit wissenschaftlichem Anspruch eintritt,[174] wohl aber eine Kritik zulässt.[175] Auch und gerade unter Zugrundelegung der Wertfreiheit steht die Rechtswissenschaft vor der Herausforderung, im Wege der Systematisierung[176] die Reichweite normativer Aussagen gegenüber empirischen und deskriptiven[177] im Einzelfall klarzustellen.[178] Nicht zuletzt in der Lösung dieser Aufgabe im Zusammenwirken mit der rechtsphilosophischen Frage der Legitimation und Erhebung des normativen Geltungsanspruchs des

169 Siehe auch *K. Popper*, Philosophische Selbstinterpretation und Polemik gegen die Dialektiker, in: Verfall der Philosophie (Hg. C. Grossner), 1971, S. 278.

170 *B. Rüthers*, Rechtstheorie, Rz. 290c.

171 Wichtig in diesem Zusammenhang *B. Rüthers*, Rechtsordnung und Wertordnung, 1986, S. 19 ff.

172 *St. Strömholm*, Allgemeine Rechtslehre, 1976, S. 34.

173 Im Unterschied dazu *G. Radbruch*, Rechtsphilosophie, 5. Auflage 1956, S. 102: „Die hier dargelegte Methode nennt sich Relativismus, weil sie die Richtigkeit jedes Werturteils nur in Beziehung zu einem bestimmten obersten Werturteil, nur im Rahmen einer bestimmten Wert- und Weltanschauung, nicht aber die Richtigkeit dieses Werturteils, dieser Wert- und Weltanschauung selbst festzustellen sich zur Aufgabe gemacht hat."

174 *U. Klug*, Thesen zu einem kritischen Relativismus in der Rechtsphilosophie, Gedächtnisschrift für G. Radbruch, 1968, S. 103; *B. Rüthers*, Rechtstheorie, Rz. 290f; *A. Brecht*, Politische Theorie, 2. Auflage 1976, S. 139.

175 *H. Albert*, Kritischer Rationalismus und Dialektik der Revolution, in: Verfall der Philosophie (Hg. C. Grosser), 1971, S. 187.

176 Zu ihr unten § 3.

177 Zu ihrer Möglichkeit etwa *H. Eidenmüller*, Rechtswissenschaft als Realwissenschaft, JZ 1999, 53.

178 *B. Rüthers*, Rechtstheorie, Rz. 291. Siehe zur soziologischen und philosophischen Seite auch *J. R. Searle*, Die Konstruktion gesellschaftlicher Wirklichkeit, 1997.

Rechts[179] begründet sich der Wissenschaftsanspruch der Jurisprudenz, der daher nicht ein- für alle Mal herzustellen, sondern stetig zu verwirklichen ist.

### 4. Ökonomische Analyse des Rechts

Im Zusammenhang mit dem zuletzt Bedachten steht noch eine weitergehende Frage, nämlich die nach dem möglichen Einfluss ökonomischer Zusammenhänge, näherhin der ökonomischen Analyse des Rechts im Hinblick auf Webers Rechtsphilosophie. Obwohl das nachgelassene Werk mit Wirtschaft und Gesellschaft überschieben ist und Weber gerade in der zuletzt behandelten Stelle Rechts- und Wirtschaftsordnung einander gegenüberstellt,[180] bleibt im Folgenden die ökonomische Analyse des Rechts weitgehend außer Betracht.[181] Zwar berücksichtigt Weber die ökonomischen Gesichtspunkte stets mit,[182] erkennt ihnen aber in den wenigsten Fällen bestimmenden Einfluss zu, der über die vertrauensbildende Stabilisierung des Marktes durch Gewährleistung von Rechtssicherheit hinausgeht, wie folgender Gedanke stellvertre-

[179] *K. Larenz*, Richtiges Recht – Grundzüge einer Rechtsethik, 1979, S. 16, unter Betonung „der Frage nach der Rechtfertigung und damit nach dem normativen Geltungsanspruch des Rechts".

[180] *M. Weber*, Wirtschaft und Gesellschaft, S. 181.

[181] *R. A. Posner*, Economic Analysis of Law, 6. Auflage 2003 (zur normativen Fundierung *ders.*, Overcomming Law, 1995; *ders.*, Frontiers of Legal Theory, 2001; *ders.*, Law, Pragmatism, and Democracy, 2003) weiterhin *M. Adams*, Ökonomische Analyse der Gefährdungs- und Verschuldenshaftung, 1985; *H.-B. Schäfer/C. Ott*, Lehrbuch der ökonomischen Analyse des Zivilrechts, 4. Auflage 2004; *H. Eidenmüller*, Effizienz als Rechtsprinzip, 3. Auflage 2005; *C. Kirchner*, Ökonomische Theorie des Rechts, 1997; kritisch *K.-H. Fezer*, Aspekte einer Rechtskritik an der economic analysis of law und am property rights approach, JZ 1986, 817; siehe aus dem neueren Schrifttum auch *E.-J. Mestmäcker*, A Legal Theory without Law. Posner, v. Hayek on Economic Analysis of Law, 2008).

[182] Siehe nur *R. Swedberg*, Max Weber and the Idea of Economic Sociology, 1998.

tend zeigt: „Ökonomische Bedingungen haben dabei, sahen wir, überall sehr stark mitgespielt, aber niemals allein ausschlaggebend, wie sich später noch bei Besprechung der politischen Herrschaft zeigen wird. Soweit sie bei der Bildung der spezifisch modernen Züge des heutigen okzidentalen Rechts beteiligt waren,[183] lag die Richtung, in welcher sie wirkten, im Ganzen in Folgendem: Für die Gütermarktinteressenten bedeutete die Rationalisierung und Systematisierung des Rechts (...): zunehmende Berechenbarkeit des Funktionierens der Rechtspflege – eine der wichtigsten Vorbedingungen für ökonomische Dauerbetriebe, speziell solche kapitalistischer Art, welche ja der juristischen ‚Verkehrssicherheit' bedürfen."[184] Gewiss „analysiert" er das Recht mitunter ökonomisch, aber eher in einem geschichtlich geprägten beschreibenden Sinne und weniger auf die Weise, in der die ökonomische Analyse heute verfährt.[185] Damit ist nicht gesagt, dass Webers Rechtssoziologie nicht auch für die ökonomische Analyse des Rechts eine Herausforderung darstellen kann,[186] doch wäre dies Gegenstand einer anderen Abhandlung, zumal ihr Stellenwert für die juristische Methodenlehre noch nicht abschließend geklärt ist.[187]

[183] Siehe dazu *W. Schluchter*, Die Entwicklung des okzidentalen Rationalismus. Eine Analyse von Max Webers Gesellschaftsgeschichte, 1979; *ders.*, Rationalismus der Weltbeherrschung. Studien zu Max Weber, 1980; ferner *H. Treiber*, Die Geburt der Weberschen Rationalismus-These: Webers Bekanntschaft mit der russischen Geschichtsphilosophie in Heidelberg. Überlegungen anlässlich der Veröffentlichung des ersten Briefbandes der Max-Weber-Gesamtausgabe: Leviathan. Zeitschrift für Sozialwissenschaft 19 (1991), 435.

[184] *M. Weber*, Wirtschaft und Gesellschaft, S. 505.

[185] *F. Kübler*, Effizienz als Rechtsprinzip, Festschrift für E. Steindorff, 1990, S. 687; *H. Eidenmüller*, Der homo oeconomicus und das Schuldrecht: Herausforderungen durch Behavioral Law, JZ 2005, 216; *ders.*, Rechtsanwendung, Gesetzgebung und ökonomische Analyse, AcP 197 (1997) 145; *M. Adams*, Ökonomische Analyse der Gefährdungs- und Verschuldenshaftung, 1985.

[186] Vgl. nur *M. Weber*, Wirtschaft und Gesellschaft, S. 466.

[187] *Th. Mayer-Maly*, Rechtswissenschaft, 2. Auflage 1981, S. 129; *Prisching*, Ökonomische Rechtslehre?, Festschrift zur 200-Jahrfeier der Rechtswissen-

## IV. Rechtsordnung als empirische Geltung

In der parallelisierenden Gegenüberstellung von juristischer und soziologischer Betrachtungsweise, im Rahmen derer die Rechtsordnung mit dem „Kosmos" der Wirtschaftsordnung „nichts zu schaffen hat",[188] ist ein unüberbrückbarer Gegensatz angelegt,[189] der dem Unterschied zwischen Sein und Sollen entspricht[190] und daher vorderhand nur vermittels eines naturalistischen Fehlschlusses überwindbar scheint.[191]

### 1. Bedeutung des Begriffs der Rechtsordnung

Indes verhält es sich mit dieser Differenz weniger rigide, als es den Anschein hat: „Wenn nun trotzdem Wirtschafts- und Rechtsordnung in höchst intimen Beziehungen zueinander stehen, so ist eben diese letztere dabei nicht in juristischem, sondern in soziologischem Sinn verstanden: als *empirische* Geltung."[192] Diese Prämisse stellt in der Tat das Gesagte auf eine neue Grundlage: „Der Sinn des Wortes ‚Rechtsordnung' ändert sich dann völlig. Sie bedeutet dann nicht einen Kosmos logisch als ‚richtig' erschließ-

schaftlichen Fakultät in Graz, 1979, S. 995; *F. Bydlinski*, Juristische Methodenlehre und Rechtsbegriff, 2. Auflage, 1991, S. 331 f. *P. Raisch*, Juristische Methoden, 1995, S. 187 ff. Neuestens dazu *Grigoleit*, in: Rechtswissenschaftstheorie (Hg. O. Lepsius/M. Jestaedt), 2008, S. 64 f.

188 *M. Weber*, Wirtschaft und Gesellschaft, S. 181.

189 Vgl. auch *M. Weber*, Archiv für Sozialwissenschaft und Sozialpolitik 24, 1907, 94 ff.: „Diese empirischen ‚Regeln', welche die adäquate ‚Wirkung' der empirischen Geltung eines Rechtssatzes aussagen, sind, logisch betrachtet, natürlich die äußersten Antipoden jener dogmatischen ‚Regeln', welche als gedankliche ‚Konsequenz' ganz desselben Rechtssatzes, wenn er als Objekt der ‚Jurisprudenz' behandelt wird, entwickelt werden können."

190 *D. Hume*, Traktat über die menschliche Natur, deutsch von T. Lipps, 1906, II. Teil, S. 245.

191 Hierzu *M. Ludwig*, Sein und Sollen – Eine Untersuchung zur Abgrenzung der Rechtsnormen von den sozialen Normen bei Max Weber und Eugen Ehrlich, 1999.

192 *M. Weber*, Wirtschaft und Gesellschaft, S. 181.

barer Normen, sondern einen Komplex von faktischen Bestimmungsgründen realen menschlichen Handelns."[193] Dementsprechend ist Recht für Weber „eine ‚Ordnung' mit gewissen spezifischen Garantien für die Chance ihrer empirischen Geltung."[194] Dieses Verständnis der Rechtsordnung muss im Folgenden immer mitbedacht werden, wenn der Versuch unternommen wird, aus Bemerkungen Webers über das Recht und die Rechtsordnung Schlüsse auf Besonderheiten der juristischen Methodenlehre zu ziehen. Denn wenn sich Weber vordringlich mit der empirischen Geltung und nicht mit dem von ihm so genannten „Kosmos" der Rechtsdogmatik beschäftigt,[195] ist auch das Erkenntnisinteresse ein anderes, so dass Folgerungen nur in aller Vorsicht, das heißt mutatis mutandis, möglich sind.

## 2. Parallelgedanken in den wissenschaftstheoretischen Aufsätzen

Eine Ausprägung dieses Gedankens findet sich auch schon in seiner Analyse des Begriffs der „Regel":[196] „Aber nicht nur jenen empirischen Regelmäßigkeiten, sondern auch diese empirische ‚Existenz' des Rechts sind natürlich etwas absolut anderes als die juristische Idee eines ‚Gelten-Sollens'. Das empirische Gelten kommt ja dem ‚juristischen Irrtum' eventuell in genau dem gleichen Maße zu wie der ‚juristischen Wahrheit', und die Frage nach dem, was in concreto ‚juristische Wahrheit' ist, d. h. gedanklich nach ‚wissenschaftlichen' Grundsätzen als solche ‚gelten' solle oder hätte ‚gelten' sollen, ist logisch gänzlich verschieden von der: was de facto empirisch in einem ähnlichen Fall oder in einer Vielheit von Fällen als kausale ‚Folge' des ‚Geltens' eines bestimmten ‚Paragraphen' eingetreten ist."[197] Es ist von besonderem Interesse,

[193] *M. Weber*, Wirtschaft und Gesellschaft, S. 181.
[194] *M. Weber*, Wirtschaft und Gesellschaft, S. 182.
[195] *M. Weber*, Wirtschaft und Gesellschaft, S. 181.
[196] *M. Weber*, Archiv für Sozialwissenschaft und Sozialpolitik 24, 1907, 94.
[197] *M. Weber*, Archiv für Sozialwissenschaft und Sozialpolitik 24, 1907, 94 ff.

dass Weber, wenn auch in der für ihn typischen Weise in Anführungsstrichen, den Begriff der juristischen Wahrheit voraussetzt, der wiederum nichts mit der bereits angesprochenen „one right answer-Thesis" zu tun haben dürfte.[198] Wahrheit bezeichnet vielmehr dasjenige, was sich wissenschaftlich in einem geordneten dogmatischen Verfahren herausarbeiten lässt. Dieser Gedanke findet sich im Übrigen mit anderen Worten, aber ebenfalls unter Rückgriff auf die wissenschaftliche Orthodoxie und die im Hintergrund stehende Wahrheitsfrage bei Nietzsche,[199] worauf hier allerdings nicht näher eingegangen werden kann.[200] Für den vorliegenden Zusammenhang ist immerhin interessant, dass sich Nietzsche an der betreffenden Stelle mit der wissenschaftlichen Methode in einer Weise auseinandersetzt,[201] die gerade auch auf die juristische Methode zutrifft.[202]

Vor diesem Hintergrund ist auch die Folgerung Webers bemerkenswert: „Die Rechtsregel ist in dem einen Fall eine ideale gedanklich erschließbare Norm, im anderen Fall ist sie eine empirisch, als mehr oder minder konsequent und häufig befolgt, feststellbare Maxime des Verhaltens konkreter Menschen. Eine ‚Rechtsordnung' gliedert sich in dem einen Fall in ein System von Gedanken und Begriffe, welches der wissenschaftliche Rechtsdogmatiker als Wertmaßstab benützt, um das faktische Verhalten gewisser Menschen: der ‚Richter', ‚Advokaten', der ‚Delinquenten', ‚Staatsbürger' usw. daran, juristisch wertend, zu messen und als der idealen Norm entsprechend oder nicht entsprechend anzuerkennen oder zu verwerfen (...)."[203] In diesem Parallelgedanken, der im Übrigen die Einheit und innere Folgerichtigkeit des Weber-

198 *R. Dworkin*, The Law's Empire, 1986; *ders.*, Taking Rights Seriously, 1977 (Bürgerrechte ernstgenommen, 1984, S. 122 ff., 145 ff.).

199 *F. Nietzsche*, Menschliches, Allzumenschliches, I, 635.

200 *J. Petersen*, Nietzsches Genialität der Gerechtigkeit, 2008, S. 12 f.

201 *F. Nietzsche*, Menschliches, Allzumenschliches, I, 635.

202 *J. Petersen*, Nietzsches Genialität der Gerechtigkeit, 2008, S. 16 f.

203 *M. Weber*, Archiv für Sozialwissenschaft und Sozialpolitik 24 (1907), S. 94 ff.

schen Denkens veranschaulicht, wie es sich insbesondere in den Aufsätzen enthüllt,[204] sind zugleich einige Leitmotive der Rechtssoziologie angesprochen, namentlich die Rolle der Logik und Rationalität, von denen im Folgenden näher die Rede sein soll.

204 *D. Henrich*, Die Einheit der Wissenschaftslehre Max Webers, 1952, S. 2, wonach „der Sammelband der Aufsätze nicht nur (...) Einzelanalysen und Meinungen eines Spezialforschers versammelt, sondern eine theoretische Einheit ausdrückt, deren Geschlossenheit um so mehr in Verwunderung setzt, weil sie nicht offen sichtbar und vielleicht nicht einmal Max Weber selbst bewusst ist". Zu diesem Gedanken, dessen Richtigkeit sich hier beispielhaft entfaltet, bereits oben im Text.

## § 2 Rationalität des Rechts

Einer der großen Verdienste der Rechtssoziologie Webers ist es, die Rationalität des Rechts in den Vordergrund gestellt zu haben. Die Rationalität der Rechtsfindung ist für das Wissenschaftsverständnis der Jurisprudenz ersichtlich von besonderer Bedeutung. Denn mit der Rationalität der juristischen Begründung[205] und ihrer Methodengerechtigkeit hängt auch der Wissenschaftsanspruch der Jurisprudenz zusammen. Davon wird am Ende der Abhandlung noch die Rede sein.[206] Auch im Übrigen zeichnet sich die Wissenschaft nach Weber durch „intellektualistische Rationalisierung"[207] aus, so dass dieser Schlüsselbegriff seines Denkens[208] hier im Mittelpunkt stehen soll. In der einschlägigen Forschungsdiskussion wird uneinheitlich beurteilt, ob Rationalität und Rationalisierung die beherrschende Thematik seines Denkens darstellen.[209] Diese Frage kann hier auf sich beruhen, weil jedenfalls für das Verhältnis zur juristischen Methodenlehre zur Rechtssoziologie die Rationalität diejenige Eigenschaft der Rechtsfindung darstellt, die für den vorliegenden Zusammenhang von besonderem

[205] Zu ihr auch *C. v. Mettenheim*, Rationalität und Recht, 1984.

[206] Unter § 5.

[207] *M. Weber*, Wissenschaft als Beruf, Geistige Arbeit als Beruf. Vier Vorträge vor dem Freistudentischen Bund, 1919, in: Gesammelte Aufsätze zur Wissenschaftslehre, 7. Auflage 1988, S. 582, 593 f.

[208] Siehe nur *T. Parsons*, Rationalität und der Prozess der Rationalisierung im Denken Max Webers, in: Max Weber und die Rationalisierung sozialen Handelns (Hg. W. Sprondel/C. Seyfarth), 1981, S. 81; *W. Schluchter*, Rationalismus und Weltbeherrschung. Studien zu Max Weber, 1980; *ders.*, Die Entstehung des modernen Rationalismus. Eine Analyse von Max Webers Entwicklungsgeschichte des Okzidents, 1998; *ders.*, Die Paradoxie der Rationalisierung. Zum Verhältnis von „Ethik" und „Welt" bei Max Weber, Zeitschrift für Soziologie 5 (1976) 256; *M. R. Lepsius*, Interessen, Ideen und Institutionen, 1977, S. 44 ff.

[209] *H.-P. Müller*, Max Weber, 2007, S. 19 ff. m.w.N.

Interesse ist. Dementsprechend hat sich auch das bisherige Schrifttum weitgehend auf die Rationalität und Rationalisierung fokussiert.[210]

## I. Rechtsfindung und Rechtsschöpfung

Bevor dies im Einzelnen unternommen wird, sei diejenige Unterscheidung vorangestellt, auf der Webers folgende Ausführungen gründen.[211] Es geht um die Differenzierung zwischen Rechtsschöpfung und Rechtsfindung, die zugleich auch die Bestimmung der nachfolgend interessierenden Rechtssätze einschließt.

### 1. Ableitung rationaler Rechtssätze

Mit seinen eigenen Worten lautet sie:[212] „Unter ‚Rechtsschöpfung' stellen wir uns heute die Satzung genereller Normen vor, deren jede in der Sprache der Juristen den Charakter eines oder mehrerer rationaler ‚Rechtssätze' annimmt. Und die ‚Rechtsfindung' denken wir uns als ‚Anwendung' jener gesatzten Normen und der

[210] Monographisch dazu *St. Uecker*, Die Rationalisierung des Rechts. Max Webers Rechtssoziologie, 2005, S. 63 ff.; *S. Aechtner*, Die Rationalität in der Rechts- und Herrschaftssoziologie Max Webers. Eine Textanalyse, 1995; zur Rationalisierungsproblematik des modernen Rechts auch *K. Eder*, in: W. Sprondel/C. Seyfarth (Hg.), Max Weber und die Rationalisierung sozialen Handelns, 1981, S. 157; *A. Febbrajo*, Kapitalismus, moderner Staat und rational-formales Recht, in: M. Rehbinder/K.-P. Tieck (Hg.), Max Weber als Rechtssoziologe, 1987, S. 55; *J. Freund*, Die Rationalisierung des Rechts nach Max Weber, in: Max Weber als Rechtssoziologe (Hg. M. Rehbinder, K.-P. Tieck), 1987, S. 9; *K. Eder*, Zur Rationalisierungsproblematik des modernen Rechts, Soziale Welt 1978, S. 247; *A. Somek*, Rationalität und Diskriminierung. Zur Bindung der Gesetzgebung an das Gleichheitsrecht, 2001.

[211] Zur Verbindung mit der zuletzt (unter § 1) behandelten Wertfreiheit siehe *M. Hartmann*, Formale Rationalität und Wertfreiheit bei Max Weber, Zeitschrift für Soziologie 17 (1988) 102.

[212] Aus diesem Grund werden die meisten Gedanken Webers im Folgenden weitgehend wörtlich wiedergegeben.

durch die Arbeit des juristischen Denkens aus ihnen abzuleitenden einzelnen ‚Rechtssätze' auf konkrete ‚Tatbestände', welche unter sie subsumiert werden."[213]

## a) Zweckrationale Vereinbarungen

Diese Definitionen entsprechen cum grano salis der dogmatischen Arbeit,[214] so dass die im Folgenden hierzu in Beziehung zu setzende juristische Methodenlehre von derselben Terminologie bezüglich der Rechtsfindung ausgeht und eine Übertragung der Einsichten nicht an der jeweiligen Fachdiktion scheitert.[215] Gleichwohl muss natürlich im Blick gehalten werden, dass etwa der Bedeutungsgehalt der Rechtsschöpfung variieren kann, je nachdem, ob es um die Rechtssoziologie geht, bei der sich die Frage stellen kann, wie überhaupt Recht entsteht, oder ob eine konkrete Frage der juristischen Methodenlehre in Rede steht, bei der man sich von vornherein auf der normativen Ebene befindet. Andernfalls ist auch hier und nicht nur in der Rechtsphilosophie die Gefahr naturalistischer Fehlschlüsse im Blick zu halten, bei denen von einem Sein auf ein Sollen geschlossen wird.[216] Zu den primären Quellen der Rechtsnormbildung gehört für Weber auch „das Typischwerden bestimmter Einverständnisse und vor allem: zweckrationaler Vereinbarungen, welche das Handeln der Einzelnen zunehmend bewusst schafft,[217] indem sie ihre Interessensphären gegeneinander, unter Mithilfe des geschulten ‚Anwalts' abgrenzen."[218] Hier begegnet zugleich – und nicht von ungefähr im Zu-

[213] *M. Weber*, Wirtschaft und Gesellschaft, S. 394.

[214] Es ist nicht zuletzt das immer wieder aufgegriffene (vgl. nur *N. Luhmann*, Rechtssystem und Rechtsdogmatik, 1974, S. 18) und auf *K. Engisch* (Logische Studien, 3. Auflage 1963, S. 15) zurückgehende Wort vom „Hin- und Herwandern des Blickes."

[215] Vgl. nur *J. Neuner*, Die Rechtsfindung contra legem, 1992.

[216] Bezüglich eines konkreten Problems *J. Petersen*, Medienrecht, 4. Auflage 2008, § 1 Rz. 11; gegen *L. Lessig*, Code and other Law of Cyberspace, 1999.

[217] Zur Rationalisierung des Handelns instruktiv die Zusammenfassung von *M. R. Lepsius*, Interessen, Ideen und Institutionen, 1977, S. 48.

[218] *M. Weber*, Wirtschaft und Gesellschaft, S. 445.

sammenhang mit der Rationalität – der Gesichtspunkt der Typizität, von dem noch näher die Rede sein wird.[219]

### b) Mitwirkung gefühlsmäßiger Determinanten

Rechtsschöpfung und Rechtsfindung können nach Weber auf rationale oder irrationale Weise verfahren.[220] Beide unterscheidet er nochmals danach, ob sie formell oder materiell (ir-)rational vorgehen.[221] Im Folgenden interessiert vor allem die rationale Vorgehensweise, weil die Rationalität des Rechts gerade die Eigenschaft ist, die auch der juristischen Methodenlehre gemäß sein muss. Webers Verständnis und Ausarbeitung der Rationalität ist freilich nicht unumstritten. So gibt Luhmann zu bedenken, dass „vor allem eine von der Einzelhandlung ablösbare Konzeption gesellschaftlicher Rationalität fehlt."[222] Aber dies kann entsprechend dem in der Einleitung Vorangestellten für den vorliegenden Zusammenhang auf sich beruhen.

Dagegen dürfen die irrationalen Momente, wie vor allem die von Weber so genannte „Mitwirkung ‚gefühlsmäßiger' Determinanten", nicht ausgeblendet werden, weil sie für die Rechtsbildung nicht ganz folgenlos ist. In der Tat hat auch die juristische Methodenlehre dem Rechtsgefühl seit jeher besondere Bedeutung beigemessen.[223] Es ist eine der besonderen Herausforderungen der juris-

219 Unter § 5.

220 Den Versuch eines wissenschaftstheoretischen Modells rationaler juristischer Begründung unternimmt *D. Buchwald*, Der Begriff der rationalen juristischen Begründung: Zur Theorie der juridischen Vernunft, 1990, mit dem Postulat teils formaler, teils inhaltlicher, teils normativ praktischer und teils empirisch deskriptiver Bedingungen; siehe auch *dens.*, Die canones der Auslegung und rationale juristische Begründung, ARSP 1993, 16. Siehe ferner *M. Herberger/D. Simon*, Wissenschaftstheorie für Juristen, 1980.

221 *M. Weber*, Wirtschaft und Gesellschaft, S. 396 f.

222 *N. Luhmann*, Rechtssoziologie, 3. Auflage 1987, S. 17 f. Siehe auch *W. Schluchter*, Handlung, Ordnung und Kultur. Studien zu einem Forschungsprogramm im Anschluss an Max Weber, 2005.

223 *R. v. Jhering*, Über die Entstehung des Rechtsgefühles (mit einer Vorbemerkung und einem anschließenden Interpretations- und Einordnungsver-

tischen Methodenlehre, das Vorverständnis des Entscheidenden von der Methode abzugrenzen,[224] womit nicht zuletzt der Rolle des Rechtsgefühls eine unleugbare Rolle zukommt.[225] Jedoch relativiert Weber diese notwendige Mitwirkung sogleich: „Aber die Beobachtung lehrt, wie außerordentlich labil das ‚Rechtsgefühl' funktioniert, soweit ihm nicht das feste Pragma einer äußeren und inneren, Interessenlage die Bahn weist."[226] Das dürfte sich nicht zuletzt gegen Eugen Ehrlichs Gefühlstheorie wenden, wonach Empörung und Entrüstung den Verletzungen von Rechts- bzw. Sittenregeln folgt.[227]

### c) Rechtssoziologie und Interessenjurisprudenz

An dieser Einschätzung ist vor allem der Rekurs auf die Interessenlage interessant, der an sich aus Sicht der Interessenjurisprudenz den Ausschlag gibt. Das ist umso bemerkenswerter, als einer ihrer herausragenden Vertreter, Max Rümelin, in einer Arbeit über das Rechtsgefühl zu bedenken gegeben hat, dass es bei guten

such von O. Behrends, 1986, S. 55–184); *E. Riezler*, Das Rechtsgefühl, 3. Auflage 1969; *H. Hubmann*, Naturrecht und Rechtsgefühl, AcP 153 (1954) 297; *R. Müller-Erzbach*, Gefühl oder Vernunft als Rechtsquelle?, ZHR 73 (1913) 429; *F. Kübel*, Das Rechtsgefühl, 1913; *A. Ehrenzweig*, Zur Phänomenologie und Psychoanalyse der Rechtswissenschaft, Festschrift für G. Husserl, 1969, S. 65; *G. Radbruch*, Über das Rechtsgefühl, Die Tat 6 (1914/15) 337; aus dem amerikanischen Schrifttum *J. Goldstein*, Psychoanalysis and Jurisprudence, Yale Law Journal 77 (1968) 1053.

224 Grundlegend *J. Esser*, Vorverständnis und Methodenwahl in der Rechtsfindung. Rationalitätsgarantien der richterlichen Entscheidungspraxis, 2. Auflage 1972. Aus dem angloamerikanischen Schrifttum *J. Frank*, Law and the Mind, 1930; *U. Moore/G. Sussman*, Legal and Institutional Methods, Yale Law Journal 40 (1930/31) 381; *dies.*, The Lawyer's Law, Yale Law Journal 41 (1931/32) 566.

225 *P. Raisch*, Juristische Methoden, 1995, S. 207: „Anklänge an das ‚Vorverständnis' Essers sind unverkennbar."

226 *M. Weber*, Wirtschaft und Gesellschaft, S. 445.

227 *E. Ehrlich*, Grundlegung der Soziologie des Rechts, 1913; 3. Auflage 1967, S. 131; dazu *H. Rottleuthner*, Ungerechtigkeiten. Anmerkungen zur westlichen Leidkultur, 2008, S. 5 mit Fußnote 3.

Juristen auf den im „Gedächtnisschatz" bewahrten „abgekürzten Denkvorgängen" gründet.[228] Das läuft auf einen vergleichsweise rationalen Erklärungsversuch des emotionalen Moments hinaus, der bei unbefangener Betrachtung eher Weber zugeordnet werden könnte, während seine Betonung der Interessenlage prima vista für die Interessenjurisprudenz kennzeichnend wäre. Hieran zeigt sich, wenngleich in einer paradox anmutenden Umkehrung, das in der Einleitung vorausgesetzte Näheverhältnis zwischen Webers Rechtssoziologie und der Interessenjurisprudenz.

## 2. Gewohnheitsrecht

Rechtsregeln können allerdings auch durch Gewohnheitsrecht,[229] mit Webers Worten „nichtgesatztes" Recht[230] – entstehen.[231] Er knüpft die Entstehung des Gewohnheitsrechts an die Voraussetzungen der tatsächlichen gemeinsamen Übung, der gemeinsamen Überzeugung von der Rechtsmäßigkeit sowie der Rationabilität[232] und befindet sich zumindest hinsichtlich der beiden ersten Momente im Einklang mit der noch heute vorherrschenden Doktrin in der juristischen Methodenlehre.[233] Bereits der Begriff der „Rationabilität" lässt indes etwas Eigenständiges aufscheinen, das zu dem soeben Behandelten passt. So stammt von Weber die

[228] *M. Rümelin*, Rechtsgefühl und Rechtsbewusstsein, 1925.

[229] Skeptisch *M. Weber*, Wirtschaft und Gesellschaft, S. 187 („Diesen wenig brauchbaren Begriff selbst kritisieren wir hier nicht."). Zur „Derogation durch Gewohnheitsrecht", von der „der Rechtsdogmatiker spricht", *M. Weber*, Wirtschaft und Gesellschaft, S. 195.

[230] *M. Weber*, Wirtschaft und Gesellschaft, S. 441.

[231] Aus dem älteren Schrifttum *Mokre*, Theorie des Gewohnheitsrechts, 1932. Siehe auch *J. Esser*, Richterrecht, Gerichtsgebrauch und Gewohnheitsrecht, Festschrift v. Hippel, 1967, S. 95.

[232] *M. Weber*, Wirtschaft und Gesellschaft, S. 441.

[233] *K. Larenz*, Methodenlehre der Rechtswissenschaft, 6. Auflage 1991, S. 345 ff.; *F. Bydlinski*, Juristische Methodenlehre und Rechtsbegriff, 2. Auflage 1991, S. 215. Aus rechtstheoretischer Sicht ferner *H. L. A. Hart*, Der Begriff des Rechts, 1973, S. 69; *H. Kelsen*, Reine Rechtslehre, 2. Auflage 1960, S. 231 ff.

Beobachtung, dass alles Gewohnheitsrecht bei Licht besehen Juristenrecht darstellt,[234] eine Erkenntnis die auch im rechtstheoretischen Schrifttum hervorgehoben wird.[235]

Allerdings zeigt sich hier paradigmatisch, wie Weber gerade auf dem Boden der zivilrechtsdogmatischen Vorüberlegungen von Zitelmann und Gierke fortschreitet[236] und den Begriff des Gewohnheitsrechts gegen die Rechtssoziologen in Schutz nimmt:[237] „Auf juristischem Gebiet ist der heftige Kampf der Rechtssoziologen (Lambert, Ehrlich) gegen ihn m. E. durchaus unbegründet und bedeutet, wenn es sich um die uns hier beschäftigende Frage handelt: inwieweit die überkommene juristische Konstruktion der Geltungsbedingungen des ‚Gewohnheitsrechts' etwas Richtiges über die *faktische* Entstehung der empirischen ‚Geltung' nicht durch Satzung geschaffenen Rechts aussage."[238] Man kann hieran beispielhaft ermessen, wie sehr Weber von der juristischen Methodenlehre seiner Zeit ausgegangen ist und wie vergleichsweise wenig ihn eine spezifisch und ausschließlich rechtssoziologische Betrachtungsweise ansprach, wie sie etwa von Eugen Ehrlich vorgestellt wurde.[239]

234 *M. Weber*, Wirtschaft und Gesellschaft, S. 508; er geht vom „halbmystischen Begriff" des Gewohnheitsrechts aus.

235 *B. Rüthers*, Rechtstheorie, 3. Auflage 2007, Rz. 233.

236 *M. Weber*, Wirtschaft und Gesellschaft, S. 441: „Auch alle seine heute üblichen Definitionen gelten als juristische Konstruktion. Für diese ist allerdings der Begriff in der sublimierten Form, die etwa Zitelmann oder auch Gierke ihm gegeben haben, nicht entbehrlich, es sei denn durch die Beschränkung des nicht statuarischen Rechts auf bindende Prinzipien." Bezüglich des Erstgenannten könnte ihm insbesondere vor Augen gestanden haben *E. Zitelmann*, Lücken im Recht, 1903.

237 Aus dem modernen Schrifttum ist insoweit zu nennen *Bechtler*, Der soziologische Rechtsbegriff, 1977.

238 *M. Weber*, Wirtschaft und Gesellschaft, S. 441; Hervorhebung auch dort.

239 *E. Ehrlich*, Freie Rechtsfindung und freie Rechtswissenschaft, 1903; *ders.*, Grundlegung der Soziologie des Rechts, Band 1, 1913.

## II. Entwicklung und „Herausläuterung" von Rechtssätzen

Der Grad der Rationalität ist für Weber bestimmend für die formellen Qualitäten des Rechts.[240] Innerhalb der Weber-Forschung herrscht Streit darüber, ob und inwieweit Weber „formell" und „formal"[241] respektive „materiell" und „material" unterscheidet.[242] Doch sind die Ergebnisse und Unterschiede dieser anspruchsvoll geführten Kontroverse für den vorliegenden Zusammenhang arm an Ertrag.[243] Wichtig ist nur, dass die Antinomie zwischen formaler und materialer Rationalität zur Geltung kommt,[244] womit die Rationalität die der Entscheidung dienlichen Rechtssätze hervorbringen kann: „Zunächst: im Sinne der (scheinbar) elementarsten Denkmanipulation: des Generalisierens, was in diesem Fall bedeutet: der Reduktion der für die Entscheidung des Einzelfalls maßgebenden Gründe auf ein oder mehrere ‚Prinzipien'."[245]

[240] *M. Weber,* Wirtschaft und Gesellschaft, S. 395.

[241] Zur formalen Rationalität und Wertfreiheit bei Weber *M. Hartmann*, Zeitschrift für Soziologie 17 (1988) 102.

[242] Vgl. nur *B. K. Quensel*, Logik und Methode in der ‚Rechtssoziologie' Max Webers, Zeitschrift für Rechtssoziologie 18 (1997) 146; *W. Schluchter*, Die Entstehung des modernen Rationalismus. Eine Analyse von Max Webers Entwicklungsgeschichte des Okzidents, 1998, S. 191; *St. Uecker*, Die Rationalisierung des Rechts. Max Webers Rechtssoziologie, 2005, S. 71 f.; *B. Peters*, Rationalität, Recht und Gesellschaft, 1991, 114. Instruktiv *H. Rottleuthner*, Einführung in die Rechtssoziologie, 1987, S. 23.

[243] Vgl. *N. Luhmann*, Rechtssoziologie, 3. Auflage 1987, S. 17: „Was damit gemeint ist, ergibt sich nicht zureichend aus den etikettierenden Begriffen ‚formal' und ‚material'. Man könnte mit diesen Kennzeichnungen ebensogut eine Gegentendenz behaupten, die im zunehmenden Abbau ritualistischer Formalismen zugunsten eines materiell-elastischen, an unvorhersehbare Situationen besser anpassbaren Rechts bestehe."

[244] *M. R. Lepsius*, Ideen, Interessen und Institutionen, 1977, S. 26.

[245] *M. Weber*, Wirtschaft und Gesellschaft, S. 395.

## 1. Reduktion auf Prinzipien

Diese Prinzipien nennt er Rechtssätze.[246] An dieser Prämisse ist zweierlei bemerkenswert. Zum einen kontrastiert sie ersichtlich mit der eingangs dargestellten Vorgehensweise des Laien, der Weber zufolge nur vom Einzelnen auf das Einzelne schließt,[247] dem mithin der Akt des Generalisierens und Abstrahierens fremd ist, weil ihm die Kenntnis fehlt, den Sachverhalt auf das rechtlich Wesentliche zu reduzieren. Hier scheint zugleich ein Moment auf, das in der Soziologie im Allgemeinen und der Rechtssoziologie im Besonderen seit Luhmann[248] eine tragende Rolle gespielt hat, nämlich die „Reduktion von Komplexität."[249] Den Begriff der Reduktion präzisiert Weber wie folgt: „Diese Reduktion ist normalerweise bedingt durch eine vorhergehende oder gleichzeitige Analyse des Tatbestandes auf diejenigen letzten Bestandteile hin, welche für die rechtliche Beurteilung in Betracht kommen."[250]

[246] Allgemein *F. Hilterhaus*, Zum Rechtsbegriff in der Soziologie Max Webers, 1965.

[247] *M. Weber*, Wirtschaft und Gesellschaft, S. 510.

[248] Außer den bisher zitierten Schriften sind zu nennen *N. Luhmann*, Grundrechte als Institution. Ein Beitrag zur politischen Soziologie, 1965; *ders.*, Legitimation durch Verfahren, 1969; *ders.*, Systemtheoretische Beiträge zur Rechtstheorie, Jahrbuch für Rechtssoziologie und Rechtstheorie 2 (1972) 255; *ders.*, Gerechtigkeit in den Rechtssystemen der modernen Gesellschaft, Rechtstheorie 4 (1973) 131: Gerechtigkeit als „adäquate Komplexität des Rechtssystems"; dazu *R. Dreier*, Zu Luhmanns systemtheoretischer Neuformulierung des Gerechtigkeitsproblems, Rechtstheorie 5 (1974) 189 (dazu wiederum *N. Luhmann*, Rechtstheorie 5, 1974, 201).

[249] Grundlegend *N. Luhmann*, Zweckbegriff und Systemrationalität: Über die Funktion von Zwecken in sozialen Systemen, 1968, S. 180 ff., Siehe dazu auch *K. F. Röhl*, Das Dilemma der Rechtstatsachenforschung, S. 76. Kritisch zum Komplexitätsbegriff *J. Habermas*, in: ders./Luhmann, Systemtheorie – Gesellschaftstheorie oder Sozialtechnologie, 1971, S. 146 ff. *W. Fikentscher*, Methoden des Rechts, Band III, 1977, S. 399 Fußnote 123, gibt zu bedenken, dass gegen den Komplexitätsbegriff Luhmanns derselbe Einwand erhoben werden kann, wie ihn *K. Larenz*, Methodenlehre der Rechtswissenschaft, S. 176 f., gegen Luhmanns Legitimationsbegriff ins Feld geführt hat, nämlich dass er gleichermaßen im faktischen wie im normativen Sinne verwendet wird, wobei freilich, wie *Fikentscher* zugibt, „die Trennung zwischen Sein und Sollen in seinem Theoriegebäude einen ganz anderen Platz einnimmt".

[250] *M. Weber*, Wirtschaft und Gesellschaft, S. 395.

Hier zeichnet sich bereits ab, dass die Rationalisierung auf ihrer ersten Stufe nichts anderes ist als ordnende Systematisierung unter größtmöglicher Reduktion des Rechtsstoffes. Es geht Weber also um die „Systematisierung und in diesem Sinn: Rationalisierung des Rechtsstoffes."[251] Für die juristische Methodenlehre bedeutsam ist in diesem Zusammenhang die Gleichsetzung der Rechtssätze mit den von Weber so genannten Prinzipien.[252] Auch wenn diese Prinzipien nicht dasselbe sind, wie diejenigen, die als gesetzgeberische Basissätze die Privatrechtsordnung durchwirken[253] und damit den Boden für die heute vorherrschende Wertungsjurisprudenz bilden,[254] ist auf einer anderen Ebene doch Entsprechendes gemeint. Der Unterschied besteht nur darin, dass die Prinzipienermittlung in der juristischen Methodenlehre auf der Ebene der Privatrechtsordnung selbst angesiedelt ist, während Weber zunächst ganz allgemein von der Sachverhaltebene ausgeht und beschreibt, wie von dieser aus die normative Ebene erreicht werden kann. Aber das ist bei Licht betrachtet die ursprüngliche Herausforderung der juristischen Methodenlehre.

[251] *M. Weber*, Wirtschaft und Gesellschaft, S. 490. Vgl. auch *J. Freund*, Die Rationalisierung des Rechts nach Max Weber, in: Max Weber als Rechtssoziologe (Hg. M. Rehbinder/K.-P. Tieck), 1987, S. 9; *G. Schöllgen*, Max *Webers* Anliegen. Rationalisierung als Forderung und Hypothek, 1985. Siehe ferner *J. Habermas*, Theorie des kommunikativen Handelns. Band 1: Handlungsrationalität und gesellschaftliche Rationalisierung, 1981.

[252] *P. Landau*, Die Rechtsquellenlehre in der deutschen Rechtswissenschaft des 19. Jahrhunderts, in: Juristische Theoriebildung und Rechtliche Einheit, Rättshistorika Studier (Hg. C. Petterson), Band XIX, 1993, S. 69, hat in einer auch für die vorliegende Fragestellung fruchtbaren Weise darauf aufmerksam gemacht, dass die frühe Begriffsjurisprudenz durchaus Züge einer von ihm treffend so genannten „Prinzipienjurisprudenz" trägt. Darauf wird noch zurückzukommen sein.

[253] Grundlegend *C.-W. Canaris*, Systemdenken und Systembegriff in der Jurisprudenz, 2. Auflage 1983.

[254] *E. Meyer*, Grundzüge einer systemorientierten Wertungsjurisprudenz, 1984; *H. Westermann*, Wesen und Grenzen der richterlichen Streitentscheidung im Zivilrecht, 1955; *J. Petersen*, Von der Interessenjuriprudenz zur Wertungsjurisprudenz, 2001, passim.

## 2. Denkmanipulation (Weber) und Denkökonomie (Mach)

Hier – wie an vielen anderen Stellen seiner Rechtssoziologie[255] – sind Webers Ausführungen unverkennbar die eines Juristen,[256] der zwar die Grenzen seiner ursprünglichen Profession überschritten,[257] aber nie den Blick für ihre immanenten Hindernisse und Schwierigkeiten verloren hat, etwa wenn er im Rahmen der Rechtsanwendung von der „(scheinbar) elementarsten Denkmanipulation" spricht,[258] die in der Praxis nicht selten schwierigste ist.[259] Zum anderen hängt damit zusammen, dass dieses die Komplexität des Einzelfalles reduzierende Vorgehen, wenn es methodengerecht erfolgt, zugleich in einem Näheverhältnis zur juristischen Theoriebildung steht.[260] Erinnert sei in diesem Zusammenhang wegen Webers auffälligen Begriffs der „Denkmanipulation" an Ernst Machs Definition der Theorie als die Zusammenfassung von Beobachtungen unter dem Prinzip der Denkökonomie,[261] der

[255] Vgl. *M. Weber*, Wirtschaft und Gesellschaft, S. 426 f.

[256] Ein anderes Beispiel bilden die Ausführungen (*M. Weber*, Wirtschaft und Gesellschaft, S. 433) zur Genossenschaftstheorie Otto von Gierkes.

[257] *H. N. Fügen*, Max Weber, S. 98: „Max Weber, der Ausbildung nach Jurist, der Berufstätigkeit nach bisher Ökonom, muss sich ab 1909 als Soziologe verstanden haben."

[258] *M. Weber*, Wirtschaft und Gesellschaft, S. 395.

[259] Aus der juristischen Methodenlehre *J. Hruschka*, Die Konstitution des Rechtsfalles. Studien zum Verhältnis von Tatsachenfeststellung und Rechtsanwendung, 1965.

[260] Zu ihr *C.-W. Canaris*, Funktion, Struktur und Falsifikation juristischer Theorien, JZ 1993, 377.

[261] Dazu *W. Heisenberg*, Der Teil und das Ganze. Gespräche im Umkreis der Atomphysik, 1969, 13. Auflage 1993, S. 81 ff., der von einem Gespräch mit Albert Einstein berichtet, der das Kriterium der Denkökonomie in einer auch für den vorliegenden Zusammenhang interessanten (weil die Einfachheit der Darstellung betreffenden) Weise kritisiert hat, indem er zu bedenken gab, dass Machs „Begriff der Einfachheit so einen verdächtig kommerziellen Charakter: Denkökonomie" erhalte (vgl. *W. Heisenberg*, Der Teil und das Ganze, S. 82). Aus dem neueren Schrifttum *R. Goeres*, Sensualistischer Phänomenalismus und Denkökonomie. Zur Wissenschaftskonzeption Ernst Machs, Journal for General Philosophy of Science, 35 (2004) 41.

auch für die juristische Methodenlehre bedeutsam ist. Die von Weber bezeichnete „Denkmanipulation" ist zwar nicht gleichbedeutend mit Machs „Denkökonomie", doch läuft beides auf dasselbe hinaus, weil es Weber ungeachtet des Wortlauts nicht um eine Verfälschung des Denkens geht, sondern vielmehr darum, das Denken um der Effizienz willen in die zielführende Richtung zu lenken, die im konkreten Einzelfall das allgemeine Prinzip erblickt – ein genuin juristisches Verfahren.

## III. Analytische Gewinnung von Rechtssätzen

Eingangs wurde hervorgehoben, dass Weber mit der Reduktion auf Prinzipien eine Gesetzmäßigkeit herausgestellt hat, die mutatis mutandis auch für die juristische Methodenlehre gilt.[262] Methodisch wichtiger noch als diese Einsicht ist vielleicht die Erkenntnis Webers, dass dieser Funktionszusammenhang nicht nur in einer Richtung besteht, sondern die Prinzipien – gleichsam *vice versa* – sich auf die Einschätzung der Besonderheiten der jeweiligen Sachverhalte auswirken können: „Und umgekehrt wirkt die Herausläuterung immer weiterer ‚Rechtssätze' wieder auf die Abgrenzung der einzelnen, möglicherweise relevanten Merkmale der Tatbestände zurück: sie beruht auf Kasuistik und fördert sie ihrerseits."[263] „Merkmale der Tatbestände" bedeutet in diesem Zusammenhang offenbar gerade nicht Tatbestandsmerkmale im Rechtssinne, sondern die Besonderheiten der Sachverhalte, ist also weniger normativ als vielmehr faktisch gemeint und entspricht somit dem, was Weber weiter oben mit dem Unterschied zwischen der juristischen und soziologischen Betrachtungsweise angesprochen hat.[264]

[262] Unter a). Siehe auch *C.-W. Canaris*, Systemdenken und Systembegriff in der Jurisprudenz, 2. Auflage 1983, passim.
[263] *M. Weber*, Wirtschaft und Gesellschaft, S. 395.
[264] *M. Weber*, Wirtschaft und Gesellschaft, S. 181 f.

## 1. Wechselwirkung zwischen Prinzipien und Tatbestandsmerkmalen

Die Beobachtung dieser möglichen Wechselwirkung ist auch vom Standpunkt der juristischen Methodenlehre weiterführend, wenn man etwa an die Entwicklung und Auslegung von Richterrecht denkt.[265] Sind demnach einmal Prinzipien im Wege der allfälligen Verallgemeinerung der für den jeweiligen Fall maßgeblichen Entscheidungskriterien ermittelt, so können anhand und unter Zugrundelegung derer in den einzelnen Fällen wieder neue Gesichtspunkte zutage treten, welche ihrerseits die Kasuistik prägen. Die Entwicklung der Rechtsprechung zur Produzentenhaftung könnte etwa in diesem Sinne verstanden werden.[266] Die dem angloamerikanischen *Case law* ähnliche Rechtsprechung gewann lange vor Inkrafttreten des Produkthaftungsgesetzes eine Richtung,[267] die bald verallgemeinerungsfähige Rechtssätze im Sinne einer Fallgruppenbildung zutage förderte[268] und andererseits mit jedem neuen Fall, der diese prinzipiellen Besonderheiten aufwies,[269] neue Sachverhaltselemente und mit ihnen eine besondere Facette ans Licht brachte,[270] die ihrerseits wiederum auf die Kasuistik zurückwirkten und sie auf diesem Wege bereicherten und so erst die Falllösung

[265] Siehe dazu nur *F. Bydlinski*, Hauptpositionen zum Richterrecht, JZ 1985, 149; *K. Langenbucher*, Die Entwicklung und Auslegung von Richterrecht, 1996.

[266] Zu ihr instruktiv *D. Medicus*, Bürgerliches Recht, 21. Auflage 2007, Rz. 650a ff.

[267] Beginnend mit BGHZ 51, 91 (Hühnerpest). Aus dem neueren Schrifttum *Ch. Fischer*, Topoi verdeckter Rechtsfortbildung im Zivilrecht, 2007, S. 167 ff. Methodisch grundlegend *J. Esser*, Grundsatz und Norm in der richterlichen Fortbildung des Privatrechts, 1956; *K. Larenz*, Wegweiser zu richterlicher Rechtsschöpfung, Festschrift für A. Nikisch, 1958, S. 275; *ders.*, Kennzeichen geglückter richterlicher Rechtsfortbildung, 1965; *ders.*, Richterliche Rechtsfortbildung als methodisches Problem, NJW 1965, 3; *U. Diederichsen*, Zur Begriffstechnik richterlicher Rechtsfortbildung im Zivilrecht, Festschrift für F. Wieacker, 1978, S. 325.

[268] *E. von Caemmerer*, Ius Privatum Gentium, Festschrift für Rheinstein, 1969, S. 659; zum Verhältnis von Generalklauseln und Fallgruppen *R. Weber*, AcP 192 (1992) 516; *A. Beater*, AcP 194 (1994) 82.

[269] Vgl. BGH NJW 1975, 1827; BGHZ 67, 359 (Schwimmerschalter).

[270] BGHZ 92, 143 (Kupolofen).

ermöglichten.[271] Ein Beispiel bildet der Hondafall,[272] in dem erstmals im Rahmen der anerkannten Grundsätze der Produzentenhaftung auch für fremdes Zubehör gehaftet wurde.[273] Auch wenn dies wohl eine Billigkeitsentscheidung war, veranschaulicht sie die auf Kasuistik beruhende Rückwirkung der Rechtssätze auf die Kasuistik.

Dabei schätzte Weber zumindest die englische Jurisprudenz in einer geradezu chauvinistisch anmutenden Weise durchaus gering: „Es fehlte bis in die jüngste Vergangenheit, jedenfalls aber bis Austin, eine englische Jurisprudenz, welche den Namen ‚Wissenschaft' verdient hätte, wenn man den kontinentalen Begriff zugrunde legt, fast ganz."[274] Ihr sprach er die Rationalität der Rechtsfindung nahezu ab: „Denn jedenfalls ist die englische Rechtsfindung dem Schwerpunkt nach nicht, wie die kontinentale, ‚Anwendung' von Rechtssätzen, welche mit Hilfe der Logik aus dem Inhalt gesetzlicher Vorschriften sublimiert ist."[275] Die Gründe für solche über den Gesetzeswortlaut hinausreichenden Entwicklungen wurden schon zu Webers Zeit uneinheitlich beurteilt; er selbst meint dazu, „dass noch jetzt die Gerichtspraxis, z. B. auch des deutschen Reichsgerichts, gerade nach dem Inkrafttreten des Bürgerlichen Gesetzbuchs, gelegentlich teils praeter legem, teils sogar contra legem ganz neue Rechtsprinzipien aufstellt, wird manchmal sogar die Überlegenheit der Präjudizien gegenüber der rationalen Satzung objektiver Normen wie die Überlegenheit des konkreten zweckrationalen Interessenausgleichs gegenüber der Schaffung und Anerkennung von ‚Normen' überhaupt abgeleitet."[276]

[271] Das entspricht in etwa der „Fallnorm" Fikentschers, die eine wechselseitige Annäherung von Sachverhalt und Norm bis zum „hermeneutischen Umkehrpunkt" vornimmt; vgl. *W. Fikentscher*, Methoden des Rechts in vergleichender Darstellung, Band IV, 1977, S. 198 f.

[272] BGHZ 99, 167.

[273] Dazu *Schmidt-Salzer*, BB 1987, 721; *Kullmann*, BB 1987, 1957.

[274] *M. Weber*, Wirtschaft und Gesellschaft, S. 510. Siehe zum Ganzen die wohl abgewogene Darstellung von *O. Lepsius*, Verwaltungsrecht unter dem Common Law, 1997.

[275] *M. Weber*, ebenda, S. 510: Bestätigend *J. C. Gray*, The Nature and the Source of Law, 2. Auflage 1927: „All the law is judge-made law."

[276] *M. Weber*, Wirtschaft und Gesellschaft, S. 508.

## 2. Analogie als „parataktisches Assoziieren"

Neben der zuletzt dargestellten Wechselwirkung zwischen Rechtssatz und Kasuistik gibt es nach Weber jedoch noch eine minder anspruchsvolle Weise der Rechtsgewinnung,[277] welche die vordem begründete Kasuistik ebenfalls erweitert, ohne dass die vergleichsweise hehre Prinzipienebene betreten werden muss: „Allein keineswegs jede entwickelte Kasuistik verläuft in der Richtung oder parallel mit der Entwicklung von logisch hoch sublimierten ‚Rechtssätzen'. Vielmehr gibt es auch auf dem Boden bloß parataktischen und anschaulichen Assoziierens: der ‚Analogie', sehr umfassende Rechtskasuistiken."[278] Dieser Befund stimmt nachdenklich, weil er eine Würdigung vorwegnimmt, die in der juristischen Methodenlehre in dieser Deutlichkeit noch nicht gesehen worden ist. Es geht damit um den Stellenwert der Analogie.[279]

Für gewöhnlich gilt der Analogieschluss als durchaus anspruchsvoller,[280] weil er neben dem Vorliegen einer Regelungslücke,[281] also

277 Instruktiv *M. Kriele*, Theorie der Rechtsgewinnung, 1967.

278 *M. Weber*, Wirtschaft und Gesellschaft, S. 395. Zu dieser Stelle auch *W. Schluchter*, Die Entstehung des modernen Rationalismus, Eine Analyse von Max Webers Entwicklungsgeschichte des Okzidents, 1998, S. 193; *St. Uecker*, Die Rationalisierung des Rechts. Max Webers Rechtssoziologie, 2005, S. 66 f.

279 Grundlegend *N. Bobbio*, Analogia, in: Novissimo Digesto Italiano, 1975, Band 1, S. 601 f.: „Der Begriff ‚Analogie', um die auf der Basis der Ähnlichkeit fußende Ausdehnung anzuzeigen, wurde erst (...) gegen Ende des 18. Jahrhunderts gebraucht, und stammt von dem Ausdruck ‚analogia legis', um den Vorgang zu bezeichnen, der nötig war, um die Lücken einer Rechtsordnung zu schließen, die als einheitliches und kohärentes System verstanden wurde." Siehe dazu auch *M. Losano*, Das „Systemdenken" in den romanischen Ländern, Festschrift für C.-W. Canaris, 2007, S. 1201, 1203 f.

280 *E. Bund*, Die Analogie als Begründungsmethode im deutschen Recht der Gegenwart, ZVglRWiss 1978, 115; *H. A. W. Langheim*, Das Prinzip der Analogie als juristische Methode, 1992; aus dem älteren Schrifttum *J. Falk*, Die Analogie im Recht, 1906.

281 *C.-W. Canaris*, Die Feststellung von Lücken im Gesetz, 1964; Siehe dazu auch *E. Schumann*, Eigenständigkeit und Vielfalt der juristischen Hermeneutik, Festschrift für C.-W. Canaris, 2007, S. 1367, 1375 ff. unter eingehender Berücksichtigung und juristischer Einordnung von *H.-G. Gadamer*, Wahrheit und Methode. Grundzüge einer philosophischen Hermeneutik, 1960.

einer planwidrigen Unvollständigkeit,[282] die Vergleichbarkeit mit Sinn und Zweck der entsprechend heranzuziehenden Regelung voraussetzt.[283] Demgegenüber nimmt sich die Analogie bei Weber vergleichsweise bescheiden und anspruchslos aus, wenn er sie „auf dem Boden bloßen parataktischen Assoziierens" ansiedelt. Gleichwohl ist diese Geringschätzung weiterführend, nicht weil sie auf die Analogie der juristischen Methodenlehre unbedingt zutrifft, sondern um ihrer deskriptiven Treffsicherheit willen: Anders als der methodisch *lege artis* gezogene Analogieschluss ist die von Weber gemeinte strukturelle Gleichachtung einander ähnlicher Fallgestaltungen in der Tat ein vergleichsweise primitives Vorgehen, wenn man es ins Verhältnis setzt zum Betreten der Prinzipienebene, weil sich dieses Prozedere auf der rein faktischen Ebene abspielt, ohne dass es auf die normative „von logisch hoch sublimierten Rechtssätzen" ankommt.[284] Gustav Boehmer hat dies in einer zeitlos gültigen Weise zusammengefasst: „So verfehlt es ist, mit Hilfe *logischer* Operationen Gebietserweiterungen der Normengeltung vollziehen zu wollen, so unablehnbar ist die *teleologische* Methode, die sich zum Ziel setzt, Rechtslücken in erster Linie mittels Erforschung der sozialen Sicherungs-, Schutz- und Ausgleichszwecke, die hinter den Gesetzesnormen stehen, auf dem Wege ausdehnender Auslegung (*extensiver Interpretation*) oder, falls diese versagt, Normenerweiterung (*Analogie*) auszufüllen."[285] Im Übrigen sind diese Überlegungen, wie sich noch zeigen wird, auch in anderer Hinsicht weiterführend, weil sie die Problematik der Logik und vermeintliche Lückenlosigkeit der Rechtsordnung betreffen,[286] von der weiter unten noch die Rede sein wird.

282 *H. Elze*, Lücken im Gesetz, 1916, S. 12.

283 *K. Larenz*, Methodenlehre der Rechtswissenschaft, 6. Auflage, 1991, S. 383.

284 *M. Weber*, Wirtschaft und Gesellschaft, S. 395. Siehe auch *C. Schmid*, Erinnerungen, 3. Band der Gesammelten Werke, 1979, S. 94: „Was ich bei der Lektüre Spenglers erlebte, hat mich für immer davor bewahrt, der Verführungskraft des assoziativen Denkens in Analogien zu erliegen."

285 *G. Boehmer*, Grundlagen der Bürgerlichen Rechtsordnung, Zweites Buch, Erste Abteilung, 1951, S. 166 f.; Hervorhebungen auch dort.

286 Hierzu auch schon *E. Zitelmann*, Lücken im Recht, 1903.

## 3. Anreicherung der Kasuistik

Es handelt sich also um Beispiele, in denen die Kasuistik schlicht dadurch angereichert wird, dass ihr ähnliche Fallgestaltungen zugerechnet werden. Ein Beispiel aus dem geltenden Recht könnte etwa die Entwicklung und Erweiterung der Verkehrspflichten darstellen,[287] die im Laufe der Jahre fortgeschrieben wurde, ohne dass jedes Mal von Neuem der prinzipielle Geltungsgrund in Frage gestanden hätte. Das wäre, um die Wendung Webers aufzugreifen und entsprechend umzukehren, ein gleichsam „hypotaktisches" Verfahren, mit dem sich die wechselseitigen Abhängigkeiten zwischen normativer und faktischer Ebene erhellen ließen.

Aber auch davon abgesehen hält die Formulierung Webers eine wertvolle Einsicht bereit: dass nämlich der Analogieschluss nicht immer gleichermaßen anspruchsvoll ist, wie es in der juristischen Methodenlehre oft den Anschein hat. Das gilt für alle Fälle, in denen auch dort – insbesondere von der Rechtsprechung[288] – mitunter der Sache nach nur mehr gefragt wird, ob die betreffende Vorschrift bzw. Rechtsfolge letztlich „passt", ohne dass eine teleologische Analyse und nicht selten auch nur eine vorrangige Lückenfeststellung erfolgt wäre.[289] In diesen Fällen handelt es sich auch unter dem Blickwinkel der juristischen Methodenlehre oftmals um nicht mehr als ein „bloß parataktisches Assoziieren". Mit dieser begrifflich scharfen Wendung und Beobachtung hat Weber somit auch der Rechtsdogmatik aufgegeben, Begründungsdefizite zu erkennen und zu beheben.

[287] Grundlegend *C. von Bar*, Verkehrspflichten, 1979.

[288] Ein Beispiel bildet wohl die mit guten Gründen bezweifelte Streupflicht des Grundstückseigentümers, deren Legitimation unter Rückgriff auf die Prinzipienebene durchaus zweifelhaft ist; eingehend *K. Larenz/C.-W. Canaris*, Lehrbuch des Schuldrechts, Band 2, 2. Halbband, 13. Auflage 1994, § 76 III 4a, S. 413; 7c), S. 429.

[289] Die Einsicht, dass diese Lückenfeststellung mitnichten ohne weiteres vorausgesetzt werden darf, sondern das Bestehen einer Lücke lege artis ermittelt werden muss, ist das Verdienst der zitierten Dissertation von *C.-W. Canaris*, Die Feststellung von Lücken im Gesetz, 1964. Siehe auch *O. A. Germann*, Gesetzeslücken und ergänzende Rechtsfindung, 2. Auflage 1967.

## IV. Synthetische Arbeit der juristischen Konstruktion

Die soeben dargestellte analytische Ermittlung von Prinzipien aus Einzelfällen betrachtet Weber nicht isoliert, sondern stellt ihr die synthetische Arbeit der juristischen Konstruktion an die Seite.[290] Es geht hierbei um die Begründung von Rechtsverhältnissen und Rechtsinstituten. Die Frage ist also zum Einen, was an einem „in typischer Art verlaufenden Gemeinschafts- und Einverständnishandeln" spezifisch *rechtlich* bedeutsam und zu würdigen ist.[291] Zum anderen – und wohl noch wichtiger – ist damit das Postulat einer widerspruchslosen Ordnung dessen gemeint. Das Postulat innerer Widerspruchslosigkeit prägt sein Denken auch in anderen Schriften, wie anhand anderer Beispiele bereits von Dieter Henrich[292] gezeigt wurde und wie folgender Hinweis Webers bestätigt: „Diese Kritik freilich kann nur dialektischen Charakter haben, d. h. sie kann nur eine formallogische Beurteilung des in den geschichtlich gegebenen *Werturteilen* und Ideen vorliegenden Materials, eine Prüfung der Ideale an dem Postulat der inneren Widerspruchslosigkeit des Gewollten sein."[293]

### 1. Vergleich mit Hecks Interessenjurisprudenz

Ordnet man dies in den methodengeschichtlichen Rahmen ein, so nimmt es nicht wunder, dass Weber, im Unterschied zu Philipp Heck[294] – und aus dessen Sicht daher auf der falschen Seite, der Begriffsjurisprudenz – wenngleich, wie zu zeigen sein wird, keineswegs unkritisch[295] – nahestand, weil er darin eine ausgefeilte Form

290 *M. Weber*, Wirtschaft und Gesellschaft, S. 395 f.

291 *M. Weber*, ebenda, S. 396. In dem zugrundeliegenden, „radikalen Rückgang auf einen subjektbezogenen Handlungsbegriff" Webers sieht *N. Luhmann*, Rechtssoziologie, 3. Auflage 1987, S. 19, „seine eigentliche Leistung".

292 *D. Henrich*, Die Einheit der Wissenschaftslehre Max Webers, 1952, S. 2.

293 *M. Weber*, Die „Objektivität" sozialwissenschaftlicher Erkenntnis, in: Archiv für Sozialwissenschaft und Sozialpolitik 19 (1904), 22, 25 f. (Hervorhebung nur hier).

294 *Ph. Heck*, AcP 142 (1936) 129, 165 f.

295 Es kommt eher unausgesprochen, also ohne ausdrückliche Bezeichnung

der Rationalisierung erblickte.[296] Interessanterweise erhob umgekehrt Heck gegen die Begriffsjurisprudenz den terminologisch auf Ernst Fuchs[297] zurückgehenden Vorwurf der „Kryptosoziologie".[298]

## a) Webers Affinität gegenüber der Begriffsjurisprudenz

Aus heutiger Sicht mutet es beinahe paradox an, dass Weber hier auf einer anderen Seite stand als Heck, der sich die Lebensforschung und Lebenswertung sowie die „Einwirkung auf das Leben"[299] im Sinne einer Hinwendung zur Wirklichkeit[300] und zum Leben[301] auf die Fahnen geschrieben hat,[302] die der Rechts-

der Begriffsjurisprudenz, zum Vorschein; vgl. *M. Weber*, Wirtschaft und Gesellschaft, S. 493.

296 *H. Schoppmeyer*, Juristische Methode als Lebensform, 2001, S. 164.

297 *E. Fuchs*, Juristischer Kulturkampf, 1912, S. 37; *ders.*, Klassische Einwendungen gegen die soziologische Methode, 1911; *ders.*, Schreibjustiz und Richterkönigtum – ein Mahnruf zur Schul- und Justizreform, 1907; *ders.*, Was will die Freirechtsschule?, 1929. Kritisch *G. Boehmer*, Grundlagen der Bürgerlichen Rechtsordnung, Zweites Buch, Erste Abteilung, 1951, S. 177, gegenüber Ernst Fuchs, „der in einer Reihe broschürenartiger Schriften immer wieder mit seinem grimmigen Zorn und Hass gegen alle logische und historische ‚Richterverbildung', gegen die ‚Rabulistik' und ‚kryptosoziologische' Heuchelei der ‚gemeinschädlichen' begriffsjuristischen Konstruktion Luft machte und dadurch die Diskussion leider auf ein nicht gerade würdiges Niveau herabzog".

298 *M. Wolf*, Philipp Heck als Zivilrechtsdogmatiker – Studien zur dogmatischen Umsetzung seiner Methodenlehre, 1996, S. 156 f., 203 m.w.N.; *J. Petersen*, Von der Interessenjurisprudenz zur Wertungsjurisprudenz, 2001, S. 23. Siehe auch *J. G. Gmelin*, Quousque? Beitrag zur soziologischen Rechtsfindung, 1910.

299 *Ph. Heck*, Das Problem der Rechtsgewinnung, 1912, S. 37; *ders.*, AcP 134 (1931) 259, 268.

300 *B. Dombek*, Das Verhältnis der Tübinger Schule zur deutschen Rechtssoziologie, 1969, S. 52; *H. Ryffel*, Rechtssoziologie. Eine systematische Orientierung, 1974, S. 29 ff.; *H. Coing*, System, Geschichte und Interesse in der Privatrechtswissenschaft, JZ 1951, 181, 184. Siehe auch *A. Heldrich*, Die Bedeutung der Rechtssoziologie für das Zivilrecht, AcP 186 (1986) 74, 76.

301 *R. Müller-Erzbach*, Die Hinwendung der Rechtswissenschaft zum Leben und was sie hemmt, 1939.

302 *Ph. Heck*, Begriffsbildung und Interessenjurisprudenz, 1932, S. 17: „Primat der Lebensforschung und Lebenswertung".

soziologie doch näher zu kommen schien als jede andere zeitgenössische Strömung[303] und für sie eine wichtige Basis wurde.[304] Immerhin ist die Interessenjurisprudenz „eine Methodenlehre mit stark soziologischem Einschlag."[305] Aber bei Licht besehen ist es deshalb nachvollziehbar, weil die Begriffsjurisprudenz mit ihrer formal rationalen Rechtsfindungslehre eine verlässlichere Kategorisierung des Entscheidungsmaterials versprach.[306] Allerdings ist diese Affinität, um es nochmals zu betonen, keine unkritische,[307] sondern eher eine den vermeintlichen Errungenschaften seiner Zeit verpflichtete, deren begrenzte Leistungsfähigkeit, vor allem was ihren Eindruck auf das allgemeine Rechtsbewusstsein macht, Weber sehr wohl sah.[308]

### aa) „Zeitbedingtheit" der Rechtssoziologie Webers?

Dessen ungeachtet findet sich im Schrifttum die „These der Zeitbedingtheit der Weberschen Rechtssoziologie: Das von ihm beschriebene Recht (Logische Konsistenz, deduktive Strenge, präzise Sprache, Berechenbarkeit) ist nichts anderes als das damals zumal im Zivilrecht vorherrschende Rechtsideal der ‚Pandektenwissenschaft'. Als das rationalste Recht erscheint Weber das der positivistischen Begriffsjurisprudenz, aus deren Geiste auch die 1900 in Kraft getretene Kodifikation des deutschen Zivilrechts, das hoch-

[303] Siehe auch *Th. Duve*, Normativität und Empirie im öffentlichen Recht und der Politikwissenschaft um 1900. Historisch-systematische Untersuchung des Lebens und Werks von Richard Schmidt (1862–1944) und der Methodenentwicklung seiner Zeit, 1998, S. 316 mit Fußnote 107.

[304] *A. Heldrich*, AcP 186 (1986) 74, 76; *B. Dombek*, Das Verhältnis der Tübinger Schule zur deutschen Rechtssoziologie, 1969, 53; *H. Hattenhauer*, Die geistesgeschichtlichen Grundlagen des deutschen Rechts, 4. Auflage 1996, Rz. 446; *H. Schoppmeyer*, Juristische Methode als Lebensaufgabe, S. 66.

[305] *H. Schoppmeyer*, Juristische Methode als Lebensaufgabe, 2001, S. 161.

[306] Vgl. nur *H. Preuß*, Zur Methode juristischer Begriffskonstruktion, Schmollers Jahrbuch 24 (1900), Band 1, S. 359 ff.

[307] *C.-W. Canaris*, Systemdenken und Systembegriff in der Jurisprudenz, S. 21 Fußnote 9.

[308] *M. Weber*, Wirtschaft und Gesellschaft, S. 506 f.

abstrakte BGB, entstammt."[309] Allerdings zeigt die zuletzt zitierte Stelle Webers,[310] dass er die Begriffs- und Konstruktionsjurisprudenz durchaus auch kritisch sah.[311]

### bb) Webers methodologische Eigenständigkeit

So richtig es ist, dass Weber aus seiner Zeit heraus den Methodenstreit innerhalb der juristischen Methodenlehre verfolgte, so sehr muss berücksichtigt werden, dass er, wie noch am Ende dieses Abschnitts ausgeführt wird,[312] immer auch über seine Zeit hinaus zu blicken vermochte und so seiner Rechtssoziologie ein zumindest vom Standpunkt der juristischen Methodenlehre zeitlos gültiges Fundament sicherte. Wenn es also so schien, als sei die von Heck favorisierte und maßgeblich ausgearbeitete Interessenjurisprudenz,[313] die mitunter auch als Rechtsrealismus bezeichnet wird,[314] dem gleichsam auf halbem Wege entgegengekommen, so bestand aus Webers Sicht womöglich dennoch eine unüberbrückbare Distanz im Ordnen des Rechtsstoffs. So finden sich auch bei Weber Stellen, wie etwa im Zusammenhang mit dem Testament, das „den Ausgleich der Interessen von Familienmitgliedern gegenüber

309 *St. Uecker*, Die Rationalisierung des Recht. Max Webers Rechtssoziologie, 2005, S. 76.

310 *M. Weber*, Wirtschaft und Gesellschaft, S. 506 f., sowie ebenda, S. 493.

311 *C.-W. Canaris*, Systemdenken und Systembegriff in der Jurisprudenz, 2. Auflage 1983, S. 21 Fußnote 9.

312 Vor § 3.

313 Früher Überblick über die einzelnen Strömungen und Vertreter bei *J. W. Hedemann*, Zivilistische Rundschau, Archiv für Bürgerliches Recht 31 (1906), 296; 34 (1909) 115. Näher *J. Edelmann*, Die Entwicklung der Interessenjurisprudenz, 1967; ferner *H. Heitmann*, Die Stellung der Interessenjurisprudenz innerhalb der Geschichte der juristischen Methodenlehre, 1936.

314 *D. Dombek*, Das Verhältnis der Tübinger Schule zur deutschen Rechtssoziologie, 1969, S. 51 f.; *W. Krawietz*, Recht als Regelsystem, S. 75, 105; *M. Baldus*, Die Einheit der Rechtsordnung. Bedeutungen einer juristischen Formel in Rechtstheorie, Zivil- und Strafrechtswissenschaft des 19. und 20. Jahrhunderts, 1995, S. 103; *H. Schoppmeyer*, Juristische Methode als Lebensaufgabe, 2001, S. 164.

ökonomischen Notwendigkeiten bezweckt."[315] Der erste Teil dieser Aussage könnte auch bei Heck stehen,[316] doch ist dies zugleich auch noch nicht mehr als ein phänotypischer Befund, in dem sich weder die eigenständige Aufgabe noch die Leistung der Interessenjurisprudenz erschöpfen kann.

### b) Unklarheiten in der frühen Interessenjurisprudenz

In der Tat war sich zumindest die frühe Interessenjurisprudenz selbst mitunter nicht völlig im Klaren darüber, auf welcher Ebene die „Lebenswertung" einsetzt, ob sie faktisch oder normativ geprägt war.[317] Dieses Defizit, das gerade die von ihm vorgestellte Ordnungsaufgabe ausmachte, mag Weber gesehen und daher eine Vorgehensweise favorisiert haben, die im Hinblick auf die rationale Ordnung erfolgversprechend schien. Dann wäre es nachvollziehbar, dass Heck und Weber ungeachtet der in der Einleitung beschriebenen Affinität einen durchaus unterschiedlichen Ausgangs- und Endpunkt hatten. Insofern sind die beiden Persönlichkeiten mit ihrem jeweiligen wissenschaftlichen Erkenntnisinteresse jede für sich paradigmatisch: der eine für die in der Begründung als wissenschaftliche Disziplin begriffene Rechtssoziologie, der andere als prononcierter Vertreter einer vergleichsweise reiferen Epoche der juristischen Methodenlehre,[318] welche die Begriffsjurisprudenz hinter sich glaubte.

### c) Würdigung der Begriffsjurisprudenz

Im methodologischen Schrifttum ist jedoch gezeigt worden, dass die Begriffs- bzw. Konstruktionsjurisprudenz auch im Zeitalter

[315] *M. Weber*, Wirtschaft und Gesellschaft, S. 400.

[316] Allerdings ist eben auch erst der zweite Teil mit seiner Gegenüberstellung ökonomischer Notwendigkeiten bezeichnend für Weber, der dem Titel des zitierten Werks entsprechend gerade die wirtschaftlichen Implikationen des Privatrechts analysierte.

[317] Eingehend *J. Petersen*, Von der Interessenjurisprudenz zur Wertungsjurisprudenz, 2001, passim.

[318] Siehe auch *M. Heitmann*, Die Stellung der Interessenjurisprudenz innerhalb der Geschichte der Methodenlehre, 1936; S. 5.

der Wertungsjurisprudenz durchaus ihr gutes Recht hat, indem sie die wertungsmäßig abzusichernden Ergebnisse zunächst konstruktiv begründet.[319] Dieses Defizit der Interessenjurisprudenz, die diese Vorzüge in ihrer Ablehnung der Begriffsjurisprudenz nicht hinreichend klar gesehen hatte, war womöglich von Weber intuitiv erkannt worden. Ähnlich äußert sich Niklas Luhmann wonach man mitunter „nur noch auf methodologischer Ebene oder gar nur ideenpolitisch gegen Begriffsjurisprudenz argumentiert."[320] Das geht wohl nicht zuletzt auf Heck zurück, der allenthalben von „Begriffsjurisprudenz der überkommenen Art" schreibt. Es setzt freilich voraus, dass es auch eine nicht überkommene Art der Begriffsjurisprudenz gibt, die gleichsam zeitlos gültig ist.[321] Der Interessenjurisprudenz stellt dies indes kein schlechtes Zeugnis aus, zumal sich einzelne ihrer Vertreter gerade auch um den Stellenwert von Begriff und Konstruktion in der Interessenjurisprudenz verdient gemacht haben.[322] Heldrich gibt zu bedenken, dass manch „naive Simplifizierung sozialer Fragestellungen" in Gerichtsurteilen „gewissermaßen der Preis sind, den wir für die Ablösung der Begriffsjurisprudenz durch eine Interessenjurisprudenz zu entrichten haben."[323]

### d) Jherings Wandel

Umgekehrt hat Rudolf von Jhering, der zunächst der Begriffsjurisprudenz verpflichtet war und die juristische Konstruktion zu einer Methode der Rechtsfindung erhoben hat, später der Interessenjurisprudenz den Weg geebnet. Luhmann hat diesen Wandel scharfsichtig kommentiert: „In der Rechtswissenschaft beginnt eine entsprechende Wendung mit Jhering. Jherings Konzept der juristischen Konstruktion verlangt in seiner Konsequenz den

319 *G. Hassold*, Rechtsfindung durch Konstruktion, AcP 181 (1981), 131.

320 *N. Luhmann*, Rechtssystem und Rechtsdogmatik, 1974, S. 30.

321 *J. Petersen*, Von der Interessenjurisprudenz zur Wertungsjurisprudenz, 2001.

322 *H. Stoll*, Begriff und Konstruktion in der Lehre der Interessenjurisprudenz, Festgabe Heck-Rümelin-Schmidt, 1931, S. 60.

323 *A. Heldrich*, Die Bedeutung der Rechtssoziologie für das Zivilrecht, AcP 186 (1986) 74, 87.

Übergang zu einem anderen Systembegriff, nämlich die Auffassung des Rechtssystems als eines Systems der sozialen Realität, als eines Teilsystems der Gesellschaft. Das Wort ‚Interesse' signalisiert diese Wendung, formuliert sie aber nicht ausreichend."[324] Die Beobachtung Luhmanns hinsichtlich des Übergangs zu einem anderen Systembegriff spricht im Übrigen für die Annahme, dass hier wissenschaftstheoretisch gesehen von einem Paradigmenwechsel gesprochen werden kann.[325] Jherings berühmter *Kampf ums Recht*[326] gründete mit den Worten Gustav Boehmers auf einem „naturalistisch-soziologischen Wertsystem" und führte zur „teleologisch-soziologischen Methode".[327] Auch in seinem *Zweck im Recht*[328] ist eine Hinwendung zur Soziologie nachweisbar,[329] obwohl es die Rechtssoziologie als Disziplin noch nicht gab.[330] Nicht von ungefähr schreibt er in der Vorrede einer anderen Schrift,[331] dass sein „Zweck im Recht" ebenso gut heißen könnte

[324] *N. Luhmann*, Rechtssystem und Rechtsdogmatik, 1974, S. 12 mit Fußnote 11; unter Hinweis auf *H. Coing*, Der juristische Systembegriff bei Rudolf von Jhering, in: J. Blühdorn/J. Ritter (Hg.), Philosophie und Rechtswissenschaft, Hg., 1969, S. 149; *H. Schelsky*, Das Jhering-Modell des sozialen Wandels durch Recht – Ein wissenschaftsgeschichtlicher Beitrag, Jahrbuch für Rechtssoziologie und Rechtstheorie 3, 1972, S. 47.

[325] *J. Petersen*, Von der Interessenjurisprudenz zur Wertungsjurisprudenz, 2001, S. 8 ff.

[326] *R. v. Jhering*, Der Kampf um's Recht, 1872. Siehe dazu auch *J. Kohler*, Shakespeare vor dem Forum der Jurisprudenz, 2. Auflage 1919.

[327] *G. Boehmer*, Grundlagen der Bürgerlichen Rechtsordnung, Zweites Buch, Erste Abteilung, 1951, S. 134.

[328] *R. v. Jhering*, Der Zweck im Recht, 1877–1883.

[329] *F. Wieacker*, Rudolf v. Jhering, 1943, S. 38, spricht von einem „geräumigen Systemaufbau, der von der Psychologie des Tieres über eine Anthropologie zur Soziologie führt."

[330] *R. Dreier*, Jherings Rechtstheorie – eine Theorie evolutionärer Rechtsvernunft, in: Privatrecht heute und Jherings evolutionäres Rechtsdenken (Hg. O. Behrends), 1993, S. 118 ff., der freilich auf interessante Bezüge und Vorwegnahmen aufmerksam macht, etwa zu *Th. Geiger*, Vorstudien zu einer Soziologie des Rechts, 1964, S. 131, oder *N. Luhmann*, Ausdifferenzierung des Rechts, 1981.

[331] *R. v. Jhering*, Der Besitzwille. Zugleich eine Kritik der herrschenden juristischen Methode, 1889, S. X.

bzw. sogar müsste: „Das teleologische System der sittlichen Weltordnung." Besonders deutlich und vor allem für den vorliegenden Zusammenhang relevant ist folgendes Bekenntnis: „Das Leben ist nicht der Begriffe, sondern die Begriffe sind des Lebens wegen da. Nicht was die Logik, sondern was das Leben, der Verkehr, das Rechtsgefühl postuliert, hat zu geschehen, möge es logisch deduzierbar oder unmöglich sein."[332] In der spektakulären Hinwendung Jherings zur Interessenjurisprudenz sind also bereits Momente einer Aufgeschlossenheit des Dogmatikers gegenüber soziologischen Elementen vorhanden. Es ist im Übrigen interessant, dass die Rechtssoziologie schon vergleichsweise früh im Archiv für die civilistische Praxis diskutiert wurde.[333] Dass dies später in den Hintergrund getreten ist,[334] könnte daran liegen, dass die Schülergeneration wieder einen rein dogmatischen Standpunkt einnahm und außerdogmatische Einflüsse auf die Rechtsfindung in die Schranken wies.[335]

### e) Aussonderung der Rechtssoziologie

Ebenso repräsentativ wie erhellend schildert Wolfgang Fikentscher die Genese der Rechtssoziologie im Wandel von der Interessenjurisprudenz zur Wertungsjurisprudenz, weshalb dieser weiträumige Gedanke wörtlich wiedergegeben zu werden verdient: „Die Interessenjurisprudenz wurde damit zu einer bewussten Vermittlerin rechtserheblicher Tatsachen für rechtsbeurteilende Wertung. Und wie auf der einen Seite die Interessenjurisprudenz sich zur (zunächst abstrakten, später konkreten) Wertungsjurisprudenz weiterentwickelte, sonderte sie auf der anderen Seite, auf der Seite der Tatsachen, die Rechtssoziologie aus sich aus."[336] Gerade die

[332] *R. v. Jhering*, Geist des römischen Rechts, III/1, S. 321.

[333] *M. Stumpf*, Was ist Rechtssoziologie?, AcP 122 (1924) 36.

[334] Allerdings nicht in den Vereinigten Staaten: *R. Pound*, Role of the Will in Law, Harvard Law Review 68 (1954) 1.

[335] *A. Merkel*, Über das Verhältnis der Rechtsphilosophie zur positiven Rechtswissenschaft, Zeitschrift für das Privat- und öffentliche Recht der Gegenwart 1 (1874) 402 ff.

[336] *W. Fikentscher*, Methoden des Rechts, Band III, 1977, S. 387, der ebenfalls bei Jhering ansetzt.

einschneidende Ablösung faktischer durch normative Kriterien spricht insoweit für einen Paradigmenwechsel.[337] So elegant jedoch die Annahme ist, dass die Rechtssoziologie gleichsam beiläufig durch die Häutung der juristischen Methodenlehre entstanden ist, die sich dabei vom Faktischen zum Normativen entwickelt hat, so erklärungsbedürftig ist sie im Hinblick auf die durchaus eigenständige Rechtssoziologie Webers. Man mag Ehrlichs genuin rechtssoziologischen Standpunkt damit erklären können,[338] doch gilt das nur bedingt für Weber, der zwar soziologische und rechtsdogmatische Betrachtung strikt trennte,[339] aber innerhalb dieser durchaus prinzipienmäßig[340] und weniger faktisch orientiert urteilte.[341]

## 2. Interdependenz von Analyse und Synthese

Diese erklärenden und den methodengeschichtlichen Zusammenhang erhellenden Anmerkungen sind nötig, um Webers synthetische Arbeit der Konstruktion in den methodologischen Zusammenhang zu stellen, aus dem heraus sie in die Methodendiskussion seiner Zeit eingeordnet werden können. Dass es sich bei dem von Weber weiter oben[342] geschilderten Vorgang wieder um eine Manipulation handelt,[343] unterstreicht Weber im Folgenden: „So eng die Manipulation mit den früheren zusammenhängt, so kann doch eine sehr hochgradige Sublimierung der Analyse mit sehr geringer konstruktiver Erfassung der rechtlich relevanten Lebensverhältnisse parallel gehen und umgekehrt: eine Synthese eines

[337] *J. Petersen*, Von der Interessenjurisprudenz zur Wertungsjurisprudenz, 2001, S. 54 ff.

[338] *E. Ehrlich*, Freie Rechtsfindung und freie Rechtswissenschaft, 1903; *ders.*, Grundlegung der Soziologie des Rechts, 1913.

[339] *M. Weber*, Wirtschaft und Gesellschaft, S. 181.

[340] Im Sinne von *P. Landau*, Die Rechtsquellenlehre in der deutschen Rechtswissenschaft des 19. Jahrhunderts, in: Juristische Theoriebildung und Rechtliche Einheit, Rättshistorika Studier (Hg. C. Petterson), Band XIX, 1993, S. 69; dazu bereits oben § 1 II 1; dazu noch öfter im Text.

[341] *M. Weber*, Wirtschaft und Gesellschaft, S. 493 f.

[342] Unter III. und IV. vor 1.

[343] Siehe bereits oben unter 2. b).

‚Rechtsverhältnisses' praktisch relativ befriedigend trotz sehr geringer Entwicklung der Analyse, zuweilen sogar infolge Einschränkung der Pflege der reinen Analyse, gelingen."[344]

### a) Bewegliches System und Typusbegriff

Es ist cum grano salis der Funktionsmechanismus, der in der juristischen Methodenlehre bei beweglichen Systemen bekannt ist.[345] Analytisches und synthetisches Element müssen also nicht gleich stark vertreten sein, sondern sind wechselseitig bzw. bedingt kompensierbar und treten im Rahmen der Rationalisierung nicht notwendigerweise parallel auf. Weber führt diese scheinbare Inkonzinität darauf zurück,[346] dass „aus der Analyse eine weitere logische Aufgabe zu entspringen pflegt, welche sich mit der synthetischen ‚Konstruktions'-Arbeit zwar prinzipiell verträgt, faktisch aber nicht selten in Spannungen zu ihr steht."[347] Nicht von ungefähr begegnet hier wieder die Voraussetzung des Logischen als Bedingung der Rationalität der Rechtsgewinnung.[348] Aber nicht nur beim beweglichen System begegnet die genannte bedingte Kom-

344 *M. Weber*, Wirtschaft und Gesellschaft, S. 396.

345 Grundlegend *W. Wilburg*, Entwicklung eines beweglichen Systems im bürgerlichen Recht, Grazer Rektoratsrede, 1950; *ders.*, Die Elemente des Schadensrechts, 1941; *ders.*, Das Zusammenspiel der Kräfte im Aufbau des Schuldrechts, AcP 163 (1963) 346; *R. Westerhoff*, Die Elemente des beweglichen Systems, 1991. Zum beweglichen System in der Rechtsgeschichte *A. Thier*, Steuergesetzgebung und Verfassung in der konstitutionellen Monarchie. Staatssteuerreformen in Preußen 1871–1893, 1999, S. 9–18; zum Unternehmensrecht *H. Eidenmüller*, Unternehmenssanierung zwischen Markt und Gesetz. Mechanismen der Unternehmensreorganisation und Kooperationspflichten im Reorganisationsrecht, 1999, S. 656 ff., 660 („heuristisches Raster"); *ders.*, ZHR 160 (1996) 343, 363; *J. Petersen*, Wilhelm von Humboldts Rechtsphilosophie, 2. Auflage 2007, S. 174.

346 Ein „Widerspruch", wie Weber (Wirtschaft und Gesellschaft, S. 396) selbst es bezeichnet, ist es dann letztlich nicht.

347 *M. Weber*, Wirtschaft und Gesellschaft, S. 396. Siehe auch *A. Somek*, Legal Formality and Freedom of Choice. A Moral Perspective on Jhering's Constructivism, Ratio Juris 15 (2002) 52.

348 Siehe soeben unter 3. b). Allgemein dazu *F. Bydlinski*, Die normativen Prämissen der Rechtsgewinnung, Rechtstheorie 1985, 1.

pensierbarkeit, sondern auch beim Typusbegriff. Das Verhältnis beider methodologischer Erscheinungsformen zueinander ist in der juristischen Methodenlehre noch nicht abschließend geklärt; am ehesten wird man festhalten können, dass sich das bewegliche System allein mit normativen Größen befasst, denen Prinzipienrang zukommt,[349] während für die Lehre vom Typus der einzelne Begriff Bezugspunkt ist.[350]

### b) Rationalität trotz Wertungsspielraum

Bei dieser vorläufigen Kennzeichnung kann es hier bewenden, zumal dem Typus ein eigener Abschnitt gewidmet ist.[351] Bereits an dieser Stelle zeigt sich aber, dass die Flexibilität, die beiden methodologischen Figuren zu eigen ist,[352] auch in der durch und durch rational ausgerichteten Rechtssoziologie Webers ihren Platz hat. Das ist nicht zuletzt deshalb aufschlussreich, weil es bezeugt, dass das Vorhandensein der damit verbundenen Wertungsspielräume der Rationalität des Rechts im Ganzen keinen Abbruch tut, weil und sofern die einzelnen Wertungsparameter mit Prinzipienrang ausgestattet sind, so dass man es im besten Sinne mit einer Prinzipienjurisprudenz zu tun hat, die auch zu Webers Zeit der Sache nach schon bestand.[353]

349 *J. Petersen*, Unternehmenssteuerrecht und bewegliches System, 1999, S. 110 f. und passim.

350 *F. Bydkinski*, Bewegliches System und Methodenlehre, in: Das bewegliche System im geltenden und künftigen Recht, 1986, S. 24 f.

351 Unten § 5.

352 Gleichermaßen anerkennend wie geringschätzig aus Sicht der Rechtssoziologie *N. Luhmann*, Rechtssystem und Rechtsdogmatik, S. 84 Anmerkung 68: „Eine bemerkenswerte Vorarbeit ist Walter Wilburg, Entwicklung eines beweglichen Systems im bürgerlichen Recht, Graz 1950, die jedoch über den einen Gesichtspunkt der (im Regel/Ausnahme-Schema angeblich zu geringen) Flexibilität nicht hinauskommt."

353 *P. Landau*, Die Rechtsquellenlehre in der deutschen Rechtswissenschaft des 19. Jahrhunderts, in: Juristische Theoriebildung und Rechtliche Einheit, Rättshistorika Studier (Hg. C. Petterson), Band XIX, 1993, S. 69; dazu noch in § 4 unter II. und IV.

## § 3 Systematisierung des Rechts

Was aber ist nun die von Weber gestellte Aufgabe, die zwar mit der systematischen Arbeit kompatibel ist, aber mitunter in einem tatsächlichen Spannungsverhältnis dazu steht? Es ist nichts anderes als die aus unserem Rechtsdenken nicht mehr hinweg zu denkende Systematisierung,[354] die freilich nach Weber „in jeder Form ein Spätprodukt ist."[355] Systematisierung bedeutet, dass die im Wege der Analyse gewonnenen Rechtssätze dergestalt zueinander in Beziehung gesetzt werden, dass sie ein „prinzipiell lückenloses System von Regeln" bilden,[356] das logisch nicht nur klar, sondern in dieser Form auch widerspruchslos ist:[357] „Nach unserer heutigen Denkgewohnheit bedeutet sie (sc. die Systematisierung): die Inbeziehungsetzung aller durch Analyse gewonnenen Rechtssätze derart, dass sie untereinander ein logisch klares, in sich logisch widerspruchsloses, und vor allem prinzipiell lückenloses System von Regeln bilden, welches also beansprucht: dass alle Tatbestände unter eine seiner Normen logisch subsumiert werden können, widrigenfalls ihre Ordnung der wesentlichen Garantie entbehrt."[358] Es verdient hervorgehoben zu werden, dass dieser zuletzt zitierte Satz Webers auch in der modernen Rechtslehre immer noch als „klassische Formulierung" gefeiert wird.[359] Es spricht für sich und

[354] Siehe nur *H. Coing*, Geschichte und Bedeutung des Systemdenkens in der Rechtswissenschaft, ÖzöR 1957/58, 257; *F. v. Hippel*, Zur Gesetzmäßigkeit juristischer Systembildung, 1930; *F. Bydlinski*, System und Prinzipien des Privatrechts, 1996; eine politische Konzeption systematischer Rechtsarbeit bietet *A. Somek*, Rechtssystem und Republik. Über die politische Funktion des systematischen Rechtsdenkens, 1992. Siehe auch *R. Alexy*, Rechtssystem und praktische Vernunft, Rechtstheorie 1987, 405.

[355] *M. Weber*, Wirtschaft und Gesellschaft, S. 396: „Das urwüchsige ‚Recht' kennt sie nicht."

[356] Aus dem älteren Schrifttum *H. Elze*, Lücken im Gesetz, 1916.

[357] *St. Uecker*, Die Rationalisierung des Rechts. Max Webers Rechtssoziologie, 2005, S. 75.

[358] *M. Weber*, Wirtschaft uns Gesellschaft, S. 396.

[359] *K. Röhl*, Allgemeine Rechtslehre, 2. Auflage 2001, § 6, S. 47.

wohl auch für die Tragweite der bisher noch nicht hinreichend gewürdigten Themenstellung, dass sich ausgerechnet in Max Webers Rechtssoziologie eine Begriffsbestimmung der Systematisierung findet, auf die das methodologisch ausgerichtete Schrifttum noch heute zurückgreift. Zu beachten ist, dass Weber auch im Rahmen dieser Begriffsbestimmung nochmals und innerhalb dessen sogar wiederholt die Logik betont,[360] die sich sowohl auf die Klarheit als auch auf die Widerspruchsfreiheit des Systems bezieht.[361] Was nach dem Bedachten tautologisch und pleonastisch erscheint, ist in Wahrheit jedes Mal aufs Neue eine Bedingung bzw. Eigenschaft des Systems.[362] Ein System von Regeln, das klar, aber nicht logisch ist, wäre ebenso wertlos wie eines, das zwar frei von Widersprüchen, aber letztlich ohne innere Logik ist.[363]

360 *C.-W. Canaris*, Systemdenken und Systembegriff in der Jurisprudenz, S. 21, hebt das Adjektiv bzw. Adverb „logisch" jeweils hervor, um das „formal-logische System" der Begriffsjurisprudenz zu kennzeichnen, der er Max Weber indes nicht zuordnet; zu dieser bemerkenswerten Einsicht bereits im letzten Abschnitt und noch weiter unten im Text.

361 Vgl. auch *R. Schmidt*, Widerspruchsfreiheit als rechtlicher Maßstab, Festschrift für C.-W. Canaris, 2007, S. 1353. Die Widerspruchsfreiheit gehört zu jenen unabdingbaren Kriterien, die *L. L. Fuller*, The Morality of Law, 3. Auflage 1967, S. 38 ff. (dazu *G. Hughes*, Positivist and Natural Lawers, Stanford Law Review 17, 1965, 547) als Mindesterfordernisse der „legality" statuiert; in diese Richtung ferner *P. Devlin*, The Enforcement of Morals, 1965.

362 Zur Einordnung nicht zuletzt im Hinblick auf den Wissenschaftsanspruch der Jurisprudenz (zu ihm noch am Ende der Abhandlung) wichtig die systemtheoretische Einbettung durch *N. Luhmann*, Rechtssystem und Rechtsdogmatik, 1974, S. 19: „Diese Stellung der Dogmatik *innerhalb* des Rechtssystems schließt es im Übrigen nicht aus, dass es außerhalb des Rechtssystems, etwa im Wissenschaftssystem und dort unter den Gesichtspunkten der Rechtstheorie, noch abstraktere Konzeptualisierungen des Rechts geben kann."

363 Die allfällige Akzentuierung mag rechtsphilosophisch betrachtet mit den anthropologischen Bedingungen zu tun haben; vgl. *F. Nietzsche*, Menschliches, Allzumenschliches, I, 32: „Wir sind von vornherein unlogische und daher ungerechte Wesen und können dies erkennen: dies ist eine der größten und unauflöslichsten Disharmonien des Daseins." Dazu *J. Habermas*, Erkenntnis und Interesse, 1973, S. 363; *J. Petersen*, Nietzsches Genialität der Gerechtigkeit, 2008, passim.

## I. Prinzipielle Lückenlosigkeit

Dass das System nach Weber *prinzipiell* lückenlos ist, bedeutet keine Statuierung der völligen Lückenlosigkeit der Rechtsordnung,[364] die etwa Hans Kelsen zugrunde gelegt hat.[365]

### 1. Webers Anspielung auf das Preußische Allgemeine Landrecht

Auch die Regelungstechnik des Preußischen Allgemeinen Landrechts[366] mit seiner in die Zigtausende von Vorschriften gehenden Überreglementierung, die ein systematisch untauglicher Versuch der Dogmatisierung der Lückenlosigkeit war[367] und diese de facto zu einer Chimäre machte, erwies sich als untauglich:[368] „Wirkliche Rechtskenntnis des Publikums konnte durch ein bändereiches

[364] *K. Bergbohm*, Jurisprudenz und Rechtsphilosophie, 1892, S. 384: „Ein Recht ist etwas allemal in lückenloser Ganzheit Dastehendes, (...) es ist jeden Augenblick voll, weil seine innere Fruchtbarkeit, seine logische Expansionskraft im eigenen Bereich jeden Bereich an Rechtsurteilen deckt."

[365] *H. Kelsen*, Reine Rechtslehre, 2. Auflage 1960 (1. Auflage 1934), S. 253; *E. Bucher*, Das subjektive Recht als Normsetzungsbefugnis, 1965; skeptisch gegenüber dem Dogma von der Lückenlosigkeit der Rechtsordnung *ders.*, Der von den Juristen verkannte apagogische Beweis, Festschrift für C.-W. Canaris, S. 991, 1003 mit Fußnote 34, 1004 ff. Für den vorliegenden Zusammenhang aufschlussreich ist auch *H. Kelsen*, Der soziologische und der juristische Staatsbegriff. Kritische Untersuchung des Verhältnisses von Staat und Recht, 1922. Wichtig ferner *H. Dreier*, Hans Kelsens Wissenschaftsprogramm, in: Die Verwaltung, Beiheft 7, 2007, S. 81, 84, zu Max Weber. Siehe auch *Ph. Heck*, Die reine Rechtslehre und ihre jungösterreichische Schule der Rechtswissenschaft, AcP 119 (1922), 173.

[366] *H. Hattenhauer*, Allgemeines Landrecht für die Preußischen Staaten von 1794, Textausgabe mit einer Einführung von Hans Hattenhauer und einer Bibliographie von Günter Berndt, 1970.

[367] Aus dem frühen Schrifttum *F. Löher*, Das System des preußischen Landrechts in deutschrechtlicher und philosophischer Begründung, 1852.

[368] *H. Conrad*, Das allgemeine Landrecht von 1794 als Grundgesetz des friederizianischen Staates, 1956; *ders.*, Richter und Gesetz im Übergang von Absolutismus und Verfassungsstaat, 1971; *ders.*, Staatsgedanke und Staatspraxis des aufgeklärten Absolutismus, 1971.

Werk mit Zehntausenden von Paragraphen am allerwenigsten erreicht werden, und wenn darunter die Emanzipation von Anwälten und anderen fachjuristischen Praktikern verstanden wurde, so war dies Ziel auch der Natur der Sache[369] nach unter den Bedingungen des modernen Rechtslebens an sich unerreichbar. Die Kodifikation sollte ‚erschöpfend' sein und glaubte, es sein zu können."[370] An anderer Stelle spricht Weber insoweit von einer „petitio principii der begrifflichen Lückenlosigkeit des Rechts".[371] Aus methodologischer Sicht lässt sich wohl sogar hinzufügen, dass die Ausfüllung etwaiger Lücken unschädlich möglich ist, wenn und weil die Lückenfeststellung auf dem Boden des Systems und damit seiner in sich widerspruchsfreien Regeln erfolgt.[372] Das setzt freilich voraus, was im beispielhaft behandelten Preußischen Landrecht fehlte, dass es neben genauen formalen Normen auch Rechtsinstitute gibt, auf deren Boden eine wissenschaftliche Jurisprudenz überhaupt nur gedeihen kann.[373]

## 2. „Intern intellektualistische Interessenkonstellation"

Insofern ist auch die Befürchtung unbegründet, dass mit der Zunahme des positiven Rechts die Arbeit des Fachjuristen entbehrlich werde, wie Weber beobachtet zu haben glaubt: „Durch die ste-

369 Skeptisch gegenüber dem Topos der „Natur der Sache" schon *E. Ehrlich*, Über Lücken im Rechte, JBl. 1888, 511; treffend *E. I. Bekker*, Ernst und Scherz über unsere Wissenschaft, 1892, S. 147 („Das schlimmste bei dem Ausdruck ist, dass er nicht zum scharfen Denken zwingt, und darum schon recht häufig als Gedankensurrogat vernutzt ist."). Aus dem weiteren Schrifttum wichtig *G. Stratenwerth*, Das rechtstheoretische Problem der „Natur der Sache", 1957; *R. Dreier*, Zum Begriff der ‚Natur der Sache', 1965; Siehe auch *A. Kaufmann*, Analogie und Natur der Sache, 2. Auflage 1982.

370 *M. Weber*, Wirtschaft und Gesellschaft, S. 494.

371 *M. Weber*, Wirtschaft und Gesellschaft, S. 509.

372 Grundlegend *C.-W. Canaris*, Die Feststellung von Lücken im Gesetz, 1964; dazu bereits oben 1. a. E.

373 *M. Weber*, Wirtschaft und Gesellschaft, S. 494. Zum historischen Hintergrund *H. Conrad*, Die geistigen Grundlagen des allgemeinen Landrechts für die preußischen Staaten von 1794, 1958. Siehe auch *W. Krawietz*, Juristische Entscheidung und wissenschaftliche Erkenntnis, 1978.

tige Zunahme des formulierten Gesetzesrechts und namentlich der systematischen Kodifikationen fühlen sich die akademischen Juristen in ihrer Bedeutung und auch in den Chancen der Bewegungsfreiheit des wissenschaftlichen Denkens empfindlich bedroht, und die rapide Zunahme der sowohl antilogischen wie antihistorischen Bewegungen in Deutschland, wo man das Los der französischen Rechtswissenschaft nach dem Code, der preußischen nach dem Allgemeinen Landrecht fürchtet, ist dadurch leicht erklärlich und insofern Produkt einer historischen, intern intellektualistischen Interessenkonstellation."[374]

Eine anspruchsvolle Gesetzgebung, so könnte man hinzufügen, hat vor der wissenschaftlichen Jurisprudenz wenig zu befürchten, weil sie als solche nach dem Bedachten niemals lückenlos ist und den Vortrag spezifisch systematischer Argumente ermöglicht.[375] Wie zutreffend auf der anderen Seite die Beobachtung Webers ist, lässt sich in dem in dieser Hinsicht bereits unvorteilhaft aufgefallenen und sogleich noch zu behandelnden Steuerrecht ersehen,[376] in dem die unsystematische Überreglementierung zwar allenthalben erkannt,[377] ihr aber mitunter wohl auch deshalb nicht entgegengewirkt wird und allfällige Vereinfachungen nur geringe Aussichten auf legislatorische Umsetzung haben, weil den einschlägig gebildeten Fachjuristen, nicht zuletzt innerhalb der Praxis, dämmert, dass man ihrer sonst nicht mehr in gewohntem Umfang bedürfen könnte.

374 *M. Weber*, Wirtschaft und Gesellschaft, S. 509.

375 Zur Bedeutung des systematischen Arguments *C.-W. Canaris*, Systemdenken und Systembegriff in der Jurisprudenz, 2. Auflage 1983; *ders.*, Das Rangverhältnis der „klassischen" Auslegungskriterien, demonstriert an Standardproblemen aus dem Zivilrecht, Festschrift für D. Medicus, 1999, S. 25 ff.

376 Unten sub II.

377 Vgl. nur *J. Petersen*, Unternehmenssteuerrecht und bewegliches System, 1999, S. 10 m. w. N.

### 3. Systematisierung als Subsumierbarkeit logisch geordneter Normen

Der Systemanspruch bedeutet nach alledem, „dass alle denkbaren Tatbestände unter eine seiner Normen müssen logisch subsumiert werden können, widrigenfalls ihre Ordnung der rechtlichen Garantie entbehre.“[378] Hier ist die Voraussetzung des Logischen keine Wiederholung, sondern es steht gleichsam vor der Klammer der Subsumtion und greift somit alle soeben behandelten Voraussetzungen zusammenfassend auf. Wie wichtig gerade das Element des Logischen ist, wird deutlich, wenn Weber betont, dass es Rechtsordnungen gibt, die sich ihre Systematisierung zu Unrecht zugute halten, weil „die logische Sublimierung des Systems äußerst unentwickelt“ ist.[379] Nicht von ungefähr erscheint in diesem Zusammenhang der Begriff der Sublimierung, der bereits bei den von Weber so bezeichneten „logisch hoch sublimierten ‚Rechtssätzen‘“ gebraucht wurde.[380] Am Beispiel der Auslegung präzisiert Weber das Vorgehen: „Streng formalistisch und am Sinnfälligen haftend, soweit die geschäftliche Verkehrssitte es verlangt, ist es (sc. das Recht) im Interesse der geschäftlichen Verkehrsloyalität unformal, soweit die logische Sinninterpretation des Parteiwillens oder die in der Richtung eines ‚ethischen Minimums‘ gedeutete ‚gute Verkehrssitte‘ es bedingen.“[381] An anderer Stelle

[378] *M. Weber*, Wirtschaft und Gesellschaft, S. 395. Wesentlich ist gerade für die dogmatische Jurisprudenz die Prämisse von *N. Luhmann*, Rechtssystem und Rechtsdogmatik, 1974, S. 24: „Die dogmatischen Begriffe, Theorien, Erkenntnisse *sind* nicht das System, sie *steuern* das System des Rechts.“ Hervorhebungen auch dort. Skeptisch *K. Larenz*, Methodenlehre der Rechtswissenschaft, 6. Auflage 1991, S. 229 ff. Siehe auch *B. Rüthers*, Rechtsdogmatik und Rechtspolitik, 2003, S. 30 ff.

[379] *M. Weber*, Wirtschaft und Gesellschaft, S. 395. Siehe auch *H. L. Kaye*, Rationalization as Sublimation: on the Cultural Analysis of Weber and Freud: Theory Culture & Society 9 (1992) 245.

[380] *M. Weber*, Wirtschaft und Gesellschaft, S. 395.

[381] *M. Weber*, Wirtschaft und Gesellschaft, S. 510. Mit der Formulierung des „ethischen Minimums“ greift Weber die berühmte Definition des Rechts von *G. Jellinek*, Die sozialethische Bedeutung von Recht, Unrecht und Strafe, 1908, S. 45, auf.

ordnet er die Systematik der logischen Rationalität gleich,[382] die wiederum zu einer „logischen Sublimierung und deduktiven Strenge des Rechts und einer zunehmend rationalen Technik des Rechtsgangs" führt.[383] Die logische Sublimierung gerät damit zur „logische(n) Sinndeutung."[384] Systematisierung ist also die Subsumierbarkeit logisch geordneter Normen.

## II. Das Steuerrecht als Paradigma mangelnder Systematisierung

Gerade der zuletzt angesprochene Gesichtspunkt, wonach der Systemanspruch mitunter fälschlich erhoben wird, betrifft nicht nur die von Weber skizzierten anderen bzw. überkommenen Rechtsordnungen, sondern muss unter dem Blickpunkt der Methodenlehre auch als stete Mahnung an Teile der eigenen Rechtsordnung begriffen werden, wie zum Beispiel namentlich das bereits angesprochene Steuerrecht, dessen fehlende Systematisierung oft und zumeist zu Recht beklagt wird, wenn diesbezüglich etwas vom „Steuerchaos" oder gleich vom „Steuerdschungel" die Rede ist.[385]

382 *St. Uecker*, Die Rationalisierung des Rechts. Max Webers Rechtssoziologie, 2005, S. 68, verweist in diesem Zusammenhang auf *J. Habermas*, Die Theorie des kommunikativen Handelns, Band 1, Handlungsrationalität und gesellschaftliche Rationalisierung, 1981, S. 348.

383 *M. Weber*, Wirtschaft und Gesellschaft, S. 505; siehe auch *E. v. Savigny*, Zur Rolle der deduktiv-axiomatischen Methode in der Rechtswissenschaft, in: Rechtstheorie (Hg. G. Jahr/W. Maihofer), 1971, S. 315.

384 *M. Weber*, Wirtschaft und Gesellschaft, S. 506, mit dem auch heute noch praktisch wichtigen Beispiel der Unterscheidung zwischen der Deutung von Rechtsnormen, also der Interpretation von Gesetzen, und der Auslegung von Rechtsgeschäfte nach Maßgabe der §§ 133, 157 BGB; dazu *J. Petersen*, Die Auslegung von Rechtsgeschäften, Jura, 2004, 536; *ders.*, Die Auslegung von letztwilligen Verfügungen, Jura 2005, 597.

385 *K. Tipke*, Steuerrecht – Chaos, Konglomerat oder System?, StuW 1971, 2; *ders.*, Steuerrechtswissenschaft und Steuersystem, Festschrift für Wacke, 1972, S. 211; grundlegend *ders.*, Die Steuerrechtsordnung, 2 Bände, 2. Auflage 2003. Zu einem Teilbereich *J. Petersen*, Unternehmenssteuerrecht und bewegliches System, 1999, S. 32 ff.

Hier begegnet die Besonderheit, dass es im Unterschied zu denjenigen Anwendungsbereichen, die Weber nennt, nicht Rechtsordnungen sind, die diesen Anspruch von vornherein nicht erheben oder ihn, wie das von ihm so bezeichnete „urwüchsige Recht“ gar nicht kennen. Vielmehr ist das gegenwärtige deutsche Steuerrecht im Unterschied dazu durch eine hypertrophe Überreglementierung gekennzeichnet,[386] die es für die Rechtssoziologie und Methodenlehre gleichermaßen interessant macht, weil vielfach weder Komplexität sinnvoll reduziert wird noch die für unerlässlich gehaltene Klarheit herrscht, da selbst Experten und Eingeweihte die mangelnde Durchschaubarkeit beklagen.[387] Das hat aber wohl nicht zum mindesten mit einem Systemdefizit zu tun, da nahezu alle Merkmale und Erfordernisse dessen, wie es Weber im oben genannten Sinne versteht,[388] fehlen oder so unzureichend ausgeprägt sind, dass sie auch nicht ohne weiteres durch andere Merkmale kompensiert werden können.

## III. Äußeres Ordnungsschema und inneres System

Wenn Weber im Folgenden in der Vergangenheit spricht, so bedeutet auch dies vom Standpunkt der juristischen Methodenlehre ein zeitlos gültiges Desiderat: „In der Regel aber war die Systematisierung vorwiegend ein äußeres Schema der Ordnung des Rechtsstoffes[389] und nur von geringem Einfluss auf die Art der analytischen Bildung der Rechtssätze sowohl wie auf die Konstruktion der Rechtsverhältnisse.“[390] Von dem besagten äußeren

[386] Rechtsvergleichend methodisch interessant *H. Bergmann Avila*, Juristische Theorie der Argumentation – Entworfen am Beispiel des brasilianischen Steuerrechts, Festschrift für C.-W. Canaris, 2007, S. 963.

[387] *P. Kirchhof*, Steuerrechtsordnung als Wertordnung, StuW 1996, 3.

[388] *M. Weber*, Wirtschaft und Gesellschaft, S. 396; dazu oben vor a).

[389] *B. Quensel*, Logik und Methode in der „Rechtssoziologie“ Max Webers, Zeitschrift für Rechtssoziologie 18 (1997) 145, spricht von der „Ausbildung einer Schablone“.

[390] *M. Weber*, Wirtschaft und Gesellschaft, S. 396.

Schema der Ordnung zu unterscheiden ist das an anderer Stelle von Weber so genannte „nur provisorische Schema der Ordnung“,[391] das einen niedrigeren Rationalitätsgrad aufweist.

## 1. Inneres und äußeres System

Wendet man diese Aussage auf die juristische Methodenlehre an, so ist mit dem dort beschriebenen und als nicht hinreichend empfundenen äußeren Ordnungsschema ein Gesichtspunkt angesprochen, der an Philipp Hecks Unterscheidung zwischen dem inneren und äußeren System erinnert,[392] die der Methodenlehre zu Recht als Entdeckung gilt.[393] Dem äußeren System, das den Rechtsstoff ordnet, indem die einzelnen Rechtsgebiete klassifiziert und innerhalb ihrer durch Untertitel und Abschnitte unterteilt, stellt Heck das innere System an die Seite, welches das Ineinandergreifen der einzelnen Regelungen auf der Prinzipienebene betrifft.[394] Gerade deshalb ist aber die systematische Argumentation aus dem inneren System derjenigen, die nur die Abfolge und äußere Ordnung der gesetzlichen Regelungen ins Feld führt, überlegen, weil jene im Unterschied zu dieser zwangläufig teleologische Züge trägt.[395] Dem äußeren System entspricht der Sache nach das von Weber gemeinte äußere Ordnungsschema; es ist jeweils nicht gering zu

[391] *M. Weber*, Archiv für Sozialwissenschaft und Sozialpolitik 24 (1907, 94, Fußnote 15. Dazu noch in § 6 zur Theoriebildung.

[392] *Ph. Heck*, Begriffsbildung und Interessenjurisprudenz, 1932, S. 139 ff.; siehe aus dem neueren Schrifttum auch *F. Bydlinski*, Zum Verhältnis von äußerem und innerem System im Privatrecht, Festschrift für C.-W. Canaris, 2007, S. 1017.

[393] *C.-W. Canaris*, Systemdenken und Systembegriff in der Jurisprudenz, 2. Auflage 1983, S. 11 ff.

[394] *Ph. Heck*, Begriffsbildung und Interessenjurisprudenz, 1932, S. 139; siehe aus dem neueren Schrifttum auch *F. Bydlinski*, Zum Verhältnis von äußerem und innerem System im Privatrecht, Festschrift für C.-W. Canaris, 2007, S. 1017.

[395] *C.-W. Canaris*, Systemdenken und Systembegriff in der Jurisprudenz, S. 91 f. mit Fußnote 23.

schätzen und wohl sogar eine notwendige Voraussetzung, aber als solches auch nicht hinreichend, um für sich allein den Systemanspruch einzulösen.

## 2. Maßgeblichkeit der Prinzipienebene

Daran zeigt sich im Übrigen mittelbar, dass die für die Rechtssoziologie essentiellen Lebenszusammenhänge vor allem für das äußere, nicht so sehr dagegen für das innere System von Bedeutung sind.[396] Weber wie Heck haben, jeder auf seinem Gebiet, erkannt, dass allein mit dem einen die Prinzipienebene nicht sinnvoll betreten werden kann. Aus diesem Grund kann nach Weber das äußere Ordnungsschema zur analytischen Bildung der Rechtssätze, also der Prinzipien,[397] ebenso wenig beitragen wie zur Konstruktion der Rechtsverhältnisse, die nach dem oben Bedachten gleichfalls den Rechtsprinzipien verpflichtet ist.[398] Dass Heck und Weber hier jeder auf seine Weise und jeder auf seinem Gebiet eine Funktionsweise gefunden haben, die letztlich auf derselben Ebene wirksam wird, macht die Gemeinsamkeiten beider hinsichtlich ihrer akademischen Herkunft doppelt interessant.[399]

396 *C.-W. Canaris*, Systemdenken und Systembegriff in der Jurisprudenz, S. 47 Fußnote 133.

397 *R. Müller-Erzbach*, Der Durchbruch des Interessenrechts durch allgemeine Rechtsprinzipien, Jherings Jahrbücher 53 (1908) 331; *M. Weber*, Wirtschaft und Gesellschaft, S. 395. Müller-Erzbach hat die Interessenjurisprudenz zum Leidwesen *Ph. Hecks* (Die Leugnung der Interessenjurisprudenz durch Hermann Isay, AcP 137, 1933, 47) später in Zweifel gezogen; vgl. *R. Müller-Erzbach*, Wohin führt die Interessenjurisprudenz?, 1932; *ders.*, Lassen sich das Recht und das Rechtsleben tiefer und sicherer erfassen?, 1934.

398 Zum Begriff des Rechtsprinzips die gleichnamige Abhandlung von *R. Alexy*, in: Argumentation und Hermeneutik in der Jurisprudenz (Hg. W. Krawietz u.a.) Beiheft zur Rechtstheorie 1979, S. 59.

399 Wie in der Einleitung dargestellt, waren beide ungefähr zur selben Zeit akademische Schüler des Handelsrechtlers Levin Goldschmidt, bei dem Weber promovierte; siehe *H. Schoppmeyer*, Juristische Methode als Lebensaufgabe, 2001, S. 160.

## IV. Folgerungen für das Verhältnis zwischen Rechtssoziologie und Interessenjurisprudenz

Eine unsichtbare Verbindungslinie zwischen beiden kommt auch in dem folgenden Satz Webers zum Ausdruck: „Die spezifisch moderne (am römischen Recht entwickelte) Systematisierung geht eben von ‚logischer Sinndeutung' sowohl der Rechtssätze wie des rechtlich relevanten Sichverhaltens aus, die Rechtsverhältnisse und die Kasuistik dagegen sträuben sich dieser Manipulation nicht selten, da sie ihrerseits zunächst von ‚anschaulichen' Merkmalen aus erwachsen sind."[400]

### 1. Primat der Lebensforschung

Es ist nämlich gerade ein Merkmal der Heckschen Interessenjurisprudenz, dass er in genau dem Sinne den Weber zunächst nennt, nämlich der logischen Sinndeutung nicht nur der Rechtssätze, sondern auch des rechtlich relevanten Sichverhaltens verfährt: Letzteres ist nichts anderes als der „Primat der Lebensforschung und Lebenswertung", von der er spricht,[401] oder – mit den Worten eines anderen prominenten Vertreters der Interessenjurisprudenz – „die Hinwendung der Rechtswissenschaft zum Leben".[402] Ersteres ist die gerade für seine Interessenjurisprudenz charakteristische Sicht,[403] wonach auch in den gesetzlichen Vorschriften „rechtlich gewertete Interessen"[404] zum Vorschein kommen. Damit werden gesetzliche Werturteile[405] zu einer „Anweisung zum Interessen-

[400] *M. Weber*, Wirtschaft und Gesellschaft, S. 396.

[401] *Ph. Heck*, Rechtsphilosophie und Interessenjurisprudenz, 1932, S. 17.

[402] *R. Müller-Erzbach*, Die Hinwendung der Rechtswissenschaft zum Leben, 1939.

[403] *J. Petersen*, Von der Interessenjurisprudenz zur Wertungsjurisprudenz, 2001, S. 5 ff.

[404] *Ph. Heck*, Gesetzesauslegung und Interessenschutz, 1932, S. 8.

[405] Aus dem frühen Schrifttum *G. Rümelin*, Werturteile und Willensentscheidungen im Civilrecht, 1891; *ders.*, Juristische Begriffsbildung, 1894.

schutz".[406] Das geht so weit, dass Heck im Einzelfall auch davon ausgeht, dass selbst „das Gesetz die unrichtige Auffassung erkennen lässt"[407] – eine für unser heutiges Verständnis zu weitgehende Interpretation.[408] So schaut die Interessenjurisprudenz eben nicht nur auf den Sachverhalt, sondern auch darauf, ob sich in den zu seiner rechtlichen Würdigung einschlägigen Regelungen eine normative Abbildung der Interessen erblicken lässt.[409] Luhmann hat das Neuartige an diesem Vorgehen wie folgt beschrieben: „Die Orientierung am Rechtssystem in einem neuartigen Sinne zeigt sich – sehr versteckt – schon daran, dass der Übergang zur Interessenjurisprudenz die Dogmatik ein gut Teil gesetzgebungsabhängiger macht als zuvor; denn sie muss nun die Wertung der Interessen durch den Gesetzgeber voraussetzen. Die Dogmatik muss nun eine rechtssystemimmanente Funktion zugewiesen erhalten."[410] Hinzu kommt, dass die Interessenjurisprudenz nach Philipp Heck „philosophielos" ist,[411] während man das wohl von der Wertungsjurisprudenz nicht ohne weiteres sagen kann, deren Entstehung vielmehr „zu einer Auseinandersetzung mit Wertvorstellungen und damit zu einer philosophischen Verankerung des Rechts zwingt".[412] An anderer Stelle hat Fikentscher diesen Übergang noch um den Gerechtigkeitsgedanken bereichert, der den Bewusstseinswandel vielleicht am deutlichsten kennzeichnet:[413]

[406] Siehe auch *R. Hönigswald*, „Begriff" und „Interesse". Eine methodologische Skizze, AcP 138 (1938) 1 ff.

[407] *Ph. Heck*, Grundriss des Schuldrechts, 1929, § 95 unter 4 a. E, S. 300.

[408] *J. Petersen*, Von der Interessenjurisprudenz, zur Wertungsjurisprudenz, S. 17.

[409] Zutreffend *N. Luhmann*, Rechtssystem und Rechtsdogmatik, 1974, S. 12: „Auch die Interessenjurisprudenz lebt, juristisch gesehen, von ihren dogmatischen Erfindungen."

[410] *N. Luhmann*, Rechtssystem und Rechtsdogmatik, 1974, S. 12.

[411] *Ph. Heck*, Rechtsphilosophie und Interessenjurisprudenz, AcP 143, 1937, 129.

[412] *W. Fikentscher*, Ein juristisches Jahrhundert, Rechtshistorisches Journal 19 (2000) 560, 567; siehe auch *H. Kronstein*, Rechtsauslegung im wertgebundenen Recht, 1957.

[413] Siehe auch *B. Rüthers*, Die Wende-Experten. Zur Ideologieanfälligkeit geistiger Berufe am Beispiel der Juristen, 2. Auflage 1995, S. 195 f. („Interes-

„Man begann zu begreifen, dass die Wahl der richtigen Methode letztlich eine Frage der Philosophie ist, die der Methode den Weg zur Werteauswahl zu weisen hat. (...) Die Erweiterung der methodischen Fragestellung zu einer philosophischen sicherte die Methode ab. Man verstand, dass Methode nicht nur falsch angewandt (‚unwahr') werden können, sondern auch falsch gewählt (‚ungerecht') sein können."[414] Nicht zuletzt diese Abkehr von der „philosophielosen" Interessenjurisprudenz veranschaulicht, dass es sich auch wissenschaftsgeschichtlich um einen Paradigmenwechsel handelt.[415]

## 2. Logische Sinndeutung und prinzipielle Konvergenz

Die „logische Sinndeutung", von der Weber spricht, ist darauf bezogen nichts anderes, als die Gesetzesanwendung, also Subsumtion, unter gleichzeitiger Heranziehung von Wortlaut und Teleologie der betreffenden Vorschriften.[416] Diese im Wortsinne prinzipielle Konvergenz wirft die im Schrifttum bereits diskutierte Frage auf,[417] wie sich Interessenjurisprudenz und Rechtssoziologie zueinander verhalten. Soweit dieser Problematik bislang nachgegangen wurde, wird soweit ersichtlich mehrheitlich davon ausgegangen, dass die Interessenjurisprudenz[418] ein maßgeblicher Wegbereiter der Rechtssoziologie gewesen ist.[419] Allerdings wird man

sen- und Wertungsjurisprudenz ohne ihre Wurzeln in der gesellschaftlichen Rechtswissenschaft gar nicht erklärbar").

414 *W. Fikentscher*, Methoden des Rechts, Band III, 1977, S. 383.

415 *J. Petersen*, Von der Interessenjurisprudenz zur Wertungsjurisprudenz, 2001, passim.

416 *N. Luhmann*, Funktionale Methode und juristische Entscheidung, AöR 1969, 1, 5, gibt zu bedenken, dass die teleologische Auslegung praktisch erst nachrangig zur Geltung kommt: „Sofern diese (sc. die Rechtsnormen) die Bedingungen bestimmter Entscheidungen nicht eindeutig definieren – und nur dann! –, wird auf der Suche nach zusätzlichen Entscheidungshilfen der Zweck oder die Funktion der Norm in Betracht gezogen."

417 *H. Schoppmeyer*, Juristische Methode als Lebensaufgabe, 2001, S. 160.

418 Zu ihr *G. Ellscheid/W. Hassemer*, Interessenjurisprudenz, 1974.

419 *B. Dombek*, Das Verhältnis der Tübinger Schule zur deutschen Rechtssoziologie, 1969; *W. Fikentscher*, Methoden des Rechts in vergleichender Dar-

diese Einschätzung einstweilen in den Rang einer Arbeitshypothese zurückverweisen müssen, weil sich gezeigt hat, dass sich umgekehrt bei Max Weber – ohne erkennbaren Rekurs auf die Interessenjurisprudenz – Prämissen von prinzipieller Bedeutung finden lassen, die darauf hindeuten, dass bei genuin unterschiedlichen Ausgangspunkten, und deshalb ohne Behauptung eines Vorrangverhältnisses in die eine oder andere Richtung, von vornherein ein gleichartiges Verständnis im Sinne prinzipieller Konvergenz zugrunde lag.

### 3. Unreflektierte Soziologisierung der Rechtsanwendung?

Bei alledem muss man sich jedoch eine Bestandsaufnahme Niklas Luhmanns vergegenwärtigen, der ein halbes Jahrhundert nach Webers Tod und ein Vierteljahrhundert, nachdem die Interessenjurisprudenz allmählich der Wertungsjurisprudenz gewichen ist,[420] ein für das Verhältnis zur Soziologie eher pessimistisch stimmendes Fazit gezogen hat: „Als Erbe der Interessenjurisprudenz haben wir einige dogmatische Gewinne zu verzeichnen, vor allem aber einen Trend zu einer massiven und unreflektierten Soziologisierung der Rechtsanwendung, ohne dass die Soziologie selbst Instrumente oder Theorien dafür anlieferte.“[421] Die damit formulier-

stellung, Band III, S. 376; zu apodiktisch *J. Petersen*, Von der Interessenjurisprudenz, zur Wertungsjurisprudenz, S. 6 Fußnote 18.

[420] Zu diesem Prozess, der ungeachtet der Allmählichkeit der Fortentwicklung als Paradigmenwechsel im Sinne Kuhns aufgefasst werden kann, *J. Petersen*, Von der Interessenjurisprudenz zur Wertungsjurisprudenz, 2001, passim.

[421] *N. Luhmann*, Rechtssystem und Rechtsdogmatik, 1974, S. 11. Siehe zu der im angloamerikanischen Rechtskreis wichtigen Parallele der sociological jurisprudence von *Roscoe Pound*, A Survey of Social Interests, Harvad Law Review 57 (1943) 1; *ders.*, A Call for a Realistic Jurisprudence, Harvard Law Review 44 (1930/31) 697 (zu ihm *K. L. Llewellyn*, Some Realism about Realism: Responding to Dean Pound, Harvard Law Review 44 (1930/31) 1222; siehe auch *W. Fikentscher*, Roscoe Pound. Von der Zweckjurisprudenz zur „Sociological Jurisprudence, Festschrift für K. Larenz, 1973, S. 93). Pound betonte im Übrigen – für den vorliegenden Zusammenhang weiterführend –,

ten Bedenken gegenüber einer unreflektierten, also die theoretischen Grundlagen der Soziologie nicht berücksichtigenden, Soziologisierung des Rechts ist in der Tat nicht von der Hand zu weisen, wenn und weil sie Gefahr läuft, einer selbstverherrlichenden Idealisierung der juristischen Methodenlehre unter dem Deckmantel der Befruchtung durch die Soziologie Vorschub zu leisten, während diese in Wahrheit nur als subalterne Hilfswissenschaft vereinnahmt wird.[422]

## V. Sinndeutende Abstraktion

Zum Schluss dieses Abschnitts, der zugleich dem des ersten Paragraphen der Rechtssoziologie Webers entspricht, können diejenigen Voraussetzungen zusammengefasst werden, die mit Webers eigenen Worten die „sinndeutende Abstraktion" ermöglichen.[423]

die lediglich instrumentelle Bedeutung des Logischen; *R. Pound*, Liberty of Contract, Yale Law Journal 18 (1909) 464. Siehe ferner *N. Reich*, Sociological Jurisprudence and Legal Realism im Rechtsdenken Amerikas, 1967; *G. Casper*, Juristischer Realismus und politische Theorie im amerikanischen Rechtsdenken, 1967. Zu nennen sind ferner die Richter bzw. Rechtstheoretiker Oliver W. Holmes, *Benjamin N. Cardozo* (The Nature of Juridical Process, 1921; *ders.*, The Paradoxes of Legal Science, 1928; *ders.*, The Growth of the Law, 1924) und Louis D. Brandeis. Bedenkenswert freilich *N. Luhmann*, Rechtssystem und Rechtsdogmatik, 1974, S. 9: „Im Streben nach ‚soziologischer Jurisprudenz' liegt die Gefahr einer Annäherung auf dem für beide Seiten niedrigsten Niveau." Zu einer ähnlichen Parallele *H. Coing*, Rudolf von Ihering und Bentham, Interessenjurisprudenz und englische utilitaristische Philosophie, in: 375 Jahre Rechtswissenschaft in Gießen (Hg. G. Weick), 1982, S. 1.

422 *H. Rottleuthner*, Richterliches Handeln. Zur Kritik der juristischen Dogmatik, 1973, S. 1: „Rationalisierungskonzepte werden mit dünnem Vokabular vertreten; die Leistungen der Rechtsdogmatik beschworen; die Bedeutung empirischen Wissens wird diskutiert." Er warnt aus gutem Grund „vor weiteren Verfilzungen der Methodendiskussion".

423 Dazu *St. Uecker*, Die Rationalisierung des Rechts. Max Webers Rechtssoziologie, 2005, S. 75, der daraus folgert: „Vollkommene Rationalität (...) besitzt folglich nur der Idealtypus des formal-rationalen, systematisch logischen Rechts."

Sie besteht in der „spezifisch systematische(n) Aufgabe, die einzelnen anerkanntermaßen geltenden Rechtsregeln durch die Mittel der Logik zu einem in sich widerspruchslosen Zusammenhang von abstrakten Rechtssätzen zusammenzufügen und zu rationalisieren."[424]

### 1. Höchstgrad methodisch-logischer Rationalität

Es ist dasjenige, was den „Höchstgrad methodisch-logischer Rationalität"[425] abbilden und damit den Standard für dasjenige setzen kann, was auch die juristische Methodenlehre voraussetzt.

#### a) Subsumtion mit den Mitteln der Rechtslogik

Das ist zunächst die Anwendung des Rechtssatzes auf den konkreten Tatbestand, also demjenigen, was herkömmlicher Weise als „Subsumtion" bezeichnet wird,[426] woraus eine Rechtsfolge abgeleitet werden kann,[427] und zwar „mit den Mitteln der Rechtslogik". Rechtssatz und Sachverhalt erfahren so – mit Karl Engischs Worten – eine „ständige Wechselwirkung, ein Hin- und Herwandern des Blicks zwischen Obersatz und Lebenssachverhalt."[428] Diesen Topos greift auch Luhmann in einer Beschreibung auf, die durchaus an Weber erinnert: „Durch Dogmatisierung des Rechtsstoffes – und das heißt zunächst: durch seine begrifflich-klassifikatorische Durcharbeitung – wird erreicht, dass jenes oft beschriebene Hin- und Herwandern des Blicks zwischen Normen und Fakten nicht ohne Führung bleibt, sich nicht nur der Entscheidungssituation, sondern auch dem Rechtssystem verpflichtet weiß

[424] *M. Weber*, Wirtschaft und Gesellschaft, S. 397.

[425] *M. Weber*, Wirtschaft und Gesellschaft, S. 397.

[426] Statt aller *J. Oechsler*, Vertragstypen, in: Staudinger/Eckpfeiler des Zivilrechts, 2005, S. 500 ff.; *J. Petersen*, Die mündliche Prüfung im ersten juristischen Staatsexamen, 2005, S. 7 ff.

[427] Rechtssoziologisch interessant *G. Lübbe-Wolff*, Rechtsfolgen und Realfolgen, 1981.

[428] *K. Engisch*, Logische Studien zur Gesetzesanwendung, 3. Auflage 1963, S. 15.

und sich nicht aus der Rechtsordnung hinausspiralt."[429] Auch das entspricht letztlich dem syllogistischen Vorgehen,[430] im Rahmen dessen der Sachverhalt dem Gesetz, also mit Webers Worten dem Rechtssatz, in der Weise subsumiert bzw. durch vermittelnde Ableitung entsprechend handhabbar gemacht wird, dass sich dadurch bruchlos, d. h. ohne Einführung weiterer Prämissen oder unzulässiger Ad-hoc-Hypothesen,[431] wohl aber unter Umständen der die Regel bestätigenden Ausnahmen,[432] die konkrete Rechtsentscheidung bewerkstelligen lässt. Durch dieses Verfahren wird zugleich verhindert, dass derjenige Fehlschluss unterläuft, den Weber, wie eingangs wiedergegeben,[433] dem Laien gemäß erachtet, nämlich dass vom Einzelnen auf das Einzelne geschlossen wird.[434]

### b) Argumentum ad absurdum

Damit zusammen hängt eine verbreitete Argumentationsweise, deren Methode – wenn man davon überhaupt sprechen kann – Weber folgendermaßen charakterisiert und die sich nur durch den Rezipientenkreis unterscheidet: „Die Methodik der publizistischen Theoretiker verfuhr von jeher und verfährt vollends heute in weitgehendem Maße so: dass sie als Konsequenz einer bekämpften juristischen Konstruktion praktisch-politisch absurd scheinende Folgerungen aus derselben aufzeigt und sie damit als erledigt betrachtet."[435] Dieses Prozedere ähnelt dem aus der juris-

[429] *N. Luhmann*, Rechtssystem und Rechtsdogmatik, 1974, S. 18.

[430] Zu ihm *W. Fikentscher*, Juristische Heuristik, Festschrift für C.-W. Canaris, 2007, S. 1091 ff.; *J. Oechsler*, Vertragstypen, in: Staudinger/Eckpfeiler des Zivilrechts, 2005, S. 501.

[431] *C.-W. Canaris*, Funktion, Struktur und Falsifikation juristischer Theorien, JZ 1993, 377.

[432] Dazu *L. G. Miller*, Rules and Exceptions, Ethics 66 (1956) 262, der davon ausgeht, dass Ausnahmen die Regel nicht diskreditieren, sondern insofern stabilisieren, als sie von nicht einzulösenden Ansprüchen entlastet wird; zustimmend *N. Luhmann*, Rechtssystem und Rechtsdogmatik, 1974, S. 83 Anmerkung 64.

[433] Zu Beginn der Abhandlung.

[434] *M. Weber*, Wirtschaft und Gesellschaft, S. 510.

[435] *M. Weber*, Wirtschaft und Gesellschaft, S. 501 f.

tischen Methodenlehre bekannten argumentum ad absurdum.[436] Es handelt sich dabei um ein im Grundsatz zulässiges Argument, soweit es aufzuzeigen vermag, dass eine konkrete Auslegungsweise zu schlechterdings nicht hinnehmbaren Konsequenzen führt und appelliert damit an einen unausgesprochenen Konsens.[437] Seine Durchschlagskraft und Legitimität steht und fällt demnach nicht nur damit, dass das gefundene Ergebnis wertungsmäßig nicht hinnehmbar ist, sondern dass auch wirklich alle Auslegungsmöglichkeiten erschöpfend ausgewertet worden sind.[438] Ähnlich verhält es sich auf rhetorisch-hermeneutischer Ebene, soweit es also etwa nicht um ein Gesetz, sondern eine als abwegig empfundene Auslegung desselben oder eine interpretatorische Ansicht handelt, so dass die Problematik mittelbar die Frage der Falsifikation juristischer Theorien berühren kann.[439] Es entspricht also dem Gebot intellektueller Redlichkeit, dass nicht von vornherein verengend eine besonders absurde Lesart manipulativ herausgegriffen wird, wie es Weber am Beispiel der publizistischen Theoretiker insinuiert.

### c) Paradoxien

Es muss also vom Allgemeinen auf das Einzelne geschlossen werden, was paradoxerweise einschließt, dass vom Einzelnen aus das Allgemeine betrachtet wird.[440] Auch letzteres ist in der juristischen Arbeit wichtig, wenn es darum geht, Einzelfallentscheidungen durch prinzipienmäßige Rückbindung abzusichern.[441] Goethe hat

436 Grundlegend *U. Diederichsen*, Die „reductio ad absurdum" in der Jurisprudenz, Festschrift für K. Larenz, 1973, S. 155; aus dem älteren Schrifttum *Schreier*, Die Interpretation der Gesetze und Rechtsgeschäfte, 1927, S. 42.

437 *F. Bydlinski*, Juristische Methodenlehre und Rechtsbegriff, 2. Auflage 1995, S. 372 f.

438 *F. Bydlinski*, ebenda, S. 457 f.

439 Zu ihr *C.-W. Canaris*, JZ 1993, 377; dazu noch unten § 6.

440 Insoweit kann man aber nicht von einem zwangsläufigen Rückschluss sprechen, wie in der Einleitung dargestellt wurde unter Verweis auf *K. Popper*, Logik der Forschung, 10. Auflage 1994, S. 4 f.

441 In gewisser Weise kann man hierin eine Ausprägung der Diskussion um die Paradoxien und die Rekursivität im Recht sehen; zu ihr *G. P. Fletcher*, Paradoxes in Legal Thought, Columbia Law Review 25 (1985), 1263; *N. Luhmann*, Reflexive Mechanismen, Soziale Welt 17 (1966) 1; *ders.*, The Third Question:

diese wichtige wissenschaftliche Einsicht in seinen *Maximen und Reflexionen* so dargestellt:[442] „Das Allgemeine und Besondere fallen zusammen: das Besondere ist das Allgemeine, unter verschiedenen Bedingungen erscheinend.“[443] Vor diesem Hintergrund erklärt sich auch das vorangehende Paradoxon: „Was ist das Allgemeine? Der einzelne Fall. Was ist das Besondere? Millionen Fälle.“[444] Im Übrigen veranschaulicht die dazwischen liegende Reflexion Goethes,[445] dass Weber mit dem eingangs zitierten Diktum über den juristischen Laien entgegen dem ersten Anschein mitnichten herablassend dessen etwa unterentwickelten Geist gemeint haben könnte, sondern dass es ihm vielmehr um einen Mangel an juristisch-handwerklicher Technik geht, die in einem methodisch-logischen Verfahren, also rational, im Einzelnen das Allgemeine erkennt, weil sie prinzipienmäßig vorgeht. Das zeigt paradoxerweise auch die gleichsam negative Umkehrung ins Irrationale, die als überbordende Folge des Rationalen erscheint: „Alle, auch und gerade die irrationalistischen Spielarten der Abkehr von der in der gemeinrechtlichen Wissenschaft entwickelten rein logischen Rechtssystematik sind aber andererseits auch wieder Konsequenzen der sich selbst überschlagenden wissenschaftlichen Rationalisierung und voraussetzungslosen Selbstbesinnung des Rechts-

The Creative Use of Paradoxes in Law and Legal History, Journal of Law and Society 15 (1988) 153.

442 Das hier und im Folgenden Dargestellte darf nicht als Bekenntnis zum so genannten „konkret-allgemeinen Begriff“ (zu ihm etwa *K. Larenz*, Zur Logik des konkreten Begriffs, DRW, Band V, 1940, S. 294) verstanden werden; dazu *H. Rottleuthner*, Rechtswissenschaft als Sozialwissenschaft, 1973, S. 239 ff.

443 *J. W. v. Goethe*, Maximen und Refelxionen, 491 (zitiert nach der Hamburger Ausgabe, Band 12, 1981).

444 *J. W. v. Goethe*, Maximen und Reflexionen, 489.

445 Sie lautet, ebenda, 490: „Der Fehler schwacher Geister ist, dass sie im Reflektieren sogleich vom Einzelnen ins Allgemeine gehen, anstatt dass man nur in der Gesamtheit das Allgemeine suchen kann.“ – Das machen, wohl gemerkt, die juristischen Laien aus Webers Sicht gerade nicht; dessen ungeachtet ist die richtige Alternative („anstatt...“) das, was Webers Rechtssoziologie ebenso vor Augen steht wie der juristischen Methodenlehre, weil sich die dort bezeichnete Gesamtheit nur durch Systematisierung gewinnen und im System abbilden lässt.

denkens. Denn soweit sie nicht selbst rationalistischen Charakter haben, sind sie doch, als Form der Flucht in das Irrationale, eine Folge der zunehmenden Rationalisierung der Rechtstechnik – eine Parallelerscheinung des Religiösen."[446]

### d) Naturrecht als Ersatz?

In dieser überraschenden Wendung liegt ein Anklang an den Schluss des Vortrags *Wissenschaft als Beruf*: „Wer dies Schicksal der Zeit nicht männlich ertragen kann, dem muss man sagen: Er kehre lieber, schweigend, ohne die übliche Renegatenreklame, sondern schlicht und einfach, in die weit erbarmend geöffneten Arme der alten Kirchen zurück. Sie machen es ihm ja nicht schwer. Irgendwie hat er dabei – das ist unvermeidlich – das ‚Opfer des Intellektes' zu erbringen, so oder so."[447] Für diesen Zusammenhang spricht, dass sich Weber in *Wirtschaft und Gesellschaft* kurz vor der soeben behandelten Stelle über das Naturrecht so geäußert hat: „Als Ersatz bietet sich teils ein religiös gebundenes Naturrecht der (katholischen) Dogmatiker an, teils der Versuch, aus dem ‚Wesen' des Rechts objektive Maßstäbe zu gewinnen."[448] Interessant ist vor diesem Hintergrund die Beobachtung Joseph Ratzingers, der auf Weber zu antworten scheint: „Die Staatslehre hat sowohl im Altertum und Mittelalter wie gerade auch in den Gegensätzen der Neuzeit an das Naturrecht appelliert, das die recta ratio erkennen kann. Aber heute scheint diese recta ratio nicht mehr zu antworten, und Naturrecht wird nicht mehr als das allein Einsichtige, sondern eher als katholische Sonderlehre betrachtet. Dies bedeutet eine Krise der politischen Vernunft, die eine Krise der Politik als solcher ist."[449] Hiermit ist bereits vorgegriffen auf Webers Blick auf das Naturrecht, von dem weiter unten noch die Rede sein wird.[450]

[446] *M. Weber*, Wirtschaft und Gesellschaft, S. 509.
[447] *M. Weber*, Gesammelte Aufsätze zur Wissenschaftslehre, 7. Auflage 1988, S. 582.
[448] *M. Weber*, Wirtschaft und Gesellschaft, S. 508.
[449] *J. Ratzinger*, Werte in Zeiten des Umbruchs, 2005, S. 25; Der letzte Satz ist im Original weitgehend hervorgehoben.
[450] § 4 II. 3. Dazu *H. Dreier*, Naturrecht und Rechtspositivismus (Lit.-Verz.), S. 127.

### e) Ansprüche und Ermächtigungen

Wichtig ist ferner, dass Weber im Rahmen der Behandlung subjektiver Rechte,[451] die für ihn „Machtquellen" sind, in Ansprüchen und Ermächtigungen denkt: „Dieser rechtlich garantierten und begrenzten Macht über deren Tun entsprechen soziologisch die Erwartungen: 1. dass Andere etwas Bestimmtes tun oder 2. dass sie etwas Bestimmtes lassen werden – die beiden Formen der ‚Ansprüche' – oder 3. dass man selbst ohne Störung durch Dritte etwas tun oder nach Belieben auch lassen dürfe: ‚Ermächtigungen'."[452] Während die letztgenannte Befugnis beispielsweise den in § 903 BGB zugunsten des Eigentümers normierten Möglichkeiten entspricht, übersetzen die beiden erstgenannten gleichsam die Legaldefinition des zivilrechtlichen Anspruchs in § 194 Abs. 1 BGB ins Soziologische. Hierin besteht eine gewisse Parallele zur Unterscheidung zwischen Primärregeln, also Verhaltensnormen, und Sekundärregeln, also Ermächtigungen im Sinne von Hart: „Im sozialen Leben spricht man von solchen Befugnissen einräumenden Regeln anders als von den verpflichtenden, man denkt anders über sie, gebraucht sie anders und schätzt sie aus anderen Gründen."[453]

## 2. Juristischer Gutachtenaufbau als Abbildung

Überträgt man diese Einsichten und Postulate auf den vielleicht praktischsten Bereich juristischer Methodenlehre, nämlich die juristische Ausbildung,[454] in der hierzulande seit jeher und damit auch zu Webers Zeit alle diejenigen unterwiesen wurden und wer-

[451] *M. Weber*, Wirtschaft und Gesellschaft, S. 397 ff. Siehe auch *N. Luhmann*, Zur Funktion der „subjektiven Rechte", Jahrbuch für Rechtssoziologie und Rechtstheorie 1 (1970) 321.
[452] *M. Weber*, Wirtschaft und Gesellschaft, S. 398.
[453] *H. L. A. Hart*, Der Begriff des Rechts, 1973, S. 65. Zustimmend *F. Bydlinski*, Juristische Methodenlehre und Rechtbegriff, 2. Auflage 1991, S. 198.
[454] Siehe etwa *H. Schlehofer*, Juristische Methodologie und Methodik der Fallbearbeitung, JuS 1992, 575.

den, die vom Laien zum Juristen werden, so zeigt sich eine nur auf den ersten Blick erstaunliche Besonderheit:[455] Was Weber mit der gehörigen Abstraktion behandelt und voraussetzt, ist im Grunde nichts anderes, als das, was die juristische Ausbildung im Gutachten schult und abbildet. Damit nicht Juristen nur über Rechtsprobleme „gepflegt parlieren",[456] sondern sie konkret lösen können, damit sie also nicht nur gleichsam über die Dinge, sondern von den Dingen reden, ist die strenge, den Gesetzen der „Rechtslogik" folgende,[457] Gutachtenmethode nicht nur sinnvoll, sondern geboten. Sie ist dann nämlich – durchaus im Sinne des bisher Behandelten – die Abbildung des inneren Systems der Privatrechtsordnung, weil sie deren innere Folgerichtigkeit und Widerspruchslosigkeit abbildet und damit dasjenige gewährleistet, was Weber der systematischen Aufgabe überantwortet, nämlich durch sie mit den eingangs zitierten Worten Webers „die einzelnen anerkanntermaßen geltenden Rechtsregeln durch die Mittel der Logik zu einem in sich widerspruchslosen Zusammenhang von abstrakten Rechtssätzen zusammenzufügen und zu rationalisieren."[458]

[455] Dass es in Nachbarländern nicht selbstverständlich ist, hat *F. Ranieri* (JZ 1997, 801, 813; zustimmend *C.-W. Canaris*, Festschrift für Medicus, 1999, S. 25, 27 Fußnote 8) herausgestellt und verdient in einem etwaigen gemeineuropäischen Angleichungsprozess Beachtung.

[456] So treffend *C.-W. Canaris*, Festschrift für Medicus, 1999, S. 25, 27.

[457] Vgl. *M. Weber*, Wirtschaft und Gesellschaft, S. 397.

[458] *M. Weber*, Wirtschaft und Gesellschaft, S. 397. Siehe aber auch *N. Luhmann*, Rechtssystem und Rechtsdogmatik, 1974, S. 54: „In Weiterführung der Analysen von Eugen Bucher kann man vermuten, dass ein Übergang von ‚Begriffsjurisprudenz' zu ‚Interessenjurisprudenz' nur möglich war in dem Maße, als ein Gesetzgeber zur Bestimmung des Schutzwertes der Interessen zur Verfügung stand – also nicht schon im Rahmen der mit historischen Materialien arbeitenden Pandektistik." Ferner *E. Bucher*, Was ist Begriffsjurisprudenz?, Zeitschrift des Bernischen Juristenvereins 102 (1966) 274. Auch diese Vermutung lässt sich für die Annahme eines Paradigmenwechsels anführen; *J. Petersen*, Von der Interessenjurisprudenz zur Wertungsjurisprudenz, 2001, S. 9 ff.

## § 4 Logik und Berechenbarkeit des Rechts

Bereits in seinem ersten Heidelberger Studiensemester hörte Max Weber „im Kolleg Kuno Fischers, morgens von sieben bis acht, Logik“, wie er im Mai 1882 nach Hause schrieb.[459] Von dieser ersten Berührung abgesehen, die zumindest sein Interesse bekundet, spielt die Logik auch in seinen späteren Schriften, insbesondere der Rechtssoziologie, eine tragende Rolle. Die Logik ist für Weber zwar kein eigenständiges Erkenntnisinteresse, wohl aber eine wichtige Hilfe der Erkenntnis,[460] wodurch zugleich eine Verbindungslinie zwischen Rechtssoziologie und Philosophie augenscheinlich wird: „Es soll hier nicht Logik getrieben, sondern es sollen bekannte Ergebnisse der modernen Logik für uns nutzbar gemacht, Probleme nicht gelöst, sondern dem Laien ihre Bedeutung veranschaulicht werden. Wer die Arbeiten der modernen Logiker kennt – ich nenne nur Windelband, Simmel, und für unsere Zwecke speziell Heinrich Rickert[461] – wird sofort bemerken, dass in allem Wesentlichen lediglich an sie angeknüpft wird.“[462]

[459] *Max Weber*, Jugendbriefe 1876–1893 (1936), S. 41.

[460] *B. Quensel*, Logik und Methode in der ‚Rechtssoziologie‘ Max Webers. Ein Beitrag zur Klärung der grundlegenden Begriffe und Perspektiven, Zeitschrift für Rechtssoziologie 18 (1997) 133.

[461] Vgl. auch *H. Rickert*, Max Webers und seine Stellung zur Wissenschaft, Logos XV (1926) 222; zum Verhältnis beider zueinander *G. Oakes*, Weber and Rickert. Concept Formation in the Cultural Sciences, 1988; *P.-U. Merz*, Max Weber und Heinrich Rickert. Die erkenntniskritischen Grundlagen der verstehenden Soziologie, 1990; *S. Wöhler*, Das Denkprinzip Heinrich Rickerts und seine Bedeutung für das Werk Max Webers, 2005. Siehe zum Dreigestirn Weber-Heck-Rickert auch *E. Dorndorf*, Zu den theoretischen Grundlagen der Interessenjurisprudenz: Die Beziehungen von Philipp Hecks allgemeiner Auslegungstheorie zu Max Weber und Heinrich Rickert, ARSP 81 (1995) 542, 555; *H. Schoppmeyer*, Juristische Methode als Lebensaufgabe, 2001, S. 163. Siehe auch *St. L. Paulson,* Erkennen und Anerkennen. Die neukantianische Urteilslehre Heinrich Rickerts, Festschrift für G. Winkler, 1997, S. 751.

[462] *M. Weber*, Die „Objektivität“ sozialwissenschaftlicher und sozialpolitischer Erkenntnis, Archiv für Sozialwissenschaft und Sozialpolitik 19 (1904), 22 Fußnote 1.

Die Stelle veranschaulicht nebenbei, dass Weber die neukantianischen Arbeiten für seine eigenen Schriften nutzbar zu machen wusste,[463] wobei Rickerts wissenschaftstheoretische Gedanken ihn besonders interessierten.[464]

## I. Logik und Widerspruchsfreiheit

Im Laufe der bisherigen Überlegungen und vor allem auch beim zuletzt Behandelten trat immer wieder Webers Betonung des Logischen in den Vordergrund. Zugleich wurde ersichtlich, dass ein unausgesprochener Zwiespalt zwischen seiner Haltung gegenüber der Begriffsjurisprudenz seiner Zeit und gegenüber der aufkommenden Interessenjurisprudenz bestand.[465]

### 1. Berechenbarkeit als Attribut des Rechts

Beides hängt miteinander zusammen und steht zugleich in einem Spannungsverhältnis zueinander: Die Akzentuierung einer logisch widerspruchsfreien Begriffsbildung kommt der Rationalität des Rechts entgegen, das jedoch von einer formal-logischen Erstarrung bedroht ist,[466] wenn die Herausforderungen der Lebensforschung und Lebenswertung unbeachtet bleiben, weil das Recht

[463] Siehe zu diesem Zusammenhang *G. Wagner*, Geltung und normativer Zwang. Eine Untersuchung zu den neukantianischen Grundlagen der Wissenschaftslehre Max Webers, 1987; *D. Suber*, Die Begründung der deutschen Soziologie zwischen Neukantianismus und Lebensphilosophie, 2002.

[464] *H. Rickert*, Die Grenzen naturwissenschaftlichen Begriffsbildung, 1902. Siehe dazu *Marianne Weber*, Max Weber: Ein Lebensbild, 1950, S. 235, 296: „Rickert habe ich aus. Er ist sehr gut, zum großen Teil finde ich darin das, was ich selbst gedacht habe."

[465] *H. Schoppmeyer*, Juristische Methode als Lebensform, 2001, S. 164, betont zu stark die Hinwendung Webers zur Begriffsjurisprudenz.

[466] Zu diesem Topos auch *W. Scheuerle*, Formalismusargumente, AcP 172 (1972) 396.

dann lebensfremd werden kann. Hier kommt schließlich auch das Postulat der Berechenbarkeit ins Spiel, das für Weber wesentlich mit dem Recht verbunden ist. Es lohnt sich, Luhmanns paraphrasierende und aktualisierende Würdigung der Rechtssoziologie Webers weitgehend ungekürzt einzubeziehen: „Weber hat dagegen eine Entwicklung im Auge, die das Gefüge der Rechtsnormen zunehmend ausdifferenziert und verselbständigt, das heißt von der Verquickung mit anderen gesellschaftlichen Strukturen und Erwartungen ablöst und im Interesse spezifischer Funktionen präzisiert. Dadurch werden Elemente der persönlichen Willkür in der Rechtshandlung (Kadijustiz) und Bindungen an traditionell überlieferte für Außenstehende nicht einsichtige Sitten- und Moralvorstellungen kleiner Gruppen abgestreift. Nur so ist es möglich, langfristige, weiträumige Investitionen auf rechtlich zuverlässig gesicherte, berechenbare Chancen zu stützen (...) Kurz: dem einzelnen müssen abstrakter berechenbare Chancen gesichert werden, deren Berechenbarkeit auch in einer komplexer werdenden gesellschaftlichen Umwelt noch standhält und für ältere Formen konkreten Vertrauens und enger Situations- und Menschenkenntnis einspringt. Erst in ein so umstrukturiertes Recht können dann sekundär wieder Wohlfahrtzwecke eingebaut werden, deren Erfüllung, wie man heute deutlich sieht, die berechenbare Maschinerie gesetzlich programmierter Verwaltung voraussetzt."[467] Gerade weil diese Würdigung vielleicht ebenso viel von Luhmanns eigener systemtheoretischer Sicht verrät, wie sie an Weber anknüpft, bestätigt sie die am Ende dieser Abhandlung nochmals aufgegriffene Prämisse Webers, dass Wissenschaft ihrem Sinn und Zweck nach überboten werden will.[468]

Das Herausdestillieren des rechtlich Relevanten bedeutet zugleich die Präparierung des rechtlich gleichartigen Kerns der unterschiedlichen Fallgestaltungen und bringt sie damit zugleich auf

[467] *N. Luhmann*, Rechtssoziologie, 3. Auflage 1987, S. 17.

[468] *M. Weber*, Wissenschaft als Beruf, Geistige Arbeit als Beruf. Vier Vorträge vor dem Freistudentischen Bund, 1919, in: Gesammelte Aufsätze zur Wissenschaftslehre, 7. Auflage 1988, S. 582, 592. Hervorhebungen auch dort.

einen normativen Nenner. Es verdient Hervorhebung, dass Weber die Widerspruchslosigkeit flankierend hervorhebt, weil dadurch neben der Forderung, gleichartige Fallgestaltungen nicht ohne sachlichen Grund ungleich zu behandeln, mittelbar zugleich das Postulat der Widerspruchslosigkeit der Rechtsordnung angesprochen ist.[469] Die synthetische Arbeit wird besonders beim Denken in und Ermitteln von Fallgruppen bedeutsam, das seit jeher eine dogmatische Herausforderung in denjenigen Bereichen darstellt, die vorderhand von blinder Faktizität geprägt sind.

## 2. Denkbarkeit des Rechtsverhältnisses

Zwei unscheinbare Worte Webers verdienen in diesem Zusammenhang hervorgehoben zu werden, da sie nicht nur wesentliche Voraussetzungen der synthetischen Arbeit schaffen, sondern auch miteinander zusammenhängen. Es ist zum einen die Prämisse, dass die rechtlichen Bestandteile als Rechtsverhältnis zu *denken* seien.[470] Es ist also nicht gleichsam ontologisch ein Rechtsverhältnis,[471] sondern dieses ist immer Produkt eines Gedankens. Das erinnert an Ota Weinbergers über Kelsen hinausgehenden „institutionellen Rechtspositivismus", wonach das Recht ein „Doppelantlitz (hat): es ist eine normative Gedankenentität und eine Tatsache des gesellschaftlichen Lebens."[472] Dieser Ansatz verlagert Kelsens Fragestellung[473] –

[469] Zu ihr grundlegend *C.-W. Canaris*, Systemdenken und Systembegriff in der Jurisprudenz, 2. Auflage 1983.

[470] *M. Weber*, Wirtschaft und Gesellschaft, S. 396.

[471] Dementsprechend ist es wohl ungeachtet einer gewissen phänotypischen Ähnlichkeit etwas fundamental Unterschiedliches gegenüber dem, was etwa *G. Husserl* (Der Rechtsgegenstand – rechtslogische Studien zu einer Theorie des Eigentums, 1933; *ders.*, Rechtskraft und Rechtsgeltung – eine rechtsdogmatische Untersuchung, 1925) im Sinn hatte.

[472] *O. Weinberger*, Norm und Institution, 1988, S. 79.; dazu *K. Larenz*, Methodenlehre der Rechtswissenschaft, S. 81 ff.

[473] *H. Kelsen*, Reine Rechtslehre, 1934, 2. Auflage 1960; *ders.*, Was ist Gerechtigkeit?, 1953; *ders.*, Was ist die Reine Rechtslehre?, Festschrift für Z. Giacometti, 1953, S. 143.

ob zu Recht oder zu Unrecht, sei hier dahingestellt[474] – auf die soziologische Ebene.[475]

Die aus den faktischen Gegebenheiten entspringende rechtliche Ordnung trägt damit für Weber Merkmale einer Fiktion im Sinne der Rationalisierung.[476] Das bedeutet zugleich, dass die rechtliche Würdigung auch anders ausfallen könnte und sich nicht notwendigerweise so darstellt, wie es aus Gründen der Rationalisierung der Fall ist. Der zweite von Weber genannte Gesichtspunkt betrifft die *logisch* widerspruchslose Weise, womit den Rechtsverhältnissen eine formale Kategorie und Funktion zugewiesen wird.[477] Damit wird implizit unterstrichen, dass es nicht notwendigerweise um eine material-inhaltliche Richtigkeit der Rechtsverhältnisse und Rechtsinstitute geht: „Innerhalb der Rechtspflege nämlich wird dem heutigen Richter teils durch positive Rechtsnormen, teils durch Rechtstheorien nicht selten zugemutet, nach materialen Grundsätzen, Sittlichkeit, Billigkeit, Zweckmäßigkeit, zu entscheiden."[478] Vielmehr ist wiederum zunächst und vor allem eine ordnende Systema-

[474] Dazu *K. Larenz*, Methodenlehre der Rechtswissenschaft, 6. Auflage 1991, S. 81 ff.

[475] Siehe auch *O. Weinberger*, Recht, Institution und Rechtspolitik, 1987.

[476] Polemisch gegenüber der Verwendung des Begriffs der Rationalisierung bei Weber *P. Crone*, Max Weber, das islamische Recht und die Entstehung des Kapitalismus, in: Max Webers Sicht des Islams (Hg. W. Schluchter), S. 296; siehe auch *St. Uecker*, Die Rationalisierung des Rechts, 2005, S. 64 f. Instruktiver Überblick bei *K.-P. Tieck*, Persönlichkeit, Ordnungen, Interessen, in: Max Weber als Rechtssoziologie (Hg. M. Rehbinder/ders.), 1987, S. 79. Siehe auch *D. Trubek*, Max Weber on Law and the Rise of Capitalism, Wisconsin Law Review 1972, 720.

[477] Im angloamerikanischen Rechtskreis wird die Logik als Voraussetzung des Rechts mitunter angezweifelt; vgl. *W. Fikentscher*, Rechtswissenschaft und Demokratie bei Justice Oliver Wendell Holmes, Jr. Eine rechtsvergleichende Kritik der politischen Jurisprudenz, Juristische Studiengesellschaft Karlsruhe, 1970. *W. Fikentscher*, Juristische Heuristik, Festschrift für C.-W. Canaris, 2007, S. 1099, nennt des Weiteren – rechtssoziologisch von besonderem Interesse – die Freirechtsschule.

[478] *M. Weber*, Wirtschaft und Gesellschaft, S. 389. Zur damit implizit angesprochenen Ausfüllung von Generalklauseln *M. Auer*, Materialisierung, Flexibilisierung, Richterfreiheit, 2005.

tisierung betroffen, von der sogleich noch näher die Rede sein wird.[479] Das Attribut des Logischen gehört also für Weber auch im Hinblick auf das Rechtsverhältnis zum Akt des Denkens.

## II. Verbindungslinien zwischen Rechtssoziologie und Rechtsphilosophie

Wenn im bisherigen Verlauf der Untersuchung von der Logik die Rede war, wurde stillschweigend vorausgesetzt, dass sie gerade in der Rechtsdogmatik und eben auch in der Rechtssoziologie ihren Platz hat, obwohl er ihr an sich vor allem in der Rechtsphilosophie zusteht. Daher muss dieser Zusammenhang im Folgenden näher berücksichtigt werden, um insoweit den Dreiklang von Rechtsdogmatik, Rechtsphilosophie und Rechtssoziologie hörbar zu machen.

### 1. Logik bei Weber und Nietzsche

Vom Einfluss Nietzsches auf Weber war bereits die Rede.[480] Es wäre interessant zu wissen, ob Weber Nietzsches Aphorismus über die Herkunft des Logischen gekannt hat,[481] der in seinem evolutionstheoretischen Ansatz[482] einerseits historisch[483] und soziologisch aufschlussreich ist,[484] andererseits auch die für die juristische

[479] Unter 4.

[480] Oben unter § 1 I 1.

[481] *F. Nietzsche*, Die fröhliche Wissenschaft, 111.

[482] Siehe auch *R. Schroeder*, Nietzsche and Weber: Two „Prophets" of the Modern World, in: Max Weber, Rationality and Modernity (Hg. S. Whimster/S. Lash) 1987, S. 207.

[483] Siehe auch *O. G. Oexle*, Von Nietzsche zu Max Weber. Objektivitätsproblem und Wertfrage der Wissenschaft im Zeichen des Historismus, in: Rechtsgeschichte und theoretische Dimension (Hg. C. Peterson), Rättshistorika Studier 15 (1990) 96.

[484] *R. Eden*, Bad Conscience for a Nietzschean Age: Weber's Calling for Science, The Review of Politics 45 (1983) 366; *ders.*, Max Weber und Friedrich Nietzsche oder: Haben sich die Sozialwissenschaften wirklich vom His-

Methodenlehre unerlässliche und auch von Weber verschiedentlich hervorgehobene Subsumtion berührt,[485] wenn auch in einer vergleichsweise atavistischen Weise. Auf die selbst gestellte Frage, woher die Logik im menschlichen Kopf entstanden sei, antwortet er: „Gewiss aus der Unlogik, deren Reich ursprünglich[486] ungeheuer gewesen sein muss. Aber unzählig viele Wesen, welche anders schlossen, als wir jetzt schließen, gingen zugrunde: (...) Wer zum Beispiel das ‚Gleiche' nicht oft genug aufzufinden wusste, in Betreff der Nahrung oder in Betreff der ihm feindlichen Tiere, *wer also zu langsam subsumierte*, zu vorsichtig in der Subsumtion war, hatte geringere Wahrscheinlichkeit des Fortlebens als der, welcher bei allem Ähnlichen sofort auf Gleichheit riet. Der überwiegende Hang aber, das Ähnliche als gleich zu behandeln, ein unlogischer Hang – denn es gibt nichts Gleiches –, hat erst alle Grundlage der Logik geschaffen."[487] Ein anderer in diesem Zusammenhang interessanter Ansatz stammt von Hermann Cohen, der die Rechtswissenschaft als Logik der Geisteswissenschaften verstand.[488] Aber alle diese philosophischen Versuche sind letztlich zu trennen von dem, was Webers rechtssoziologische Betrachtung an der Rechtsordnung interessierte.

torismus befreit?, in: Max Weber und seine Zeitgenossen ( Veröffentlichungen des Deutschen Historischen Instituts London 21, 1988 (Hg. W. J. Mommsen/ W. Schwentker) S. 557.

485 *M. Weber*, Wirtschaft und Gesellschaft, S. 395 f.

486 Zur Bedeutung dieses für Nietzsches (Rechts-)Denken so wichtigen Wortes *J. Petersen*, Nietzsches Genialität der Gerechtigkeit, 2008, 2. Kapitel. Zu Berührungspunkten zwischen Max Webers Rechtssoziologie und Nietzsches Verständnis der Gerechtigkeit siehe ebenda, S. 93 f.

487 *F. Nietzsche*, Die fröhliche Wissenschaft, 111; Hervorhebung nur hier. Siehe dazu im weiteren Sinne auch *G. Stauth/B. S. Turner*, Nietzsche in Weber oder die Geburt des modernen Genius' im professionellen Menschen, Zeitschrift für Soziologie 15 (1986) 81; *L. Cortella*, Crisi e razionalita. Da Nietzsche ad Habermas (Nietzsche, Weber, Habermas), 1981; *R. Eden*, Political Leadership and Nihilism, A Study of Weber and Nietzsche, 1984.

488 *H.-G. Gadamer*, Philosophische Lehrjahre, 1977, S. 61.

## 2. Webers Rezeption der Logik

Es wurde bereits dargestellt,[489] dass Weber an die logischen Studien seiner Zeit anknüpft. Hierin liegt ein grundlegender Unterschied zur dogmatischen Jurisprudenz, die es mit Sollenssätzen zu tun hat, die gelten oder nicht gelten,[490] aber nicht dem Gesichtspunkt von wahr bzw. falsch unterliegen.[491]

### a) Tertium non datur?

Allerdings bedarf auch dieses im Sinne eines Alternativitätsverhältnis[492] formulierte Entweder-Oder („tertium non datur")[493], das für die klassische Logik gilt, seinerseits der Präzisierung, wie im Übrigen auch Weber, wenn auch nicht in seiner Rechtssoziologie im engeren Sinne, sondern in seiner anfänglichen Begriffsbestimmung und methodologischen Einführung zugrunde gelegt hat: „Die für die juristische Betrachtungsweise unvermeidliche Alternative: dass ein Rechtssatz bestimmten Inhalts entweder (im Rechtssinn) gelte oder nicht, ein Rechtsverhältnis entweder bestehe oder nicht, gilt für die soziologische Betrachtung also nicht."[494] Denn Sollenssätze haben zwar formal („logisch") die

[489] Oben vor I.

[490] Dazu auf rechtssoziologischer Ebene bezogen auf Weber *H. Treiber*, Im ‚Schatten' des Neukantianismus: Norm und Geltung bei Max Weber, Festschrift für E. Blankenburg, 1998, S. 245.

[491] *C.-W. Canaris*, Systemdenken und Systembegriff in der Jurisprudenz, S. 123.

[492] Siehe dazu *J. Rödig*, Die Denkform der Alternative in der Jurisprudenz, 1969.

[493] *E. Husserl*, Logische Untersuchungen, Band I, 2. Auflage 1913, S. 114: „Ein Satz ist entweder wahr oder er ist es nicht, ein drittes gibt es nicht." Siehe bereits *M. T. Cicero*, De fato.

[494] *M. Weber*, Wirtschaft und Gesellschaft, S. 14. Dazu *W. Schluchter*, in: Rechtssoziologie am Ende des 20. Jahrhunderts (Hg. H. Dreier) 2000, S. 8, 26: „In jeder Rechtsordnung gelten Rechtssätze mehr oder weniger. Auch diese gradualistische Sichtweise widerspricht dem rechtsdogmatischen Ideal." Zu diesem Befund sogleich im Text unter b).

Eigenschaft der Geltung oder eben Nichtgeltung.[495] Inhaltlich unterscheiden sie sich darüber hinaus aber durch ihre jeweilige Überzeugungskraft, wodurch die Rechtsanwendung einerseits erschwert, andererseits aber erst so anspruchsvoll wird, dass die Jurisprudenz den Wissenschaftsanspruch überhaupt erheben kann.[496] Ginge es nur um das formal-logische Ineinandergreifen der Normen ohne ihre historische, systematische und teleologische Gewichtung,[497] so wäre die Jurisprudenz eine bloße Technik[498] und die Methodenlehre nicht mehr als eine Anleitung dazu. Nicht zuletzt darin bestand die Unzulänglichkeit der nicht wertungsorientierten „reinen" Begriffs- und Konstruktionsjurisprudenz, die mit diesem Defizit noch nicht den Namen der Prinzipienjurisprudenz verdient.[499] Weiter unten wird sich zeigen,[500] dass Weber eher diese als jene gemeint hat und sich so als methodologisch „aufgeklärter" erweist als die Befürworter einer „ungewerteten" Konstruktionsjurisprudenz.

### b) Unterschiedliche Überzeugungskraft von Sollenssätzen

Die über die logische Geltung oder Nichtgeltung hinausgehende Frage der unterschiedlichen Überzeugungskraft der Sollenssätze ermöglicht zugleich Abstufungen. Gewiss können Vorschriften nicht „mehr oder weniger" gelten, sondern sie gelten eben oder sie gelten nicht. Bei der Beantwortung der Frage, ob sie im Einzel-

495 Aus dem neueren Schrifttum *J. Joerden*, Logik im Recht, 2005; *E. Schneider/F. E. Schnapp*, Logik für Juristen, 6. Auflage 2006.

96 Dazu am Ende unter § 6.

497 Zu ihr *C.-W. Canaris*, Das Rangverhältnis der „klassischen" Auslegungskriterien, demonstriert an Standardproblemen aus dem Zivilrecht, Festschrift für D. Medicus, 1999, S. 25.

498 Mahnend bereits *L. Nelson*, Die Rechtswissenschaft ohne Recht, 1917, 2. Auflage 1949.

499 Prägnant *P. Landau*, Die Rechtsquellenlehre in der deutschen Rechtswissenschaft des 19. Jahrhunderts, in: Juristische Theoriebildung und Rechtliche Einheit, Rättshistorika Studier (Hg. C. Petterson), Band XIX, 1993, S. 69; dazu bereits oben § 1 II 1. Der Sache nach ähnlich *G. Hassold*, Rechtsfindung durch Konstruktion, AcP 181 (1981) 131.

500 Unter IV. a. E.

fall – oder besser: in einer bestimmten Art von Fällen – anwendbar sind, kann jedoch durchaus, wie noch weiter unten im Rahmen der Behandlung des Typus deutlich wird,[501] eine Abstufung und Gewichtung einzelner teleologisch nachvollziehbarer Merkmale erforderlich sein.[502] Das bedeutet im Übrigen keine unzureichend legitimierte Eigenmächtigkeit des Rechtsanwendenden, weil die Rechtsanwendung gerade in der richtigen, das heißt etwa teleologisch und systematisch orientierten Gewichtung besteht.[503] So entspricht es einem althergebrachten Grundsatz der Methodenlehre, dass systemwidrige Normen, denen ja deshalb nicht pauschal die Geltung versagt wird, einschränkend ausgelegt werden. Es geht also in der Rechtsdogmatik weniger um das logische Folgern als die Herstellung innerer Folgerichtigkeit, wie Canaris mit Recht hervorgehoben hat: „Denn die innere Sinneinheit des Rechts, die es im System zu erfassen gilt, ist entsprechend ihrer Ableitung aus dem Gerechtigkeitsgedanken nicht logischer, sondern wertungsmäßiger, also axiologischer Natur. Wer wollte denn auch im Ernst behaupten, das Gebot, Gleiches gleich und Ungleiches nach dem Maße seiner Verschiedenheit ungleich zu *bewerten*, ließe sich mit den Mitteln der Logik erfüllen?"[504] Hierin besteht also prima vista ein markanter Unterschied zwischen Webers Rechtssoziologie und der juristischen Methodenlehre.

[501] Sub 5; *D. Leenen*, Typus und Rechtsfindung, 1971, passim.

[502] Dementsprechend verhält es sich im Übrigen beim beweglichen System, das eine normative Korrespondenz zum Typus darstellt und gleichfalls das unterschiedliche Wirken von – als solchen unabdingbar erkannten und ermittelten – Prinzipien betrifft (*J. Petersen*, Unternehmenssteuerrecht und bewegliches System, 1999, S. 55 ff. und passim).

[503] Siehe zum Ganzen auch *K. Larenz*, Grundformen wertorientierten Denkens in der Jurisprudenz, Festschrift für W. Wilburg, 1975, S. 217.

[504] *C.-W. Canaris*, Systemdenken und Systembegriff in der Jurisprudenz, S. 21 f.; Hervorhebung auch dort. Grundlegend zur wissenschaftstheoretischen Seite des Problems *G. H. von Wright*, The Logic of Preference, 1963; *ders.*, The Varieties of Goodness, 1963.

### c) Das zugrunde liegende Verständnis der Logik

Jedoch wird diese Differenz zumindest teilweise wieder aufgehoben, wenn auch Weber implizit dasjenige zugrunde gelegt hat, was soeben angenommen wurde, nämlich, dass die Logik im Sinne der Jurisprudenz weniger streng verfährt als im Sinne eines strikten Entweder-Oder.[505] Das ist deshalb nicht selbstverständlich, weil Weber in der soeben zitierten Stelle[506] „lediglich" – aber eben auch immerhin – an die moderne Logik anknüpft, und zwar „im wesentlichen",[507] wobei das Wesentliche, so könnte man argumentieren, gerade im strikten Alternativitätsverhältnis ohne dritten Weg besteht. Dabei sollte man jedoch seine übrigen sozialwissenschaftlichen Schriften, insbesondere den hier zitierten Aufsatz zur Objektivität sozialwissenschaftlichen Erkenntnis, nicht in der Weise streng determinierend auslegen, dass sie auch in der Rechtssoziologie nicht anders verstanden werden könnten. Zwar bilden sie eine wichtige Auslegungshilfe und führen, wie z.B. bei dem Aufsatz über die Analyse des Begriffs der „Regel",[508] dasjenige näher aus, worauf in der Rechtssoziologie nur verwiesen werden kann.[509] Jedoch muss im Rahmen der Interpretation der Rechtssoziologie berücksichtigt werden, dass Weber hier auch – die Jurisprudenz gleichsam imitierend und beschreibend – ein Verständnis der Logik zugrunde legen kann, das weniger streng ist, weil es sich den Eigengesetzlichkeiten des beschriebenen Gegenstandes angleicht.

[505] Siehe dazu auch *H.-J. Koch/H. Rüßmann*, Juristische Begründungslehre, 1983, § 18; *R. Alexy*, Die logische Analyse juristischer Entscheidungen, ARSP Beiheft 14, 1980, 181. Zur Logik *W. V. O. Quine*, Methods of Logic, 1950 (8. Auflage 1993; deutsch: Grundzüge der Logik, 1969), *E. Tugendhat/U. Wolf*, Logisch-semantische Propädeutik, 1983.

[506] Oben 2 vor a).

[507] *M. Weber*, Archiv für Sozialwissenschaft und Sozialpolitik 19 (1904), 22.

[508] *M. Weber*, Archiv für Sozialgeschichte XXIV (1907) 94.

[509] *M. Weber*, Wirtschaft und Gesellschaft, S. 182 (zu dieser Stelle oben unter § 1), mit dem bei Weber zitierten Fußnotenverweis auf seinen genannten Archiv-Beitrag, der im Übrigen einer der ganz wenigen expliziten Nachweise innerhalb der Rechtssoziologie ist, was für das im Text Gesagte spricht.

### d) Unterschied zum Common Law

Darin liegt im Übrigen ein markanter Unterschied zu dem, wie noch zu zeigen sein wird, von Weber überaus kritisch verfolgten angloamerikanischen Rechtsdenken, das am besten in der berühmten Aussage zur Geltung kommt, die Oliver Wendell Holmes seinem *Common Law* vorangestellt hat: „Das Leben des Rechts ist nicht Logik, sondern Erfahrung. Die gefühlten Notwendigkeiten der Zeit, die herrschenden moralischen und politischen Anschauungen, bewusste und unbewusste, und die Vorurteile, welche die Richter mit ihren Mitmenschen gemeinsam haben, sie haben die Regeln des Rechts, durch die Menschen geleitet werden sollen, weit stärker bestimmt als logische Ableitungen im Sinne des Syllogismus."[510] Diese anscheinend „lebensnähere" Vorstellung und erfrischende Feststellung ist wohl das akkurate Gegenteil dessen, was Weber im Sinn hatte.[511] Bei ihm liest sich das so: „Und ebenso wirkt der ‚Regel'-Charakter der ‚empirischen Rechtsordnung', d. h. der als Faktum feststellbare und als solches auch einer Vielheit von Menschen bekannte Umstand, dass die ‚Maxime' der ‚Richter' dahin geht, an gewisse generell bestimmte Tatbestände eine generell gleiche Entscheidung von Interessenkonflikten zu knüpfen und zu erzwingen, – der Umstand also, dass die ‚Rechtsnormen' eben den Charakter generalisierter Sätze: ‚Rechtsregeln', besitzen *und in dieser Form als ‚Maximen' in den Köpfen der Richter leben*, – dieser Umstand wirkt teils direkt, teils indirekt zur Erzeugung empirischer Regelmäßigkeiten im faktischen Verhalten der Menschen zueinander und den Sachgütern mit."[512] Diese

[510] *O. W. Holmes*, The Common Law, 1881, S. 1 (deutsch: Das gemeine Recht Englands und Nordamerikas: in elf Abhandlungen dargestellt, 1. Auflage 1912, zuletzt 2006.

[511] Vgl. auch *M. Weber*, Wirtschaft und Gesellschaft, S. 493: „Nicht nur vieles in seiner Systematik und zahlreiche einzelne Rechtsinstitute weisen die Spuren davon auf, sondern auch die Definition der Quellen des Common Law: richterliche Präjudizien und ‚legal principles', zeugt davon, so ungeheuer allerdings der Unterschied in der inneren Struktur blieb."

[512] *M. Weber*, Analyse des Begriffs der „Regel", Archiv für Sozialwissenschaften und Sozialpolitik 24, 1907, 94 ff.; Hervorhebung nur hier.

strikt rationale Betrachtung veranschaulicht wiederum, dass die Logik für Weber ein unerlässliches Attribut des Rationalen ist.[513]

### e) Bedeutungsdifferenz

Damit würde dann der soeben behandelte Strukturunterschied – logisches Folgern ist nicht gleichbedeutend mit der Herstellung innerer Folgerichtigkeit – wenn auch nicht eingeebnet, so doch in den Auswirkungen relativiert. So spricht viel dafür, dass Webers Darstellung der juristischen Arbeit in der Rechtssoziologie von der logischen Methode der Begriffsjurisprudenz ausging und sie abbildete, wobei ein dem Gegenstand der Rechtserkenntnis gemäßer eingeschränkter Begriff der Logik zugrunde gelegt wurde. Er beschrieb also die juristische Vorgehensweise seiner Zeit, welche die Logik akzentuierte, ohne sie notwendigerweise wissenschaftstheoretisch exakt zugrunde zu legen. Die Bedeutungsdifferenz besteht damit ziemlich genau in der Distanz des juristisch gebildeten Soziologen zum von ihm beschriebenen „idealtypischen" Juristen.

## 3. Naturrechtsdogmen und „Macht der Logik im Rechtsdenken"

Aber noch in anderer Hinsicht ist der soeben referierte, von Weber selbst aufgezeigte Zusammenhang zwischen Rechtsphilosophie und Logik des Rechts aufschlussreich. Es handelt sich um das Naturrecht,[514] jenen „Inbegriff der unabhängig von allem positiven Recht und ihm gegenüber präeminent geltenden Normen, welche ihre Dignität nicht von willkürlicher Satzung zu Lehen tragen, sondern umgekehrt deren Verpflichtungsgewalt erst legitimieren."[515]

513 *M. Weber*, Wirtschaft und Gesellschaft, S. 493 ff.; 501 ff.
514 Zu ihm *L. Strauss*, Naturrecht und Geschichte, 1953.
515 *M. Weber*, Wirtschaft und Gesellschaft, S. 497; zu dieser Stelle auch *H.-P. Müller*, Max Weber, 2007, S. 239.

## a) Kontraintuitive Verbindungslinien

Überraschenderweise sind es nämlich ausgerechnet die Naturrechtsdogmen, von denen man es wohl am wenigsten erwartet hätte, die seines Erachtens „die Neigung zum logisch abstrakten Recht, überhaupt die Macht der Logik im Recht formal steigerten."[516] Im Sinne des in der Einleitung Vorangestellten ist es wichtig, diese kontraintuitiv anmutenden Verbindungslinien zwischen Rechtsdogmatik, Rechtsphilosophie und Rechtssoziologie in Erinnerung zu rufen, um die grundsätzliche Trennung zwischen den Disziplinen nicht zu einer wechselseitigen Erstarrung werden zu lassen, die den Blick auf die interdisziplinäre Verbindung dort verstellt, wo sie bereits entdeckt wurde. Zu nennen ist in diesem Zusammenhang Friedrich Kessler,[517] der für die allfällige Naturrechtsbestimmung[518] nicht nur auf Fries,[519] Cassirer[520] und Dilthey verwies,[521] sondern gerade auch auf Max Webers Rechtssoziologie,[522] deren wissenschaftlicher Rationalitätsanspruch ihm entgegen gekommen sein dürfte.[523] Anders als Weber warnte er die Jurispru-

[516] *M. Weber,* Wirtschaft und Gesellschaft, S. 501. Das ist interessant im Hinblick auf die von Seiten der katholischen Theologie geforderte Rückbesinnung auf das Naturrecht. Siehe auch *L. Honnefelder*, Rationalization and natural law. Max Weber's and Ernst Troeltsch's interpretation of the medieval doctrine of natural law, Review of Metaphysic. A Philosophical Quarterly 49 (1995/96) 275.

[517] *F. Kessler*, Theoretic Basis of Law, University of Chicago Law Review 9 (1941) 98, 99; zu ihm *H. Bernstein*, Friedrich Kessler's American Contract Scholarship and its Political Subtext, 1993, S. 85; *W. Fikentscher*, Methoden des Rechts, Band II, 1975, S. 417 f.

[518] Zum aus vorliegender Sicht (vgl. unten § 5) besonders interessierenden Typendenken bezüglich des Naturrechts auch *Neumann*, Types of Natural Law, Studies in Philosophy and Social Sciences 8 (1940) 338.

[519] *Fries*, Philosophische Rechtslehre, 1803.

[520] *E. Cassirer*, Die Philosophie der Aufklärung, 1932, S. 313 ff.; zu ihm *M. Scherer*, Vom Apriori der Prägnanz. Vortheoretische Sinnerschlossenheit als zentrales Motiv der Kulturphilosophie Ernst Cassirers, 1996.

[521] *W. Dilthey*, Einleitung in die Geisteswissenschaften, 2. Auflage 1933, S. 54 ff.

[522] *M. Weber*, Wirtschaft und Gesellschaft, S. 496 ff.

[523] *F. Kessler*, Natural Law, Justice, and Democracy: Some Reflections in

denz freilich ausdrücklich davor, sich hinter begrifflichen Syllogismen zu verschanzen.[524] Das Beispiel zeigt, dass die Betonung der Rationalität der Rechtsfindung nicht mit einem Bekenntnis zur von Weber so genannten Logisierung einhergehen muss.

### b) Vernünftigkeit des positiven Rechts und Naturrechtsrenaissance

Der Grund für den Einfluss der Naturrechtsdogmen liegt für Weber nicht zuletzt in der „Vernünftigkeit" des gesetzten Rechts.[525] Dass dieses Paradoxon so wenig wahrgenommen und vor allem nicht wirksam wird, liegt darin begründet, dass der naturrechtliche Einfluss umgehend wieder beseitigt wurde: „Einen direkten Einfluss auf die Rechtsprechung haben aber diese materialen Naturrechtsdogmen nicht erlangen können, schon weil sie, ehe sie überhaupt dazu befähigt gewesen wären, schon wieder durch die zunehmend rasch arbeitende positivistische und relativistisch-evolutionäre Skepsis eben dieser Intellektuellenschichten zersetzt wurden."[526] Diese Zersetzung geht auch nach Weber nicht zuletzt auf den Positivismus von Auguste Comte zurück.[527] Eben um dieser Neutralisierung willen ist es aber so wichtig, gegenwärtig zu halten,

Three Types of Thinking about Law and Justice, Tulane Law Review 19 (1944) 32, 61 („to push the rationality of scientific method further and further").

524 *F. Kessler*, Arthur Linton Corbin – A Tribute, Yale Law Journal 64 (1954) 164.

525 Auch dieser Gesichtspunkt ist aufschlussreich für den seitens der katholischen Kirche postulierten möglichen Gleichklang von Vernunft und Glaube (*Benedikt XVI.*, Glaube und Vernunft. Die Regensburger Vorlesung, Text der Vorlesung und Kommentare, 2006, S. 29 f.), dem auf das Recht bezogen das Verhältnis von Vernunftrecht und Naturrecht entsprechen könnte (siehe dazu andeutungsweise *J. Petersen*, Wilhelm von Humboldts Rechtsphilosophie, 2. Auflage 2007, S. 121). Interessanterweise macht auch *M. Weber* (Wirtschaft und Gesellschaft, S. 508) darauf aufmerksam, dass „sich als Ersatz teils ein religiös gebundenes Naturrecht der (katholischen) Dogmatiker anbietet"; dazu bereits weiter oben im Text.

526 *M. Weber*, Wirtschaft und Gesellschaft, S. 501.

527 Nach dem in den letzten Anmerkungen Bedachten verwundert es nicht, dass die Theologie hier einen Hauptgegner ausmachte; vgl. *J. Ratzinger*, Glaube, Wahrheit, Toleranz, 4. Auflage 2005, S. 143 mit Fußnote 125.

dass es diesen Einfluss gerade dort gegeben hat, wo man ihn am wenigsten erwartete, weil er von daher möglicherweise wiederbelebt werden kann. Man denke nur an die so genannte „Naturrechtsrenaissance" nach den Erfahrungen der nationalsozialistischen Diktatur,[528] die eine partielle, wenn auch unbefriedigend gebliebene Aufarbeitung des Unrechts ermöglichen sollte und so potentiell auch in die Rechtsdogmatik Einzug halten konnte, indem sie etwa in die Rechtsprechung des Bundesgerichtshofs eingegangen ist.[529] Allerdings wird Weber auch durch die Naturrechtsrenaissance, langfristig betrachtet, nicht in seiner Einschätzung widerlegt,[530] dass „der Rechtspositivismus in vorläufig unaufhaltsamem Vordringen ist".[531]

[528] Vgl. nur BGHZ 8, 243 (Lues), wonach die Rechtsgüter im Sinne des § 823 Abs. 1 BGB, insbesondere Leben und Gesundheit, „von Schöpfung und Natur vorausgegeben" seien; *H. Weinkauff*, Der Naturrechtsgedanke in der Rechtsprechung des Bundesgerichtshofs, NJW 1960, 1689; *H. U. Evers*, Zum unkritischen Naturrechtsbewusstsein in der Rechtsprechung der Gegenwart, JZ 1961, 241.

[529] Nachweise bei *A. Künnecke*, Auf der Suche nach dem Kern des Naturrechts. Ein Vergleich der schwachen säkularen Naturrechtslehren Radbruchs, Coings, Harts, Welzels und Fullers ab 1945, 2003; *W. Maihofer* (Hg.), Naturrecht oder Rechtspositivismus?, 1962; *K. Kühl*, Rückblick auf die Renaissance des Naturrechts nach dem 2. Weltkrieg, Freundesgabe A. Söllner, 1990, S. 331. Eine erneute Hinwendung zum Naturrecht gab es freilich auch in den Vereinigten Staaten; vgl. *L. L. Fuller*, The Law in Quest of Itself, 1940; *ders.*, American Legal Philosophy at Mid-Century, Journal of Legal Education 6 (1954) 457; zu ihm *W. Fikentscher*, Methoden des Rechts, Band III, 1975, S. 411 f. Es ist vor dem Hintergrund des hier Behandelten – gerade auch im Hinblick auf den eingangs (§ 1) erörterten Werturteilsstreit – interessant, dass Fuller inbesondere von Ernst Nagel vorgeworfen wurde, er vermenge Tatsache und Werturteil; vgl. *E. Nagel*, On the Fusion of Fact and Value: A Reply to Professor Fuller, Natural Law Forum 3 (1958) 77; dagegen *L. L. Fuller*, A Rejoinder to Prof. Nagel, Natural Law Forum 3 (1958) 83; hiergegen wiederum *E. Nagel*, Fact, Value and Human Purpose, Natural Law Forum 4 (1959) 26; zwischenzeitlich zu dieser Kontroverse *J. P. Witherspoon*, The Relation of Philosophy and Jurisprudence, Natural Law Forum 3 (1958) 105.

[530] So wohl auch *H.-P. Müller*, Max Weber, 2007, S. 240 f.

[531] *M. Weber*, Wirtschaft und Gesellschaft, S. 502. Aus dem rechtsphilosophischen Schrifttum für den Positivismus und gegen das Naturrecht *J. Raz*, Practical Reasons and Norm, 2. Auflage 1990.

## III. Verabsolutierung des „logisch richtigen" Rechts

Es ist nicht nur rechtsgeschichtlich, sondern auch dogmengeschichtlich aufschlussreich, wie Weber aus der Rezeption des römischen Rechts[532] Folgerungen für die Begriffsjurisprudenz seiner Zeit zieht, ohne diese beim Namen zu nennen.

### 1. Webers Skepsis gegenüber der Begriffsjurisprudenz

War im bisherigen Verlauf der Untersuchung im Einklang mit der wohl herrschenden Lehre innerhalb der Rechtssoziologie zugrunde gelegt worden, dass Weber eher der Begriffsjurisprudenz nahe stand, obwohl die Rechtssoziologie an sich in einem engen genetischen Verhältnis zur Interessenjurisprudenz steht, so darf nicht ausgeblendet werden, dass es in Webers Rechtssoziologie Stellen gibt, die eine gewisse Distanz gegenüber der Begriffsjurisprudenz erkennen lassen:[533] „Ansätze zu dem Grundsatz, dass, was der Jurist nicht ‚denken' und ‚konstruieren' könne, auch rechtswirksam nicht existieren könne, finden sich in der Tat bereits bei den römischen Juristen."[534] Hier scheint bereits eine kritische Stellungnahme zur Begriffsjurisprudenz auf, die zu bedenken gibt, dass eine derart eingeschränkte Sicht der Lebenswirklichkeit nicht gerecht werden kann. Weber erklärt im Einklang mit Eugen Ehrlich, den man zum besseren Verständnis der Rechtssoziologie Webers mit berücksichtigen muss,[535] das Überleben des römischen Rechts nicht zuletzt dadurch, dass „unsystematische Gelegenheitsproduktionen abstrakter

[532] Grundlegend *M. Kaser*, Zur Methode der römischen Rechtsfindung, 1962.

[533] *C.-W. Canaris*, Systemdenken und Systembegriff in der Jurisprudenz, 2. Auflage 1983, S. 21 mit Fußnote 9. Zur Begriffsjurisprudenz wichtig *H.-P. Haferkamp*, Georg Friedrich Puchta und die „Begriffsjurisprudenz", 2004; ferner *U. Falk*, Ein Gelehrter wie Windscheid. Erkundungen auf den Feldern der Begriffsjurisprudenz, 1989.

[534] *M. Weber*, Wirtschaft und Gesellschaft, S. 492. Siehe zum Ganzen neuestens auch *G. Dilcher*, JZ 2007, 105, der Webers Weg von der Rechtsgeschichte zur Soziologie nachzeichnet, sowie *B. Quensel*, Max Webers Konstruktionslogik, 2007.

[535] *N. Luhmann*, Rechtssoziologie, 3. Auflage 1987, S. 21.

Rechtslogik“ über den jeweiligen Fall, zu dem sie ergingen, hinaus unter gleichzeitiger Verschiebung in das formal Logische auch „zum ‚logisch richtigen‘ Recht schlechthin verabsolutiert“ wurden:[536] „Was den römischen Juristen in starkem Maß gefehlt hatte: die rein systematischen Kategorien, wurde nun geschaffen: Begriffe, wie etwa der des ‚Rechtsgeschäfts‘ oder der ‚Willenserklärung‘, für welche in der antiken Jurisprudenz selbst die einheitlichen Namen fehlten, wurden konstruiert.“[537] Hierin besteht wohl weniger ein Zugeständnis gegenüber der Freirechtsbewegung, die Ehrlich mitbegründete,[538] als vielmehr eine Referenz an den gelernten Romanisten Ehrlich,[539] doch gelangte er wohl auch durch romanistische und methodische Vorarbeiten zu seiner freieren Sicht auf das Recht.[540]

## 2. Rechtsgeschäftslehre als Paradigma

Es ist interessant, dass Weber just diese beiden, die Rechtsgeschäftslehre in der Tat prägenden Begriffe zum Beispiel für die Begriffsbildung nimmt.[541] Er setzt damit als selbstverständlich

[536] Mit dieser „Verabsolutierung“ dürfte nicht zuletzt *F. C. von Savigny* (Vom Beruf unserer Zeit für Gesetzgebung und Rechtswissenschaft, 1814; gegen *A. F. Thibaut*, Über die Notwendigkeit eines allgemeinen bürgerlichen Rechts für Deutschland, 1814) gemeint sein; vgl. auch *P. Caroni*, Savigny und die Kodifikation, ZRG, Germ. Abt. 86 (1969) 97; *H. Hattenhauer*, Thibaut und Savigny. Ihre pragmatischen Schriften, 1973; *H. Kiefner*, Thibaut und Savigny, Festschrift für R. Gmür, 1983, S. 53.

[537] *M. Weber*, ebenda, S. 492: „Vor allem aber gewann jetzt der Satz, dass, was ein Jurist nicht denken kann, auch rechtlich nicht interessiert, *wirklich* praktische Bedeutung.“ (Hervorhebung nur hier). Eine parallele Stelle zu der im Text zitierten findet sich ebenda, S. 466: „Dagegen die Bildung des Begriffs ‚Rechtsgeschäft‘ hat sie (sc. praktische Folgen) direkt wenigstens nicht: sie dient uns zunächst systematischen Bedürfnissen.“ Auch zur Lehre vom Rechtsgeschäft und der Willenserklärung bei Weber *B. Quensel*, Max Webers Konstruktionslogik, 2007.

[538] *E. Ehrlich*, Freie Rechtsfindung und freie Rechtswissenschaft, 1903.

[539] *P. Raisch*, Juristische Methoden, 1995, S. 111.

[540] *E. Ehrlich*, Über Lücken im Recht, Juristische Blätter (Österreich/Ungarn), 1888, 447.

[541] Ähnlich im Übrigen *N. Luhmann*, Rechtssystem und Rechtsdogmatik, 1974, S. 30.

voraus, was in der modernen Rechtsgeschäftslehre unbeachtet, begrifflich eingeebnet und gleichsam verschüttet wurde,[542] nämlich dass es sich dabei um kategorial unterschiedliche, selbstständige Begriffe handelt, denen nicht nur ein jeweiliger Bedeutungsgehalt zukommt, sondern der sich gerade aus der systematischen Fügung innerhalb der Rechtsgeschäftslehre des Bürgerlichen Gesetzbuchs exakt aufschlüsseln lässt.[543] Man muss dies stets hinzufügen und als kontinuierliche dogmatische Herausforderung begreifen, weil andernfalls das geläufige Verdikt von der überkommenen Begriffsjurisprudenz als Freischein begriffen werden kann für einen sorglosen Umgang mit den Begriffen des Gesetzes, die nicht dort gering geschätzt werden dürfen, wo sie die jeweilige interpretatorische Ansicht nicht zu legitimieren vermögen. Daher ist nochmals hervorzuheben, dass auch die richtig verstandene Wertungsjurisprudenz Begriff und Konstruktion nicht pauschal abqualifiziert, sondern einen harmonischen Gleichlauf durch wertungsmäßige Fundierung erstrebt.[544]

542 *L. Enneccerus/H. C. Nipperdey*, Allgemeiner Teil des Bürgerlichen Rechts, 15. Auflage 1960, Zweiter Halbband, § 145 I, S. 895; *H. Schack*, BGB – Allgemeiner Teil, 11. Auflage 2006, Rz. 177; *R. Bork*, Allgemeiner Teil des Bürgerlichen Gesetzbuchs, 2. Auflage 2006, Rz. 404.

543 Grundlegend *D. Leenen*, Willenserklärung und Rechtsgeschäft in der Regelungstechnik des BGB, Festschrift für C.-W. Canaris, 2007, S. 699. Auf die juristische Gutachtenmethode, die nach dem oben Vorausgesetzten das innere System zur Geltung bringen und abbilden soll, hat er seine Theorie ebenfalls folgerichtig angewandt; vgl. *D. Leenen*, Jura 2007, 739; sowie in wichtigen Teilbereichen bereits *ders.*, Jura 1991, 393; *ders.*, FamRZ 2000, 863. Eine auf den Vertragsschluss bezogene ähnliche dogmatische Leistung bildet der Beitrag von *D. Leenen*, Abschluss, Zustandekommen und Wirksamkeit von Verträgen, AcP 188 (1988) 381.

544 *G. Hassold*, Rechtsfindung durch Konstruktion, AcP 181 (1981), 131; *J. Petersen*, Von der Interessenjurisprudenz zur Wertungsjurisprudenz, 2001; das schwingt auch mit bei der Beobachtung einer „Prinzipienjurisprudenz" durch *P. Landau*, Die Rechtsquellenlehre in der deutschen Rechtswissenschaft des 19. Jahrhunderts, in: Juristische Theoriebildung und Rechtliche Einheit, Rättshistorika Studier (Stockholm), Band XIX, 1993.

## IV. Zwischen Logisierung und Freirechtsbewegung

Die sonach im Mittelpunkt der Rechtsanwendung stehende und sie regelrecht dominierende widerspruchsfreie Konstruktion ist möglicherweise mit der Hypothek belastet, den Bedürfnissen des Lebens nicht hinlänglich gerecht zu werden: „Jetzt bei der Übertragung dieses Rechts auf ganz fremdartige, der Antike unbekannte Tatbestände trat die Aufgabe: den Tatbestand widerspruchsfrei juristisch zu ‚konstruieren', fast alleinherrschend in den Vordergrund, und damit wurde die heute vorherrschende Auffassung des Rechts als eines in sich logisch widerspruchslos und lückenlos geschlossenen Komplexes von ‚Normen', die es ‚anzuwenden gilt', allein maßgebend für das Rechtsdenken."[545]

### 1. Verdrängung des „Primats der Logik"?

Die darin mitschwingende Kritik nimmt etwas vorweg,[546] das jenseits des zeitgenössischen Streits zwischen Begriffs- bzw. Konstruktionsjurisprudenz und Interessenjurisprudenz, die heute ihrerseits als überkommen gilt, von ganz grundsätzlichem Interesse ist, weil darin eine Einsicht enthalten ist, die heute zur allgemeinen Ansicht geworden ist. Das gilt richtigerweise aber nur mit der Maßgabe, dass in Mehrpersonenverhältnissen potentielle Drittinteressen durch eine reine Interessenjurisprudenz schwerlich Rechnung zu tragen ist, so dass in zweigliedrigen Rechtsverhältnissen auch die Interessenjurisprudenz ohne weiteres zu tragfähigen Ergebnissen gelangen kann.[547] Die Konzeption eines formal-logischen Systems der Rechtsordnung ist mindestens so überkommen,[548] wie es Be-

[545] *M. Weber*, Wirtschaft und Gesellschaft, S. 492 f.

[546] Auch wenn es keine so markante Kritik ist, wie diejenige, welche Ehrlich an der pandektistischen Begriffsjurisprudenz übte; vgl. *E. Ehrlich*, Grundlegung der Soziologie des Rechts, 1913; instruktiv *U. Wesel*, Geschichte des Rechts, 3. Auflage 2006, Rz. 293. Siehe auch *G. Dilcher*, JZ 2007, 105 ff.

[547] *J. Petersen*, Von der Interessenjurisprudenz zur Wertungsjurisprudenz, 2001, S. 38 ff., 42 f.

[548] *S. Simitis*, Zum Problem einer juristischen Logik, Ratio 3 (1960) 76; *H. Coing*, Zur Geschichte des Privatrechtssystems, 1962, S. 27; *J. Esser*, Grund-

griffs- und Interessenjurisprudenz sind,[549] weil sich die maßgeblichen Wertungen den Kategorien der formalen Logik entziehen.[550] Hierin bestand ein berechtigtes Anliegen Hecks, der zwar einerseits der Freirechtsbewegung wegen der gefährdeten Rechtssicherheit eine Absage erteilte,[551] andererseits aber der Begriffsjurisprudenz die „Illusion eines ganz objektiven Verfahrens“[552] zu rauben versuchte.[553] Vor diesem Hintergrund lässt sich nunmehr besser verstehen, was bislang bewusst verkürzend zitiert wurde als der von ihm postulierte „Primat der Lebensforschung und Lebenswertung“, dem sich die Interessenjurisprudenz verschrieben hatte. Denn im Zusammenhang postulierte er: „Der *Primat der Logik*

satz und Norm, 2. Auflage 1964, S. 221; *T. Viehweg*, Topik und Jurisprudenz, 3. Auflage 1963, S. 53; *K. Engisch*, Sinn und Tragweite juristischer Systematik, Studium Generale 12 (1950) 173; *C. A. Emge*, Philosophie der Rechtswissenschaft, 1961, S. 289; *C. Perelman*, Justice et raison, 1963, S. 206; siehe auch *D. Horn*, Studien zur Rolle der Logik bei der Anwendung des Gesetzes, 1962; *Fiedler*, Juristische Logik in mathematischer Sicht, ARSP 52 (1966) 93.

549 Freilich mit den soeben gemachten Einschränkungen.

550 *C.-W. Canaris*, Systemdenken und Systembegriff in der Jurisprudenz, S. 22. Siehe auch *A. Podlech*, Wertungen und Werte im Recht, AöR 1970, 185.

551 *E. Ehrlich*, Freie Rechtsfindung und freie Rechtswissenschaft, 1903; *H. Kantorowicz* (Pseudonym: „Gnaeus Flavius“, nach dem scriba des Appius Claudius Caecus, der durch Veröffentlichung geheimen juristischen Wissens das Geheimnisgebaren des Juristenstandes decamouflierte), Der Kampf um die Rechtswissenschaft; zur Freirechtsschule *K. Riebschläger*, Die Freirechtsbewegung: Zur Entwicklung einer soziologischen Rechtsschule, 1968; *R. Ogorek*, Richterkönig oder Subsumtionsautomat?, 1968, S. 260 ff. Ähnliche Forderungen nach einer soziologisch gefärbten Jurisprudenz bei *E. Fuchs*, Recht und Wahrheit in unserer heutigen Justiz, 1908; zu ihm *A. S. Foulkes/Arthur Kaufmann*, Gerechtigkeitswissenschaft – Ausgewählte Schriften zur Freirechtslehre von Ernst Fuchs, 1965.

552 Zur Objektivität bei Max Weber *T. Parsons*, Wertgebundenheit und Objektivität in den Sozialwissenschaften. Eine Interpretation der Beiträge Max Webers, in: Max Weber und die Soziologie heute. Verhandlungen des 15. deutschen Soziologentages (Hg. O. Stammler), 1965, S. 39.

553 *Ph. Heck*, Das Problem der Rechtsgewinnung, 1912 (Nachdruck 1968), S. 22: „Zauber, der nur demjenigen hilft, der an ihn glaubt“; programmatisch *ders.*, Was ist diejenige Begriffsjurisprudenz, die wir bekämpfen?, DJZ 1909, 1456.

wird verdrängt durch den Primat der Lebensforschung und Lebenswertung."[554] Die vorherrschende Logisierung des Rechts, um es mit Webers Worten zu sagen,[555] sollte abgelöst werden durch eine angemessene Berücksichtigung der Lebenswirklichkeit, ohne richterlicher Willkür Vorschub zu leisten.[556]

## 2. Bedenken gegen die Freirechtsschule

Darin lag wohl die Befürchtung gegenüber der Freirechtsbewegung,[557] die einem überspitzten und über das Ziel hinausschießenden Wort von Kantorowicz zufolge,[558] in „verzweifelt verwickelten" nicht nur „nach freiem Recht", sondern sogar nach „Willkür entscheiden" dürfe.[559] Weber sah dies demgegenüber mit der gebotenen Klarheit, indem er der Rationalität des Rechts die Irrationalität der Tatsachen gegenüberstellte: „Die ‚freirechtliche' Doktrin unternimmt den Nachweis, dass dies Versagen das prinzipielle Schicksal aller Gesetze gegenüber der Irrationalität der Tatsachen, dass also in zahlreichen Fällen die Anwendung der bloßen Interpretation nur Schein sei und die Entscheidung nach konkreten Wertabwägungen, nicht nach formalen Normen, erfolge und erfol-

[554] *Ph. Heck*, Begriffsbildung und Interessenjurisprudenz, 1932, S. 17; Hervorhebung nur hier.

[555] *M. Weber*, Wirtschaft und Gesellschaft, S. 493. Siehe auch *G. Dilcher*, JZ 2007, 105, 109 ff.

[556] Als Vorläufer einer soziologischen Jurisprudenz ist *O. Bülow*, Gesetz und Richteramt, 1885, zu nennen. Siehe auch *A. Nussbaum*, Die Rechtstatsachenforschung, 1917. Aus dem vergleichsweise jüngeren Schrifttum *M. Rehbinder*, Die Rechtstatsachenforschung im Schnittpunkt von Rechtssoziologie und soziologischer Jurisprudenz, Jahrbuch für Rechtssoziologie 1 (1970) 334.

[557] Zu ihr *E. Stampe*, Die Freirechtsbewegung, 1911; *E. Baumgarten*, Die Freirechtsbewegung, DJZ 1911, Nr. 16; *H. Kantorowicz*, Aus der Vorgeschichte der Freirechtsschule, 1925; *H. Reichel*, Zur Freirechtsbewegung, DJZ 1910, 463; *ders.*, Zum Problem des freien Ermessens, Festschrift für E. Zitelmann, 1913; *P. E. W. Oertmann*, Gesetzeszwang und Richterfreiheit, 1909.

[558] *M. Frommel*, Hermann Ulrich Kantorowicz (1877–1940), Ein Rechtstheoretiker zwischen allen Stühlen, in: Deutsche Juristen jüdischer Herkunft (Hg. H. Heinrichs u.a.) 1993, S. 631.

[559] *H. Kantorowicz*, Der Kampf um die Rechtswissenschaft, S. 13, 21 f., 34.

gen müsse."[560] Darin erblickte er den berechtigten Kern der Kritik gegenüber dem Richter als „Subsumtionsautomaten": „Die Situation des an die bloße Interpretation von Paragraphen und Kontrakten gebundenen Rechtsautomaten, in welchen man oben den Tatbestand nebst den Kosten einwirft, auf dass er unten das Urteil nebst den Gründen ausspeie, erschien den modernen Rechtspraktikern subaltern und wird gerade mit Universalisierung des kodifizierten formalen Gesetzesrechts immer peinlicher empfunden."[561] Andererseits entgeht auch der in diesem Zusammenhang stets beschworene und auch von Weber der Vollständigkeit halber mitbehandelte Art. 1 des Schweizerischen Zivilgesetzbuchs diesen Einwänden nicht.[562] Danach ist der Richter in Ermangelung einer eindeutigen Auskunft des Gesetzes ermächtigt,[563] nach der Regel zu entscheiden, die er selbst als Gesetzgeber erlassen würde.[564] Weber räumt die an den kategorischen Imperativ gemahnende kantische Prägung „formal" ein:[565] „Der Sache nach würde aber

[560] *M. Weber*, Wirtschaft und Gesellschaft, S. 507.

[561] *M. Weber*, Wirtschaft und Gesellschaft, S. 507.

[562] Diese Vorschrift hatte insbesondere *E. Ehrlich*, Freie Rechtsfindung und freie Rechtswissenschaft, 1903 (Nachdruck 1973), im Sinn. Siehe auch *O. A. Germann*, Präjudizielle Tragweite höchstrichterlicher Urteile, insbesondere der Urteile des schweizerischen Bundesgerichts, Zeitschrift für schweizerisches Recht, 1949, 297. Zur dahinter stehenden Problematik auch *W. Hassemer*, Rechtssystem und Kodifikation: Die Bindung des Richters an das Gesetz, in: Einführung in Rechtsphilosophie und Rechtstheorie (Hg. A. Kaufmann/ders.), 6. Auflage 1994.

[563] Sehr weitgehend *G. Boehmer*, Grundlagen der Bürgerlichen Rechtsordnung, Zweites Buch, Erste Abteilung, 1951, S. 174 f.: Wenn das Gesetz nicht durch Generalklauseln etc. „den richtigen Weg leitet" durch „generelle gesetzliche Direktive, so gilt auch bei uns der vorbildlich gefasste Art. 1 II, III des SchweizZGB".

[564] Optimistisch *M. Gmür*, Die Anwendung des Rechts nach Art. 1 des schweizerischen Zivilgesetzbuches, 1908, S. 100, wonach „das Institut der freien Rechtsfindung auf feste Füße gestellt ist; sein Gebiet und seine Methode sind mit kurzen aber festen Strichen vorgezeichnet."

[565] Vgl. auch *J. Petersen*, Kants „Metaphysische Anfangsgründe der Rechtslehre" – kritisches Spätwerk oder „Erzeugnis eines gewöhnlichen Erdensohns"?, Festschrift für C.-W. Canaris, 2007, S. 1243.

eine Judikatur, welche den gedachten Idealen entspräche, angesichts der Unvermeidlichkeit von Wertkompromissen, von einer Bezugnahme auf solche abstrakten Normen sehr oft ganz abgesehen und mindestens im Konfliktfall ganz konkrete Wertungen, also nicht nur unformale, sondern auch irrationale Rechtsfindung zulassen müssen."[566]

### 3. Richterliche Eigenwertung und ihre Grenzen

Weber hat also die besonderen Probleme richterlicher Eigenwertung klar gesehen.[567] Die Betonung des Problematischen liegt hier ersichtlich auf den zu gewärtigenden „Wertkompromissen" und „Wertungen", die nicht nur einer irrationale Rechtsfindung,[568] sondern schlimmstenfalls auch der Richterwillkür Tür und Tor öffnen können.[569] Denn als gedachte Normen wären sie zwar abstrakt, also vom konkreten Fall losgelöst, doch wären die – wenn auch nicht zugrundeliegenden, so doch mit berücksichtigten – Wertungen „konkret", also gerade auf den zu entscheidenden Fall bezogen, und damit der Rationalität des Rechts entzogen. Dieser Befund ist deswegen wesentlich und weiterführend, weil damit zugleich unausgesprochen vorausgesetzt ist, was die heutige Wertungsjurisprudenz zugrunde legt, nämlich dass die maßgeblichen

[566] *M. Weber*, Wirtschaft und Gesellschaft, S. 506. Zu den besonderen Bedenken, die sich erst nach Webers Tod durch das Unrecht des Nationalsozialismus ergeben haben *O. Behrends*, Von der Freirechtsbewegung zum konkreten Ordnungs- und Gestaltungsdenken, in: Recht und Justiz im „Dritten Reich" (Hg. R. Dreier/W. Sellert), 1989, S. 34.

[567] Wichtig aus dem neueren Schrifttum *C.-W. Canaris*, Richtigkeit und Eigenwertung in der richterlichen Rechtsfindung, Grazer Universitätsreden 50, 1993.

[568] Vgl. *F. Berolzheimer*, Die Gefahren einer Gefühlsjurisprudenz, ARWPh 1911, 595.

[569] *G. Boehmer*, Grundlagen der Bürgerlichen Rechtsordnung, Zweites Buch, Erste Abteilung, 1951, S. 189, zutreffend gegen *H. Isay*, Rechtsnorm und Entscheidung, 1929, S. 61. Siehe auch *J. W. Hedemann*, Die Flucht in die Generalklauseln. Eine Gefahr für Recht und Staat, 1933, S. 66 ff., der „Rechtsverweichlichung, Rechtsunsicherheit und Rechtswillkür" befürchtet.

Wertungen nur begrenzt[570] die des Richters sein und seinen Wertvorstellungen gehorchen dürfen,[571] sondern notwendigerweise die Wertungen des Gesetzes sein müssen.[572] Das bedeutet nicht, dass richterliche Eigenwertungen generell unzulässig wären.[573] Die damit eröffnete „Richterinitiative", wie Heck sie nennt,[574] steht aber stets im Spannungsfeld einer rationalen Gesetzesanwendung. Hinsichtlich der Werturteile macht Schoppmeyer auf einen interessanten Zusammenhang zu Hecks Interessenjurisprudenz aufmerksam: „In Übereinstimmung mit Webers Forderung nach Werturteilsfreiheit liegt hier eine der tieferen Ursachen für die Bindung an die gesetzgeberischen Werturteile und für den Verzicht auf nähere Aussagen über die richterliche Eigenwertung."[575]

## 4. Verhältnis von Rechtssoziologie und Rechtsdogmatik

Bei dieser impliziten Gegenüberstellung Hecks und Ehrlichs muss man jedoch noch einen tiefgreifenden strukturellen Unterschied beider Prämissen berücksichtigen, der auch uns gerade für Webers Rechtssoziologie in ihrem Widerstreit zwischen begriffsjuristischer Prägung und interessenjuristischer Öffnung und Hinwendung zum Leben Beachtung verdient.

570 *C.-W. Canaris*, Richtigkeit und Eigenwertung in der richterlichen Rechtsfindung, Grazer Universitätsreden 50, 1993, S. 23.

571 Das ist die Gefahr richterlicher Eigenwertungen; beispielhaft hierzu *K. Larenz/C.-W. Canaris*, Schuldrecht II/2, 13. Auflage, § 84 III 1 d, S. 621 f., gegen BGHZ 115, 84, 84, 87 ff. Allerdings hat man mit dem Wandel in der Methodenlehre von der Begriffs- über die Interessen- bis hin zur Wertungsjurisprudenz noch nicht notwendigerweise eine entsprechende Wandlung in der Justiz festgestellt, wie zutreffend zu bedenken gegeben wird von *H. Rottleuthner*, Richterliches Handeln, Zur Kritik der juristischen Dogmatik, 1973, S. 2.

572 *J. Petersen*, Von der Interessenjurisprudenz zur Wertungsjurisprudenz, 2001, S. 62 ff.

573 *F. Bydlinski*, Juristische Methodenlehre und Rechtsbegriff, S. 125 f.

574 *Ph. Heck*, Gesetzesauslegung und Interessenbegriff, AcP 112 (1914) 160.

575 *H. Schoppmeyer*, Juristische Methode als Lebensaufgabe, S. 163 f.

### a) Ehrlichs vergleichsweise radikale Rechtssoziologie

Ehrlich erkannte die Grenzen reiner Begriffsjurisprudenz, so wie Heck und Jhering sie erkannten, ohne aber dieselben Konsequenzen daraus zu ziehen. Während diese sich – mit Niklas Luhmanns Worten – „mit einer soziologisierenden Rechtswissenschaft, die bei der Auslegung von Normen auf Interessen abstellt, begnügen“[576], beschritt Ehrlich einen vergleichsweise und im Wortsinne radikaleren Weg, indem er den Versuch unternahm, die Rechtswissenschaft auf der Basis der Rechtssoziologie gründen zu lassen.[577] Das war allerdings in soziologischer Hinsicht noch nicht hinreichend ausgereift,[578] sondern unwillkürlich eher rechtsdogmatisch aufschlussreich.[579]

Weber stand, wie erinnerlich, in diesem Widerstreit paradoxerweise der dogmatischen Jurisprudenz näher, als man es von einem der Mitbegründer der Soziologie als eigenständiger Wissenschaft annehmen könnte. Nicht nur seiner Provenienz nach (denn gleiches würde für den Juristen Ehrlich zutreffen), sondern wohl nicht zuletzt im Hinblick auf die größere Anpassungsfähigkeit gegenüber seinem Rationalitätskonzept kam ihm der Begriffs- und Konstruktionsjurisprudenz eher entgegen, ohne ihr unkritisch zu begegnen,[580] als einer Richtung, die unbedingt auf der Rechtssoziologie basiert. Hierin dürfte der Grund für Webers besondere Nähe zur Rechtsdogmatik liegen, die Weber einerseits gerade für den vorlie-

576 *N. Luhmann*, Rechtssoziologie, 3. Auflage 1987, S. 21.

577 *E. Ehrlich*, Grundlegung der Soziologie des Rechts, 1913 (Neudruck 1967); dazu *M. Rehbinder*, Die Begründung der Rechtssoziologie durch Eugen Ehrlich, 1967.

578 *N. Luhmann*, Rechtssoziologie, S. 22 („theoretisch unzulänglich begründet und relativ unergiebig“).

579 *E. Ehrlich*, Die richterliche Rechtsfindung auf Grund des Rechtssatzes, Jherings Jahrbücher 67 (1917) 1. Treffend *K. Larenz*, Methodenlehre der Rechtswissenschaft, Teil I, Kapitel 3: „Rechtswissenschaft als Rechtssoziologie“; ihm zustimmend *W. Fikentscher*, Methoden des Rechts, Band III, S. 388.

580 *C.-W. Canaris*, Systemdenken und Systembegriff in der Jurisprudenz, 2. Auflage 1983, S. 21 mit Fußnote 9. *G. Dilcher*, JZ 2007, 105, 109, spricht von einer „verdeckten Abrechnung mit der Historischen Rechtsschule.“

genden Zusammenhang interessant macht, ihn andererseits aber in der reinen Rechtssoziologie,[581] wie bereits in der Einleitung zitiert, in einen gewissen Misskredit gebracht hat.[582]

### b) Luhmann und Weber

Allerdings erklärt die Konvergenz von Rationalität und Konstruktionsjurisprudenz auch die Bedenken, die Luhmann sowohl gegenüber Webers Rationalitätskonzept als auch gegenüber seinem stark von der Rechtsdogmatik geprägten rechtssoziologischen Ansatz hegte; Webers Verständnis der Rationalität entbehrte seines Erachtens einer „von der Einzelhandlung ablösbaren Konzeption gesellschaftlicher Rationalität“[583] so wie er bei Weber eine genuin und spezifisch soziologische Konzeption des Rechts vermisste: „Umgekehrt (sc. wie bei Durkheim)[584] scheint es bei Weber zu liegen. Seine Rechtssoziologie hat prägnantere Form gewonnen, nimmt aber in dieser engeren Fassung den theoretischen Beitrag Webers zu einer soziologischen Konzeption des Rechts nicht auf.“[585] Der tiefere Grund für diese Kritik dürfte darin liegen, dass Luhmann zufolge Webers große theoretische Leistung in der Rückführung auf einen subjektbezogenen Handlungsbegriff liegt, der jedoch seinen in der „Rechtssoziologie“ vertretenen Rechtsbegriff unterlaufe.[586] Dieser Zusammenhang wiederum ist der Grund für das Paradoxon Luhmanns: „Webers ‚Rechtssoziologie‘ ist nicht Webers Rechtssoziologie.“[587]

581 Anders aber, wie ebenfalls bereits in der Einleitung zitiert, *T. Parsons*, Wertgebundenheit und Objektivität in den Sozialwissenschaften. Eine Interpretation der Beiträge Max Webers, in: Max Weber und die Soziologie heute. Verhandlungen des 15. Deutschen Soziologentages, 1965, S. 39, 54.

582 *G. Gurvitch*, Grundzüge der Soziologie des Rechts, 1960, S. 37 ff.; tendenziell auch *N. Luhmann*, Rechtssoziologie, S. 19 mit Fußnote 18.

583 *N. Luhmann*, Rechtssoziologie, S. 18.

584 Gemeint ist *E. Durkheim*, Die Regeln der soziologischen Methode, 1895.

585 *N. Luhmann*, Rechtsssoziologie, S. 18 f.

586 *N. Luhmann*, Rechtssoziologie, S. 19.

587 *N. Luhmann*, Rechtssoziologie, S. 19.

Setzt man diesen Befund in Beziehung mit dem in der Einleitung Vorgestellten, so ist interessant zu sehen, wie zwei der größten Soziologen juristischer Provenienz bei gleichmäßiger Vertrautheit mit der juristischen Methodenlehre dieser einen durchaus unterschiedlichen Stellenwert einräumen. Luhmann war auch dort in erster Linie Soziologe, wo er über die Rechtsdogmatik urteilte und gab dieser nur unter der Bedingung eine Zukunft, dass sie sich zumindest auch auf eine gesellschafts- und systemtheoretische Fundierung einlassen würde: „Die Analyse ist zugleich exemplarisch gemeint für die Frage nach der Zukunft juristischer Dogmatik. Das soll nicht etwa heißen, dass die Rechtsdogmatik mit dem Eigentum steht oder fällt. Stehen und fallen wird sie mit der Frage, ob es noch möglich ist, juristische Abstraktions- und Reflexionsleistungen auf ein der gesellschaftlichen Lage entsprechendes Niveau zu bringen oder ob die weitere Entwicklung des Rechts auf die Gesetzgebung und damit in weitem Umfang auf die Politik übergehen wird."[588] Bei dieser vergleichenden Betrachtung kann es hier einstweilen bewenden, weil auf die Postulate Luhmanns an späterer Stelle nochmals eingegangen wird.[589]

### c) Rechtssoziologie und „soziologisierende" Rechtswissenschaft

Webers Rechtssoziologie ging demgegenüber noch stärker von der juristischen Dogmatik seiner Zeit aus, die auch dort, wo sie die Begriffsjurisprudenz in die Richtung der Interessenjurisprudenz zu überwinden glaubte, eher einer „soziologisierenden Rechtswissenschaft" das Wort redete, als genuin soziologisch zu argumentieren.[590] Gerade das macht sie aber aus Sicht der juristischen Methodenlehre so interessant – nicht weil es ein nicht zu rechtfertigendes Primat dieser gegenüber der Rechtssoziologie zu begrün-

588 *N. Luhmann*, Rechtssystem und Rechtsdogmatik, 1974, S. 76.

589 § 5 am Ende.

590 In diese Richtung zielen wohl auch die gewichtigen Einwände von *H. Rottleuthner*, Richterliches Handeln. Zur Kritik der juristischen Dogmatik, 1973, S. 1 f. Zum Folgenden wichtig *G. Dilcher*, JZ 2007, 105, 109, der überzeugend nachweist, dass bestimmte Positionen in Webers Rechtssoziologie bereits in seiner Dissertation angelegt gewesen sind.

den vermöchte, sondern weil Webers Rechtssoziologie am Scheitelpunkt zwischen Rechtswissenschaft und aufkeimender eigenständiger Soziologie stand und auf diese Weise über die methodengeschichtliche Lozierung hinaus Erkenntnisse über das tiefere Verhältnis zwischen beiden Disziplinen möglich sind.

## V. Lebensfremdheit des logischen Rechts

Weber hat erkannt, dass eine Überbetonung der logischen Konstruktion dem allgemeinen Rechtsbewusstsein widerstrebt und daher die fehlende Akzeptanz droht: „Nun aber haben wir gesehen, dass die rein fachjuristische Logik, die juristische ‚Konstruktion‘ der Tatbestände des Lebens an der Hand abstrakter ‚Rechtssätze‘ und unter der beherrschenden Maxime: dass dasjenige was der Jurist nach Maßgabe der durch wissenschaftliche Arbeit ermittelten ‚Prinzipien‘ nicht denken könne, auch rechtlich nicht existiere, unvermeidlich immer wieder zu Konsequenzen führen muss, welche die ‚Erwartungen‘ der privaten Rechtsinteressenten auf das Gründlichste enttäuschen.“[591] Der ökonomische Sinn eines Rechtssatzes, der den Laien interessiert, ist „rechtslogisch angesehen, irrational“. Es dürfte eine argumentative Herausforderung für die hier außer Betracht bleibende ökonomische Analyse des Rechts darstellen,[592] wenn Weber in diesem Zusammenhang von einer „Disparatheit logischer Eigengesetzlichkeiten jedes formalen Rechtsdenkens überhaupt gegenüber den auf ökonomischen Effekt abzweckenden (...) Handlungen der Interessenten“ spricht.[593]

591 *M. Weber*, Wirtschaft und Gesellschaft, S. 506. Siehe dazu auch *B. Quensel*, Max Webers Konstruktionslogik. Sozialökonomik zwischen Geschichte und Theorie, 2007.

592 Vgl. oben unter § 1. Außer den dort zitierten Autoren *S. Utzig*, Die Rolle des Rechts in der modernen ökonomischen Theorie, AcP 189 (1989) 158.

593 Siehe aber auch den Vorschlag von *P. Raisch*, Juristische Methodik, 1995, S. 189: „Die aus einer ökonomischen Analyse des Rechts resultierenden Argumente können also Elemente der Auslegung einzelner Normmerkmale sein, vor allem solcher, die vage sind und deshalb Wertungen verlangen.“

### 1. Paradoxe Irrationalität aus Sicht der Verkehrsinteressenten

Gleichwohl liegt in Webers Beschreibung der Vorherrschaft in der juristischen Methodenlehre seiner Zeit ungeachtet aller partiellen Kritik weder eine vollständige Ablehnung noch vorbehaltlose Zustimmung,[594] wie teilweise angenommen wird.[595] Es ist eher als nüchterne Bestandsaufnahme zu verstehen, wenn er der Konstruktionsjurisprudenz, von der er der Sache nach spricht attestiert: „Bei dieser spezifischen Art von Logisierung des Rechts waren aber keineswegs, wie bei der Tendenz zum formalen Recht an sich Bedürfnisse des Lebens, etwa der bürgerlichen Interessenten nach einem ‚berechenbaren' Recht, entscheidend beteiligt."[596]

Zwei unscheinbare Worte sind es, die diese Aussage erst recht erklärlich machen. Zum einen ist es die Vergangenheitsform („waren"), die davon kündet, dass für Weber die Begriffsjurisprudenz nicht die Krone der Entwicklung der Epochen juristischer Methodenlehre darstellt. Zum anderen ruht die Tonstelle ersichtlich auf der *entscheidenden* Beteiligung. Die Bedürfnisse des Lebens waren durchaus beteiligt, nur eben nicht „entscheidend". Das ist allerdings nicht nur formal, sondern auch inhaltlich – nämlich im Wortsinne – eine deutliche Einschränkung. Indem der Rechtsfall nicht maßgeblich nach den Bedürfnissen des Lebens entschieden wurde, verlor das Recht für die „bürgerlichen Interessenten", also nicht zuletzt diejenigen, für die das Bürgerliche

[594] Ebenso *C.-W. Canaris*, Systemdenken und Systembegriff in der Jurisprudenz, 2. Auflage 1983, S. 21 Fußnote 9, wonach „Max Weber dieser Art Jurisprudenz (sc. der Begriffsjurisprudenz) durchaus kritisch gegenüberstand." Siehe auch *G. Dilcher*, JZ 2007, 105, 109, der sogar (oben Fußnote 580), in der Rechtssoziologie mit guten Gründen eine verdeckte Abrechnung mit der Historischen Rechtsschule erblickt

[595] Für letzteres aber *M. Rheinstein*, Preface and Introduction to Max Weber on Law and Society, in: ders., Gesammelte Schriften. Band 1. Rechtstheorie und Soziologie (Hg. H. G. Leser), 1979, S. 27, 52; *D. M. Trubek*, Max Weber über das Recht und die Entstehung des Kapitalismus, in: Zur Rechtssoziologie Max Webers. Interpretation, Kritik, Weiterentwicklung (Hg. St. Breuer/ H. Treiber), 1984, S. 152, 168; *St. Uecker*, Die Rationalisierung des Rechts. Max Webers Rechtssoziologie, 2005, S. 76.

[596] *M. Weber*, Wirtschaft und Gesellschaft, S. 493.

Gesetzbuch gedacht war, seine Berechenbarkeit und konnte sich in letzter Konsequenz als ökonomisch ineffizient erweisen:[597] „Die Konsequenzen der rein logischen begrifflichen Konstruktion verhalten sich vielmehr zu den Erwartungen der Verkehrsinteressenten ungemein häufig gänzlich irrational und geradezu disparat; die vielberedete ‚Lebensfremdheit' des rein logischen Rechts hat hier ihren Sitz."[598] Das eingangs dieser Abhandlung vorangestellte Diktum Webers beschreibt dieses Dilemma eindrücklich.[599] Was demnach für den Fachjuristen logisch-rational anmutet, erscheint aus Laiensicht paradoxerweise gerade aufgrund seiner logischen Prägung irrational. Es erinnert freilich auch an die Aufgabe der Dogmatik, die mit Wieackers Worten auch den „Gerechtigkeitserwartungen der Rechtsgenossen" entgegenzukommen habe.[600]

## 2. Rechtsbindung an Präjudizien?

Es ist wohl eine Referenz gegenüber dem lebensnäheren Fallrecht angloamerikanischer Provenienz, wenn er über das Bedürfnis der Bürger nach einem berechenbaren Recht zugibt:[601] „Denn dieses

597 Siehe auch *D. M. Trubek,* Max Weber über das Recht und die Entstehung des Kapitalismus, in: Zur Rechtssoziologie Max Webers. Interpretation, Kritik, Weiterentwicklung (Hg. S. Breuer/H. Treiber), 1984, S. 152.

598 *M. Weber*, Wirtschaft und Gesellschaft, S. 493. Interessanterweise ist danach „das Verlangen nach einer von juristischen Spitzfindigkeiten und Formalismen gesäuberten, materialen Gerechtigkeit erstrebenden Rechtspflege an sich (...) jedem fürstlichen Patriarchalismus eigen." Es ist dann die hinzunehmende und zu tragende Konsequenz des „Strebens nach materialer Gerechtigkeit statt nach formaler Schärfe" (*M. Weber*, Wirtschaft und Gesellschaft, S. 494).

599 *Max Weber*, Wirtschaft und Gesellschaft, S. 510, ähnlich S. 506: „Niemals wird ein ‚Laie' verstehen, dass es einen ‚Elektrizitätsdiebstahl' bei der alten Definition des Diebstahlsbegriffs nicht geben konnte."

600 *F. Wieacker*, Zur praktischen Leistung der Rechtsdogmatik, Festschrift für H.-G. Gadamer, Band 2, 1970, S. 311, 332.

601 Überblick bei *I. Zajtay*, Begriff, System und Präjudizien in den kontinentalen Rechten und im Common Law, AcP 165 (1965) 97. Methodisch instruktiv vor allem *O. Lepsius*, Verwaltungsrecht unter dem Common Law, 1997; *St. Vogenauer*, Die Auslegung von Gesetzen in England und auf dem Kontinent, 2001; siehe ferner *P. S. Atiyah*/*R. S. Summers*, Form and Sub-

Bedürfnis wird, wie alle Erfahrung zeigt, ganz ebenso gut oder besser durch ein formales empirisches, an Präjudizien gebundenes Recht gewahrt."[602] Dieses allerdings hat seinerseits Grenzen, zumindest, was die Bindungswirkung für künftige Fallgestaltungen betrifft, so dass Webers Sympathie ihm gegenüber nicht aus dem Blick verliert, dass das gründlichere Eingehen auf die konkreten Lebensverhältnisse der Eröffnung von Wertungsmöglichkeiten geschuldet ist, die in anderen Fällen mit anderen Lebensumständen nicht unbedingt sachgerecht sein müssen: „Der Vorliebe für die mit dem Rechtsleben, d. h. aber: mit dem Leben des Rechts*praktikers,* in Berührung gebliebenen Präjudizienrechte zuungunsten der Gesetzesrechte tritt nun aber wieder der Anspruch entgegen: dass auch die Präjudizien zugunsten der freien Abwägung zwischen den unvermeidlich stets konkreten Wertungsmöglichkeiten nicht über den Einzelfall bindend sein dürfen."[603] Das vermeintlich lebensnähere Präjudizienrecht läuft also immer Gefahr, in dem Maße, wie es der Lebenswirklichkeit entgegenkommt, an Rationalität zu verlieren.

### 3. Drittschützende Wertungen

Auch wenn Weber die Begriffsjurisprudenz aufgrund ihres vergleichsweise formal-rationalen Charakters entgegenkam und er der Interessenjurisprudenz trotz ihrer Hinwendung zur Lebens-

stance in Anglo-American Law, 1987; *J. Benedict*, Consideration: Formalismus und Realismus im Common Law of Contracts, RabelsZ 69 (2005), 1; *T. Lundmark*, Juristische Technik und Methodik des Common Law, 1990; *E. Bucher*, England und der Kontinent. Juristische Andersartigkeit des Vertragsrechts – die Gründe, und zu consideration, ZVerglRWiss 105 (2006) 164; *P. Melin*, Gesetzesauslegung in den USA und in Deutschland, 2005.

602 *M. Weber*, Wirtschaft und Gesellschaft, S. 493. Näher zu den Präjudizien *W. Fikentscher*, Präjudizienbildung, ZVglRWiss 1985, 163; *K. Larenz*, Über die Bindungswirkung von Präjudizien, Festschrift für H. Schima, 1969, S. 247. Allgemein zur Rechtssoziologie im Rechtsvergleich *A. Heldrich*, Sozialwissenschaftliche Aspekte der Rechtsvergleichung, RabelsZ 34 (1970) 427.

603 *M. Weber*, Wirtschaft und Gesellschaft, S. 508. Siehe zu der im Text von Weber angesprochenen Problematik von Wertung und Abwägung auch *H. Hubmann*, Wertung und Abwägung im Recht, 1977; sowie *B. Schlink*, Abwägung im Verfassungsrecht, 1976.

wirklichkeit nicht so viel abgewinnen konnte, wie man hätte erwarten können, macht man es sich, wie mehrfach betont, zu einfach, wenn man ihn nur als Produkt seiner Zeit versteht, die eben die Konstruktionsjurisprudenz zur Blüte gebracht habe.[604]

### a) Drittschutz bei Webers Ermächtigungsnormen

Wie sehr Weber unausgesprochen die Begrenzungen der Interessenjurisprudenz sah, veranschaulicht eine Stelle, in der er die Ordnung der von ihm so genannten Ermächtigungsnormen behandelt. „Sie greift nämlich in gewissen Fällen notwendig über die bloße Sphäre bloßer Abgrenzung des gegenseitigen individuellen Freiheitsbereichs grundsätzlich hinaus. Denn die zugelassenen Rechtsgeschäfte schließen in aller Regel die Ermächtigung zugunsten der Interessenten in sich, auch *Dritte*, an dem betreffenden Akt nicht Beteiligte, zu binden."[605] Diese lapidare Erkenntnis ist deshalb umso höher zu schätzen, als sie etwas für selbstverständlich nimmt, das die zeitgleich entwickelte Interessenjurisprudenz wenn nicht übersehen, so doch eher stiefmütterlich behandelt hat. Dass Weber dies mitberücksichtigt hat, folgt auch daraus, dass er die von ihm selbst hervorgehobenen Dritten gegenüber den Interessenten abgrenzt.[606]

604 So etwa – unter Verweis auf *P. Crone*, Max Weber, das islamische Recht und die Entstehung des Kapitalismus, in: Max Webers Sicht des Islam. Interpretation und Kritik (Hg. W. Schluchter), 1987, S. 294, 322 Fußnote 19, – *St. Uecker*, Die Rationalisierung des Recht. Max Webers Rechtssoziologie, 2005, S. 76 „Zum Ideal der Rechtsrationalität, des formal-rationalen Rechts, dem Höchstmaß an Generalisierung und Systematisierung stilisiert der deutsche Zivilrechtler Weber also ausgerechnet das damals aktuelle (Zivil-)Recht des Deutschen Reiches und dessen Methodenlehre!" Wie hier auch *G. Dilcher*, JZ 2007, 105.

605 *M. Weber*, Wirtschaft und Gesellschaft, S. 409; Hervorhebung auch dort.

606 Der Gedanke begegnet auch in verbandsrechtlichem Zusammenhang und erläutert dort zugleich den Zusammenhang mit der Rationalisierung des Rechts: „Die technische Form andererseits, in welcher Ermächtigungen zu solchen rechtlichen Verfügungen, welche, wie etwa die Gründung einer Aktiengesellschaft, die Interessen Dritter sonderrechtsmäßig berühren, gegeben werden, ist die Aufstellung entsprechender Vertragsschemata, deren Normen jede Vereinbarung von Interessenten als zwingend zugrunde legen muss, um

### b) Beschränkungen der Interessenjurisprudenz

In der Tat hat sich die Interessentenjurisprudenz nämlich vielfach darauf beschränkt, die Interessen der Vertragsparteien erschöpfend zu würdigen, ohne die notwendige Berührung mit den Interessen Dritter, nicht am jeweiligen Rechtsgeschäft Beteiligter in Rechnung zu stellen. Das macht die Interessenjurisprudenz in Zweipersonenverhältnissen wertvoll, lässt sie jedoch bei unmittelbarer oder mittelbarer Drittbetroffenheit, insbesondere wenn die gesetzlichen Wertungen notwendig auf Dritte ausstrahlen, an ihre Grenzen gelangen.[607] Weber hat dies gesehen: „In irgendeinem Maß und Sinn wirkt fast jedes Rechtsgeschäft zwischen zwei Personen, indem es die Art der Verteilung der rechtlich garantierten Verfügungsgewalten verschiebt, auf die Beziehungen zu unbestimmt vielen Dritten zurück."[608] Weber hat also, wie sogleich noch beispielhaft zu veranschaulichen ist, die widerstreitenden Interessen im konkreten Rechtsfall gesehen, wie er sie auch soziologisch als Triebfeder des Handelns erkannte, aber – wichtiger noch – auch zu den Ideen ins Verhältnis zu setzen wusste, wie folgender für sein Denken zentrale Satz bezeugt:[609] „Interessen (ma-

rechtswirksam zu sein, und das heißt in diesem Fall: um vom Rechtszwang auch jedem Dritten gegenüber garantiert zu werden. Denn im Verhältnis unter den Vereinbarenden selbst kann sie, wenn nicht andere Gründe ihre Wirksamkeit ausschließen, Rechtswirkungen entfalten, auch wo sie Dritte nicht bindet. Diese moderne Form, den Interessenten zu überlassen, durch Benutzung bestimmter Schemata von Vereinbarungen und Erfüllung der vom Recht geforderten sachlichen Voraussetzungen sich mit Wirkung gegen Dritte die Vorteile eines Sonderrechtsinstituts zu verschaffen, weicht nun von der Art, wie die Vergangenheit Sonderrecht gegenüber den allgemeinen Rechtsregeln zuließ, erheblich ab und ist Produkt der Vereinheitlichung und Rationalisierung des Rechts in Verbindung mit der offiziellen Monopolisierung der Rechtsschöpfung durch die modernen, anstaltmäßig organisierten politischen Verbände." (*M. Weber*, Wirtschaft und Gesellschaft, S. 416).

[607] Eingehend mit Beispielen aus der damaligen Dogmatik *J. Petersen*, Von der Interessenjurisprudenz zur Wertungsjurisprudenz, 2001, S. 42 ff.

[608] *M. Weber*, Wirtschaft und Gesellschaft, S. 409.

[609] *M. R. Lepsius*, Max Weber (1864–1920) Begründer der modernen Sozialwissenschaften, in: München leuchtet für die Wissenschaft: berühmte Forscher und Gelehrte (Hg. U. Leutheusser/H. Nötz), 2007, S. 64, 73, erblickt in dieser Aussage eine Verallgemeinerung von Webers grundlegender These,

terielle und ideelle), nicht: Ideen beherrschen unmittelbar das Handeln der Menschen. Aber: die ‚Weltbilder', welche durch Ideen geschaffen wurden, haben sehr oft als ‚Weichensteller' die Bahnen bestimmt, in denen die Dynamik der Interessen das Handeln fortbewegte."[610]

### c) Zuordnung zur Prinzipienjurisprudenz?

Es ist bemerkenswert, dass Weber diese Auswirkungen nicht nur gesehen und gewichtet hat, sondern sie unmittelbar mit den Interessen in Einklang bringt, indem er insoweit von den „Interessen der Nachbarn",[611] „Interessen Dritter" bzw. den „Interessen der

wonach die protestantische Ethik mit ihrer innerweltlichen Askese die Entstehung des Kapitalismus als ideeller Faktor begünstigt hat; vgl. *M. Weber*, Die protestantische Ethik und der „Geist des Kapitalismus", Archiv für Sozialwissenschaft und Sozialpolitik 20 (1904) 1; *ders.*, Die Berufsidee des Protestantismus, 21 (1905) 1; dazu aus dem früheren Schrifttum *H. K. Fischer*, Protestantische Ethik und „Geist des Kapitalismus". Replik auf Herrn Prof. Max Webers Gegenkritik, Archiv für Sozialwissenschaft und Sozialpolitik 26 (1908) 270. Siehe auch *T. Parsons*, Der Begriff des Kapitalismus in den Theorien von Max Weber und Werner Sombart, 1929 (= „Capitalism" in recent German Literature: Sombart and Weber, Journal of Political Economy 36 (1928) 641; 37 (1929) 31; *H. Marcuse*, Industrialisierung und Kapitalismus im Werk Max Webers, in: Max Weber und die Soziologie heute, Verhandlungen des 15. deutschen Soziologentages (Hg. Otto Stammler), 1965, S. 161.

610 *M. Weber*, Gesammelte Aufsätze zur Religionssoziologie I, S. 252.

611 Was sie betrifft, so ist zwar im Ausgangspunkt einzuräumen, dass die Interessenjurisprudenz gerade im Nachbarrecht wegen der deutlich konfligierenden Interessen einen ursprünglichen Anwendungsbereich sah (vgl. bereits *R. v. Jhering*, Zur Lehre von den Beschränkungen des Grundeigentums im Interesse des Nachbarn, Jherings Jahrbücher 6, 1863, 81; *Ph. Heck*, Grundriss des Sachenrechts, § 50, S. 215). Aber auch die Wertungsjurisprudenz hat gerade das Nachbarrecht zu einer Domäne erklärt (vgl. *H. Westermann*, Die Funktion des Nachbarrechts, Festschrift für K. Larenz, 1973, S. 1003, 1008: „insofern ein besonders interessantes Objekt, als die Wertmaßstäbe besonders verhältnismäßig offen zu Tage treten"), wobei die entscheidende Thematik der Drittbetroffenheit auch von den früheren Vertretern der Wertungsjurisprudenz nur rudimentär gesehen wurde (dazu aus neuerer Sicht *J. Petersen*, Duldungspflicht und Umwelthaftung, 1996, passim; *ders.*, Von der Interessenjurisprudenz zur Wertungsjurisprudenz, 2001, S. 72 ff.

etwaigen Gläubiger“ spricht.[612] Weber hat diese Gesichtspunkte zwar als „faktisch mögliche Reflexwirkungen“ bezeichnet und damit noch einen eher am Lebenssachverhalt orientierten als spezifisch normativen Standpunkt eingenommen. Er sieht aber, dass auch „die Rechtsordnungen sie keineswegs immer ignorieren“.[613] Das entspricht der Linie der Heckschen Interessenjurisprudenz, die von „gesetzlich gewerteten Interessen“ spricht.[614] Im Vergleich zu ihr hat Weber jedoch in dem besonderen Bereich der Drittbetroffenheit auf Anhieb mehr gesehen, so dass man, wenn er überhaupt einseitig der Begriffs- und Konstruktionsjurisprudenz zugerechnet werden soll, bei ihm Ansätze finden kann, die in die moderne Wertungsjurisprudenz weisen, ohne sie freilich vorwegzunehmen: „Und es ist ferner klar, dass diese Art von Beeinflussung der Rechtslage Dritter diejenigen ‚Reflexwirkungen‘, welche im Gefolge fast jeden Rechtsgeschäfts irgendwie über den Kreis der Beteiligten hinaus eintreten können, überschreitet, weil sie von sonst geltenden Rechtsregeln abweicht.“[615] Das spricht dafür, ihn

[612] *M. Weber*, Wirtschaft und Gesellschaft, S. 409 f.: „Soweit es nur zwischen denjenigen, welche es (sc. das Rechtsgeschäft) abschließen, Ansprüche und Verbindlichkeiten schafft, scheint dies (sc. die Betroffenheit Dritter) rein äußerlich überhaupt nicht der Fall zu sein, denn hier scheint in der Tat nur die Chance, dass das Zugesagte, rechtlich erfüllt wird, rechtlich garantiert. In Wahrheit ist diese Unberührtheit der Interessen Dritter stets nur eine relative. So werden die Interessen der etwaigen Gläubiger eines jeden, der eine Schuldverpflichtung eingeht, durch dessen vermehrte Belastung mit Verbindlichkeiten berührt.“

[613] *M. Weber*, Wirtschaft und Gesellschaft, S. 410.

[614] *Ph. Heck*, Gesetzesauslegung und Interessenschutz, 1932, S. 8.

[615] *M. Weber*, Wirtschaft und Gesellschaft, S. 410 f.; zusammenfassend unter dem Gesichtspunkt der Vertragsfreiheit ebenda, S. 411: „Jedenfalls bedeutet ‚Vertragsfreiheit‘ im Sinn der Ermächtigung zur gültigen, nur durch relativ wenige, das Interesse der ‚Dritten‘ schützende Bestimmungen eingeengten Eingehung solcher Rechtsgeschäfte, die über die internen Beziehungen der Vertragsschließenden nicht nur reflexmäßig, sondern kraft speziellen Sonderrechts hinausgreifen, mehr als die bloße Einräumung des ‚Freiheitsrechts‘ im Sinne einer bloßen Ermächtigung zum beliebigen Tun oder Unterlassen konkreter Handlungen.“

jener aufgeklärten Form der Konstruktionsjurisprudenz zuzuordnen, die in Wahrheit – mit den Worten Peter Landaus – schon eher eine „Prinzipienjurisprudenz" darstellt.[616]

## VI. Ausblick

Weber hat hier über seine Zeit hinausgeblickt. Mit der Erkenntnis der Genese der Konstruktionsjurisprudenz, die ihm zugleich ihre Unzulänglichkeit der Herauslösung von nicht losgelöst zu betrachtenden Sentenzen aus dem historischen Kontext unter gleichzeitiger Verabsolutierung gezeigt hatte, wusste er, dass die aufkeimende Interessenjurisprudenz zwar das Ende einer Epoche kündete,[617] aber selbst noch keine hinreichende Rechtserkenntnis würde gewährleisten können.

### 1. Weitblick auf die Epochen der Jurisprudenz

Wenn die Konstruktionsjurisprudenz die Bedürfnisse des Lebens vergleichsweise zu gering achtete und die Interessenjurisprudenz sie womöglich überbewertete, indem sie sie den gesetzlichen Wertungen als Interessen an die Seite stellte,[618] war zu erwarten, dass

[616] *P. Landau*, Die Rechtsquellenlehre in der deutschen Rechtswissenschaft des 19. Jahrhunderts, in: Juristische Theoriebildung und Rechtliche Einheit, Rättshistorika Studier (Hg. C. Petterson), Band XIX, 1993, S. 69; dazu bereits oben § 1 II 1. *R. Dreier*, Jherings Rechtstheorie – eine Theorie evolutionärer Rechtsvernunft, in: Privatrecht heute und Jherings evolutionäres Rechtsdenken (Hg. O. Behrends), 1993, S. 125, hat demensprechend die begriffsjuristische Geschlossenheitsthese im Sinne einer Prinzipientheorie interpretiert und beruft sich auf die ersten drei Kapitel von *R. Dworkin*, Taking Rights Seriously, 2. Auflage 1978; sowie *F. Bydlinski*, Fundamentale Rechtsgrundsätze, 1988; *R. Alexy*, Begriff und Geltung des Rechts, 1992, S. 108 ff., 148 ff.

[617] Allerdings berühmte sich *Ph. Heck*, Begriffsbildung und Interessenjurisprudenz, S. 3, dass die von Weber als dominierend zugrunde gelegte Begriffsjurisprudenz durch die Interessenjurisprudenz abgelöst worden sei.

[618] Vgl. *M. Weber*, Wirtschaft und Gesellschaft, S. 494, zwar nicht über die Interessenjurisprudenz, sondern die gleich nach Inkrafttreten des Preußi-

noch eine Epoche der juristischen Methodenlehre folgen würde, die – gleichsam als Synthese – die Entgegensetzung von Konstruktion und Interesse aufheben und vereinigen würde. Dass Weber zeitgemäß von der Begriffs- und Konstruktionsjurisprudenz ausging und diese ihm wegen ihrer prima vista vergleichsweise rationalen Vorgehensweise entgegenkam, bedeutet also nicht, wie mitunter angenommen wird, dass er sie als der Weisheit letzter Schluss erachtete. Das gilt um so mehr, als Weber wie keinem seiner Zeitgenossen gegenwärtig war, dass Wissenschaft niemals zu einem Endpunkt kommt und nachgerade „überboten werden will", ist es doch gerade nicht nur ihr Schicksal, sondern ihr Sinn und Zweck überboten zu werden.[619] Dass dies konkret die Wertungsjurisprudenz sein würde, konnte er freilich nicht vorhersehen, spielt aber für seine Rechtssoziologie auch keine Rolle, die gleichwohl in vieler Hinsicht hellsichtiger urteilte als der überwiegende Teil der Literatur der juristischen Methodenlehre seiner Zeit und gerade dadurch für die jetzige juristische Methodenlehre zeitlos aktuell ist.

## 2. Zweckrationale Revolution rationalen Rechts

Als weitsichtig erweist sich vor allem die Schlusspassage seiner Rechtssoziologie, in der er nicht von ungefähr von den „ideologisch begründeten Machtansprüchen des Juristenstandes" ausgeht und die „zunehmende Wertung des jeweils geltenden Rechts" einbezieht.

schen Allgemeinen Landrechts eintretende „Gebundenheit an den Begriffsvorrat und die Methodik des römischen Rechts", aber gleichwohl programmatisch mutatis mutandis für die Interessenjurisprudenz bedeutsam: „Da endlich die Systematik zum Teil nicht von formal juristischen Begriffen, sondern von praktischen Beziehungen der Interessenten zum Recht ausging, zerriss sie vielfach die Erörterung der Rechtsinstitute und schuf dadurch trotz ihres Bestrebens nach Deutlichkeit Unklarheiten."

619 *M. Weber*, Wissenschaft als Beruf, in: Geistige Arbeit als Beruf. Vier Vorträge vor dem Freistudentischen Bund, 1919, Erster Vortrag, in: Gesammelte Aufsätze zur Wissenschaftslehre, 7. Auflage 1988, S. 582, 592.

### a) Missbrauchsanfälligkeit der juristischen Methode

Insbesondere die Einsicht, dass die Rationalität des Rechts es mit sich bringt, dass es jederzeit zweckrational umzubilden ist, kann vor dem Hintergrund der zwischenzeitlichen Erfahrung mit einer Terrordiktatur, deren Markenzeichen es nicht zuletzt war, eine hohe Justizförmigkeit vorzutäuschen,[620] nicht ernst genug genommen werden, weil sie veranschaulicht, dass einerseits auch die juristische Methodenlehre missbrauchsanfällig ist bzw. am Missbrauch mitwirken kann,[621] andererseits aber auch eine noch so ausdifferenzierte juristische Methodenlehre rechtspolitische Versäumnisse und verhängnisvolle Fehleinschätzungen nicht verhindern kann.[622] Ein erschreckendes Beispiel bildet etwa § 1 Abs. 1 des Steueranpassungsgesetzes der Nationalsozialisten, wonach bei der Auslegung des gesamten Steuerrechts die nationalsozialistische Ideologie zugrunde zu legen ist; damit musste das „rationale" Steuerrecht selbst nicht geändert werden, weil es gleichsam vor der Klammer „zweckrational" pervertiert wurde.

### b) Gefahr der „De-Institutionalisierung von Rationalitätskriterien"

Von besonderer Wichtigkeit ist deshalb die Mahnung von Rainer Lepsius: „Im übrigen sollte gerade die Erfahrung mit dem Nationalsozialismus vor solchen Programmen (sc. der De-Institutionalisierung von Rationalitätskriterien) warnen. Das nationalsozialisti-

620 Näher *M. Stolleis*, Recht im Unrecht, 1994; *U. Wesel*, Geschichte des Rechts, 3. Auflage 2006, Rz. 298 ff.

621 Grundlegend *B. Rüthers*, Die unbegrenzte Auslegung – Zum Wandel der Privatrechtsordnung im Nationalsozialismus, 6. Auflage 2005; *O. Lepsius*, Die gegensatzaufhebende Begriffsbildung. Methodenentwicklungen in der Weimarer Republik und ihr Verhältnis zur Ideologisierung der Rechtswissenschaft unter dem Nationalsozialismus, 1994; *D. Simon*, Waren die NS-Richter „unabhängige Richter" im Sinne des § 1 GVG?, Rechtshistorisches Journal 2 (1985) 102; *M. Stolleis*, Gemeinwohlformeln im nationalsozialistischen Recht, 1974; *B. Schlink*, Vergangenheitsschuld und gegenwärtiges Recht, 2002.

622 *B. Rüthers*, Rechtstheorie, 3. Auflage 2007, Rz. 997.

sche System zeichnete sich ja gerade durch einen Prozess der De-Institutionalisierung von Rationalitätskriterien aus und wurde getragen von einem blinden Vertrauen in die charismatische Sonderqualifikation des Führers, dem Glauben an die Kraft des Willens – auch gegen alle Vernunft –, der Vorstellung von einer höheren Effizienz einer verfahrensmäßig nicht bestimmten und kontrollierten Handlungsorientierung an materialen Zielen. (…) Der Nationalsozialismus ist ein eindrucksvolles Beispiel dafür, wie durch die Veränderung des Rationalitätsgrades in einzelnen institutionellen Komplexen und durch die damit einhergehende Veränderung der Konstellation von Institutionen und ihrer Beziehungen untereinander, das Kultur- und Sozialsystem einer ganzen Gesellschaft innerhalb kurzer Zeit seinen Charakter ändert."[623]

Weber selbst hat die Gefahren der zweckrationalen Pervertierung des Rechts beim ersten deutschen Soziologentag im Jahre 1910,[624] anlässlich dessen er, wie erinnerlich, wieder mit Heck zusammentraf, pointiert zusammengefasst, indem er prophezeite, was sich unter anderen Vorzeichen unglücklicherweise keine zweieinhalb Jahrzehnte später bewahrheitete: „so könnte jeder einzelne Paragraph des Bürgerlichen Gesetzbuches völlig unverändert, wie wir uns auszudrücken pflegen, in Geltung bleiben (…) und dennoch könnte die Wirtschaftsordnung sich dergestalt verändert haben, dass kein Mensch behaupten würde, sie sei noch dieselbe wie früher. Meine Herren, es wäre sogar nicht ausgeschlossen, dass bei vollem Bestehenbleiben des Bürgerlichen Gesetzbuchs eine sozialistische Wirtschaftsordnung entstehen könnte."[625]

623 *M. R. Lepsius*, Interessen, Ideen und Institutionen, 1977, S. 49. Zu Webers institutioneller Differenzierungstheorie auch *ders.*, Eigenart und Potenzial des Weber-Paradigmas, in: Das Weber-Paradigma. Studien zurWeiterentwicklung von Max Webers Forschungsprogramm (Hg. G. Albert/A. Bienfait/S. Sigmund/C. Wendt) 2003, S. 32 ff.

624 *M. Weber*, in: Verhandlungen des Ersten Deutschen Soziologentages (1910), Tübingen 1911, S. 269 f.

625 Zutreffend *B. Rüthers*, Rechtstheorie, Rz. 36: „Allerdings wurde nicht nur die Wirtschaftsordnung, sondern das gesamte politische System gleich mehrfach umgestürzt. Der NS-Staat ließ das BGB mit wenigen Ausnahmen (…)

In diesem Sinne haben auch die letzten Sätze von Webers Rechtssoziologie einen buchstäblich fatalistischen Unterton:[626] „Wie immer aber sich unter diesen Einflüssen das Recht und die Rechtspraxis gestalten mögen, unter allen Umständen ist als Konsequenz der technischen und ökonomischen Entwicklung, allem Laienrichtertum zum Trotz, die unvermeidlich zunehmende Unkenntnis des an technischem Gehalt stetig anschwellenden Rechts, und die zunehmende Wertung des jeweils geltenden Rechts als eines rationalen, daher jederzeit zweckrational Umzuschaffenden, jeder inhaltlichen Heiligkeit entbehrenden,[627] technischen Apparats sein unvermeidliches Schicksal. Dieses Schicksal kann durch die aus allgemeinen Gründen vielfach zunehmende Fügsamkeit in das einmal bestehende Recht zwar verschleiert, nicht aber wirklich von ihm abgewendet werden. Alle die kurz erwähnten modernen, wissenschaftlich oft höchst wertvollen Darlegungen rechtssoziologischer und rechtsphilosophischer Art werden nur dazu beitragen, diesen Eindruck zu verstärken, mögen sie ihrerseits Theorien über die Natur des Rechts und die Stellung des Richters vertreten, welchen Inhalts immer."[628]

fortbestehen." Lesenswert auch *ders.*, Wir denken die Rechtsbegriffe um... Weltanschauung als Auslegungsprinzip, 1987.

626 Zum ideengeschichtlichen Hintergrund und im Hinblick auf die Umbildungsproblematik bei Weber weiterführend *H. Berman*, Law and Revolution, 1983 (deutsch: Recht und Revolution, 1991, S. 267); dazu *P. Landau*, Rezension „Harold Berman, Law and Revolution", Harvard University Press 1983, The University of Chicago Law Review 51 (1984) 937.

627 Es dürfte Webers Einschätzung eher bestätigen als Lügen strafen, dass das Grundgesetz in Art. 79 Abs. 3 als Reaktion auf die Erfahrungen der Terrordiktatur eine „Ewigkeitsklausel" enthält, mit der es insbesondere die Menschenwürde gleichsam heiligt. Diese muss jedoch nicht naturrechtlich gedeutet werden, sondern kann auch als eine Art „ultimate rule" im Sinne von *H. L. A. Hart*, The Concept of Law, 1962 (Der Begriff des Rechts, 1973, S. 128 f., 154 ff.) gedeutet werden (*B. Rüthers*, Rechtstheorie, Rz. 480a).

628 *M. Weber*, Wirtschaft und Gesellschaft, S. 513.

## § 5 Typus und Rechtsfindung

Kaum etwas bringt selbst der soziologische Laie mit Max Weber so rasch in Verbindung wie den Begriff des Typus, näherhin des Idealtypus.[629] Er ist nicht nur prägend für Webers Methode,[630] sondern auch wegweisend für die spezifisch rechtssoziologischen Ausführungen.[631] Da die Typizität des Handelns seine rationale Erfassung ermöglicht,[632] steht dies zugleich in einem Bedingungsverhältnis zu dem im ersten Abschnitt Behandelten. Darüber hinaus – und für den vorliegenden Zusammenhang bedeutsam – ist der Typus,[633] seine Funktion und sein Verständnis, auch ein zentrales Instrument der juristischen Methodenlehre im Allgemeinen und der Rechtsfindung im Besonderen.[634] Darüber hinaus ist Webers Idealtypus noch in einem anderen Sinne für die juristische Methodenlehre fruchtbar gemacht bzw. auf einen Zusammenhang aufmerksam gemacht worden, nämlich wiederum im Verhältnis zu

[629] Grundlegend *M. Weber*, Die ‚Objektivität' sozialwissenschaftlicher und sozialpolitischer Erkenntnis, Archiv für Sozialwissenschaft und Sozialpolitik 19 (1904) 22. Instruktiv dazu *W. J. Mommsen*, ‚Verstehen' und ‚Idealtypus'. Zur Methodologie einer historischen Sozialwissenschaft, in: Max Weber. Gesellschaft, Politik und Geschichte, 1974, S. 208 ff.

[630] Kritisch *J. Janoska-Bendl*, Methodologische Aspekte des Idealtypus, 1965, S. 17 ff. Siehe auch *B. Quensel*, Logik und Methode in der ‚Rechtssoziologie' Max Webers. Ein Beitrag zur Klärung der grundlegenden Begriffe und Perspektiven, Zeitschrift für Rechtssoziologie 18 (1997) 133.

[631] *M. Weber*, Wirtschaft und Gesellschaft, S. 456, § 4: „Die Typen des Rechtsdenkens". *T. Burger*, Theory of Concept Formation. History, Laws, and Idealtypus, 1987.

[632] Vgl. auch *S. Kalberg*, Max Webers Typen der Rationalität: Grundstein für eine Analyse von Rationalisierungsprozessen in der Geschichte, in: Max Weber und die Rationalisierung sozialen Handelns (Hg. W. Sprondel/C. Seyfarth), 1981, S. 9.

[633] Zum Begriff *J. E. Heyde*, Typus. Ein Beitrag zur Bedeutungsgeschichte des Wortes Typus, Forschungen und Fortschritte 17 (1941) 220; *ders.*, Typus. Ein Beitrag zur Typologik, Studium Generale 5 (1952) 235.

[634] Grundlegend *D. Leenen*, Typus und Rechtsfindung, 1971.

Hecks Interessenjurisprudenz.[635] Die Bedeutungsvarianten, die Heck zur Auslegung des objektiven Sinns des Gesetzes angibt,[636] weisen immerhin eine Nähe zu Webers Unterscheidung des objektiven Sinnes auf,[637] womit zugleich Webers Idealtypus in Erscheinung tritt.[638] Dieser Zusammenhang kann schon deshalb nicht ganz zufällig sein,[639] weil auch Heck selbst gelegentlich auf den Idealtypus Webers Bezug nimmt.[640] Kurioserweise warf die marxistische Rechtstheorie der Interessenjurisprudenz vor, dass der „apolitische Rechtsgelehrte, den die Untersuchung der schweren Störungen des Lebensprozesses durch die Wirtschaftskrisen[641] und deren Zusammenhang mit dem gesetzten Recht als politische Angelegenheit nichts angeht" ihr „Idealtyp" sei.[642]

635 Zu ihr auch *W. Kallfass*, Die Tübinger Schule der Interessenjurisprudenz, 1972; *F. v. Hippel*, Die Tübinger Schule der Interessenjurisprudenz, Festschrift für R. Reinhard, 1972, S. 83.

636 *Ph. Heck*, Gesetzesauslegung und Interessenjurisprudenz, AcP 112 (1914) 1, 41 ff.

637 *H. Schoppmeyer*, Juristische Methode als Lebensaufgabe, 2001, S. 163.

638 *E. Dorndorf*, Zu den theoretischen Grundlagen der Interessenjurisprudenz: Die Beziehungen von Philipp Hecks allgemeiner Auslegungstheorie zu Max Weber und Heinrich Rickert, ARSP 1995, 542, 555.

639 Das gilt auch für den Zusammenhang mit dem bereits mehrfach behandelten inneren Systems im Sinne Hecks. Zutreffend *H. Rottleuthner*, Rechtswissenschaft als Sozialwissenschaft, 1973, S. 240: „Typologisches Denken setzt aber Grundstrukturen, z. B. rechtliche Sinnzusammenhänge (das ‚innere System'), und einen graduierbaren Maßstab voraus."

640 *Ph. Heck*, AcP 128 (1928) 112, 116; *ders.*, Begriffsbildung und Interessenjurisprudenz, 1932, S. 64.

641 Aus ökonomischer Sicht *H. Haller*, Typus und Gesetz in der Nationalökonomie. Versuch zur Klärung einiger Methodenfragen der Wirtschaftswissenschaften, 1950.

642 *Such*, NJ 1947, 229; 1948, 63; partiell zustimmend *G. Boehmer*, Grundlagen der Bürgerlichen Rechtsordnung, Zweites Buch, Erste Abteilung, 1951 S. 193 f. Fußnote 1.

## I. Methodische Grundlegung des Idealtypus

Bereits in den methodischen Grundlagen des hier behandelten Werkes definiert Weber den „Sinn“ insbesondere als den „in einem begrifflich konstruierten reinen Typus von dem oder den als Typus gedachten Handelnden subjektiv gemeinten Sinn.“[643]

### 1. Ausschluss irrationaler Elemente

Es geht ihm erklärtermaßen um die „*typen*bildende wissenschaftliche Behandlung.“[644] Dabei hat die Ermittlung von Typen und der Vergleich mit dem Idealtypus zu tun mit der möglichst rationalen Erfassung des Lebens[645] und daher dem Ausschluss abweichender irrationaler Momente:[646] „Die Konstruktion eines streng zweckrationalen Handelns also dient in diesen Fällen der Soziologie, seiner evidenten Verständlichkeit und seiner – an der Rationalität haftenden – Eindeutigkeit wegen, als *Typus* (‚Idealtypus‘), um das reale, durch Irrationalitäten aller Art (Affekte, Irrtümer) beeinflusste Handeln als ‚Abweichung‘ von dem bei rationalem Verhalten zu gegenwärtigenden Verlaufe zu verstehen.“[647] Es ist zur Vermeidung von Missverständnissen und zugleich im Sinne des bisher Behandelten wichtig zu betonen, was damit nicht gemeint war: „Zur Debatte steht also nicht die Dichotomie zwischen

643 *M. Weber*, Wirtschaft und Gesellschaft, S. 1.

644 *M. Weber*, ebenda, S. 2; Hervorhebung auch dort.

645 Zur Berücksichtigung des Logischen in Verbindung mit dem Idealtypus aus dem früheren Schrifttum *A. v. Schelting*, Die logische Theorie der historischen Kulturwissenschaft von Max Weber und im besonderen sein Begriff des Idealtypus, Archiv für Sozialwissenschaft und Sozialpolitik 49 (1922) 623.

646 *B. Pfister*, Die Entwicklung des Idealtypus. Eine methodologische Untersuchung über das Verhalten von Theorie und Geschichte bei Schmoller und Max Weber, 1928.

647 *M. Weber*, ebenda, S. 3; Hervorhebung auch dort. Siehe auch *G. Oakes*, The Verstehen-Thesis and the Foundation of Max Webers Methodology, 1977.

Rationalität und Irrationalität, wie sie in der gegenwärtigen Diskussion oft vorherrscht, sondern die Frage nach der ‚Eigenart des okzidentalen Rationalismus'."[648] Das Abstellen auf den jeweiligen Typus dient also der Rationalität, die ihrerseits ein methodisches Mittel der von Weber so genannten „verstehenden" Soziologie ist: „Insofern und nur aus diesem methodischen Zweckmäßigkeitsgrunde ist die Methode der ‚verstehenden' Soziologie ‚rationalistisch'."[649] Verstehen bedeutet insbesondere die „deutende Erfassung (…) des für den *reinen* Typus (Idealtypus) einer häufigen Erscheinung wissenschaftlich zu konstruierenden (‚idealtypischen') Sinnes oder Sinnzusammenhangs."[650] Der Typus wird also methodisch konstruiert:[651] „Die Soziologie bildet (…) *Typen*-Begriffe und sucht generelle Regeln des Geschehens."[652]

## 2. Herstellung vollständiger Sinnadäquanz

Der Idealtypus ermöglicht die Bildung soziologischer Kasuistik, auch wenn er womöglich in der Weise realiter nicht vorfindbar ist: „Die Soziologie muss ihrerseits reine (*Ideal-*)Typen von Gebilden jener Arten entwerfen, welche je in sich die konsequente Einheit möglichst vollständiger Sinnadäquanz zeigen, eben deshalb aber in dieser absolut idealen *reinen* Form vielleicht ebenso wenig je in der Realität auftreten wie eine physikalische Reaktion, die unter Voraussetzung eines absolut leeren Raums errechnet ist."[653] Vom Standpunkt der juristischen Methodenlehre verdient allerdings ein

648 *M. R. Lepsius*, Interessen, Ideen und Institutionen, 1977, S. 45.

649 *M. Weber*, Wirtschaft und Gesellschaft, S. 3.

650 *M. Weber*, Wirtschaft und Gesellschaft, S. 4; Hervorhebung auch dort; zu Beispielen aus der Nationalökonomie *M. Weber*, Archiv für Sozialwissenschaften 19 (1904), 22, 64.

651 Thematisch aus vorliegender Sicht interessant, weil die Trias von Typus, System und Rationalität angesprochen ist: *H. Lenk*, Typen und Systematik der Rationalität, Festschrift für K. Hübner, 1986, S. 11.

652 *M. Weber*, Wirtschaft und Gesellschaft, S. 9; Hervorhebung auch dort.

653 *M. Weber*, Wirtschaft und Gesellschaft, S. 10; Hervorhebungen auch dort."

Postulat von Karl Larenz Berücksichtigung,[654] der im Hinblick auf Webers Unterscheidung zwischen subjektiv-gemeintem und objektiv-gültigem Sinn – und damit bezüglich der Rechtssoziologie einerseits und Rechtsdogmatik andererseits – zu bedenken gegeben hat, dass eine verstehende Soziologie[655] auch die „objektiven Sinngehalte der Rechtsinstitute und rechtlichen Strukturtypen als mitgestaltende Faktoren des gesellschaftlichen Lebens" einbeziehen müsse.[656]

## II. Ideal als Maßstab der Dogmatik

Es bedarf im Kern keiner Begründung, dass dies auch für die juristische Methodenlehre von hohem Interesse ist. Gerade die zuletzt zitierte Präzisierung von Larenz veranschaulicht, dass die objektivrechtlichen Vorgaben nicht außer Betracht bleiben dürfen.

### 1. Typenbildung in der Dogmatik

Die Typenbildung ist in verschiedenen Bereichen seit jeher eine besondere Herausforderung der juristischen Methodenlehre.[657]

654 Im Anschluss an *A. v. Schelting*, Max Webers Wissenschaftslehre, 1934, S. 400, der wiederum R. Stammler gegen Weber verteidigt, und unter Berücksichtigung von *H. Ryffel*, Rechtssoziologie, 1974, S. 186 ff., der von einer „verstehend-nachkonstruierenden" Richtung der Rechtssoziologie ausgeht. Siehe auch *F. Loos*, Zur Wert- und Rechtslehre Max Webers, 1970, S. 17 ff.

655 Zu ihr auch *P. A. Munch*, Empirical Science and Max Weber's ‚Verstehende Soziologie', American Sociological Review 22 (1957) 26.

656 *K. Larenz*, Methodenlehre der Rechtswissenschaft, 6. Auflage 1991, S. 64 Fußnote 78. Zum Zusammenhang zwischen Jurisprudenz und verstehender Soziologie auch *S. Marck*, Substanz- und Funktionsbegriff in der Rechtsphilosophie, 1925, S. 73 ff.

657 *D. Leenen*, Typus und Rechtsfindung, 1971, S. 5 ff.; siehe auch *W. Hassemer*, Tatbestand und Typus. Untersuchungen zur strafrechtlichen Hermeneutik, 1968; *K.-D. Drüen*, Typus und Typisierung im Steuerrecht, StuW 1997, 261; *M. Strahl*, Die typisierende Betrachtungsweise im Steuerrecht, 1996; *C. G. Hempel/P. Oppenheim*, Der Typusbegriff im Lichte der neuen Logik, 1936; *H. J. Wolff*, Typen im Recht und in der Rechtswissenschaft, Studium Generale 5 ( 1952) 195.

Aber auch der Maßstab des Idealen begegnet in der Rechtsdogmatik verschiedentlich. Auf phänotypischer Ebene veranschaulicht dies eine Parallele im Haftungsrecht, wo gleichfalls an verschiedenen Stellen eine am Ideal orientierte Betrachtungs- und Bewertungsweise vorgenommen wird. Dabei darf freilich nicht übersehen werden, dass es im Ausgangspunkt um etwas strukturell Verschiedenes geht. Während Weber damit das gesellschaftliche Sein klassifiziert, geht es denjenigen Fallgestaltungen, in denen das Ideal in der Rechtsdogmatik eine Rolle spielt, um ein Sollen. Hiermit ist freilich nicht im strengen Sinne die verschiedentlich behandelte Disparität von Sein und Sollen angesprochen,[658] sondern vielmehr nur der Klarstellung halber die Ebene bezeichnet, auf der die Problematik in der Rechtsdogmatik zum Tragen kommt.[659]

## 2. Der „ideale" Fahrer als Paradigma

So orientiert sich die Rechtsprechung für die Frage, ob aus Sicht des Fahrers eines Kraftfahrzeugs ein unabwendbares Ereignis im Sinne des § 7 Abs. 2 Straßenverkehrsgesetz vorliegt, am Leitbild des „idealen" Halters bzw. Fahrers,[660] der etwa auf der Autobahn die Richtgeschwindigkeit einhält.[661] Im Unterschied zum Idealtypus Weberscher Prägung gibt es den idealen Fahrer durchaus, doch geht es eben nicht um die statistische Häufigkeit, sondern letztlich um eine Risikozuordnung. So muss auch der ideale Fahrer nicht damit rechnen, dass hinter jedem im Straßenverkehr hal-

[658] Zu ihr etwa *H. Kelsen*, Über Grenzen zwischen juristischer und soziologischer Methode, 1911; *ders.*, Der juristische und der soziologische Staatsbegriff, 2. Auflage 1928; *ders.*, Hauptprobleme der Staatsrechtslehre, 1911. *H.-L. Schreiber*, Der Begriff der Rechtspflicht, 1966, S. 144, gibt zu bedenken, dass die von Kelsen postulierte Unableitbarkeit des Sollens aus dem Sein geradewegs in die bloße Faktizität führe; zustimmend *K. Larenz*, Methodenlehre der Rechtswissenschaft, 6. Auflage 1991, S. 73 Fußnote 97.

[659] Vgl. *M. Weber*, Wirtschaft und Gesellschaft, S. 181 f.

[660] BGHZ 113, 164, 166.

[661] BGHZ 117, 337, 342.

tenden Auto plötzlich ein kleines Kind auf die Straße treten kann.[662] Sieht er jedoch in einer schmalen Ortsdurchfahrt ein Kind, das auf einem schmalen Bürgersteig seitwärts vor ihm herfährt, so muss er gewärtigen, dass es die Balance verlieren könnte.[663] Dem entspricht es, dass die genannte Rechtsprechung nicht auf den ordentlichen, gleichsam durchschnittlichen Verkehrsteilnehmer abstellt,[664] sondern eben den idealen abstellt.

## III. Rationalisierung in Rechtssoziologie und Dogmatik

Auf den ersten Blick scheint gerade die zuletzt betrachtete Parallele zu der Vermutung Anlass zu geben, dass die Rechtsdogmatik von der Rechtssoziologie wenig lernen kann[665] und der phänotypische Befund sich in der gleich klingenden Gegenüberstellung von Idealtypus und idealem Fahrer bzw. Hersteller erschöpft.

### 1. Rechtssoziologie als *ancilla iuris*?

Immerhin wird gerade nicht auf den Durchschnitt abgestellt, der rechtssoziologisch womöglich leichter zu ermitteln wäre, womit die Rechtssoziologie zu einer Art Hilfswissenschaft der Dogmatik in schwierigen Abgrenzungsfragen des täglichen Lebens werden könnte.[666] Eine solchermaßen beschränkte Rolle der Rechtssoziologie als *ancilla iuris*[667] wäre wohl aber nicht im Sinne Webers. Sie

662 BGH NJW 1985, 1950, 1951.

663 BGH VersR 1987, 1034, 1035.

664 Zustimmend *K. Larenz/C.-W. Canaris*, Lehrbuch des Schuldrechts, Band 2, Halbband 2, 13. Auflage 1994, § 84 III 1. e), S. 622 f.; ebenso im Produkthaftungsrecht; vgl. *dies.*, ebenda, § 84 VI 1b.

665 Weiterführend *N. Luhmann*, Rechtssystem und Rechtsdogmatik, 1974.

666 In diesem Sinne gibt *H. Schoppmeyer*, Juristische Methode als Lebensaufgabe, 2001, S. 164, das Verständnis Philipp Hecks wieder; gegen eine Übernahme der soziologischen Begriffe sperrte er sich; vgl. *Ph. Heck*, AcP 138 (1934) 129, 134 Anmerkung 11. Siehe auch *W. Naucke*, Über die juristische Relevanz der Sozialwissenschaften, 1972.

667 *W. Fikentscher*, Methoden des Rechts, Band III, 1977, S. 389: „Dabei soll hier nicht jenen das Wort geredet werden, die unter der Rechtssoziologie mit

würde auch der Dogmatik weniger bringen, als es zunächst den Anschein haben könnte, wenn sie nicht gar zu einem bloßen Ornament verkommen würde.[668] Denn vor der jeweiligen Überantwortung des Forschungsauftrags würde und müsste in erster Linie die rein dogmatisch zu bestimmende Ermittlung des in Frage kommenden Maßstabs stehen, ob es also unter dem Gesichtspunkt der Risikozuweisung erforderlich ist, dass die Sorgfalt eines idealen Fahrers oder eines durchschnittlichen in Betracht kommt. Wenn vom idealen Fahrer verlangt wird, dass er „zwar nichts Menschenunmögliches zu leisten braucht, aber eine erheblich überdurchschnittliche Aufmerksamkeit, Geschicklichkeit und Umsicht sowie geistesgegenwärtiges und sachgemäßes Verhalten im Augenblick der Gefahr an den Tag legt",[669] so ist dieser hohe Richtwert in der realen Welt ersichtlich selten und womöglich wirklichkeitsfremd, trotzdem aber unter Umständen von Rechts wegen geboten, weil sich aus dem inneren System ergibt,[670] dass das Abstellen auf ein lediglich durchschnittliches Verhalten die Risikozuweisung stören würde.

## 2. Die unterschiedlichen Erkenntnisinteressen

Berücksichtigt man dies für die Beantwortung der Ausgangsfrage, so ergibt sich, dass Weber hierfür mehr als nur einen Begriff, eben den des Idealtypus, geschaffen hat, sondern zugleich auch den

dem Unterton des Despektierlichen eine Hilfswissenschaft oder ‚Service-Wissenschaft' verstehen. Beurteilung von tatsächlichen Verhältnissen ohne ihre Kenntnis ist sinnlos."

668 Treffend *A. Heldrich*, AcP 186 (1986) 74, 109: „Eine Rechtstatsachenforschung nach dem Motto: ‚Schmücke Dein Heim!', wie sie auch in manchen zivilrechtlichen Dissertationen und Habilitationsschriften üblich zu werden scheint, ist aber ohne besonderen Nutzen."

669 *K. Larenz/C.-W. Canaris*, Lehrbuch des Schuldrechts, Band 2, Halbband 2, 13. Auflage 1994, § 84 III 1e, S. 623.

670 Zu ihm bereits weiter oben; vgl. *Ph. Heck*, Begriffsbildung und Interessenjurisprudenz, 1932, S. 139; *C.-W. Canaris*, Systemdenken und Systembegriff in der Jurisprudenz, 2. Auflage 1983, S. 40 f.; *F. Bydlinski*, Zum Verhältnis von äußerem und innerem System im Privatrecht, Festschrift für C.-W. Canaris, 2007, S. 1017.

Rahmen für den wissenschaftsspezifischen Erkenntnisfortschritt gesetzt hat. Denn so wie die Orientierung am Idealtypischen zur soziologischen Erkenntnis führen kann,[671] also auf die Rechtssoziologie bezogen, einen Rationalitätsgewinn verbuchen kann, verhilft die Orientierung am Idealmaßstab – jedoch nicht als Imitation, sondern unter Berücksichtigung des systematisch Gebotenen – dem jeweiligen Ausschnitt der Rechtsordnung zur Rationalität der juristischen Begründung. Es geht also weniger um eine vorgebliche Hilfsfunktion der Rechtssoziologie überhaupt, die so auch gar nicht pauschal zu begründen wäre, als vielmehr um gerade Webers Blick auf das Recht, der von Rationalität geprägt ist, die seine Methoden kennzeichnet. Darin besteht zugleich das gemeinsame Erkenntnisinteresse, dessen Mittel jeweils unterschiedliche sind: In Webers Rechtssoziologie ist es die am idealtypischen Maßstab orientierte, trennende Säuberung des Tatsachenstoffes durch Aussonderung,[672] dessen was in concreto zufällig auch der Fall, aber nicht verallgemeinerungsfähig ist, also dessen, was Luhmann in anderem Zusammenhang die „erfolgreiche Ausschließung von Irrelevanzen" genannt hat.[673] In der Dogmatik ist es die am inneren System orientierte Herausarbeitung der maßgeblichen Wertungen des Gesetzes,[674] denen der Fall mitunter nur dann bruchlos subsumiert werden kann, wenn konkretisierende Zwischenwertungen, wie etwa der Maßstab des „idealen" Fahrers auf der Grundlage der gesetzlichen Risikozuweisung gefunden worden sind. Nicht von ungefähr, sondern methodisch vorher bestimmt, ist es aber in beiden Disziplinen die Rationalisierung, welche die jeweilige Wissenschaft bestimmt und damit ihren Rang als Wissenschaft ausmacht.

671 *M. Weber*, Wirtschaft und Gesellschaft, S. 9 f.

672 Das entspricht der Sache nach dem, was in der Methodenlehre etwa *A. Somek*, Rechtliches Wissen, 2006, S. 41, sehr treffend bezeichnet als „Generierung von Normativität kraft Elimination von methodisch als irrelevant durchschauten Entscheidungsgesichtspunkten"; unter Verweis auf *J. Raz*, Practical Reasons and Norm, 2. Auflage 1990.

673 *N. Luhmann*, Rechtssystem und Rechtsdogmatik, 1974, S. 95 Fußnote 167.

674 Näher dazu *J. Petersen*, Von der Interessenjurisprudenz zur Wertungsjurisprudenz, 2001, S. 15 ff.

## IV. Typisierung als Mittel der Rechtsanwendung und Reduktion von Komplexität

Der Blick der juristischen Methodenlehre auf gerade Webers Rechtssoziologie ist deshalb von besonderem Interesse, weil er einerseits mit ihr wissenschaftlich aufgewachsen ist – das allein wäre aber eine fruchtlose Selbstbespiegelung –, andererseits aber auf dieser Basis die methodischen Grundlagen einer seinerzeit vergleichsweise jungen Wissenschaft gelegt hat.[675] Die beiden Disziplinen gemeinsame Herausforderung der „Reduktion von Komplexität"[676] bewältigte er binnen kurzem durch Rationalisierung, die es mit sich brachte, einen Maßstab zu entwickeln, den (Ideal-) Typus eben. So ist nicht nur er mutatis mutandis für die Rechtsfindung wichtig, sondern die Entwicklung der Weberschen Methode enthält so in nuce viel von dem, was sich in der juristischen Methodenlehre erst allmählich von der Begriffs- über die Interessenjurisprudenz zur Wertungsjurisprudenz vervollkommnete.[677] Der Typus

[675] *F. K. Ringer*, Max Webers's Methodology. The Unification of the Cultural and Social Sciences, 1997; *T. Burger*, Max Weber's Methodology and ist Place, International Journal of Politics, Culture, and Society 12 (1998) 277; *P. Rossi*, Max Weber und die Methodologie der Geschichts- und Sozialwissenschaften, in: M. Weber, der Historiker (Hg. J. Kocka) 1986, S. 28; *F. H. Tenbruck*, Das Werk Max Webers: Methodologie und Sozialwissenschaft, Kölner Zeitschrift für Soziologie und Sozialpsychologie 38 (1986) 13; *ders.*, Max Webers Wissenschaftslehre, 1994, S. 367; *H. Baier*, Soziologie als Handlungswissenschaft. Eine wissenschaftsgeschichtliche Studie über die Erkenntnis- und Methodenlehre Max Webers, 1969.

[676] *N. Luhmann*, Zweckbegriff und Systemrationalität: Über die Funktion von Zwecken in sozialen Systemen, 1968, S. 180 ff. Siehe aber auch *dens.*, Rechtssystem und Rechtsdogmatik, 1974, S. 19: „Durch dogmatische Analysen kann daher die Unbestimmtheit gesetzlicher Regeln nicht nur reduziert, sondern auch gesteigert werden, wenn nämlich die Dogmatik Normen zur Einbeziehung anderer Entscheidungsmöglichkeiten generalisieren und problematisieren muss."

[677] Dabei handelt es sich jeweils um einen Paradigmenwechsel im Sinne von *Th. Kuhn*, The Structure of Scientific Revolutions, 2. Auflage 1970 (Die Struktur wissenschaftlicher Revolutionen, 12. Auflage 1993); näher *J. Petersen*, Von der Interessenjurisprudenz zur Wertungsjurisprudenz, 2001, S. 19 ff. Siehe auch *N. Luhmann*, Das Recht der Gesellschaft, 1995, S. 398, der den

ist also jeweils ein methodisch wichtiges Hilfsmittel der Rechtsfindung bzw. Reduktion von Komplexität. Das konvergiert im Übrigen mit der Einsicht Luhmanns, wonach „die Folgenorientierung die Klassifikationsinstrumente zersetzt. Die zur Klassifikation von Tatbeständen und Rechtsproblemen erforderliche Typisierung geht verloren, sobald man fallweise nach Folgen fragt."[678] Auf dieser Grundlage kann nun im Einzelnen betrachtet werden, wie sich Typus und Rechtsfindung zueinander verhalten.[679]

## V. Typenarten

Weber unterscheidet den Idealtypus vom Durchschnittstypus, der wissenschaftlich vergleichsweise unergiebig ist, weil er keine hinreichend verallgemeinerungsfähigen wissenschaftlichen Aussagen erlaubt.[680]

### 1. Durchschnittstypus

Der Durchschnittstypus hat für Weber eher „empirisch-statistischen" Wert und wird daher nur gelegentlich gebraucht.[681] Insofern ist der Gesichtspunkt der bloßen Häufigkeit für ihn noch keine hinreichende wissenschaftliche Kategorie. Diese Differenzie-

Unterschied betont, dass durch den Übergang von der Interessen- zur Wertungsjurisprudenz nicht mehr die Interessen, sondern die Wertungen der vom Richter anzuwendenden Rechtsvorschriften in den Vordergrund rücken. Ferner *N. Luhmann*, Interesse und Interessenjurisprudenz im Spannungsfeld von Gesetzgebung und Rechtsprechung, ZNR 12 (1990) 1.

678 *N. Luhmann*, Rechtssystem und Rechtsdogmatik, 1974, S. 30. Siehe zur Folgenberücksichtigung vor allem *K. Arrow*, Social Choice and Individual Values, 1951 (2. Auflage 1963).

679 Aus dem älteren Schrifttum *W. Bergfeld*, Der Begriff des Typus, 1933.

680 *M. Weber*, Wirtschaft und Gesellschaft, S. 10.

681 *M. Weber*, ebenda, S. 10: „Man muss sich klar sein, dass auf soziologischem Gebiete ‚Durchschnitte' und ‚Durchschnittstypen' sich nur da einigermaßen eindeutig bilden lassen, wo es sich nur um Gradunterschiede qualitativ gleichartigen sinnhaft bestimmten Verhaltens handelt."

rung zwischen Ideal- und Durchschnittstypus findet in der juristischen Methodenlehre eine interessante Entsprechung in der Unterscheidung zwischen dem Normstrukturtypus und dem Häufigkeitstypus.[682] Die letztgenannte Unterscheidung wird bedeutsam im Rahmen der sogleich noch näher zu behandelnden Frage, ob und inwieweit sich neuartige („atypische") Parteivereinbarungen einem bestimmten gesetzgeberischen Regelungstypus zuordnen lassen.[683] Normstrukturtypen bezeichnen etwa die gesetzlich geregelten Vertragstypen des Kauf-, Miet- oder Werkvertrags,[684] während Häufigkeitstypen die im Wirtschaftsleben öfter vorkommenden Parteivereinbarungen sind, die, wie etwa der Leasingvertrag,[685] gesetzlich nicht geregelt sind.[686] Die typologische Zuordnung vollzieht sich in einer von Leenen prägnant so genannten „Ähnlichkeitsprüfung".[687]

## 2. Häufigkeitstypus

Überwiegend geht man davon aus, dass die Parteivereinbarung mit dem Häufigkeitstypus verglichen wird, der wiederum im gesetzlich geregelten Normstrukturtypus seine positiv-rechtliche Ausprägung erfahren hat.[688] Sachgerechter erscheint aber der Ver-

682 Zu dieser Unterscheidung *F. Bydlinski*, Juristische Methodenlehre, 2. Auflage 1991, S. 547 f.

683 Exemplarisch *T. Becker*, Die Auslegung des § 9 Abs. 2 AGB-Gesetz, 1986, S. 94.

684 *K. Larenz*, Methodenlehre der Rechtswissenschaft, 6. Auflage 1991, S. 461; *J. Oechsler*, Vertragliche Schuldverhältnisse, 2. Auflage 2007, Rz. 15.

685 *J. Oechsler*, Vertragliche Schuldverhältnisse, Rz. 17.

686 *K. Larenz/C.-W. Canaris*, Methodenlehre, 3. Auflage 1995, S. 290 ff.; *J. Oechsler*, Vertragstypen, in: Staudinger/Eckpfeiler des Zivilrechts, 2005, S. 502. Zu dogmatischen Konsequenzen aus der jeweiligen typologischen Zuordnung grundlegend *C.-W. Canaris*, AcP 190 (1990) 410, 452.

687 *D. Leenen*, Typus und Rechtsfindung, 1971, S. 183; zustimmend *J. Oechsler*, Staudinger/Eckpfeiler, S. 503.

688 *K. Larenz*, Methodenlehre der Rechtswissenschaft, 6. Auflage 1991, S. 468; *ders.*, NJW 1963, 737, 740; *ders./C.-W. Canaris*, Methodenlehre, 3. Auflage 1995, S. 298.

gleich der Parteivereinbarung direkt mit dem Normstrukturtypus,[689] so dass sich der Umweg über den Häufigkeitstypus erübrigt, der, soweit er nicht ohnehin im konkreten Fall identisch ist mit der Parteivereinbarung,[690] an sich keinen eigenständigen wissenschaftlichen Erklärungswert besitzt und insofern mit Webers Durchschnittstypus vergleichbar ist. Der Durchschnittstypus der Rechtssoziologie hat somit einen ebenso limitierten wissenschaftlichen Erklärungswert wie der Häufigkeitstypus der juristischen Methodenlehre, weil beide eher faktisch geprägt sind und daher nur begrenzte normative Verallgemeinerungen erlauben.[691]

## VI. Typus und Ermächtigungsnorm

Mitunter finden sich in Webers Rechtssoziologe ganze Absätze, die ebenso gut in einem großen juristischen Lehrbuch ihren Platz haben könnten, womit abermals unterstrichen wird, wie groß und wissenschaftlich interessant die Schnittmenge zwischen der juristischen Dogmatik und Methodenlehre mit der Methode Webers in der Rechtssoziologie ist, der auch über juristische Feinheiten sachverständig zu berichten wusste.

### 1. Vertragsfreiheit und Typus

Ein solcher Abschnitt betrifft die Unterscheidung zwischen zwingendem und dispositivem Recht.[692]

689 *D. Leenen*, Typus und Rechtsfindung, 1971, S. 179.

690 Zu dieser Möglichkeit *J. Oechsler*, Vertragstypen, in: Staudinger Eckpfeiler, S. 502 Fußnote 41.

691 *J. Oechsler*, Vertragliche Schuldverhältnisse, Rz. 19, macht für die Rechtsdogmatik aufmerksam auf „folgenden höchst problematischen ‚juristischen Dreisatz' (...): Der Häufigkeitstyp X ist dem Normstrukturtyp Y zugeordnet, deshalb muss X das Recht *Y im Zweifel* Anwendung finden." Eingehend *ders.*, Gerechtigkeit im modernen Austauschvertrag 1997, S. 303 ff.

692 Siehe auch *H. P. Westermann*, Vertragsfreiheit und Typengesetzlichkeit im Recht der Personengesellschaften, 1970, S. 102 ff.; *R. Zippelius*, Der Typenvergleich als Instrument der Gesetzesauslegung, Jahrbuch für Rechtssoziologie

### a) Typen von Vertragsvereinbarungen

Im Ausgangspunkt stellt Weber fest, dass es erst eine späte Errungenschaft der Rechtsentwicklung darstellt, dass die Parteien grundsätzlich selbst kraft eines Vertrags formfrei Recht schaffen können:[693] „Wenn nun trotz dieser heute generell bestehenden Vertragsfreiheit die moderne Gesetzgebung sich durchweg nicht mit der Feststellung begnügt: dass man vorbehaltlich besonderer Einschränkungen prinzipiell gültig vereinbaren könne, was immer man wolle, sondern durch allerlei spezielle Ermächtigungssätze[694] einzelne *Typen von Vertragsvereinbarungen* speziell dergestalt regelt, dass die gesetzlichen Folgen eintreten, wo die Parteien nichts anderes vereinbaren, (dispositives Recht), so sind dafür zunächst und im allgemeinen reine Bequemlichkeitsgesichtspunkte entscheidend: die Parteien denken in aller Regel nicht daran, alle möglichen relevanten Punkte wirklich ausdrücklich zu regeln, und es entspricht auch reiner Bequemlichkeit, sich an erprobte und vor allem bekannte Typen halten zu können."[695] Der Satz verdient nicht nur deshalb wörtlich zitiert zu werden, weil er die zivilrechtsdogmatische Präzision veranschaulicht, mit der Weber zu Werke geht, sondern weil er einen Bereich behandelt, in dem Rechtsdogmatik und Rechtssoziologie gleichsam Hand in Hand gehen. Instruktiv und nicht von ungefähr ebenfalls unter dem Gesichtspunkt der Vertragsfreiheit wird dies zusammengefasst von Niklas Luhmann: „Innerhalb der Rechtswissenschaft vollzieht sich seit etwa hundert Jahren eine Rebellion gegen diese Grundorientierung. Entwicklungsgeschichtlich gesehen hängt dies zusammen mit der Abnahme des Vertrauens in das Prinzip der Vertragsfrei-

und Rechtstheorie 2 (1972) 482, 486 ff.; *ders.*, Die Verwendung von Typen in Normen und Prognosen, Festschrift für K. Engisch, 1969, S. 224.

693 Vor dem Hintergrund der hier interessierenden Problematik aufschlussreich *W. Kilian*, Rechtssoziologische und rechtstheoretische Aspekte des Vertragsabschlusses, Festschrift für Wassermann, 1985, S. 715.

694 Als Oberbegriff spricht *M. Weber* (ebenda, S. 398) von „Ermächtigungen"; teilweise aber auch von „Ermächtigungsnormen" (S. 409; dazu gleich im Text).

695 *M. Weber*, Wirtschaft und Gesellschaft, S. 409; Hervorhebung nur hier.

heit als eines Instruments der Folgenkontrolle."[696] Hier scheint bereits der Zusammenhang mit dem von Weber zur Vertragsfreiheit Gesagten auf.

### b) Das Desiderat des „theoretischen Bezugsrahmens"

Interessant ist darüber hinaus aber die Folgerung, die Luhmann daraus zieht, weil sie die bereits mehrfach behandelte Interessenjurisprudenz und ihre angloamerikanischen Ausprägungen und Abwandlungen betrifft: „Interessenjurisprudenz, soziologische Jurisprudenz, teleologische Auslegungsmethode, ‚social engineering' approach, realistisches Rezeptdenken, die Sorge um die Effektivität des Rechts und neuestens die Forderung eines gesellschaftspolitischen Engagements der Juristen liegen insofern auf einer Linie und akkumulieren sich heute zu einem rasch verstärkenden und radikalisierenden Trend. Es fehlt jedoch ein theoretischer Bezugsrahmen, der die Reflexion und Kontrolle dieses Trends ermöglichte. Es genügt nicht, Radikalität schon als Reflexion auszugeben; man schafft damit nur ein Symptom mehr für das offensichtliche Defizit."[697] Die Rechtswissenschaft sollte dieses Monitum nicht ohne weiteres übergehen, weil der vermisste „theoretische Bezugsrahmen" daran erinnert, dass die von Luhmann genannten Ausprägungen im bisherigen rechtsdogmatischen und methodologischen Schrifttum weithin schon als hinreichend theoretisch fundiert angesehen werden. Damit ist auch die am Ende der Abhandlung noch erörterte Problematik der juristischen Theoriebildung angesprochen.[698] Wenn aber ein profilierter Vertreter einer Nachbarwissenschaft, der seinerseits von der Rechtswissenschaft herkommt, diese Prämisse nicht teilt, so deutet es

[696] *N. Luhmann*, Rechtssystem und Rechtsdogmatik, 1974, S. 29.
[697] *N. Luhmann*, Rechtssystem und Rechtsdogmatik, 1974, S. 29.
[698] Wichtige Arbeiten in diese Richtung sind *C.-W. Canaris*, JZ 1993, 377; *D. Medicus*, Theorien im modernen Zivilrecht, Festschrift für W. Thiele, S. 38. *R. Dreier*, Zur Theoriebildung in der Jurisprudenz, in: ders., Recht-Moral-Ideologie, 1981, S. 82 ff. Siehe auch *O. Lepsius*, in: Rechtswissenschaftstheorie (Hg. M. Jestaedt/ders.), 2008, S. 1, 25 f.

zumindest auf mögliche Divergenzen im zugrunde liegenden Wissenschaftsverständnis hin, welche die Jurisprudenz um ihrer Wissenschaftlichkeit willen ernst nehmen sollte.[699]

### c) Rechtsrationalität und Formenreichtum

Indem das dispositive Recht Typen bereithält und damit Ermächtigungsnormen eröffnet, wird nicht nur – soziologisch betrachtet – dem beschriebenen Hang der Rechtsgenossen zur Bequemlichkeit Rechnung getragen, sondern zugleich – dogmatisch gesehen – das Prinzip der Privatautonomie verwirklicht. Weber hat indes noch tiefer geblickt, indem er die Vertragsfreiheit und ihre allfällige Beschränkung aufgreift: „Aber allerdings spielte unter anderem auch der Umstand mit, dass jenem noch nicht logisch rationalisierten Recht die Maxime der spezifisch ‚wissenschaftlichen' Behandlung des Rechts: dass was der Jurist mit seinem Begriffsvorrat nicht ‚konstruieren', also nicht ‚denken' könne, auch rechtlich nicht zu existieren vermöge, noch fremd war."[700] Im Zusammenhang mit der im ersten Kapitel behandelten Rationalität des Rechts führt dies in einem anderen Sinne, als bisher zugrunde gelegt, zu einer Reduktion: „Der Rechtsrationalismus bedeutet in der Tat – so leicht dieser Gesichtspunkt auch übertrieben wird – unter Umständen eine Verarmung an ‚Formenreichtum'."[701]

## 2. Vertragstypen und typenfremde Verträge

Die zuletzt zitierten Stellen Webers bedürfen im Unterschied zu vielen anderen Aussagen praktisch keiner Übersetzung in rechtsdogmatische Kategorien, weil sie einerseits, wie eingangs hervorgehoben, teilweise selbst in einem juristischen Lehrbuch ihren Platz finden könnten, andererseits damit ein geradezu klassisches dogmatisches Problem angesprochen ist. Näher betrachtet sind es

[699] Dazu noch unter § 6. Einen wichtigen Schritt in diese Richtung unternehmen die Autoren des zitierten Sammelbandes Rechtswissenschaftstheorie (Hg. M. Jestaedt/O. Lepsius) 2008.

[700] *M. Weber*, Wirtschaft und Gesellschaft, S. 412.

[701] *M. Weber*, Wirtschaft und Gesellschaft, S. 412.

zwei miteinander zusammenhängende dogmatische Fragen. Zum einen wirft Weber die grundsätzliche Problematik von zwingendem und dispositivem Recht auf.[702] Zum anderen geht es um die Zuordnung und Behandlung gemischttypischer[703] und typenfremder Verträge.[704] Hier stehen sich bekanntlich die Absorptionstheorie,[705] die Theorie der analogen Anwendung des Vertragsrechts[706] und die Kombinationstheorie,[707] die man besser als Kombinationsmethode bezeichnet,[708] gegenüber.[709] Es ist jedoch müßig, diesen komplexen Streit hier näher darzustellen, weil einstweilen nur festzuhalten ist, dass die typenbildende Methode hier ihre Berechtigung hat,[710] zumal die Grundproblematik schon zu Webers Zeit bekannt war. Wichtiger ist die Gegenüberstellung von juristischem Typus und demjenigen, den Weber im Blick hatte.

[702] Zu ihr *H. Köhler*, BGB. Allgemeiner Teil, 31. Auflage 2007, § 3 Rz. 23 ff.; *D. Medicus*, Allgemeiner Teil des BGB, 9. Auflage 2006, Rz. 470; *F. Faust*, Bürgerliches Gesetzbuch. Allgemeiner Teil, 2. Auflage 2007, § 1 Rz. 5.

[703] Grundlegend *H. Hoeniger*, Vorstudien zum Problem der gemischten Verträge, 1906. Siehe ferner aus dem älteren Schrifttum *H. Charmatz*, Zur Geschichte und Konstruktion der Vertragstypen im Schuldrecht, 1937 (Neudruck 1968).

[704] *K. Larenz/C.-W. Canaris*, Lehrbuch des Schuldrechts, II/2, 13. Auflage 1994, § 63.

[705] *Ph. Lotmar*, Der Arbeitsvertrag, Band 1, 1902, S. 176 ff.; 686 ff.

[706] *O. Schreiber*, Gemischte Verträge im Reichsschuldrecht, Jherings Jahrbücher 60 (1912) 106.

[707] *H. Hoeniger*, Gemischte Verträge in ihren Grundformen, 1910, S. 57 ff.

[708] *K. Larenz/C.-W. Canaris*, Schuldrecht II, § 63 I 3. b). Vgl. auch unten § 6 zur Theoriebildung. Die hier so genannten „Theorien" sind schwerlich mehr als interpretatorische Ansichten.

[709] *D. Leenen*, Typus und Rechtsfindung, 1971, S. 169 f.

[710] *F. Bydlinski*, Juristische Methodenlehre und Rechtsbegriff, 2. Auflage 1991, S. 552: „Die gemischten Verträge machen besonders evident, dass auf den ‚Typenvergleich' als Methode der Rechtsgewinnung nicht verzichtet werden kann. Hier ist schon die ‚klassische Typuskonzeption' zu ihren wichtigsten Teilergebnissen gekommen, die von ihren modernen Kritikern samt dem ganzen Problem der gemischten Verträge der Einfachheit halber ignoriert werden." Siehe auch *H. Rottleuthner*, Rechtswissenschaft als Sozialwissenschaft, 1973, S. 240 f.

## VII. Begriff und Typus

Bezeichnend für den Typenbegriff im Sinne der juristischen Methodenlehre ist seine Offenheit,[711] so dass bei ihm – anders als beim klassifikatorischen Begriff – nicht alle Merkmale seiner Definition vorliegen müssen, sondern bedingt kompensierbar, das heißt austauschbar und abstufbar sind.[712] Er ist ein „elastisches Merkmalsgefüge".[713]

### 1. Bedingte Kompensierbarkeit

Es kann demnach ausreichen, dass der zu beurteilende Sachverhalt dem Typus im Ganzen entspricht,[714] ohne dass alle auf ihn zutreffenden Merkmale gleichermaßen vorliegen.[715] Es kommt dann auf das Gesamtbild an.[716] Anders als beim klassischen juristischen Tatbestand müssen also nicht alle Merkmale vorliegen.[717] So kann man etwa, um nur ein Beispiel zu nennen,[718] den Begriff

711 *F. Bydlinski*, Juristische Methodenlehre und Rechtsbegriff, 2. Auflage, S. 544.

712 Vgl. *A. Kaufmann*, Analogie und Natur der Sache. Zugleich ein Beitrag zur Lehre vom Typus, 2. Auflage 1982.

713 *D. Leenen*, Typus und Rechtsfindung, 1971, S. 34; kritisch *B. Rüthers*, Rechtstheorie, Rz. 933.

714 *K. Larenz*, Methodenlehre der Rechtswissenschaft, 6. Auflage 1991, S. 200.

715 *D. Leenen*, Typus und Rechtsfindung, 1971, S. 28, 34 ff.

716 *K. Larenz*, Methodenlehre der Rechtswissenschaft, S. 451; *ders.*, ARSP 34 (1940/41), 20.

717 *K. H. Strache*, Das Denken in Standards. Zugleich ein Beitrag zur Typologie, 1967; *L. Kuhlen*, Typuskonzeptionen in der Rechtstheorie, 1977; *ders.*, Die Denkform des Typus in der juristischen Methodenlehre, in: Juristische Methodenlehre und analytische Philosophie (Hg. Koch), 1976, S. 53; *R. Zippelius*, Die Verwendung von Typen in Normen und Prognosen, Festschrift für K. Engisch, 1969, S. 224; *ders.*, Der Typenvergleich als Instrument der Gesetzesauslegung, Jahrbuch für Rechtssoziologie und Rechtstheorie II, 1972, S. 482.

718 Aus dem Gesellschaftsrecht *A. Koller*, Grundfragen einer Typenlehre im Gesellschaftsrecht, 1967; *W. Ott*, Die Problematik einer Typologie im Gesellschaftsrecht, 1972; *Meier-Hayoz-Schluep-Ott*, Zur Typologie im schweizerischen Gesellschaftsrecht, ZSR 90 (1971), I. Halbband, S. 293.

der Person der Zeitgeschichte im Sinne des § 23 Abs. 1 KUG als Typusbegriff ansehen, bei dem die beiden prägenden Merkmale in Gestalt der Prominenz des Abgebildeten und des objektiven Nachrichtenwerts der Veröffentlichung austauschbar und bedingt kompensierbar sind,[719] ohne dass es auf die im Schrifttum und in der Rechtsprechung[720] vertretene Unterscheidung in absolute und relative Personen der Zeitgeschichte mehr ankommt.[721]

## 2. Primäre und sekundäre Wertungen

Eine besondere Herauforderung der juristischen Methodenlehre lag allerdings darin begründet, dass sich gezeigt hatte,[722] dass einund derselbe Gesetzesbegriff gleichermaßen Typusbegriff wie auch „normaler" Begriff sein kann, so dass sich die Frage nach der Unterscheidbarkeit stellte. Leenen entwickelt eine Lösung und zugleich einen Ausweg aus diesem Dilemma, indem er auf zwei verschiedene Wertentscheidungen aufmerksam macht.[723] Dem Gesetz lägen nicht nur „primäre" (sachliche), sondern auch „sekundäre" Wertungen zugrunde, welche letztere im Interesse der Zweckmäßigkeit und Rechtssicherheit den Objektbereich der betreffenden Regelung präzisierten.[724] Primäre und sekundäre Wertungsarten verhielten sich komplementär und stehen zueinander

[719] *J. Petersen*, Medienrecht, 4. Auflage 2008, § 3 Rz. 18 ff.

[720] Allerdings bahnt sich seit einiger Zeit eine andere Bewertung an, die auf eine umfassende Abwägung hinausläuft. Auch die umstrittene Rechtsprechung des Europäischen Gerichtshofs für Menschenrechte zu Art. 8, 10 EMRK zielt unausgesprochen eher in die hier vertretene Richtung.

[721] Insoweit grundlegend *H. Neumann-Duesberg*, Bildberichterstattung über absolute und relative Personen der Zeitgeschichte, JZ 1960, 114, 115.

[722] Namentlich wurde es herausgearbeitet von *D. Leenen*, Typus und Rechtsfindung, 1971, S. 57, 92.

[723] Er bezieht sich ebenda, S. 112, u.a. auf eine Unterscheidung von *F. C. v. Savigny*, System des heutigen römischen Rechts, Erster Band, 1840, S. 217.

[724] *D. Leenen*, Typus und Rechtsfindung, S. 109, 114. Er macht auf eine interessante Parallele bei *Ph. Heck* (Gesetzesauslegung und Interessenjurisprudenz, AcP 114 (1912) 1, 18) aufmerksam, der den psychologischen Vorgang der Gesetzesentstehung in gleichfalls zwei Schritte gliedert, womit die Differenzierung zwischen „Lebensinteressen" und „rechtstechnischen Interes-

in einem „variablen Mischverhältnis“.[725] Diese Erkenntnis bildet zugleich einen wesentlichen Fortschritt im Rahmen der Entwicklung der Wertungsjurisprudenz.[726]

## VIII. Folgerungen

Verallgemeinert man die vorstehenden Überlegungen im Hinblick auf die vorliegende Problemstellung, so soll damit nicht um jeden Preis eine Parallele zu den Idealtypen Weberscher Prägung gefunden werden; das würde nicht weiterführen, weil nicht übersehen werden darf, dass beide auf verschiedenen Ebenen anzusiedeln sind und eine beliebige Vermengung nur Verwirrung in beiden Wissenschaften erzeugen könnte. Interessanter ist vielmehr aufzuzeigen, dass durch das rechtstechnische Mittel des Typus eine neue Einsicht über die Jurisprudenz, näherhin die Wertungsjurisprudenz, ermöglicht wurde, die ihr eine neue Dimension eröffnete. Das hat die Typus-Forschung mit der Betrachtung des soziologischen Idealtypus gemeinsam, der als Darstellungsmittel gleichfalls einen genuin neuen Zugang geschaffen hat, die Wirklichkeit abzubilden.[727] Weber selbst hat dies in einem noch zu wenig beachteten Exkurs über die Rechtsgeschichte in einer Weise eingeordnet, die deshalb wörtlich wiedergegeben werden sollte: „Wir werden in diesem letztgenannten Fall natürlich sorgsam zu konstatieren

sen“ (*Ph. Heck*, Begriffsbildung und Interessenjurisprudenz, 1932, S. 40 f.) abgemildert wird.

[725] *D. Leenen*, Typus und Rechtsfindung, S. 175.

[726] *F. Bydlinski*, Juristische Methodenlehre und Rechtsbegriff, S. 547 Fußnote 358 („sollten diejenigen zur Kenntnis nehmen, die dazu neigen, die ‚Wertungsjurisprudenz‘ in Richtung auf Auflösung des geltenden Rechts misszuverstehen.“). In diesem Sinne wichtig auch die Folgerung von *D. Leenen*, Typus und Rechtsfindung, 1971, S. 177: „Nur wenn auf die hinter den Denkformen jeweils stehenden *Wertungen* zurückgegriffen wird, kann die ‚Typenjurisprudenz‘ den Kardinalfehler der Begriffsjurisprudenz vermeiden, aus bloßen Denkformen materiale Ergebnisse deduzieren zu wollen.“

[727] Vgl. auch *N. Luhmann*, Rechtssystem und Rechtsdogmatik, 1974, S. 33. „Bei der Zuordnung – sei es zur Regel, sei es zu einer zuzulassenden Ausnahme – kann eine Orientierung an Typen hilfreich sein.“

suchen, inwieweit die eine oder die mehreren von uns als möglich entwickelten ‚Theorien' dem empirischen ‚Rechtsbewusstsein' der Zeitgenossen entsprechen, – die eigene ‚Theorie' dient uns nur als provisorisches Schema der Ordnung. Aber das ‚Rechtsbewusstsein' der Zeitgenossen ist eben ganz und gar nicht notwendig etwas eindeutiges, noch weniger etwas in sich widerspruchslos Gegebenes. In jedem Fall verwenden wir unsere *dogmatische Konstruktion als ‚Idealtypus'* in dem von mir an anderer Stelle entwickelten Sinn. Ein solches Gedankengebilde ist nie Endpunkt der empirischen Erkenntnis, sondern stets entweder *heuristisches* oder *Darstellungs-Mittel* (oder beides)."[728] Obwohl oder gerade weil der juristische Typus sich vom Tatbestand in einem wesentlichen Punkt gelöst hat, indem er davon entbunden hat, dass nicht mehr alle Merkmale vorliegen müssen,[729] hat er ebenso wie der Idealtypus, der sich von dem in der Realität Vorfindbaren abgewendet hat, um zu verallgemeinerbaren Aussagen zu gelangen, der jeweiligen Wissenschaft ein erkenntnisleitendes Prinzip vermittelt.

## 1. Leistungsfähigkeit

Für den vorliegenden Zusammenhang aufschlussreich ist, dass der Typusbegriff der juristischen Methodenlehre wie auch der Idealtypus Webers, wie er ihn beispielhaft in seiner Konstruktion der

[728] *M. Weber*, Archiv für Sozialwissenschaft und Sozialpolitik 24, 1907, 94 ff. Fußnote 15. Weiterführend *G. Dilcher*, JZ 2007, 105, 112: „Seine Lehrlingszeit in der Historischen Rechtsschule hat offenbar auch dafür (sc. die Entwicklung des Idealtypus) die Grundlage gelegt. Weber nahm die Fruchtbarkeit des breiten, Empire und Normativität verbindenden, kulturgeschichtlichen Ansatzes, dessen Wirkung sich für die Jurisprudenz erschöpft hatte, in die sich neu begründenden Sozialwissenschaften hinüber."

[729] Es ist mutatis mutandis dasjenige, was Weber in der Rechtssoziologie als Anknüpfung „von Rechtsfolgen an unformale Tatbestände" bezeichnet; vgl. *M. Weber*, Wirtschaft und Gesellschaft, S. 506. Nicht von ungefähr nennt Weber dort „bona fides, dolus" als Ausprägung der „Gesinnung", was daran erinnert, dass auch in der Dogmatik im Rahmen der Arglist („dolus") oder der Bestimmung von Generalklauseln die Typenbildung ihren Platz haben kann; vgl. *C.-W. Canaris*, Systemdenken und Systembegriff in der Jurisprudenz, S. 152.

Rationalitätsstufen vorstellt, Einwänden ausgesetzt ist, die eine gewisse Parallelität zeigen. Die Einwände gegen den Typusbegriff der juristischen Methodenlehre wurden bereits vorgestellt und lassen sich dahingehend zusammenfassen, dass seine Leistungsfähigkeit bestritten wird und klare Maßgaben für die Operationalisierbarkeit fehlten bzw. von den Befürwortern nicht angegeben werden könnten.[730] Ähnlichen Bedenken ist Webers Idealtypus im Hinblick auf die von ihm begründeten Entwicklungsstufen von der charismatischen „prophetischen" Rechtsoffenbarung über die Rechtsschöpfung durch Honoratioren im Wege der Kautelar- und Präjudizienrechtsschöpfung bis zur Rechtspflege durch Fachjuristen ausgesetzt.[731] Man hat darin eine „spekulative Geschichtsmetaphysik" gesehen,[732] die angesichts der Komplexität der Rechtsgeschichte nicht leistungsfähig sei.[733] Das ist insofern nicht ganz gerecht, als Weber selbst in einer für seinen Idealtypus geradezu bezeichnenden Weise konzediert, „dass die hier theoretisch konstruierten Rationalitätsstufen in der historischen Realität weder überall gerade in der Reihenfolge des Rationalitätsgrades aufeinander gefolgt, noch auch nur überall, selbst im Okzident, alle vorhanden gewesen sind."[734] Es ist Weber also durchaus klar gewesen, was ihm gleichwohl entgegengehalten wird, dass es sich um eine „eindeutig gesteigerte Eindeutigkeit der Idealtypen" handele, wenn die „rein begrifflich konstruierte Typologie mit rechtshistorisch gewonnenen Anschauungen" angereichert werde.[735]

[730] *L. Kuhlen*, Typuskonzeptionen in der Rechtstheorie, 1977; *ders.*, Die Denkform des Typus in der juristischen Methodenlehre, in: Juristische Methodenlehre und analytische Philosophie (Hg. Koch), 1976, S. 53; *W. Ott*, Die Problematik einer Typologie im Gesellschaftsrecht, 1972.

[731] *M. Weber*, Wirtschaft und Gesellschaft, S. 504.

[732] *W. Gephart*, Gesellschaftstheorie und Recht. Das Recht im soziologischen Diskurs der Moderne, 1993, S. 531.

[733] *St. Uecker*, Die Rationalisierung des Rechts. Max Webers Rechtssoziologie, 2005, S. 80. Siehe aus rechtsgeschichtlicher Sicht aber auch *G. Dilcher*, JZ 2007, 105.

[734] *M. Weber*, Wirtschaft und Gesellschaft, S. 505.

[735] *B. Quensel*, Logik und Methode in der „Rechtssoziologie" Max Webers, Zeitschrift für Rechtssoziologie 18 (1997) 149; vgl. auch *ders.*, Max Webers Konstruktionslogik, 2007.

## 2. Zusammenfassung von Beobachtungen unter dem Prinzip der Denkökonomie

Die Einwände richten sich also sowohl im Falle des Typusbegriffs als auch bezogen auf Webers Idealtypus der Evolution der Rechtsgewinnung nicht nur gegen ein explizites Zugeständnis, sondern nachgerade die Besonderheit der jeweiligen Methode. Dass im einen Fall der Typus indes gerade kein subsumtionsfähiger Tatbestand ist und im anderen Fall die Komplexität wegen des notwendigerweise approximativen Charakters des Idealtypus nicht *restlos* reduziert werden kann,[736] diskreditiert also nicht die Methode, zumal die betreffende Einordnung ohne ihre Anwendung schwerer gelingt und sie somit innerhalb ihres vorgegebenen und behaupteten Anspruchs durchaus leistungsfähig ist. Es soll eben wie im Rahmen der Theoriebildung nicht jeder Fall voraussetzungslos aufs neue bedacht und bewertet werden müssen, wenn durch die Abstraktion von vielfältigen Fallgestaltungen eine theoretische Hilfestellung gefunden worden ist, die nicht nur der Einfachheit, sondern auch der Wertungsgerechtigkeit halber Kategorisierungen ermöglicht und damit den jeweiligen Fall zu lösen bzw. einzuordnen hilft.[737] Bringt man es mit dem weiter oben Bedachten in Verbindung,[738] so ist es jeweils in wissenschaftstheoretischer Hinsicht nichts anderes als die „Zusammenfassung von Beobachtungen unter dem Prinzip der Denkökonomie", die Werner Heisenberg dem Physiker und Philosophen Ernst Mach zugeschrieben hat.[739]

736 *M. R. Lepsius*, Max Weber (1864–1920) Begründer der modernen Sozialwissenschaften, in: München leuchtet für die Wissenschaft: berühmte Forscher und Gelehrte (Hg. U. Leutheusser/H. Nötz), 2007, S. 64, 68 f.: „es ging ihm mit diesen ‚Idealtypen' darum, Modelle zu entwickeln, mit deren Hilfe die empirisch vorkommenden Mischverhältnisse von Strukturelementen genauer erfasst werden können."

737 *C.-W. Canaris*, Funktion, Struktur und Falsifikation juristischer Theorien, JZ 1993, 377.

738 § 1 sub 2.

739 *W. Heisenberg*, Der Teil und das Ganze. Gespräche im Umkreis der Atomphysik, 1969, 13. Auflage 1993, S. 81 ff.

### 3. Bezug zum Wissenschaftsanspruch der Jurisprudenz

Eine solche Betrachtungsweise hat aber, indem sie Typen zueinander ins Verhältnis setzt, die vorderhand wenig miteinander zu tun zu haben und auf anderen Ebenen anzusiedeln zu sein scheinen, auch noch einen weiteren Vorzug, der letztlich dem bereits in der Einleitung zum Leitgesichtspunkt erhobenen Problem des Wissenschaftsanspruchs[740] der Jurisprudenz entspricht.[741] Die bisherigen Überlegungen verdeutlichen, dass sich die Rechtssoziologie Webers – nicht zuletzt im Hinblick auf Typus und Idealtypus – für die Rechtswissenschaft noch insoweit operationalisierbar darstellt, als ihr auch eine – wenngleich von der soziologischen Betrachtungsweise strikt zu trennende[742] – juristische Betrachtungsweise zugrunde liegt bzw. diese mit berücksichtigt wird. Darin unterscheidet sie sich insbesondere von der rechtssoziologischen Usurpation Ehrlichs, die ihr Programm so versteht: „Da das Recht eine gesellschaftliche Erscheinung ist, so gehört jede Art der Jurisprudenz den Geisteswissenschaften an, aber die eigentliche Rechtswissenschaft ist ein Teil der theoretischen Gesellschaftswissenschaft der Soziologie. Die Soziologie des Rechts ist die wissenschaftliche Lehre vom Recht.“[743] Mit Recht hat sich Hans Kelsen überaus

[740] *A. Kaufmann*, Über die Wissenschaftlichkeit der Rechtswissenschaft – Ansätze einer Konvergenztheorie der Wahrheit, in: Über Gerechtigkeit (Hg. ders.) 1993, 259; zuletzt *W. Ernst*, Gelehrtes Recht, in: W. Schön (Hg.), Das Proprium der Rechtswissenschaft, 2007, S. 3 ff.; *U. Diederichsen*, Einführung in das wissenschaftliche Denken, 1970. Der Wissenschaftsanspruch hängt aufs engste mit dem Systemgedanken zusammen; vgl. *J. Binder*, Der Wissenschaftscharakter der Rechtswissenschaft, Kantstudien XXV (1921) 321, 356; auch insoweit kritisch *E. Ehrlich*, Die juristische Logik, 2. Auflage 1925, S. 121 ff. Aus dem wichtigen Band „Rechtswissenschaftstheorie (Hg. M. Jestaedt/O. Lepsius), 2008, *O. Lepsius*, S. 1, 36 ff.; *H. C. Grigoleit*, S. 52, 66 f.

[741] Zur Rechtswissenschaft als hermeneutischer Wissenschaft *H. Coing*, Grundzüge der Rechtsphilosophie, 5. Auflage 1993, S. 319; *K. Obermayer*, Rechtswissenschaft als Geisteswissenschaft, JZ 1987, 694.

[742] *M. Weber*, Wirtschaft und Gesellschaft, S. 181.

[743] *E. Ehrlich*, Grundlegung der Soziologie des Rechts, 1913, S. 19. Ähnlich wie zuvor Ehrlich später *F. W. Jerusalem*, Kritik der Rechtswissenschaft, 1948; *ders.*, Die Zersetzung der Rechtswissenschaft, 1968; dagegen zutreffend *K. Larenz*, Methodenlehre der Rechtswissenschaft, 6. Auflage 1991, S. 67 ff.

kritisch zu dieser Konzeption geäußert, indem er sie als „Synkretismus der Methode normativer Jurisprudenz und explikativer Rechtssoziologie" bezeichnete.[744]

Allerdings ist zu der damit aufgeworfenen Frage nach der Wissenschaftlichkeit der Jurisprudenz auch noch Luhmanns Einschätzung zu berücksichtigen, die ebenso wie diejenige Webers immer zugleich Innen- wie Außensicht ist: „Ihre (sc. der Jurisprudenz) Wissenschaftlichkeit ist umstritten. Sie kann nur behauptet werden, wenn man eindeutig zwischen den begrifflichen, dogmatischen, normativen Selbstabstraktionen der gesellschaftlichen Realität, hier also des Rechtssystems, und deren wissenschaftlicher Analyse unterscheidet. Diese Unterscheidung ist Voraussetzung dafür, dass im Zusammenhang wissenschaftlicher Forschung unter nichtdogmatischen Gesichtspunkten nach der rechtssystematischen und der gesellschaftlichen Funktion und nach der Zukunft juristischer Dogmatik gefragt werden kann."[745] Dann kann sie nämlich beispielhaft und zumindest annäherungsweise etwas gewährleisten, das einer weiteren wichtigen Feststellung Niklas Luhmanns zufolge eine notwendige Bedingung des Wissenschaftsanspruchs darstellt, indem zwischen Rechtsdogmatik und Rechtstheorie[746] dergestalt unterschieden wird,[747] dass letztere die Abs-

[744] *H. Kelsen*, Archiv für Sozialwissenschaften 41 (1914) 840 f.

[745] *N. Luhmann*, Rechtssystem und Rechtsdogmatik, 1974, S. 13. Vgl. dazu *A. v. Aaken*, in: Rechtswissenschaftstheorie (Hg. M. Jestaedt/O. Lepsius) 2008, S. 79, 84.

[746] *M. Weber*, Wirtschaft und Gesellschaft, S. 458, ordnet die Rechtstheorie gleich mit der rationalen Rechtsschulung.

[747] *N. Luhmann*, Rechtssystem und Rechtsdogmatik, 1974, S. 13: „Die Notwendigkeit, in dieser Weise juristische Dogmatik und Rechtstheorie (oder auch: Jurisprudenz und Rechtswissenschaft) zu unterscheiden, findet heute zunehmend Anerkennung." (unter Hinweis auf *O. Ballweg*, Rechtswissenschaft und Jurisprudenz, 1970; *A. Peczenik*, Towards the Juristic Theory of Law, Österreichische Zeitschrift für öffentliches Recht 21, 1971, 167; *K. Adomeit*, Zivilrechtstheorie und Zivilrechtsdogmatik – mit einem Beitrag zur Theorie des subjektiven Rechts, Jahrbuch für Rechtssoziologie und Rechtstheorie 2, 1972, 503).

traktionen nochmals losgelöst betrachtet,[748] hier also etwa zwischen den Rechtsanwendungsfragen des Typus und seiner Funktion im Hinblick auf den bzw. im Vergleich mit dem Idealtypus unterschieden wird. Allerdings braucht man den Wissenschaftsanspruch nicht von einem Bekenntnis zur Systemtheorie abhängig zu machen, wie dies im Übrigen wohl auch Weber fremd gewesen wäre.[749] So spiegelt sich in dieser Frage ein Grundproblem der juristischen Methodenlehre, das die Frage berührt, ob sie zwangsläufig auf einer bestimmten Rechtstheorie basiert oder sie wenigstens einschließt.[750] Gerade die Flexibilität des Typusbegriffs ermöglicht wertungsmäßige Abstufungen, die der Wertungsgerechtigkeit Rechnung tragen können. Gerechtigkeit ist eben doch mehr als die „adäquate Komplexität des Rechtssystems."[751]

[748] *N. Luhmann*, Rechtssystem und Rechtsdogmatik, 1974, S. 13: „Die Rechtstheorie bildet Abstraktionen von Abstraktionen; sie fragt zum Beispiel nach der Funktion von Klassifikationen. Und erst auf dieser Ebene kann jene Autonomie der Erkenntnis beansprucht werden, die mit der neuzeitlichen Entwicklung der Wissenschaften durchgesetzt ist." Ähnlich *B. Rüthers*, Rechtstheorie, 3. Auflage 2007, Rz. 23 („Rechtstheorie ist also eine Art Meta-Dogmatik."). Siehe auch die Kontroverse in dem zitierten Band „Rechtswissenschaftstheorie" (2008) zwischen *C. Möllers*, S. 151 ff. und *M. Jestaedt* (S. 175 ff.).

[749] Siehe nochmals den bereits am Ende der Einleitung zitierten wichtigen Hinweis von *M. R. Lepsius*, Max Weber (1864–1920) Begründer der modernen Sozialwissenschaften, in: München leuchtet für die Wissenschaft (Hg. U. Leutheusser/H. Nötz), 2007), S. 64, 69: „Weber war kein Systemtheoretiker und sah in der Nutzenabwägung nicht die elementaren Antriebe der Sebstdomestizierung des Menschen."

[750] *K. Larenz*, Methodenlehre der Rechtswissenschaft, 6. Auflage 1991, Vorwort; *F. Bydlinski*, Juristische Methodenlehre und Rechtsbegriff, 2. Auflage 1991, S. 184 Fußnote 3.

[751] *N. Luhmann*, Gerechtigkeit in den Rechtssystemen der modernen Gesellschaft, Rechtstheorie 4 (1973) 131, 142.

## § 6 Rechtswissenschaft als Beruf

Max Webers Rechtssoziologie ist für die Rechtsdogmatik nicht zuletzt deshalb so interessant, weil Weber das Recht und die juristische Methode inwendig kannte und von daher, gleichsam auswendig, deutend verstehen konnte. Die juristische Methodenlehre betrifft den Ausgangspunkt seines Denkens und eröffnet somit einen Zugang zu Max Webers Rechtssoziologie.[752] Diese erweist sich umgekehrt für die juristische Methodenlehre buchstäblich als Fundgrube in jenem heuristischen Sinne, der zwar die logisch rationale Rechtsfindung, von der Weber ausging, nicht hervorzubringen vermag,[753] dafür aber Fragen an die Jurisprudenz stellt, deren Beantwortung etwas über ihre Wissenschaftlichkeit im Verhältnis zu anderen Disziplinen aussagt. Die Rechtswissenschaft sollte sich – auch soweit sie der Rechtssoziologie im Einzelnen fernsteht – dem Werk Webers nicht länger verschließen[754] und sich in der methodologischen Durchdringung den Umstand zu eigen machen, dass er, der die deutsche Soziologie im Ausland wie kein anderer repräsentiert[755] und den kein Geringerer als Karl Jaspers 1932 als den „größten Deutschen unseres Zeitalters" genannt hat,[756] ebenso wie später Niklas Luhmann als Jurist begonnen hat.

[752] *St. P. Turner/R. A. Factor*, The Lawyer as Social Thinker, 1994.

[753] *W. Fikentscher*, Juristische Heuristik, Festschrift für C.-W. Canaris, 2007, S. 1091.

[754] Aus dem bisherigen Schrifttum immerhin *W. Brugger*, Menschenrechtsethos und Verantwortungsethik. M. Webers Beitrag zur Analyse und Begründung der Menschenrechte, 1980.

[755] *M. R. Lepsius*, Interessen, Ideen und Institutionen, 1977, S. 22: „Weber gilt als der wesentliche Vertreter dessen, was man – international – die ‚deutsche Soziologie' nennt: die Verbindung von systematischer Gegenwartskritik mit universalhistorisch vergleichender Gesellschaftsanalyse, die Erforschung von Kulturordnungen und sozialökonomischen Interessenkonflikten in komplexen Handlungskonstellationen, das Bemühen, in methodologischer ‚Wertfreiheit' den subjektiven Sinn des jeweils Handelnden zu verstehen."

[756] *K. Jaspers*, Max Weber. Politiker, Forscher, Philosoph, 1932, S. 7. Umgekehrt legt *M. Weber*, Wirtschaft und Gesellschaft, S. 1, *K. Jaspers*, Allgemeine

So könnte die Jurisprudenz die von Talcott Parsons[757] herausgestellte Zentralität der Rechtssoziologie in Webers Werk als Chance begreifen und damit zu einer Verständigung innerhalb der Geisteswissenschaften beitragen, die mehr wäre als die in der Rechtssoziologie verständlicherweise geargwöhnte „interdisziplinäre Attitude".[758] Das könnte zumindest reflexiv auch der Wissenschaftlichkeit der Jurisprudenz zugute kommen.[759]

Webers Rechtssoziologie setzt die juristische Methodenlehre seiner Zeit voraus, ohne dass sich aus dieser Voraussetzung ein Vorrangverhältnis ergibt. Die Rationalität der Rechts, die Weber zugrunde legt, gilt auch und setzt mutatis mutandis einen Maßstab für die Rechtsdogmatik. Wenn die Rechtstheorie eine universelle juristische Theorie der Rechtswissenschaft und des Rechts darstellen soll, bedarf sie des Bezugs zur Rechtsdogmatik.[760] Das hängt mit dem zugrunde liegenden Rechtsbegriff zusammen, der entsprechend der überwiegenden Ansicht im methodenrechtlichen Schrifttum ein spezifisch rechtswissenschaftlicher und kein rechtsphilosophischer oder rechtssoziologischer ist.[761] Ebenso wenig wie die juristische Methodenlehre „philosophielos" bestehen kann,[762]

Psychopathologie, 1913, zugrunde. Siehe auch *D. Henrich*, Karl Jaspers: Denken im Blick auf Max Weber, in: Max Weber und seine Zeitgenossen (Hg. W. J. Mommsen/W. Schwentker) 1988, 722.

757 *T. Parsons*, Wertgebundenheit und Objektivität in den Sozialwissenschaften. Eine Interpretation der Beiträge Max Webers, in: Max Weber und die Soziologie heute. Verhandlungen des 15. deutschen Juristentages (Hg. O. Stammler), 1965, S. 39, 54 f.

758 *H. Rottleuthner*, Richterliches Handeln. Zur Kritik der juristischen Dogmatik, 1973, S. 1.

759 *N. Luhmann*, Rechtssystem und Rechtsdogmatik, 1974, S. 13.

760 *R. Alexy/R. Dreier*, The Concept of Jurisprudence, Ratio Juris 3 (1990) 1 ff.

761 *F. Bydlinski*, Juristische Methodenlehre und Rechtsbegriff, S. 184 Fußnote 3; *H.-M. Pawlowski*, Methodenlehre für Juristen, 1981, S. 146 ff.

762 *K. Larenz*, Rechtswissenschaft und Rechtsphilosophie, AcP 143 (1937) 257; a. A. *Ph. Heck*, Rechtsphilosophie und Interessenjurisprudenz, AcP 143 (1937) 129. Wichtig zum historischen Hintergrund dieser Kontroverse *B. Rüthers*, Rechtstheorie, Rz. 534 f.

braucht sie die Rechtssoziologie kategorisch auszuklammern,[763] weil sie sonst zwar zu in sich konsistenten, aber entsprechend dieser Selbstbeschränkung eben auch zwangsläufig begrenzten Ergebnissen gelangen würde. Der Blick auf Webers Rechtssoziologie schärft so zugleich die Sicht auf den Epochenwandel in der juristischen Methodenlehre. Gerade die Überwindung der von Heck behaupteten Philosophielosigkeit der Interessenjurisprudenz veranschaulicht, dass man ihre Ablösung durch die Wertungsjurisprudenz wissenschaftstheoretisch[764] als Paradigmenwechsel würdigen kann.[765] Weber verhielt sich gegenüber der Interessenjurisprudenz reservierter, als man es von einem Soziologen annehmen könnte,[766] stand aber auch der Konstruktions- und Begriffsjurisprudenz kritischer gegenüber,[767] als im bisherigen Schrifttum vertreten wird, es sei denn, man begreift sie als Prinzipienjurisprudenz.[768]

Webers Rechtssoziologie ist nicht allein die Anwendung der von ihm maßgeblich ausgearbeiteten soziologischen Methode auf das Recht, sondern zugleich – wenn auch damit nicht konstitutiv für die Soziologie – Rückbesinnung auf die juristische Methode. So kann die Jurisprudenz von ihm lernen, dass die Frage nach ihrer Wissenschaftlichkeit nicht nur eine theoretische, sondern dadurch gerade auch eine praktische ist,[769] so dass der Wissenschaftsanspruch immer aufs Neue behauptet und eingelöst wird durch die jeweilige

[763] *A. Heldrich*, Die Bedeutung der Rechtssoziologie für das Zivilrecht, AcP 186 (1986) 74, 76; *ders.*, JuS 1974, 281.

[764] *Th. Kuhn*, The Structure of Scientific Revolutions, 2. Auflage 1970.

[765] *J. Petersen*, Von der Interessenjurisprudenz zur Wertungsjurisprudenz, 2001, freilich noch ohne zureichende Berücksichtigung der rechtsphilosophischen Dimension, so dass dort nur ein abgeschwächter Paradigmenwechsel festgestellt wurde.

[766] *H. Schoppmeyer*, Juristische Methode als Lebensaufgabe, 2001, S. 160 f.

[767] *M. Weber*, Wirtschaft und Gesellschaft, S. 506; *C.-W. Canaris*, Systemdenken und Systembegriff in der Jurisprudenz, S. 21 Fußnote 9.

[768] *P. Landau*, Die Rechtsquellenlehre in der deutschen Rechtswissenschaft des 19. Jahrhunderts, in: Juristische Theoriebildung und Rechtliche Einheit, Rättshistorika Studier (Hg. C. Petterson), Band XIX, 1993, S. 69.

[769] Vgl. *I. Kant*, Über den Gemeinspruch: Das mag in der Theorie richtig sein, taugt aber nicht für die Praxis, Band IX der von W. Weischedl herausgegebenen Werkausgabe.

Rationalität der Methode der Gesetzesanwendung. Webers Ausarbeitung der Rationalität des Rechts kann der Jurisprudenz auf diese Weise die Teilhabe an den Maßstäben anderer Wissenschaften vermitteln.[770] Implizit verbunden ist damit die stetige Aufgabe der juristischen Methodenlehre, Leitgesichtspunkte für die Theoriebildung zu entwickeln, die den Maßstäben anderer Wissenschaften standhalten[771] und die eigene Wissenschaftlichkeit begründen.[772] Das ist vor allem einer angloamerikanischen Strömung innerhalb der Methodenlehre entgegenzuhalten, die den Nutzen der juristischen Theoriebildung überhaupt in Frage stellt.[773] Gerade vor dem Hintergrund des Werturteilsstreits in den Sozialwissenschaften, in den Weber maßgeblich eingegriffen hat,[774] verdient auch in der rechtswissenschaftlichen Diskussion der Vorschlag Interesse, angesichts bestehender Strukturunterschiede zwischen Geistes- und Naturwissenschaften vom Kriterium der Prüfbarkeit abzusehen,[775] auch wenn ein solcher Dispens das Problem zumindest aus juristischer Sicht nicht vollständig lösen würde. Er entspricht aber wohl auch Webers Wissenschaftsverständnis, der im Anschluss an Rickerts Sicht der Wirklichkeit als „unübersehbarer, extensiv un-

[770] *B. Rüthers*, Rechtstheorie, Rz. 282: „Es geht um die Teilnahme der Jurisprudenz an der Rationalität der Wissenschaften und deren besonderen Erkenntnismethoden."

[771] Exemplarisch *C.-W. Canaris*, Funktion, Struktur und Falsifikation juristischer Theorien, JZ 1993, 377.

[772] *K. Larenz*, Über die Unentbehrlichkeit der Jurisprudenz als Wissenschaft, 1966.

[773] *St. L. Fish*, Dennis Martinez and the Uses of Theory, in: Doing What Comes Naturally, 1989, S. 372 ff.

[774] *M. Weber*, Die Objektivität sozialwissenschaftlicher und sozialpolitischer Erkenntnis, Archiv für Sozialwissenschaft und Sozialpolitik 19 (1904) 22; *ders.*, Der Sinn der ‚Wertfreiheit' der soziologischen und ökonomischen Wissenschaften, Logos 7 (1917) 40.

[775] *J. Habermas*, Gegen einen positivistisch halbierten Rationalismus, in: Der Positivismusstreit in der deutschen Soziologie (Hg. Th. Adorno u. a.), 13. Auflage 1989, S. 235; a. A. *H. Albert*, Kritischer Rationalismus, 2000, S. 74; siehe auch *R. Dreier*, Zur Theoriebildung in der Jurisprudenz, in: ders., Recht-Moral-Ideologie, 1981, S. 82 ff.

endlicher Mannigfaltigkeit“[776] die Sozialwissenschaft als Wirklichkeitswissenschaft verstand[777] – ein Verständnis, das auch auf die Rechtswissenschaft angesichts der Mannigfaltigkeit der rational zu lösenden Fälle passt.[778] An die Stelle der Prüfbarkeit tritt in der Rechtswissenschaft die Rationalität der Argumentation auf der Grundlage der gesetzgeberischen Basiswertungen, das heißt die Systemrationalität.[779] Im Rahmen der juristischen Theoriebildung erweist sich eher Ernst Machs Theoriedefinition der Zusammenfassung von Beobachtungen unter dem Prinzip der Denkökonomie[780] sowohl im Sinne Webers Rationalitätskonzepts als auch vom Standpunkt der juristischen Methodenlehre als weiterführend. Die damit vorausgesetzte und postulierte begriffliche Sparsamkeit entspricht nicht nur Webers Rechtssoziologie, sondern eignet sich auch zur Unterscheidung juristischer Theorien, die diesen Namen verdienen,[781] von bloßen interpretatorischen Ansichten.[782] Solche „Theorien“ wären für Weber wohl „nur provisorisches Schema der Ord-

[776] *H. Rickert*, Die Grenzen der naturwissenschaftlichen Begriffsbildung, 1902, S. 34.

[777] *M. Weber*, Die „Objektivität sozialwissenschaftlicher und sozialpolitischer Erkenntnis, Archiv für Sozialwissenschaft und Sozialpolitik 19 (1904) 22 ff.: „Die Sozialwissenschaft, die wir treiben wollen, ist eine Wirklichkeitswissenschaft.“ Siehe auch *H. Freyer*, Soziologie als Wirklichkeitswissenschaft, 1930, 2. Auflage 1964.

[778] *H. Eidenmüller*, Rechtswissenschaft als Realwissenschaft, JZ 1999, 53; *A. Heldrich*, AcP 186 (1986) 74, 78: Rechtssoziologie als Wirklichkeitswissenschaft vom Recht.

[779] Eingehend *C.-W. Canaris*, JZ 1993, 377. Zustimmend: *H. C. Grigoleit*, in: Rechtswissenschaftstheorie, 2008 (Hg. M. Jestaedt/O. Lepsius), S. 51, 66.

[780] *E. Mach*, Erkenntnis und Irrtum, 1905; *ders.*, Die Analyse der Empfindungen und das Verhältnis des Physischen zum Psychischen, 6. Auflage 1911, S. 256; dazu *W. Heisenberg*, Der Teil und das Ganze. Gespräche im Umkreis der Atomphysik, 1969, 13. Auflage 1993, S. 81 ff.

[781] *J. W. v. Goethe*, Maximen und Reflexionen, 428: Theorien sind Übereilungen eines ungeduldigen Verstandes, der die Phänomene gern los sein möchte und an ihre Stelle deswegen Bilder, Begriff, *ja oft nur Worte* verschiebt.“ Hervorhebung nur hier.

[782] *D. Medicus*, Theorien im modernen Zivilrecht, Festschrift für W. Thiele, S. 38, unterscheidet dementsprechend zwischen großen und kleinen Theorien.

nung".[783] Es geht also zumindest um Theorien mittlerer Reichweite, wie sie Robert K. Merton forderte.[784]

Daher kann sich die Aufgabe der dogmatischen Jurisprudenz nicht darin erschöpfen nur vorherzusagen, was der Richter entscheiden wird.[785] Das würde auch Auguste Comtes – freilich zu engem – Wissenschaftskriterium nicht gerecht.[786] Gerade Weber erinnert die Jurisprudenz daran, dass ihre Fragestellung sein muss, „was als Recht ideell gilt. Das will sagen: welche Bedeutung, und dies wiederum heißt: welcher *normative* Sinn einem als Rechtsnorm auftretenden sprachlichen Gebilde logisch *richtiger*weise zukommen *sollte.*"[787] Webers strenge Unterscheidung der den Rechtsdogmatiker betreffenden *ideellen Geltung* von der soziologischen Betrachtungsweise des Rechts erweist sich zugleich als wegweisend für die eigentliche Aufgabe der dogmatischen Jurisprudenz. So bildet der Wissenschaftsanspruch der Jurisprudenz eine beständige Herausforderung und ist immer aufs neue zu erheben, aber nicht ein- für allemal einlösbar, sondern stetig von der Dogmatik unter Berücksichtigung der Methodenlehre zu verwirklichen. Auf diese Weise behauptet der Wissenschaftsanspruch der Jurisprudenz kein Lippenbekenntnis, sondern ein einlösbares und einzulösendes Postulat. Die Selbstbesinnung der Methodenlehre kann womöglich einen Fingerzeig geben, wie Jürgen Habermas in anderem Zusammenhang festgestellt hat: „Allein, sobald Methodologie auf sich selber reflektiert, muss sie wiederum, wie das Beispiel des konsequent denkenden Popper lehrt,[788] zu einer Theorie

[783] *M. Weber*, Archiv für Sozialwissenschaft und Sozialpolitik 24 (1907, 94, Fußnote 15.

[784] *R. K. Merton*, Social Theory and Social Structure, 1957, S. 5; ebenso *O. Lepsius*, in: Rechtswissenschaftstheorie, S. 1, 26.

[785] So aber *O. W. Holmes*, The Path of the Law, Harvard Law Review 10 (1897) 457: „The prophecies of what the courts will do in fact, and nothing more pretentious, are what I mean by the law."

[786] *A. Comte*, Soziologie, 1923, Band III, S. 614: „Sehen um vorherzusehen: das ist das dauernde Unterscheidungsmerkmal der wahren Wissenschaft."

[787] *M. Weber*, Wirtschaft und Gesellschaft, S. 181; Hervorhebung auch dort.

[788] *K. Popper*, The Poverty of Historicism, 1957.

des wissenschaftlichen Fortschritts Zuflucht nehmen."[789] Das passt zu Webers These, wonach Wissenschaft geradezu überboten werden will und dies nicht ihr Schicksal, sondern ihr Zweck ist.

Nicht zuletzt im unausgesprochenen Dialog mit der juristischen Methodenlehre seiner Zeit besteht einer der wesentlichen Orientierungspunkte von Webers Rechtssoziologie für die Jurisprudenz. So verdient zum Schluss dasjenige Hervorhebung, was Weber in seinem epochalen Vortrag *Wissenschaft als Beruf*,[790] in zeitloser Gültigkeit über die Aufgabe und Beschränkung der Jurisprudenz sagt: „Sie stellt fest, was, nach den Regeln des teils zwingend logisch, teils durch konventionell gegebene Satzung gebundenen juristischen Denkens gilt, also: *wenn* bestimmte Rechtsregeln und bestimmte Methoden ihrer Deutung als verbindlich anerkannt sind. *Ob* es Recht geben solle, und ob man gerade diese Regeln aufstellen solle, darauf antwortet sie nicht; sondern sie kann nur angeben: wenn man den Erfolg will, so ist diese Rechtsregel nach den Normen unseres Rechtsdenkens das geeignete Mittel, ihn zu erreichen."[791] Doch auch die Rechtswissenschaftler ereilt früher oder später die Bestimmung,[792] der letztlich nicht einmal Max Weber

[789] *J. Habermas*, Erkenntnis und Interesse, 1973, S. 95, unter Verweis auf *A. Wellmer*, Methodologie als Erkenntnistheorie, 1967.

[790] Siehe dazu *K. Löwith*, Max Webers Stellung zur Wissenschaft, in: Max Webers Werk und seine Wirkung (Hg. D. Käsler) 1972, S. 310; zum unmittelbaren Eindruck des Vortrags auf die Zuhörer *ders.*, Mein Leben in Deutschland vor und nach 1933. Ein Bericht, 1940 (1989) S. 16: „Er sprach vollkommen frei und ohne Stockung, sein Vortrag wurde mitstenographiert und ist wörtlich so, wie er gesprochen wurde, veröffentlicht worden."

[791] *M. Weber*, Wissenschaft als Beruf, Geistige Arbeit als Beruf. Vier Vorträge vor dem Freistudentischen Bund, 1919, in: Gesammelte Aufsätze zur Wissenschaftslehre, 7. Auflage 1988, S. 582, 600 f; Hervorhebungen auch dort.

[792] Allerdings nicht im Hinblick auf das Bonmot von *J. v. Kirchmann*, Die Wertlosigkeit der Jurisprudenz als Wissenschaft, 1848, S. 17 („Drei berichtigende Worte des Gesetzgebers und ganze Bibliotheken werden zu Makulatur."); dagegen zutreffend *C.-W. Canaris*, Systemdenken und Systembegriff in der Jurisprudenz, S. 32 Fußnote 63. Ferner *C. Möllers*, S. 165; *M. Jestaedt*, S. 179, in: Rechtswissenschaftstheorie (2008).

entgangen ist:[793] „Jeder von uns dagegen in der Wissenschaft weiß, dass das, was er gearbeitet hat, in 10, 20, 50 Jahren veraltet ist. Das ist das Schicksal, ja: das ist der *Sinn* der Arbeit der Wissenschaft".[794]

[793] *N. Luhmann*, Rechtssoziologie, 3. Auflage 1987, S. 18, zufolge ist die Ausarbeitung des Handlungsbegriffs die wichtigste Errungenschaft der Rechtssoziologie Webers; vgl. *M. Weber*, Wissenschaft und Gesellschaft, S. 1; *ders.*, Über einige Kategorien der verstehenden Soziologie Logos 4 (1913) 253.

[794] *M. Weber*, Wissenschaft als Beruf, in: Gesammelte Aufsätze zur Wissenschaftslehre, 7. Auflage 1988, S. 582, 592 f., Hervorhebung auch dort. Treffend *M. R. Lepsius*, Juristen in der sozialwissenschaftlichen Emigration, 1993, S. 19: „Die Wissenschaft aber ist ein Prozess des unaufhörlichen Selbstverzehrs von Leistungen, Neues verdrängt altes in zunehmender Geschwindigkeit, vor allem in den Naturwissenschaften."

## Literaturverzeichnis

*Abramowski, G.*, Das Geschichtsbild Max Webers. Universalgeschichte am Leitfaden des okzidentalen Rationalisierungsprozesses, 1966.

*Adams, M.*, Ökonomische Analyse der Gefährdungs- und Verschuldenshaftung, 1985.

*Adomeit, K.*, Zivilrechtstheorie und Zivilrechtsdogmatik – mit einem Beitrag zur Theorie des subjektiven Rechts, Jahrbuch für Rechtssoziologie und Rechtstheorie 2 (1972) 503.

*Adorno, Th. W.*, Zur Logik der Sozialwissenschaft, in: Der Positivismusstreit in der deutschen Soziologie (Hg. ders./Habermas/Dahrendorf/Popper/Albert/Pilot), 1969, 14. Auflage 1991.

*Aechtner, S.*, Die Rationalität in der Rechts- und Herrschaftssoziologie Max Webers. Eine Textanalyse, 1995.

*Albert, H.*, Traktat über kritische Vernunft, 1968.

- *ders.*, Kritischer Rationalismus und Dialektik der Revolution, in: Verfall der Philosophie (Hg. Grosser, C.), 1971.
- *ders.*, Plädoyer für einen kritischen Rationalismus, 1971.
- *ders.*, Kritischer Rationalismus, 2000.
- *ders./Topitsch, E.* (Hg.), Werturteilsstreit, 3. Auflage 1990.
- *ders.*, Theorie und Praxis. Max Weber und das Problem der Wertfreiheit und der Rationalität, Festschrift für S. Moser, 1967, S. 264.
- *ders.*, Probleme der Wissenschaftslogik in der Sozialforschung, in: Handbuch der empirischen Sozialforschung, Band I, ed. König, 1962, S. 38.

*Alexy, R.*, Begriff und Geltung des Rechts, 1992.

- *ders.*, in: Argumentation und Hermeneutik in der Jurisprudenz (Hg. Krawietz, W. u. a.) Beiheft zur Rechtstheorie 1979.
- *ders.*, Rechtssystem und praktische Vernunft, Rechtstheorie 1987.
- *ders.*, Theorie der juristischen Argumentation, 1976.
- *ders./Dreier, R.*, The Concept of Jurisprudence, Ratio Juris 3 (1990) 1.
- *ders.*, Die logische Analyse juristischer Entscheidungen, ARSP Beiheft 14, 1980, 181.

*Arrow, K.*, Social Choice and Individual Values, 1951 (2. Auflage 1963).

*Atiyah, P. S./Summers, R. S.*, Form and Substance in Anglo-American Law, 1987.

*Auer, M.*, Materialisierung, Flexibilisierung, Richterfreiheit, 2005.

*Austin, J. L.*, Zur Theorie der Sprechakte, 2. Auflage 1974.

*Baier, H.*, Soziologie als Handlungswissenschaft. Eine wissenschaftsgeschichtliche Studie über die Erkenntnis- und Methodenlehre Max Webers, 1969.

– *ders.*, Die Gesellschaft – ein langer Schatten des toten Gottes. Friedrich Nietzsche und die Entstehung der Soziologie aus dem Geist der décadence, Nietzsche-Studien 10/11 (1981/82) 1.
– *ders./Lepsius, M. R./Mommsen, W. J./Schluchter, W.*, Zur Edition von „Wirtschaft und Gesellschaft". Allgemeine Hinweise der Herausgeber der Max Weber-Gesamtausgabe. Max Weber-Gesamtausgabe, Abteilung I: Schriften und Reden, Band 22-5: Max Weber, Wirtschaft und Gesellschaft. Die Wirtschaft und die gesellschaftlichen Ordnungen und Mächte. Nachlass. Teilband 5: Die Stadt (Hg. W. Nippel), 1999, S. VII–XVII.
*Baldus, L.*, Die Einheit der Rechtsordnung. Bedeutungen einer juristischen Formel in Rechtstheorie, Zivil- und Strafrechtswissenschaft des 19. und 20. Jahrhunderts, 1995.
*Ballweg, O.*, Rechtswissenschaft und Jurisprudenz, 1970.
*Bar, C. v.*, Verkehrspflichten, 1979.
*Baumgarten, E.*, Die Freirechtsbewegung, DJZ 1911, Nr. 16.
*Baumgarten, Ed.*, Max Weber. Werk und Person, 1964
*Baurmann, M.*, Grundzüge der Rechtssoziologie Max Webers, JuS 1991, 97.
*Beater, A.*, Generalklauseln und Fallgruppen, AcP 194 (1994) 82.
*Bechtler, T. W.*, Der soziologische Rechtsbegriff, 1977.
*Becker, T.*, Die Auslegung des § 9 Abs. 2 AGB-Gesetz, 1986.
*Behrends, O.*, Von der Freirechtsbewegung zum konkreten Ordnungs- und Gestaltungsdenken, in: Recht und Justiz im „Dritten Reich" (Hg. Dreier, R./Sellert, W.), 1989, S. 34.
*Bekker, E. I.*, Ernst und Scherz über unsere Wissenschaft, 1892.
*Bendix, R.*, Max Weber, An Intellectual Portrait, 1960 (deutsch: Max Weber – Das Werk. Darstellung, Analyse, Ergebnisse, 1964).
*Benedict, J.*, Consideration: Formalismus und Realismus im Common Law of Contracts, RabelsZ 69 (2005) 1.
*Bergbohm, K.*, Jurisprudenz und Rechtsphilosophie, 1892.
*Berger, J.*, Die Grenzen des handlungstheoretischen Paradigmas am Beispiel der „soziologischen Grundbegriffe" Max Webers, in: Materialien aus der soziologischen Forschung (Hg. Bolte, K. M.) 1978, S. 108.
*Bergfeld, W.*, Der Begriff des Typus, 1933.
*Bergmann Avila, H.*, Juristische Theorie der Argumentation – Entworfen am Beispiel des brasilianischen Steuerrechts, Festschrift für C.-W. Canaris, 2007, S. 963.
*Berman, H.*, Law and Revolution, 1983 (deutsch: Recht und Revolution, 1991).
*Bernstein, H.*, Friedrich Kessler's American Contract Scholarship and its Political Subtext, in : Der Einfluss deutscher Emigranten auf die Rechtsentwicklung in den USA und in Deutschland (Hg. Lutter, M./Stiefel, E. C./ Hoeflich, M. H.) 1993, S. 85.
*Berolzheimer, F.*, Die Gefahren einer Gefühlsjurisprudenz, ARWPh 1911, 595.

*Binder, J.*, Der Wissenschaftscharakter der Rechtswissenschaft, Kantstudien XXV (1921) 321.

*Bobbio, N.*, Analogia, in: Novissimo Digesto Italiano, 1975, Band 1, S. 601.

*Boehmer, G.*, Grundlagen der Bürgerlichen Rechtsordnung, Zweites Buch, Erste Abteilung, Dogmengeschichtliche Grundlagen des Bürgerlichen Rechts, 1951.

*Bork, R.*, Allgemeiner Teil des Bürgerlichen Gesetzbuchs, 2. Auflage 2006.

*Bouman, P. J.*, Kausalität und Funktionszusammenhang in der Soziologie Max Webers, Zeitschrift für die gesamte Staatswissenschaft 1949.

*Brandom, R. B.*, Articulating Reasons. An Introduction of Inferentialism, 2000.

– *ders.*, Making it explicit. Reasoning, Representing & Discursive Commitment, 1994.

*Brecht, A.*, Politische Theorie, 2. Auflage 1976.

*Breuer, St.*, Bürokratie und Charisma. Zur politischen Soziologie Max Webers, 1994.

*Brugger, W.*, Menschenrechtsethos und Verantwortungsethik. M. Webers Beitrag zur Analyse und Begründung der Menschenrechte, 1980.

*Bruun, H. H.*, Science, Values and Politics in Max Weber's Methodology, 1972.

*Bucher, E.*, Das subjektive Recht als Normsetzungsbefugnis, 1965.

– *ders.*, Der von den Juristen verkannte apagogische Beweis, Festschrift für C.-W. Canaris, 2007, S. 991.

– *ders.*, England und der Kontinent. Juristische Andersartigkeit des Vertragsrechts – die Gründe, und zu consideration, ZVerglRWiss 105 (2006) 164.

– *ders.*, Was ist Begriffsjurisprudenz?, Zeitschrift des Bernischen Juristenvereins 102 (1966) 274.

*Buchwald, D.*, Der Begriff der rationalen juristischen Begründung: Zur Theorie der juridischen Vernunft, 1990.

– *ders.*, Die canones der Auslegung und rationale juristische Begründung, ARSP 79 (1993) 16.

*Bund, E.*, Die Analogie als Begründungsmethode im deutschen Recht der Gegenwart, ZVglRWiss 1978, 115.

*Burger, Th.*, Max Weber's Methodology and its Place, International Journal of Politics, Culture, and Society 12 (1998) 277.

– *ders.*, Max Weber's Theory of Concept Formation. History, Laws, and Idealtypus, 1987.

*Bülow, O.*, Gesetz und Richteramt, 1885.

*Bydlinski, F.*, Die normativen Prämissen der Rechtsgewinnung, Rechtstheorie 1985.

– *ders.*, Fundamentale Rechtsgrundsätze, 1988.

– *ders.*, Hauptpositionen zum Richterrecht, JZ 1985, 149.

– *ders.*, Juristische Methodenlehre und Rechtbegriff, 2. Auflage 1991.

– *ders.*, Zum Verhältnis von äußerem und innerem System im Privatrecht, Festschrift für C.-W. Canaris, 2007, S. 1017.
– *ders.*, System und Prinzipien des Privatrechts, 1996.
– *ders.*, Bewegliches System und Methodenlehre, in: Das bewegliche System im geltenden und künftigen Recht, 1986, S. 24.
*Caemmerer, E. v.*, Ius Privatum Gentium, Festschrift für Rheinstein, 1969.
*Canaris, C.-W.*, Interessenlage, Grundprinzipien und Rechtsnatur des Finanzierungsleasing, AcP 190 (1990) 410.
– *ders.*, Das Rangverhältnis der „klassischen" Auslegungskriterien, demonstriert an Standardproblemen aus dem Zivilrecht, Festschrift für D. Medicus, 1999, S. 25.
– *ders.*, Die Feststellung von Lücken im Gesetz, 1964.
– *ders.*, Funktion, Struktur und Falsifikation juristischer Theorien, JZ 1993, 377.
– *ders.*, Richtigkeit und Eigenwertung in der richterlichen Rechtsfindung, Grazer Universitätsreden 50, 1993, S. 23.
– *ders.*, Systemdenken und Systembegriff in der Jurisprudenz, 2. Auflage 1983.
*Cardozo B. N.*, The Nature of Juridical Process, 1921.
– *ders.*, The Paradoxes of Legal Science, 1928.
– *ders.*, The Growth of the Law, 1924.
*Caroni, P.*, Savigny und die Kodifikation, ZRG, Germ. Abt. 86 (1969) 97.
*Casper, G.*, Juristischer Realismus und politische Theorie im amerikanischen Rechtsdenken, 1967.
*Cassirer, E.*, Die Philosophie der Aufklärung, 1932.
*Charmatz, H.*, Zur Geschichte und Konstruktion der Vertragstypen im Schuldrecht, 1937 (Neudruck 1968).
*Christensen, R./Kudlich, H.*, Theorie richterlichen Begründens, 2001.
*Cicero, M. T.*, De fato.
*Cohn, J.*, Die Erkenntnis der Werte und das Vorrecht der Bejahung. Betrachtungen, angeknüpft an Max Webers Lehre von der Wertfreiheit der Wissenschaft, in: Logos 10 (1921/22) 195.
*Coing, H.*, Der juristische Systembegriff bei Rudolf von Jhering, in: Blühdorn, J./Ritter, J. (Hg.), Philosophie und Rechtswissenschaft, 1969, S. 149.
– *ders.*, Geschichte und Bedeutung des Systemdenkens in der Rechtswissenschaft, ÖzöR 1957/58, 25.
– *ders.*, Rudolf von Ihering und Bentham, Interessenjurisprudenz und englische utilitaristische Philosophie, in: 375 Jahre Rechtswissenschaft in Gießen (Hg. G. Weick), 1982, S. 1.
– *ders.*, System, Geschichte und Interesse in der Privatrechtswissenschaft, JZ 1951, 181.
– *ders.*, Zur Geschichte des Privatrechtssystems, 1962.
– *ders.*, Grundzüge der Rechtsphilosophie, 5. Auflage 1993.

*Comte, A.*, Soziologie, 1923.
*Conrad, H.*, Das allgemeine Landrecht von 1794 als Grundgesetz des friederizianischen Staates, 1956.
– *ders.*, Die geistigen Grundlagen des allgemeinen Landrechts für die preußischen Staaten von 1794, 1958.
– *ders.*, Richter und Gesetz im Übergang von Absolutismus und Verfassungsstaat, 1971.
– *ders.*, Staatsgedanke und Staatspraxis des aufgeklärten Absolutismus, 1971.
*Cortella, L.*, Crisi e razionalita. Da Nietzsche ad Habermas (Nietzsche, Weber, Habermas), 1981.
*Crone, P.*, Max Weber, das islamische Recht und die Entstehung des Kapitalismus, in: Max Webers Sicht des Islam. Interpretation und Kritik (Hg. Schluchter, W.), 1987, S. 294.
*Dahrendorf, R.*, Homo Sociologicus, 11. Auflage 1972.
*Devlin, P.*, The Enforcement of Morals, 1965.
*Diederichsen, U.*, Die „reductio ad absurdum" in der Jurisprudenz, Festschrift für K. Larenz, 1973, S. 155.
– *ders.*, Zur Begriffstechnik richterlicher Rechtsfortbildung im Zivilrecht, Festschrift für F. Wieacker, 1978, S. 325.
– *ders.*, Einführung in das wissenschaftliche Denken, 1970.
*Dilcher, G.*, Von der Rechtsgeschichte zur Soziologie. Max Webers Auseinandersetzung mit der Historischen Rechtsschule, JZ 2007, 105.
*Dilthey, W.*, Die Entstehung der Hermeneutik, 1910.
– *ders.*, Einleitung in die Geisteswissenschaften, 2. Auflage 1933.
*Dombek, B.*, Das Verhältnis der Tübinger Schule zur deutschen Rechtssoziologie, 1969.
*Dorndorf, E.*, Zu den theoretischen Grundlagen der Interessenjurisprudenz: Die Beziehungen von Philipp Hecks allgemeiner Auslegungstheorie zu Max Weber und Heinrich Rickert, ARSP 81 (1995) 542.
*Dreier, H.*, Hans Kelsens Wissenschaftsprogramm, in: Die Verwaltung, Beiheft 7, 2007, S. 81.
– *ders.*, Naturrecht und Rechtspositivismus. Pauschalurteile, Vorurteile, Fehlurteile, in: „Vom Rechte, das mit uns geboren ist" (Hg. W. Härle/B. Vogel), 2007, S. 127.
– *ders.*, (Hg.), Rechtssoziologie am Ende des 20. Jahrhunderts. Gedächtnissymposium für E. M. Wenz, 2000.
*Dreier, R.*, Jherings Rechtstheorie – eine Theorie evolutionärer Rechtsvernunft, in: Privatrecht heute und Jherings evolutionäres Rechtsdenken (Hg. Behrends, O.), 1993.
– *ders.*, Zur Theoriebildung in der Jurisprudenz, in: ders., Recht-Moral-Ideologie, 1981.
– *ders.*, Zum Begriff der ‚Natur der Sache', 1965.

– *ders.*, Zu Luhmanns systemtheoretischer Neuformulierung des Gerechtigkeitsproblems, Rechtstheorie 5 (1974) 189.

*Drüen, K.-D.*, Typus und Typisierung im Steuerrecht, StuW 1997, 261.

*Durkheim, E.*, Die Regeln der soziologischen Methode, 1895.

*Duve, Th.*, Normativität und Empirie im öffentlichen Recht und der Politikwissenschaft um 1900. Historisch-systematische Untersuchung des Lebens und Werks von Richard Schmidt (1862–1944) und der Methodenentwicklung seiner Zeit, 1998.

*Dux, G.*, Gegenstand und Methode. Am Beispiel der Wissenschaftslehre Max Webers, Festschrift für H. Plessner, 1974, S. 187.

*Dworkin, R.*, Taking Rights Seriously, 2. Auflage 1978.

– *ders.*, The Law's Empire, 1986.

*Edelmann, J.*, Die Entwicklung der Interessenjurisprudenz, 1967.

*Eden, R.*, Political Leadership and Nihilism, A Study of Weber and Nietzsche, 1984.

– *ders.*, Bad Conscience for a Nietzschean Age: Weber's Calling for Science, The Review of Politics 45 (1983) 366.

– *ders.*, Max Weber und Friedrich Nietzsche oder: Haben sich die Sozialwissenschaften wirklich vom Historismus befreit?, in: Max Weber und seine Zeitgenossen ( Veröffentlichungen des Deutschen Historischen Instituts London 21, 1988 (Hg. Mommsen, W. J. /Schwentker, W.) S. 557.

*Eder, K.*, in: Sprondel, W./Seyfarth, C. (Hg.), Max Weber und die Rationalisierung sozialen Handelns, 1981.

– *ders.*, Zur Rationalisierungsproblematik des modernen Rechts, Soziale Welt 1978, 247.

*Ehrenzweig, A.*, Zur Phänomenologie und Psychoanalyse der Rechtswissenschaft, Festschrift für G. Husserl, 1969, S. 65.

*Ehrlich, E.*, Die richterliche Rechtsfindung auf Grund des Rechtssatzes, Jherings Jahrbücher 67 (1917) 1.

– *ders.*, Die juristische Logik, 1918 (2. Auflage 1925).

– *ders.*, Freie Rechtsfindung und freie Rechtswissenschaft, 1903.

– *ders.*, Grundlegung der Soziologie des Rechts, 1913 (3. Auflage 1967).

– *ders.*, Über Lücken im Recht, Juristische Blätter (Österreich/Ungarn), 1888, 447.

*Eidenmüller, H.*, Unternehmenssanierung zwischen Markt und Gesetz. Mechanismen der Unternehmensreorganisation und Kooperationspflichten im Reorganisationsrecht, 1999.

– *ders.*, Die Banken im Gefangenendilemma: Kooperationspflichten und Akkordstörungsverbot im Sanierungsrecht, ZHR 160 (1996) 343, 363.

– *ders.*, Der homo oeconomicus und das Schuldrecht: Herausforderungen durch Behavioral Law, JZ 2005, 216.

– *ders.*, Effizienz als Rechtsprinzip, 3. Auflage 2005.

– *ders.*, Rechtswissenschaft als Realwissenschaft, JZ 1999, 53.

– *ders.*, Rechtsanwendung, Gesetzgebung und ökonomische Analyse, AcP 197 (1997) 80.

*Ellscheid, G./Hassemer, W.*, Interessenjurisprudenz, 1974.

*Elze, H.*, Lücken im Gesetz, 1916.

*Emge, C. A.*, Philosophie der Rechtswissenschaft, 1961.

*Engel-Reimers, Ch.*, Der Methodenstreit in der Soziologie, Schmollers Jahrbuch für Gesetzgebung, Verwaltung und Volkswirtschaft im Deutschen Reiche 56 (1932) 87.

*Engisch, K.*, Logische Studien zur Gesetzesanwendung, 3. Auflage 1963.

– *ders.*, Max Weber als Rechtsphilosoph und Rechtssoziologe, in: ders./Pfister, B./Winckelmann, J. (Hg.), Max Weber. Gedächtnisschrift der Ludwigs-Maximilians-Universität München zur 100. Wiederkehr seines Geburtstags 1964, 1966, S. 67.

– *ders.*, Sinn und Tragweite juristischer Systematik, Studium Generale 12 (1950) 173.

– *ders.*, Wahrheit und Richtigkeit im juristischen Denken, 1963.

*Enneccerus, L./Nipperdey, H. C.*, Allgemeiner Teil des Bürgerlichen Rechts, 15. Auflage 1960, Zweiter Halbband.

*Ernst, W.*, Gelehrtes Recht, in: Schön, W. (Hg.), Das Proprium der Rechtswissenschaft, 2007, S. 3.

*Esser, J.*, Grundsatz und Norm in der richterlichen Fortbildung des Privatrechts, 2. Auflage 1964.

– *ders.*, Richterrecht, Gerichtsgebrauch und Gewohnheitsrecht, Festschrift für v. Hippel, 1967, S. 95.

– *ders.*, Vorverständnis und Methodenwahl in der Rechtsfindung. Rationalitätsgarantien der richterlichen Entscheidungspraxis, 2. Auflage 1972.

*Evers, H. U.*, Zum unkritischen Naturrechtsbewusstsein in der Rechtsprechung der Gegenwart, JZ 1961, 241.

*Falk, J.*, Die Analogie im Recht, 1906.

*Falk, U.*, Ein Gelehrter wie Windscheid. Erkundungen auf den Feldern der Begriffsjurisprudenz, 1989.

*Faust, F.*, Bürgerliches Gesetzbuch. Allgemeiner Teil, 2. Auflage 2007.

*Febbrajo, A.*, Kapitalismus, moderner Staat und rational-formales Recht, in: Rehbinder, M./Tieck, K.-P. (Hg.), Max Weber als Rechtssoziologe, 1987, S. 55.

– *ders.*, Per una rilettura della sociologia del diritto weberiana, Sociologia del diritto 3 (1976) 1.

*Fezer, K.-H.*, Aspekte einer Rechtskritik an der economic analysis of law und am property rights approach, JZ 1986, 817.

*Fiedler, H.*, Juristische Logik in mathematischer Sicht, ARSP 52 (1966) 93.

*Fikentscher, W.*, Ein juristisches Jahrhundert, Rechtshistorisches Journal 19 (2000) 560.

– *ders.*, Juristische Heuristik, Festschrift für C.-W. Canaris, 2007, S. 1091.

– *ders.*, Methoden des Rechts in vergleichender Betrachtung, Band III, 1975; Band IV, 1977.
– *ders.*, Präjudizienbildung, ZVglRWiss 1985, 163.
– *ders.*, Rechtswissenschaft und Demokratie bei Justice Oliver Wendell Holmes, Jr. Eine rechtsvergleichende Kritik der politischen Jurisprudenz, Juristische Studiengesellschaft Karlsruhe, 1970.
– *ders.*, Roscoe Pound. Von der Zweckjurisprudenz zur „Sociological Jurisprudence“, Festschrift für K. Larenz, 1973, S. 93.
*Fischer, Ch.*, Topoi verdeckter Rechtsfortbildung im Zivilrecht, 2007.
*Fischer, H. K.*, Protestantische Ethik und „Geist des Kapitalismus“. Replik auf Herrn Prof. Max Webers Gegenkritik, Archiv für Sozialwissenschaft und Sozialpolitik 26 (1908) 270.
*Fish, St. L.*, Dennis Martinez and the Uses of Theory, in: Doing What Comes Naturally, 1989, S. 372.
*Fletcher, G. P.*, Paradoxes in Legal Thought, Columbia Law Reiview 25 (1985) 1263.
*Flitner, E. H.*, Revolte gegen den Rationalismus. Beziehungen zwischen Max Webers und Hegels Analysen zur Dialektik der Verwissenschaftlichung, Kölner Zeitschrift für Soziologie und Sozialpsychologie 35 (1983) 255.
*Foulkes, A. S./Kaufmann, A.*, Gerechtigkeitswissenschaft – Ausgewählte Schriften zur Freirechtslehre von Ernst Fuchs, 1965.
*Frank, J.*, Law and the modern Mind, 1930.
*Freund, J.*, Die Rationalisierung des Rechts nach Max Weber, in: Max Weber als Rechtssoziologe (Hg. Rehbinder, M./K.-P. Tieck), 1987.
*Freyer, H.*, Soziologie als Wirklichkeitswissenschaft, 2. Auflage 1964.
*Fries, J.*, Philosophische Rechtslehre, 1803.
*Frommel, M.*, Hermann Ulrich Kantorowicz (1877–1940), Ein Rechtstheoretiker zwischen allen Stühlen, in: Deutsche Juristen jüdischer Herkunft (Hg. Heinrichs, H., u. a.) 1993, S. 631.
*Fuchs, E.*, Juristischer Kulturkampf, 1912.
– *ders.*, Klassische Einwendungen gegen die soziologische Methode, 1911.
– *ders.*, Recht und Wahrheit in unserer heutigen Justiz, 1908.
– *ders.*, Schreibjustiz und Richterkönigtum – ein Mahnruf zur Schul- und Justizreform, 1907.
– *ders.*, Was will die Freirechtsschule?, 1929.
*Fuller, L. L.*, The Morality of Law, 3. Auflage 1967.
– *ders.*, The Law in Quest of Itself, 1940.
– *ders.*, American Legal Philosophy at Mid-Century, Journal of Legal Education 6 (1954) 457.
– *ders.*, A Rejoinder to Prof. Nagel, Natural Law Forum 3 (1958) 83.
*Gabriel, K.*, Analysen der Organisationsgesellschaft. Ein kritischer Vergleich der Gesellschaftstheorien Max Webers, Niklas Luhmanns und der phänomenologischen Soziologie, 1979.

*Gadamer, H.-G.*, Philosophische Lehrjahre, 1977.
- *ders.*, Wahrheit und Methode. Grundzüge einer philosophischen Hermeneutik, 1960.

*Geiger, Th.*, Vorstudien zu einer Soziologie des Rechts, 1964.

*Gephart, W.*, Gesellschaftstheorie und Recht. Das Recht im soziologischen Diskurs der Moderne, 1998.

*Germann, O. A.*, Gesetzeslücken und ergänzende Rechtsfindung, 2. Auflage 1967.
- *ders.*, Präjudizielle Tragweite höchstrichterlicher Urteile, insbesondere der Urteile des schweizerischen Bundesgerichts, Zeitschrift für schweizerisches Recht, 1949, 297.
- *ders.*, Probleme und Methoden der Rechtsfindung, 2. Auflage 1967.

*Gmelin, J. G.*, Quousque? Beitrag zur soziologischen Rechtsfindung, 1910.

*Gmür, M.*, Die Anwendung des Rechts nach Art. 1 des schweizerischen Zivilgesetzbuches, 1908.

*Goeres, R.*, Sensualistischer Phänomenalismus und Denkökonomie. Zur Wissenschaftskonzeption Ernst Machs, Journal for General Philosophy of Science, 35 (2004) 41.

*Goethe, J. W. v.*, Maximen und Reflexionen (Hamburger Ausgabe, Band 12, 1981).

*Goldstein*, Psychoanalysis and Jurisprudence, Yale Law Journal 77 (1968) 1053.

*Gray, J. C.*, The Nature and the Source of Law, 2. Auflage 1927.

*Grigoleit, H. C.*, Anforderungen des Privatrechts an die Rechtstheorie, in: Rechtswissenschaftstheorie, 2008, (Hg. O. Lepsius/M. Jestaedt), S. 51.

*Grimm, K.*, Niklas Luhmanns „soziologische Aufklärung“ oder Das Elend der aprioristischen Soziologie. Ein Beitrag zur Pathologie der Systemtheorie im Licht der Wissenschaftslehre Max Webers, 1974.

*Günther, K.*, Der Sinn für Angemessenheit, 1988.

*Gumplowicz, L.*, Grundriss der Soziologie, 1885.

*Gurvitch, G.*, Grundzüge der Soziologie des Rechts, 1960.

*Habermas, J.*, Die Theorie des kommunikativen Handelns, Band 1, Handlungsrationalität und gesellschaftliche Rationalisierung, 1981.
- *ders.*, Erkenntnis und Interesse, 1973.
- *ders.*, Faktizität und Geltung. Beiträge zur Diskurstheorie des Rechts und des demokratischen Rechtsstaates, 1992.
- *ders.*, Strukturwandel der Öffentlichkeit, 1962.
- *ders.*, Wahrheit und Rechtfertigung, 2000.
- *ders.*, Gegen einen positivistisch halbierten Rationalismus, in: Der Positivismusstreit in der deutschen Soziologie (Hg. Adorno, Th. W. u. a.), 13. Auflage 1989, S. 235.
- *ders.*, Zur Logik der Sozialwissenschaften, 5. Auflage 1982.
- *ders.*, Theorie und Praxis. Sozialphilosophische Studien, 1971 (1963).

– *ders./Luhmann, N.*, Systemtheorie – Gesellschaftstheorie oder Sozialtechnologie, 1971.
*Haller, H.*, Typus und Gesetz in der Nationalökonomie. Versuch zur Klärung einiger Methodenfragen der Wirtschaftswissenschaften, 1950.
*Hart, H. L. A.*, The Concept of Law, 1962 (Der Begriff des Rechts, 1973).
*Hartmann, M.*, Formale Rationalität und Wertfreiheit bei Max Weber, Zeitschrift für Soziologie 17 (1988) 102.
*Hassemer, W.*, Rechtssystem und Kodifikation: Die Bindung des Richters an das Gesetz, in: Einführung in Rechtsphilosophie und Rechtstheorie (Hg. Kaufmann, A./ders.), 6. Auflage 1994.
– *ders.*, Tatbestand und Typus. Untersuchungen zur strafrechtlichen Hermeneutik, 1968.
*Hassold, G.*, Rechtsfindung durch Konstruktion, AcP 181 (1981) 131.
*Hattenhauer, H.*, Die geistesgeschichtlichen Grundlagen des deutschen Rechts, 4. Auflage 1996.
– *ders.*, Allgemeines Landrecht für die Preußischen Staaten von 1794, Textausgabe mit einer Einführung von Hans Hattenhauer und einer Bibliographie von Günter Berndt, 1970.
– *ders.*, Thibaut und Savigny. Ihre pragmatischen Schriften, 1973.
*Haferkamp, H.-P.*, Georg Friedrich Puchta und die Begriffsjurisprudenz, 2004.
*Heck, Ph.*, Grundriss des Schuldrechts, 1929.
– *ders.*, Gesetzesauslegung und Interessenschutz, 1932.
– *ders.*, Begriffsbildung und Interessenjurisprudenz, 1932.
– *ders.*, Gesetzesauslegung und Interessenjurisprudenz, AcP 112 (1914) 1.
– *ders.*, Die reine Rechtslehre und ihre jungösterreichische Schule der Rechtswissenschaft, AcP 119 (1922) 173.
– *ders.*, Binder, Philosophie des Rechts, AcP 128 (1928) 112.
– *ders.*, Max v. Rümelin, AcP 134 (1931) 259.
– *ders.*, Die Leugnung der Interessenjurisprudenz durch Hermann Isay, AcP 137 (1933) 47.
– *ders.*, Die logische Analyse des juristischen Methodenstreits durch Richard Hönigswald, AcP 138 (1934) 129.
– *ders.*, Die Interessenjurisprudenz und ihre neuen Gegner, AcP 142 (1936) 129; 297.
– *ders.*, Rechtsphilosophie und Interessenjurisprudenz, AcP 143 (1937), 129.
– *ders.*, Das Problem der Rechtsgewinnung, 1912, Nachdruck 1968, DJZ 1909, 1456.
*Hedemann, J. W.*, Die Flucht in die Generalklauseln. Eine Gefahr für Recht und Staat, 1933.
– *ders.*, Zivilistische Rundschau, Archiv für Bürgerliches Recht 31 (1906) 296; 34 (1909) 115.

*Hegenbarth, R.*, Juristische Hermeneutik und linguistische Pragmatik, 1982.
*Heisenberg, W.*, Der Teil und das Ganze. Gespräche im Umkreis der Atomphysik, 1969, 13. Auflage 1993.
*Heitmann, H.*, Die Stellung der Interessenjurisprudenz innerhalb der Geschichte der juristischen Methodenlehre, 1936.
– *ders.*, Die Stellung der Interessenjurisprudenz innerhalb der Geschichte der Methodenlehre, 1936.
*Heldrich, A.*, Die Bedeutung der Rechtssoziologie für das Zivilrecht, AcP 186 (1986) 74.
– *ders.*, Sozialwissenschaftliche Aspekte der Rechtsvergleichung, RabelsZ 34 (1970) 427.
– *ders.*, Das Trojanische Pferd in der Zitadelle des Rechts?, Überlegungen zur Einbeziehung der Sozialwissenschaften in die juristische Ausbildung, JuS 1974, 281.
*Hempel C. G./Oppenheim, P.*, Der Typusbegriff im Lichte der neuen Logik, 1936.
*Henke, W*, Kritik des kritischen Rationalismus, 1974.
*Hennis, W.*, Max Webers Fragestellung. Studien zur Biographie des Werks, 1987.
– *ders.*, Die Spuren Nietzsches im Werk Max Webers, Nietzsche-Studien 16 (1987) 382.
*Henrich, D.*, Die Einheit der Wissenschaftslehre Max Webers, 1952.
– *ders.*, Die Situation der Historie und Max Webers Methodenlehre, Archiv für Philosophie 3 (1949) 400.
– *ders.*, Karl Jaspers: Denken im Blick auf Max Weber, in: Max Weber und seine Zeitgenossen, Veröffentlichungen des Deutschen Historischen Instituts London 21 (Hg. Mommsen, W. J./Schwentker, W.) 1988, 722.
*Herberger, M./Simon, D.*, Wissenschaftstheorie für Juristen, 1980.
– *ders./Koch, H.-J.*, Juristische Methodenlehre und Sprachphilosophie, JuS 1978, 810.
*Hesse, H. A.*, Die Relevanz der Soziologie Max Webers für die juristische Praxis und Juristenausbildung, Zeitschrift für vergleichende Rechtswissenschaft 84 (1982) 242.
*Heyde, J. E.*, Typus. Ein Beitrag zur Bedeutungsgeschichte des Wortes Typus, Forschungen und Fortschritte 17 (1941) 220.
– *ders.*, Typus. Ein Beitrag zur Typologik, Studium Generale 5 (1952) 235.
*Hilgendorf, E./Kuhlen, L.*, Die Wertfreiheit der Jurisprudenz, 2000.
*Hilterhaus, F.*, Zum Rechtsbegriff in der Soziologie Max Webers, 1965.
*Hippel, F., v.*, Die Tübinger Schule der Interessenjurisprudenz, Festschrift für R. Reinhard, 1972, S. 83.
– *ders.*, Zur Gesetzmäßigkeit juristischer Systembildung, 1930.
*Hoeniger, H.*, Gemischte Verträge in ihren Grundformen, 1910.
– *ders.*, Vorstudien zum Problem der gemischten Verträge, 1906.

*Holmes, O. W.*, The Path of the Law, Harvard Law Review 10 (1897) 457.
- *ders.*, The Common Law, 1881 (deutsch: Das gemeine Recht Englands und Nordamerikas: in elf Abhandlungen dargestellt, 1. Auflage 1912, zuletzt 2006).

*Honnefelder, L.*, Rationalization and natural law. Max Weber's and Ernst Troeltsch's interpretation of the medieval doctrine of natural law, Review of Metaphysic. A Philosophical Quarterly 49 (1995/96) 275.

*Hopt, K.*, Rechtssoziologische und rechtsinformatorische Elemente im Wirtschaftsrecht, BB 1972, 1017.

*Horn, D.*, Studien zur Rolle der Logik bei der Anwendung des Gesetzes, 1962.

*Hönigswald, R.*, „Begriff“ und „Interesse“. Eine methodologische Skizze, AcP 138 (1938) 1.

*Hruschka, J.*, Die Konstitution des Rechtsfalles. Studien zum Verhältnis von Tatsachenfeststellung und Rechtsanwendung, 1965.

*Hubmann, H.*, Wertung und Abwägung im Recht, 1977.
- *ders.*, Naturrecht und Rechtsgefühl, AcP 153 (1954) 297.

*Hume, D.*, A Treatise of Human Nature: Beeing an Attempt to introduce the experimental Method of Reasoning into Moral Subjects, 1739–1749 (Traktat über die menschliche Natur, deutsch von T. Lipps, 1906).
- *ders.* An Enquiry Concerning Human Understanding, 1748 (deutsch: Eine Untersuchung über den menschlichen Verstand; übersetzt von R. Richter, Hg. J. Kulenkampff, 12. Auflage 1993).

*Hughes, G.*, Positivist and Natural Lawyers, Stanford Law Review 17, 1965, 547.

*Husserl, E.*, Logische Untersuchungen, Band I, 2. Auflage 1913.

*Husserl, G.*, Der Rechtsgegenstand – rechtslogische Studien zu einer Theorie des Eigentums, 1933.
- *ders.*, Rechtskraft und Rechtsgeltung – eine rechtsdogmatische Untersuchung, 1925.

*Isay, H.*, Rechtsnorm und Entscheidung, 1929.

*Jäger, C.*, Der Rücktritt vom Versuch als zurechenbare Gefährdungsumkehr, 1996.
- *ders.*, Zurechnung und Rechtfertigung als Kategorialprinzipien des Strafrechts, 2006.

*Janoska-Bendl, J.*, Methodologische Aspekte des Idealtypus, 1965.

*Jaspers, K.*, Allgemeine Psychopathologie, 1913.
- *ders.*, Max Weber. Politiker, Forscher, Philosoph, 1932.

*Jellinek, G.*, System der subjektiven öffentlichen Rechte, 2. Auflage, 1905.
- *ders.*, Allgemeine Staatslehre, 3. Auflage 1959.
- *ders.*, Die sozialethische Bedeutung von Recht, Unrecht und Strafe, 1908, S. 45.

*Jestaedt, M.*, Perspektiven der Rechtswissenschaftstheorie, in: Rechtswissenschaftstheorie (Hg. O. Lepsius/ders.), 2008, S. 185.

*Jhering, R. v.*, Der Besitzwille. Zugleich eine Kritik der herrschenden juristischen Methode, 1889.
- *ders.*, Der Kampf um's Recht, 1872.
- *ders.*, Der Zweck im Recht, 1877–1883.
- *ders.*, Über die Entstehung des Rechtsgefühles (mit einer Vorbemerkung und einem anschließenden Interpretations- und Einordnungsversuch von O. Behrends), 1986.
- *ders.*, Zur Lehre von den Beschränkungen des Grundeigentums im Interesse des Nachbarn, Jherings Jahrbücher 6 (1863) 81.

*Jerusalem, F. W.*, Kritik der Rechtswissenschaft, 1948.
- *ders.*, Die Zersetzung der Rechtswissenschaft, 1968.

*Joerden, J.*, Logik im Recht, 2005.

*Kalberg, S.*, Einführung in die historisch-vergleichende Soziologie Max Webers, 2001.
- *ders.*, Max Webers Typen der Rationalität: Grundstein für eine Analyse von Rationalisierungsprozessen in der Geschichte, in: Max Weber und die Rationalisierung sozialen Handelns (Hg. Sprondel, W./Seyfarth, C.), 1981, S. 9.

*Kallfass, W.*, Die Tübinger Schule der Interessenjurisprudenz, 1972.

*Kantorowicz, H.*, Aus der Vorgeschichte der Freirechtsschule, 1925.
- *ders.*, Der Kampf um die Rechtswissenschaft, 1906.
- *ders.*, Rechtswissenschaft und Soziologie. Verhandlungen des Ersten Deutschen Soziologentages 1910, Tübingen 1911.

*Kaser, H.*, Zur Methode der römischen Rechtsfindung, 1962.

*Kaufmann, A.*, Analogie und Natur der Sache. Zugleich ein Beitrag zur Lehre vom Typus, 2. Auflage 1982.
- *ders.*, Über die Wissenschaftlichkeit der Rechtswissenschaft – Ansätze einer Konvergenztheorie der Wahrheit, in: Über Gerechtigkeit (Hg. ders.) 1993, 259.
- *ders.*, Rechtsphilosophie zum Mitdenken, Einführung in die juristische Methodenlehre, Jura 1992, 346.

*Kaye, H. L.*, Rationalization as Sublimation: on the Cultural Analysis of Weber and Freud: Theory Culture & Society 9 (1992) 245.

*Kelsen, H.*, Der juristische und der soziologische Staatsbegriff, 1922, 2. Auflage 1928.
- *ders.*, Reine Rechtslehre, 2. Auflage 1960 (1. Auflage 1934).
- *ders.*, Über Grenzen zwischen juristischer und soziologischer Methode, 1911.
- *ders.*, Hauptprobleme der Staatsrechtslehre, 1911.

*Kessler, F.*, Theoretic Basis of Law, University of Chicago Law Review 9 (1941) 98.
- *ders.*, Natural Law, Justice, and Democracy: Some Reflections in Three Types of Thinking about Law and Justice, Tulane Law Review 19 (1944) 32.

– *ders.*, Arthur Linton Corbin – A Tribute, Yale Law Journal 64 (1954) 164.
– *ders.*, Was ist Gerechtigkeit?, 1953.
– *ders.*, Was ist die Reine Rechtslehre?, Festschrift für Z. Giacometti, 1953, S. 143.
*Kiefner, H.*, Thibaut und Savigny, Festschrift für R. Gmür, 1983, S. 53.
*Kilian, W.*, Rechtssoziologische und rechtstheoretische Aspekte des Vertragsabschlusses, Festschrift für Wassermann, 1985, S. 715.
*Kirchmann, J. v.*, Die Wertlosigkeit der Jurisprudenz als Wissenschaft, 1848.
*Kirchner, C.*, Ökonomische Theorie des Rechts, 1997.
*Kißler, L.*, Recht und Gesellschaft. Einführung in die Rechtssoziologie, 1984.
*Klug, U.*, Thesen zu einem kritischen Relativismus in der Rechtsphilosophie, Gedächtnisschrift für G. Radbruch, 1968, S. 103.
*Knauthe, K.*, Kausales Rechtsdenken und Rechtssoziologie, 1968.
*Koch, H.-J./Rüßmann, H.*, Juristische Begründungslehre, 1983.
*Köhler, H.*, BGB. Allgemeiner Teil, 31. Auflage 2007.
*Kohler, J.*, Shakespeare vor dem Forum der Jurisprudenz, 2. Auflage 1919.
*Koller, A.*, Grundfragen einer Typuslehre im Gesellschaftsrecht, 1967.
*Koller, P.*, Theorie des Rechts, 2. Auflage 1997.
*Krawietz, W.*, Juristische Entscheidung und wissenschaftliche Erkenntnis, 1978.
– *ders.*, Juristische Entscheidung und wissenschaftliche Erkenntnis. Eine Untersuchung zum Verhältnis von dogmatischer Kausalwissenschaft und rechtswissenschaftlicher Grundlagenforschung, 1978.
– *ders.*, Recht als Regelsystem, 1984.
*Kriele, H.*, Theorie der Rechtsgewinnung, 1967.
– *ders.*, Kriterien der Gerechtigkeit, 1963.
*Kries, J. v.*, Über den Begriff der objektiven Möglichkeit und einige Anwendungen desselben, Vierteljahresschrift für wissenschaftliche Philosophie 12 (1888) 179.
*Kronstein, H.*, Rechtsauslegung im wertgebundenen Recht, 1957.
*Kübel, F.*, Das Rechtsgefühl, 1913.
– *ders.*, Effizienz als Rechtsprinzip, Festschrift für E. Steindorff, 1990, S. 687.
*Kühl, K.*, Rückblick auf die Renaissance des Naturrechts nach dem 2. Weltkrieg, Freundesgabe A. Söllner, 1990, S. 331.
*Kuhlen, L.*, Die Denkform des Typus in der juristischen Methodenlehre, in: Juristische Methodenlehre und analytische Philosophie (Hg. Koch), 1976.
– *ders.*, Typuskonzeptionen in der Rechtstheorie, 1977.
*Kuhn, Th.*, The Structure of Scientific Revolutions, 2. Auflage 1970 (Die Struktur wissenschaftlicher Revolutionen, 12. Auflage 1993).
*Kullmann, H. J.*, Die Produktbeobachtungspflicht des Kraftfahrzeugherstellers im Hinblick auf Zubehör, BB 1987, 1957.
*Künnecke, A.*, Auf der Suche nach dem Kern des Naturrechts. Ein Vergleich

der schwachen säkularen Naturrechtslehren Radbruchs, Coings, Harts, Welzels und Fullers ab 1945, 2003.
*Landau, P.*, Die Rechtsquellenlehre in der deutschen Rechtswissenschaft des 19. Jahrhunderts, in: Juristische Theoriebildung und Rechtliche Einheit, Rättshistorika Studier (Hg. Petterson, C.), Band XIX, 1993.
– *ders.*, Rezension „Harold Berman, Law and Revolution“, Harvard University Press 1983, The University of Chicago Law Review 51 (1984) 937.
*Langenbucher, K.*, Die Entwicklung und Auslegung von Richterrecht, 1996.
*Langheim, H. A. W.*, Das Prinzip der Analogie als juristische Methode, 1992.
*Larenz, K.*, Über die Unentbehrlichkeit der Jurisprudenz als Wissenschaft, 1966.
– *ders.*, Rechtswissenschaft und Rechtsphilosophie, AcP 143 (1937) 257.
– *ders.*, Typologisches Rechtsdenken. Bemerkungen zu V. Tuka: Die Rechtssysteme, ARSP 34 (1940/41) 20.
– *ders.*, Rechtswissenschaft und Rechtsphilosophie, AcP 143 (1937) 257.
– *ders.*, Das Problem der Rechtsgeltung, 1929.
– *ders.*, Kennzeichen geglückter richterlicher Rechtsfortbildung, 1965.
– *ders.*, Methodenlehre der Rechtswissenschaft, 6. Auflage 1991.
– *ders.*, Ergänzende Vertragsauslegung und dispositives Recht, NJW 1963, 737.
– *ders.*, Richtiges Recht, – Grundzüge einer Rechtsethik 1979.
– *ders.*, Über die Bindungswirkung von Präjudizien, Festschrift für H. Schima, 1969, S. 247.
– *ders.*, Wegweiser zu richterlicher Rechtsschöpfung, Festschrift für A. Nikisch, 1958, S. 275.
– *ders.*, Zur Logik des konkreten Begriffs, DRW, Band V (1940) 294.
– *ders.*, Richterliche Rechtsfortbildung als methodisches Problem, NJW 1965, 3.
– *ders.*, Grundformen wertorientierten Denkens in der Jurisprudenz, Festschrift für W. Wilburg, 1975, S. 217.
– *ders.*/Canaris,C.-W., Lehrbuch des Schuldrechts 13. Auflage 1994.
– *ders./Canaris, C.-W.*, Methodenlehre der Rechtswissenschaft (Studienausgabe), 3. Auflage 1995.
*Leenen, D.*, Abschluss, Zustandekommen und Wirksamkeit von Verträgen, AcP 188 (1988) 381.
– *ders.*, Die Heilung fehlender Zustimmung gemäß § 110 BGB, FamRZ 2000, 863.
– *ders.*, Die Anfechtung von Verträgen, Jura 1991, 393.
– *ders.*, Willenserklärung und Rechtsgeschäft, Jura 2007, 721.
– *ders.*, Typus und Rechtsfindung, 1971.
– *ders.*, Willenserklärung und Rechtsgeschäft in der Regelungstechnik des BGB, Festschrift für C.-W. Canaris, 2007, S. 699.
*Lenk, H.*, Typen und Systematik der Rationalität, Festschrift für K. Hübner, 1986, S. 11.

*Lepsius, M. R.*, Die Soziologie in der Zwischenkriegszeit: Entwicklungstendenzen und Beurteilungskriterien, in: Soziologie in Deutschland und Österreich 1918–1945, Materialien zur Entwicklung, Emigration und Wirkungsgeschichte (Hg. ders.), Sonderheft 23 der Kölner Zeitschrift für Soziologie und Sozialpsychologie, 1981.
– *ders.*, Interessen, Ideen und Institutionen, 1990.
– *ders.*, Max Weber (1864–1920) Begründer der modernen Sozialwissenschaften, in: München leuchtet für die Wissenschaft: berühmte Forscher und Gelehrte (Hg. Leutheusser, U./Nötz, H.), 2007, S. 64.
– *ders.*, Eigenart und Potenzial des Weber-Paradigmas, in: Das Weber-Paradigma. Studien zur Weiterentwicklung von Max Webers Forschungsprogramm (Hg. Albert, G./Bienfait, A./Sigmund, S./Wendt, C.) 2003, S. 32.
– *ders.*, Juristen in der sozialwissenschaftlichen Emigration, in: Der Einfluss deutscher Emigranten auf die Rechtsentwicklung in den USA und in Deutschland (Hg. Lutter, M./Stiefel, E. C./Hoeflich, M. H.) 1993, S. 19.
*Lepsius, O.*, Die gegensatzaufhebende Begriffsbildung. Methodenentwicklungen in der Weimarer Republik und ihr Verhältnis zur Ideologisierung der Rechtswissenschaft unter dem Nationalsozialismus, 1994.
– *ders.*, Verwaltungsrecht unter dem Common Law, 1997.
– *ders.*, Themen einer Rechtswissenschaftstheorie, in: Rechtswissenschaftstheorie (Hg. ders./M. Jestaedt) 2008, S. 1.
*Lessig, L.*, Code and other Law of Cyberspace, 1999.
*Llewellyn, K. L.*, Some Realism about Realism: Responding to Dean Pound, Harvard Law Review 44 (1930/31) 1222.
*Löher, F.*, Das System des preußischen Landrechts in deutschrechtlicher und philosophischer Begründung, 1852.
*Loos, F.*, Max Webers Wissenschaftslehre und die Rechtswissenschaft, in: Max Weber als Rechtssoziologe (Hg. Rehbinder, M./K.-P. Tieck), 1987, S. 169 (= JuS 1982, 87).
– *ders.*, Zur Wert- und Rechtslehre Max Webers, 1970.
*Lorenzen, P.*, Konstruktive Wissenschaftstheorie, 1974.
*Losano, H.*, Das „Systemdenken" in den romanischen Ländern, Festschrift für C.-W. Canaris, 2007, S. 1201.
*Lotmar, P.*, Der Arbeitsvertrag 1902.
*Löwith, K.*, Max Webers Stellung zur Wissenschaft, in: Max Webers Werk und seine Wirkung (Hg. Käsler, D.) 1972.
– *ders.*, Mein Leben in Deutschland vor und nach 1933. Ein Bericht, 1940 (1989) S. 16.
*Lübbe, W.*, Legitimität kraft Legalität. Sinnverstehen und Institutionenanalyse bei Max Weber und seinen Kritikern, 1991.
*Lübbe-Wolff, G.*, Rechtsfolgen und Realfolgen, 1981.
*Ludwig, M.*, Sein und Sollen – Eine Untersuchung zur Abgrenzung der

Rechtsnormen von den sozialen Normen bei Max Weber und Eugen Ehrlich, 1999.
*Luhmann, N.*, Grundrechte als Institution. Ein Beitrag zur politischen Soziologie, 1965.
– *ders.*, Legitimation durch Verfahren, 1969.
– *ders.*, Ausdifferenzierung des Rechts, 1981.
– *ders.*, Ausdifferenzierung des Rechtssystems, Rechtstheorie 7 (1976) 121.
– *ders.*, Das Recht der Gesellschaft, 1995.
– *ders.*, Funktionale Methode und juristische Entscheidung, AöR 1969, 1.
– *ders.*, Interesse und Interessenjurisprudenz im Spannungsfeld von Gesetzgebung und Rechtsprechung, ZNR 12 (1990) 1.
– *ders.*, Rechtssoziologie, 3. Auflage 1987.
– *ders.*, Rechtssystem und Rechtsdogmatik, 1974.
– *ders.*, Zur Funktion der „subjektiven Rechte", Jahrbuch für Rechtssoziologie und Rechtstheorie 1 (1970) 321.
– *ders.*, Zweckbegriff und Systemrationalität: Über die Funktion von Zwecken in sozialen Systemen, 1968.
– *ders.*, Reflexive Mechanismen, Soziale Welt 17 (1966) 1.
– *ders.*, The Third Question: The Creative Use of Paradoxes in Law and Legal History, Journal of Law and Society 15 (1988) 153.
– *ders.*, Systemtheoretische Beiträge zur Rechtstheorie, Jahrbuch für Rechtssoziologie und Rechtstheorie 2 (1972) 255.
– *ders.*, Gerechtigkeit in den Rechtssystemen der modernen Gesellschaft, Rechtstheorie 4 (1973) 131.
*Lundmark, T.*, Juristische Technik und Methodik des Common Law, 1990.
*Mach, E.*, Die Analyse der Empfindungen und das Verhältnis des Physischen zum Psychischen, 6. Auflage 1911.
– *ders.*, Erkenntnis und Irrtum, 1905.
*Marck, S.*, Substanz- und Funktionsbegriff in der Rechtsphilosophie, 1925.
*Marcuse, H.*, Industrialisierung und Kapitalismus im Werk Max Webers, in: Max Weber und die Soziologie heute, Verhandlungen des 15. deutschen Soziologentages (Hg. Otto Stammler), 1965, S. 161.
*Mayer-Maly, Th.*, Rechtswissenschaft, 2. Auflage 1981.
*Medicus, D.*, Allgemeiner Teil des BGB, 9. Auflage 2006.
– *ders.*, Bürgerliches Recht, 21. Auflage 2007.
– *ders.*, Theorien im modernen Zivilrecht, Festschrift für W. Thiele, S. 38.
*Meier-Hayoz, A./Schluep, W. R./Ott, W.*, Zur Typologie im schweizerischen Gesellschaftsrecht, ZSR 90 (1971) 293.
*Melin, P.*, Gesetzesauslegung in den USA und in Deutschland, 2005.
*Merkel, A.*, Über das Verhältnis der Rechtsphilosophie zur positiven Rechtswissenschaft, Zeitschrift für das Privat- und öffentliche Recht der Gegenwart 1 (1874) 402.

*Merton, R. K.*, Social Theory and Social Structure, 1957.
*Merz, P.-U.*, Max Weber und Heinrich Rickert. Die erkenntniskritischen Grundlagen der verstehenden Soziologie, 1990.
*Mestmäcker, E.-J.*, A Legal Theory without Law. Posner, v. Hayek on Economic Analysis of Law, 2008.
*Mettenheim, C. v.*, Rationalität und Recht, 1984.
*Meyer, E.*, Grundzüge einer systemorientierten Wertungsjurisprudenz, 1984.
*Miller, L. G.*, Rules and Exceptions, Ethics 66 (1956) 262.
*Möllers, C.*, Vorüberlegungen zu einer Wissenschaftstheorie des öffentlichen Rechts, in: Rechtswissenschaftstheorie (Hg. O. Lepsius/M. Jestaedt), 2008, S. 151.
*Mommsen, W. J.*, ‚Verstehen' und ‚Idealtypus'. Zur Methodologie einer historischen Sozialwissenschaft, in: Max Weber. Gesellschaft, Politik und Geschichte, 1974, S. 208.
*Moore, U./Sussman, G.*, Legal and Institutional Methods, Yale Law Journal 40 (1930/31) 381.
– *dies.*, The Lawyer's Law, Yale Law Journal 41 (1931/32) 566.
*Mokre, H.*, Theorie des Gewohnheitsrechts, 1932.
*Müller, H.-P.*, Max Weber, 2007.
*Müller-Erzbach, R.*, Der Durchbruch des Interessenrechts durch allgemeine Rechtsprinzipien, Jherings Jahrbücher 53 (1908) 331.
– *ders.*, Die Hinwendung der Rechtswissenschaft zum Leben und was sie hemmt, 1939.
– *ders.*, Lassen sich das Recht und das Rechtsleben tiefer und sicherer erfassen?, 1934.
– *ders.*, Wohin führt die Interessenjurisprudenz?, 1932.
– *ders.*, Gefühl oder Vernunft als Rechtsquelle?, ZHR 73 (1913) 429.
*Munch, P. A.*, Empirical Science and Max Weber's ‚Verstehende Soziologie', American Sociological Review 22 (1957) 26.
*Nagel, E.*, On the Fusion of Fact and Value: A Reply to Professor Fuller, Natural Law Forum 3 (1958) 77.
– *ders.*, Fact, Value and Human Purpose, Natural Law Forum 4 (1959) 26.
*Naucke, W.*, Über die juristische Relevanz der Sozialwissenschaften, 1972.
*Nelson, L.*, Die Rechtswissenschaft ohne Recht, 1917, 2. Auflage 1949.
*Neumann, F.*, Types of Natural Law, Studies in Philosophy and Social Sciences 8 (1940) 338.
*Neumann, U.*, Juristische Fachsprache und Umgangssprache, in: Sprachkultur als Rechtskultur (Hg. Grewendorf, G.), 1992, S. 110.
*Neumann-Duesberg, H.*, Bildberichterstattung über absolute und relative Personen der Zeitgeschichte, JZ 1960, 114.
*Neuner, J.*, Die Rechtsfindung contra legem, 1992.
*Nietzsche, F.*, Der Wille zur Macht (Kröner-Ausgabe).
– *ders.*, Die fröhliche Wissenschaft 1882.

– *ders.*, Menschliches, Allzumenschliches. Ein Buch für freie Geister, Band I/II, 1878–1880.

*Nusser, K.-H.*, Kausale Prozesse und sinnerfassende Vernunft. Max Webers philosophische Fundierung der Soziologie und der Kulturwissenschaften, 1986.

*Nussbaum, A.*, Die Rechtstatsachenforschung, 1917.

*Oakes, G.*, The Verstehen Thesis and the Foundation of Max Webers Methodology, 1977.

– *ders.*, Weber and Rickert. Concept Formation in the Cultural Sciences, 1988.

*Obermayer, K.*, Rechtswissenschaft als Geisteswissenschaft, JZ 1987, 694.

*Oechsler, J.*, Gerechtigkeit im modernen Austauschvertrag 1997.

– *ders.*, Vertragliche Schuldverhältnisse, 2. Auflage 2007.

– *ders.*, Vertragstypen, in: Staudinger/Eckpfeiler des Zivilrechts, 2005.

*Oertmann, P. E. W.*, Gesetzeszwang und Richterfreiheit, 1909.

– *ders.*, Rechtsordnung und Verkehrssitte, 1914.

*Oexle, O. G.*, Von Nietzsche zu Max Weber, in: ders., Geschichtswissenschaft im Zeichen des Historismus, 1996.

*Ogorek, R.*, Richterkönig oder Subsumtionsautomat?, 1968.

*Oh, I.-J.*, Das Kausalproblem bei Max Weber und in der neueren Wissenschaftstheorie, 1998.

*Oksaar, E.*, Alltagssprache, Fachsprache, Rechtssprache, Zeitschrift für Gesetzgebung 3 (1989), 210.

*Ott, W.*, Die Problematik einer Typologie im Gesellschaftsrecht, 1972.

*Owen, D.*, Maturity and Modernity. Nietzsche, Weber, Foucault and the Ambivalence of Reason, 1994;

– *ders.*, Autonomy and „inner distance“: a trace of Nietzsche in Weber, History of the Human Sciences 4 (1991) 79.

*Parsons, T.*, Der Begriff des Kapitalismus in den Theorien von Max Weber und Werner Sombart, 1929 (= „Capitalism“ in recent German Literature: Sombart and Weber, Journal o Political Economy 36 (1928) 641; 37 (1929) 31.

– *ders.*, Evolutionary Universals in Society, American Sociological Review 29 (1964) 339.

– *ders.*, Rationalität und der Prozess der Rationalisierung im Denken Max Webers, in: Max Weber und die Rationalisierung sozialen Handelns (Hg. Sprondel, W./Seyfarth, C.), 1981, S. 81.

– *ders.*, Societies. Evolutionary and Comparatives Perspectives, 1966.

– *ders.*, The Place of Ultimate Values in Social Theory, The International Journal of Ethics 45 (1935) 282.

– *ders.*, The Structure of Social Action, 1937.

– *ders.*, The System of Modern Societies, 1971.

– *ders.*, Unity and Diversity in the Modern Intellectual Disciplines: the Role

of the Social Science, in: ders., Sociological Theory and Modern Society, 1967, S. 166.
- *ders.*, Wertgebundenheit und Objektivität in den Sozialwissenschaften. Eine Interpretation der Beiträge Max Webers, in: Max Weber und die Soziologie heute, Verhandlungen des 15. Deutschen Soziologentages (Hg. Stammer, O.), 1965, 39.
- *ders.*, On the Relation of Action to Max Weber's „Verstehende Soziologie", in: Verhalten, Handeln und System. Talcott Parsons' Beitrag zur Entwicklung der Sozialwissenschaft (Hg. Schluchter, W.) 1980, S. 150.

*Patterson, D. M.*, Recht und Wahrheit, 1999.

*Paulson, St. L.*, Erkennen und Anerkennen. Die neukantianische Urteilslehre Heinrich Rickerts, Festschrift für G. Winkler, 1997, S. 751.
- *ders.*, The Weak Reading of Authority in: Hans Kelsen's Pure Theory of Law, Law and Philosophy 19 (2000) 131.

*Pawlowski, H.-M.*, Methodenlehre für Juristen, 1981.

*Peczenik, A.*, Towards the Juristic Theory of Law, Österreichische Zeitschrift für öffentliches Recht 21 (1971) 167.

*Perelman, C.*, Justice et raison, 1963, S. 206.

*Peters, B.*, Rationalität, Recht und Gesellschaft, 1991.

*Petersen, J.*, Wilhelm von Humboldts Rechtsphilosophie, 2. Auflage 2007.
- *ders.*, Nietzsches Genialität der Gerechtigkeit, 2008.
- *ders.*, Die Auslegung von letztwilligen Verfügungen, Jura 2005, 597.
- *ders.*, Die Auslegung von Rechtsgeschäften, Jura 2004, 536.
- *ders.*, Die mündliche Prüfung im ersten juristischen Staatsexamen, 2005.
- *ders.*, Duldungspflicht und Umwelthaftung, 1996.
- *ders.*, Kants „Metaphysische Anfangsgründe der Rechtslehre" – kritisches Spätwerk oder „Erzeugnis eines gewöhnlichen Erdensohns"?, Festschrift für C.-W. Canaris, 2007, S. 1243.
- *ders.*, Medienrecht, 4. Auflage 2008.
- *ders.*, Unternehmenssteuerrecht und bewegliches System, 1999.
- *ders.*, Von der Interessenjurisprudenz zur Wertungsjurisprudenz, 2001.

*Pfister, B.*, Die Entwicklung des Idealtypus. Eine methodologische Untersuchung über das Verhalten von Theorie und Geschichte bei Schmoller und Max Weber, 1928.

*Philipps, L.*, Zur Ontologie der sozialen Rolle, 1963.

*Plessner, H.*, Der Weg der Soziologie, 1960.
- *ders.*, in: Max Weber zum Gedächtnis (Hg. König, R./Winckelmann, J.) 1963, S. 30.

*Podlech, A.*, Wertungen und Werte im Recht, AöR 1970, 185.

*Popper, K.*, Logik der Forschung, 10. Auflage 1994.
- *ders.*, The Poverty of Historicism, 1957.
- *ders.*, Philosophische Selbstinterpretation und Polemik gegen die Dialektiker, in: Verfall der Philosophie (Hg. Grossner, C.) 1971, S. 278.

– *ders.*, Objektive Erkenntnis, 4. Auflage 1984.
*Posner, R. A.*, Economic Analysis of Law, 6. Auflage 2002.
– *ders.*, Overcoming Law, 1995.
– *ders.*, Frontiers of Legal Theory, 2001.
– *ders.*, Law, Pragmatism, and Democracy, 2003.
*Pound, R.*, A Survey of Social Interests, Harvad Law Review 57 (1943) 1.
– *ders.*, Liberty of Contract, Yale Law Journal 18 (1909) 464.
– *ders.*, Role of the Will in Law, Harvard Law Review 68 (1954) 1.
– *ders.*, A Call for a Realistic Jurisprudence, Harvard Law Review 44 (1930/31) 697.
*Preuß, H.*, Zur Methode juristischer Begriffskonstruktion, Schmollers Jahrbuch 24 (1900), Band 1, S. 359.
*Prisching, M.*, Ökonomische Rechtslehre?, Festschrift zur 200-Jahrfeier der Rechtswissenschaftlichen Fakultät in Graz, 1979, S. 995.
*Putnam, H.*, The Collapse of the Fact/Value Dichotomy and Other Essays, 2004.
*Quante, M.*, Allgemeine Ethik, 2003.
*Quensel, B. K.*, Logik und Methode in der ‚Rechtssoziologie' Max Webers. Ein Beitrag zur Klärung der grundlegenden Begriffe und Perspektiven, Zeitschrift für Rechtssoziologie 18 (1997) 133.
– *ders.*, Max Webers Konstruktionslogik. Sozialökonomik zwischen Geschichte und Theorie, 2007.
*Quine, W. V. O.*, Methods of Logic, 1950 (8. Auflage 1993; deutsch: Grundzüge der Logik, 1969).
*Radbruch, G.*, Rechtsphilosophie, 5. Auflage 1956.
– *ders.*, Die Lehre von der adäquaten Verursachung, N. F. Band 1, Heft 3, 1902.
– *ders.*, Über das Rechtsgefühl, Die Tat 6 (1914/15) 337.
*Ranieri, F.*, Juristen für Europa, JZ 1997, 801.
*Raisch, P.*, Juristische Methoden, 2. Auflage 1995.
*Raiser, Th.*, Grundlagen der Rechtssoziologie, 4. Auflage 2006.
*Ratzinger, J./Benedikt XVI.*, Glaube, Wahrheit, Toleranz, 4. Auflage 2005.
– *ders.*, Werte in Zeiten des Umbruchs, 2005.
– *ders.*, Glaube und Vernunft. Die Regensburger Vorlesung, Text der Vorlesung und Kommentare, 2006.
*Raz, J.*, Practical Reasons and Norm, 2. Auflage 1990.
*Rehbinder, M.*, Die Begründung der Rechtssoziologie durch Eugen Ehrlich, 1967.
– *ders.*, Die Rechtstatsachenforschung im Schnittpunkt von Rechtssoziologie und soziologischer Jurisprudenz, Jahrbuch für Rechtssoziologie 1 (1970) 333.
– *ders.*, Max Weber und die Rechtswissenschaft, in: Max Weber als Rechtssoziologie (Hg. ders./Tieck, K.-P.) 1987.

– *ders.*, Max Webers Rechtssoziologie: Eine Bestandsaufnahme, in: Max Weber zum Gedächtnis. Materialien und Dokumente zur Bewertung von Werk und Persönlichkeit 1963, S. 470.
– *ders.*, Recht und Rechtswissenschaft im Werk von Max Weber, in: Max Weber heute (Hg. Weiß, J.), 1989, S. 497.
– *ders.*, Rechtssoziologie, 1977.
– *ders.*, Weber und die Rechtswissenschaft, 1986.
*Reich, N.*, Sociological Jurisprudence and Legal Realism im Rechtsdenken Amerikas, 1967.
*Reichel, H.*, Zum Problem des freien Ermessens, Festschrift für E. Zitelmann, 1913.
– *ders.*, Zur Freirechtsbewegung, DJZ 1910, 463.
*Rheinstein, M.*, Preface and Introduction to Max Weber on Law in Economy and Society, in: ders., Gesammelte Schriften, Band 1. Rechtstheorie und Soziologie. Rechtsvergleichung und Common Law (Hg. Leser, H. G.) 1979, S. 27.
*Rickert, H.*, Die Grenzen naturwissenschaftlichen Begriffsbildung, 1902.
– *ders.*, Max Weber und seine Stellung zur Wissenschaft, Logos XV (1926) 222.
*Riebschläger, K.*, Die Freirechtsbewegung: Zur Entwicklung einer soziologischen Rechtsschule, 1968.
*Riezler, E.*, Das Rechtsgefühl, 3. Auflage 1969.
*Ringer, F. K.*, Max Webers's Methodology. The Unification of the Cultural and Social Sciences, 1997.
– *ders.*, Max Weber. An intellectual biography, 2004.
*Rödig, J.*, Die Denkform der Alternative in der Jurisprudenz, 1969.
*Röhl, K. F.*, Das Dilemma der Rechtstatsachenforschung, 1974.
*Roellecke, G.*, Wende der deutschen Rechtsphilosophie?, ARSP 1991, Beiheft 44, S. 287.
*Rossi, P.*, Max Weber und die Methodologie der Geschichts- und Sozialwissenschaften, in: M. Weber, der Historiker (Hg. Kocka, J.) 1986, S. 28.
*Rothenfußer, C.*, Kausalität und Nachteil, 2003.
*Rottleuthner, H.*, Einführung in die Rechtssoziologie, 1987.
– *ders.*, Rechtswissenschaft als Sozialwissenschaft, 1973.
– *ders.*, Ungerechtigkeiten. Anmerkungen zur westlichen Leidkultur, 2008.
– *ders.*, Zur Rezeptivität der Rechtswissenschaft gegenüber soziologischem Wissen, Soziologie, Mitteilungsblatt der Deutschen Gesellschaft für Soziologie 2 (1978) 17.
– *ders.*, Richterliches Handeln, 1973.
*Rümelin, G.*, Juristische Begriffsbildung, 1894.
– *ders.*, Werturteile und Willensentscheidungen im Civilrecht, 1891.
– *ders.*, Rechtsgefühl und Rechtsbewusstsein, 1925.

*Runciman, W. G.*, A Critique of Max Weber's Philosophy of Social Science, 1972.
*Rüthers, B.*, Die unbegrenzte Auslegung – Zum Wandel der Privatrechtsordnung im Nationalsozialismus, 6. Auflage 2005.
– *ders.*, Die Wende-Experten. Zur Ideologieanfälligkeit geistiger Berufe am Beispiel der Juristen, 2. Auflage 1995.
– *ders.*, Rechtstheorie. Begriff, Geltung und Anwendung des Rechts, 3. Auflage 2007.
– *ders.*, Das Ungerechte an der Gerechtigkeit, 2. Auflage 1993.
– *ders.*, Wissenschaft und Weltanschauung am Beispiel der Jurisprudenz, 1995.
– *ders.*, Wir denken die Rechtsbegriffe um... Weltanschauung als Auslegungsprinzip, 1987.
– *ders.*, Institutionelles Rechtsdenken im Wandel der Verfassungsepochen, 1970.
– *ders.*, Rechtsordnung und Wertordnung, 1986.
– *ders.*, Rechtsdogmatik und Rechtspolitik, 2003.
– *ders.*, Methodenrealismus in Jurisprudenz und Justiz, JZ 2006, 53.
*Ryffel, H.*, Rechtssoziologie. Eine systematische Orientierung, 1974.
*Säcker, F.-J.*, Grundprobleme der kollektiven Koalitionsfreiheit, 1969.
*Savigny, E. v.*, Zur Rolle der deduktiv-axiomatischen Methode in der Rechtswissenschaft, in: Rechtstheorie (Hg. Jahr, G./Maihofer, W.), 1971, S. 315.
– *ders.*, Die Philosophie der normalen Sprache, 1974.
*Savigny, F. C. v.*, System des heutigen römischen Rechts, 1840.
– *ders.*, Vom Beruf unserer Zeit für Gesetzgebung und Rechtswissenschaft, 1814.
*Schacht, R.*, Philosophy as Linguistic Analysis: A Nietzscheau Critique, Philosophical Studies 25 (1974) 153.
*Schack, H.*, BGB – Allgemeiner Teil, 11. Auflage 2006.
*Schäfer, G. H.*, Die Rechtsontologie Werner Maihofers: Möglichkeiten und Grenzen einer Rechtsphilosophie im Anschluss an Martin Heidegger, 2004.
*Schäfer, H.-B./Ott, C.*, Lehrbuch der ökonomischen Analyse des Zivilrechts, 4. Auflage 2004.
*Schelsky, H.*, Das Jhering-Modell des sozialen Wandels durch Recht – Ein wissenschaftsgeschichtlicher Beitrag, Jahrbuch für Rechtssoziologie und Rechtstheorie, Bd. 3 (1972) 47.
– *ders.*, Nutzen und Gefahren der sozialwissenschaftlichen Ausbildung von Juristen, JZ 1974, 410.
– *ders.*, Soziologiekritische Bemerkungen zu gewissen Tendenzen der Rechtssoziologen, Jahrbuch für Rechtssoziologie und Rechtstheorie 3 (1972) 603.
*Schelting, A. v.*, Max Webers Wissenschaftslehre, 1934.
– *ders.*, Die logische Theorie der historischen Kulturwissenschaft von Max

Weber und im besonderen sein Begriff des Idealtypus, Archiv für Sozialwissenschaft und Sozialpolitik 49 (1922) 623.
*Scherer, M.*, Vom Apriori der Prägnanz. Vortheoretische Sinnerschlossenheit als zentrales Motiv der Kulturphilosophie Ernst Cassirers, 1996.
*Scheuerle, W.*, Formalismusargumente, AcP 172 (1972) 396.
*Schlehofer, H.*, Juristische Methodologie und Methodik der Fallbearbeitung, JuS 1992, 575.
*Schlink, B.*, Abwägung im Verfassungsrecht, 1976.
– *ders.*, Vergangenheitsschuld und gegenwärtiges Recht, 2002.
*Schluchter, W.*, Aspekte bürokratischer Herrschaft, 1972.
– *ders.*, Die Entwicklung des modernen Rationalismus. Eine Analyse von Max Webers Gesellschaft, 1979 (Die Entstehung des modernen Rationalismus. Eine Analyse von Max Webers Entwicklungsgeschichte des Okzidents, 1998).
– *ders.*, Handlung, Ordnung und Kultur. Studien zu einem Forschungsprogramm im Anschluss an Max Weber, 2005.
– *ders.*, Rationalismus und Weltbeherrschung. Studien zu Max Weber, 1980.
– *ders.*, Wertfreiheit und Verantwortungsethik, 1971.
– *ders.*, Max Webers hinterlassenes Hauptwerk: Die Wirtschaft und die gesellschaftlichen Ordnungen und Mächte. Entstehung und gedanklicher Aufbau, 1986.
– *ders.*, Die Paradoxie der Rationalisierung. Zum Verhältnis von „Ethik" und „Welt" bei Max Weber, Zeitschrift für Soziologie 5 (1976) 256.
– *ders.*, „Wirtschaft und Gesellschaft" – Das Ende eines Mythos, in: Max Weber heute. Erträge und Probleme der Forschung (Hg. J. Weiß), 1989, S. 55.
– *ders.*, Rechtssoziologie als empirische Geltungstheorie, in: Rechtssoziologie am Ende des 20. Jahrhunderts (Hg. H. Dreier) 2000, S. 8.
*Schmid, C.*, Erinnerungen, 3. Band der Gesammelten Werke, 1979.
*Schmid, M.*, Rationalität und Theoriebildung. Studien zu Karl R. Poppers Methodologie der Sozialwissenschaften, 1966.
*Schmidt, K.*, Levin Goldschmidt (1829–1897). Der Begründer der modernen Handelsrechtswissenschaft, in: Deutsche Juristen jüdischer Herkunft (Hg. Heinrichs, H. u. a.), 1993, S. 215.
*Schmidt, R.*, Widerspruchsfreiheit als rechtlicher Maßstab, Festschrift für C.-W. Canaris, 2007, S. 1353.
*Schmidt-Salzer, J.*, Zum Umfang der Herstellerhaftung, BB 1987, 721.
*Schneider, E./Schnapp, F. E.*, Logik für Juristen, 6. Auflage 2006.
*Schoppmeyer, H.*, Juristische Methode als Lebensaufgabe, 2001.
*Schöllgen, G.*, Max Webers Anliegen. Rationalisierung als Forderung und Hypothek, 1985.
*Schreiber, H.-L.*, Der Begriff der Rechtspflicht, 1966.

*Schreiber, O.*, Gemischte Verträge im Reichsschuldrecht, Jherings Jahrbücher 60 (1912) 106.
*Schreier, F.*, Die Interpretation der Gesetze und Rechtsgeschäfte, 1927.
*Schroeder, R.*, Nietzsche and Weber: Two „Prophets" of the Modern World, in: Max Weber, Rationality and Modernity (Hg. Whimster, S./Lash, S.) 1987, S. 207.
*Schumann, E.*, Eigenständigkeit und Vielfalt der juristischen Hermeneutik, Festschrift für C.-W. Canaris, 2007, S. 1367.
*Searle, J. R.*, Die Konstruktion gesellschaftlicher Wirklichkeit, 1997.
– *ders.*, Sprechakte, 1971.
*Seibel, H. D.*, Bürokratie und Charisma. Systemrationalität und Systemwandel, Jahrbuch für Sozialwissenschaft 27 (1976) 342.
*Seidenfeld, M.*, A Civic Republican Justification for the Bureaucratic State, Harvard Law Review 105 (1992) 1511.
*Sica, A.*, Weber, Irrationality, and Social Order, 1988.
*Simitis, S.*, Zum Problem einer juristischen Logik, Ratio 3 (1960) 76.
*Simon, D.*, Waren die NS-Richter „unabhängige Richter" im Sinne des § 1 GVG?, Rechtshistorisches Journal 2 (1985) 102.
*Sinzheimer, H.*, Die Aufgabe der Rechtssoziologie, 1935.
– *ders.*, Die soziologische Methode in der Privatrechtswissenschaft, 1909.
– *ders.*, Über die soziologische und dogmatische Methode der Arbeitsrechtswissenschaft, 1922.
*Somek, A.*, Der Gegenstand der Rechtserkenntnis – Epitaph eines juristischen Problems, 1996.
– *ders.*, Gesetzesbindung als Problem der Demokratie, Journal für Rechtspolitik 6 (1998) 41.
– *ders.*, Juristische Expertise, Rechtshistorisches Journal 20, 2001, S. 698.
– *ders.*, Legal Formality and Freedom of Choice. A Moral Perspective on Jhering's Constructivism, Ratio Juris 15 (2002) 52.
– *ders.*, Rationalität und Diskriminierung. Zur Bindung der Gesetzgebung an das Gleichheitsrecht, 2001.
– *ders.*, Rechtliches Wissen, 2006.
– *ders.*, Rechtssystem und Republik. Über die politische Funktion des systematischen Rechtsdenkens, 1992.
*Speer, H.*, Herrschaft und Legitimität. Zeitgebundene Aspekte in Max Webers Herrschaftssoziologie, 1978.
*Stammler, R.*, Wirtschaft und Recht nach der materialistischen Geschichtsauffassung, 2. Auflage 1906.
– *ders.*, Theorie der Rechtswissenschaft, 1923.
*Stampe, E.*, Die Freirechtsbewegung, 1911.
*Starck, C.*, Empirie in der Rechtsdogmatik, JZ 1972, 609.
*Stauth, G./Turner, B. S.*, Nietzsche in Weber oder die Geburt des modernen Genius' im professionellen Menschen, Zeitschrift für Soziologie 15 (1986) 81.

*Stoll, H.*, Begriff und Konstruktion in der Lehre der Interessenjurisprudenz, Festgabe Heck-Rümelin-Schmidt, 1931, S. 60.
*Stolleis, M.*, Recht im Unrecht, 1994.
– *ders.*, Gemeinwohlformeln im nationalsozialistischen Recht, 1974.
*Strache, K.-H.*, Das Denken in Standards. Zugleich ein Beitrag zur Typologie, 1967.
*Strahl, M.*, Die typisierende Betrachtungsweise im Steuerrecht, 1996.
*Stratenwerth, G.*, Das rechtstheoretische Problem der „Natur der Sache“, 1957.
*Strauss, L.*, Naturrecht und Geschichte, 1953.
*Strong, T. B.*, „What have we to do with the morals?“ Nietzsche and Weber on history and ethics, History of the Human Sciences 5 (1992) 9.
*Strömholm, St.*, Allgemeine Rechtslehre, 1976.
*Stumpf, M.*, Was ist Rechtssoziologie?, AcP 122 (1924) 36.
*Suber, D.*, Die Begründung der deutschen Soziologie zwischen Neukantianismus und Lebensphilosophie, 2002.
*Swedberg, R.*, Max Weber and the Idea of Economic Sociology, 1998.
*Tenbruck, F. H.*, Die Genesis der Methodenlehre Max Webers, Kölner Zeitschrift für Soziologie und Sozialpsychologie 11 (1959) 573.
– *ders.*, Das Werk Max Webers: Methodologie und Sozialwissenschaft, Kölner Zeitschrift für Soziologie und Sozialpsychologie 38 (1986) 13.
*Thibaut, A. F.*, Über die Notwendigkeit eines allgemeinen bürgerlichen Rechts für Deutschland, 1814.
*Thier, A.*, Steuergesetzgebung und Verfassung in der konstitutionellen Monarchie. Staatssteuerreformen in Preußen 1871–1893, 1999.
*Tieck, K.-P.*, Persönlichkeit, Ordnungen, Interessen, in: Max Weber als Rechtssoziologie (Hg. Rehbinder, M./ders.), 1987.
*Tiemeyer, J.*, Zur Methodenfrage der Rechtssoziologie, mit einem Vorwort von Ernst E. Hirsch, 1969.
*Tipke, K.*, Die Steuerrechtsordnung, 2. Bände, 2. Auflage 2003.
– *ders.*, Steuerrecht – Chaos, Konglomerat oder System?, StuW 1971, 2.
– *ders.*, Steuerrechtswissenschaft und Steuersystem, Festschrift für Wacke, 1972, S. 211.
*Topitsch, E.* (Hg.), Logik der Sozialwissenschaften, 12. Auflage 1993.
– *ders.*, Das Wertfreiheitsproblem seit Max Weber, Zeitschrift für Nationalökonomie 13 (1952) 158.
*Treiber, H.*, Im ‚Schatten‘ des Neukantianismus: Norm und Geltung bei Max Weber, Festschrift für E. Blankenburg, 1998, S. 245.
– *ders.*, Die Geburt der Weberschen Rationalismus-These: Webers Bekanntschaft mit der russischen Geschichtsphilosophie in Heidelberg. Überlegungen anlässlich der Veröffentlichung des ersten Briefbandes der Max-Weber-Gesamtausgabe: Leviathan. Zeitschrift für Sozialwissenschaft 19 (1991) 435.
– *ders.*, Zur Genealogie einer „Science positive de la morale en Allemagne“.

Die Geburt einer r(é)ealistischen Moralwissenschaft" aus der Idee einer monistischen Naturkonzeption, Nietzsche-Studien 22 (1993) 165.
*Trubek, D. M.*, Max Weber on Law and the Rise of Capitalism, Wisconsin Law Review 1972, 720.
– *ders.*, Max Weber über das Recht und die Entstehung des Kapitalismus, in: Zur Rechtssoziologie Max Webers. Interpretation, Kritik, Weiterentwicklung (Hg. Breuer, S./Treiber, H.), 1984, S. 152.
*Tugendhat, E./Wolf, U.*, Logisch-semantische Propädeutik, 1983.
*Turner, B. S.*, Lebensphilosophie und Handlungstheorie. Die Beziehungen zwischen Talcott Parsons und Max Weber innerhalb der Entwicklung der Soziologie, in: Max Webers Wissenschaftslehre. Interpretation und Kritik (Hg. Wagner, G./Zipprian, H.) 1994, S. 310.
*Turner, St. P./Factor, R. A.*, The Lawyer as Social Thinker, 1994.
*Udy, S. H.*, „Bureaucracy" and „Rationality" in Weber's Organization Theory, American Journal of Sociology 24 (1959) 791.
*Uecker, St.*, Die Rationalisierung des Recht. Max Webers Rechtssoziologie, 2005.
*Utzig, S.*, Die Rolle des Rechts in der modernen ökonomischen Theorie, AcP 189 (1989) 158.
*Viehweg, T.*, Topik und Jurisprudenz, 3. Auflage 1963.
*Vogenauer, St.*, Die Auslegung von Gesetzen in England und auf dem Kontinent, 2001.
*Wagner, G.*, Geltung und normativer Zwang. Eine Untersuchung zu den neukantianischen Grundlagen der Wissenschaftslehre Max Webers, 1987.
*Weber, M.*, Analyse des Begriffs der „Regel", Archiv für Sozialwissenschaft und Sozialpolitik 24 (1907).
– *ders.*, Kritische Studien auf dem Gebiet der kulturwissenschaftlichen Logik, Archiv für Sozialwissenschaften und Sozialpolitik 22 (1906) 143.
– *ders.*, Der Sinn der ‚Wertfreiheit' der soziologischen und ökonomischen Wissenschaften, Logos 7 (1917) 40.
– *ders.*, Die ‚Objektivität' sozialwissenschaftlicher und sozialpolitischer Erkenntnis, Archiv für Sozialwissenschaft und Sozialpolitik 19 (1904) 22.
– *ders.*, Die drei Typen der legitimen Herrschaft, 1952.
– *ders.*, Lehre von der Wertfreiheit der Wissenschaft, Logos X (1921) 195.
– *ders.*, Objektive Möglichkeit und adäquate Verursachung in der historischen Kausalbetrachtung, Archiv für Sozialwissenschaften und Sozialpolitik 22 (1906) 143.
– *ders.*, Wirtschaft und Gesellschaft, 1. Auflage 1922, 5. revidierten Auflage, 1980.
– *ders.*, Wissenschaft als Beruf, Geistige Arbeit als Beruf. Vier Vorträge vor dem Freistudentischen Bund, 1919, Gesammelte Aufsätze zur Wissenschaftslehre, 7. Auflage 1988.
– *ders.*, Zur Geschichte der Handelsgesellschaften im Mittelalter, Schriften

1889–1894 (Hg. Dilcher, G./Lepsius, S.), Max Weber-Gesamtausgabe I 1, 2008.
– *ders.*, Über einige Kategorien der verstehenden Soziologie Logos 4 (1913) 253.
– *ders.*, Die protestantische Ethik und der „Geist des Kapitalismus“, Archiv für Sozialwissenschaft und Sozialpolitik 20 (1904) 1.
– *ders.*, Die Berufsidee des asketischen Protestantismus, Archiv für Sozialwissenschaft und Sozialpolitik 21 (1905) 1.
*Weber, Marianne*, Max Weber: Ein Lebensbild, 1950.
*Weber, R.*, Einige Gedanken zur Konkretisierung von Generalklauseln durch Fallgruppen, AcP 192 (1992) 516.
*Weigelin, E.*, Sitte, Recht und Moral, 1919.
*Weinberger, O.*, Norm und Institution, 1988.
– *ders.*, Recht, Institution und Rechtspolitik, 1987.
*Weinkauff, H.*, Der Naturrechtsgedanke in der Rechtsprechung des Bundesgerichtshofs, NJW 1960, 1689.
*Weisser, G.*, Zur Erkenntniskritik der Urteile über den Wert sozialer Gebilde und Prozesse. Weiterführung der „Werturteilsdebatte“, Kölner Zeitschrift für Soziologie und Sozialpsychologie 6 (1953/54) 16.
*Wellmer, A.*, Methodologie als Erkenntnistheorie, 1967.
*Wesel, U.*, Geschichte des Rechts, 3. Auflage 2006.
*Westerhoff, R.*, Die Elemente des beweglichen Systems, 1991.
*Westermann, H. P.*, Vertragsfreiheit und Typengesetzlichkeit im Recht der Personengesellschaften, 1970.
*Westermann, H.*, Die Funktion des Nachbarrechts, Festschrift für K. Larenz, 1973, S. 1003.
– *ders.*, Interessenkollisionen und ihre richterliche Wertung bei den Sicherungsrechten an Fahrnis und Forderungen, 1954.
– *ders.*, Wesen und Grenzen der richterlichen Streitentscheidung im Zivilrecht, 1955.
*Weyhe, L.*, Levin Goldschmidt. Ein Gelehrtenleben in Deutschland – Grundfragen des Handelsrechts und der Zivilrechtswissenschaft in der zweiten Hälfte des 19. Jahrhunderts, 1996.
*Wieacker, F.*, Rudolf v. Jhering, 1943.
– *ders.*, Zur praktischen Leistung der Rechtsdogmatik, Festschrift für H.-G. Gadamer, Band 2, 1970, S. 311, 332.
*Wilburg, W.*, Das Zusammenspiel der Kräfte im Aufbau des Schuldrechts, AcP 163 (1963) 346.
– *ders.*, Die Elemente des Schadensrechts, 1941.
– *ders.*, Entwicklung eines beweglichen Systems im bürgerlichen Recht, Grazer Rektoratsrede, 1950.
*Winckelmann, J.*, Legitimität und Legalität in Max Webers Herrschaftssoziologie, 1952.

*Witherspoon, J. P.*, The Relation of Philosophy and Jurisprudence, Natural Law Forum 3 (1958) 105.

*Wöhler, S.*, Das heterologische Denkprinzip Heinrich Rickerts und seine Bedeutung für das Werk Max Webers, 2005.

*Wolf, M.*, Philipp Heck als Zivilrechtsdogmatiker – Studien zur dogmatischen Umsetzung seiner Methodenlehre, 1996.

*Wolff, H. J.*, Typen im Recht und in der Rechtswissenschaft, Studium Generale 5 (1952) 195.

*Wright, G. H. v.*, The Logic of Preference, 1963.

– *ders.*, The Varieties of Goodness, 1963.

*Zajtay, I.*, Begriff, System und Präjudizien in den kontinentalen Rechten und im Common Law, AcP 165 (1965) 97.

*Zingerle, A.*, Max Webers Historische Soziologie. Aspekte und Materialien zur Wirkungsgeschichte, 1981.

*Zippelius, R.*, Der Typenvergleich als Instrument der Gesetzesauslegung, Jahrbuch für Rechtssoziologie und Rechtstheorie 2 (1972) 482.

– *ders.*, Die Verwendung von Typen in Normen und Prognosen, Festschrift für Engisch, K., 1969, S. 224.

*Zitelmann, E.*, Lücken im Recht, 1903.

## Personenverzeichnis

Die kursiv gedruckten Zahlen verweisen auf den Text, die normal gedruckten auf Fußnoten.


Aaken, Anne van 157
Abramowski, Günther 11
Adams, Michael 35 f.
Adomeit, Klaus 157
Adorno, Theodor W. 29, 162
Aechtner, Silke 42
Albert, Hans 29 ff., 34, 51, 130, 162
Alexy, Robert 20, 69, 78, 101, 127, 160
Arrow, Kenneth J. 143
Atiyah, Patrick S. 121
Auer, Marietta 95
Austin, John Langshaw 20, *54*

Baier, Horst 1, 12, 142
Baldus, Manfred 61
Ballweg, Ottmar 157
Bar, Christian von 57
Baumgarten, Eduard *13*
Baumgarten, Edwin 112
Baurmann, Michael 24
Beater, Axel 53
Bechtler, Thomas W. 47
Becker, Thomas 144
Behrends, Okko 45, 64, 114, 127
Bekker, Ernst Immanuel 72
Bendix, Reinhard 26
Benedict, Jörg 122
Bergbohm, Karl 71
Berger, Johannes 22
Bergfeld, Werner 143
Bergmann Avila, Humberto 76
Bernstein, Herbert 104
Berman, Harold J. 131
Berolzheimer, Fritz 114
Binder, Julius 156
Bobbio, Norberto 55
Boehmer, Gustav 27, *56*, 59, *64*, 113 f., 134
Bork, Reinhard 109
Brandom, Robert B. 19
Brecht, Arnold 34
Breuer, Stefan 7, 120 f.
Brugger, Winfried 159
Bucher, Eugen 71, 90, 122
Buchwald, Delf 44
Bülow, Oskar 112
Burger, Thomas 133, 142
Bydlinski, Franz 6, 37, 46, 53, 67, 69, 77, 86, 89, 115, 127, 140, 144, 149 f., 152, 158, 160

Caemmerer, Ernst von 53
Canaris, Claus-Wilhelm 18, 24, 50 ff., 55, 57, 60 f., 70, 72 f., 77 f., 85 f., 90, 94, 98 f., *100*, 107, 111, 114 ff., 120, 139 f., 144, 147, 149, 153, 155, 161 ff., 165
Cardozo, Benjamin N. 83
Caroni, Pio 108
Casper, Gerhard 83
Cassirer, Ernst *104*
Charmatz, Hans 149
Christensen, Ralph 20
Cicero, Marcus Tullius 98
Cohn, Jonas 4, 30
Coing, Helmut 59, 64, 69, 83, 106, 110, 156
Comte, Auguste *105*, *164*
Conrad, Hermann 71 f.
Cortella, Lucio 97
Crone, Patricia 95, 123

Dahrendorf, Ralf 27
Devlin, Patrick 70
Diederichsen, Uwe 53, 86, 156
Dilcher, Gerhard 1, 4, 9, 107, 110, 112, 116, 118, 120, 123, 153 f.

Dilthey, Wilhelm 3, *104*
Dombek, Bernhard 59 ff., 81
Dorndorf, Eberhard 16, 91, 134
Dreier, Horst 26, 71, 88, 98
Dreier, Ralf 49, 64, 72, 114, 127, 147, 160, 162
Drüen, Klaus-Dieter 137
Durkheim, Emile 8, *117*
Duve, Thomas 60
Dux, Günter 29
Dworkin, Ronald *18*, 39, 127

Edelmann, Johann 61
Eden, Robert 96 f.
Eder, Klaus 42
Ehrenzweig, Albert A. 45
Ehrlich, Eugen *45*, *47*, *66*, 72, *107 f.*, 110 f., *115 f.*, *156*
Eidenmüller, Horst 5, 14, 18, 27, 34 ff., 67, 163
Ellscheid, Günter 81
Elze, Hans 56, 69
Emge, Carl August 111
Engel-Reimers, Charlotte 29
Engisch, Karl 12, 18, 43, *84*, 111
Enneccerus, Ludwig 109
Ernst, Wolfgang 156
Esser, Josef 32, 45 f., 53, 110
Evers, Hans Ulrich 106

Falk, Johann 55
Falk, Ulrich 107
Faust, Florian 149
Febbrajo, Alberto 25, 42
Fezer, Karl-Heinz 35
Fiedler, Herbert 111
Fikentscher, Wolfgang 6, 25, 49, 54, *65*, *80*, 81 f., 85, 95, 104, 106, 116, 122, 139, 159
Fischer, Christian 53
Fischer, Hans Karl 125
Fish, Stanley L. 162
Fletcher, George P. 86
Flitner, Elisabeth H. 26
Foulkes, Albert S. 111
Frank, Jerome 45
Freund, Julien 42, 50
Freyer, Hans 163
Fries, Jakob Friedrich *104*
Frommel, Monika 112
Fuchs, Ernst *59*, 111
Fuller, Lon L. 70, 106

Gabriel, Karl 8
Gadamer, Hans-Georg *11*, 55, 97, 121
Geiger, Theodor 64
Gephart, Werner 154
Germann, Oskar Adolf 31, 57, 113
Gmelin, Johannes G. 59
Gmür, Max 113
Goeres, Ralf 51
Goethe, Johann Wolfgang von *86 f*, 163
Goldstein, Joseph 45
Gray, John Chipman 54
Grigoleit, Hans Christoph 37, 156, 163
Grimm, Klaus 9
Gumplowicz, Ludwig 31
Günther, Klaus 20
Gurvitch, Georges 27, 117

Habermas, Jürgen 17, 19, *20*, 21, *30*, 31, 49 f., 70, 75, 162, *164*, 165
Haferkamp, Hans-Peter 107
Haller, Hans 134
Hart, Herbert Lionel Adolphus 46, *89*, 105, 131
Hartmann, Michael 42, 48
Hassemer, Winfried 81, 113, 137
Hassold, Gerhard 63, 99, 109
Hattenhauer, Hans 60, 71, 108
Heck, Philipp *3 f.*, 5, *16*, 31, *58 f.*, *61 ff.*, 71, *77 ff.*, *111*, 112, *115 f.*, 125 ff., *126*, *130*, *134*, 139 f., 151 f., 160, *161*
Hedemann, Justus Wilhelm 61, 114
Hegenbarth, Rainer 21
Heisenberg, Werner 51, *155*, 163
Heitmann, Hermann 61 f.
Heldrich, Andreas 25, 59 f., *63*, 122, 140, 161, 163
Hempel, Carl 137

Henke, Wilhelm 30
Hennis, Wilhelm 13, 28
Henrich, Dieter *28*, 40, *58*, 160
Herberger, Maximilian 19, 44
Hesse, Albrecht 25
Heyde, Johannes Elrich 133
Hilgendorf, Eric 33
Hilterhaus, Friedhelm 49
Hippel, Fritz von 69, 134
Hoeniger, Heinrich 149
Holmes, Oliver Wendell *102*, 164
Hönigswald, Richard 80
Honnefelder, Ludger 104
Hopt, Klaus 25
Horn, Dieter 111
Hruschka, Joachim 51
Hubmann, Heinrich 45, 122
Hughes, Graham 70
Hume, David 3, 37
Husserl, Edmund 98
Husserl, Gerhart 94

Isay, Hermann 114

Jäger, Christian 15
Jánoska-Bendl, Judith 133
Jaspers, Karl *159*
Jellinek, Georg 24, 74
Jerusalem, Franz Wilhelm 156
Jestaedt, Matthias 158, 165
Jhering, Rudolf von 3, 44, *63 ff.*, *116*, 125
Joerden, Jan C. 99

Kalberg, Stephen 12, 133
Kallfass, Wilfried 134
Kantorowicz, Hermann *4*, 111, *112*
Kaser, Max 107
Kaufmann, Arthur 14, 72, 111, 150, 156
Kaye, Howard L. 74
Kelsen, Hans 46, *71*, *94*, 138, *156*, 157
Kessler, Friedrich *104*, 105
Kiefner, Hans 108
Kilian, Wolfgang 146
Kirchmann, Julius von 165
Kirchner, Christian 35
Kißler, Leo 25
Klug, Ulrich 34
Knauthe, Karlheinz 14
Koch, Hans-Joachim 19, 101
Köhler, Helmut 149
Kohler, Josef 64
Koller, Arnold 150
Koller, Peter 18
Krawietz, Werner 14, 61, 72
Kriele, Martin 30, 55
Kries, Johannes von *15*, 16
Kronstein, Heinrich 80
Kübel, Friedrich 45
Kudlich, Hans 20
Kühl, Kristian 106
Kuhlen, Lothar 33, 150, 154
Kuhn, Thomas 31, 82, 142, 161
Kullmann, Hans Josef 54
Künnecke, Arndt 106

Landau, Peter 50, 66, 68, 99, 109, *127*, 131, 161
Langenbucher, Katja 18, 53
Langheim, Heinrich A. W. 55
Larenz, Karl 2, 6, 18, 35, 46, 49, 53, 56 f., 74, 87, 94 f., 100, 115 f., 122, *137*, 138 ff, 144, 14 f., 156, 158, 160, 162
Leenen, Detlef 7, 100, 109, 133, 137, *144*, 145, 149 f., *151*, 152
Lenk, Hans 136
Lepsius, Mario Rainer 1, *7*, 8 f., 16, *26*, 28, 41, 43, 48, 124, *129*, 130, 136, 155, 158 f., 166
Lepsius, Oliver 54, 121, 129, 147, 156, 164
Lepsius, Susanne 4
Lessig, Lawrence 43
Llewellyn, Karl N. 82
Löher, Franz von 71
Loos, Fritz 5, 137
Lorenzen, Paul 30
Losano, Mario G. 55
Lotmar, Philipp 149
Löwith, Karl 165
Lübbe, Weyma 7

Lübbe-Wolff, Gertrude 84
Ludwig, Markus 37
Luhmann, Niklas 1 f., *3*, *8 f.*, *12*, *22*, 23, 27, 43 f., *44*, 48, *49*, 58, *63 f.*, 68, 70, 74, *80*, 81, *82*, 83, *84*, 85 f., 89 f., *93*, 107 f., *116 ff.*, 139, *141*, 142, *143*, *146 f.*, 152, *157*, 158, *159*, 160, 166
Lundmark, Thomas 122

Mach, Ernst *51 f.*, 155, 163
Marck, Siegfried 137
Marcuse, Herbert 125
Mayer-Maly, Theo 36
Medicus, Dieter 53, 147, 149, 163
Meier-Hayoz, Arthur 150
Melin, Patrick 122
Merkel, Adolf 65
Merton, Robert K. *164*
Merz, Peter-Ulrich 91
Mestmäcker, Ernst-Joachim 35
Mettenheim, Christoph von 41
Meyer, Ernst 50
Miller, Leonard G. 85
Mokre, Hans 46
Möllers, Christoph 158, 165
Mommsen, Wolfgang Justin 1, 97, 133
Moore, Underhill 45
Müller, Hans-Peter 11, 13, 41, 103, 106
Müller-Erzbach, Rudolf 45, 59, 78 f.
Munch, Peter A. 137

Nagel, Ernst 106
Naucke, Wolfgang 139
Nelson, Leonard 99
Neumann, Franz 104
Neumann, Ulfrid 2
Neumann-Duesberg, Horst 151
Neuner, Jörg 43
Nietzsche, Friedrich *12 f.*, *20 f.*, *39*, 70, *96*, 97
Nipperdey, Hans Carl 109
Nussbaum, Arthur 112
Nusser, Karl-Heinz 14

Oakes, Guy 91, 135
Obermayer, Klaus 156
Oechsler, Jürgen 84 f., 144 f.
Oertmann, Paul Ernst Wilhelm 3, 112
Oexle, Otto Gerhard 12, 96
Ogorek, Regina 111
Oh, In-Je 14
Oksaar, Els 2
Oppenheim, Paul 137
Ott, Claus 35
Ott, Walter 150, 154
Owen, David 13

Parsons, Talcott *8*, 22, 30, 41, 111, 117, 125, *160*
Patterson, Dennis M. 18
Paulson, Stanley L. 18, 91
Pawlowski, Hans-Martin 160
Peczenik, Aleksander 157
Perelman, Chaim 111
Peters, Bernhard 48
Pfister, Bernhard 135
Philipps, Lothar 17
Plessner, Helmuth 11, 28
Podlech, Adalbert 111
Popper, Karl R. 2, 19, 34, 86, *164*
Posner, Richard A . 35
Pound, Roscoe 65, 82 f.
Preuß, Hugo 60
Prisching, Manfred 36
Putnam, Hilary 30

Quante, Michael 30
Quensel, Bernhard K. 48, 76, 91, 107 f., 119, 133, 154
Quine, Willard Van Orman 101

Radbruch, Gustav 15, 34, 45
Raisch, Peter 6, 37, 45, 108, 119
Raiser, Thomas 24
Ranieri, Filippo 90
Ratzinger, Joseph/ Benedikt XVI. *88*, 105
Raz, Joseph 106, 141
Rehbinder, Manfred 5, 11, 15, 23 f., 112, 116

Reich, Norbert 83
Reichel, Hans 112
Rheinstein, Max 15, 120
Rickert, Heinrich *91 f.*, *162*, 163
Riebschläger, Klaus 111
Riezler, Erwin 45
Ringer, Fritz K. 28, 142
Rödig, Jürgen 98
Roellecke, Gerd 2
Röhl, Klaus Friedrich 2, 33, 49, 69
Rossi, Pietro 142
Rothenfußer, Christoph 15
Rottleuthner, Hubert 27 f., 32, 45, 48, 83, 87, 115, 118, 134, 149, 160
Rümelin, Gustav *45*, 46, 79
Runciman, Walter Garrison 28
Rüßmann, Helmut 101
Rüthers, Bernd 1 f., 14, 18, 21, 27, 30 ff., 47, 74, 80, 129 ff., 150, 158, 160, 162
Ryffel, Hans 59, 137

Säcker, Franz-Jürgen 33
Savigny, Eike von 20, 75
Savigny, Friedrich Carl von *5*, 151
Schacht, Richard 20
Schack, Haimo 109
Schäfer, Gunther Hermann 17
Schäfer, Hans-Bernd 35
Schelsky, Helmut 25, 64
Schelting, Alexander von 3, 28, 135, 137
Scherer, Martin 104
Scheuerle, Wilhelm 92
Schlehofer, Horst 89
Schlink, Bernhard 122, 129
Schluchter, Wolfgang 1, 7, 26, 36, 41, 44, 48, 55, 98
Schluep, Walter R. 150
Schmid, Carlo 56
Schmid, Michael 19
Schmidt, Karsten 4
Schmidt, Reiner 70
Schmidt-Salzer, Joachim 54
Schnapp, Friedrich E. 99
Schneider, Egon 99
Schöllgen, Gregor 50
Schoppmeyer, Heinrich 4 f., 59 ff., 78, 81, 91 f., *115*, 134, 139, 161
Schreiber, Hans-Ludwig 138
Schreiber, Otto 149
Schreier, Fritz 86
Schroeder, Ralph 96
Schumann, Ekkehard 55
Searle, John R. 19, 34
Seibel, Hans Dieter 7
Seidenfeld, Mark 6
Sica, Alan 14
Simitis, Spiros 110
Simon, Dieter 44, 129
Sinzheimer, Hugo 3, 27
Somek, Alexander 6, 17, 20, 42, 67, 69, 141
Speer, Heino 7
Stammler, Rudolf 3, 33, 137
Stampe, Ernst 112
Starck, Christian 5
Stauth, Georg 97
Stoll, Heinrich 63
Stolleis, Michael 129
Strache, Karl-Heinz 150
Stratenwerth, Günter 72
Strauss, Leo 103
Strong, Tracy B. 12
Strömholm, Stig 34
Stumpf, Max 65
Suber, Daniel 92
Summers, Robert S. 121
Sussman, Gilbert 45
Swedberg, Richard 35

Tenbruck, Friedrich H. 28, 142
Thibaut, Anton Friedrich 108
Thier, Andreas 67
Tieck, Klaus-Peter 95
Tiemeyer, Jürgen 30
Tipke, Klaus 75
Topitsch, Ernst 29
Treiber, Hubert 12, 36, 98
Trubek, David M. 95, 120 f.
Tugendhat, Ernst 101
Turner, Bryan 8, 97
Turner, Stephen 5, 159

Udy, Stanley H. 7
Uecker, Stefan 25, 42, 48, 55, 61, 69, 75, 83, 95, 120, 123, 154
Utzig, Siegfried 119

Viehweg, Theodor 111
Vogenauer, Stefan 121

Wagner, Gerhard 92
Weber, Marianne 92
Weigelin, Ernst 3
Weinberger, Ota *94*, 95
Weinkauff, Hermann 106
Weisser, Gerhard 30
Wellmer, Albrecht 165
Wesel, Uwe 110, 129
Westerhoff, Rudolf 67
Westermann, Harm Peter 145
Westermann, Harry 32, 50, 125
Weyhe, Lothar 4
Wieacker, Franz 64, *121*
Wilburg, Walter 67
Winckelmann, Johannes 1, 6
Witherspoon, Joseph P. 106
Wöhler, Sven 91
Wolf, Manfred 3, 59
Wolf, Ursula 101
Wolff, Hans Julius 137
Wright, George Henrik von 100

Zajtay, Imre 121
Zingerle, Arnold 11
Zippelius, Reinhold 145, 150
Zitelmann, Ernst *47*, 56

www.ingramcontent.com/pod-product-compliance
Lightning Source LLC
LaVergne TN
LVHW092114300926
849161LV00002B/135
*9783899495348*